# AMERICAN
# EXTREMISTS

# AMERICAN EXTREMISTS

## MILITIAS, SUPREMACISTS, KLANSMEN, COMMUNISTS, & OTHERS

## JOHN GEORGE & LAIRD WILCOX

Prometheus Books

59 John Glenn Drive
Amherst, New York 14228-2197

Cover photo courtesy AP/Wide World Photos

Published 1996 by Prometheus Books

00 99 98 97 96     5 4 3 2 1

Library of Congress Cataloging-in-Publication Data

George, John, 1936–
    [Nazis, communists, klansmen, and others on the fringe]
    American extremists : militias, supremacists, klansmen, communists, & others / John George, Laird Wilcox.
        p.    cm.
    Originally published: Nazis, communists, klansmen, and others on the fringe, 1992.
    Includes bibliographical references and index.
    ISBN 1–57392–058–4 (pbk.)
    1. Political clubs—United States.  2. Political parties—United States. 3. Radicalism—United States.  4. Left-wing extremists—United States. 5. Right-wing extremists—United States.  I. Wilcox, Laird M.  II. Title.
[HS2325.G46     1996]
324.273—dc20                                          96–16425
                                                          CIP

Printed in the United States of America on acid-free paper

# Contents

## Part III: The Far Right

# Preface

We are always asked: "How did you get interested in political extremism?" This is a reasonable question because the subject admittedly is somewhat arcane. Yet political extremism has a mystique all its own, combining elements of superstition, urban legend, and political utopianism. While, by definition, extremists roam about the fringes of our culture, they also pay close attention to our culture. Agreeing with them little, nonetheless, we can learn a lot from them and their social and political concerns.

For John George, it was the blustering of Soviet dictator Nikita Khrushchev in the late 1950s and commensurate praise for this behavior by Communist Party USA members and their fellow travelers that piqued his interest. How, he wondered, could they admire one such as Khrushchev? Further study answered the question: For the alienated and "ideologically prone," identification with a figure like Khrushchev or any other power figure plays an important psychological role. It frees one from the anxieties of reflection and doubt, at least for a while. For American Communists, the leader of the Soviet Union (the "great socialist motherland") embodied all their fantasies, utopian ideals, and hopes for the future. This phenomenon is repeated over and over with other causes, figures, and followers.

In the early 1960s, when it became known that John Birch Society founder Robert Welch had written that President Dwight Eisenhower and Secretary of State John Foster Dulles were Communist agents and part of a master conspiracy to subvert the American way of life, it was as if a door had been opened into a strange and fascinating world. For not only do extremists tend to believe things supported by little or no evidence, but many of them have a strong proclivity toward "conspiracy theories," that is, the belief that events are controlled by a small group of insiders who, with the assistance of their allies throughout society, are working for their advantage and our doom.

John George found that extremists tend to regard those who disagree with them as enemies, or worse. This is well-illustrated by former Italian Communist party leader Ignazio Silone's complaint about Lenin, Trotsky, and other important early Soviet officials. Silone wrote of their

> utter incapacity to be fair in discussing opinions that conflicted with their own. The adversary, simply for daring to contradict, became a traitor, an opportunist, a hireling. An adversary in good faith is inconceivable . . .[1]

7

The impetus for Laird Wilcox's interest came from another source. He grew up in a family that included a wide range of political tendencies, Communist to staunch Republican. He listened in on their discussions and arguments, watching passions ignite and tempers flare over ideological abstractions. At age fourteen he encountered Eric Hoffer's book *The True Believer,*[2] which he now regards as a "virtual owner's manual to all the nuttiness and fanaticism" he had observed. Later, he read John Howard Griffin's *Black Like Me,*[3] an account of a white man who moved freely in the black community, having had his skin cosmetically treated so that he could pass for black. It was by reading Griffin that Laird Wilcox developed his modus operandi: Get to know and mingle freely with extremists of all kinds. That's the way to get to understand the ideas and feelings that motivate them.

Laird became active in the antiwar and radical student movements of the 1960s, but he became disturbed by the increasing violence and intolerance, so he dropped out in 1966 and began developing what has become one of the largest collections on U.S. extremist movements (now housed at the University of Kansas in the Kenneth Spencer Research Library).

*   *   *

This book discusses American political extremism in some detail with the discussion filtered, naturally, through our experiences with hundreds of people who fall into the extremist "category," such as it is. We have talked with them in their homes and at public meetings, demonstrations, and debates; in restaurants over coffee; in the classroom; and sometimes while just walking along a busy thoroughfare. Some of our contacts have been deep and very personal and have extended over many years, while others were more on the order of single interview situations. Over the years we have encountered approximately six hundred individual extremists between us, and it is from this pool of experience that we draw our conclusions, which are necessarily tentative and subject to further evidence.

In our study of extremism we have become very aware that all human beings have biases and tend to see events from certain perspectives. We recognize the "Rashomon" principle, whereby individuals tend to interpret, and even distort, events in order to preserve their own integrity and sense of self-esteem. We found considerable support for Leon Festinger's theory of cognitive dissonance[4] in this regard. According to Festinger:

> This theory centers around the idea that if a person knows various things that are not psychologically consistent with one another, he will, in a variety of ways, try to make them more consistent. Two items of information that psychologically do not fit together are said to be in a dissonant relationship to each other. The items of information may be about behavior, feelings, opinions, things in the environment and so on . . .
>
> Such items can of course be changed. A person can change his opinion; he can

change his behavior, thereby changing the information he has about it; he can even distort his perception and his information about the world around him.[5]

Political extremists tend to be very prone to both conscious and unconscious distortions of various kinds. Simply put, they prefer to believe what they prefer to be true. The extremist tends to be the ideologue in purest form, i.e., the a priori thinker who believes what he "must" believe, regardless of evidence to the contrary. Extremists usually attempt to deduce the facts of an issue from a set of principles, often in the form of a political ideology, rather than determine the facts of an issue and then induce the principles that necessarily derive from them. It is this primacy of belief over knowledge that accounts for the often bizarre and impractical systems they create.

Largely because of the nature of their reasoning processes, extremists are often, but not always, "wrong" in terms of their understanding of the facts of an issue. Simply put, they seldom think things through clearly and objectively, their concept of logic and rationality is often under-developed, and they usually have poor insight into their psychological motives. Sometimes there are situations in which there is no "right' or "wrong," but rather positions or solutions which favor this interest group or that. "Right" or "wrong" in this case involves compromise and give and take, another area where extremists have difficulty.

The difference between the average person and the political extremist is largely one of degree and not of kind. If one is conscious of the problems and issues involved, the tendency toward bias and distortion can be tempered considerably, but not completely. We regard human beings as fallible, including ourselves. Consequently, while we cannot claim anything approaching complete objectivity, we make an honest and diligent attempt to be fair and even-handed in our treatment of this subject.

There are many books covering "extremism" or "extremists" on the market today, and not a few of them have their own agenda—often to provide a rationale for persecuting or doing away with certain "extremists." This is not our goal. We hope to provide understanding of a human problem, not a basis for one more round of persecutions. So, if you're an ideologue looking for another hate book to confirm your prejudices about "enemies" on the left or the right, this isn't it. Still, we hope you'll hear us out, because we have some insights that might make a difference for you.

Other tactics we hope to avoid are the "guilt-by-association," ad hominem techniques refined by the now discredited House Un-American Activities Committee (HUAC), which actively persecuted extremists (primarily on the far left) until its demise in 1974. This is not to say that associations are unimportant, but merely that of themselves they may mean relatively little. If substantial evidence of extremism exists, the case should be made on the basis of direct evidence and primary material, not on questionable inferences based upon acquaintances, hearsay, or presumed alliances and associations. Indeed, it is a characteristic of extremists themselves to attempt to make the case for their conspiracy theories by developing complex networks of "links" and "ties" among individuals, organizations, and beliefs.

On the other hand, where extremists are in the business of accusing other extremists of various kinds of perfidy on the basis of ad hominem, we feel free to mention their own "links" and "ties" simply to illustrate how weak and hypocritical these arguments frequently are. Also, it is often necessary to relate an organization or person with another in order to develop a context in which to explain the ins and outs of various "splinter groups" and the like. We caution you not to take this for more than it is, and to remember these associations may be circumstantial and fleeting. Alliances and agreements among extremists are quite often transient, and to assume that A must agree with B as evidenced by the fact that they both know C, or any variation of this kind of reasoning may very well be unwarranted.

*    *    *

A common error in dealing with extremists is to assume that if two or more extremists are alike in some respects, they must be alike in all or at least most respects. This fallacy of stereotyping is structurally similar to ethnic or religious prejudice, where an observation that "they're all alike" is a recognizable slur. We make the case that extremists only tend to have certain behavioral traits in common, and that these represent *relative* inclinations. By no means are they absolute criteria. Both of us have found surprising exceptions to virtually any generalization we might make. We have known extremists who were miserable, hateful individuals, who were virtually everything their enemies might say they were, and who would easily fulfill the stereotype of the hate-filled bigot or the wild-eyed revolutionary nihilist. But we have also known extremists who we felt were basically good people struggling with issues and problems, and who, once they were outside their conflict area, were decent and well-meaning. Generalizations may have a certain limited validity, but it must constantly be borne in mind that extremists are individual human beings.

Although the characteristics we have mentioned are hardly exclusive to extremists and are found widely in the general population to a certain extent, among extremists they may seem more strikingly evident. None of these traits, which can be profoundly distressing to many people, means that extremists are less deserving of civil liberties than the rest of us. They should have the same protections, privileges, and respect as those of us who are more often, but not always, "right."

*    *    *

"He who defines the terms wins the argument," the old axiom goes. In dealing with the subject of "extremism," an arbitrary and unfair definition can have far-reaching effects. We can see from observing dictatorships of the left and right that concepts like "justice," "freedom," and "equality" can be distorted and twisted to mean quite nearly the opposite of what the words actually denote. This is also the case with "extremism." We will propose a definition that will go a long way toward eliminating these abuses.

There are several different ways of looking at "extremism." The normative or "statistical" way is to frame the spectrum on a linear scale, as in a Gallup poll, and arbitrarily determine that beyond a certain point on each end of the spectrum lie the "extremists"; that is, the 2 percent, say, on the far "left" and far "right" of the political spectrum are the "extremists." This has a kind of utility and makes a kind of sense. Visualize a "bell curve," with the great mass toward the center and the "extremes" on the fringes. The problem is that there are too many examples of beliefs or behavior that most of us would agree are "extremist" and yet they are held by a considerable percentage of the population. Many dictators, for example, have a large following. When an "extreme" belief originally held by a small minority becomes popular, does it cease to be "extreme"? If a Nazi won an election is he no longer an "extremist"? Conversely, is a belief "extreme" simply because it is unpopular? We don't think the unpopularity of a particular belief is sufficient to prove its "extreme" nature.

Another view of "extremism" is that it is essentially a social definition agreed upon by collective fiat, i.e., what is "extreme" is what the masses collectively decide is "extreme." This is the "popularity contest" theory of extremism, and one that reeks of an intolerance that allows a majority to gang up on the minority, whoever that happens to be—people who dress funny, have dark skin or a strange religion, have subversive ideas, or are just "different." This approach places excessive power in social and political elites, particularly in the opinion-molding sector. It's also the perennial temptation of the newly empowered to use their position to marginalize those who they feel are responsible for their own former marginalization.

Finally, there's the behavioral model of "extremism," defined in terms of certain behaviors, particularly behavior toward other human beings. This is the model we prefer, and it is explained in some detail in chapter 2, "What Is Extremism?" We feel that this approach best preserves the integrity of individuals and the values of an open and democratic system. It also helps to define our social responsibilities to one another and protects against the dangers inherent in the other models we have described.

There is a certain danger in the notion that we should be "intolerant of intolerance." It is almost always those who are definitionally "intolerant" who are most often targets of persecution themselves. Advocacy of *any* strident position implies intolerance—intolerance, perhaps, of persecution, unfairness, double standards, denial of due process, or prejudice, as seen through the eye of the beholder. "Intolerance of intolerance" has a kind of "death to fanatics" character, and it reminds one of Thomas Bailey Aldrich's statement in the *Pongkapog Papers* where he speaks of the person who "is opposed to the death penalty but . . . would willingly have any electrocuted who disagreed with him on the subject." It also smacks of Orwellian "doublethink" in that it consists of two mutually exclusive values, a way of reframing the concept of tolerance so that it justifies intolerance.

\*   \*   \*

In a book concerned with politics, it is fair for the reader to ask where on the political spectrum the authors fit. Our positions are a bit difficult to pin down. Temperamentally, we're more or less "liberals," and this is evident in the way we approach our subject. The necessity of pragmatism is apparent to both of us, although we each have a touch of the idealist as well. Both of us have been attached to the civil rights movement and both of us are considered strong civil libertarians and champions of the underdog. At one time these traits would have put us on the moderate left, but this is less clear today. Because we have a very wide range of friends and associations, it would be possible to find bits of evidence to "link" us with any position on the political spectrum, only to have these canceled out by other "links" in the opposing direction. Right-wingers tend to view us as leftists, and many left-wingers think we're rightists. We often differ with one another on various issues, but our mutual respect and tolerance make this collaboration possible. Perhaps we might be most accurately described as pragmatists with libertarian tendencies.

We hope that, similarly, the tone of our book could be called "pragmatic with a touch of idealism." In this work we will attempt to delineate the characteristics of extremism and extremists *as we have experienced them* and give many examples. We will also try to summarize the pre-1960 historical background of American extremist movements, discuss conspiracy theories and their validity, offer our insight on what motivates extremists, and discuss a number of contemporary groups on the "far left" and "far right" based principally on our personal contacts and their own writings.

So, we invite you to accompany us on our summary of what we have learned about political extremism. If you're open to it, it can be an enlightening experience and may well alter the way you've thought about this issue. If your position is fixed, you'll find much in this book to get your juices flowing, and we welcome that, too.

John George
Laird Wilcox

## Notes

1. Richard Crossman, ed. *The God That Failed* (New York: Harper & Row, 1949), 101.

2. Eric Hoffer, *The True Believer* (New York: Harper & Row, 1951).

3. John Howard Griffin, *Black Like Me* (New York: Houghton-Mifflin, 1961).

4. Leon Festinger, *A Theory of Cognitive Dissonance* (Stanford, Calif.: Stanford University Press, 1957).

5. Leon Festinger, "Cognitive Dissonance," in *Readings About the Social Animal,* Elliot Aronson, ed. (San Francisco: Freeman, 1973), 100–101.

# Part I. Background, Characteristics, Motivations, and Other Considerations

# 1. It's Not New: Historical Perspective on American Extremism Prior to 1960

*Extremism,* broadly defined, existed in America virtually from the moment it was inhabited by humans. Wars among Native American tribes, rivalries within those tribes, and even altercations among individuals all undoubtedly had extremist characteristics. Fanaticism, prejudice toward other Native Americans, and unfairness no doubt marked early American history with distressing regularity.

In 1980 Larry Zimmerman, professor of anthropology at the University of South Dakota, helped in unearthing and studying a mass grave containing the skeletons of at least 486 men, women, and children by the conjunction of Elm Creek and Crow Creek near the Missouri River in South Dakota. He proceeded to chronicle the forensic evidence of a horror the likes of which we tend to associate with the extremism of a Nazi or Stalinist dictatorship.

According to reports, "Between 1325 and 1400, apparently during a prolonged drought that forced severe competition for food, one group of Indians attacked and massacred another. Most of the skulls were bashed in, and knife marks indicate that nearly all were scalped. Many skeletons were missing hands and feet. Some noses were hacked off." Zimmerman noted, "People have tended to idealize Indian life in the past. It goes all the way back to Rousseau's noble savage." Of the skeletons that could be assigned an age and sex, 152 were children under the age of fourteen, hardly "military' threats. Of the victims between fifteen and thirty-nine years of age, seventy-eight were men and twenty-eight were women. The disparity between the sexes may be accounted for by the common practice of forcing women into slavery when captured.[1]

American Indians played a part in numerous revolts and insurrections after the settlers came from Europe. Britain's victory over France in the 1760s triggered the great revolt of the eastern tribes known by the extremist-sounding name of "Pontiac's Conspiracy." American independence from Great Britain was followed by Little Turtle's War, the Blackhawk War, the revolt of the Creeks and Cherokees, and the Seminole War. As Richard E. Rubenstein notes in *Rebels In Eden*:

> Calling these conflicts "wars" against Indian "nations," of course, does not alter their character: they were armed *insurrections* [emphasis ours] by domestic groups denied the privileges of citizenship, as well as the perquisites of nationhood . . .[2]

15

Recent books on American extremism, particularly on the American "right wing," have attempted to attach the concept of "nativism" to white European society, primarily in the early nineteenth century. Was not "nativism" expressed by the "native Americans" when they resisted the incursion by European explorers? There are many recorded cases of violence, massacre, and brutality toward settlers. The very first settlement of Europeans in the new world, Jamestown, in Virginia, was the site of a murderous Indian massacre in 1622 that wiped out the colony. The Jamestown massacre was clearly the result of "nativism," or resentment toward "foreigners" and "aliens." Europeans replied in kind with extremism of their own, including massacres and random killing of Indians.

Indeed, it was a boatload of religious extremists who landed at Plymouth Rock in Massachusetts. Refugees from "persecution" in England and Holland, undoubtedly from other "extremists," the pilgrims sought refuge in the New World not for religious freedom in the generic sense, but freedom to practice their own form of intolerance and dogmatism, a characteristic not uncommon in persecuted minorities. Not only did they not get along with their home society, but they were a quarrelsome lot among themselves, as extremists often are. They bickered, fought, and even had a "mutiny" on the Mayflower itself.[3]

Extremism flourished throughout early American history in one form or another, as it has in Europe and everywhere else on the globe throughout history. Wars, revolutions, social movements, religions, crusades, and "causes" have exhibited elements of "extremism," including those which we recognize today as "good." Not the least of these was the American Revolution, which was preceded by a number of radical pamphleteers and seditious propagandists, not to mention traitors and subversives, and even a smattering of people who would today be described as terrorists. If one were to describe the American Revolution as a seditious conspiracy fomented by a band of extremists, misfits, malcontents, and troublemakers dedicated to the overthrow of recognized authority, one might well be right on the mark. For many people, the words used to describe behavior have a lot to do with how they view it.

American vigilante movements were present as early as 1769 (and probably before), when a group known as "Regulators" was formed in South Carolina. According to *Assassination and Violence*, a "Staff Report to the National Commission on the Causes and Prevention of Violence" issued by the U.S. Government in 1969:

> Included in a "Who's Who" of American Vigilantism would be United States senators and congressmen, governors, judges, wealthy capitalists, generals, lawyers, and even clergymen. Presidents of the United States have not been immune to the vigilante infection. During his presidency, Andrew Jackson once approved the vigilante methods of Iowa pioneers pending the clarification of their territorial status. As a young cattle rancher in North Dakota, Theodore Roosevelt was refused admittance to a vigilante band that was being formed to deal with rustlers and horse thieves.[4]

Even in more-or-less normal times, extremism has been practiced in this country by one group or individual against another; retaliation has also been common. There are few things more characteristic of human beings than their predilection to extremism, which is not alien to human society but an integral part of it. In certain forms, it may have been responsible for great inventions, exploration, and other achievements. In other forms, it has been responsible for horrible suffering and pointless loss of life. If we are to understand extremism, we must accept its apparent naturalness; only then can we learn how to cope with its destructive aspects.

## The Nineteenth Century

Organized "extremism," as judged by today's standards, made its appearance early in the young United States. Before the first third of the nineteenth century was over, one well-organized "right-wing" group was in existence. This was the Anti-Masonic movement, which eventually reorganized as a political party and in 1830 staged America's first national convention.

As is often the case, these extremists were, no doubt, responding to what *they* regarded as extremism. The Masonic lodge was a secret fraternal organization. Its meetings were private and its rituals, involving elaborate handshakes, passwords, oaths, and ceremonies, themselves aroused suspicion. Most importantly, it was in the interest of the Masonic lodge to seek members from among the social elite, i.e., physicians, lawyers, businessmen, and military officers. Consequently, and perhaps for good reason, the Masons were regarded as a secret society with powers far beyond their numbers and, consequently, inimical to any kind of democratic process.

Mixed with these fairly reasonable objections were a variety of conspiracy theories, bolstered by the behavior of the Masons themselves who, not surprisingly, exhibited conduct one would expect from an unaccountable elite. It was a normal part of Masonic life to give preference to other Masons, and when non-Masonic businessmen fell upon misfortune, it wasn't entirely unreasonable to suspect a "conspiracy." In military ranks, men with Masonic connections seemed to fare better than non-Masons. Entrance into professional schools and clerkships also seemed more available to the well-connected. What the Anti-Masonic movement was responding to, then, was what they regarded as an abusive, unfair, secret society bent upon their own enrichment. This, in itself, may not have been an extremist response. In fact, when all elements are considered, a case can be made that the Masonic lodge itself was "extremist" in nature. In September 1830 delegates from eleven states met in Philadelphia for the United States Anti-Masonic Convention. They heard earnest pleas for liberal democracy and an open society:

> Free inquiry, free discussion, free communication are essential requisites to the most valuable knowledge. In the arts and sciences, in ethics and theology, all liberal minds acknowledge their indispensable importance. In the political conduct of life, their

importance is, if possible, still more manifest. They are the living foundations of our government, which would be speedily dissolved, in blood, without them. No man has ever yet sufficiently valued them: for they alone can safely be relied upon, to open and illuminate all the paths, in which the majestic power of public opinion displays itself. But freemasonry is opposed to free inquiry, free discussion, and free communication. Its greatest fear is publicity, its best virtue, silence. It professes to have inestimable treasures of social benefits, which it refuses to disclose to any but the small number of its devoted followers.[5]

' The Anti-Masonic movement grew as more and more individuals felt abused by the Masonic lodge; complaints escalated into full-blown conspiracy-mongering. The tone was set for the rise of the Anti-Masons in the mid-1820s, when some religious books attacking Masonry were published. Masons, of course, responded with charges of their own. Anti-Masonic literature was directed at Masonic secrecy, bizarre rituals, and admitted preoccupation with influence and power—all of which suggested a "conspiracy." Mixed with this was a heavy dose of literalist religious doctrine that was popular at the time. A major element of the Anti-Masonic argument was that one could not be both a Christian and a Mason, and they pointed to the fact that Masons accepted Jews and deists as evidence that the lodge was actually anti-Christian.

The factor that sparked Anti-Masonic excesses was the abduction from jail and probable murder of one William Morgan. A former Mason, Morgan had broken his secrecy oath and was in the process of writing a book, *Illustrations of Masonry by One of the Fraternity Who Has Devoted Thirty Years to the Subject,* which would have put Masonry in a very bad light indeed. Arrested on the presumably trumped-up charge of theft, Morgan was accused of stealing a shirt and tie. The question of Morgan's death came up at the United States Anti-Masonic Convention in 1830. The question of who the real extremists were arises again and, as we shall see, the "good guys versus bad guys" paradigm becomes less clear as more is known of the actual controversy.[6]

James H. Billington, director of the Woodrow Wilson International Center for Scholars, notes:

"Free" masonry was . . . a moral meritocracy—implicitly subversive within any static society based on a traditional hierarchy. Men of intelligence and ambition in the eighteenth century often experienced within Masonic lodges a kind of brotherhood among equals. . .

The rituals leading to each new level of membership were . . . awesome rites of passage into new types of association, promising access to higher truths of Nature once the blindfold was removed in the inner room of the lodge.

Masonry ritualized fraternity and provided upward mobility more easily than outside society.[7]

Probably the major impetus to start their own party was the Anti-Masonic movement's conviction that most office-holders were Masons. Although they held anti-elitist beliefs, the Anti-Masons made an alliance of convenience with the elitist

National Republicans. By the mid-1830s these two groups had coalesced into the Whig party. As is so often the case when relatively radical groups merge with less radical groups, the result is much closer to what might be called the "mainstream" of the period. There have been many examples of this in American history. (In modern times quite respectable religious bodies have condemned Masonic practices on somewhat similar grounds. In 1985 in London a committee of the relatively liberal Methodist church issued a report that said: "There is great danger that the Christian who becomes a Freemason will find himself compromising his Christian beliefs or his allegiance to Christ, perhaps without realizing what he is doing.")[8]

The political sociologists Lipset and Raab described the Anti-Masons as "perhaps the first example in the United States of a preservatist anti-elitist mass movement based on the more provincial and traditional elements in society" and called this "a sociological precursor of movements like the Ku Klux Klan and McCarthyism."[9] This conclusion would certainly have shocked the Anti-Masons, who saw their movement as an alternative to a secret, antidemocratic and definitionally extremist clique having, in many respects—including ritual, secrecy, professions of brotherhood, and mutual aid—a certain structural similarity to the Klan itself.

The observation by Lipset and Raab is troublesome. If one uses the qualifier "sociological," it's probably true that the Anti-Masonic movement was a precursor to the Ku Klux Klan. For one thing, the KKK developed not too many years after the Anti-Mason movement was in deep decline, and some Ku Klux Klansmen had previously been active in Anti-Masonic causes. It's worth noting that while the Klan opposed one kind of "elitism," it advocated another. As is so often the case, a crusade against one form of abuse became an advocate of another form of abuse, and the cycle continued.

The allusion to McCarthyism is also unconvincing. McCarthy, a Roman Catholic, was obviously not a Mason. However, his relationships with Masons were quite cordial, as would be the case with almost any successful politician. If what Lipset and Raab suggest is that the Anti-Masonic movement and McCarthy were similar because they were both opposed to a group that embraced elements of secrecy and were suspected of conspiratorial activity, an analogy might be sustained. There is, however, no demonstrable chain of events leading from Anti-Masonism to McCarthyism. Had the Anti-Masonic movement never existed, McCarthyism would still most probably have occurred. There is no evidence that Senator McCarthy was even aware of the Anti-Masonic movement of the early nineteenth century. Lacking any evidence of causality, Lipset and Raab's term "precursor" is now relegated to mean "antecedent." In other words, the Anti-Masonic movement is a "precursor" to McCarthyism and the Ku Klux Klan merely because it came before them. And so did a lot of other things with little or no more causal relationship than the Anti-Masonic movement.

By the middle of the nineteenth century another large "rightist"[10] group, the American party, was well established. The organization was better known as the "Know Nothings," because when asked about their business they would reply,

"I know nothing." This appellation was no great help to their activities, by the way, because it confirmed to many people with no real knowledge of their reasoning that they were so named because they were ignorant or stupid, a notion not entirely without merit.

The group, which drew some of its early membership from a variety of secret nativist societies, was a powerful bane to newly arriving immigrants (some of whom originated secret societies of their own) and managed to develop a significant degree of political organization. For example, when the 34th Congress assembled in 1855, five senators and forty-three representatives were publicly declared members of the American party. As a minority party they had little influence on legislation, and the movement was essentially defunct by the end of the Civil War, a victim of ridicule, internal dissent, and the desertion of its leaders.[11]

The party has been described as an awkward confederation of conservative elite and bigoted workers. This means in part that they didn't share the prejudices of their critics, supporting instead what they perceived as their own interests rather than those of others—particularly the foreign born (many of whom were Irish Catholics), who did precisely the same thing. For example, in 1834 mobs of Roman Catholics assaulted speakers and sacked the hall at a public meeting sponsored by the New York Protestant Association because the topic was unpleasing to them.[12] Famine in Ireland from 1845 to 1850 brought some 400,000 aliens into the United States during each of the peak years, and this caused severe disruption of basic services, including housing and sanitation.[13]

The tendency of extremist groups to develop in opposition to one another is illustrated again in this instance. Opposing the Know Nothing movement were the Molly Maguires, an openly terrorist organization of Irish Catholic origins formed in 1843 in Ireland for the purpose of intimidating or terrorizing bailiffs and process servers. Organized in the coal fields of Pennsylvania as an inner group of the secret Irish society, the Ancient Order of Hibernians, they were as ethnically exclusive or "racist" as the Know Nothings, with membership totally composed of Roman Catholics. Molly Maguire activity peaked following the Civil War, shortly after the Know Nothing movement evaporated. Unlike the Know Nothings and the American Party—a legitimate political party—the Molly Maguires remained secret and were responsible for a large number of murders, maimings, bombings, and arsons. In 1874 the Pinkerton detectives were called in. One of their operatives, posing as a common criminal, joined the terrorist group and became secretary of his division. The organization disbanded in 1877 after several leading members of the group were arrested, jailed, and sometimes executed.[14]

\*    \*    \*

The premier extremist organization of the nineteenth century was the Ku Klux Klan. The Klan initially appeared after the Civil War during the Reconstruction period when the federal government sent troops into the South to enforce the acts of Congress giving blacks equal political and civil rights, which in many cases simply involved appointing them to otherwise elective offices. Although originally a fraternal organization, the Klan soon developed into a secret society complete with bizarre rituals reminiscent of those of the Masons, whom it opposed. In the summer of 1867 delegates from several states attended a Klan convention held in Nashville, Tennessee. Written precepts were adopted, officers appointed, and the Invisible Empire of the Ku Klux Klan was officially proclaimed. Former Confederate general Nathan Bedford Forrest was the first Grand Wizard.

Between 1867 and 1871 the KKK was a potent factor in intimidating blacks and overthrowing the black rule which had been imposed by federal authorities in North Carolina, Tennessee, and Georgia. Faced with growing evidence of KKK violence, President Ulysses S. Grant, under the authority of the Ku Klux Klan Act of April 1871, suspended the writ of habeas corpus in nine South Carolina counties. Authorities rounded up Klansmen and suspected Klansmen, holding some of them for long periods without formal charges. Some 1,250 Klansmen were convicted of various offenses in proceedings of dubious constitutionality. The Ku Klux Klan was disbanded, only to reappear in somewhat modernized form in 1915.[15]

Yet another "rightist" organization formed before the end of the nineteenth century. The American Protective Association was founded in Clinton, Iowa, in 1887 and within ten years it had more than two million members (nearly 4 percent of the population). The APA essentially picked up where the Know Nothing movement left off; in fact, many of its older members had been active in the American party. Its focus was primarily on restricting further immigration into the United States; Roman Catholics were especially unwanted.[16] Interestingly, a major plank in the APA's platform is embraced today by people of all political persuasions, namely, opposition to any government aid to Catholic schools. Other issues included alleged political corruption, violations of the U.S. Constitution by public officials, opposition to an increase in untaxed church property, opposition to Roman Catholicism as "an un-American ecclesiastical institution," and defense of "true Americanism."[17]

APA membership skyrocketed as social tensions increased during the financial panic of 1893, growing rapidly in New York, Pennsylvania, Massachusetts, Connecticut, Rhode Island, California, Washington, and Oregon, and peaking in 1896. It declined steadily after that as the economic situation improved, becoming virtually inactive after the turn of the century, and folded in 1911.[18]

\*    \*    \*

One man linked the "right-wing" extremism of the late nineteenth century with that of the twentieth. Southerner Tom Watson did not begin his career as an outspoken racial supremacist, but he certainly ended up that way. As a leader of the "left-wing" People's party, better known as the Populist party, Watson was adamantly opposed to racism and anti-Catholicism in the 1890s. In one of those remarkable conversions where an individual attached to one set of views switches and becomes attached to an opposing set, by the 1910s Watson launched *Watson's Magazine* and began attacking blacks, Roman Catholics, and Jews.[19]

Watson was particularly incensed about the immigrant problem, which was causing major disruptions in social conditions and community life. "The scum of creation has been dumped on us," he said. "Some of our principal cities are more foreign than American. The most dangerous and corrupting hordes of the Old World have invaded us. The vice and crime which they have planted in our midst is terrifying." To counter these conditions Watson called for the formation of "another Ku Klux Klan."[20]

What about the "left wing" in the nineteenth century? As with the "right," it depends upon what and whom you include. There were numerous communal groups practicing a kind of "communism," but they tended toward a live-and-let-live existence and were generally uninvolved in the political process. A particularly well-known example was Harmonie, a utopian communal settlement in Indiana that lasted from 1815 until 1824. In 1825 the property was purchased by Robert Owen and another utopian society was attempted—New Harmony—which folded in 1828. There were others, but most ended after a brief period of time.[21]

Prior to the Civil War there arose a network of abolitionists whose primary interest was the destruction of slavery. The movement took shape in 1833 when William Lloyd Garrison and others formed the American Anti-Slavery Society in Philadelphia. They were well organized, contained both moderate and extreme elements, and became a significant political force.[22] One could say, perhaps, that the egalitarian social doctrines of the communal societies and the abolitionists were the "sociological precursors" of the socialist and Marxist left that began to coalesce in the late nineteenth century. We, however, aver no such connection.

The first significant socialist party was established in 1877 with the Workingman's party, which became the Socialist Labor party in 1890. Its membership was largely European ethnics, including many Germans, and early meetings were conducted in the language of each group's local members. It achieved modest electoral success early in its history and in 1878–79 managed to elect an Illinois state senator, three representatives, and four Chicago city councilmen. The party's mentor until his death in 1914 was Columbia University economics professor Daniel DeLeon, and SLP members were often referred to as "DeLeonists."[23]

Stressing what they described as "pure Marxism," the SLP was never violence-oriented; they felt violence was simply counterproductive in the United States. SLP doctrine was largely an extension of DeLeon's interpretation of Marx and Engels, a sectarian mixture of industrial unionism and utopian socialism. DeLeon was contemptuous of what he considered "sham" socialists and their false leaders and produced lengthy polemics against them. The organization's history was marked by alliances, splits, factionalism and expulsions and, like many Marxist organizations, had some of the characteristics of a religious cult.

The major organ of the SLP was originally called the *Daily People,* which subsequently became the *Weekly People* and eventually the *People,* appearing monthly. Membership may have peaked at around eight thousand in the late 1890s and then settled down to less than five thousand, where it remained for several decades. Many individuals who subsequently became members of the

Communist Party USA had their first indoctrination to socialist theory in the SLP. The SLP regularly ran candidates for president and as recently as 1972 actually received 53,831 votes in the limited number of states where it was on the ballot. The organization exists today, but is only a shadow of its former self. Several small groups have split off to form their own "parties," and 1990 SLP membership was down to about two hundred. Having lasted a hundred years with relatively little doctrinal change, the SLP may well be gone by the year 2000.

## Twentieth Century

The concepts of "right wing" and "left wing" became more clearly defined in the early twentieth century. Generally speaking, "right wing" became associated with conservativism, religiosity, patriotism, nationalism, and racism. "Left wing" became associated with "liberalism," secularism, internationalism, collectivism, and egalitarianism. There have been exceptions to this paradigm but it has remained for the most part constant.

*    *    *

Prior to the three decades emphasized in this book (1960–1990), there were three main periods when extreme left- and/or right-wing groups flourished during the twentieth century. The first period came during World War I and continued into the early 1920s when extremists of both the left and right battled it out in their own little corner while the rest of the nation watched. Termed by many as the "Red Scare," this period involved activity on both the far left and far right, as well as the "anti-extremist" activity of the government itself. The second period, taking in the Great Depression of the 1930s up to the end of World War II, included the rapid growth of the Communist movement in America as well as the right-wing reaction to it, including not only superpatriots and "conservatives" but American Nazis and fascists as well. The third period, dating from the early-to-mid 1950s, was characterized by Senator Joe McCarthy's infamous crusade against "subversives."

It's worth noting before focusing on modern extremist groups that virtually all of them have considered themselves anti-extremist, in that they have opposed other obviously extremist groups from the other end of the political spectrum. This is not to say that they don't have enemies who are not extremists. Obviously they do, but in their skewed view, nonextremists can easily be seen as extremists. Hence, we have the John Birch Society claim that President Eisenhower was a Communist agent, or the Communist party insinuating that Senator Barry Goldwater was a fascist.

One's perspective, of course, makes all the difference. If one has been steeped in a Marxist-Leninist environment for a period of time, as a member of the Communist party, for example, then the question of what is right, left, or center becomes badly distorted, and in a practical sense what is or is not "extremism" is very difficult for the individual in question to determine with any degree of objectivity. The same is true with the far right or any other interest group where issues are polarized, as in race, sex, or religion.

Another key factor is semantic: extremists tend to use metaphor rather generously. To accuse one of "selling us out to the Commies" is not to mean that such a person literally accepts payment for betraying the United States; usually that accusation can refer to any number of things, ranging from being duped to harboring Communist sympathies. To accuse the current administration of "racism" does not literally mean that it promotes classical theories of racial superiority, but rather that it is insensitive to minority concerns or perhaps opposed to expanding affirmative action programs. The promiscuous use of metaphor is so commonplace among extremists, and many of their critics, that each particular case should be taken in context in order to determine what is actually meant, which is often rather different than what has been said. This can be confusing and difficult, and it underscores the importance of plain, straightforward language in discussing controversial issues.

The tendency of extremist groups to feed upon one another and form a strange, symbiotic relationship, each justifying the existence of the other, is plainly evident. Many extremist groups are formed expressly to oppose a particular kind of "extremism." The case of some militant anti-Klan groups with Marxist-Leninist origins whose underlying ideologies are hardly a less extreme alternative to the extremism they purportedly oppose furnishes a good example.

Generally, extremists of the right have been far more successful in persecuting extremists of the left than the other way around: up until recently the right more often received help from the government. But right-wingers had their turn at the stake during World War II when some thirty of their number were indicted in the Great Sedition Trial of 1944. Both the "Red Scare" period of the late teens and early 1920s and the McCarthy period of the 1950s were eras of considerable persecution of leftists. From the mid-1960s on the left became less unpopular in some quarters and leftist "anti-racist" groups pushed repressive legislation against their ideological adversaries. During the 1980s laws prohibiting "paramilitary training," which could include instruction in karate, were enacted in about twenty states, and "anti-hate" legislation proliferated on state and local levels, all aimed at extremists of the far right. In 1988 a group of twenty-three far-rightists including neo-Nazis and Ku Klux Klansmen were acquitted in a widely publicized sedition trial in Ft. Smith, Arkansas.[24]

The twentieth century began with considerable organization by the socialist left. Formally founded in 1901 by Victor L. Berger, Job Harriman, Morris Hilquit and Eugene V. Debs, the Socialist party comprised numerous tendencies. Many of its early members, like Morris Hilquit, were defectors from the Socialist Labor party, which accommodated moderate, radical, and even revolutionary members, although most of the latter quit in 1919 to join the Communist party, which was founded that year.

The Socialist party had to deal with several handicaps. First, at the 1894 convention of the American Federation of Labor, AFL leader Samuel Gompers prevented the organization from endorsing socialism and continued to do so throughout his career. This kept the party from acquiring legitimacy among working class Americans and especially from the skilled trade unionists who bolstered its European counterparts. Secondly, the pacifism of the party and its leaders during World War I cost it substantial public support, particularly among intellectuals. Finally, the party faced rivalry from other socialist organizations, including the older Socialist Labor party, the Industrial Workers of the World (the IWW, or "Wobblies") and eventually the Communist party.[25]

In spite of this, the Socialist party acquired nearly 100,000 dues-paying members by 1912, its peak year. Only about one American in nine hundred was a member, which says something of its marginality. Socialist publications remained fairly popular, however. The *Jewish Daily Forward,* for example, reached a circulation of some 200,000 by 1919. Other nonparty ethnic socialist publications abounded. The Slovakian *Rovnost Ludu* claimed a readership of nearly 10,000 and the Bohemian *Spraredulust* approached 12,000.

In 1910 Victor Berger became the first socialist elected to Congress and Eugene V. Debs won nearly a million votes for president in 1912. The 1917 Socialist party candidate for mayor of New York City finished second, an event that called attention to the growing popularity of the party in isolated areas as membership declined elsewhere. Many party members were active in trade and industrial unions, particularly the various garment workers unions. Like the Socialist Labor party, the Socialist party had a large foreign-born contingent, comprising about 40 percent of the membership in its early days.[26]

Debs, incidentally, began as a conservative-minded labor writer, editor of the journal of the Brotherhood of Locomotive Firemen, who spoke strongly against strikes and condemned the Haymarket "martyrs" in no uncertain terms. Over several years he became progressively more radical as he gained experience. He was quoted as saying:

> I am not a capitalist soldier; I am a proletarian revolutionist. I am opposed to every war but one; I am for that war with heart and soul, and that is the world wide war of the social revolution. In that way, I am preparing to fight in any way the ruling class may make necessary, even to the barricades.

Debs quickly found the martyrdom he was seeking with that kind of rhetoric in the last year of World War I, and in June 1918 he was arrested for sedition after a militant antiwar speech in Canton, Ohio. He was eventually convicted and sentenced to ten years in federal prison at the age of sixty-three. It was while in prison that Debs polled 901,000 votes for president, slightly less than his 1912 total. He was pardoned by Warren Harding in 1921; he died in 1926.[27]

In 1928 Socialist party membership hit a low of 8,000. Norman Thomas, who would become the perennial Socialist party candidate for president, generated considerable publicity, and membership doubled by 1932, in the midst of the Great Depression. Norman Thomas, born in 1884 into a family of clergymen, graduated from Princeton University and was ordained a Presbyterian minister at Union Theological Seminary in 1911. He almost immediately became a Christian socialist and a pacifist. He entered the Socialist party in 1918 and left the clergy. He ran for president on the Socialist ticket six times (1928–1948) and was the party's public spokesmen until his death in 1968. In 1952 he began supporting Democratic presidential candidates. Thomas was, most of all, an ardent civil libertarian and championed the First Amendment more than any other figure on the American socialist left.[28] Thomas received 892,000 votes in the presidential election of 1932, but this dropped to less than 190,000 in 1936. By the late 1930s membership slipped below 10,000 and continued to decline steadily thereafter. In 1938 a group of members supporting Trotskyism were expelled and formed the Socialist League, although many of the rebels rejoined the party in 1957 during a period of reconciliation.[29]

In 1972 a breakaway group formed Social Democrats USA, a strongly anti-communist organization. A second wing split off to form the Democratic Socialist Organizing Committee, a more radical group that in 1982 merged with the New American Movement to form Democratic Socialists of America. Small factions exist to the present day with a combined membership of a few thousand. Interestingly, many present-day "neoconservatives" served their leftist apprenticeship in Social Democrats USA, considered by many to be the "extreme right" of the Social Democratic complex.[30]

Among socialist organizations, the Socialist party and the Socialist Labor party were unique in espousing a nonviolent and generally non-confrontational policy. It is largely because of their seminal role in the early American left and the fact that they were significant in the various splits and schisms that racked the left from time to time that they are included in this book on extremism.

The Industrial Workers of the World (IWW) is another story. Founded in 1905 by the Western Federation of Miners and a number of other labor organizations, its early leaders included Debs and DeLeon, although they soon left in a dispute over the group's growing militancy. Elizabeth Gurley Flynn, later a primary Communist Party USA functionary, was associated with the IWW for a time. The organization soon became known for its revolutionary tactics and confrontational nature. For one thing, the IWW refused to sign contracts with management. During World War I the organization took a stridently pacifist position, which raised questions of loyalty in the minds of many officials.

In September 1917 the U.S. government raided IWW offices nationwide with warrants that accused the entire leadership, some two hundred individuals, of subversion. In the trial that followed nearly one hundred "wobblies" were sentenced to federal prison terms of up to twenty years. Members were implicated in numerous acts of violence and strike-related sabotage, but they were also persecuted with trumped-up charges and police abuse. Unconstitutional syndicalism laws were widely used to harass IWW members. So significant were the free speech cases in which the organization was continually embroiled that American Civil Liberties Union founder Roger Baldwin considered their contribution to civil liberties quite significant. IWW agitation about prison abuses helped to bring about prison reform.[31]

Although membership peaked around 1920 at about 100,000, the IWW quickly dwindled as government harassment took its toll and as members faded away into mainstream labor unions or joined other revolutionary groups, such as the new Communist party. By the 1930s the organization had become largely ineffectual. Interestingly, the IWW exists to this day, still operating out of its traditional Chicago headquarters with a membership in the neighborhood of five hundred. Its newspaper, *Industrial Worker,* appears monthly.[32]

During the years following World War I, there was a period of over-reaction and fear of domestic radicalism brought about in part by the Bolshevik Revolution in Russia and leftist opposition to the draft. Considerable prejudice against ethnic Germans ("the Hun") coupled with widespread Jewish and other European ethnic participation in domestic radical politics contributed to this climate.

Of particular concern were communists, anarchists, socialists, and militant trade unionists. All were lumped together as potential perpetrators of violence, as though being similar in some respects made them alike in all respects. A few were bombers, but they comprised a tiny minority of such groups. (Whether one is dealing with extremists of the far left or the far right, nearly all of the violence is committed by a very small percentage of the activists.) Although minute in comparison to the vast majority of the membership, the "bomber" element was responsible for helping to confirm this stereotype and bringing considerable wrath down upon left-wing radicals.

Still, there was reason for federal authorities to be nervous. In the spring of 1919 alone, thirty-six bombs were sent through the mail. Among the intended victims were two U.S. senators, the postmaster general, and the secretary of labor. Bombs were also destined for Attorney General R. Mitchell Palmer, Justice Oliver Wendell Holmes, and financiers John D. Rockefeller and J. P. Morgan. Postal authorities discovered thirty-four of the explosive packages and prevented their reaching their destinations. The two other bombs did not kill their intended victims, but one seriously burned an ex-senator's wife and her maid lost both hands. Newspapers played up the bombings as a "Red plot," while radical left-wing publications wrote of a frame-up designed to "get" radicals and labor leaders.

In a memorandum dated August 12, 1919, to "all special agents and employees," Palmer issued orders to launch

> a vigorous and comprehensive investigation of anarchistic and similar classes, Bolshevism and kindred agitations advocating change in the present form of government by force and violence, the promotion of sedition, bomb throwers, and similar activities.[33]

The "Palmer Raids," referring to a series of raids on Communist and other left-wing radical groups by Attorney General Palmer, commenced in November 1919; hundreds of "extremists," including most of the members of the Union of Russian Workers, were arrested. Forty-three of these, along with two hundred "anarchists," were subsequently deported in December 1919 on the ship *Buford* to the newly formed Soviet Russia.[34]

The Palmer Raids provide an example of an antiextremist group with extremist tendencies forming an alliance with government law enforcement in order to promote its own interests. The American Protective League, a superpatriotic group and private intelligence network, which actually functioned in an "advisory" capacity with the government, ushered in an especially troublesome practice. So effective was the league in targeting extremists that in his annual report for 1917 the attorney general noted, "The American Protective League has proven to be invaluable and constitutes a most important auxiliary and reserve force for the Bureau of Investigations. . . ." Similar, although somewhat less effective, groups included the National Security League and the American Defense Society.

Were it not for the fact that one of the bombs had been addressed to him, Palmer might not have responded so harshly. Prior to the bombs he had agreed to disband the APL, having observed that "espionage conducted by private individuals and organizations is entirely at variance with our theories of government." During the war, strong social pressures favoring unquestioning loyalty had been generated by organizations encouraging right-wing "superpatriots and self-styled spy-chasers [who spread] rabid propaganda which maximized the dangers of wartime sabotage and sedition," wrote Robert Murray in *Red Scare*.[35]

Coinciding with this period of leftist activity, the right-wing camp was also abuzz. Ralph Easley, who could be called the spiritual father of twentieth century right-wing extremists,

> persistently invented fantastic conspiracies and imminent bloody revolutions. . . In the late spring of 1919, Easley ran a series of startling exposes on communism in the schools, press, churches, universities, and organized labor, and subsequently led a movement to scrutinize textbooks . . . for breaches of loyalty.[36]

Groups ranging from those already mentioned to the larger and more respectable American Legion, a veteran's organization founded in 1919, engaged in this practice. The American Legion's membership consisted largely of World War I veterans and probably came close to representing a reasonable cross-section of the American public, including a certain percentage of extremists who, as extremists are wont to do, rose to positions of influence. Although not nearly as militant as other groups, the legion promoted a kind of conservatism and jingoistic superpatriotism, including an active antiextremist program aimed at what they considered radicals and subversives. Yet another group, the Daughters of the American Revolution, originally organized along hereditary and genealogical lines, was active in antiextremist work as well. Of course, the practice of screening textbooks and policing institutions for ideological orthodoxy is hardly unique to Ralph Easley—or even to the right wing, for that matter. Virtually all extremist groups engage in this kind of policing, and have for many years.

(To put this issue in perspective, it's worth noting that at the present time there are at least two hundred organizations, both left and right, who regularly police and attempt to censor textbooks, movies, and other media for "offensive" material and views that are "insensitive" to their prejudices. These include ethnic, religious, and racial groups of all types, as well as feminist, homosexual, and environmental organizations. Christian fundamentalist groups are especially active in policing books, movies, and other media for what they consider anti-Christian and immoral material.)

In 1905 the Ku Klux Klan was popularized anew in Thomas W. Dixon's book *The Clansman.* D. W. Griffith's cinematic adaptation, *Birth of a Nation,* made in 1915, increased interest in the organization. It was then that Tom Watson's dream was realized, and a new Ku Klux Klan was founded in Atlanta. Its creator was William J. Simmons, a former circuit-riding minister and veteran of the Spanish-American War. Simmons's father had been an officer in the Ku Klux Klan of the post-Civil War era.

By 1920 the new Klan had several thousand members plus chapters in Atlanta, Birmingham, Mobile, and Montgomery, Alabama. Part of this new extremist organization's effort was "antiextremist" work in reporting on leftists of varying kinds. Simmons submitted reports on "untrustworthy" individuals to the Citizens Bureau of Investigation and actively worked against the influence of "the Hun." It was during this period of endeavor against extremists that Simmons changed his organization from a relatively open and public order to a secret society.[37]

The early history of the new Klan involves a study in the kind of squabbling, rivalries, personality conflicts, and ego trips that have become characteristic of nativist right-wing movements. By utilizing the talents of two natural promoters, Edward Clarke and Elizabeth Tyler, whom Simmons had met in the summer of 1920, the Klan flourished; within fifteen months it had reached 100,000 members. Tyler subsequently resigned from the order following a scandal involving sexual improprieties with Clarke, who was married. Various prominent Klansmen demanded that Simmons dismiss Clarke, but this suggestion was rejected amid a flurry of unfavorable publicity. A "palace revolt" ensued and Simmons was persuaded to step aside in favor of Hiram Wesley Evans, an outgoing dentist from Texas. Simmons, who had been given the powerless position of Klan "Emperor," began rebelling, and before long, defamatory charges and counter-charges filled the pages of Klan papers. Simmons accused Evans of misappropriating Klan funds. Simmons was labeled a "pirate" and "traitor to the cause." After receiving a severance payment of $146,500 Simmons allowed himself to be expelled from the Klan. Edward Clarke, who faced criminal charges for violating the Mann Act (transporting a female across a state line for immoral purposes) and carrying whiskey in his suitcase, was eventually expelled as well.[38]

Under Evans, the Ku Klux Klan took on something of the program of the Know Nothings and the American Protective Association, adding its own innovations on nativist and racist themes. Klan publications included *The Firey Cross, The Courier,* and *The Imperial Hawk,* titles still used in the 1990s by the minuscule Klan groups that still exist. The organization targeted Roman Catholics, Jews, and aliens, with a peculiar emphasis on Catholics. Of particular interest, however, was the terror campaign conducted against blacks, probably unparalleled in American history.

As with most nativist movements, Klan appeal was explicitly antielitist. In a moment of remarkable candor, Klan leader Evans noted:

We are a movement of the slain people, very weak in the matter of culture, intellectual support, and trained leadership. We demand a return of power into the hands of the everyday, not highly cultured, not overly intellectualized but entirely unspoiled and not de-Americanized average citizens of the old stock.[39]

The actual size of the 1920s Ku Klux Klan is uncertain, but estimates range from 1.5 million to 6 million members. Unfortunately, the organization left no national records and only partial local records exist. Sensational organizations tend to make sensational claims and have such claims made about them, so the more conservative figures are probably nearer the mark. In some parts of the country, Klan influence was considerable and in others it was virtually nonexistent. A great many accounts exist of Klan influence in various states, particularly throughout the South and in Michigan, Indiana, and Illinois. Even Kansas had a very active Klan which controlled several city governments. One thing is certain: after the national office was moved to Washington in 1925, its popularity plummeted, although not for that reason. The Indiana Grand Dragon, David C. Stephenson, then thirty-five years old, had achieved prominence rivaling that of Evans himself and when he was charged in a particularly sordid crime of rape and murder against one Madge Oberholtzer, it devastated the entire movement. Membership dropped dramatically and by 1928 the Klan was a mere shadow of its former self. By 1944 federal tax collectors forced the formal disbanding of the order.[40]

The 1920s Klan was the largest twentieth-century extremist group, and probably the most intolerant and violence-prone overall. As usual, only a very small percentage of members were involved in illegal activities, and the group was active for a relatively short period of time.

*    *    *

The depression that struck the United States in 1929 was the impetus for a number of extremist groups to broaden their base and organize. Whether it was disillusionment with conditions that developed during those stark years or the awakening of some predisposition toward extremism, many Americans drifted into the ranks of the Communist party, including a number of intellectuals. Communist theory and jargon invoked utopian images and promised solutions to what seemed at the time to be overwhelming problems. The phrase "Marxism, the opiate of the intellectuals" was coined by critics.

A number of extreme-right groups flourished briefly, some of which were openly fascist and, in some cases, even pro-Nazi. Harsh and hateful criticism of Jews was commonplace along with scapegoating and occasional acts of violence. By the late 1930s groups like the American Destiny Party, Paul Revere Sentinels, the Gray Shirts, the Citizens Protective League, and American Women Against Communism had appeared. Most were small and transient, never having more than a few thousand members and disappearing after World War II began. Others, like the America First committee supported by aviation hero Charles Lindbergh,

Car belonging to H. H. Darks, great-uncle of one of the authors, in Wetumka, Oklahoma, 1925. Bullet holes were made by a Ku Klux police chief who was brought in from Texas by a Klan-dominated city council and given instructions to kill Darks and two others with him. One man was indeed killed, another wounded. Darks escaped unscathed but badly shaken; one friend's partially blown-off head ended up in his lap. All this occurred in broad daylight. Darks was targeted because he had spoken out forcefully against the Klan and also because "they say I'm too friendly with the colored." The Klan didn't bother Darks after this episode due to what could only be construed as threats against Klansmen by his brother "Chancy" (Chauncey actually) who was armed, fearless, and reputed to be a man who would do "just about anything."

and Father Charles Coughlin's organization, the Christian Front, attracted large, sympathetic followings, although they, too, quickly faded by World War II.

One of the more colorful, if objectively minor, figures of the Depression-era right wing was Court Asher. Author of a poem entitled *The Jew-Nited Nations Red Rag,* Asher was a crude Jew-hater. He believed that Jews were trying to steal back copies of his publication *The X-Ray,* which was published in Muncie, Indiana. The November 1, 1941, issue had attacked democracy with zeal:

> The word "democracy" is the weapon of scoundrels and the refuge of fools. Every political pap-sucker seeking public office takes it to this breast—every war monger and public liar uses it to deceive the unwary.

Compare this to John Birch Society founder Robert Welch's 1959 statement that "Democracy is the weapon of demagoguery and perennial fraud" (*The Blue Book,* 159). Asher was obsessed with Jewish power and influence as he saw it. Before his death in 1967, one of his last pronouncements was that the Mayo Clinic, where he had been treated, had become "Jew dominated."

Another rightist who began his career in the Depression era was Merwin K. Hart. A John Birch Society chapter leader until his death in 1962, Hart headed the National Economic Council in the 1940s and 1950s, a group branded as anti-Semitic by the Anti-Defamation League. Among other things, Hart was a defender of Spanish dictator Francisco Franco and was characterized by U.S. Supreme Court Justice Robert Jackson as "pro-fascist."

A notable far-right movement of the Depression era was the Black Legion, headed by Virgil Effinger who, along with other legionnaires, had been a Klansman in the 1920s. Founded in Ohio in 1931, the legion's base of support was in the Detroit area; by 1936 some 40,000 members rived in that locality. Having exchanged their former white robes for black ones to demonstrate their break from the Ku Klux Klan, Black Legionnaires took an oath that they would support God, the U.S. Constitution, and their organization. The legion claimed that they were in a holy war against aliens, blacks, Communists, Catholics, and Jews. Strongly opposed to trade unions, although some of their members belonged to them, the Legion looked with favor upon European fascist organizations.[41]

The German-American Bund, formed in Chicago in 1930 as "Friends of the New Germany," was comprised primarily of ethnic Germans who identified with the National Socialist movement, although some non-German rightists were members as well. Fritz Kuhn, who assumed leadership of the Bund in 1936, was a German army veteran of World War I and a Nazi party member since the 1920s. Membership peaked at about 20,000 with 40 percent of its members residing in New York City. FBI penetration of the Bund was so thorough that when Germany declared war against the United States in 1941, the Bund was incapable of rendering any assistance to the Nazis.[42]

Among the far-right books of the period was *The Coming American Fascism* by Lawrence Dennis, one of the few fascist intellectuals born on American soil. Among the more active native fascist organizations were the Black Legion, Silver

Shirts, Defenders of the Christian Faith, and the Christian Front. An early associate of Hart and Dennis was Harold Lord Varney, who later wrote for the John Birch Society magazine *American Opinion.* Varney and Dennis edited a far-right magazine, *The Awakener,* whose executive editor, Joseph P. Kamp, "urged 'patriots' to withhold information 'regarding Communist activities' from the FBI and submit it, instead, either to Martin Dies or to him"—yet another example of an extremist organization attempting to take on investigative and law-enforcement-type functions.[43]

We tend to assume that most of the great legal victories for civil liberties and freedom of the press have involved socialists, communists, anarchists, or free-love advocates. This was often the case, but occasionally extreme rightists were involved in important cases as well. In 1927 the publisher of *Rip-Saw,* Jay M. Near, whose muckraking newspaper indulged his anti-Semitic, antiblack, anti-Catholic, and antilabor prejudices, was put out of business by a Minnesota gag law not dissimilar in kind to the regulations that have appeared on college campuses in recent years. This law allowed a single judge to bar publication of any newspaper found "malicious, scandalous, or defamatory," setting a dangerous precedent for prior restraint and curtailment of freedom of the press. Near's case was eventually taken up by Colonel Robert McCormick, the powerful publisher of the *Chicago Tribune,* who paid for the appeal to the U.S. Supreme Court. In 1931 *Near v. Minnesota* was decided 5 to 4 in Near's favor—a decision that bears directly on freedom of the press today.[44]

\*　　\*　　\*

Other Depression-era extreme rightists are of note because of the amount of influence and popularity they achieved. Three of these were ultimately defendants in the Great Sedition Trial of 1944 (*U.S.* v. *McWilliams*): William Dudley Pelley, head of the Nazi Silver Shirt Legion; Elizabeth Dilling, a leader of the isolationist "mother's movement" and author of books attacking Jewish beliefs and influence (both real and imagined); and Gerald B. Winrod, founder of Defenders of the Christian Faith.[45] Also important were Father Charles Coughlin, the "radio priest" of Royal Oaks, Michigan, and Gerald L. K. Smith, consort of Louisiana Governor Huey Long and founder of Christian Nationalist Crusade.

William Dudley Pelley, born in 1890, son of a Methodist minister, had a lifelong preoccupation with religious and metaphysical themes. He was a reporter for the *Springfield Homestead* and the *Boston Globe.* His visit to the newly formed Soviet Union in 1918 was an experience that led to his strong anti-Communism. He worked as a Hollywood writer during the 1920s, and in 1928 had a profound mystical experience that accounted for his ultimate conversion to fascism. After publishing an occult journal for two years, in 1933 Pelley founded the Silver Shirt Legion, better known as the Silver Shirts. In 1936 he was a presidential candidate on the Christian Party of America ticket and received 1,600 votes. With a peak membership of 15,000, the organization folded in 1940 after having perturbed fascist-watchers for seven years.[46]

Pelley's heresy was not to be forgiven, however. In April 1942, he was arrested for subversion during the World War II antifascist "Brown Scare," convicted, and sentenced to fifteen years imprisonment. Pelley was also indicted in the Great Sedition Trial of 1944, which ended in a mistrial. He was released from prison in 1950 and returned to Indiana to pursue his metaphysical interests. He died in Noblesville, Indiana, in 1965, survived by his daughter, Adelle Pelley Pearson, who was still selling his "soulcraft" metaphysical tapes and writings through the mail in the 1990s.[47]

Elizabeth Kirkpatrick Dilling was born in 1894 and attended the University of Chicago. Like Pelley, she visited the Soviet Union in 1919, with somewhat the same results. A fanatic anti-Communist and Jew-hater, in 1932 she founded the Chicago-based Paul Reveres, whose purpose was to ferret out subversives and promote "Americanism." In 1934 she published *The Red Network: A Who's Who of Radicals*, which listed some 500 organizations and 1,300 individuals Dilling considered unsavory, including H. L. Mencken and Eleanor Roosevelt. In 1936 she published *The Roosevelt Red Record and Its Background*, in which she castigated F.D.R.

Dilling was characterized by friends and foes alike as a strident zealot, a true believer, and an articulate propagandist. Her anti-Jewish sentiments were evident in many of her writings, not the least of which was her book *The Plot Against Christianity*, which reprinted large sections of the Talmud along with conspiratorial and alarmist commentary on the Jewish "menace." Although Dilling's influence was greater than Pelley's, it rapidly faded as World War II got underway and support for domestic fascism evaporated. Dilling was arrested in 1941 during a demonstration against the lend-lease program, which transferred large amounts of military goods to England, and fined fifteen dollars. In 1944 she was one of the primary defendants in the Great Sedition Trial.

After the war Dilling resumed her stridency and continued her work in the small *Patriotic Research Bulletin* and in Mrs. Lyrl Clark Van Hyning's group, We the Mothers Mobilize for America. Van Hyning was the principle source of the charge that postal zip codes are part of an international Jewish plot to code the nation for final takeover. Instead of a zip code, her return address always featured "No!!!" Dilling refused to endorse General Douglas MacArthur's presidential hopes in 1952, much to his relief, because of his alleged Jewish ancestry. She died in Lincoln, Nebraska, in 1966. Her son, Kirkpatrick Dilling, a Chicago attorney, occasionally represents far-right clients such as the Liberty Lobby.[48]

Gerald Burton Winrod was born in Wichita, Kansas, in 1900. His father was a Christian evangelist. At the age of twenty-five he established his lifelong organization, Defenders of the Christian Faith, and began publishing his monthly journal, *The Defender*. The original orientation of the group was simple "back to the Bible" Christianity, and by 1936 his journal had a circulation of 100,000 or approximately one reader per 1,300 Americans. Winrod claimed to have prophetic powers, and he saw the rise of fascism and Communism as two heads of the same beast.

In the early 1930s Winrod adopted a belief in a Jewish world conspiracy and began promoting the notorious anti-Semitic fabrication, the *Protocols of the Learned Elders of Zion,* which he called an accurate representation of Jewish plans. In 1938 he was a candidate for U.S. senator from Kansas on the Republican ticket and managed to garner 22 percent of the vote, coming in third. Staunchly opposed to American involvement in World War II, he was a major defendant in the 1944 Great Sedition Trial for allegedly conspiring to cause insubordination in the armed forces. His case ended in a mistrial. Returning to Wichita, he appealed to dwindling numbers of supporters and dabbled in crackpot medical theories. Winrod died there in 1957, but his organization continued well into the 1970s, eventually becoming little more than a mail-order ministry.[49]

Gerald Winrod's son, Gordon, a former Lutheran minister, still follows in his father's footsteps through his anti-Semitic publication, *The Winrod Letter.* His radio program, "The Winrod Hour," was banned from several stations following protests by the Anti-Defamation League. In the early 1960s he was National Chaplain of the neo-Nazi National States Rights party for six months. He is currently minister at Our Savior's Church in Gainesville, Missouri.[50] Gordon's son, David Winrod, has followed in the family footsteps. In May 1991 he was embroiled in a controversy in Alaska, where he was attempting to establish a branch of his father's church. Lurid newspaper reports told of anti-Semitic literature appearing in Ketchikan mailboxes and alleged neo-Nazi and paramilitary goings-on in the nearby woods.[51]

\* \* \*

The Great Sedition Trial of 1944 (*U.S.* v. *McWilliams*), alluded to previously, deserves some amplification. It was significant in a number of ways, aside from the fact that it ended in a mistrial when the judge died before it was completed. Although directed at extremists of the far fight, it was this case that established the political precedent for the postwar persecution of unpopular dissidents of the far left, including the Smith Act prosecutions of American Communists during the 1950s.

On July 21, 1942, a U.S. grand jury charged twenty-eight individuals with conspiring to bring about insubordination in the armed forces as part of a Nazi plot. This indictment, originally known as *United States* v. *Winrod,* marked the beginning of the "Brown Scare" prosecutions. By the time the case came to trial on April 17, 1944, it was known as *United States* v. *McWilliams* and embraced thirty defendants, including Gerald Winrod, William Dudley Pelley, Joseph E. McWilliams, George E. Deatherage, Robert E. Edmondson, Elizabeth Dilling, Colonel Eugene Nelson Sanctuary, Lawrence Dennis, and George Sylvester Viereck, among others. Pelley and Viereck were already serving sentences for previous convictions. Two individuals readily identified with the far right conspicuously absent from the indictment were Father Charles E. Coughlin and Gerald L. K. Smith.

A fascinating and detailed account of the trial and the Brown Scare is found in Leo P. Ribuffo's *The Old Christian Right: The Protestant Far Right From the Depression to the Cold War.* In particular, Ribuffo deals extensively with the civil liberties implications of the trial, including the responses from the civil liberties commmunity.

The basic thrust of the prosecution's argument was that the defendants were engaged in propaganda and other activities in the furtherance of a worldwide Nazi conspiracy. The government used the obvious and strident anti-Semitism of most of the defendants as evidence of Nazi connections, and insisted that communications among the defendants indicated a criminal conspiracy of sorts. According to Lawrence Dennis, one of the defendants, and Maximillian St. George, one of their attorneys:

> What the people behind the trial wanted to have judicially certified to the world was that anti-Semitism is a Nazi idea and that anyone holding this idea is a Nazi who is thereby violating the law—in this instance by causing insubordination in the armed forces—through his belief in or advocacy of this idea.[52]

No overt act of sabotage was alleged against any defendant, only the promotion of values, opinions, and beliefs. With some exceptions, the reaction of civil libertarians was ambivalent. According to Ribuffo:

> The sedition indictment divided prominent civil libertarians. Zechariah Chafee, Jr., the premier authority on freedom of speech, called them "indefensible." Roger N. Baldwin, executive director of the ACLU, considered the case "monstrous," and ACLU General Counsel Arthur Garfield Hayes drafted a protest against this "sort of attack on free speech, once removed." On the other side, ACLU General Counsel Morris L. Ernst, who had persistently urged President Roosevelt to take action against the far right, refused to sign Hayes's statement. After months of wavering, the ACLU decided in early 1943 to stand aside, a majority of directors believing that the accused "were cooperating or acting on behalf of the enemy."[53]

In addition, Socialist party leader Norman Thomas and the leadership of the Socialist Workers party (which had also been prosecuted under the Smith Act), spoke out against the government's case. The remainder of the American left for the most part rejoiced in the prosecutions, particularly the Communist party and its various front groups, refusing to realize that prosecution of one type of dissident represents a danger to all dissidents.

After the case ended in a mistrial following the death of the judge, Chief Justice Edward C. Eicher of the United States District Court for the District of Columbia, it lingered in the courts until 1947. On June 12, 1947, the U.S. Supreme Court ruled in favor of the defendant in a similar case, *United States* v. *Keegan.* Realizing that a sedition case would be reversed on appeal, the government dropped the matter, thus ending a sorry chapter in American legal history.

*    *    *

Father Charles Coughlin was born into a devout Canadian Roman Catholic family in 1891 and entered the seminary as a young man. In 1926 he was assigned to the parish in Royal Oak, Michigan, where he began his broadcasting career over station WJR, Detroit, direct from his office at the Shrine of the Little Flower. A cross had been burned on the lawn there by the Ku Klux Klan, presumably as a protest against Roman Catholicism. Coughlin began his radio career with an essentially unremarkable religious message. By 1930, early in the Great Depression, his resounding voice began delivering an explicitly political message, replete with the moralizing and righteousness so common to extremists of all kinds. Eventually he reached an audience of some forty million listeners.

Coughlin's early messages contained primarily leftist social welfare-religious themes, as exemplified by the idea that government should protect the workers against exploitation. In 1931 he attacked the international bankers for taking advantage of the Versailles Treaty to profit themselves. Coughlin supported Franklin D. Roosevelt's 1932 presidential bid and in 1933 he began promoting various New Deal programs, with great enthusiasm, in a manner that suggested a strident anticapitalist populism. Even his later pronouncements sounded collectivist, although increasingly anti-Jewish. In fact, Coughlin's self-made ideology was a curious blend of the far-left and far-right beliefs of the day, embracing anti-elitist elements of both.

In 1934 he founded the National Union for Social Justice, which embraced a kind of populism, and proceeded to denounce the New Deal for its allegedly communist tendencies and for serving the interests of the rich while the poor suffered. He supported various monetary schemes, promoted silver coinage, and opposed the League of Nations and the World Court. In 1936 he began his weekly newspaper, *Social Justice,* which at one point published extracts from the anti-Semitic *Protocols.* Coughlin supported Congressman William Lemke of North Dakota and his Union Party, along with Dr. Francis Townsend of "Townsend Plan" old age insurance fame, and also formed an alliance with Gerald L. K. Smith, one of the most notorious Jew-baiters of the twentieth century. In one of his famous radio broadcasts Coughlin had to say:

> Thus . . . America, instead of rescuing from the hands of the international bankers the right to coin and regulate the value of money, instead of limiting the accumulation of wealth by the favored law, instead of bending her efforts to rescue the impoverished farmer, instead of guaranteeing a just and living wage to every laborer who is willing to contribute his honest work—America is ready to join hands with the Rothchilds and Lazerre Freres, with the Warburgs and Morgans and Kuhn-Loebs to keep the world safe for the inevitable slaughter.[54]

Coughlin supported Lemke's Union party presidential candidacy in 1936 and promised to quit broadcasting if he did not receive at least nine million votes. Lemke received less than 10 percent of that and Coughlin kept his promise—but only for two months; in January 1937 he resumed broadcasting. He had dissolved the National Union the month before. As time went on. Coughlin became more and more strident and began openly supporting an Italian-style fascist system for the United States. In July 1938 he formed the Christian Front organization.[55]

Coughlin was eventually suppressed by the U.S. Post Office, which, in an act of dubious constitutionality, banned *Social Justice* from the mails (alleging that it was in violation of the Espionage Act of 1942). Coughlin's archbishop also ordered him to stop all "public pronouncements." The U.S. attorney general had warned that Coughlin would face federal indictment for sedition. Coughlin dutifully returned to full-time priesthood and retired in 1966. He died in 1979 in Bloomfield Hills, Michigan, having been virtually silenced for thirty-seven years.[56]

Gerald L. K. Smith is widely regarded as the arch-bigot of all anti-Semites and certainly qualifies by any reasonable standard as a florid example of a political extremist. Born in Wisconsin in 1898, Smith was the son of a preacher. He attended college and received a degree in oratory from Valparaiso University. He became a minister in an evangelical denomination and found himself in charge of the King's Highway Christian Church in Shreveport, Louisiana, at the age of thirty-one. It was then that he met the highly controversial populist governor of Louisiana, Huey P. Long, and became an administrator of Long's "Share Our Wealth" clubs.[57]

Smith's oratorical skills were legend. H. L. Mencken called him "the gutsiest and goriest, the loudest and lustiest, the deadliest and damnedest orator" he had ever heard. In 1934 he joined William Dudley Pelley's Silver Shirt Legion, but later rejected it as too extreme even for him. After Long was assassinated in 1935, Smith worked for the Old Age Revolving Pension Plan of Dr. Francis Townsend. From there he joined William Lemke, Rev. Charles Coughlin, and Townsend in promoting Lemke's ill-fated Union party presidential campaign that same year. In 1937 he founded the "Committee of One Million," whose goals included the destruction of Communism and the promotion of a white, Christian nation. The committee, which briefly caused the usual panic in anti-fascist circles, met the fate of virtually all groups of this type and folded shortly after it was formed. Smith then worked with Gerald Winrod for a time before moving on to Detroit to establish the Federation of Americanization, but this organization collapsed, too, and Smith moved on to work with other extremist leaders, becoming more stridently racist and anti-Jewish as time passed.

In 1942 Smith began publishing *The Cross and the Flag,* a monthly magazine that survived until shortly after his death in 1976, and he ran as an independent for U.S. senator in Michigan, managing to garner 32,000 votes. In 1944 he founded the America First party and became its presidential candidate, gaining ballot status only in Michigan and Texas, receiving a mere 1,530 and 250 votes respectively.

In 1947 Smith established Christian Nationalist Crusade and in 1953 moved his entire operation from St. Louis to Los Angeles, where he continued to upset opponents with *The Cross and the Flag,* which maintained a circulation in the 1960s and 1970s of between 20,000 and 25,000, or approximately one reader per 8,000 Americans. Smith also published a torrent of pamphlets and tracts with such endearing titles as *The Jew Created Communism* and *Jews Strive For World Control.* In the late 1960s Smith attracted media attention with his plans to build a theme park, including a huge statue of Jesus, near Eureka Springs, Arkansas.

Complaints centered on the fact that federal funds would be used to construct roads leading to the location. The completed project features a seven-story "Christ of the Ozarks" statue. After Smith's death in 1976 his magazine continued only briefly. A few of his old pamphlets were being sold out of a Eureka Springs post office box in the early 1990s, but otherwise his life could only be described as a relic, having no perceptible mark on our society.[58]

There are numerous interesting anecdotes regarding Smith, but one of the more revealing has to do with his personal relationships with Jews. Smith was fond of antique sales and moved freely in those circles where he used the alias of Ken Smith. In the Los Angeles area many antique dealers and purchasers are Jewish and Smith conducted himself in such a way as to imply he was Jewish himself, joking and generally having a very congenial time with Jewish people. This is in stark contrast with his pronouncements to followers, to whom he declared, "I'm holding the line with blistered hands against the Jew-Communist conspiracy."

One element of Gerald L. K. Smith's career that remains troublesome was a technique used by opponents to counter his activities, the "quarantine" treatment, whereby an interest group pressures news media to refrain from reporting or giving publicity to a particular individual, organization, or point of view. The Anti-Defamation League led a particularly effective campaign against Smith that remains a model for this questionable practice. According to Glen Jeansonne, this policy was advanced by Rabbi S. R. Fineberg of the American Jewish Committee and eventually adopted by the Anti-Defamation League. While one can rejoice at the defeat of a bigot, one must be vigilantly aware that the tactics used—including manipulation of the news media—are critically important. Means tend to influence ends, and means that we would recognize as unconscionable and unfair if used against ourselves do not lose their character when used against enemies. Uncompromising extremism, and its mirror image, uncompromising anti-extremism, are perilously alike in certain respects. If we fail to realize this, we may only injure ourselves. Double standards have no place in an open society.[59]

*       *       *

There were many other important personalities in the Depression-era right wing, but we restrict ourselves to these and move on to the far left, which achieved its greatest respectability during the mid-forties. (The extreme right was relatively quiescent during World War II.) By the late 1930s the Communist party (CP) had reached a membership of roughly 65,000 and attained a fairly wide following among intellectuals on college campuses and in various sectors of the country, particularly large urban areas like New York and Chicago. The Spanish Civil War became a Communist party cause célèbre: most of the members of the Abraham Lincoln Brigade who fought against Franco in Spain had Communist party ties or connections. As the Nazi and fascist enemies of the great socialist experiment (the USSR) began to mobilize, party membership grew even more, and by 1942 it rose to over 80,000, in spite of the defections that had followed the Hitler-Stalin pact.

During World War II, respectability soared and the Communist party influenced Hollywood, labor circles, and the Jewish community, in particular, and American cultural life, in general. By the war's end in 1945, about one-fifth of the membership in the Congress of Industrial Organizations (CIO) was in unions controlled by Communists or pro-Communists. In addition, the Communist party had helped form the Progressive party, which was to support Henry Wallace's presidential candidacy in 1948. Many well-meaning non-Communists lent support to the Progressive party.[60]

Beginning in 1946 the Communist party made several particularly inept tactical moves, which tended to alienate it from the American public and which contributed to its precipitous decline. First, the party maintained strict adherence to the Soviet line on foreign policy; second, the party failed to cultivate and maintain close contact with non-Communists in "popular front" activities after the war; and third, while the American public drifted somewhat to the right ideologically, the Communist party line propelled it further to the left. Communist influence in American labor unions was fading. By the spring of 1950 Communist influence in the CIO was all but eliminated. Other factors that helped to decimate Communist influence were United States participation in the Korean War, the arrest and prosecution of several Soviet spies, and general government persecution of domestic Communists and their organizations. With respect to this last item, there were two particular institutions that deserve some special attention: the House Committee on Un-American Activities and Senator Joseph R. McCarthy.[61]

The House Un-American Activities Committee (popularly known as HUAC), a standing committee of the House of Representatives, had actually been around for several years in one form or another busily fighting "extremism." The first chairman and guiding spirit of the committee was Martin Dies, a Democratic congressman from Texas who acquired his position in 1938. The committee became permanent in 1946 and was mandated to investigate "subversive and un-American propaganda activities." It had the power to issue subpoenas and to enforce its rules with criminal sanctions. From the late 1940s until its demise in 1975, the committee, under various chairmen, paraded hundreds of communists, suspected communists, radicals, nonconformists, and even a few Ku Klux Klansmen through its hearings. It produced almost no legislation. The sole purpose of the hearings was a kind of ritual defamation. Thousands upon thousands of pages of testimony produced some interesting reading, but little of substantive value otherwise. On the other hand, it cost scores of people their jobs, reputations, and in some cases their families and even their lives.[62]

Of particular interest to HUAC was the Los Angeles area and the role of "extremists" and "subversives" in the movie industry. In 1947 the committee, with the cooperation of the FBI, began a veritable witch hunt in Hollywood that culminated in the prosecution of the "Hollywood Ten," a group of mostly Communist writers and directors who refused to answer HUAC questions on First Amendment grounds. When the U.S. Supreme Court refused to reverse their convictions they were sentenced to prison, careers in shambles. According to the *Encyclopedia of the American Left:*

Between 1936 and 1946, approximately 300 movie studio employees joined the Communist Party (about 1 percent of the work force). They joined for various reasons and stayed for varying lengths of time. Screenwriters predominated (146); there were 60 actors, 20 directors and producers, and somewhere between 50 and 100 backlot, sound stage, or front-office workers.[63]

A "blacklist" emerged in the movie industry that effectively denied employment to anyone else who had run afoul of the committee or private anti-Communist screening and investigation groups, such as Aware, Inc., and American Business Consultants. This last group published the book *Red Channels,* which listed some 151 actors, producers, and so on, along with appropriate damaging citations. Listees included Edward G. Robinson, Jose Ferrer, Gypsy Rose Lee, and Lee J. Cobb. The American Civil Liberties Union estimates that by 1952 the Hollywood blacklist had extended to about 250 people. The *New York Times* later calculated the figure at 1,500.[64]

The privatization of the antiextremist "loyalty-security" program was particulalry distressing and remains so today. Although the type of target has changed, the basic defamation and blacklisting tactics remain the same. The concept of "politically correct" is not new by any means. The case of John Henry Faulk demonstrates the damage that private vigilante-type groups can inflict.[65]

Faulk was an outspoken soft-core leftist but certainly no Communist party member nor fellow traveler. He had been a strong supporter of FDR and the New Deal, worked for liberal causes, and had a widely followed commentary program over WCBS radio in New York. A member of the American Federation of Television and Radio Artists, he had opposed the pro-Aware faction within the AFTRA on civil liberties grounds. For this he was branded as having "a significant Communist record," and in August 1957 he was fired by WCBS. He soon discovered that he was effectively black-balled from employment in the entertainment industry. Faulk hired Louis Nizer, an eminently successful attorney, and sued Aware, Vincent Hartnett, and Laurence Johnson, blacklisters who had pressured Faulk's sponsors to withdraw. The case finally came to trial in April 1962 and Faulk was eventually awarded $550,000 in damages, an event which brought about the end of blacklisting.[66]

The House Un-American Activities Committee continued its campaign against extremists of the left, and occasionally of the right, into the 1970s. Its name was changed to the House Committee on Internal Security in 1969, and in 1975 it was abolished. The Committee's files on some 750,000 suspected "subversives" are sealed away in the National Archives, a relic (we hope) of the bygone past.

*     *     *

One issue that has come up again and again with respect to the Communist Party USA is whether or not it is a bona fide American organization or an arm of the "international Communist conspiracy," as many rightists term it. Most writers have deemed it an American organization but one that has been a strong supporter of the Soviet Union and which models itself after other Communist parties in western countries, such as England. It is usually denied that the Communist Party USA has been financed by the Soviet Union and that charge has been relegated to the status of a "right-wing canard" and an expression of anti-Communist paranoia.

The truth of the matter, however, represents one of those few cases where rightist suspicions may well have been correct. The evidence for this is revealed in David J. Garrow's *The FBI and Martin Luther King,* where he discusses the work of Morris and Jack Childs, brothers and veteran Communist party members who worked as financial couriers for the party and as undercover operatives for the FBI. Morris Childs, who had been treated badly in an inner-party squabble in 1947 when he was removed as editor of the *Daily Worker,* had become embittered by the experience. When the brothers were visited by the FBI in 1952, they agreed to become informants.[67]

"Solo," the code name for the Childs's project, was, over the next twenty-five years, to become the FBI's most successful undercover operation in the Communist Party USA. Not only did Morris Childs take part in the secret transfer of an annual one million dollars from the Soviet Union to the CPUSA, but he was privy to most of the goings-on within party inner circles. Morris Childs met with Boris Pomarev, a high Soviet official, and other Soviet party leaders, and traveled widely on behalf of party business. Jack Childs followed domestic party affairs closely and reported on developments. The Childs brothers kept the FBI fully informed on daily party activities. The FBI operation was finally terminated in the late 1970s when the brothers' health had deteriorated so badly that they could no longer continue their work as informants.

"Solo" aside, the role of the Federal Bureau of Investigation in suppressing political dissent has been the subject of numerous books, so we won't devote much space to it here. It's important to understand that suppression of political extremism is impossible without law enforcement involvement at some level—and this was the role the FBI provided. It was estimated that at one time the FBI was the largest single financial contributor to the Communist Party USA—in the form of its dues-paying informants. In the case of "Solo," the FBI chose to refrain from interceding in the illegal transfer of money to the CPUSA, in effect allowing it to be funded. Garrow explains the FBI's reasoning:

> The Soviet subsidy, most bureau officials felt, made the American CP relatively lazy and content, and less of a domestic threat than if it had to support itself rather than merely "launder" the Soviet funds that Jack Childs administered.[68]

The FBI role in attempting to suppress antiwar sentiment in the 1960s is still coming to light, as more and more individuals acquire their FBI files under the Freedom of Information Act. On the other hand, an account of the Indiana Ku Klux Klan in the 1960s reveals that virtually *all* of its officers were informants for the FBI or other police agencies. Other extreme right-wing groups have experienced the same kind of harassment. Surveillance of far-left groups has been greatly reduced.[69]

The FBI's COINTELPRO (Counter-Intelligence Program), initiated against domestic extremist movements, mainly during the 1960s, has been well-documented in numerous books on the bureau, as well as in dozens of tracts published by the target organizations themselves. According to Phillip Finch, author of *God, Guts, and Guns: A Close Look at the Radical Right:*

> "Counterintelligence" is a tepid term, actually, for a variety of tactics to harass, disrupt, confuse and impede the Bureau's targets. Acts against left-wing groups—principally the Communist Party USA and the Socialist Workers Party—comprised roughly 85 percent of COINTELPRO, according to FBI statistics. . . . The remaining 15 percent, against what the FBI termed "white hate groups," have received less attention.[70]

Finch offers a brief review of COINTELPRO as it was used against the radical right in order to help explain some of the movement's wholesale paranoia:

> Beginning in 1964, FBI headquarters or field offices proposed 404 different programs of action against 17 (Ku Klux) Klan groups and 9 white racist groups then under investigation by the bureau. Of the 404 proposals, 289 were actually approved and used. Many were legal—like a series of interview programs to show Klan members that their affiliation was not secret. Some were petty disruptions—like mailing 850 copies of a faked letter, apparently from the national office of the Minutemen, requesting that members of the group withhold their dues and contributions because of a security leak. Some were of questionable legality and of even more questionable morality.[71]

Finch details some of the COINTELPRO activities against the far right, including the setting up of a phony right-wing organization and the publishing of counterfeit far-right periodicals. He notes that a September 2, 1965, letter from the FBI to a White House assistant mentioned

> nearly two thousand of our informants and sources . . . being operated to obtain up-to-date intelligence data concerning racial matters which we disseminate on a continuing basis. . . . Particularly significant has been the high-level penetration we have achieved of Klan organizations. At the present time, there are 14 Klan groups in existence. We have penetrated every one of them through informants and currently are operating informants in top-level positions of leadership in seven of them.[72]

As in the case of the Communist Party USA, the FBI may have been the largest single source of funds for the Ku Klux Klan through its dues-paying informants. Such penetration of the KKK continues to this day. In the early 1980s it was revealed that Bill Wilkinson, Imperial Wizard of the Invisible Empire, Knights of the Ku Klux Klan, had been an FBI informant for years. Other Klan leaders have been similarly suspected.

\*    \*    \*

In 1950 another antiextremist movement emerged, somewhat in alliance with the HUAC and the private blacklisters, although not necessarily the FBI, and it bore the name of its standard-bearer: Senator Joseph R. McCarthy of Wisconsin. McCarthy hated extremists. Not all extremists, mind you, for antiextremists are usually quite selective in whom they trust. Joe McCarthy hated extremists of the left, particularly Communists and fellow travelers. On the other hand, he was quite comfortable with the extremists of the right who rallied around him, for he was on a divine mission to expose "Reds" and do them in. Paradoxically, the legacy of McCarthyism has been just the opposite of what the senator intended. "McCarthyism" has become a slogan to rally the far left against opposition; in the end, McCarthy's ill-advised tactics backfired against him. As the old cliche goes, had McCarthy not existed it would have been necessary to invent him.[73]

The phenomenon of McCarthyism was described by sociologist Talcot Parson in 1955 as "both a movement supported by certain vested interest elements and a popular revolt against the upper classes." Parsons further commented in his essay that this movement

> is best understood as a symptom of the strains attendant on a deep-seated process of change in our society, rather than as a "movement" representing a policy or a set of values for the American people to act on. Its content is overwhelmingly negative, not positive. It advocates "getting rid" of undesirable influences, and has amazingly little to say about what should be done.[74]

Senator McCarthy galvanized the press in Wheeling, West Virginia, on February 9, 1950, when he claimed to have in his possession a list of names of subversives in sensitive governmental positions. The number of names on this (and subsequent) lists changed in later speeches, ranging from a high of 205 subversives to a low of 57. The senator's attacks were not merely confined to lists of unnamed people. Among his illustrious targets were such personages as Professor Phillip Jessup, General George C. Marshall, Senator Millard Tydings, and Anna Rosenberg.[75]

McCarthy accused Jessup (a former United Nations ambassador) of belonging to a Communist front group called the China Aid Society, an accusation which was wrong on two counts. First, this organization helped Nationalist Chinese orphans, and second, the professor himself had never belonged to the group; rather his wife had joined at the urging of Madame Chiang Kai-shek, wife of the anti-Communist Chinese leader who had wisely fled mainland China to Taiwan in 1949. When these facts were brought to his attention, McCarthy refrained from apologizing and asked why Jessup did not belong to any anti-Communist organizations. (It was precisely this kind of bad judgment that plagued Joe McCarthy from the beginning, much to the delight of his opponents.) For this unsubtle insinuation, McCarthy was called to account. Jessup's American Legion post in Utica, New York, passed a resolution declaring that such "reckless and despicable conduct in this instance cannot be condoned by any right-thinking American."

In the case of Anna Rosenberg, McCarthy found himself on the same side as the anti-Semitic former Jew Benjamin Freedman in an effort to prevent her confirmation as assistant secretary of defense. McCarthy charged that she had been a Communist for many years and was active in the John Reed Clubs. A tedious investigation revealed a different woman with the same name. He eventually wound up voting for her confirmation.[76]

Perhaps McCarthy's most ambitious undertaking was an investigation of the U.S. Army, including close scrutiny of Secretary of the Army Robert Stevens. Unfortunately for McCarthy, the hearings were nationally televised and the senator wound up looking like a bully and a fool. More than any of his other mistakes, this led to his undoing and in late 1954 McCarthy was condemned by his fellow senators.

McCarthy's impact on the Communist party itself was most interesting. While it's probably true that his actions influenced some not to join the party, it is also feasible that his bludgeoning tactics were influential in causing others to become members or fellow travelers. A certain kind of person is attracted to "outlaw" movements in the first place, and in the eyes of some people the party gained status for having withstood McCarthy's attempts to destroy it. His harassment apparently caused much more discomfort for moderates and liberals (and even a few conservatives) than for homegrown Reds. Herbert Philbrick, the FBI informant whose career became the subject of a popular 1950s TV series, *I Led Three Lives,* commented on the senator's impact:

> According to the leaders of the Communist Party, McCarthy has helped them a great deal. The kind of attacks he has made do three things the comrades like: They add greatly to the confusion, putting up a smokescreen for the party and making it more difficult than ever for people to discern just who is a Communist and who is not; they make the party appear a lot stronger than it is; and they do considerable damage to some of the "stupid liberals" whom the party hates.[77]

According to mid-1954 Gallup polls, 14 percent of the general public held a high opinion of Senator McCarthy, while another 20 percent expressed mild or qualified approval. Thus, one-third demonstrated at least qualified endorsement of the senator. It should be remembered, however, that these individuals were largely responding to an image they held of the senator, as is the case of all opinion polls of this type. They may have had no clear idea as to his methods or the reliability of his accusations.

McCarthy's tendency to shoot himself in the foot became legendary, and this was well-illustrated during the mid-1953 testimony before his committee of James Wechsler, political columnist and editorial page editor of the *New York Post.* Wechsler had joined the Young Communist League (YCL) while at Columbia, but had resigned at the age of twenty-two in 1937 and in ensuing years had become a mainstay of the anti-Communist left. Much of what follows consists of quotes and paraphrases from Wechsler's book *The Age of Suspicion.*[78]

Wechsler wrote that he thought he had been prepared for anything, but

McCarthy surprised him with his audacity and he had to resist the competing emotions of anger and hopelessness. Wechsler read into the record an attack on him by the National Committee of the Communist Party and commented that he considered it a tribute and was rather fond of it. But McCarthy stunned him:

> McCarthy: Did you have anything to do with the passage of that resolution?
> Wechsler: Is that a serious question?
> McCarthy to stenographer: Will you read the question to the witness?
> Wechsler: Sir. I have not been in any way affiliated with the Communist movement since 1937. . . . That resolution was adopted by the Communist Party as a tribute to the militant and vigorous anti-Communism of the *New York Post* which has, in my judgment, been more effective in leading people away from Communism, Senator, than those who prefer to identify liberalism with Communism.
> McCarthy: Will you now answer the question?
> Wechsler: The answer is no, Senator.
> McCarthy: The answer is no. Do you know whether anyone on your staff took part in promoting that resolution?
> Wechsler: Senator, to the best of my knowledge, no one on my staff is a member of the Central Committee of the Communist Party or identified with it in any way.
> McCarthy: Now will you answer the question?
> Wechsler: I have answered it as best I can.
> McCarthy: You have said that you didn't think anyone on your staff was a part of the committee. That was not the question. Read the question to the witness.
>
> . . . . . . . . . . . . . . . . .
>
> Wechsler: I do not know that anyone on my staff took any part in promoting the passage of that resolution.

Wechsler commented on the preceding by saying that McCarthy had astounded him.

> Thus, within ten minutes after the hearing had begun, I found myself in the preposterous position of denying under oath that I had inspired the long series of Communist attacks against me, climaxed by the denunciation of the Central Committee.
>     With that single stroke of what Philip Graham, publisher of the *Washington Post,* later described as "brute brilliance," McCarthy had virtually ruled out the whole structure of evidence which I had wide-eyedly assumed would resolve the issue once and for all. Here indeed was a daring new concept in which the existence of evidence of innocence becomes the damning proof of guilt. This is the way it must feel to be committed to a madhouse through some medical mistake; everything is turned upside down. What had heretofore constituted elementary reasonableness is viewed by everyone else as a quaint eccentricity; the most absurd remark becomes the commonplace.

Wechsler had further comments on the foregoing:

> There it was again, and not for the last time; and each time he said it I had a feeling of rage tinged with futility . . . but how could one break through the ring

of fantasy that McCarthy was constructing? If each exhibit of my anti-Communism were merely additional evidence that I had led a truly gigantic political double life, what remained to be said that had any meaning?

Occasionally I glanced at (ex-Communist McCarthy staff member Howard) Rushmore, who never turned my gaze; he . . . knew the magnitude of the fraud and was perfectly willing to be an accomplice to it. . . . He reminded me of a Communist enjoying what he knows is a demonstration trial of an alleged Trotskyist accused of being a fascist agent.

There were moments during the interrogation when I thought of the Moscow trials, and what it must have been like to be a defendant. Suppose Joe McCarthy were dictator and I had been trying to undermine his tyranny, and now he had brought me in and accused me of all sorts of heinous and implausible crimes in addition to the single offense of being against him. If there were no way of communicating the truth to the contrary, might not a man 'confess' to the most wicked absurdities and the most fanciful charges in the hope that people would detect the burlesque?

McCarthy's conspiratorial bent was evident in many of the questions he asked Wechsler.

McCarthy: Mr. Wechsler, let me ask you this. If you or I were a member of the Communist Party and we wanted to advance the Communist cause, perhaps the most effective way of doing that would be to claim that we deserted the party and, if we got in control of the paper, use that paper to attack and smear anybody who actually was fighting Communism. Now, without saying whether you have done it, you would agree that would be a good tactic, would you now?

Wechsler's rejoinder was that he strongly doubted that this was part of Communist strategy and raised an interrogative regarding Howard Rushmore's position as a McCarthy committee staff member. Did this prove the Reds had "infiltrated the McCarthy operation"? When Senator Henry Jackson expressed surprise at the presence of an ex-Communist on the staff, McCarthy quickly explained that Rushmore had truly reformed because he had, on many occasions, voluntarily testified before congressional committees. There was more:

Wechsler: Senator, let's face it. You are saying that an ex-Communist who is for McCarthy is a good one and an ex-Communist who is against McCarthy is suspect. I will stand on that distinction.

McCarthy denied this and said that the real measure of ex-Red sincerity was how many former comrades he helped to uncover. Wechsler pointed out that he did not see all ex-Communists as being alike and had come to the defense of Whittaker Chambers, whom he felt had been victim of a smear.

One of Wechsler's more interesting insights was that he thought McCarthy did not truly believe him to be sympathetic to Communism. He said,

I was dead tired; no ordeal is more exacting than the systematic suppression of one's temper. And there was also an element of despair. Often the Communists had said that democratic debate is a sham because reaction owns all the weapons. I was too old to believe that nonsense. But for a moment I had to fight the awful fear that this was the century of the demagogues, and that only eighteenth-century romantics could believe that truth always triumphs in the end. I am sure some lunatics on the rightist fringe consider me subversive; at no time did I believe McCarthy was overcome by that theory. . . . I am certain that he would have been happy to shake my hand and forget the whole thing if I had merely indicated that I had misjudged him and was prepared henceforth to write kinder things about him.

Researchers who have written on the McCarthy phenomenon indicate that his followers differed to some extent from those who comprised the extreme right of later decades. In this regard it should be noted that virtually all right-wing extremists of the sixties, seventies, and eighties looked back on the senator as a martyred hero. The difference is that during his era McCarthy had the acquiescence of millions of Americans who were not extremists themselves. Thus, McCarthy was partially a product of the temper of the time and partially of his own making. As Daniel Bell summarized: "[He] has to be understood in relation to the people behind him and the changed political temper which these groups . . . brought. He was the catalyst, not the explosive force. These forces still remain."[79]

Numerous studies were done to explain McCarthyism and the social basis for his support, almost always by individuals aligned against him. McCarthy raises strong emotions in writers, and an aura of passionate intensity permeates most of the books and articles on him, even when they're written in scholarly tones. Many of these studies represent second-guessing, and a few are exercises in extremism themselves, having been penned by the kind of far leftist McCarthy victimized. Others have been written by academics with an almost congenital disdain for McCarthy's style and tactics. Whatever theories are offered, and there are many, they all contain these elements in common: (1) they attempt to explain a belief that the end justifies the means; (2) that given the right enemies, almost anything is permissible against them; (3) and that there are "correct" attitudes, opinions, and beliefs, and whoever contradicts them must be punished. This may be more of a moral problem than a problem of "status anxiety" or "relative depriva- tion," as some studies have claimed.[80]

McCarthyism existed on a half-truth. There were Communists in the United States and some of them were entirely anti-American and would have liked to do in our system of government. For the most part, however, the Communists, real or imagined, were of no significant security threat to our country. What was a greater threat was the witch-hunting and official and unofficial persecution of these people as heretics. One of the worst things extremists can do to a society, usually without even intending to, is to cause it to overreact and burn down the barn to catch the rat, so to speak. The net effect of domestic extremism has been negligible. The net effect of attempts to exterminate it have been quite telling, a legacy that haunts us to this day.[81]

The 1950s ended with McCarthyism in disarray but with a viable base for future right-wing extremism still intact. There were numerous groups operating, and right-wing influence was strong in organizations ranging from the American Legion and Daughters of the American Revolution to the Republican party. The radical left was in a state of considerable decline. It has been estimated that by 1960 Communist party membership had dropped to 6,000. Other leftist groups were in similar circumstances. The civil rights movement was just building its base for the explosion of civil rights activity that was to come in the years ahead and absolutely no one predicted the radical student revolts that were to rock college campuses in the late sixties.

## Notes

1. *New York Times* News Service, May 29, 1980.

2. Richard E. Rubenstein, *Rebels in Eden: Mass Political Violence in the United States* (Boston: Little, Brown, 1970), 25.

3. Francis R. Stoddard, *The Truth About the Pilgrims* (Baltimore, Md.: Genealogical Publishing Co., 1973); George F. Willison, *Saints and Strangers* (New York: Reynal & Hitchcock, 1945).

4. James F. Kirkham, Sheldon G. Levy, and William J. Crotty, *Assassination and Political Violence,* vol. 8 (Washington, D.C.: National Commission on the Causes and Prevention of Violence, 1969), 173.

5. Quoted in David Biron Davis, *The Fear of Conspiracy* (Ithaca, N.Y.: Cornell University Press, 1971), 78.

6. Charles McCarthy, *The Antimasonic Party: A Study of Political Anti-Masonry in the United States, 1827–1840,* American Historical Association, Annual Report for 1902 (Washington, D.C.: U.S. Government Printing Office, 1903).

7. James H. Billington, *Fire in the Minds of Men: Origins of the Revolutionary Faith* (New York: Basic Books, 1980), 92.

8. Associated Press, Albany (Ore.) *Democrat-Herald* (June 13, 1985).

9. Seymour M. Lipset and Earl Raab, *The Politics of Unreason* (New York: Harper and Row, 1970), 39–40.

10. The use of the term (epithet?) "rightist" to describe nativist or ethnocentric organizations is questionable but common. There are examples of ethnocentrism and even frank racism among groups nominally "leftist," particularly those populated by ethnic minorities.

11. J. Desmond Humphrey, *The Know-Nothing Party* (Washington, D.C.: New Century Press, 1904).

12. Ray Billington, *The Protestant Crusade, 1800–1860* (Chicago: Quadrangle Books, 1964), 54–60.

13. Louis D. Scisco, *Political Nativism in New York State* (New York, 1901).

14. Wayne G. Broehl, *The Molly Maguires* (Cambridge, Mass.: Harvard University Press, 1964).

15. Arnold S. Rice, *The Ku Klux Klan in Politics* (Washington, D.C.: Public Affairs Press, 1961); John M. Mecklin, *The Ku Klux Klan: A Study of the American Mind* (New York: Harcourt, Brace, 1924); David W. Chalmers, *Hooded Americanism: The First*

*Century of the Ku Klux Klan* (Garden City, N.Y.: Doubleday, 1965).

16. Donald L. Kinzer, *An Episode in Anti-Catholicism: The American Protective Association* (Seattle: University of Washington Press, 1964).

17. See Humphrey Desmond, *The APA Movement* (Washington: New Century Press, 1912), 38–43; Gustavus Myers, *History of Bigotry in the United States* (New York: Capricorn Books, 1960).

18. Desmond, *The APA Movement.*

19. C. Vann Woodward, *Tom Watson: Agrarian Rebel* (Savannah, Ga.: Beehive Press, 1973).

20. Richard Hofstadter, *The Age of Reform: From Bryan to F.D.R.* (New York: Knopf, 1955), 82.

21. Mark Holloway, *Heavens on Earth: Utopian Communities in America, 1680–1880* (New York: Library Publishers, 1951).

22. Anthony Craven, *The Coming of the Civil War* (Chicago: University of Chicago Press, 1957); Allen Nevins, *The War Against Proslavery Religion* (Ithaca, N.Y.: Cornell University Press, 1984).

23. *The Socialist Labor Party, 1890–1930* (New York: New York Labor News, 1931); L. Glen Seretan, *Daniel DeLeon: The Odyssey of an American Marxist* (Cambridge, Mass.: Harvard University Press, 1979).

24. Associated Press, April 9, 1988.

25. David A. Shannon, *Third Parties in American Politics* (Washington, D.C.: Public Affairs Press, 1959); *The Socialist Party in America: A History* (New York: Macmillan, 1955).

26. Drew Egbert and Stow Parsons, *Socialism and American Life* (Princeton, N.J.: Princeton University Press, 1952); Frank A. Warren, *An Alternative Vision: The Socialist Party in the 1930s* (Bloomington: University of Indiana Press, 1974).

27. Ray Ginger, *The Bending Cross: A Biography of Eugene Victor Debs* (New Brunswick, N.J.: Rutgers University Press, 1949); Nick Salvatore, *Eugene V. Debs: Citizen and Soldier* (Urbana: University of Illinois Press, 1982).

28. Harry Fleischman, *Norman Thomas: A Biography, 1884–1968* (New York: W. W. Norton, 1969); Swanberg, *Norman Thomas: The Last Idealist.*

29. W. A. Swanberg, *Norman Thomas: The Last Idealist* (New York: Charles Scribner's, 1976); Bernard K. Johnpoll, *Pacifist's Progress: Norman Thomas and the Decline of American Socialism* (Westport, Conn.: Greenwod Press, 1970).

30. Social Democrats USA has consistently taken a strong anti-Communist position.

31. Fred Thompson, *The IWW: Its First Seventy Years: 1905–1975* (Chicago: Industrial Workers of the World, 1976); Melvyn Dubofsky, *We Shall Be All* (New York: Quadrangle, 1969); Philip Foner, *The Industrial Workers of the World—1915–1917* (New York: International Publishers, 1965).

32. Mari Jo Buhle, Paul Buhle, and Dan Georgakas, *The Encyclopedia of the American Left* (New York: Garland Publishing, Inc., 1990).

33. Quoted in Frank J. Donner, *The Age of Surveillance* (New York: Vantage, 1981), 34.

34. Stanley Cohen, *A. Mitchell Palmer: Politician* (New York: Columbia University Press, 1963).

35. Robert Murray, *Red Scare: A Study in National Hysteria, 1919–1920* (New York: McGraw-Hill, 1955), 12; Joan M. Jensen, *The Price of Vigilance* (Chicago: Rand McNally, 1968); Frank J. Donner, *The Age of Surveillance* (New York: Random House, 1981).

36. Murray, 88.

37. David H. Bennett, *The Party of Fear* (New York: Vintage, 1990).

38. Robert L. Duffus, "Salesmen of Hate: The Ku Klux Klan," *World's Work* 46 (May 1923); Winfield Jones, *Knights of the Ku Klux Klan* (New York: Tocsin Publishers, 1941).

39. Hiram Wesley Evans, "The Klan's Fight for Americanism," *North American Review* 123 (March 1926).

40. Chalmers, *Hooded Americanism;* Mccklin, *The Ku Klux Klan: A Study of the American Mind;* Charles C. Alexander, *The Ku Klux Klan in the Southwest* (Lexington: University Press of Kentucky, 1966); Kenneth Jackson, *The Ku Klux Klan in the City: 1915–1930* (New York: Oxford University Press, 1967).

41. Morris Janowitz, "Black Legions on the March," in Daniel Aaron, ed., *America in Crisis* (New York: Alfred P. Knopf, 1952).

42. Sander A. Diamond, *The Nazi Movement in the United States, 1924–1941* (Ithaca, N.Y.: Cornell University Press, 1974); Bennett, *The Party of Fear.*

43. John Roy Carlson, *Undercover* (New York: E. P. Dutton, 1943), 470–71.

44. Fred W. Friendly, *Minnesota Rag* (New York: Vintage Books, 1982).

45. Over thirty persons were tried in three trials (1942–1944). One judge died. According to Morris Janowitz in *Political Conflict* (Chicago: Quadrangle Books, 1970), 170: "The unwieldy nature of such a large-scale proceeding (was a factor which) prevented the completion" of this case.

46. William Dudley Pelley, "Seven Minutes in Eternity—The Amazing Experience That Made Me Over," *American Magazine* 107 (March 1929).

47. J. M. Werley, *The Millenarian Right: William Dudley Pelley and the Silver Shirt Legion of America* (Syracuse University MA thesis, 1972); Phillip Rees, *Biographical Dictionary of the Extreme Right Since 1890* (New York: Simon & Schuster, 1990); Leo P. Ribuffo *Protestants on the Right: William Dudley Pelley, Gerald Winrod and Gerald L. K. Smith* (Yale University thesis, 1976).

48. Rees, *Biographical Dictionary;* Donald S. Strong, *Organized Anti-Semitism in America* (Washington, D.C.: American Council on Public Affairs, 1941); Leo P. Ribuffo, *The Old Christian Right: The Protestant Far Right from the Depression to the Cold War* (Philadelphia: Temple University Press, 1983).

49. Ribuffo, *The Old Christian Right;* G. H. Montgomery, *Gerald Burton Winrod* (Wichita, Kan.: Defenders of the Christian Faith, 1965); Ralph Lord Roy, *Apostles of Discord* (Boston: Beacon Press, 1953); Rees, *Biographical Dictionary;* G. A. Sindel, *Gerald B. Winrod and the Defender* (Case Western Reserve University Ph.D. thesis, 1973); David H. Bennett, *The Party of Fear* (New York: Vintage Books, 1988).

50. Anti-Defamation League, *Extremism on the Right: A Handbook* (New York: Anti-Defamation League, 1988).

51. Tom Miller, *Ketchikan Daily News,* "Neo-Nazis Solicit POW Followers" (April 27–28, 1991); "All in the Family?" (May 4–5, 1991); "Anti-Semitic Packets Mailed to Ketchikan" (May 22, 1991).

52. Lawrence Dennis and Maximillian St. George, *A Trial on Trial: The Great Sedition Trial of 1944* (Chicago: National Civil Rights Committee, 1945), 37.

53. Ribuffo, 194.

54. Charles E. Coughlin, radio address of 27 January 1935, in *A Series of Lectures on Social Justice Published by the Radio League of the Little Flower* (Royal Oak, Mich.: 1935).

55. David H. Bennett, *Demagogues in the Depression: American Radicals and the Union Party, 1932–1936* (New Brunswick, N.J.: Rutgers University Press, 1969).

56. Sheldon Marcus, *Father Coughlin: The Tumultuous Life of the Priest of the Little*

*Flower* (Boston: Little, Brown, 1973); Rees; Alan Brinkley, *Voices of Protest: Huey Long, Father Coughlin and the Great Depression* (New York: Alfred P. Knopf, 1982).

57. Raymond Gram Swing, *Forerunners of American Fascism* (New York: Julian Mesner, 1935).

58. Brinkley, *Voices of Protest;* Rees; Ribuffo; Bennett, *Demagogues in the Depression;* Elna M. Smith and Charles F. Robertson, *Besieged Patriot: Autobiographical Episodes Exposing Communism, Traitorism and Zionism in the Life of Gerald L. K. Smith* (Eureka Springs, Ark.: Elna M. Smith Foundation, 1978); Glen Jeansonne, *Gerald L. K. Smith* (New Haven, Conn.: Yale University Press, 1988); Leo Lowenthal and Norbert Guterman, *Prophets of Deceit* (New York: Harper & Row, 1949).

59. Glen Jeansonne, "The Case of Gerald L. K. Smith," in David A. Gerber (ed.), *Anti-Semitism in American History* (Chicago: University of Illinois Press, 1986).

60. David A. Shannon, *The Decline of American Communism: A History of the Communist Party Since 1945* (New York: Macmillan, 1955), 45; Harvey Klehr, *The Heyday of American Communism: The Depression Decade* (New York: Basic Books, 1984); Maurice Isserman, *Which Side Are You On?: The American Communist Party and the Second World War* (New York: Basic Books, 1987).

61. David J. Saposs, *Communism in American Politics* (Washington, D.C.: Public Affairs Press, 1960); Shannon, *The Decline of American Communism,* 35, 217; Joseph Starobin, *American Communism in Crisis, 1943-1957* (Cambridge, Mass.: Harvard University Press, 1972); William L. O'Neill, *A Better World* (New York: Simon & Schuster, 1982).

62. Walter Goodman, *The Committee* (New York: Farrar, Straus and Giraux, 1968); Eric Bentley, *Thirty Years of Treason* (New York: Viking, 1971); Robert K. Carr, *The House Committee on Un-American Activities, 1945-1950* (Ithaca, N.Y.: Cornell University Press, 1952); Raymond Ogden, *The Dies Committee, 1938-1944* (Washington, D.C.: Catholic University of America Press, 1945); Telford Taylor, *Grand Inquest* (New York: Ballantine, 1961); Frank J. Donner, *The Un-Americans* (New York: Ballantine, 1961). For a sympathetic view see William F. Buckley and L. Brent Bozell, *The Committee and Its Critics* (Chicago: Henry Regnery, 1954).

63. Buhle, Buhle, and Georgakas, *Encyclopedia of the American Left,* 331.

64. Victor S. Navasky, *Naming Names* (New York: Penguin Books, 1980); Gordon Kahn, *Hollywood on Trial* (New York: Boni & Gaer, 1948); Robert Vaughn, *Only Victims: The Story of Show Business Blacklisting* (New York: G. P. Putnam, 1972); *New York Times,* April 28, 1962. American Business Consultants, *Red Channels: The Report on Communist Influence in Radio and TV* (New York: Counterattack, 1950).

65. John Cogley, *Report on Blacklisting* (New York: Fund for the Republic, 1956).

66. John Henry Faulk, *Fear on Trial* (New York: Simon & Schuster, 1964).

67. David J. Garrow, *The FBI and Martin Luther King* (New York: Penguin, 1981).

68. Garrow, *The FBI and Martin Luther King,* 38.

69. Books critical of the FBI include: Fred J. Cook, *The FBI Nobody Knows* (New York: Macmillan, 1964); Frank J. Donner, *The Age of Surveillance* (New York: Alfred P. Knopf, 1980); David J. Garrow, *The FBI and Martin Luther King* (New York: W. W. Norton, 1981); William W. Turner, *Hoover's FBI: The Men and the Myth* (New York: Dell, 1971); Richard Powers, *Secrecy and Power: The Life of J. Edgar Hoover* (New York: Free Press, 1987).

Books sympathetic to the FBI include: Ralph DeToledano, *J. Edgar Hoover: The Man in His Time* (New York: Arlington House, 1973); Mark Felt, *The FBI Pyramid* (New York: G. P. Putnam's, 1979); J. Edgar Hoover, *Masters of Deceit* (New York: Henry

Holt, 1958); Max Lowenthal, *The Federal Bureau of Investigation* (New York: William Sloane, 1950); Don Whitehead, *The FBI Story* (New York: Random House, 1956).

70. Phillip Finch, *God, Guts and Guns: A Close Look at the Radical Right* (New York: Seaview/Putnam, 1983), 157–58.

71. Ibid.

72. Ibid., 160.

73. Earl Latham, *The Communist Controversy in Washington* (Cambridge, Mass.: Harvard University Press, 1966); Michael Rogin, *The Intellectuals and McCarthy: The Radical Specter* (Cambridge, Mass.: M.I.T. Press, 1967).

74. Talcott Parsons in Daniel Bell, ed., *The Radical Right* (Garden City, N.Y.: Doubleday Anchor, 1964), 226–27.

75. Fred J. Cook, *The Nightmare Decade: The Life and Times of Senator Joe McCarthy* (New York: Random House, 1971); Richard Rovere, *Senator Joe McCarthy* (New York: Harcourt, Brace, 1959); Senator Joe McCarthy, *The Fight for America* (New York: Devin Adair, 1952).

76. Jack Anderson and Ronald May, *McCarthy: The Man, the Senator, the Ism* (Boston: Beacon Press, 1956), 29.

77. *The Progressive,* March, 1952; also Anderson and May, *McCarthy.*

78. James Wechsler, *The Age of Suspicion* (New York: Random House, 1953).

79. Wechsler; Bell.

80. Numerous studies have been done to explain the social psychology of McCarthyism. Many of these are discussed in Daniel Bell, *The Radical Right,* previously footnoted. For a sympathetic view of McCarthy, see William F. Buckley and L. Brent Bozell, *McCarthy and His Enemies* (Chicago: Henry Regnery, 1954).

81. Herbert Mitgang, *Dangerous Dossiers* (New York: Donald I. Fine, 1988).

## 2. What Is Extremism? Style and Tactics Matter More Than Goals

### Laird Wilcox

If it's a despot you would dethrone, see first that his throne erected within you is destroyed.

Kahlil Gibran, 1923

In *A Dictionary of Political Thought* (1982) Roger Scruton defines "extremism" as:

> 1. Taking a political idea to its limits, regardless of unfortunate repercussions, impracticalities, arguments, and feelings to the contrary, and with the intention not only to confront, but to eliminate opposition.
> 2. Intolerance toward all views other than one's own.
> 3. Adoption of means to political ends which show disregard for the life, liberty and human rights of others.[1]

This definition basically reflects my own experience, that extremism is more an issue of style than of content. In the twenty-five years that I have been investigating political groups of the left and right, I have found that most people can hold radical or unorthodox views and still entertain them in a more or less reasonable, rational, and nondogmatic manner. On the other hand, I have met people whose views were fairly close to the political mainstream but were presented in a shrill, uncompromising, bullying, and distinctly authoritarian manner. The latter demonstrated a starkly extremist mentality while the former demonstrated only ideological unorthodoxy, which is hardly to be feared in a relatively free society such as ours.

This view of extremism, which may seem novel to many people since in today's climate the term is usually used as an epithet, is held by many writers and authorities, especially those who approach the issue from a relatively even-handed and nonideological point of view. Milton Rokeach, whose book *The Open and Closed Mind* is a classic in the field of dogmatic thinking, prejudgment, and authoritarianism, has this to say about it:

> To study the organization of belief systems, we find it necessary to concern ourselves with the structure rather than the content of beliefs. The relative openness or closed-

ness of a mind cuts across specific content; that is, it is not uniquely restricted to any particular ideology, or religion, or philosophy, or scientific viewpoint. A person may adhere to communism, existentialism, Freudianisn, or the "new conservatism" in a relatively open or relatively closed manner. Thus, a basic requirement is that concepts to be employed in the description of belief systems must not be tied to any one particular belief system; they must be constructed to apply equally to all belief systems.[2]

Rokeach goes on to say "authoritarianism and intolerance in belief and interpersonal relations are surely not a monopoly of fascists, anti-Semites, Ku Klux Klanners, or conservatives."[3] I agree, and would add that the same behaviors merely take different forms and utilize different vocabulary on the "left" side of the political spectrum. The essential characteristics remain quite similar. The choice of adjectives used to describe the behavior in question often derives more from the biases and interests of the observer than from the objective facts of the situation. Daniel Bell, the eminent sociologist, tends to support this view. He says:

> The way you hold beliefs is more important than what you hold. If somebody's been a rigid Communist, he becomes a rigid anti-Communist—the rigidity being constant.[4]

In my opinion, most strident opponents of right-wing or left-wing "extremism" exhibit significant ideological bias, and many are actually representatives of the opposing extreme. The fact that an extremist hates and agitates against other extremists doesn't mitigate his or her own character in this regard. In fact, opposing extremists often form a vague bond or symbiotic relationship with one another, each justifying the other's existence in a peculiar kind of way.

In focusing on the style rather than the content of a belief system, I don't mean to imply that content is entirely irrelevant. People who tend to adopt the extremist style most often champion causes and adopt ideologies that are essentially "fringe" positions. But mere advocacy of "fringe" positions gives our society the variety and vitality it needs to function as an open democracy, to discuss and debate all aspects of an issue, and to deal with problems that otherwise have been ignored. The extremist style is another issue altogether, however, in that it hampers our understanding of important issues, muddies the waters of discourse with invective, defamation, self-righteousness, fanaticism, and hatred, and impairs our ability to make intelligent, well-informed choices.

Another point is that the extremist style is not only found at the fringes of the political or religious spectrum, but sometimes in the "middle" as well. An individual who is uncompromisingly, intolerantly "centrist" may be far more dogmatic and prejudiced than someone who adopts more radical views but does so in an open and tolerant manner. Consequently, a guarded middle-of-the-road position doesn't necessarily provide a solution to extremism, and in some cases may only serve as a mask to conceal it. In fact, it could be argued that those beliefs that are accorded legitimacy by consensus, which is to say that everyone unthinkingly accepts them, may be even more prone to appear on the extremist agenda and more difficult to challenge or effectively debate.

When the word "extremist" is used as an epithet it usually represents points of view with which we disagree, advocated by someone we dislike (but usually don't know) and whose interests are contrary to our own. Political ideologues and special interests often attempt definitions of "extremism" that specifically condemn the views of their critics and opponents while leaving their own equally strident and intolerant behavior untouched. In the debate over abortion, for example, one side or the other will condemn opponents as "extremists" while describing themselves as valiant defenders of human life or champions of freedom. In fact, bona fide extremist elements exist on both sides of this controversy, as do relatively calm, fairminded, honest, evenhanded, and rational advocates. It is not the position they take, but *how* they take it that matters. The ability to define the terms, as Milton Rokeach suggests, goes a long way in deciding how a particular belief system or set of values is viewed. The use of loaded terms including slogans, buzzwords, and cliches, and selective vocabulary that are biased toward certain forms of authoritarianism, bigotry, and prejudice while exempting others from criticism, is but an example of the pervasive double standards one encounters in this area.

## The Traits of "Extremists"

The late Senator Robert F. Kennedy wrote:

> What is objectionable, what is dangerous about extremists is not that they are extreme, but that they are intolerant. The evil is not what they say about their cause, but what they say about their opponents.[5]

In analyzing the rhetoric and propaganda of several hundred militant "fringe" political and social groups across the political spectrum, I have identified a number of specific traits or behaviors that tend to represent the extremist "style." Other writers have delineated various extremist traits and where their criteria have been objective, I have included them. I am especially indebted to Dr. John George and also to Gordon Hall for their suggestions. Please let me caution you with the admonition that we are all fallible human beings, and anyone, without bad intentions, may resort to some of these behaviors from time to time. With bona fide extremists, however, these lapses are not occasional. Rather, they are a habitual and strongly established part of their repertoire, so much so that in some cases their entire belief system is expressed in these terms, including a political style that is fairly easy to identify.

1. *Character assassination.* Extremists often attack the character of an opponent rather than deal with the facts or issues raised. They will question motives, qualifications, past associations, alleged values, personality, looks, and mental health as a diversion from the issues under consideration.

Some of these matters are not entirely irrelevant, but they should not serve to avoid the real issues. Extremists object strenuously when this is done to them, of course!

2. *Name calling and labeling.* Extremists are quick to resort to epithets (subversive, pervert, racist, hatemonger, nut, crackpot, degenerate, un-American, anti-Semite, Red, commie, Nazi, kook, fink, liar, bigot, and so on) to label and condemn opponents in order to divert attention from their arguments and to discourage others from hearing them out. These epithets don't have to be proved to be effective; the mere fact that they have been said is often enough.

3. *Irresponsible sweeping generalizations.* Extremists tend to make sweeping claims or judgments on the basis of little or no evidence, and they have a tendency to confuse similarity with sameness. That is, they assume that because two (or more) things, persons, or events are alike in some respects, they must be alike in most or all respects. The sloppy use of analogy is a treacherous form of logic and has a high potential for false conclusions.

4. *Inadequate proof for assertions.* Extremists tend to be very fuzzy about what constitutes proof, and they also tend to get caught up in logical fallacies, such as *post hoc ergo propter hoc* (assuming that a prior event explains a subsequent occurrence simply because of their before-and-after relationship). They tend to project wished-for conclusions and to exaggerate the significance of information that confirms their beliefs while derogating or ignoring information that contradicts them. They tend to be motivated by feelings more than facts, what "ought to be" rather than what is. Extremists do a lot of wishful and fearful thinking.

5. *Advocacy of double standards.* Extremists generally tend to judge themselves or their interest group in terms of their intentions, which they tend to view generously, and their critics and opponents by their acts, which they tend to view very critically. They would like you to accept their assertions on faith, but they demand proof for yours. They tend to engage in special pleading on behalf of themselves or their interests, usually because of some alleged special status, past circumstance, or present disadvantage.

6. *Tendency to view opponents and critics as essentially evil.* To the extremist, opponents hold opposing positions because they are bad, immoral, dishonest, unscrupulous, mean-spirited, hateful, cruel, prejudiced, or whatever, and not merely because they simply disagree, see matters differently, or are mistaken.

7. *Manichaean worldview.* Extremists have a tendency, to see the world in terms of absolutes of good and evil, for them or against them, with no middle ground or intermediate positions. All issues are ultimately moral issues of right and wrong, good and bad, with the "right" and "good" position coinciding with their interests. Their slogan is often "those who are not with me are against me."

8. *Advocacy of some degree of censorship or repression of their opponents and/or critics.* This may include a very active campaign to keep opponents

from media access and a public hearing, as in the case of blacklisting, banning, or "quarantining" dissident spokespersons. It may include lobbying for legislation against speaking, writing, teaching, or instructing "subversive" or forbidden information or opinions. It may even include attempting to keep offending books out of stores or off of library shelves, discouraging advertising with threats of reprisals, and keeping spokespersons for "offensive" views off the airwaves or certain columnists out of newspapers. In each example the goal is some kind of information control. Extremists would prefer that you listen only to them. They feel threatened if someone talks back or challenges their views.

9. *Tendency to identify themselves in terms of who their enemies are.* Accordingly, extremists may become emotionally bound to their opponents, who may be competing extremists themselves. Because they tend to view their enemies as evil and powerful, they tend, perhaps subconsciously, to emulate them, adopting the same tactics to a certain degree. For example, anti-Communist and anti-Nazi groups often behave surprisingly like their opponents. Anti-Klan rallies often take on much of the character of the stereotype of Klan rallies themselves, including an orgy of emotion, bullying, screaming epithets, and even acts of violence. To behave the opposite of someone is to actually surrender your will to them, and "opposites" are often more like mirror images that, although they have "left" and "right" reversed, look and behave amazingly alike.

10. *Tendency to use argument by intimidation.* Extremists tend to frame their arguments in such a way as to intimidate others into accepting their premises and conclusions. To disagree with them is to "ally oneself with the devil" or to give aid and comfort to the enemy. They use a lot of moralizing and pontificating, and tend to be very judgmental. This shrill, harsh rhetorical style allows them to keep their opponents and critics on the defensive, cuts off troublesome lines of argument, and allows them to define the parameters of debate.

11. *Use of slogans, buzzwords, and thought-stopping cliches.* For many extremists, shortcuts in thinking and in reasoning matters out seem necessary in order to avoid troublesome facts and compelling counter-arguments. Extremists generally behave in ways that reinforce their prejudices and alter their own consciousness in a manner that bolsters their false confidence and sense of self-righteousness.

12. *Assumption of moral superiority over others.* Most obvious would be claims of general racial or ethnic superiority—a master race, for example. Less obvious are claims of ennoblement because of alleged victimhood, a special relationship with God, membership in a special "elite" or "class" with the accompanying entitlements, and a kind of aloof "highminded" snobbishness that accrues because of the weightiness of their preoccupations, their altruism, and their willingness to sacrifice themselves (and others) to their cause. (After all, who can bear to deal with common people and their petty concerns when one is trying to save the world!)

Extremists can show great indignation when one is "insensitive" enough to challenge these claims.

13. *Doomsday thinking.* Extremists often predict dire or catastrophic consequences from a situation or from a failure to follow a specific course, and they tend to exhibit a kind of "crisis-mindedness." It can be a Communist takeover, a Nazi revival, nuclear war, earthquakes, floods, or the wrath of God. Whatever, it's just around the corner unless we follow their program and listen to their special insight and wisdom, to which only the truly enlightened have access. For extremists, any setback or defeat is "the beginning of the end!"

14. *Belief that it's okay to do bad things in the service of a "good" cause.* Extremists may deliberately lie, distort, misquote, slander, defame, or libel their opponents and/or critics, engage in censorship or repression, or undertake violence in "special cases." This is done with little or no remorse as long as it's in the service of defeating the Communists or Fascists or whomever. Defeating an "enemy" becomes an all-encompassing goal to which other values are subordinate. With extremists, the end justifies the means.

15. *Emphasis on emotional responses and, correspondingly, a de-emphasis on reasoning and logical analysis.* Extremists have an unspoken reverence for propaganda, which they may call "education," "sensitivity training," or "consciousness-raising." Symbolism plays an exaggerated role in their thinking, and they tend to think imprecisely and metaphorically. Harold D. Lasswell, in his book *Psychopathology and Politics,* says, "The essential mark of the agitator is the high value he places on the emotional response of the public."[6] Effective extremists tend to be effective propagandists. Propaganda differs from education in that the former teaches one what to think, and the latter teaches one how to think clearly.

16. *Hypersensitivity and vigilance.* Extremists perceive hostile innuendo in even casual and innocuous comments, imagine rejection and antagonism concealed in honest disagreement and dissent, and see "latent" subversion, anti-Semitism, perversion, racism, disloyalty, and so on in innocent gestures and ambiguous behaviors. Although few extremists are actually clinically paranoid, many of them adopt a paranoid style with its attendant projective mechanisms, hostility and distrust.

17. *Use of supernatural rationales for beliefs and actions.* Some extremists, particularly those involved in "cults" and religious movements—such as fundamentalist Christians, militant Zionist extremists, and members of mystical and metaphysical organizations—claim some kind of supernatural rationale for their beliefs and actions; their movement or cause, they believe, is ordained or looked upon favorably by God. In this case, stark extremism may become reframed in a "religious" context, which can have a legitimizing effect for some people. It's surprising how many people are reluctant to challenge "religiously" motivated extremism because it represents "religious belief" or because of the sacred-cow status of some

religions in our culture.

18. *Problems tolerating ambiguity and uncertainty.* Indeed, the ideologies and belief systems to which extremists tend to attach themselves often represent grasping for certainty in an uncertain world, or an attempt to achieve absolute security in an environment that is naturally unpredictable or perhaps populated by people with agendas and interests opposed to their own. Extremists exhibit a kind of risk-aversiveness that compels them to engage in controlling and manipulative behavior, both on a personal level and in a political context, to protect themselves from the unforeseen and unknown. The more laws or rules there are that regulate the behavior of others—particularly their "enemies"—the more secure extremists feel.

19. *Inclination toward "groupthink."* Extremists, their organizations, and their subcultures are prone to a kind of inward-looking group cohesiveness that leads to what Irving Janis describes as "groupthink." Groupthink involves a tendency to conform to group norms and to preserve solidarity and concurrence at the expense of distorting members' observations of facts, conflicting evidence, and disquieting observations that would call into question the shared assumptions and beliefs of the group. Right-wingers (or left-wingers), for example, talk mostly to one another, read only material that reflects their own views, and can be almost phobic about the "propaganda" of the "other side." The result is a deterioration of reality-testing, rationality, a sense of perspective and moral judgment. With groupthink, shared illusions of righteousness, superior morality and persecution remain intact, and those who challenge them are viewed with skepticism and hostility.[7]

20. *Tendency to personalize hostility.* Extremists often wish for the personal bad fortune of their "enemies," and celebrate when it occurs. When a critic or an adversary dies or has a serious illness, a bad accident, or personal legal problems, extremists often rejoice and chortle about how he or she "deserved" it. I recall seeing right-wing extremists celebrate the assassination of Martin Luther King and leftists agonizing because George Wallace survived an assassination attempt. In each instance their hatred was not only directed against ideas, but also against individual human beings.

21. *Extremists often feel that the system is no good unless they win.* For example, if they lose an election, then it was "rigged." If public opinion turns against them, it is because of "brainwashing." If their followers become disillusioned, it's because of "sabotage." The test of the rightness or wrongness of the system is how it has an impact upon them.

22. *Extremists tend to believe in far-reaching conspiracy theories.* Many extremists claim that there is a secret conspiracy by some hidden elite to control the world. Both leftists and rightists have their own versions of conspiracy theories. Sometimes claims by extremists may have an element of truth to them, however tenuous and ephemeral, and every claim must be judged on the basis of its evidence. However, extremists

are prone to jump to conclusions, disregard evidence to the contrary, and grasp at the most insubstantial and elusive facts and theories to support their case.

Thus, extremists tend to have these things in common:

1. They represent some attempt to distort reality for themselves and others. Extremism tends to be "feeling-based" rather than "evidence-based," although the selective use of evidence may obscure that fact.
2. They try to discourage critical examination of their beliefs by a variety of means, usually by false logic, rhetorical trickery, or some kind of censorship, intimidation, or repression.
3. Extremism usually represents some attempt to act out private personal grudges or to rationalize the pursuit of special interests in the name of public welfare, morality, duty, or social consciousness. Extremists often have motives they themselves do not recognize.

Human beings are imperfect and fallible. Even an honest, rational, and well-intentioned person may resort to some of these tactics from time to time. Everyone has strong feelings about some issues and anyone can become excited and "blow up" once in a while. Most of us still retain our basic common sense, good will, and sense of humor. My purpose is not to establish some impossible standard that almost no one can meet, but simply to suggest a better direction. The difference between true extremists and others is that this general kind of behavior is the extremist's normal and usual way of relating their values and feelings, and they usually feel no guilt or sense that anything is wrong when they behave this way. The extremist subculture, such as it is, rewards and reinforces these behaviors, while the society of thoughtful and fair-minded people discourages it.

## One Final Note

The truth of a proposition cannot be inferred merely from the manner in which arguments are presented in its behalf, from the fact that its adherents may censor or harass their opponents, or because they practice any other behavior or combination of behaviors suggested in this article. Ultimately, the truth of any proposition or claim must rest upon the evidence for it. Moreover, the intensity of a conviction has nothing whatsoever to do with whether or not it is true. To dismiss a proposition out of hand merely because it is advocated by obvious extremists is to dismiss it *ad hominem,* that is, because of *who* advocates it and not on its merits.

Extremists sometimes fulfill a "watchdog" function in society in that they're especially sensitive to issues concerning their particular interests. They often deal with the "hot" issues, the controversial issues many people choose to avoid. Many social problems were first identified by extremists, whose agitating and propagandizing forced society to take a closer look and then apply more moderate and realistic solutions. In point of fact, extremists are sometimes correct. Before you write people off as extremists, take a look at their evidence. However unlikely it may seem, it might be that they're actually on to something important after all.

## Notes

1. Roger Scruton, *A Dictionary of Political Thought* (New York: Hill & Wang, 1982), 164.

2. Milton Rokeach, *The Open and Closed Mind: Investigations Into the Nature of Belief Systems and Personality Systems* (New York: Basic Books, 1969), 6.

3. Rokeach, 13.

4. Daniel Bell, quoted in Rushworth M. Kidder, "A Lifetime of Looking at Life," *The Christian Science Monitor* (March 12, 1991), 14.

5. Theodore J. Lowe, ed., *The Pursuit of Justice* (New York: Harper & Row, 1964).

6. Harold D. Lasswell, *Psychopathology and Politics* (New York: Viking Press, 1960), 78.

7. Irving L. Janis, *Victims of Groupthink* (Boston: Houghton-Mifflin, 1972).

# 3. **Motivations: Why They Join, Stay, Leave**

The purpose of this chapter is to discuss some of the sociopsychological theories of extremist behavior and to consider the weaknesses and pitfalls of this approach. We begin with a skeptic's view of the field in order to encourage free thinking and debate, and then move on to current beliefs about extremist behavior, i.e., the views that are quoted over and over again in scholarly books and journals.

We have provided a definition of political extremism and the characteristics of political extremists in another chapter. When we speak of political extremists, of course, we are almost always speaking of people who adopt particular political ideologies of the far right or left. Here, we will offer several definitions of "ideology."

[Political ideology] is a more or less integrated system of values and norms, rooted in society, which individuals and groups project on the political plane in order to promote the aspirations and ideals they have come to value in social life.[1]

Political ideology is a form of thought that presents a pattern of complex political ideas simply and in a manner that inspires action to achieve certain goals.[2]

An ideology is an integrated set of beliefs about the social and political environment. . . . An ideology assimilates information in ways that preserve its basic integrity; it consists of a system of mutually reinforcing beliefs which appear plausible when viewed from within.[3]

Ideology is the conversion of ideas into social levers. . . . It is the commitment to the consequence of ideas. . . . What gives ideology its force is its passion. . . . For the ideologue, truth arises in action, and meaning is given to experience by the "transforming moment."[4]

An ideology . . . is a system of beliefs, held in common by the members of a collectivity, i.e., a society or a subcollectivity of one—including a movement deviant from the main culture of the society. . . .[5]

Ideologies are characterized by a high degree of explicitness of formulation over a very wide range of objects with which they deal. . . . All adherents to the ideology are urgently expected to be in complete agreement with each other. . . .[6]

As propositions [ideologies] become epigrams and slogans to mobilize and confuse groups or individuals. They polarize hostility, justify social oppression and persecution, rationalize yet another national or international crisis and confrontation, or generate loyalty and cohesion.[7]

A political ideology is a belief system that explains and justifies a preferred political order for society, either existing or proposed, and offers a strategy (processes, institutions, programs) for its attainment.[8]

An ideology is a way of twisting facts and theories into neat little packages for the comfort of the believer. An ideology is essentially what the believer wishes were

63

true and which "becomes" true for him, in a manner of speaking, if he believes it hard enough. Above all, an ideology is an exercise in "a priori" thinking. "Ideology" can easily become another name for bullshit.[9]

Ideologue: A person who uses ideas as incantations. True Believer: A person who accepts incantations as ideas. Skeptic: A person who assumes that ideas are incantations until proven otherwise.[10]

An even more complete definition of ideology is given by Herbert A. Kampf:

Ideology is usually defined as a group of generally related thoughts that forms a belief system for viewing the world. This belief system provides its adherents with value judgments about society, economics, government, and most other aspects of life, and with a course of action for coping with problems in these fields. . . . Followers of various ideologies can derive intense emotional satisfaction from them and can even become fanatical believers in them. Consequently, some ideologies have been characterized as "secular religions" that provide for their adherents, in a modern setting, psychological satisfactions similar to those traditionally provided by religion.[11]

Over the years in classrooms, public lectures, and on radio and television programs we often have been asked why people become involved in extremist groups. The reasons are, of course, both varied and complex and most believers and activists probably have motives which they themselves do not recognize. Social psychologists would say that an individual becomes involved in social and political movement due to an interaction of his or her psychological make-up and the social situation in which he or she is involved. This is true, of course, for all kinds of activism, extremist or not. Indeed, many of the forces which may push one person into florid political extremism may have no such effect upon another person. The notion of the political extremist as a separate and unique psychological type may not be especially well-founded, although it's certainly suggested in the literature on the subject. The problem with the "extremist" prototype is that it attempts to define a population "at risk," as though they cannot be trusted to make their own decisions. We feel there is a potential danger in such a stereotype. The appeal of such a prototype is that it helps to answer a puzzling question: Why *do* some people get involved in extremist groups?

When we observe someone who appears different and strange, or who behaves in ways that flout conventions and prejudices, it's a common sense assumption that something different and strange must account for it. In the political sphere, we may have reasons for believing this beyond mere common sense and, indeed, we too may have motives we ourselves do not recognize that influence our *evaluation* of this phenomenon. This is not an easy, simply defined subject area. Problems related to subjectivity abound.

Virtually all of us assume that our own values, opinions, and beliefs are quite sensible. After all, we read books, have friends, mix in social groups and, perhaps, belong to organizations that confirm this view of the world. Our contact with those who feel "otherwise" is limited and we tend not to listen to them very much anyway. In some way, we all exercise a kind of "milieu control," limiting our access to challenging and disturbing ideas. We may also have a tendency to define ideas in terms of "right" and "wrong," which tends to polarize us and hardens our opinions, making them relatively impervious to new information or new ways of looking at issues. Finally, when we have believed something for a long time, we tend to make a strong ego investment in it, so much so that it becomes part of our identity, part of what we stand for.

Attributing psychological motives to ideologues and activists is, however, full of perils and pitfalls. An informal school of thought assumes that once you have imputed an alleged unconscious psychological motive to account for your opponent's arguments, you have rendered these irrelevant, reducing him or her to a mere psychological organism reacting to stimuli. Then the issue becomes one's state of mind rather than the facts in question. This is a clever ploy and is often successful.

If we think in terms of "good guys" and "bad guys" in dealing with extremists (or anyone) we set ourselves up for a kind of distorting process similar to that experienced by extremists themselves. Further, not wishing to be "wrong," or even having to reexamine our cherished beliefs, we find that if we can convince ourselves that the political values, opinions, and beliefs we find so distressing in others have a pathological basis, it relieves us of the burden of dealing with the person expressing them as a normal human being. This person now becomes an object, a phenomenon, an abstraction, and no longer a real, whole person like ourselves. This process is called *dehumanization* and one element of it is name-calling or labeling. It happens when a black person becomes a "nigger," when a gay person becomes a "pervert," when a right-winger becomes a "hate-monger," when a left-winger becomes a "subversive," and when a Jew becomes a "kike."

This, for example, was done with the early feminists. Women who complained about their status relative to men were said to be experiencing "penis envy" or were "hysterical." There are many examples of psychological reductionism of this sort, where legitimate issues of fairness and discrimination were reduced to questions of temperament and mental health. It's easy to dismiss communists or extreme rightists on grounds that their beliefs are so overlaid with emotional projections and hang-ups that their assertions are irrational and essentially pointless. However, aside from being an instance of nothing less than stereotyping, this view is also intellectually unsound. Each argument advanced, by an extremist or anyone else, has to be considered on its merits. History has recorded too many instances where radicals and wild-eyed nonconformists brought long-overdue matters to public attention. This "watchdog" function that political extremists sometimes serve actually may be facilitated by a drive for original and creative expression, even in its more eccentric forms. If there are flaws in perception or logic of extremist assertions, these will evidence themselves to a critical observer anyway, and psychologizing and name-calling become unnecessary.

One of the major problems has been the tendency of writers to attempt to differentiate a set of motives and influences applicable to each end of the spectrum. That is, right extremists are accounted for by this set of circumstances, while left extremists are accounted for by another set. Among theories that have been offered are the role of status anxiety, downward mobility and the "authoritarian personality" in predisposing one toward a particular form of extremism. If there are social and psychological influences that account for extremism, and we feel that there are to a certain extent, it may be simply that they account for extremism in a generic sense, rather than for any *particular* kind of extremism. Both of us have had the feeling many times that the Bircher with whom we were talking could just as easily have been a communist and vice-versa. It may be merely a question of who "gets to them" first. We tend to view the existence of an extremism-prone personality as a more reasonable hypothesis than attempts to account for the "pathology" of a particular point of view.

A possible consequence of the social-psychologizing approach is that it tends to diminish the significance of the individuals' responses to their own experiences along with the judgments they may make on the basis of those experiences. Rather, it substitutes the experiences of the social scientists who, while questioning the validity of the conclusions drawn by the individual, often refuse to see themselves as a source of bias and preconception as well.

For those who believe in free will, social-psychologizing also minimizes personal responsibility for one's values, opinions and beliefs. These are often seen as the involuntary product of circumstances and social forces as viewed by the social scientists, and not necessarily as the result of any rational cognitive process. To recognize that individuals make conscious choices is to acknowledge their existential autonomy and independence, which many social scientists are reluctant to do. Rather, the individual is seen merely as an organism reacting to stimuli rather than as a thinking, judging, choosing human being.

Extremists are troublesome to social scientists in that they reduce predictability and increase ambiguity—somewhat like a joker in a deck of cards. Under certain circumstances extremists can dramatically increase the number of possible outcomes of an otherwise relatively predictable situation. Extremists often don't follow "rules," nor are they particularly controllable—except those extremists who are in vogue with the current intellectual elite. For some social scientists the extremist that they like is a prophet, while the extremist they don't like is a potentially dangerous nut case.

One way of looking at extremists is as random mutations who, if their mutated traits are adaptive, may thrive and usher in social change. In this sense they can serve a social evolutionary function, a harbinger of an idea whose time has come. Far more often, of course, they represent nothing of the kind, although the resistence generated against them may lead to innovation itself.

We posit the notion that extremists are potentially useful, usually of little consequence, and rarely dangerous. The social-psychologizing approach to extremists basically tends to deny this and reduces them to examples of psychopathology on the one hand, or a police matter on the other.

One vociferous critic of psychologizing is the psychiatrist Thomas Szasz, author of several books on psychiatric abuses and a collection of his aphorisms entitled *The Untamed Tongue,* from which we quote here:

Declaring that one does not like Jones is much weaker than diagnosing him as mentally sick. If we describe our adversary in plain English—as hostile and threatening—we continue to recognize him as fully human; but if we diagnose him in the defamatory rhetoric of psychiatry . . . then we no longer recognize him as fully human. Herein lies the appeal of madness-mongering imagery. . . .[12]

Psychiatric diagnoses are stigmatizing labels phrased to resemble medical diagnoses, applied to persons whose behavior annoys or offends others.[13]

Finally, one must be aware that scholarly researchers themselves may have agendas that bias their work. Theodore W. Adorno, the originator of the view that right-wingers are prone to "authoritarianism" while left-wingers are not, was widely recognized as a Marxist and undoubtedly harbored Marxist disdain for right-wingers, whom he tended to identify with fascists and Nazis. Yet Adorno's study, *The Authoritarian Personality,*[14] is still cited as a pioneering explanation of right-wing behavior, although other scholars have criticized it on numerous grounds. It is our view that studies attempting to correlate political ideology and personality type should pay scrupulous attention to questions of objectivity and bias.

A refreshing alternative to Adorno's hypothesis has been the work of Milton Rokeach, author of *The Open and Closed Mind,*[15] who notes that authoritarianism is not relegated only to right-wingers but to leftists as well. For those of us who have studied both extremes, this is somewhat obvious, yet resistance to this belief remains in some quarters. The concept of authoritarianism has tended to lose its objective value as a description and has become to many an epithet. As one wag put it, an authoritarian is a right-winger you disagree with; a subversive is a left-winger who is after your money; and a paranoid is someone who is out to get you.

The appearance of *The Authoritarian Personality* brought about numerous rebuttals. *Studies in the Scope and Methods of the "Authoritarian Personality"* appeared a few years later. Responding to Adorno's so-called "F-scale" to measure authoritarianism (fascism), Edward Shils, one of the contributors to the volume, wrote of

political attitudes masquerading as personality dispositions . . . designed to disclose not the authoritarian personality as such but rather the "right"—nativist—fundamentalist authoritarian.[16]

Another scholar with doubts about Adorno's concept of authoritarianism is James A. Aho, professor of sociology at Idaho State University, who has found that some right-wingers are explicitly anti-authoritarian. Aho's recent book on the Idaho Christian Patriot Movement, *The Politics of Righteousness,* is a detailed study of the Idaho far right and his findings may surprise most extremist-watchers.[17] Aho found the divorce rate far lower among "Christian patriots" than among all Idahoans, and that the patriots also had attended college in slightly higher percentages. Aho notes, however, that while there were graduates of such institutions as Columbia and Harvard among the patriots, 92 percent "attended either state universities of moderate or little distinction or denominational institutions of comparable repute."[18] Although political activists are better educated than the general public, many have assumed this would not be true of right extremists. A clarifying statement for consideration would be this: Far-right activists may be less educated than activists in mainstream organizations.

In chapter 10 Aho discusses the ideas of Seymour Martin Lipset and Earl Raab, whose *The Politics of Unreason* has been highly regarded on this subject. He recognizes the contribution these two gentlemen have made and indicates approval for many of their ideas:

> The ranks of extremist movements are not filled with basically evil types, Lipset and Raab remind the reader, but with ordinary people caught in certain kinds of stress: the terrifying specter of losing their position in the world. The disconcerting elements of right-wing ideology—Manichaenistic dualism, conspiratorialism, historical simplism, moralistic advocacy of violence and bigotry—are less neurotic symptoms than the "cultural baggage," as Lipset calls it, that any American political group must adopt if its commodity is to be marketed successfully. . . .[19]

Nevertheless, Aho critiques Lipset and Raab on several points, finding many of their concepts incomplete and lacking. One weakness, he notes, is that Lipset and Raab's theory of "status displacement" is never explicitly defined. Indeed, the authors admit as much, claiming that the comprehensiveness of their model "defies . . . any particularistic definition." In general terms status displacement refers to a loss or change in the status of an individual or class of individuals, usually because of economic factors such as recession or depression, and its accompanying anxieties. He further notes that Lipset and Raab are open to criticism for circular reasoning. With respect to status displacement, for example, Aho notes that the peak of postwar anti-Communist hysteria came during a time of prosperity. According to Aho:

> Lipset and Raab handle this evident incongruity by arguing that the new wealth of the postwar period produced new status anxieties: "With the possession of status comes the fear of dispossession." . . . My point is not that what the authors say is necessarily untrue, although they never do provide concrete evidence of status insecurity for any of the movements they study. It is rather that the concept is so vaguely posed that virtually nothing is excluded.[20]

We can hardly review the particular chapter here, but serious readers are advised to acquire a copy of Aho's excellent study and determine this for themselves.

One element that suggests hostility toward the far right or left is the use of pejorative terms in describing them. If a subject is described as "virulent," which suggests the medical model of a virus, the point should be clear. Other examples include "hatemonger"—one who peddles mere hate devoid of any intellectual content; "rabid"—one who is diseased and out of control; "subversive"— one whose goal is to undermine and destroy the existing system; and so on.

When, for example, is a "subversive" only "rabid" and not "virulent"? Is a "hatemonger" still a "hatemonger" when he loves his family and friends, but hates Nazis and/or communists? The whole language of psychologizing about extremists is full of this kind of expression and needs thoughtful reworking.

In some attempts at psychologizing there is even an element of what can only be called superstitious belief. An example of this is the belief that the cause necessarily resembles the effect, or vice versa. If one is raised in a religious and authoritarian environment, one is destined to be religious and authoritarian, right? Not necessarily. Any particular environment is capable of producing rebels as well as clones. If this kind of determinism is used in attempting to explain why one becomes an extremist, then one must account for the reasons others who experience essentially the same environment fail to become extremists or why the majority of people who have embraced some form of extremism eventually abandon it. All determinist explanations suffer from this dilemma, whether they deal with religious or authoritarian upbringing, status, or mobility. Every one of these factors is filtered through an individual psyche, and many other factors impinge upon the outcome.

Any theory which attempts to establish a relationship between two or more events must explain precisely *what* that relationship is, *why* it exists, and *what* accounts for it, but it also must explain the situations in which the relationship *does not* occur. This last is most important, and it's there that most fine theories falter. When examined in this critical light many relationships turn out to be far more tenuous and fleeting than would initially appear. As Henry Ward Beecher said, "Whatever is almost true is quite false and among the most dangerous of errors."

This problem exists among historians who attempt to explain the events of history, what caused them, and so on. Pitfalls abound, yet the temptation to be intuitive is strong. So often is this the case that in 1970 an excellent volume appeared attempting to deal with this problem. *Historians' Fallacies,* by David Hackett Fischer, is a critical account of errors of judgment and logical fallacies of which historians have been guilty. Subtitled *Toward a Logic of Historical Thought,* it's really a text on informal logic and rhetoric. Fischer has this to say about selected fallacies on motivation:

> *The fallacy of the one-dimensional man* selects one aspect of the human condition and makes it into the measure of humanity itself. . . . In one of its forms it mistakes people for political animals who are moved mainly by a desire for power. It reduces the complex psychic condition of men merely to their political roles and shrinks all the components of the social calculus to a simple equation of power, ambition, and interest.[21]
>
> *The fallacy of the universal man* assumes that people are intellectually and psychologically the same in all times, places, and circumstances. It is an error that has ruined the designs of innumerable utopians, revolutionaries, prophets, preachers, psychiatrists, mystics, cranks, and social scientists of every shape and hue.[22]
>
> *The historians' fallacy* is . . . the error of assuming that a man who has a historical experience knows it, when he has it, to be all that a historian would know it to be, with the advantage of historical perspective.[23]

Similar fallacies and fallacy complexes exist in all the social sciences and we alluded to a few of them previously. They are most prone to appear when dealing with subjects of great controversy.

In their provocative book *Human Inference: Strategies and Shortcomings of Social Judgment,* two social psychologists, Robert Nisbett and Lee Ross, contend that many mistakes arise out of the excessive use of intuition as a problem-solving technique. According to Mort LaBrecque, who reviewed the book, Nisbett and Ross explain:

> We interpret events according to our perceptions. When we meet people, our reactions to them can be greatly influenced by our deeply held . . . stereotypes.
>
> We vastly overestimate the role of people's dispositions as a cause of their behavior.
>
> . . . objects or events are judged as frequent or probable, or infrequent or improbable, depending upon the readiness with which they come to the judge's mind.
>
> We persevere in our judgments even when the evidence is overwhelming that they are wrong.[24]

In an interesting aside, LaBrecque relates a conversation with Nisbett in which he offers a suggestion that may be relevant to the issue of political extremism.

> I think we owe change in society to people with an erroneous belief about the probability of change—that a little effort produces enormous change. If they hadn't had those wildly inflated beliefs, they might not have acted the way they did, and we might not have seen any change.[25]

To conclude this line of thought let us state the obvious: It is our view that studies attempting to correlate political ideology with personality, or character structure, or social circumstance, or any other factor, may have merit, but they have to be undertaken with care, preferably by individuals with as little interest in the outcome as possible.

Psychological or sociological reductionism is the perennial temptation of the extremist-watcher. It's useful in the sense that any ideological construct is useful, i.e., it provides an a priori framework that tends to supply the answers we have hypothesized (and may privately desire) in the first place. The question "Who watches the watchman?" is relevant here.

Having belabored this point, let us add one more admonition: Basically the issue boils down to fairness. Do not subject the values, opinions, and beliefs of another human being to a process you would find objectionable if applied to yourself or to those with whom you agree. Human beings are fallible, and neurotic or sociopathic processes may well account for almost as many outcomes we would recognize as "good" as for those we recognize as "bad." Extremists are not necessarily demons, monsters, or madmen. In most respects they are much like nonextremists. With that we will take a quick look at some current thinking on the subject.

## A Summary of Motivation Theories

Most social psychologists and sociologists feel that one of the more important elements related to psychological make-up causing one to join a movement is desire for recognition and favorable regard by others. For some people, if favorable attention is unattainable, perhaps notoriety will do. If what is desired is to be noticed (and thus to demonstrate one's importance or effectiveness), then "bad" attention will serve the function equally as well as "good" attention.

The longshoreman philosopher Eric Hoffer noted that this desire seems to stem from frustration and boredom, and according to several studies can be related to downward social mobility or the experience of failure. Thus, it is suggested, many people join an extremist group because they feel that it will cause a great and glorious (or at least interesting) change in their lives. Hoffer notes:

> A rising mass movement attracts and holds a following not by doctrine and promises, but by the refuge it offers from the anxieties, barrenness, and meaninglessness of an individual existence.[26]

Social "misfits" and persons with unhappy relationships may be attracted to extremist movements due to frustration and unhappiness in their personal lives. Hoffer adds:

> By embracing a holy cause and dedicating their energies and substance to its advancement, they find a new life full of purpose and meaning.[27]

Gabriel Almond made a similar statement:

> The Communist militant merges himself in the corpus mysticism of the party, acquires a large identity from it and even a sense of immortality.[28]

Guenter Lewy, author of *The Cause That Failed: Communism in American Political Life,* notes the propensity of intellectuals to dogmatic ideological themes:

> Intellectuals, it appears, are especially vulnerable to the totalitarian temptation. They see themselves as the moral conscience of society and therefore find it easy to justify the use of the coercive power of the state to free ordinary folks from "false consciousness." Intellectuals are fond of social engineering and, to use Rousseau's classic phrase, they have little difficulty countenancing schemes that "force people to be free."[29]

It should be remembered that psychological make-up, or temperament, also may have another important effect. If a person is generally predisposed toward personal conservatism he or she may be more easily led into a politically conservative or rightist group. If predispositions are liberal or perhaps utopian in nature, one may be more easily influenced to join a leftist group. It's important to realize, however, that this is relative to the society or to the subculture within the society.

For example, in a Marxist-Leninist nation a "conservative" would be more likely to become a member of the Communist party, because it represents (or has represented) the "conservatism" of the ruling oligarchy. An organization's tendency toward "liberalism" or "conservatism," then, is not necessarily a function of the particular sector of the ideological spectrum it occupies. There are very "conservative" socialists and communists, and very "liberal" free market advocates. Libertarians, for example, are a mix of "right-wing" economics and "left-wing" social attitudes. Consequently, the old "liberalism" vs. "conservatism" scales are often inadequate today.[30]

The terms "liberal" and "conservative" are probably more descriptive of temperament than ideology, although certain ideologies are more congenial to one or the other. "Right" and "left" describe a complex of values, opinions, and beliefs. Precise definitions are difficult and a certain precision is actually necessary, since there is considerable ambiguity in practice. Gray areas, contradictions, and paradoxes are common.

Gordon J. DiRenzo, in *Personality and Politics,* deals with the relationship (or lack of it) between the content of an ideology and the style of its followers. Drawing from the work of Alex Inkeles,[31] he says:

> The formal or explicit "content" of a political ideology, and general political orientations, such as left or right, conservative or radical, as well as political party preference, may be related more to, and determined mainly by, "extrinsic" social characteristics, such as social class and other social background variables; but the form or style of the political ideology—favoring force or persuasion, compromise or arbitrary dictation, being tolerant or narrowly prejudiced, flexible or highly dogmatic in policy—is largely determined by personality considerations.[32]

There is some indication that situational circumstances, such as the influence of parents and peers, may be an even stronger factor than psychological make-up with respect to an actual decision to join an extremist organization, or any sort of group. According to Hans Toch, in *The Social Psychology of Social Movements:*

> Although there undoubtedly exist some people whose personalities are so constituted that they become equally susceptible to almost every proposition they encounter, most people would feel responsive only to certain types of solutions at particular stages of their lives and in particular situations. . . . A Chinese peasant is not likely to find himself involved in a health fad or in the Christian Science Church.[33]

Ted Robert Gurr, author of the fascinating volume on the psychology of political extremism and violence, *Why Men Rebel,* notes:

> Some of the most general explanations of the origins of revolution and other forms of collective violence attribute it to the loss of ideational coherence: men's loss of faith in, or lack of consensus about, the beliefs and norms that govern social interaction.[34]

Gurr's book is largely an account of the role of "relative deprivation" in political and social rebellion and violence. Pulling together the work of numerous scholars, he makes the case that relative deprivation (RD) is a major factor in motivating individuals and collectives toward action of one kind or another, including violence and rebellion (although none of the extremists we've known seem to be aware of it). Gurr defines RD as

> actors' perception of discrepancy between their value expectations and their value capabilities. Value expectations are the goods and conditions of life to which people believe they are rightfully entitled. Value capabilities are the goods and conditions they think they are capable of getting and keeping.[35]

Gurr makes a number of poignant observations in *Why Men Rebel,* some of which seem rather self-evident. Consider this, where he quotes Karl W. Deutch:

> [If a set of beliefs] prescribes a corresponding code of conduct, if the believer has internalized this code, and if he now perceives himself as living up to it, he is also likely to experience a gain in his own feelings of righteousness. . . .[36]

One detailed study of a religious movement, the Divine Principle Movement (forerunner of the Unification Church), found strong indication that the decision to join results from "a social or situational process rather than an individual or primary psychological event."[37] Three examples that emphasize the importance of social situation follow:

> 1. A young man went to work for a major oil company. His parents were nominal Democrats who had voted for Roosevelt, Truman, and Kennedy (albeit with some trepidation regarding Catholicism). His own political ideas were not well founded. Two men in the particular department where he worked were members of the John Birch Society and others were sympathetic to Birch ideas. After a few months association with these persons, the young man became a Birch Society fellow traveler, if not a member, and began to purvey the Birch line regularly.

> 2. Speaking of a young man who joined the (then Maoist) Progressive Labor Party, former communist-turned-rightist Phillip Luce illustrated a clear example of peer group influence: "He joined the Communist set because his friends were members, because it gave him a somewhat self-fulfilling role, and because it was the 'cool' thing to do."[38]

> 3. A young man in a medium-sized southern city obtained a job at a body shop. He quickly learned that several fellow workers, including his boss, were members of a local Ku Klux Klan klavern. Although he had no strong feelings about racial issues he joined the Klan because he felt it would help him keep his job and fit in better at work.[39]

\*    \*    \*

Among students of political psychology, the work of Harold Lasswell has been held in special regard. The author of several books on propaganda and its analysis, Lasswell has been instructive about political extremism. In his fascinating, if somewhat dated, *Psychopathology and Politics,* he offers the following:

> The essential mark of the agitator is the high value he places on the emotional response of the public. Whether he attacks or defends social institutions is a secondary matter. . . . The agitator easily infers that he who disagrees with him is in communion with the devil, and that opponents show bad faith or timidity. Agitators are notoriously contentious and undisciplined; many reforming ships are manned by mutineers.[40]
>
> Agitators show many traits which are characteristic of primitive narcissism in the exaggerated value which they put on the efficacy of formulas and gestures in producing results in the world of objective reality.[41]

Another work by Lasswell is *Power and Personality,* in which he discusses the formation of what he terms the "democratic personality" and its antithesis, the paranoid:

> All mankind might be destroyed by a single paranoid in a position of power who could imagine no grander exit than using the globe as a gigantic funeral pyre. And the paranoid need not be the leader of a great state. He can be the head of a small state or even of a small gang.
>
> Even a modicum of security under present-day conditions calls for the discovery, neutralization and eventual prevention of the paranoid. And this calls for the overhauling of our whole inheritance of social institutions for the purpose of disclosing and eliminating the social factors that create these destructive types.[42]

This last item is one to consider: the paranoids are out to get us and we must discover and neutralize them. And what do we become in the process of hunting down the last paranoid? We can visualize—without much effort, sad to say—the "Paranoia Police" dragging him, kicking and screaming, from under his bed so that he can be relieved of his delusions that someone is out to get him.

What are some of the factors that would cause an individual to be attracted to a left extremist group? In Almond's classic study, emotional maladjustment and neurotic needs were high in his sample of 224 people who joined the Communist party in the United States, United Kingdom, France, and Italy. Almond stated, in *The Appeals of Communism,* that most members were not aware of the esoteric side of the party when they joined and, in fact, were not familiar with Marxist-Leninist writings. Some middle class intellectuals even viewed joining the party as something exciting and dangerous, even as an adventure. Almond wrote that one of the most important appeals of the party as perceived by joiners was *militancy.* This probably holds true for most leftist and, indeed, many rightist groups. A considerable percentage of those who became CP members

> were persons with strong compulsive needs to attack authority and the established order. The American and British respondents in particular included a large proportion

of emotionally maladjusted individuals who were seeking to solve their emotinal problems by attacking society rather than face up to their personal inadequacies and conflicts.[43]

Unconscious hostility in the neurotic person, wrote Almond, could be a major factor in influencing his or her decision to join the Communist party:

> In a normal individual experiencing a society or social situation which rejects him, which disqualifies him from certain kinds of roles and participations may create a readiness to join the party. . . . The neurotic person will join the party in response to the pressure of internal needs, and often in defiance of the model patterns of his social grouping. The normal person who has suffered some situational damage will join the party in response to the situation and often (but by no means always) in conformity with patterns prevailing in his social grouping.[44]

Self-oriented interests were important to Communist party joiners. Twenty percent of Almond's respondents were influenced strongly by needs for group relationships. One American woman stated that her social life had been quite unstable and the CPUSA offered group relationships around ethical themes. Group-related interests were also important to joiners. For instance, the Communist party always claimed to be the only organization truly interested in the well-being of African-Americans as a group.[45]

Ideological interests also were quite important, Almond emphasized. The Communist party was opposed to specific social ills and in favor of such goals as ethnic equality, economic and social equality, internationalism, and "freedom from oppression." Almond commented that there were instances where ideological interests were merely rationalizations for personal motives, but in other cases he believed these interests were genuine.[46]

A high proportion of members of the CPUSA during the 1930s and 1940s were either foreign born or were first-generation U.S. citizens. Almond suggested that for many of these the party played a major role in the process of assimilation. A considerable number probably felt alienated from the cultural patterns of their parents, yet concomitantly rejected by their new environment.[47]

Why do people leave left extremist groups? Longtime FBI Director J. Edgar Hoover gave six reasons why people leave the Communist party in *Masters of Deceit*[48] (which was actually ghostwritten):

1. The absence of freedom inside the Party.
2. The inability to live a normal life.
3. The Party's callous disregard of members' personal problems.
4. Discrepancy between Party practices and claims.
5. Communist tyranny in Russia and behind the Iron Curtain.
6. Communist opposition to religion.

What Hoover does not mention, of course, was widespread FBI harassment of Communists. The goal of the FBI, aside from a small legitimate counter-espionage concern, was to create a state of paranoia among domestic radicals and to disrupt their legal activities through its now-discredited domestic COINTELPRO (counter-intelligence program). This worked to a certain extent and, undoubtedly, some radicals simply could not pay the enormous personal and social price associated with continued membership in the Communist party or its various fronts. Overall, however, the CP and other targeted groups managed to function in spite of it.

To these should be added one other factor that not only suggests why people quit left extremist groups, but also why so few in western democracies joined such groups after the 1940s: many of the stated ends of which Marxist-Leninists spoke have come into existence through reform with no bloodshed, no loss of civil liberties, and no suppression and subjugation of the upper middle and upper classes.

Almond found that American ex-Communists' political attitudes varied, but that more than one-third eventually held "moderate left" opinions. An interesting sidebar, the explanation of which extends beyond our expertise, is Almond's finding that half of the former CP members came from homes where religion was important and only one in twenty came from antireligious homes. A clue to this might be found in the quasi-religious nature of Marxism-Leninism, which, like all utopian belief systems, envisions a heaven on earth.[49]

A number of themes expounded upon by Almond have appeared in the writings by and about former Communist intellectuals. This is especially true of an exceptional work called *The God That Failed,* edited by former British MP Richard Crossman. In this revealing book, six ex-Communists tell what attracted them to Marxism-Leninism, why they joined the party or fellow-traveled, what caused their disillusionment, and why they dropped out. These were African-American novelist Richard Wright, French author Andre Gide, Hungarian-born British author Arthur Koestler, Italian novelist and journalist Ignacio Silone (who knew both Lenin and Trotsky), British poet and critic Stephen Spender, and American journalist Louis Fischer.[50]

Concerning their experience, two of the contributors had the following to say:

Spender: With the Communist intellectuals I was always confronted by the fact that they had made a calculation when they became Communists which changed the whole reality for them into the crudest black and white. . . . The Revolution was the beginning and the end of all sums. Someday, somewhere, everything would add up to the happy total which was the dictatorship of the Proletariat and a Communist society.[51]

Koestler: All true faith is uncompromising, radical, purist; hence the true traditionalist is always a revolutionary zealot in conflict with a pharisian society. . . . To say that one had "seen the light" is a poor description of the mental rapture which only the convert knows. . . . There is now an answer to every question; doubts and conflicts are a matter of the tortured past.[52]

Another interesting study of Communist party members is Harvey Klehr's *Communist Cadre,* a detailed account of the social background of 212 people who served on the Central Committee of the Communist Party USA between

1921 and 1961. Klehr notes a variety of reasons why people joined the party, including one Almond overlooked:

> Some joined because of neurotic needs. Others were attracted by such self-oriented considerations as career opportunities or the need of social companionship or the need for intellectual clarity. . . . Finally, the party had an ideological attraction for most people. One factor not mentioned by Almond is that for some people, joining the party was not out of the ordinary. Indeed, many party members grew up in Communist households.[53]

There are several other works that attempt to explain the psychological and sociological reasons for Communist party membership. Some of the more interesting are Nathan Glazer's *The Social Basis of American Communism* and, for a right-wing view by a former Communist turned conservative, Frank Meyer's *The Moulding of Communists.* Numerous books have been published on the radical student movement of the 1960s but most noteworthy, as well as controversial, are Stanley Rothman and S. Robert Lichter's *Roots of Radicalism,* and Lewis Feuer's *Conflict of Generations.*[54]

Regarding the general subject of political psychology, there is an absolute wealth of literature available. Two small, poignant books are L. B. Brown's *Ideology*[55] and Fred I. Greenstein's *Personality and Politics.*[56] Both books discuss numerous studies attempting to correlate specific personality traits with political preferences. Of the two, Greenstein's is probably the most comprehensive, while Brown's is more recent and slightly more readable. Yet another book, also entitled *Personality and Politics,*[57] edited by Gordon J. DiRenzo, is somewhat more comprehensive than Brown or Greenstein.

Most observers of extremist politics have noted that bona fide hard-core extremists such as neo-Nazis or Marxist-Leninists rarely attempt participation in conventional electoral politics. Moreover, when they do they inevitably fail miserably, and a casual examination of their rhetorical and personality style strongly suggests their temperamental unfitness for it. Rarely, as in the case of David Duke, an extremist achieves surprising results by abandoning the rhetoric of his past and claiming a conversion to more moderate positions.

Assuming that the ranks of political extremists are heavily laden with psychological misfits, a view shared by several observers, the following observation by Lester W. Milbrath may be in order:

> Persons with great neurotic or psychotic problems are not attracted to normal democratic political action. The chaotic, rough-and-tumble environment of competitive politics carries few rewards for thin-skinned, neurotic personalities. . . . Political gladiators are persons who are particularly well equipped to deal with their environment . . . they are not burdened by a load of anxiety and internal conflict.[58]

One theory of group behavior applicable to all groups, right or left, political or not, is Irving Janis's "groupthink." To explain this theory Janis uses examples from the field of international affairs, including the 1961 Bay of Pigs fiasco in Cuba, the Japanese attack at Pearl Harbor in 1941, and the Cuban missile crisis in 1962, among others. Janis's excellent book on the subject, *Victims of Groupthink,* explains his theory:

> I use the term "groupthink" as a quick and easy way to refer to a mode of thinking that people engage in when they are deeply involved in a cohesive in-group, when the members' strivings for unanimity override their motivation to realistically appraise alternative courses of action. . . . "Groupthink" refers to a deterioration of mental efficiency, reality testing, and moral judgment that results from in-group pressures.[59]

In Janis's examples, "groupthink" was cited as a key factor in the decision-making processes that led to some major foreign policy blunders. Specifically, Janis cites the reluctance of members of the policy team, including advisors, to buck the current that was flowing and to question assumptions and policy goals. The cohesiveness of the group and the pressure on its members to conform under stress superseded independent thinking and reevaluation.

The relevance of "groupthink" to extremist group behavior is obvious and we feel that it is a powerful factor in the operations of these groups. The sad phenomenon of ideologically motivated true believers isolating themselves into little enclaves is all too common.

*     *     *

The behavior of some extremists suggests paranoid-like thinking, as evidenced in some cases by a kind of megalomania. The term "paranoid" is a clinical diagnosis which very few of us are qualified to make, however, and should not be used lightly or as an epithet. Historian Richard Hofstadter, author of *The Paranoid Style in American Politics and Other Essays,* discusses "political paranoids":

> We are all sufferers from history, but the paranoid suffers twice—first from real problems and second from his fantasies. He doesn't see social conflicts as problems to be mediated. He is not willing to compromise. The enemy is totally evil and so must be eliminated.[60]

Professor Hofstadter also asserts that the paranoid amasses "mountains of documentation [which] keeps him from considering other interpretations of history."[61] This is hardly a diagnostic characteristic, however. It also could be true of nonparanoids diligently accumulating information to support particular causes. Although Hofstadter speaks quite generally, other writers have not been so restrained. Defined broadly, it would appear that evidence of paranoid thinking is common in the writings of both the extreme left and extreme right, as well as in the writings of the various "monitor" groups obsessed with extremists. Indeed, the argument could be made that we have paranoids monitoring other paranoids. The equivalent of a small industry thrives, dedicated to keeping a watchful eye on "paranoids."

A more objective account of the political "paranoid" is given in *The Paranoid*, a scholarly volume authored by David W. Swanson, Philip J. Bohnert, and Jackson A. Smith, all of whom are professors of psychiatry in medical schools. Their findings include the following:

> Singleness of purpose, intense motivation and great energy are necessary in the social reformer who detects inequity in a social system. . . . Even in the successful reformer, prominent psychological conflicts may exist; but this does not diminish the contribution of the reformer who can operate to some degree in the established social system and offer constructive alternatives to the inequities he perceives.[62]

> The aggressiveness of a person with a paranoid style may be masked, but no less powerful, when it is expressed in intellectual or ideological terms. In such a subtle and controlled form it usually has a greater impact on others. . . . As individuals, extremist reformers utilize psychological mechanisms which resemble those observed in the paranoid individual. One cannot say such a person is clinically paranoid without adequate examination, however.[63]

Perhaps the bottom line on the subject is this: it's very likely that some political extremists are clinically paranoid simply because the moralizing, good guys vs. bad guys atmosphere of a political crusade tends to attract such people. However, aside from being unkind and unfair, it is also irresponsible to promiscuously use "paranoid" to describe political extremists. This represents psychologizing at its worst and most destructive, and only encourages dehumanizing of political dissidents.

Related to the issue of paranoia is the problem of conspiracies and conspiracy theories. Here, again, we find an issue where there is considerably more heat than light. To describe a statement as a "conspiracy theory" is a rather effective put-down, yet anyone who is familiar with the illogical and irresponsible claims that are made with reference to alleged conspiracies finds it necessary to do precisely that from time to time. The real question, as usual, is what one considers as evidence for conspiracy claims. In our view, if a conspiracy is suggested in a tentative, open-minded way, or as an admitted speculation, one is obligated to give it a fair hearing. On the other hand, when presented with an obviously unfounded, irrational, or fantastic claim, one may have reasonable grounds to dismiss it. Two elements are important: the manner in which the assertion is made, and the nature of the evidence for it.

## Sinister Plots Abound

Far Leftist:    "It's the fascist-racist cabal."
Far Rightist:   "It's the Illuminati."
Far Leftist:    "It's the Council on Foreign Relations and Trilateral Commission."
Far Rightist:   "You're right about that! But the international Jews and the Rockefellers and Kennedys are behind both of them."

Far Leftist:    "What about the Wall Streeters and the liberals?"
Far Rightist: "They're part of it, but of course it's satanic. Satan controls it all."
Far Leftist:    "I don't buy that one."

This imaginary conversation could well be real. We have both heard more-or-less these identical words, if never all at the same time. The general consensus among American political extremists is that the United States (to many, even the entire planet) is controlled by a powerful conspiratorial group—a hidden ruling elite. There are some differences in the way the far right and far left envision this conspiracy. The extreme left does not postulate a huge, well-constructed, all-encompassing, overarching, centuries-old plot. Their conspiracy theories revolve around economic, class, racial, and lately, sexual themes. The extreme right, on the other hand, tends to speak in terms of a grandiose conspiracy throughout history, and a few even take the "big one" back three thousand years to Egyptian Isis worshippers and bring it forward in time through such groups as Greek Mystery Cults, the Gnostics, the Knights Templar, the Rosicrucians, to Freemasons, the Illuminati, and international Jewish bankers.

The central theme to conspiracy theories is that few events occur by chance, and that most events are the product of some plan or plot, i.e., they are "willed" by a person or group of persons. Randomness or the unforeseen are unlikely occurrences, at least as far as the major issues are concerned. The appeal of this mode of thinking is obvious: it renders the incomprehensible much easier to understand. The propensity some have toward conspiracy theories can be explained in part by cognitive dissonance theory, where the drive to reduce dissonance may involve altering one's perception of the facts, or by creating a new way of interpreting them, or by inventing new facts. Conspiracy theories, therefore, may be a first step in reducing feelings of helplessness, by identifying a "cause" and possibly a course of action.

## Major Conspiracies

### Catholics

Big in the nineteenth century, this one began to lose adherents in the twentieth. The presidential candidacies of Al Smith (1928) and John F. Kennedy (1960) gave it a shot in the arm, so to speak, but anti-Catholicism has declined enormously since Pope John and the Second Vatican Council of the early 1960s. Due greatly to Kennedy's popularity and notable changes in the church, believers in Catholic conspiracies are now few.

Today's primary anti-Catholic conspiracy theorist is Jack Chick, a fundamentalist Protestant whose Chick Publications continues to grind out nasty anti-Catholic screeds, in comic book form. The most widely known of these is *Alberto*, which purports to be the story of an ex-priest, even worse, a *Jesuit* named Alberto Rivera, who joined forces with Chick. As it so often happens in cases like this,

Rivera was never a priest of any variety whatsoever.[64] According to George Johnson, in *Alberto* and other comics:

> Rivera rehashes age-old legends of priests keeping nuns as concubines and seducing girls in confession boxes. Throughout the comics, cartoons of the contorted faces of priests, nuns, and victims of the Inquisition capture the fear and hatred Rivera believes is the essence of the Catholic Church.[65]

Another Chick comic, *Angel of Light*, promotes the Illuminati conspiracy theory, beginning with Lucifer and the Garden of Eden.

## The Illuminati

The conspiracy idea on the far right was simpler before 1966 when Robert Welch, founder of the John Birch Society, spoke only of the "Communist Conspiracy." After all, there were well-armed Soviets with their satellites, and the Chinese, and the sneaky Cubans. The problem was that Welch believed that the Sino-Soviet split wasn't real, but simply part of the Red plot. And, his followers insisted, this was also true with respect to Yugoslavia. Communism was one giant monolithic conspiracy directed by Moscow. Time has shown this to have been a rather ridiculous belief by at least the early 1960s. But the whole picture became more complicated when an *American Opinion* (November 1966) article by Welch demonstrated that he had pretty well adopted the Illuminati idea, although he preferred the term "Insiders."

The Illuminati was an actual group that existed from 1776 until 1785, when it was abolished by the Elector (somewhat like a governor) of Bavaria. Founder Adam Weishaupt's purpose was to promote what have been called anticlerical Enlightenment doctrines. He foresaw an educational system independent of the church and evidently believed in deism, a religious philosophy popular among eighteenth century intellectuals, including Thomas Jefferson and Thomas Paine. A few of his followers were atheists but the majority were deists or nondogmatic, free-spirited Christians. Given the fact that Weishaupt's ideas ran counter to the authoritarian, church-intertwined-with-state power structure, he was forced to keep his Illuminati secret and work through Masonic lodges. He was not successful.[66]

People who today believe in the existence of the Illuminati (almost entirely far rightists) insist that the group was *not* destroyed; it went underground, instead. They claim that this secret, powerful group was responsible for the French Revolution, the War of 1812, the American Civil War, World War I, World War II, the Korean War, and the Vietnam War. The organization also controls the Federal Reserve system, the Interstate Commerce Commission, and almost every organization of any importance. Anti-Semites believe that Jews control the Illuminati and that the latter control world Communism.

## International Jewish Bankers

Supposedly started by the Rothschild family in Europe, this group purportedly controls the Illuminati, manipulates the world's money supply and starts wars when such actions are economically beneficial to them. Most anti-Semitic belief systems promulgate some version of this legend. The fabricated document, *The Protocols of the Learned Elders of Zion,* is held up as "proof" of this nefarious Jewish plot. (See *Protocols* in Appendix I on fake quotations and fabricated documents.)

\*    \*    \*

Many formal ideologies contain elements of a conspiracy theory: an explanation of the victims (good guys), the victimizers (bad guys), and a detailed account of the evil-doings of the latter as well as a course of action to right the wrongs committed by the conspirators, which may take the form of a counter-conspiracy. This is certainly true of Marxism-Leninism and National Socialism as well as their variations. L. B. Brown alludes to this:

> Social power rests with those who can control and implement an ideology, whether by persecution and torment or by education and propaganda, while each society contains deviants from whom there is much to be learned about that society. An attack on another's ideology may reflect a pungent ideology in the attacker, especially if either attacked or attacker occupies a minority position.[67]

Accordingly, some conspiracies are directed at defeating other conspiracies, real or imagined. The oppressed engage in a conspiracy to undo the conspiracy that enslaved them, and then the original conspirators cook up another conspiracy to defeat the conspiracy of the uprising, and so on. It would be funny if it didn't so often have such tragic consequences, as history has shown.

John Birch Society founder Robert Welch's article "The Truth in Time,"[68] in which he discusses the plotting of the "INSIDERS," is one of many examples of uncompromising conspiratorial thinking, as are the writings of the extreme left, which speak of such things as "The Racist Masters of the U.S.A."[69]

The far right has produced a number of books alleging massive conspiracies. One of the most widely circulated of these was John A. Stormer's *None Dare Call It Treason,*[70] in which the author offers "the carefully documented story of America's retreat from victory." Chapter titles include: "The Origin of Communism"; "Subverting Our Religious Heritage"; "The Press, Radio and TV"; "Mental Health"; "Economics and Government"; and "Internationalism." Published in 1964, the book was immensely popular, with a total printing of over seven million copies. It became a major issue in the 1964 Goldwater-Johnson presidential campaign and was widely distributed by right-wing Republicans and members of the John Birch Society. Stormer has published a sequel to it titled *None Dare Call It Treason: Twenty-Five Years Later.*[71]

A somewhat related book, *None Dare Call It Conspiracy,* by Gary Allen,[72] appeared in 1973. Allen blamed the Rockefeller family for bankrolling the Bolshevik Revolution" and funding several radical groups, including SDS and the Black Panthers. Some five million copies are in print.[73]

One approach to this issue has been taken by George Johnson, whose *Architects of Fear* is a very detailed study of primarily right-wing conspiracy theories. Johnson's preoccupation with the nefariousness of the right in this regard is so profound that the book smacks slightly of a conspiracy theory about right-wing conspiracy theories. In fact, Johnson acknowledges, "In writing this book I have tried to avoid becoming a conspiracy theorist myself."[74] His book, nevertheless, is a fascinating and informative account of a murky subject. Johnson offers this insight:

> Who runs the world? Is there a mysterious they, a group of secret conspirators who manipulate world events? Almost as soon as we ask the question, we dismiss it as absurd. We are taught to believe that the world works in more complex and subtle ways. . . .
> In other words, there are no final answers. History and economics are not puzzles to solve. There are no "right" solutions, but only models to help us understand. . . . [We] learn to absorb into our world view the idea that there are a number of different ways to interpret events—that there is not a single all-embracing system.[75]

Two other books demand attention. *The Fear of Conspiracy,*[76] edited by David Brion Davis, is a collection of articles on conspiracy theories from the American Revolution to the 1960s. He deals with such diverse examples as the French Revolution, the anti-Masonic movement, the abolitionists, anti-Semitism, McCarthyism, and the Ku Klux Klan. Most of the book is on conspiracy theories of the right, but there are several leftist examples as well. Consider this one from Earl Browder, former head of the Communist Party USA:

> There is ample cause for uneasiness and alarm. Reactionary forces, moving toward fascism, within our land, are not accepting their defeat in the last elections. . . .
> The reactionaries, the fascists, the warmakers, have tremendous resources on their side. They have control of the great trustified industries, the heart of the national economy, in each of the capitalist nations. They are the economic royalists, the "sixty families." They control the bloody dictatorships of Germany, Italy, and Japan, which regiment whole peoples into the military machine. They work internationally, in concert, despite their sharp struggle among themselves, on a worldwide plan, to gobble up and assimilate the world, piecemeal, bite by bite, leading toward world anarchy.[77]

Yet another account of conspiracies merits consideration, too. As in *The Fear of Conspiracy,* the preponderance of examples are conspiracy theories associated with the American far right. In this case, however, examples on the left are given slightly more attention. *Conspiracy: The Fear of Subversion in American History,*[78] edited by Richard O. Curry and Thomas M. Brown, contains articles on subjects ranging from the "Copperhead conspiracy" of Abraham

Lincoln's administration to an essay on "The McCarthyism of the Left," by James Hitchcock. The authors quote Richard Hofstadter:

> It would of course be misleading to imply that there are no such things as conspiracies in history. Anything that partakes of political strategy may need, for a time at least, an element of secrecy, and is thus vulnerable to being dubbed conspiratorial. . . . Indeed, what makes conspiracy theories so widely acceptable is that they usually contain a germ of truth. But there is a great difference between locating conspiracies *in* history and saying that history *is,* in effect, a conspiracy, between singling out those conspiratorial acts that do on occasion occur and weaving a vast fabric of social explanation out of nothing but skeins of evil plots."[79]

Curry and Brown also make the significant observation that fears of conspiracies are not solely the work of right-wing extremists and that sociological and psychological interpretations that suggest this are open to objection.

Among extremists, fanatic dedication for one's cause and mission, bordering on a kind of megalomania, appears to be exhibited more than just occasionally. A considerable number of extremists always seem to view themselves as the only forces standing fearlessly between the United States and a takeover by communists or fascists; they nearly always seem to see themselves as very important in shaping the forces of history. For example, the Workers World party, a small Marxist-Leninist organization which, with their youth group included, probably has never had more than five hundred members, has seen itself as the most effective and principal force aiding the oppressed and preventing a seizure of the United States by Nazis. Radical anti-Klan groups often portray themselves as frontline fighters against racial genocide, although the Ku Klux Klan today has shrunk to minuscule proportions in spite of the publicity given it by such groups.

A good example of megalomania on the far right is the following quotation from an undated, one-page plea by the Patriot Legal Defense Committee, a front group of the Minutemen:

> If we lose this case the very heart will be torn out of the Minutemen organization. Our "last line of defense" may easily fall apart into separate ineffective groups—the Patriotic Party will falter—and the American people may ultimately be enslaved by Communism as a result.

Extremists tend to believe the wild, unfounded charges made by their leaders because they *want* to believe them, i.e., because the beliefs themselves have a certain psychological utility regardless of whether they are true or not. They need something on which to blame their lack of personal satisfaction. They seek excuses and escapes. They want to be shown the way—the way to freedom from themselves. Eric Hoffer notes:

> Propaganda serves more to justify ourselves than to convince others; and the more reason we have to feel guilty, the more fervent our propaganda.[80]

   Extremists are quite unhappy with the current state of political affairs and are certain that our nation is being taken down the road to communism or fascism by those in power. According to Hans Toch:

> In addition to providing a concrete target for tensions, conspiracies can simplify the believer's system of reasoning and his conception of social causation . . . [causation] becomes centralized (in that all events can be blamed on one group of plotters), and it is also integrated (because the plotters presumably know what they are doing and intend the consequences of the actions).[81]

*   *   *

As we have seen many studies of the relationship between personality and political persuasion have focused on the issue of power—that is to say, how particular political "types" relate to having and using political power, the implication being that this is predictable on the basis of ideological factors. Yet, this may not be quite as predictable as it would seem. David Spitz notes that the response of a particular "type" may be largely circumstantial:

> Personality is as much molded by the situation in which a person finds himself as it is by the imputed compulsiveness or aggressiveness of his neurotic nature. If, then, a so-called "authoritarian" personality is thrust into a "democratic" environment, it does not necessarily follow that his personality will remain unchanged.[82]

   Spitz also says that it is not clear exactly what a "democratic" or an "authoritarian" personality actually is. He says that many of the character traits attributed to each type are "for the most part, tautologous terms; they hide rather than reveal meanings," and that nearly every person "exhibits a complex of both 'democratic' and 'authoritarian' traits." With respect to power in particular, he says:

> It gives its holders a new importance, a new set of habits. . . . This is why it is foolish to assume, as the theorists of "democratic" personality are too often inclined to do, that a man out of power will remain the same man when in power.
>    This is one of the reasons why extreme radicals and reactionaries, when out of power and with relatively little chance of getting into power, are so often men of inflexible principle. They are incorruptible because, in part, no one seeks to corrupt them. They are inflexible because, in part, no one seeks to compromise their differences in order to enlist their support.[83]

   J. Allen Broyles's study, *The John Birch Society: Anatomy of a Protest,* illustrates some of the sociopsychological appeals he feels are probably applicable to almost all extremist groups, both left and right. In the mid-1960s, Broyles administered Milton Rokeach's dogmatism and opinionation questionnaires to members of the John Birch Society, and found that all were high on general authoritarianism, very high on general intolerance, and therefore, high in the more inclusive concept of dogmatic closed-mindedness of which the foregoing are components.[84]

In discussing the appeals of the society, he stated that a distinctive appeal is to be found in ideology and stressed three main points:

1. The base for certainty: "The ideology of the Society provides certainty of understanding because it is a fairly simple framework of interpretation through which to view world and national events."

2. The perception of self-righteousness: "This . . . serves to override any sense of guilt for personal sins by providing members of the Society with . . . assurance that they are on the right side of the 'really' important issues."

3. The perception of superiority: Since they are on the "right" side, Birch members "can feel superior to opponents with higher educational attainment and higher social status."

Thus, according to Broyles:

The ideology of the Birch Society leads its members to express their aggressions directly against the sources of their frustration in the form of irrational conflict and in a mood of certainty, self-righteousness and superiority. Therein lie its social-psychological appeals. Because of the psychological satisfactions offered by these appeals, it is almost impossible to "wean" a member away from the logic-tight and closed-minded ideology of the Birch Society.[85]

This kind of analysis, while well-meaning and not without merit, could use some criticism. Broyles's concepts would give great comfort to any advocate of psychologizing. In some respects his analysis resembles the ideology he attempts to account for, especially with regard to the needs it would appear to fill in items one through three above, as follows:

1. Birchers are reduced to a readily defined and easily understood psychological phenomenon: they believe what they believe for nonrational reasons—reasons that smack of psychopathology.

2. This view of Birchers, whose beliefs and philosophy are profoundly distressing to "right-thinking" people, provides us with a sense of "self-righteousness" in seeing them thusly. We can camouflage our dehumanization of them in academic terms and regard them almost as mental patients or the subjects of an experiment.

3. Having exposed their fraudulent attempt at feeling superior, we can now reclaim it for ourselves. Who do these people think they are, anyway?

Again, all this is not to say that Broyles is totally wrong, but merely to raise a caution sign with respect to such pronouncements. Most political movements, extremist or otherwise, contain elements from contradictory sources and a whole range of inconsistencies in their beliefs and doctrines. Also, there is a difference between studying a movement or an organization and studying the *stereotype* of a movement or organization. Researchers wanting to confirm a hypothesis, from any perspective, can find subjects who will assist them. The way in which questions arc worded may have a profound effect on the outcome of any survey, as would countless other elements of setting, context, and interviewer technique.

A study by John J. Ray of the University of New South Wales, Australia, entitled "Half of All Racists Are Left Wing," calls into question some conventional beliefs about authoritarianism, conservatism, and racism. Dealing with prejudice toward Asians among white Australians, Ray found that individuals with traditional "left-wing" values were just as likely to be prejudiced against Asians as individuals with traditional "right-wing" values.

In discussing Adorno's *The Authoritarian Personality*, Ray says that it has "a particularly paranoid and misanthropic flavor. . . ." He also says that Adorno's suggestion that conservatism, authoritarianism, paranoia, misanthropy, rigidity, or some combination of these all go together "cannot, unfortunately, any longer be accepted." He adds,

> Ethnocentrism may be present on the political Right but is not confined to it. Any theory that links ethnocentrism with the political Right alone is therefore fundamentally faulty.[86]

The purpose in mentioning these findings by Ray is not to endorse them. Indeed, they may be as prone to bias and error as any other we have mentioned. The point is that there is no final authority on this issue nor any other issue associated with political extremism, and that much work needs to be done, or redone, as the case may be.

Orrin Klapp, author of *The Collective Search for Identity*, discusses nonspecific political extremism in the context of the "crusading" type of individual:

> The goal of a crusade is to defeat an evil, not merely to solve a problem. This gives it the sense of righteousness, of nobility . . . ; thus the crusader may think of himself as a hero and define his opponents as villains. Indeed, the crusade classifies as a kind of vilifying movement. . . .[87]
> . . . the crusader role has an unusual capacity for giving the feeling of "rightness"— more so, even, than rational certification procedures, such as court decisions, licensing, conferring of diplomas, or professional promotion. The crusades' power of conferring rightness resembles that of a cult in giving a deep moral, rather than a technical, sense of rightness, and in making life more exciting. . . .[88]

Klapp's thesis that crusaders attempt to capture the moral high ground is consistent with our own observations.

Eric Hoffer's book, *The True Believer*, has been mentioned previously. His companion volumes, *The Passionate State of Mind* and *The Ordeal of Change* are also well worth reading. Hoffer provides a wealth of insight into extremist motivation. An unschooled longshoreman, Hoffer has been regarded with disdain by some scholars and his own contempt for pompous intellectuals is legend. Nevertheless, he produced such insights as the following:

> The uncompromising attitude is more indicative of inner uncertainty than of deep conviction. The implacable stand is directed more against the doubt within than the assailant without.[89]

> The substitute for self-confidence is faith; the substitute for self-esteem is pride; and the substitute for individual balance is fusion with others into a compact group.[90]

In putting together a basic list of the most common motives political extremists may have, we suggest the following (some of which have already been addressed by others we have mentioned):

> To experience a sense of "moral superiority," or a feeling of being better than others who believe otherwise.

> To exercise power over others, directly or indirectly, by propaganda, manipulation, or by brute force. . . .

> To lose oneself in a movement . . . to relieve a sense of personal worthlessness and insecurity by being absorbed in a movement of noble aspirations far greater than one's flawed and imperfect self. . . .

> Propaganda addiction. Some people are stimulus-bound to stirring propaganda or emotional appeals. . . .

> Envy. Jealousy and envy of the success of other individuals, races, or classes, and their possessions, culture power, etc. . . .

> As a substitute for one-to-one relationships. . . . The psychic energy that would normally be expended in a love (or other personal) relationship is diverted to a cause, a group, a church, a movement, or a belief system.[91]

## The Democratic Personality

Having focused on the psychopathology of political extremism and the traits and behaviors that may account for it, let's now consider its antithesis—the democratic personality. It seems reasonable that if there is an extremist personality there should also be a "nonextremist" personality as well, or at least a complex of traits and behaviors that would mitigate in this direction. Many writers have discussed this concept, including several of those mentioned in this chapter (Lasswell, Greenstein, and Lane). Harold Lasswell used the term "democratic personality" to describe the antithesis of the authoritarian personality, and the concept shares some of the same problems, not the least of which is that it represents a stereotype which may reflect the interests and biases of the individuals defining it. Michael B. Binford discusses this democratic personality at length and contends that

The democratic personality has far greater ego strength, flexibility, tolerance, and more developed cognitive abilities. . . . These characteristics facilitate a much broader range of political behavior; this breadth of acceptable political behavior is also a distinguishing characteristic of a democratic political environment.[92]

Binford accounts for three basic subtypes of the democratic personality— the *socially adaptive,* the *cognitive,* and the *character-rooted*—and explains how they differ.

The *socially adaptive* subtype, according to Binford, focuses on and is deeply affected by peer group relations. With far less ego strength than the other two subtypes, the socially adaptive person depends upon considerable reinforcement from others. The level of political reasoning is rather simplistic and embraces the "good guys vs. bad guys" dichotomy to a large extent. Regarding this subtype Binford observes:

The existence of appropriate reference groups and of personal aspirations becomes very important, although the process of imitation, identification, and internalization of values and attitudes is not necessarily a conscious one.[93]

Of the three subtypes, this is the most problematic. Whether or not this kind of "democratic" personality actually contributes to democracy is questionable. (We have observed that the ranks of extremist groups contain a considerable number of impressionable and easily swayed individuals who can degenerate into mush at the hands of a charismatic extremist fanatic or be thoroughly bamboozled by any cause that promises to perfume their existence with nobility and goodness.) What is clear, however, is its differentiation from the authoritarian personality.

The *cognitive* subtype, on the other hand, is better grounded in reasoning abilities and more strongly attached to democratic norms. Its distinguishing characteristic is that these attachments are basically cognitive rather than emotional, and "drawn to traditional symbols and political activities but not to extreme or unconventional varieties."[94] Binford observes:

The cognitive democratic personality corresponds quite closely to what Berkowitz and Lutterman[95] . . . call the traditionally socially responded personality. They describe this personality type as having the cognitive ability to learn and accept the traditional norms and values of society, using them as a guide for social behavior. The traditional socially responsible personality is unalienated and participatory, a team player. . . . In reflecting the core values of American culture, he or she may appear conservative or status quo oriented.[96]

What Binford seems to be describing here is basically a conformist. Whether or not compulsive conformity is conducive to a democratic society is also questionable, although there's little doubt that conformity keeps social stresses to a minimum. As with the previous subtype, we have encountered more than a few individuals of this type in extremist circles. According to Binford:

This type of person differentiates a societal point of view from interpersonal motives and takes the point of view of the system, which defines roles and rules.[97]

The example of the cognitive personality subtype cited by Binford, appropriately named "Oliver," is a kind of idealized, well-socialized citizen who gives lip service to the symbols of a free society but doesn't want to get carried away with actually observing them.

> Oliver supports free speech in principle, but he sees nothing wrong with restricting the speech of inflammatory or violent groups. While acknowledging that demonstrations were necessary in "Dr. King's time," Oliver feels that such tactics have run their course and are no longer useful in bringing about social change. Disruptive and unconventional political practices apparently make him uncomfortable, and he does not support such activity.[98]
>
> He takes comfort from the social order, acting as an agent who enforces that social order on others. Disruptive or unconventional behavior, political or otherwise, is threatening to him, and, he believes, to society. He is quite knowledgeable about politics and can clearly justify his own beliefs and actions.[99]

So far the democratic personality described by Binford makes us a little nervous, but all is not lost. There is still the *character-rooted* subtype, which we believe is the genuine antithesis of the political extremist. According to Binford, the character-rooted democratic personality

> fuses cognitive and affective personal linkages with political beliefs. The democratic beliefs and values are congruent with the personality structure and psychological characteristics of the individual.
>
> The character-rooted democratic personality has a sophisticated and complex style of political reasoning. A good deal of contextual information is readily available and easily articulated. Such a personality is quite sensitive to the inherent paradoxes in most political problems.[100]
>
> He or she recognizes and supports the individual's right to oppose social norms, practices, and laws, when the opposition is based on universal principles. Given deeply internalized values and the support received from a congruent personality structure and ideology, this person is quite capable of opposing superiors, institutions, or groups, when personally valued, ethical principles are threatened.[101]

Binford notes that among the characteristics separating the character-rooted style of reasoning from the other subtypes is the appreciation of and ability to reason dialectically about a political problem. The example Binford cites is named "Alice," who escribes this ability:

> Ultra-conservative I see as wrong and ultra-radical movements, or whatever, are very wrong. But . . . philosophically, I feel like they both have to exist. In that, you've got to have the radical . . . to forge ahead and call our attention to (problems) like the Viet Nam war. . . . On the other hand, you've got to have your die-hard conservatives to hold us back from moving too fast. What I am saying is that the

two groups allow the rest of us to end up in the middle, which is where most of us ought to be. . . . I can tolerate . . . extreme points of view. . . . I can see diametrically opposing views existing at the same time as totally necessary.[102]

Thus, the character-rooted personality appears to represent the best embodiment of tolerance, civil libertarianism, and the principles of liberal democracy. Binford acknowledges that

The tolerance of opposing viewpoints and the appreciation of the utility of such views for social change is an important organizing principle for the character-rooted democratic personality.[103]

It is clear to us that the antidote to political extremism is not counter-extremism or "hating back," but rather to show a better way. Many people, in the quest to combat what they perceive to be some form of extremism, have become extremists themselves by adopting their very style and tactics.

We could go on, but we believe we have covered many of the major themes in the area of the psychology and sociology of political extremism and their attendant controversies. There is a wealth of material available but the reader must remain aware of problems of bias and of the availability of alternative points of view.

## Notes

1. Leon Dion, "Political Ideology as a Tool of Functional Analysis in Socio-Political Dynamics: An Hypothesis," *Canadian Journal of Political Science* 25 (February 1959): 49.

2. Max J. Skidmore, *Ideologies: Politics in Action* (New York: Harcourt, Brace, 1989), 7.

3. William E. Connolly, *Political Science and Ideology* (New York: Atherton, 1967).

4. Daniel Bell, *The End of Ideology* (Glencoe: The Free Press, 1960).

5. Talcott Parsons, *The Social System* (New York: The Free Press, 1951).

6. Edward Shils, "Ideology," in *The International Encyclopedia of the Social Sciences* (New York: Macmillan, 1968).

7. L. B. Brown, *Ideology* (Baltimore: Penguin Books, 1973).

8. Reo M. Chistianson, et al., *Ideologies and Modern Politics* (New York: Dodd, Mead, 1975).

9. Laird Wilcox, oral presentation (Marquette, Mich.: Western Michigan University, April 11, 1989).

10. Thomas Szasz, *The Untamed Tongue: A Dissenting Dictionary* (LaSalle, Ill.: Open Court, 1990), 54.

11. Herbert A. Kampf, "The Challenge of Marxist-Leninist Propaganda," *Political Communication and Persuasion* 4 (1987): 104. See also Lyman T. Sargent, *Contemporary Political Ideologies* (Homewood, Ill.: The Dorsey Press, 1969, 1972), 1–11; William Ebenstein, *Today's Isms* (Englewood Cliffs, N.J.: Prentice-Hall, 1973).

12. Szasz, 79.

13. Szasz, 115.

14. Theodore W. Adorno, Else Frenkel Brunswick, Daniel J. Levinson, and R. Nevitt

Sanford, *The Authoritarian Personality* (New York: Harper, 1950).

15. Milton Rokeach, *The Open and Closed Mind* (New York: Basic Books, 1960). An earlier response to Adorno was: Milton Rokeach, "Political and Religious Dogmatism: An Alternative to the Authoritarian Personality," *Psychology Monographs* 70 (no. 18, whole no. 425, 1956).

16. Richard Christie and Marie Jahoda, eds., *Studies in the Scope and Method of the "Authoritarian Personality"* (Glencoe, Ill.: The Free Press, 1954).

17. James A. Aho, *The Politics of Righteousness: Idaho Christian Patriotism* (Seattle: University of Washington Press, 1990).

18. Aho, 145.

19. Aho, 213.

20. Aho, 215.

21. David Hackett Fischer, *Historians' Fallacies: Toward a Logic of Historical Thought* (New York: Harper & Row, 1970), 200.

22. Fischer, 203.

23. Fischer, 209.

24. Mort LaBrecque, "On Making Sounder Judgments: Strategies and Snares," *Psychology Today* (June 1980), review of Robert Nisbett and Lee Ross, *Human Inference: Strategies and Shortcomings of Social Judgment* (Englewood Cliffs, N.J.: Prentice-Hall, 1980).

25. LaBrecque.

26. Eric Hoffer, *The True Believer* (New York: Harper & Row, 1951), 44.

27. Hoffer, 54.

28. Gabriel Almond, *The Appeals of Communism* (Princeton, N.J.: Princeton University Press, 1954), 272.

29. Guenter Lewy, *The Cause That Failed: Communism in American Political Life* (New York: Oxford University Press, 1990), 303.

30. William S. Maddocks and Stuart A. Lilie, *Beyond Liberal and Conservative: Reassessing the Political Spectrum* (Washington, D.C.: Cato Institute, 1984); David Boaz, ed., *Left, Right and Babyboom* (Washington, D.C.: Cato Institute, 1986).

31. Alex Inkeles, "National Character and Modern Political Systems," in F. L. K. Hsu, ed., *Psychological Anthropology* (Homewood, Ill.: The Dorsey Press, 1961).

32. Gordon J. DiRenzo, ed., *Personality and Politics* (New York: Doubleday Anchor, 1974), 157.

33. Hans Toch, *The Social Psychology of Social Movements* (Indianapolis, Ind.: Bobbs-Merrill, 1965), 13.

34. Ted Robert Gurr, *Why Men Rebel* (Princeton, N.J.: Princeton University Press, 1970).

35. Gurr, 24.

36. Gurr, 137.

37. John Lofland, *The Doomsday Cult* (Englewood Cliffs, N.J.: Prentice-Hall, 1966), advertisement.

38. Phillip Abbott Luce, *The New Left* (New York: David McKay, 1966), 35.

39. Laird Wilcox, oral presentation, *The Psychology of Ideological Belief Systems* (Bellingham, Wash.: Western Washington University, November 13, 1986).

40. Harold D. Lasswell, *Psychopathology and Politics* (New York: Viking Press, 1930), 78.

41. Lasswell, 125.

42. Harold D. Lasswell, *Power and Personality* (New York: Viking Press, 1948), 184.

43. Almond, 216.

44. Almond, 236.

45. Almond, 237–40.

46. Almond, 240–41.

47. Almond, 201–206.

48. J. Edgar Hoover, *Masters of Deceit: The Story of Communism in America* (London: Dent, 1958), 113 16.

49. For commentary on the essentially chiliastic character of Marxism see: Eric Hobsbawn, *Primitive Rebels* (Manchester: University Press, 1959), and *Revolutionaries* (London: Weidenfeld and Nicolson, 1973).

50. Richard Crossman, ed., *The God That Failed* (New York: Bantam Books, 1952).

51. Crossman, 255.

52. Crossman, 16, 23.

53. Harvey E. Klehr, *Communist Cadre: The Social Background of the American Communist Party Elite* (Stanford: Hoover Institution Press, 1978), 5.

54. Nathan Glazer, *The Social Basis of American Communism* (New York: Harcourt, Brace, 1962); Frank S. Meyer, *The Moulding of Communists: The Training of the Communist Cadre* (New York: Harcourt, Brace, 1962); Stanley Rothman and S. Robert Lichter, *Roots of Radicalism: Jews, Christians and the New Left* (New York: Oxford University Press, 1982); Lewis Feuer, *Conflict of Generations* (New York: Basic Books, 1969).

55. Brown, *Ideology.*

56. Fred I. Greenstein, *Personality and Politics: Problems of Evidence, Inference and Conceptualization* (New York: W. W. Norton, 1969).

57. Gordon J. DiRenzo, *Personality and Politics* (New York: Doubleday, 1974).

58. Lester W. Milbrath, in Leroy N. Rieselbach and George I. Balch, *Psychology and Politics: An Introductory Reader* (New York: Holt, Rinehart and Winston, 1969), 164–65.

59. Irving L. Janis, *Victims of Groupthink* (Boston: Houghton Mifflin, 1972), 9.

60. Walt Murray, "Hofstadter Talks on Paranoia," *The Dixon Line* (November 1966). See also Richard Hofstadter, *The Paranoid Style in American Politics and Other Essays* (New York: Knopf, 1965).

61. Murray.

62. David W. Swanson, MD, Philip J. Bohnert, MD, and Jackson A. Smith, MD, *The Paranoid* (Boston: Little, Brown & Co., 1970), 441.

63. Swanson, et al., 443.

64. *Christianity Today* (March 13, 1982, and October 23, 1981).

65. George Johnson, *Architects of Fear* (New York: Jeremy Tarcher, 1983), 87.

66. The Birch Society's proof for the Illuminati legend comes primarily from John Robison's *Proofs of a Conspiracy* (Belmont, Mass.: Western Islands, 1973). Originally published in the eighteenth century, it was republished by the society as part of its series. J. M. Roberts, *The Mythology of Secret Societies* (London: Secker & Warburg, 1972) traces the Illuminati legend in Germany and France. Vernon Stauffer, "New England and the Bavarian Illuminati," *Studies in History and Public Law,* vol. 82, no. 1 (New York: Columbia University Press, 1918), deals with the Illuminati in early American history.

67. Brown, 12–13.

68. Robert Welch, *American Opinion* (November 1966).

69. *Workers World* (February 25, 1965).

70. John A. Stormer, *None Dare Call It Treason* (Florissant, Mo.: Liberty Bell Press, 1964).

71. John A. Stormer, *None Dare Call It Treason: Twenty-five Years Later* (Florissant, Mo.: Liberty Bell Press, 1990).

72. Gary Allen, *None Dare Call It Conspiracy* (Rossmoor, Calif.: Concord Press, 1972).

73. Johnson, 135.

74. Johnson, 15.

75. Johnson, 11–12.

76. David Brion Davis, *The Fear of Conspiracy: Images of Un-American Subversion from the Revolution to the Present* (Ithaca, N.Y.: Cornell University Press, 1971).

77. Davis, 276–77, quoting from Earl Browder, *Report of the Tenth National Convention of the Communist Party of the U.S.A., on Behalf of the Central Committee* (1938), 7–8.

78. Richard O. Curry and Thomas M. Brown, *Conspiracy: The Fear of Subversion in American History* (New York: Holt, Rinehart, 1972).

79. Curry and Brown, 101, quoting from Richard Hofstadter, *The Age of Reform* (New York: Alfred A. Knopf, 1955).

80. Hoffer, *The True Believer,* 99.

81. Toch, *The Social Psychology of Social Movements,* 52.

82. David Spitz, "Power and Personality: The Appeal to the 'Right Man' in Democratic States," *American Political Science Review* 52 (1958).

83. Spitz.

84. J. Allen Broyles, *The John Birch Society: Anatomy of a Protest* (Boston: Beacon Press, 1964), 176.

85. Broyles, 151–53.

86. John J. Ray, "Half of All Racists are Left Wing," *Political Psychology* 5 (no. 2, 1984).

87. Orrin Klapp, *Collective Search for Identity* (New York: Holt, Rinehart, 1969), 274.

88. Klapp, 296–97.

89. Eric Hoffer, *The Passionate State of Mind* (New York: Harper & Row, 1954), 43.

90. Eric Hoffer, *The Ordeal of Change* (New York: Harper & Row, 1963), 5.

91. Laird Wilcox, oral presentation before the Kansas City Association for Holistic Health (Kansas City, Mo.: February 15, 1984).

92. Michael B. Binford, "The Democratic Political Personality: Functions of Attitudes and Styles of Reasoning," *Political Psychology* 4(4): 669 (December 1983).

93. Binford, 668–69.

94. Binford, 673.

95. L. Berkowitz and K. Lutterman, "The Traditionally Socially Responsible Personality," *Public Opinion Quarterly* 32: 169–85 (1968–69).

96. Binford, 673.

97. Binford, 675.

98. Binford, 674.

99. Binford, 676.

100. Binford, 676.

101. Binford, 677.

102. Binford, 678.

103. Binford, 678.

# Part II. The Far Left

The far left in America consists principally of people who believe in some form of Marxism-Leninism, i.e., some form of Communism. A small minority of extreme leftists adhere to "pure" Marxism or collectivist anarchism. Most far leftists scorn reforms (except as a short-term tactic), and instead aim for the complete overthrow of the capitalist system including the U.S. government. In Lenin's view, the battle for an eight-hour work day was nothing more than a "tactical maneuver to improve the power position of the party" and those who saw it as something more were guilty of vulgar reformism.[1]

Recent developments in the Soviet bloc and elsewhere have complicated the international Marxist-Leninist picture, and the impact of these enormous changes is only now being felt on groups in the United States. Generally, orthodox Marxism-Leninism is in increasing disfavor.

In the traditional form, virtually all Marxist-Leninists may be categorized as follows: Soviet, Trotskyist, Maoist/Kimist/Hoxhaist, or Independent. The pro-Soviet types, for example, include the Communist Party USA and the Young Communist League, who always regarded the USSR as the way, the truth, and the light until the Gorbachev reforms.

Trotskyists are those communing with the ghost of Leon Trotsky (1877–1940), who was expelled from the Soviet Union by Joseph Stalin in 1928. Stalin and Trotsky had many differences, but the main one was over building Marxian socialism in one country (Stalin) v. bringing revolutions in all nations as rapidly as possible (Trotsky). More realistically, Stalin's expulsion of Trotsky was a matter of eliminating a rival and the ideological considerations were a convenient rationalization. A Stalinist agent, Spanish Communist Ramon Mercador, assassinated Trotsky in Mexico in 1940. The Socialist Workers Party was the main Trotskyist organization in America until 1985, when its leaders abandoned their commitment to Trotsky's ideas in favor of a more flexible line.

The Maoists/Kimists/Hoxhaists could be accurately termed neo-Stalinists. After Nikita Khrushchev's denunciation of Stalin in 1956, these die-hards wrote off the Soviet Union as hopelessly revisionist and came to adopt the views of the Chinese leader Mao Tse-tung, or his avid follower, the late Albanian dictator Enver Hoxha, or the aging North Korean strongman Kim Il Sung. The first well-organized American Maoist group (1962) was the Progressive Labor Party, which later denounced Mao in 1971 over his backing of Pakistan against the Mukti Bahini guerrillas in East Pakistan (now Bangladesh).

Independent Communists are those who claim to follow the line of no nation or group except their own. Independents have never cared for the Soviet Union, while some have given "critical support" to Cuba or even China. American groups of this nature include the Workers World party (originally Trotskyist) and the Progressive Labor party (originally Maoist).

Inasmuch as political extremism is more a matter of style rather than content, it's not the case that the only left extremist groups are the Marxist-Leninists. Any group identified with nominally "leftist" political positions may be "extremist" to some extent. Extreme radical feminists or environmentalists, for example, may be as "extreme" in their behaviors as the most dedicated Marxist-Leninist. One of the modern innovations of Marxist-Leninist theory has been the increasing transformation of ethnic and gender oppression to overshadow the traditional role of working-class oppression in its worldview. However, for the purposes of this book we have focused on groups that espouse distinct political ideologies.

## Note

1. Gabriel Almond, *The Appeals of Communism* (Princeton, N.J.: Princeton University Press, 1965), 17–18.

# 4. Communist Party USA

The Communist Party USA, commonly referred to as the CP, is the best known as well as the largest and best-funded of all left extremist groups in the United States. Founded in 1919 as one of two rival Communist parties, the Workers Party, as it was then known, came upon the American scene in the years following the Russian revolution and managed to pull several thousand members together in competition with other socialist and Marxist organizations.

According to its own publication, *Communist* (September 1939), the party reached a claimed membership of 100,000 that year. This figure seems a bit high. At any rate, party membership remained above the 50,000 mark until the 1950s, when it plummeted dramatically, not rebounding until the mid-1960s and then only modestly so.

Figures on membership vary enormously. David A. Shannon in *The Decline of American Communism* estimates CP membership in the summer of 1957 at 10,000. Richard Gid Powers in *Secrecy and Power: The Life of J. Edgar Hoover* puts December 1957 membership at 3,474, which would be a remarkable decline over so few months. Richard Starr in the *Yearbook on International Communist Affairs, 1969–1987* estimates CP membership in 1968 at 13,000 and in 1971 at 15,000. The CP's *Daily World* of October 10, 1972, stated that membership was 16,500. Harvey Klehr in *The Heyday of American Communism* estimates 1988 CP membership at 15,000. That same year Gus Hall claimed a membership of 20,000. On the other hand, Stephen Schwartz of the Institute for Contemporary Studies estimated the 1988 figure between 5,000 and 6,000.[1]

Few things in extremist politics are more controversial, more "secret," and more lied about than membership figures. Part of this comes from organizations wanting to inflate their image and give the impression of a large following. Paradoxically, some antiextremist groups tend to exaggerate their opponents' "threat," and inflating membership figures is one way to do it. Generally, we have found membership claims to be exaggerated. Our estimate of current Communist Party USA membership is in the neighborhood of 4,000 to 5,000 or one Communist for every 50,000 to 60,000 Americans.[2]

Several factors led to the decline of the CPUSA. Among these were the 1956 Hungarian uprising and Khrushchev's revelations about Stalin, both of which brought numerous defections from the party. Perhaps most important, however, was the government's steady campaign of surveillance and harassment. The McCarthy period took a heavy toll on party members, as did the House Un-American Activities Committee hearings of the 1950s and 1960s. The Rosenberg spy case and widely publicized loyalty-security cases such as the Hiss-Chambers affair helped foster an alien and subversive image of the party. By 1960 it was almost impossible to recruit new members. This onus remained until the radical student movement grew on college campuses in the mid and late 1960s, when the CP began to grow significantly again. Nevertheless, the CP never regained any substantial base among American intellectuals or the working class. Like other Marxist-Leninist groups, it remained highly marginalized and small.[3]

Several Communist party "front" organizations from the 1950s and before continue in one form or another to the present day. Among these are Veterans of the Abraham Lincoln Brigade, which numbered about 350 in 1986. The official name was the Abraham Lincoln Battalion of the 15th International Brigade. Steven Nelson, national commander of the group in 1986 and once a prominent CP member, noted, "The burning issue then was the danger of Fascism." Of the some 3,000 brigaders, about 60 percent were members of either the Communist party or the Young Communist League. On April 7, 1986, the remnants of the brigade assembled in New York City to commemorate their role in the Spanish Civil War. Abe Smorodin, then sixty-nine years old, said:

> My parents and grandfather were radicals. It was as natural for me to be a radical as it was for other Jewish kids to have a bar mitzvah. The volunteers all came out of various political activities of the time, out of the Depression. We were all in the Young Communist League.[4]

Other front organizations surviving into the 1960s were the American Committee for the Protection of Foreign Born, the Labor Research Association, the National Council of American-Soviet Friendship, and the U.S. Peace Council. Other groups with less direct present-day "links" to the CPUSA and its allies are the National Lawyers Guild, the National Emergency Civil Liberties Committee, and the Center for Constitutional Rights—all of whose commitment to civil liberties consists of defending only those causes and individuals congenial to their politics.[5]

The National Lawyers Guild is probably the most influential of all present-day groups with past CPUSA ties. By 1990 it reached approximately 8,000 members, about a third of whom were law students. NLG president Paul Harris has said:

> The role of U.S. multi-national corporations, the action of the U.S. Government abroad—these are our responsibilities, as we live in what Che Guevara accurately called "the belly of the beast."[6]

Doris Brin Walker, an NLG member since 1941 and a past president (1970), has stated that it had been the struggle of the working class that

> has been both the keystone of my adult beliefs and the touchstone of my professional and organizational life. It is this commitment which makes me so proud to be a member of the Communist Party.[7]

John Quigley, an NLG vice president (1978), appears to have embraced some of the tenets of Marxist-Leninist revolutionary dogma. He has stated:

> The Guild is not Amnesty International. Its aim is not to ferret out human rights violations wherever they exist. As an anti-imperialist organization, its aim is to aid national liberation struggles.[8]

The NLG remains a member of the Soviet-run International Association of Democratic Lawyers, founded in 1946. According to Clive Rose:

> In October, 1949, after the break between Stalin and Tito, the IADL expelled the Yugoslav delegation. The NLG representatives at the IADL meeting voted for this resolution, but the Guild repudiated this step and urged that the Yugoslav section be restored to membership. In the years since, the IADL has continued to be a faithful supporter of Soviet foreign policy, including the invasions of Hungary, Czechoslovakia, and Afghanistan, but the NLG no longer dissociates itself from these positions.[9]

The National Lawyers Guild is one of the many bridges linking the old left with the new. Many of the leading activists in the student radical left of the 1960s were NLG members and active in terrorist groups such as the Weather Underground or the May 19th Communist Organization. These included Bernardine Dohrn, NLG national student organizer in 1967 and a former federal fugitive, and Judith Clark, now serving a prison term for her part in the Brinks robbery and murder in Nyack, New York, in 1981. Another prominent NLG member whose span of activism ranges from the 1960s to the present day is Chip Berlet, researcher for Political Research Associates and a founding member of Chicago Friends of Albania.[10]

\*     \*     \*

In the mid-1960s the CP attempted a comeback by trying to attract more young people, and it had some success through the now-defunct W. E. B. DuBois Clubs of America, a party affiliate that was the ideological successor to the Young Communist League. The CP also stepped up its recruiting among women and minorities.

In the summer of 1966, the CP held a national convention, its first since 1959. The convention report hailed gains among youth, but voiced displeasure over the party's predominantly white membership. Kind words were directed toward the Student Non-violent Coordinating Committee (SNCC), Students for a Democratic Society (SDS), and the DuBois Clubs, but "ultraleft" groups such as Youth Against War and Fascism (YAWF), Young Socialist Alliance (YSA) and Progressive Labor (PL) were taken to task, mainly on the grounds that they were allegedly influencing young people to take narrow and sectarian positions.

The DuBois Clubs of America were named after the late W. E. B. DuBois, a respected sociologist and historian who helped to found the NAACP. He later became pro-Communist, moved to Ghana, and renounced his American citizenship. There, at the age of ninety-three, he joined the Communist party.

The national founding convention of the DuBois Clubs was held in June 1964, but the Berkeley, California, DuBois Club existed for about three years before this convention. Among those who were instrumental in the founding were Terrence and Matthew Hallinan, sons of Vincent Hallinan, a wealthy lawyer who ran for president on the CP-backed Progressive party ticket in 1952. Better known by their nicknames, Kayo and Dynamite, the Hallinan brothers developed a reputation for their quick tempers and proficiency at boxing and brawling. Others who were present at the founding convention were such party regulars as Alva Buxenbaum, Mike Zagarell, Eugene Dennis (son of former CP general secretary Eugene Dennis, Jr.), Marvin Markman, Bettina Aptheker (daughter of party theoretician Herbert Aptheker), and Carl Bloice, who became editor of the DuBois Clubs' publication, *Insurgent*. A number of CP regulars were invited as observers. These included Douglas Wachter, Mickey Lima (chairman of the Northern California CP), Roscoe Porter , and Al Richmond, editor of the West Coast CP newspaper, *People's World.* Despite the presence of their well-known guests, the DuBois Clubs tried to act as though they were independent of the CP. Ex-Maoist Phillip Luce commented:

> As a "voting delegate" at their founding convention I know that they are the youth arm of the CPUSA. . . the undeniable fact is that they are controlled, financed, and led by Gus Hall and his cronies. The DuBois Clubs are about as independent of Communist Party influence as the Buick Motor Car Company is of General Motors.[11]

At the end of the summer of 1965, four of the five top leaders of the DuBois Clubs participated in a meeting with several leading party members, including Gus Hall and Mike Zagarell. This meeting was supposedly secret. Hall criticized the DuBois Clubs for appearing to be nothing more than a CP youth organization and said that they should try to change their image by broadening their leadership and enlarging their membership. Hall was apparently saying that they should try not to look like what they actually were—a CP youth group.

The Communist party's outreach to young people has a long history. The Young Communist League was formed in April 1922. By 1925 the organization claimed to have 4,000 members. The circulation for their publication, *Young Worker,* was perhaps twice that. During the Depression era, when Communist party membership grew considerably, YCL membership may have hit 10,000. A majority of the Communists who fought in the Abraham Lincoln Brigade in the Spanish Civil War were YCL members. During the "Popular Front" period, when Communists cooperated broadly with liberals and nonparty leftists, the YCL claimed to have 10,000 members in New York City alone; that figure is probably somewhat exaggerated.

In 1943 the Communist party dissolved the YCL into American Youth for Democracy, which four years later was succeeded by Young Progressives for America, largely for the purpose of supporting Henry Wallace's Progressive party presidential bid. This group folded when Wallace was defeated, and in 1949 the Labor Youth League was formed. By the early 1950s the LYL claimed a memberhip of 5,000. According to Paul Buhle in the *Encyclopedia of the American Left:*

> It did not grow into a mass movement so much as train its activists for intellectual, social, cultural, and organizational contributions to the civil rights, antiwar, and other movements in later decades. Former members loomed especially large in campus life of the 1960s, as senior advisers to the New Left.[12]

The Communist party folded the Labor Youth League in 1957 shortly after the Khrushchev revelations at the 20th Soviet Congress. It was not until 1965 that the CP attempted to field another youth-oriented organization. As the civil rights movement was gathering steam and the antiwar movement was starting up, the DuBois Clubs were founded, although they later proved to be ill-equipped to compete with the burgeoning radical student movement in the late sixties and folded in 1971. Nevertheless, the CP established the Young Workers Liberation League that same year, although it actually amounted to little more than a name change. This, in turn, was dissolved, and once again the Young Communist League (refounded in the spring of 1983) emerged on the American scene. Membership in 1990 probably was less than a thousand.

In late 1966, two Trotskyists and two Maoists informed us that it was common knowledge among young leftists that the CP started the DuBois Clubs in order to eventually recruit more young members from the student left. As one of the "Trots" put it: "The CP looked around one day and noticed their average age was over fifty. That's when they decided to start the DuBois Clubs." This analysis, though simply put, was evidently accurate, since the clubs eventually became nonexistent, while, according to the young radical grapevine, several hundred former DuBois Club members joined the CP.

The majority of young left extremists long have considered the CP to be made up of tired old people knowing little about revolution and only able to talk of the way they "almost had one going back in the thirties." In fact, the fascists were probably closer to success in the late 1930s than were the Communists. The CP had been called "a bunch of old ladies who live in the Bronx" by some of the young radical leftists. The compliments that the party once paid to Students for a Democratic Society (SDS) were never returned. SDS members and young Marxist-Leninists generally have looked upon the CP with contempt and have considered party publications to be boring at best.

\*    \*    \*

The 22nd National Convention of the Communist Party USA was held August 23-26, 1979, in Detroit—a city that has been one of the party's strongholds along with New York City, Chicago, Philadelphia, Cleveland, and Los Angeles. This was also the occasion of the CPUSA's sixtieth anniversary. A total of 369 delegates attended the convention from thirty-nine states and the District of Columbia.

Of these 24 percent were black, 36 percent were female, 29 percent were under thirty, and 53 percent had been party members for fewer than ten years. Representatives of some forty-seven foreign Communist parties were present, including a member of the Central Committee of the Communist Party of the Soviet Union, Peter Fedoseyev.

At the 1983 National Convention 17 percent were black, 43 percent were female, 7 percent Mexican-American or Puerto Rican, and 17 percent other racial or ethnic minorities, 21 percent had been party members for less than five years, 32 percent were between the ages of eighteen and thirty-four, and 25 percent were over the age of sixty-five. These figures are in contradistinction to the Depression-era Communist party, in which the party membership was predominantly white males. In 1983 only 25 percent of the party were white males.[13]

The most widely read CP publication is the *People's Weekly World* (formerly the *People's Daily World, The Daily Worker, The Worker,* and the *Daily World*). For decades the quarterly *Political Affairs* has been their theoretical journal. Although many of the statements found in the publications are considered extreme by most Americans, they appear moderate and even stodgy when compared to those found in ultraleft publications like *Progressive Labor,* the *Revolutionary Worker* or *Worker's World.*

In 1988, Gus Hall, chairman of the CPUSA since 1959, surprised observers by not running for president. He had been the party's candidate for every election since 1972. The CP had never done well at the polls, although some of its failure is undoubtedly due to requirements that effectively keep third parties off the ballot in many states. Hall received 25,595 votes in 1972; 58,992 in 1976; 45,023 in 1980, and 35,561 in 1984.[14]

Although thousands of people have quit the CP, others have remained year after year. Why? One answer is that people do not like to admit they have been wrong. Some have excused the brutality and terror perpetrated in the name of Communism by blaming Joseph Stalin for everything bad, never considering that the core philosophy of Marxism-Leninism might be at fault. Gabriel Almond, writing prior to Khrushchev's revelations about Stalin and before the Hungarian uprising, gave still another reason why people stay in the CP:

> Because of the dangers of disbelief, the fully initiated Communist clings to the party even though he is deeply troubled by its actions. He escapes from risks by taking cover within the party's system of ethical and political perception, rejoices in the enormity of the evils of the world outside since it renders more bearable the evils of his own, fingers his ideological beads, and walks forward soberly cultivating the tactical virtues.[15]

The CP has always occupied a special place among large sectors of America's leftist intellectual establishment, especially since the "Great War" when the United States and the Soviet Union were allied against Nazism and fascism. However, the crimes of Marxism-Leninism have not been particularly hidden. They are, in fact, common knowledge. Yet, in spite of this there is a convention among some leftist intellectuals that Arthur Schlesinger calls "anti-anti-Communism."

This label applies to those who think it fine to be anti-fascist, anti-Republican, or anti-Democratic but who squirm and wince when someone in exactly the same sense is anti-Communist. All forms of baiting are okay for the "anti-anti-Communist" except red-baiting. Some of the "anti-anti-Communists" are not substantially pro-Stalinist. They just have a feeling that a Communist is a rather noble, dedicated fellow who deserves special consideration in a harsh and reactionary world.[16]

A split in the party was narrowly averted in 1968 when a resolution backing the Soviet invasion of Czechoslovakia passed by only one vote (according to insiders). Dorothy Healey, a CP functionary on the West Coast, and Al Richmond, editor of the West Coast equivalent of the *Daily Worker,* the *People's World* (which merged with the *Daily Worker* to become the *People's Daily World* in 1986), were among the leaders of the faction opposing the resolution. Always somewhat of a maverick, Healey was relieved of her position as chairman of the southern district of the California branch of the party as punishment for her heresy; along with Richmond, she was expelled in 1973. Later, Peggy Dennis, widow of former CPUSA general secretary Eugene Dennis, resigned in protest of the treatment meted out to Healey and Richmond.

Although the government had kept close watch on the Communist party almost from its inception, and especially during the late 1940s and early 1950s, systematic FBI harassment of the party and its members through its Counter-Intelligence Program (COINTELPRO) was started in 1956 and continued into the late 1960s. The purpose of COINTELPRO was to destroy the party with a campaign of "dirty tricks," which included the planting of destructive rumors about party officials and members, encouraging dissension, and so on. It was marginally effective and undoubtedly played some role in the party's fortunes. The bureau continues to "monitor" the party to this day, although not nearly as intensely as previously.

In the fall of 1969 and twice in the summer of 1970, the party was again in the news. The focus of attention was on Angela Davis, a young black philosophy teacher at UCLA and an admitted Communist who became a controversial media figure as the result of being fired from her teaching position and her indirect connection with a kidnapping and murder. Shortly after Davis was hired at the university it became known that she was a CP member who had deep sympathies for the Black Panther party. When pressure was exerted to have her removed, she brought legal action and eventually a California court found in her favor. She taught the 1969–70 term at UCLA. In the summer the California regents announced that her contract would not be renewed—not, they said, because of her party membership, but because of certain public speeches she had made. Civil libertarians were highly disturbed, especially Montgomery Furth, chairman of the UCLA philosophy department, who stated:

The allegations that she used her teaching position to indoctrinate students, or that her work as a faculty member is in any way impaired by her political activities, have been conclusively disproved, as the board admits. . . . The true reason for their action is that she is a Communist, and the board's disclaimer of this point is hypocritical and dishonest.[17]

The CP was, no doubt, overjoyed with this type of publicity, but both they and the civil libertarians were quite unprepared for the next time Angela Davis made the news.

In August 1970, a heavily armed seventeen-year-old Black Panther party sympathizer named Jonathan Jackson barged into a Marin County, California, courtroom, handed firearms to three San Quentin inmates and took five hostages, including the judge. He planned to use the hostages to secure release of three people, including his older brother George, from Soledad Prison. In the shoot-out that ensued, Jackson, two of the three San Quentin convicts, and the judge were killed.

What was Angela Davis's connection with this incident? She had allegedly purchased four of the firearms used in the attempt and given them to Jackson. Under California law an accomplice to a crime is as guilty as the person who actually commits the crime. Thus, a warrant was issued for kidnapping and murder, and Davis became one of the FBI's "Ten Most Wanted." She disappeared amid speculation that she had left the country, but in October 1970 she was arrested in New York. After her arrest, Gus Hall stated that the charges were a "fraud and a frame-up," and the CP released a statement that referred to Davis as a "brilliant Black Communist and freedom fighter."

The Angela Davis case became a cause célèbre for leftists the world over, especially in the Soviet Union, where the question "Why are you persecuting Angela Davis?" was asked of all U.S. officials. Meetings were held in the Soviet Union to "protest against the trial of the courageous daughter of the American people." But when Soviet officials were questioned about the cases of Leningrad Jews accused of plotting to hijack an airplane, they stoutly maintained that these cases were an "internal affair." Hence the double standard: "Your trials are our business—ours are internal matters." It is not difficult to see why adulators of the Soviet Union always have been low on American popularity lists. Incidentally, after a short deliberation, the jury acquitted Angela Davis.

Guenter Lewy has commented on the role Angela Davis plays in promoting the image of American Communism as a benign force:

Communist leader Angela Davis has found praise as a person of significant achievements from the most unexpected quarters. In October 1988, Dartmouth College celebrated the anniversary of fifteen years of coeducation, and Angela Davis was the principal speaker. For reasons best known to the Dartmouth administration, the press was not permitted to record the speech, but one reporter took notes. The introduction was given by a Dartmouth dean who included among Davis's accomplishments the award of the Lenin Peace Prize in Moscow. The dean went on: "Angela Davis' life is an example of how one committed black woman activist has chosen to make a difference."[18]

Lewy notes that recently there has been a general prohibition against attacking anyone for their Communist party affiliations or membership, while individuals with membership in right-wing groups are readily identified.

> If during the years of McCarthyism all too many Americans suspected a Communist under every bed, the conviction now appears to be equally widespread that there are no Communists under any bed. A substantial segment of the American intellectual community today embraces a philosophy of anti-anticommunism no less reflexive than the obsessive anticommunism that did exist in some circles during the 1950s.[19]

Anti-anticommunism was clearly the motive behind a three-day conference held at Harvard University in November 1988, where 1,200 people heard lectures on the conference theme, "Anticommunism and the U.S.: History and Consequences." Among the speakers was Gus Hall, who characterized anticommunism as

> the biggest hoax ever perpetrated against a whole people . . . (Anticommunism) . . . remains the main ideological justification for imperialist aggression and U.S. world domination. . . .The rich and the powerful will continue to benefit and the American people will suffer until we rid society of the anticommunist myth.[20]

*    *    *

Since 1940, the Communist party has claimed to be an American party, strictly independent of the Soviet Union. Recent revelations about Soviet funding of the CPUSA dispute that claim. In November 1991, Alexander A. Drosdov, editor of the Soviet newspaper *Rossiya,* revealed that seized Soviet Communist party records confirmed that "the Communist movement in the United States had been regularly supported by the annual stipend (of $2 million) with an occasional supplement of $1 million more."[21] Also, to our knowledge, the party has never opposed the Soviet line on any significant issue. This shows signs of changing, as it seems that some CPUSA leaders have not been at all enamored with a number of the Soviet reforms that have been enacted since 1989. According to an inside source, by the beginning of 1991 the CP National Committee (formerly the Central Committee) was split over the concept of democratic centralism; the hardliners held a bare majority. The National Committee also voted to take some power away from the National Board (Politburo). The CP no longer runs recruiting ads in their publications and no active recruiting is taking place. Our source also stated that CP membership was 4,000 as of January 1991. He further asserted that Gus Hall's recent directives have been generally ignored, that "what Hall writes is no longer sacrosanct," and that "there is more debate within the Communist Party USA today than ever before in its history."

It's difficult to predict the precise future of the CPUSA. Given its tenaciousness it would seem likely, however, that the party will be around in some form for a while, and remain small and highly marginal. However, the recent breakup of the Soviet Union complicates even that prognosis. As we write, splits and factions have formed in party ranks and major defections and expulsions have occurred. It must be heartbreaking to be a dedicated, hardcore American Communist today.

Whatever threat to our society this group may have represented at one time in our history, we believe it has remained far less of a threat than the ill-advised attempts to suppress it. A society that is willing to let extremist groups function openly is probably safer than one that attempts to ban or persecute them. It is one thing to investigate and persecute bona fide acts of violence or espionage, and when extremist groups engage in illegal activities the individuals involved should be held accountable. It is quite another to harass and intimidate advocates of unpopular ideas. A society that vigilantly persecutes its critics and opponents is no longer a free society.

# Notes

1. David A. Shannon, *The Decline of American Communism: A History of the Communist Party of the United States* (Chatham, N.J.: Chatham Bookseller, 1971); Richard Gid Powers, *Secrecy and Power: The Life of J. Edgar Hoover* (New York: Free Press, 1987); Richard Starr, ed., *Yearbook on International Communist Affairs, 1969–1987* (Stanford, Calif.: Hoover Institution Press, 1970–87); Harvey Klehr, *The Heyday of American Communism: The Depression Decade* (New York: Basic Books, 1984); Sam Roberts, "Top Communist in U.S. Is Taking 'Fever' in Stride," *New York Times* (December 8, 1988); Stephen Schwartz, quoted in Henrik Bering-Jensen, "This Time, No Comrade Candidate," *Insight* (January 18, 1988).

2. This estimate is based upon what was known of the party before the collapse of the Soviet Union in late 1991.

3. William L. O'Neill, *A Better World: The Great Schism, Stalinism and the American Intellectuals* (New York: Simon & Schuster, 1982); Joseph R. Starobin, *American Communism in Crisis, 1943–1957* (Berkeley: University of California Press, 1972); David A. Shannon, op. cit.; Guenter Lewy, *The Cause That Failed: Communism in American Political Life* (New York: Oxford University Press, 1990).

4. Richard F. Shepard, "Lincoln Brigade Veterans Assemble," *New York Times* (April 7, 1986).

5. Harvey Klehr, *Far Left of Center: The American Radical Left Today* (New Brunswick, N.J.: Transaction Books, 1988); Guenter Lewy, *The Cause That Failed: Communism in American Political Life.*

6. Ann Fagan Ginger and Eugene M. Tobin, eds., *The National Lawyers Guild: From Roosevelt Through Reagan* (Philadelphia: Temple University Press, 1988), 341.

7. Ginger and Tobin, 359.

8. *Congressional Record* (March 3, 1978), p. E1023.

9. Clive Rose, *Campaigns Against Western Defense: NATO's Adversaries and Critics* (New York: St. Martin's, 1985), 262, quoted in Lewy, 286.

10. Klehr, 162; flyer, Chicago Friends of Albania, 1987.

11. Phillip A. Luce, *The New Left* (New York: David McKay, 1966), 114 and 138.

12. Mari Jo Buhle, Paul Buhle, and Dan Georgakas, *Encyclopedia of the American Left* (New York: Garland Publishing, 1990), 874.

13. Arnold Bechetti, "CPUSA Convention"; John Pittman, "For Peace, Jobs and

Equality," *World Marxist Review* (February 1984).

14. Klehr, 13.

15. Gabriel A. Almond, *The Appeals of Communism* (Princeton, N.J.: Princeton University Press, 1965), 379.

16. Arthur Schlesinger, Jr., in the *New York Post* (May 4, 1952), quoted in Victor Navasky, *Naming Names* (New York: Viking, 1980), 54.

17. "Red Prof Plans Suit Over Job," *Oklahoma Journal* (June 21, 1970).

18. Lewy, 132.

19. Ibid.

20. Lewy, 131.

21. "Kremlin Financed Communist Party in U.S., Editor Says," *Kansas City Star* (December 1, 1991), A-26.

# 5. Socialist Workers Party

For decades the Socialist Workers party (SWP) was the official Trotskyist party in the United States and a part of the international movement started by followers of Leon Trotsky after he was expelled from the Soviet Communist party near the end of 1927. Early American Trotskyist leaders included James P. Cannon, Karl Skoglund, Martin Abern, Rose Karsner, V. R. Dunne, and Max Shachtman, and others who took Trotsky's side in his power struggle with Stalin and were expelled from the Communist Party USA for their trouble. They founded the Communist League of America in 1928. CLA publications included *The Militant* (weekly) newspaper and a theoretical journal, *International Socialist Review* —titles used by current SWP periodicals.[1]

In 1934 the CLA merged with A. J. Muste's American Workers party to form the Workers Party of the United States, which in 1936 merged with Norman Thomas's Socialist Party of America. However, when the Trotskyists tried to take over the Socialist party—at Trotsky's direction—they were tossed out in 1937, taking many young Socialist party members with them, who together formed the Socialist Workers party the next year. They had 1,200 supporters at the time.[2]

Following their exclusion from the SP, the Trotskyists complained of the "reformist" nature of the organization. The SP, in turn, complained of the "disruptive" nature of the Trotskyists. After establishing as the SWP the Trotskyists appropriately joined Leon Trotsky's newly created Fourth International, which in turn had emerged from Trotsky's International Left Opposition organization.

A significant Trotskyist split also occurred in 1935, when Hugo Ohler and some two hundred of his followers were expelled from the CLA for opposing the entry of Trotskyists into social democratic parties. Ohler went on to form the Chicago-based Revolutionary Workers League, whose official publication was the *Fighting Worker*. In 1941 the leadership of the RWL was assumed by Sidney Lens; that group folded in the early 1950s.[3]

James Cannon remained a lifelong Trotskyist, while Max Shachtman, a former editor of *The Militant,* founder of Pioneer Press, and Trotsky's "commissar of foreign affairs," became a strongly anticommunist social democrat.[4] A well-known conservative writer who left the SWP in 1940 with Shachtman was James Burnham, who became an editor of *National Review* for many years. His book, *The Managerial Revolution,* has been compared to George Orwell's *1984* in its depiction of a totalitarian collectivist society.[5]

Each of the many splits and schisms in the SWP drained it of its most creative members. Shachtman took some five hundred members with him in 1940, and

Bert Cochran, who left in 1953, took another two hundred. Most prominent figures in the American left had been members of the Socialist Workers party at one time, including Harry Braverman, C. L. R. James, Hal Draper, Staughton Lynd, and Murray Weiss.[6]

Two groups split from the SWP in late 1963 and early 1964—the Spartacist League and the Workers League. The former had fewer than one hundred members and published *Spartacist,* a tabloid. The Workers League (referred to derisively as the "Wohlforth Family Circle," after its leader, Tim Wohlforth), had less than a hundred members and published the weekly *Bulletin.* Both groups spent much time in mutual denunciation and in arguments with the SWP concerning strategy and tactics—i.e., how Trotsky would have interpreted a particular political situation, or some obscure point of Marxian ideology. A WL pamphlet, *Black Nationalism and Marxist Theory,* has skewered other viewpoints, particularly those of the SWP and its youth group, the Young Socialist Alliance.[7] A former leftist has commented that at least Jim Robertson, a former Spartacist leader, "has a sense of humor, which is what keeps him from going mad when he reads his own material."[8] It is not for nothing that the term "Trotskyist" or "Trotskyite" has come to mean a contentious and nit-picking ideologue.

The SWP tended to believe that although the Soviet Union had many shortcomings and that its leadership (along with the leadership of China and other Marxist-Leninist dictatorships) had "sold out" the workers, it was still fairly close to a "worker's state" (the SWP term has been a "degenerate worker's state") and therefore should be defended against "reactionary forces." Far more impressed with Cuba, the SWP has lavished praise on the Castro regime. In fact, their uncritical worship of Cuba led them to basically ignore the fact that Castro persecuted and jailed a number of Cuban Trotskyists.

The general line of the SWP is that racial minorities and the white working class are ripe for revolution, but that they are held back by their leaders. They believe that a "revolution" ultimately will be necessary to destroy capitalism in the United States and elsewhere.

The SWP's youth group is the Young Socialist Alliance, founded in 1960. Although represented on many college campuses, it has failed to attract a very large membership. For example, the 1969 YSA convention in Minneapolis drew about seven hundred participants. However, not all attendees were members and this was the peak year of its membership. At that gathering, spokesmen for the group claimed a figure of nine thousand members, a transparently fantastic exaggeration. In fact, the 1970 membership was in the neighborhood of five hundred, and it has gradually declined over the years to a figure of approximately half that today.

In the mid-sixties the YSA made a number of attempts to gain control of several Students for a Democratic Society (SDS) chapters around the nation—with very limited success. Another strategy was to form the National Mobilization Committee to End the War in Vietnam on numerous campuses. The founders and leaders of most of these committees were either SWP/YSA members or Trotskyist fellow travelers. During the late 1960s the SWP and YSA began to take on some of the membership demographics of the "New Left," with a dramatic increase in female membership.

The *Young Socialist,* a professionally done monthly tabloid of twenty or more pages, is the official organ of the YSA. In addition to numerous articles on Marxist-Leninist analysis of gender and ethnic issues, the tabloid rhapsodizes about the accomplishments of numerous third-world, one-party Marxist-Leninist dictatorships. Despite occasional claims of independence, the YSA is simply a junior version of the SWP, and its policies are those of the parent body.

A prominent SWP spokesman in the sixties and seventies, Paul Boutelle, a taxi driver, was the party's candidate for vice president in 1968. On one of the several occasions we observed Mr. Boutelle, he utilized the phrase "international bankers," a stock buzzword of the extreme *right,* in delineating his various conspiracy theories. On another occasion Boutelle spoke heatedly, quoting from Lenin's *Imperialism: The Highest State of Capitalism.* The audience was informed that World Wars I and II were merely wars between thieves for the raw materials of the world. The simplistic, moralizing "good guys vs. bad guys" rhetorical style of Marxism-Leninism is clearly evident in SWP and YSA propaganda.

The SWP candidate for president in 1968 was Fred Halstead, whose mother was a follower of Eugene Debs. His father was in the IWW and was also an early member of the SWP. Halstead joined the party in 1947 when he was twenty, and in 1955 moved to New York from California to become a staff writer for *The Militant.* He is a cloth-cutter by trade.

*    *    *

According to Paul LeBlanc in the *Encyclopedia of the American Left:*

> In the early 1980's—as the new SWP leadership put forward a far-reaching critique of Trotsky's theory of permanent revolution—about 200 veteran members were driven out for resisting the abandonment of major aspects of the SWP program. Many more drifted away in demoralization, though the SWP remained one of the major organizations on the American left, with perhaps 700 members.[9]

The SWP has been involved in numerous violent scuffles. On a few occasions they were attacked by extreme rightists, but more often by other Marxist-Leninist groups. Almost from the beginning, head Trotskyist James Cannon was forced to form a defense guard to protect his followers from attacks by Communist party members. In the sixties and seventies SWP and YSA members were attacked by Progressive Labor party members, Black Panthers, and others. The volatile National Caucus of Labor Committees, headed by Lyndon LaRouche, also committed battery against the SWP on occasion. In the mid-1970s a grand jury indicted one Thomas Stewart, a member of the rightist Legion of Justice, for armed robbery and aggravated battery in connection with an attack on the SWP Chicago headquarters. The Los Angeles and Austin SWP offices were also attacked. In Austin a bomb was involved, but it did not explode. Also in mid-

1970, a group of Progressive Laborites attempted to break into an SWP front-group meeting without first registering as required. A PL spokesperson stated, "If people attack us on the way in we intend to defend ourselves."[10]

Adopted by the Congress in 1940, the Smith Act made it a criminal act to advocate or encourage the overthrow of the U.S. government. It was first used against members of the Socialist Workers party. Twenty-eight defendants were brought to trial in 1941, including SWP national secretary James P. Cannon; national labor secretary Farrell Dobbs; SWP attorney Albert Goldman; editor of *The Militant,* Felix Morrow; and Teamsters Union Local 544 leaders V. R. Dunne and Karl Skoglund. The defendants were convicted and served from twelve to eighteen months during 1944–45.[11]

One of the more frightening examples of harassment of domestic radicals occurred in May 1963: Monroe County (Bloomington, Indiana) Prosecutor Thomas A. Hoadley indicted three Indiana University students—James Bingham, Tom Morgan, and Ralph Levitt, all officers of the Young Socialist Alliance chapter at IU—for assembling on March 25 and advocating the "violent overthrow" of the state of Indiana and the United States government in violation of the 1951 Indiana Communism Act.

In March 1964, Monroe County Circuit Court Judge Nat Hill ruled the 1951 Indiana law unconstitutional and dismissed the indictments against the students. Hoadley appealed this decision to the Indiana Supreme Court where, in January 1965, in a split decision, the court reversed Hill's ruling and upheld the law.

The unconstitutionality of this law derives from two U.S. Supreme Court rulings delivered in the cases of Pennsylvania v. Nelson (1956) and Yates v. United States (1957). The former decision, involving a state statute similar to the Indiana act, held that prosecution of "subversion" is preempted by federal legislation, allowing no such action by state authorities. In the latter case, brought under the federal Smith Act, the Court opined that even advocacy of the violent overthrow of the government as an abstract doctrine, and not as an appeal or incitement to immediate action, is protected by the guarantees of the First Amendment to the Constitution.

The 1951 Indiana law reads, in part, as follows:

It shall be unlawful for any person to be a member of the Communist Party or any party, group, or organization which advocates in any manner the overthrow, destruction, or alteration of the constitutional form of Government of the United States or the State of Indiana, or any political subdivision thereof by revolution, force, violence, sedition, or which engages in any un-American activities.

It shall be unlawful for any person by word of mouth or writing to advocate, advise, or teach the duty, necessity, or propriety of overthrowing or overturning the Government of the United States or of the State of Indiana or any political subdivision thereof by force or violence; or print, publish, edit, issue, or knowingly circulate, sell, distribute, or publicly display any book, paper, document, or written or printed matter in any form for the purpose of advocating, advising, or teaching the doctrine that the Government of the United States, or of the State of Indiana, shall be overthrown by force, violence, or any unlawful means.[12]

The law also provides penalties "whenever two or more persons assemble for the purpose of advocating or teaching" in much the same way as currently popular antiparamilitary legislation directed at the extreme right does for "whoever assembles with one or more persons for the purpose of training with, practicing with, or being instructed in. . . ."

Finally, in 1968, after a four-and-a-half-year battle, attorneys for the defendants received the order dismissing the charges against all three students. Signed by Hoadley's successor, it dismissed the charges with prejudice, which means that the three cannot be indicted for the same "offense" again.

*    *    *

In the early 1970s the SWP began a complex legal action against the FBI for decades of harassment and surveillance of SWP members and leaders. Having obtained detailed records of the FBI's counterintelligence program (COINTEL-PRO) against the party under the Freedom of Information Act, SWP attorneys discovered an "SWP Disruption Program." The trial, in which the SWP asked for $40 million in damages and an injunction preventing the FBI from monitoring the party, commenced in April 1981. *Cleveland Plain Dealer* staff writer James Neff reported:

> According to documents, the FBI kept watch over the SWP since 1940, opening and copying mail, planting informants in leadership ranks, wiretapping members' homes, bugging conventions, and breaking into party offices.
>
> Between 1960 and 1976 . . . the FBI paid $358,648 to 1,300 informants, including 300 party members, for information on the 2,000-member party and its affiliate, the Young Socialist Alliance.[13]

Among the specific actions detailed in the lawsuit were incidents in which the FBI threatened an SWP member with arrest by local police for traffic violations unless that member became an informant, sending bomb threats over the telephone to an SWP office, breaking into an SWP office and taking a typewriter and a $100 case, and tossing smoke bombs at a Young Socialist Alliance meeting. The government did not dispute this information and, in fact, tried to settle out of court—but the SWP refused, hoping to garner much publicity and increase the ultimate settlement.

According to Neff:

> "The issue in this case," U.S. Atty. John S. Martin, Jr., said in a pretrial statement, "is whether the government has a right to keep itself informed of the activities of groups that openly advocate revolutionary change in the structure and leadership of the government . . . even if such advocacy might be within the letter of the law."
>
> Despite decades of investigation, the government says it has been unable to find evidence of criminal wrongdoing by the SWP.[14]

In August 1986 U.S. District Judge Thomas P. Greisa ruled against the FBI and awarded the SWP a total of $246,000. In August 1987 Judge Greisa issued an injunction against the FBI's use of an estimated one million pages of investigative documents compiled on the SWP and its members since 1940 for any reason whatsoever, without the judge's personal consent, due to the illegal activities involved in the gathering of the material.[15]

The Socialist Workers party has run candidates for countless national, state, and local elections, fielding U.S. presidential candidates in every election since 1940. In 1988 James MacWarren received 15,604 votes, or .02 percent of the total cast for president.

Next to the Communist Party USA, the SWP is the largest functioning Marxist-Leninist political party in America today. Membership remains well under a thousand and at last report was declining.

## Notes

1. George Breitman, ed., *The Founding of the Socialist Workers Party* (New York: Monad Press, 1982); James P. Cannon, *The History of American Trotskyism* (New York: Pathfinder Press, 1972).

2. Paul LeBlanc, *Trotskyism in America, The First Fifty Years* (New York: Fourth International Tendency, 1987).

3. Sidney Lens, *Unrepentant Radical* (Boston: Beacon Press, 1983).

4. Alan Wald, *The New York Intellectuals* (Chapel Hill: University of North Carolina Press, 1987).

5. James Burnham, *The Managerial Revolution* (New York: John Day, 1941). Also see: Burnham, *The Machiavellians* (New York: John Day, 1943), and *The Struggle for the World* (New York: John Day, 1947).

6. Paul LeBlanc, in Mari Jo Buhle, Paul Buhle, and Dan Georagakas, *Encyclopedia of the American Left* (New York: Garland Publishing, 1990), 727–28.

7. Tim Wohlforth, *Black Nationalism and Marxist Theory* (New York: Labor Publications, 1970).

8. Phillip A. Luce, *The New Left* (New York: David McKay, 1966), 170.

9. Paul LeBlanc, op. cit.

10. *The Militant* (June 12, 1970).

11. James P. Cannon, *Letters From Prison* (New York: Merit Publishers, 1968); Cannon, *Socialism on Trial* (New York: Pathfinder Press, 1973).

12. *Indiana Burns Statutes,* Chapter 226, H. 72, Approved March 5, 1951, Communism Act.

13. James Neff, "Workers' Party Drive to Launch FBI Trial Comes to Fruition," *Cleveland Plain Dealer* (March 29, 1981), 3-AA.

14. Ibid.

15. For the SWP's account of this event see: Margaret Jayko, ed., *FBI on Trial: The Victory in the Socialist Workers Party Suit Against Government Spying* (New York: Pathfinder Press, 1988); and Cathy Perkus, ed., *The FBI's Secret War on Political Freedom* (New York: Monad Press, 1975).

# 6. Black Panther Party

The Black Panther party was founded in 1966 by Huey Newton, Bobby Seale, and David Hilliard, students at Merritt College in Oakland, California. They had been influenced by the writings of Frantz Fanon, Malcolm X, Robert F. Williams, and Mao Tse Tung, and drafted a ten-point program, the last of which contained approximately the first 250 words of the Declaration of Independence. This program included demands for the power to determine the destiny of the black community, full employment for blacks, an end to capitalist exploitation, decent housing, exemption from military service for all blacks, freedom for all black prisoners, and a UN-sponsored plebiscite "in which only black colonial subjects will be allowed to participate, for the purpose of determining the will of black people as to their national destiny."[1]

The program immediately raised questions as to method of implementation, but perhaps the most interesting point deals with the power to determine the destiny of the black community. It is likely that the early Panthers, who felt themselves to be the "vanguard of the proletariat," assumed that such an awesome responsibility should fall upon their shoulders. Thus, if their program were implemented, they could become virtual dictators of countless black communities. The Panthers no doubt believed they were nearer to the people, understood their needs, and had their best interests at heart—the claim of all twentieth-century dictators.

Newton and Seale did most of their recruiting on street corners rather than campuses. Talk of violence was heard from the very beginning of the organization. Though self-proclaimed revolutionaries, the two founders proved better-than-average capitalists and made money to buy guns by purchasing Mao's *Red Book* for thirty cents apiece and then selling them on the Berkeley campus for a dollar. Soon they commanded a small but well-armed group.

The first Panther program involved patrolling the black community in Oakland with weapons in plain sight, to keep "tabs" on the police. According to Gene Marine, in his sympathetic account entitled *The Black Panthers,* when police stopped a black the Panthers sometimes intervened to advise the suspect of his rights. Furthermore, Marine claims that incidents of police brutality and harassment, as well as entering homes without warrants, definitely lessened under these circumstances.[2]

After his release from prison in 1967, the author of the 1969 bestseller *Soul On Ice,* Eldridge Cleaver—who maligned the assassinated Robert Kennedy as "another dead pig"—joined the Panthers. Cleaver, Newton, and Seale published

114

the first issue of the organization's tabloid, *The Black Panther*. Later involved in a fracas with the police, Cleaver had his parole revoked. In 1968, the Panthers leader vanished from the country, going to Cuba through Canada. During the next seven years he lived in or paid extended visits to Algeria, North Korea, the Soviet Union, a few subsaharan African nations, and France.

During the seventies, Cleaver underwent a number of changes in sociopolitical and religious position: Algerian-oriented revolutionary, Kim II Sung admirer, born-again Christian, Mormon, and Moonie. Add to these the short enchantment with the rightist Nation of Islam (Black Muslims) before becoming a Panther, and the saga of Eldridge Cleaver becomes even more complex.[3] In an interview with *Reason* magazine, Cleaver mentioned the beginning of his disillusionment with Marxism-Leninism:

> To go to a country like Cuba or Algeria and see the nature of control that those state apparatuses have had over the people—it was shocking to me. I didn't want to believe it.[4]

In 1986 Cleaver was in Eugene, Oregon, on behalf of CAUSA-USA, an anti-Communist organization sponsored by the Unification Church. Although he once called Dr. Martin Luther King an "Uncle Tom" for his nonviolent teachings, Cleaver said he now felt different:

> I can tell you that I have no hesitation in saying that if we could turn back the clock, I would support Dr. Martin Luther King, as opposed to being very eager to go down to the OK Corral and shoot it out with the police.
>     I really believe the peaceful way is the best way, and I feel that an appreciation of our own history and goals should be our guide.[5]

Several other former Panthers have retracted their previous ideological allegiances. Anthony Bryant hijacked an airliner to Havana in 1968, hoping that Fidel Castro would supply him with weapons to initiate guerrilla warfare in the United States. Instead, Castro threw him in jail. Released in 1980, Bryant became an anti-Communist making the rounds of the John Birch Society's American Opinion Speaker's Bureau in 1987. In an interview that year he said:

> I've lived in the belly of the beast. . . . While there in Cuba, I witnessed three executions. I watched them dance around the bodies. They placed guards on us and beat us excessively. But I had to go there to find these things out.[6]

Capping his ideological conversion, Bryant supported Pat Robertson in the 1988 presidential elections.

\*     \*     \*

In May 1967 thirty Panthers, twenty carrying unloaded weapons, entered the California State Assembly to protest a bill that would criminalize the carrying of loaded weapons within incorporated areas. The action brought national media attention, although in retrospect it appears that coverage was somewhat distorted. Later the same year (in October), Huey Newton got entangled in a shoot-out with two policemen; one was killed, the other wounded. Newton also sustained a wound.[7]

The exact circumstances of the incident will probably never be known; as might be expected, Newton and the surviving officer, Herbert Heanes, told decidedly conflicting stories. During Newton's trial there was agitation (via signs and shouting) to "Free Huey," but he was sentenced to two-to-fifteen years. In August 1970 the California Supreme Court upheld a lower court reversal of his murder conviction on grounds that the jury had not been properly charged, and the Panther leader was freed on $50,000 bail. After two trials for voluntary manslaughter ended in hung juries, the state dropped all charges against Newton in the fall of 1971.

Newton was also tried twice in the late seventies for the 1974 murder of a young prostitute, but both ended in hung juries and the charges were dropped. In addition, Newton was implicated in the brutal beating of a middle-aged tailor, Preston Collins. On the witness stand, Collins said he remembered the beating but couldn't be sure who his assailant was. It was later revealed that Newton had paid Collins $6,000.[8]

In August 1989 Newton was gunned down in Oakland. His murderer evidently was an apolitical thug. Claybourne Carson and David Malcolm Carson have noted:

> Upon his return to the U.S. [from Cuba], Newton remained a controversial figure. Although he completed a doctorate and remained politically active, he was also involved in the drug trade. He was shot to death in the summer of 1989 in a drug-related incident.[9]

*    *    *

Bobby Seale, originally a defendant in the "Chicago 8" trial (in connection with actions during the 1968 Democratic convention), disrupted courtroom proceedings to such an extent that a mistrial was declared in his case. Later tried for involvement in the torture-murder of one Alex Rackey (whom the Panthers claim had been a police informant), Seale was acquitted. He ran for mayor of Oakland in 1974 and lost. In 1979 he moved to Washington, D.C., where he founded Advocates Scene, Inc., a non-profit consulting organization for community groups. A detailed account of his experiences and difficulties is contained in *A Lonely Rage: The Autobiography of Bobby Seale*. In the late seventies, his political views moderated, and his cookbook, *Barbecue'n with Bobby*, has sold fairly well.[10]

In 1985 Seale was traveling the campus lecture circuit debating with Stuart Pringle, a South African citizen who contended black South Africans were not yet ready for democracy. At the University of Portland Seale said, "I can talk to him. I believe I'm changing his mind about things." Pringle responded, "I intend to win Bobby Seale's heart. I'm three-fourths of the way there."[11]

*     *     *

A December 1969 pre-dawn Chicago police raid on a Panther apartment left Fred Hampton and Mark Clark dead and four other Panthers wounded. Previous police-Panther shootouts had left questions as to who had "started it" or what the facts were, or it had appeared that evidence was on the side of the police. This Chicago case was different. Evidence did not bear out the police version that the police were fired upon repeatedly without provocation. The *Chicago Tribune* published the police version of the incident, while the *Sun-Times* and the *Daily News* of Chicago gave equal coverage to conflicting stories.[12] *Newsweek* commented:

> Actually both the *Sun-Times* and the *Daily News* reflected in their coverage what was plain to every reporter who inspected the Panther flat after the shooting: there were no bullet holes in any wall where there should have been if the Panthers had been firing.[13]

After a four-month investigation, a federal grand jury found that over eighty shots were fired by police and only one by a Panther. Furthermore, the grand jury report stated that police testimony was inconsistent with the physical evidence of the case. The Panthers were criticized for their refusal to testify before the grand jury. In typical stubborn manner they had declined because the jury was not "composed of their peers." By this time it was evident to the observer that police-Panther mutual hatred had spawned the whirlwind.

More than one and a half years later the Supreme Court of Illinois ordered a Chicago judge to release a grand-jury indictment of those involved in the aforementioned raid in which Fred Hampton and Mark Clark were killed. The good judge had been keeping the document "under wraps." Among those named in the indictment were four policemen who investigated the tragedy, eight who made the raid, an assistant state's attorney, and Mayor Daley protégé Edward V. Hanrahan, state attorney for Cook County. Hanrahan was accused of providing false information to the news media, giving false information to obtain indictments against the Panthers, and authorizing a TV reenactment of the raid by police.

In spite of their revolutionary rhetoric and behavior and the constant thread of criminal activities that ran through the group almost from its inception, the Black Panther party was still the victim of political repression. Clayborne Carson and David Malcolm Carson describe the actions taken against the party by the FBI:

> Police raids and covert efforts of the FBI's counterintelligence program contributed to the tendency of Panther leaders to suspect the motives of black militants who did not fully agree with the party's strategy or tactics. In August 1967 the FBI targeted

the Panthers when it launched its COINTELPRO operations designed to prevent "a coalition of militant black nationalist groups" and the emergence of a "black messiah" who might unify and electrify these "violence-prone elements." FBI misinformation, infiltration by informers, and numerous police assaults contributed to the Panthers' siege mentality.[14]

Paradoxically, the FBI and other federal agencies have undertaken in recent years an almost identical program against white racist groups, such as the Ku Klux Klan. The COINTELPRO program was formally discontinued in 1971, but a "reasonable facsimile" has been in use to the present day, only this time directed almost exclusively against the extreme right.

Ward Churchill and Jim Vander Wall detail the COINTELPRO program against the Black Panther party and the American Indian Movement in *Agents of Repression*. They describe a December 3, 1970, memorandum from the Los Angeles field office to FBI headquarters that recommends a letter be forged and mailed—supposedly by a disgruntled party member—to Eldridge Cleaver, then in exile in Algeria. The letter should attempt to

provoke Cleaver to openly question Newton's leadership. . . . It is felt that distance and lack of personal contact between Newton and Cleaver do offer a counterintelligence opportunity that should be probed. . . . (Additionally) each division (of the FBI) should write numerous letters (under similar circumstances) to Cleaver criticizing Newton's leadership. It is felt that, if Cleaver received a sufficient number of complaints regarding Newton it might . . . create dissension that later could be more fully exploited.[15]

FBI headquarters approved this COINTELPRO deception—one of a dozen similar and well-documented correspondence efforts taken with regard to the Newton-Cleaver factional fight alone.[16] Apparently it worked. According to Peter L. Zimroth:

During the next several months, the rift in the Party widened. Two Black Panther Parties emerged—one led by Newton and (Bobby) Seale, and one led by Cleaver in Algeria. . . . On March 8, 1971, Robert Webb, a Panther loyal to Cleaver, was shot in New York. One month later, Samuel Napier, loyal to Newton, was scalded, shot to death, and then set on fire in the Party's office in Queens.[17]

Another detailed account of FBI disinformation and destabilization operations against black militants is Kenneth O'Reilly's *Racial Matters,* which also documents FBI operations against the Communist Party USA, Martin Luther King's Southern Christian Leadership Conference, the Black Muslims, the Student Non-Violent Coordinating Committee, and the Ku Klux Klan.[18]

Ideologically, the Panthers always were a confusing mess. Many spouted Marxist-Leninist rhetoric and tried to indoctrinate with theories they evidently didn't understand. Theoreticians they were not. Several Panthers carried Mao's *Red Book* and quoted it frequently, but they denounced most domestic Maoist organizations. And although they yelled "fascist" at many who opposed them, it's doubtful that more than a handful could have even discussed the essential characteristics of fascism. However, haphazard theories didn't deter them from sponsoring a United Front Against Fascism in July 1969, which was attended by left extremists of all varieties. Requirements for attendance had been set forth by the deputy minister of information, Masai Hewitt: "First you've got to be against fascism, and second, you can't be anticommunist."[19] Speechmakers at the conference included attorneys Charles Garry and William Kunstler, who often defended Panthers, and Communist party theoretician Herbert Aptheker.

Contrary to many reports, the Black Panthers *as a group* were not racists, black nationalists, or separatists, although some individual members had leanings in these directions. However, they did become self-proclaimed "communists" with emphasis on the small "c." They followed no party line but their own and took no orders from the Communist party, China, the Soviets, or anyone else. The Workers World party, then a Maoist group which voiced support without giving a lot of advice, was able to stay on good terms with the Panthers.

*     *     *

One group, no longer very active, that merged for a short time (from February until August 1968) with the Black Panthers was SNCC—the Student National Coordinating Committee (formerly Student Nonviolent Coordinating Committee). An entirely different type of organization than when it first appeared on the political scene, SNCC went through five stages, the fifth being advocacy of revolutionary violence.

Jack Newfield described SNCC's other four stages. When the group came into being in 1960, the majority were civil-rights activists with a general religious motivation. The second stage (1962) involved nonviolent protests, voter registration, and community organization projects in slums. The third stage (1964) emphasized freedom and participatory democracy.[20] The fourth stage involved growing pains in late 1965, but reached full bloom in May 1966, when Stokely Carmichael became chairman. This phase emphasized "independent black power, race pride, black dignity, and the third world," and SNCC released a statement that rejected participation in the White House Conference on Civil Rights. Part of the statement read:

> We cannot in good conscience meet with the chief policy maker of the Vietnam War to discuss human rights in this country when he flagrantly violates the human rights of colored people in Vietnam.

From that time it wasn't long until Carmichael was speaking typical Marxist-Leninist jargon and Rap Brown was threatening the nation with flames. Brown, supposed to stand trial in Maryland in March 1970, disappeared that same month. The next time he appeared was during an October 1971 armed robbery attempt at a New York bar. He was arrested, tried, convicted, and sentenced to five-to-fifteen years in prison.

Although some informed commentators believe that the organization had covert links with Cuba as early as 1964, SNCC's first overt move into the violent-revolution camp seems to have begun sometime in 1966, when chairman Stokely Carmichael began having contact with Max Stanford, then leader of the Revolutionary Action Movement (RAM), a secretive Maoist organization of fewer than one hundred people. Stanford was arrested in mid-1967 as part of an alleged plot to assassinate Roy Wilkins of the NAACP and Whitney Young of the Urban League.

*    *    *

In mid-1967 Stokely Carmichael abdicated leadership of SNCC to H. Rap Brown —louder and wilder than his predecessor, and lacking Carmichael's finesse and all-around smoothness. (Brown later passed the torch to Phil Hutchings.) With that, Stokely decided to visit a few "revolutionary" countries. He started by going to Havana for the Conference of the Organization for Latin American Soldiarity (OLAS), where a number of his statements revealed familiarity with Marxist-Leninist revolutionary terminology, if not theory:

> We want to destroy capitalism economically because this system always goes hand in hand with racism and exploitation. It is no secret that wherever capitalism has been kept up these two characteristics are certain to be seen. Consequently, it is our duty to destroy the capitalist system which enslaves us at home and enslaves the peoples of the Third World abroad.[21]

Carmichael was asked his opinion of other black organizations in the United States, such as Martin Luther King's Southern Christian Leadership Conference. He answered that at present he supported a united front against "the most fascist regime in the world":

> But the time will come very soon when there will be no reason to discuss and nothing to discuss and when we will simply eliminate all those who put obstacles in the way of the real liberation of the black people.[22]

In answer to a question regarding the type of struggle to be used against U.S. imperialism, Carmichael replied:

> Let me make it quite clear that the only solution is a black revolution and that we are not interested in peaceful coexistence. Armed struggle is the only way, not only for us but for all the oppressed people in the world. The people who talk about peaceful coexistence today are talking about maintaining the status quo because the only way to destroy an imperialist system is through force, since talking doesn't get you anywhere. That is something that is especially clear to us.[23]

Carmichael elaborated:

We are organizing urban guerrillas in the United States according to the tactics inspired by [Che] Guevara of creating two or three more Vietnams to bring the collapse of capitalism and imperialism.

As we develop our revolutionary conscience, we must begin to develop urban guerrilla warfare. We are ready to meet the savagery of the white United States with arms.[24]

After Havana, Carmichael visited Hanoi, then Algiers, where he was quoted by the Algerian news agency as saying, "It is clear that the only solution for Negroes in the United States is revolution. That is why we have come to see what we can learn from our brothers in Africa."

In February 1968 Carmichael challenged Cleaver's role as the main spokesman for the party. Carmichael's sophisticated pan-African perspective, emphasizing black racial unity, was at odds with that of other Panther leaders, who emphasized the Marxist-Leninist concept of the class struggle and working with white leftists. Carmichael resigned as the party's "prime minister" in the summer of 1969. The SNCC-Panther alliance soon fell apart.[25]

At a June 1968 staff meeting the SNCC representatives voted not to adopt the Panthers' ten-point program. Later meetings between the two groups almost ended in violence, and one SNCC member stated, "I can't work with anybody I don't feel right turning my back on."[26] (At this time SNCC probably had no more than a hundred members, the Panthers no more than a thousand.)

Don A. Schanche followed the Panthers' exploits closely and wrote several articles and a book (*The Panther Paradox*) on them. He believes that they had a Samsonian thirst for "retributive suicide" which showed up in almost everything they did "from their children's breakfast program," which was actually

only a front, like the Cubs and Brownies, for implanting party dogma in ever younger minds, to the deliberately self-defeating courtroom tactics of the Panther 21 or Bobby Seale, an impassioned man of extremely limited vision and intelligence.[27]

Schanche maintained that the Panthers were not only ungrateful to civil libertarians who tried to ensure their rights, but strongly disliked these people; in fact, they did not want their liberties within the existing judicial system because they aimed to destroy the system itself. The liberal journalist further contended that the Panthers often challenged the courts to deprive them of their liberties. By taking this course of action these militants had "become the leading anti-civil-libertarians in this country, and every dime sent to their legal fund simply strengthened that destructive cause" and enabled them to purchase more guns and spend more time in the "indoctrination of aggrieved and therefore malleable little children."[28]

Although many left extremists condemned all criticism of the Black Panthers as originating in reactionary or fascist quarters, Don Schanche's credentials as a liberal always seemed in order. Consider this commentary on the Panthers:

Their totalitarian ideology and obsession with violence are not minor matters. They are not merely psychological tendencies apparent only among a minority of Panther members. Nor do they spring only from a need for black self defense against police oppression in the ghetto. They are a central element in a consciously held, rigorously enforced and militarily aggressive political philosophy. One may, perhaps, explain the rise of the Panthers in terms of the injustice of ghetto life, just as one can explain the rise of Fascism in terms of the wartime humiliation and post-war economic collapse of the German nation. But to explain is not to justify. All genuine liberals and democratic radicals must vigorously oppose the Panthers' political program.

This excerpt is from an April 1970 statement by the national committee of the Socialist party—hardly a reactionary organization.

*    *    *

Two important developments occurred in early and mid-1971. The first of these was a split in the Black Panther party involving Huey Newton on one side and Eldridge Cleaver on the other. They expelled each other from the party, then threatened violence.

The second development was Newton's announcement in late May that the Panthers had been using incorrect tactics. He admitted they had lost favor with the black community, and he stated that in the future they would become involved in church and community affairs. From now on, he announced, the party would work within the system. The Black Panthers, evidently trapped by their own rhetoric, behaved in a provocative manner and utilized questionable strategy. No American organization would be likely to gain a large following by quoting Mao's *Red Book* or praising North Korean dictator Kim Il Sung. Nor would cartoons urging the murder of police officers be conducive to producing a mass movement. (But these cartoons were of questionable origin. In fact, according to FBI documents released under the FOIA, they were actually published and distributed by the FBI in a COINTELPRO disinformation attempt.)

For all practical purposes, the Black Panthers ceased to exist in the early 1980s. However, in March 1991 the tabloid newspaper, *The Black Panther,* reappeared in Oakland, California. According to an Associated Press dispatch:

> The revived newspaper, subtitled *Black Community News Service,* is a quarterly but otherwise much the same as the old *Black Panther.* . . .
>
> Policy will still be guided by the party's 10-point platform, which lists a series of goals including decent housing and free health care. Demonstrating the party's more radical side, the platform also says that "all black and oppressed people would be armed for self-defense of our homes and communities against these Fascist Police Forces."
>
> The new paper, which costs $1 a copy, is published by a non-profit group and will carry a financial statement in each issue.[29]

# Notes

1. Bobby Seale, *Seize the Time: The Story of the Black Panther Party and Huey P. Newton* (New York: Random House, 1970).

2. Gene Marine, *The Black Panthers* (New York: Signet Books, 1969).

3. Eldridge Cleaver, *Soul On Ice* (New York: Dell, 1969); with Lee Lockwood, *Conversation with Eldridge Cleaver: Algiers* (New York: McGraw-Hill, 1970); *Soul On Fire* (Waco, Tex.: Word Books, 1978).

4. *Reason* (February 1986).

5. Dana Tims, "Cleaver Talks Change, Without Violence," *The Oregonian* (June 23, 1986), B3.

6. Steve Penn, "Ex-Black Panther Now a Capitalist," *Kansas City Times* (October 5, 1987).

7. Huey Newton, *Revolutionary Suicide* (New York: Harcourt Brace Jovanovich, 1973).

8. Kate Coleman and Paul Avery, "The Party's Over," *New Times* (July 10, 1978), 34–35.

9. Mari Jo Buhle, Paul Buhle, and Don Georgakas, *Encyclopedia of the American Left* (New York: Garland Publishing, 1990), 97.

10. Bobby Seale, *A Lonely Rage: The Autobiography of Bobby Seale* (New York: Times Books, 1978); *Barbecue'n with Bobby* (San Francisco: Ten Speed Press, 1988); Donald Freed, *Agony in New Haven: The Trial of Bobby Seale, Ericka Huggins, and the Black Panther Party* (New York: Simon & Schuster, 1973).

11. Nancy McCarthy, " '60s Warrior Bobby Seale Wages New Battle in '80s," *The Oregonian* (October 16, 1985).

12. Earl Anthony, *Picking Up the Gun* (New York: Dial, 1970).

13. *Newsweek* (December 22, 1969), 91.

14. Buhle, et al., 97.

15. Quoted in Ward Churchill and Jim Vander Wall, *Agents of Repression: The FBI's Secret Wars Against the Black Panther Party and the American Indian Movement* (Boston: South End Press, 1990), 40.

16. Sanford Ungar, *FBI* (New York: Little, Brown & Co., 1976), 41.

17. Peter L. Zimroth, *Perversion of Justice: The Prosecution and Acquittal of the Panther 21* (New York: Viking Press, 1974).

18. Kenneth O'Reilly, *Racial Matters: The FBI's Secret File on Black America, 1960–1972* (New York: The Free Press, 1989). For yet another account see M. Karenga, *The Roots of the US/Panther Conflict* (San Diego: Kawaida Publications, 1976).

19. *Guardian* (June 21, 1969), 3.

20. Jack Newfield, *A Prophetic Minority* (New York: New American Library, 1966).

21. *World Outlook* (October 6, 1967), 803.

22. Ibid., 804–805.

23. Ibid., 806.

24. David Lawrence, "Agitators Are Screened," *Oklahoma City Times* (August 5, 1967).

25. Buhle, et al., 97.

26. *Guardian* (August 24, 1968), 15.

27. Don A. Schanche, "Panthers Against the Wall: Liberty, Fraternity, Insanity," *Atlantic* (May 1970): 56.

28. Ibid., 61. Before reading Schanche's writings we held views quite similar to his.

Ours were formed by reading the party's newspaper, *The Black Panther, Guardian, Daily World, Workers World,* Gene Marine's *The Black Panthers,* and several articles in *Ramparts*—none of which drew the same conclusions that Schanche and we did.

29. "Black Panther Back on Stands, Says 'The Struggle Continues,' " Associated Press, March 21, 1991.

# 7. Students for a Democratic Society

It will be most instructive to discuss Students for a Democratic Society under two headings: "Early SDS" and "Late SDS."

## Early SDS

The organization originally descended from a group called the Student League for Industrial Democracy (SLID), which was formed in 1930 by members of the League for Industrial Democracy (LID), itself founded in 1905 as the Intercollegiate Socialist Society by Jack London, Upton Sinclair, and other radicals of the time. LID had always worked closely with (and had overlapping membership in) the Socialist party. According to Joseph Conlin:

> LID's history paralleled that of the larger party. With the waxing of American Communism during the late 1920s and 1930s, the Socialist Party, and LID with it, drifted into an anti-revolutionary reformist politics, filling a niche between the mainstream liberals and the revolutionist, pro-Soviet Communists. Like Norman Thomas, its leader for almost forty years, the party functioned somewhat as the conscience of the liberals. Socialist policies did not really differ from what the New Dealers preached. Simply, the Socialists believed in ideas the New Dealers found merely useful.[1]

SLID was perhaps the main student group on the anticommunist left during the 1930s and represented the Socialist opposition to the National Student Union, a Communist-controlled organization active on many campuses. These two groups later "merged to form the American Student Union, which died a few years later, torn apart by an internal struggle between Socialists and Communists."[2]

After World War II, SLID was temporarily revived, but it soon faltered again, due in part to the political climate of the McCarthy era. In 1960 it was revived again by young activists who oriented it toward direct-action tactics. This was accomplished principally by students from the University of Michigan, who officially formed SDS in the summer of 1962 at Port Huron. Predominant among these students was Al Haber. Although Haber quickly fell out with the increasing radicalization of SDS, it was his vision of direct action as an organizing tool that shaped the course of the organization.

He fixed on the organization and the Movement it spearheaded certain patterns of behavior that evolved directly into the patent nonsense of Yippie and the pathos of the Weather underground. Chief among these was Haber's assumption that action, any action, was constructive, desirable, progressive, radical in and of itself. . . . Haber encouraged SDSers around the country to attach themselves to the innumerable single-issue protests that were erupting on campuses, including campus political parties.[3]

Although SDS maintained contact with LID for several years, the beliefs of the two organizations continually diverged, finally culminating in a break at the beginning of 1966.

In the view of SDS, LID, once an active and vital socialist education organization, [had become] dominated by aging trade unionists whose anticommunism [outweighed] old commitments to socialism. In turn, SDS's radical critique of American policy [went] too far for most of the LID board, especially since SDS [did] not frame its analysis from an anticommunist premise.[4]

It should be noted that while early SDS was not explicitly anticommunist, the majority of its members had no faith in communism of the Soviet variety. Their *Port Huron Statement*—a broad, general statement of policy written in 1962—includes the following passage:

Communist parties throughout the world are generally undemocratic in internal structure and mode of action. Moreover, in most cases they subordinate radical programs to requirements of Soviet foreign policy. The communist movement has failed, in every sense, to achieve its stated intentions of leading a worldwide movement for human emancipation.[5]

Many people felt that this statement was not strong enough; in order to maintain contacts with elements of the democratic left in America, the SDS should take a clear stand in opposition to all forms of totalitarianism. The League for Industrial Democracy, on the other hand, expressed its anti-Communism with an exclusion clause that was probably more stringent than any government loyalty oaths:

Advocates of dictatorship and totalitarianism and of any political system that fails to provide for freedom of speech, of press, of religion, of assembly, and of political, economic, and cultural organization; or of any system that would deny civil rights to any person because of race, color, creed, or national origin are not eligible for membership.[6]

It was largely the issue of opposition to totalitarianism that caused LID and SDS to part ways in February 1965, after many years of grumbling about the increasing friendliness of SDS members with the Marxist-Leninist left.

In October 1967, the FBI released a statement showing that SDS was allied with the Communist party through the CP youth organization, the W. E .B. DuBois Clubs. The newspapers made much of this, but they failed to note that SDS chapters were autonomous and that such cooperation with the Communist party could exist only on campuses that had both SDS and DuBois Club chapters or where there was an SDS chapter on one campus and a DuBois Club close by. Most observers of SDS activities noted that the Communist party is the far-left organization with which SDS cooperated least. The Maoist (at that time) Progressive Labor party received the greatest cooperation; it had members in many SDS chapters and even gained control of a few. One of the three 1969 SDS splinter groups, the Worker Student Alliance, was a Progressive Labor party front. Of course, the Communist party tried to gain control of SDS and Gus Hall once remarked that this young group was among the things the party had going for it, but like the overwhelming majority of young radicals, most SDS members viewed the CP with scorn. As one SDS leader remarked to us in 1966, "The CP? They haven't had a new idea in thirty years."

Nevertheless, there was a small amount of CPUSA influence in SDS. Known as the "red diaper syndrome," several of the more radical SDS members were the sons and daughters of Communists and "progressives" of various stripes. Michael Klonsky, later to lead the Revolutionary Youth Movement II (RYM II) faction and eventually the Communist Party, Marxist-Leninist, was the son of a party functionary. Kathy Boudin was the daughter of Leonard Boudin, who, if not a party member, was extremely close to the organization and its New York City subculture. Moreover, the schools that seemed to produce the greatest SDS following were pretty much what the right wing would call "hotbeds of radicalism." Consider the University of Wisconsin:

> A large number of CP stalwarts sent their heirs to the University of Wisconsin where they took a leading part in the loquacious, heady discussions that were the regimen of the leftist community. These heirs were not merely second generation in the cause . . . but they had been conceived, delivered, nursed, and weaned during the party's Popular Front period.[7]

According to political scientists Stanley Rothman and S. Robert Lichter, Robb Ross described the situation at the University of Wisconsin in the early 1960s thus:

> My impression is that the left at Madison is not a new left, but a revival of the old . . . with all the problems that entails. I am struck by the lack of Wisconsin-born people (in the left) and the massive preponderance of New York Jews. The situation at the University of Minnesota is similar.[8]

Rothman and Lichter, both political science professors and well-credentialed in their fields, have raised a controversial issue in calling attention to the role of youth from Jewish families in SDS and 1960s radicalism generally.

> Americans of Jewish background were disproportionately represented among the leadership and cadres of the Movement until the mid-1960s. At that time they constituted under 3 percent of the population of the United States, and about 10 percent of the students at colleges and universities. Yet, they provided a majority of its most active members and perhaps even a larger proportion of its leadership.[9]

Rothman and Lichter cite other studies. Among these were Richard Braungart's 1966 survey of leading SDS activists—60 percent of those whose religious background could be identified were Jewish.[10] Even as late as 1971 only 25 percent of non-Jewish freshmen at Berkeley considered themselves to be on the left, compared with 58 percent of Jewish freshmen.[11] A 1970 Harris survey showed that 23 percent of all Jewish college students termed themselves "far left," compared with only 4 percent of Protestant students and 2 percent of Catholics.[12]

The Rothman and Lichter study is complicated and contains numerous qualifiers and reservations, so it is important that it be carefully read and fully understood before conclusions are drawn from it.

Another interesting aspect of the demographics of SDS is that while most of its membership were clearly post-WWII "babyboomers," relatively few of its leaders were. SDS leaders and their year of birth include Al Haber (1936), Tom Hayden (1940), Todd Gittlin (1943), Paul Potter (1940) and Carl Ogelsby (1935). Other 1960s radicals not explicitly associated with SDS include Abbie Hoffman (1936), Jerry Rubin (1939), Stokely Carmichael (1941), H. Rap Brown (1943), and Angela Davis (1944).[13]

\*    \*    \*

"Early SDS" was such an ideologically garbled mixture that all sorts of beliefs could often be found in the same chapter. Many people who attended SDS meetings during the sixties had very little political sophistication, and only a very few possessed what could be termed a coherent ideology. Indeed, there was a kind of "ideological hunger" among SDS members that was noticeable even to the casual observer. There was much talk about morality and a kind of fanatic "holier than thou" moralizing emerged—a kind of precursor to the political correctness of the late 1980s. In fact, a number of SDS members considered cooperation with such groups as SANE or NAACP to be immoral. Yet, some of these same people did not consider it immoral to cooperate with the wildest of Maoists. This "compartmentalized" thinking led the late Bayard Rustin to remark that

> The difference between expediency and morality in politics is the difference between selling out a principle and making smaller concessions to win larger ones. The leader who shrinks from this task reveals not his purity, but his lack of political sense.[14]

But even "early SDS" was not about to listen to such talk, for although they had little knowledge of history, they, like extremists of all types, had the TRUTH! This kind of thinking caused democratic socialist Steve Kelman to observe that,

> The New Left's most significant contribution to modern political paranoia is their increasingly prominent belief (strangely parallel to that of the John Birch Society) that The System against which they are railing is none other than American liberalism.[15]

Rothman and Lichter add:

By 1965 the Movement was a vanguard in search of a mass following. More precisely, the search was for issues of such transcendent significance that they could generate a broad-based nationwide social movement. The civil rights struggle was turning away from the patronage of white students, as more radical blacks developed the notion of black power. . . . . All the issues that had impelled and sustained the Movement— civil rights, poverty, the impersonal university—seemed incapable of broadening it.[16]

In February 1965 that issue came along. Lyndon Johnson dramatically escalated the war in Vietnam, directing the first bombing of North Vietnam and rapidly increasing the number of American support troops. These new manpower requirements also mandated enlarged draft calls. The campus response was quick in coming. The antiwar phase of SDS began in earnest.

The antiwar movement, which embraced elements from virtually the entire left, was the primary focal point of student radicals. If one paid attention to only "movement" publications, sympathetic columnists, a handful of politicians who identified with them, and the North Vietnamese, one could have developed a sense of great purpose and power during 1969 and 1970. A survey of seventy-eight prominent universities found that 430 protests occurred during academic year 1966–67.[17]

As the movement built up steam, it appeared from the myopic perspective of SDS that the people were "with it." This was not true. Public opposition to the war had little to do with the antiwar crowd but rather with more practical concerns. Almost everyone knew someone who had died in Vietnam, and the media campaign against the war was beginning to have an effect. It had gone on too long with no end in sight and the public was getting tired of it. The sense of effectiveness the antiwar movement eventually claimed was a self-aggrandizing delusion and a classical example of the post-hoc fallacy.

> But the delusion that they possessed real power was by no means restricted to people who found themselves in the midst of hundreds of thousands of anti-war marchers. In addition to the exhilaration of that kind of experience, black, student, and SDS leaders and troops were convinced by media attention, the dependable hysteria of the far right, and the prattlings of the intellectuals and politicians who rooted them on that they were part of a great movement very near to success.[18]

With regard to a specific governmental system, "early SDS" was a bit hazy, but they strongly emphasized "participatory democracy," which became one of their most effective buzzwords. One of their favorite slogans, "Let the people decide," has implications of direct democracy of the New England town-meeting variety. Oddly enough, it never seemed to occur to SDSers that if decisions were made in this sort of setting, "the people" would probably vote to send them or anyone else with remotely similar characteristics into exile. Even the poor, in which the young radicals seemed to have so much faith, probably would have turned on them. According to Jack Newfield:

The poor are the most anti-Communist class in America: they were the major constituency of Fascism in Germany and Italy and of Peronism in Argentina.[19]

Slogans aside, the *Port Huron Statement* reveals that SDS originally favored "the establishment of a democracy of individual participation governed by two central aims: that the individual share in those social decisions determining the quality and direction of his life; that society be organized to encourage independence in men and provide a medium for their common participation." The statement also asserts that the "American political system is not the democratic model of which its glorifiers speak. In actuality it frustrates democracy by confusing the individual citizen, paralyzing policy discussion, and consolidating the irresponsible power of military and business interests." Actually the idea of participatory democracy appears to encompass several types of political theory. The following are basic principles from the *Port Huron Statement:*

> . . . that decision making of basic social consequence be carried on by public groupings; that politics has the function of bringing people out of isolation and into community, thus being a necessary, though not sufficient, means of finding meaning in personal life; that work should involve incentives worthier than money or survival. It should be educative, not stultifying; creative, not mechanical; self directed, not manipulated, encouraging independence, a respect for others, a sense of dignity and a willingness to accept social responsibility, since it is this experience that has crucial influence on habits, perceptions and individual ethics; that the economy itself is of such social importance that its major resources and means of production should be open to democratic participation and subject to democratic social regulation.[20]

A number of value systems are integrated into the statement, including direct democracy with overtones of guild socialism; the belief that man finds his best self in participation in affairs of state; a view of work championed by Catholic political theorists Hilaire Belloc and Antonio Salazar; and ideas that could easily have been expressed by a Fabian socialist, among others.

It may be fallacious to attribute too much importance to the *Port Huron Statement.* "Official" documents often look far better than the reality they encourage and the more lofty and idealistic they appear the more they tend to engender shortcuts and compromises in achieving altruistic and noble ends. In the end SDS virtually formalized its position: as long as one was fighting racism, fascism, sexism, imperialism, poverty, or war, *anything goes.* This was most evident in the Marxist-Leninist rhetoric that characterized the group in its last years. In short, the end justifies the means—a trait so characteristic of extremist groups across the political spectrum that it constitutes the basis for a kind of symbiotic kinship. More than one observer has noted that these groups are far more alike than they had imagined. To use a loose analogy, political extremists are a bit like football players. Which particular team they play for is of secondary importance with respect to their essential character. They're in the same game and follow (or break) the same rules.

This does not mean that SDS, or other extremists, do not address legitimate issues, or that the solutions they suggest are not without some validity. Each case has to be decided on its respective merits. In general, however, SDS wound up vulgarizing virtually everything it originally stood for and did so by embracing a nihilistic, extremist style not entirely unlike its most extreme opponents, the Nazis and the Ku Klux Klan.

Although against all injustice in principle, the early SDSers did not seem to be nearly so concerned about the oppression suffered in such places as China, North Korea, Albania, and Cuba as they were about the least sign of oppression in Western nations, especially the United States. Typically, many had a much stronger feeling of disgust for Lyndon Johnson, Hubert Humphrey, Richard Nixon, and Gerald Ford than for Mao Tse-tung or Leonid Brezhnev.

This incredible alienation from American society caused a kind of automatic rejection of anything they regarded as "normal." Drug use—almost universally condemned outside of "the movement"—skyrocketed as did other symbolic forms of rebellion, from long hair and beards to bizarre dress, language regarded as obscene, and extreme sexual freedom. The movement developed a lexicon of buzzwords, slogans, and cliches. The term "national liberation" had a romantic quality and suggested fearless, honest, selfless champions of the people concerned only with freedom and justice. Into this category of national liberators they lumped some of the most corrupt and fanatical totalitarian thugs, like Fidel Castro and Pol Pot.

Because they seemed to be making little political progress, more and more SDSers became discontented and frustrated. The feelings of in-group solidarity and shared prejudices they derived from attending meetings and picketing with like-minded people began to fade when they realized how little they were accomplishing. Some began to talk in terms of revolutionary violence, though few seemed to have much idea how to implement such drastic measures. But throughout 1967 and 1968, people who had previously spoken only of nonviolent demonstrations and bringing about quick reforms began to talk of "the revolution" and those who had favored this approach all along began to make more sense to the frustrated reformers. One young radical just back from a late 1967 SDS convention informed us that "more and more people are beginning to look at things from a Marxist perspective." Not long after that he, too, was talking of revolution, but when queried about whether he would take part in the violence that would be necessary, he backed away from a revolutionary stance. His reaction, we found, was typical. Nevertheless, revolution *is* an integral part of radical leftist rhetoric and it isn't that easy to shake it. Alan Adelson explains the problem:

> The Left's whole approach to analyzing society and bringing about change is based on a concept of opposites in conflict. Marx and Engels call it "Dialectical Materialism." Mao Tse-tung calls it "contradiction." The world is made up of two groups, they say: the forces that rule and the forces that are oppressed and must fight for liberation. Any significant force in the world works either in the interest of one group or another, they say.[21]

One of the appeals of Marxist-Leninist rhetoric is that it promises simple solutions to complex problems and instant gratification to aggressive and hostile impulses. Most of all, it conveys a sense of profound importance to its adherents for they are now in the vanguard of history. Indeed, the fate of humanity rests upon them for they alone possess the correct solutions to mankind's most pressing problems. For this reason, Marxism-Leninism has a rather obvious appeal to the narcissistic, self-aggrandizing personality that numerous studies have suggested tends to characterize radical youth.

## Late SDS

The beginning of the end for the reformers in SDS came in June 1968, at the National Convention in East Lansing, Michigan, attended by some eight hundred delegates. Although an attempt by the Progressive Labor party faction to take over the organization was defeated, it became clear that revolutionaries were now in control at the national level. Two of those elected to national office, Bernardine Dohrn and Mike Klonsky, described themselves as "revolutionary Communists." A third, Fred Gordon, was a graduate student studying under Marxist philosopher Herbert Marcuse at the University of California in San Diego.

Nineteen sixty-eight was a watershed year for SDS and for sixties radicalism generally. Several major events occurred. Most important were the assassinations of both Robert Kennedy and Martin Luther King and the rash of urban riots that followed. On the campus, the takeover of Columbia University on March 27 by SDS members and sympathizers provided an inspiration for similar takeovers elsewhere. This event prompted Columbia President Grayson Kirk to comment:

> Our young people, in disturbing numbers, appear to reject all forms of authority, from whatever source derived, and they have taken refuge in a turbulent and inchoate nihilism whose sole objectives are destruction. I know of no time in our history when the gap between the generations has been wider or more potentially dangerous.[22]

The "Columbia uprising," as it was called, "signaled four important transformations in the student movement," according to former SDS leader Todd Gitlin:

> First, deference and civility were resoundingly dumped. . . . Second, the festival moved onto the authorities' home grounds. Counterculture and New Left met. . . . Third, the powers did not cede graciously. After eight days of oscillation and failed negotiations, Kirk called in the police. . . . Finally . . . the press built a containing wall against the radical students.[23]

The "uprising" was no small thing. Five buildings were seized by the students. When the police came in after five days they arrested 712 individuals and the official injured count was 148. Following the arrests Columbia was hit with a strike for the remainder of the school year. Possibly equally significant was the riot at the Chicago convention of the Democratic party from August 25 to 30. Years later Gitlin analyzed:

> Chicago confirmed that no centers were going to hold, no wisdom was going to prevail. It wiped out any lingering doubt that the logic of the Sixties—of both the movement and the mainstream—was going to play itself out to a bitter end. Two decades later, the polarizations etched into the common consciousness that week are still working their way through American politics.[24]

The big split in the SDS occurred at their convention in Chicago the following year (June 1969). Of the 1,500 delegates, about a third were allied with the Progressive Labor party, and another third with what would become known as the "Weatherman" faction and the Revolutionary Youth Movement II, a rival group. The remaining third was a collection of puzzled newcomers, shocked old stalwarts, and a small collection of anarchist and other obscure tendencies. The Progressive Labor party and its front, the Worker-Student Alliance, were ousted from the organization. A statement prepared by RYM leaders, including Bernardine Dohrn and Bill Ayers read, in part:

> Progressive Labor Party, because of its positions and practices, is objectively racist, anti-communist, and reactionary. PLP has also in principle and practice refused to join the struggle against male supremacy. It has no place in SDS, an organization of revolutionary youth.[25]

The PLP dated from 1962, when a small group of Communist party members and former members joined to form their own Stalinist organization. PLP sided with the Communist Chinese in the Sino-Soviet split and claimed to represent the "true" Communist revolutionary position while the Soviet Communists (and their American allies) were selling out their principles in making accommodations to capitalism. Master ideologues and genuine true believers, Joseph Conlin observed that "the PLers were masters of Marxian hairsplitting."[26] Anyone who was susceptible to this kind of thinking was susceptible to the PLP.

Following Dohrn's dramatic announcement, the anti-PL group then walked out of their own convention site and convened elsewhere. The PL people later released the following statement to the press:

> Last night, a minority-group faction of the SDS national convention split off the original. This faction included a majority of the previous leadership whose anti-working-class politics and practices have been exposed and defeated. . . . They walked out of the convention hall, held their own meeting and declared that the PLP was purged from SDS. This fallacious attempt to cover up their political defeat was coupled with the false claim that they legitimately represent SDS.[27]

Thus, the Progressive Labor party asserted that they were the true SDS. Few people accepted this claim. The main group of SDS (anti-PL faction) split into the Revolutionary Youth Movement 1 (RYM 1), later known as Weathermen (or Weather Underground), and the RYM 2, which eventually underwent multiple splits and led to the formation of several radical groups, including the Revolutionary Communist party and the Communist party, Marxist-Leninist.

Before the walkout, the convention had been characterized by bitter squabbles with the two RYM factions trying to prove (via chanting) that they interpreted Mao's teachings more accurately than the PL faction did. Thus was SDS split into three rival factions: RYM, Worker-Student Alliance, and the Weathermen (a name derived from lyrics of a Bob Dylan song: "You don't need a weatherman to know which way the wind blows"). After this debacle, SDS chapters on campuses around the nation were left with a dilemma—which group represented them? More than a few solved the problem in the manner of the University of Oklahoma chapter. They simply denounced all three factions as "Stalinists," announced they were no longer affiliated with SDS, and formed an independent radical organization not aligned with any other.

The spirit of this wind of sectarianism was captured by Tom Nairn in a commentary on the May 1968 radical movement in France:

> Where ideas are all, the upholder of a contrary thesis becomes automatically an enemy —indeed, the most vicious of enemies, since his "position" is the most direct contestation of the vital truths. Where the revolution is reduced to poverty, every scrap matters: every opinion, every attitude, every individual adhesion to this or that idea must be fought over like a bone. Antagonism becomes hatred, and polemic is turned into degenerate abuse.[28]

The RYM 2 group included former SDS National Secretary Mike Klonsky, son of a Communist party functionary; Carl Davidson, also a former SDS national secretary; Noel Ignatin, leader of the Chicago Revolutionary League; Bob Avakian, leader of the Bay Area Revolutionary Union; and Lyn Wells, associated with the Southern Student Organizing Committee and later the Communist Party, Marxist-Leninist.

Weathermen included Bill Ayers, son of the chairman of the board of Commonwealth Edison; David Gilbert, son of the mayor of New Rochelle; Kathy Boudin, daughter of National Lawyers Guild attorney Leonard Boudin; Diana Oughton, daughter of an Illinois Republican state legislator and great-granddaughter of the founder of the Boy Scouts of America; Cathy Wilkerson, daughter of a radio station owner; and Bernardine Dohrn, a National Lawyers Guild activist and daughter of an appliance dealership owner. Todd Gitlin summarized the developments:

> The no-longer-new Left trapped itself in a seamless loop: growing militancy, growing isolation, growing commitment to The Revolution, sloppier and more frantic attempts to imagine a revolutionary class, growing hatred among the competing factions with their competing imaginations.[29]

Of the three groups that evolved from SDS, the Weathermen faction received the most notoriety, due in part to the wild pronouncements of the group's leaders, and perhaps even more to involvement in brawls with the police and in bombings. In October 1969, a few hundred Weathermen (many of whom were women) "attacked Chicago" in what became known as "Four Days of Rage." They broke windows in cars and buildings and many were involved in a battle with riot police.

> Seventy-three policemen had been injured during the action. Some three hundred Weatherpeople had been arrested, many of them on charges ranging up to attempted murder. Their bail totaled over $2.6 million. One city official, Richard Elrod, was paralyzed from the neck down when he attempted to tackle a demonstrator and struck his head on a curb.[30]

While most of those involved were injured or jailed, a few of them insisted on calling the encounter a victory. In a headline describing the battle, *Guardian,* the independent Marxist-Leninist newsweekly, stated: "Weatherman-SDS goes it (very much) alone in 'kick-ass' brawl." Dan Georgakas in the *Encyclopedia of the American Left* describes an element of Weathermen strategy that has been a part of Marxist-Leninist doctrine for some time:

> Weathermen set out to create incidents that would result in police repression. They believed a persecuted movement would then split and the most militant fighters would become part of the Weather underground.[31]

While we have not dwelt on it in this chapter, SDS and its various factions were the subject of enormous legal and illegal FBI infiltration and surveillance. For example, four years after the "Days of Rage" convictions occurred they were voided because the FBI had used burglaries, mail openings, and illegal wiretaps in obtaining them. There is a large body of literature available on questionable government surveillance and harassment of SDS and related groups. According to Barnard L. Collier, the FBI long had dossiers on all the important SDSers and, in addition, had undercover informants inside the majority of chapters.[32] Also, in 1969 the House Committee on Internal Security published the findings of its own investigations of SDS, largely utilizing FBI sources.[33]

\*      \*      \*

In late December of 1969 some four hundred people attended a "war council" held in Flint, Michigan. The leadership, known as the "Weather Bureau," gave the word on how to bring about a revolution in the United States. The key, they stated, is armed struggle, a large component of which is terrorism—including bombing and political assassination. Bernardine Dohrn emphasized that they should be "crazy mother-fuckers" and should "scare the shit out of honky America." Dohrn also referred to the recent Charles Manson murders this way:

Dig it. First they killed those pigs; then they ate dinner in the same room with them; then they even shoved a fork into a victim's stomach! Wild![34]

Another Weather Bureau member, John Jacobs, stated that the Weathermen were "against everything that's good and decent in honky America. We will loot and burn and destroy. We are the incubation of your mother's nightmare."[35] According to Alan Adelson, in *SDS: A Profile,*

For a great many of the 400 peoole who attended that War Council what the Weathermen were outlining sounded terribly like fascism. Someone dared tell Ted Gold. . . . "Well," Ted shrugged, "if it will take fascism, we'll have to have fascism."[36]

The Weathermen were back in the news again on March 6, 1970, when three of their number died in a bomb blast in a Greenwich Village townhouse that was, from all available evidence, a bomb factory. Those killed were Diana Oughton, Ted Gold (mentioned above), and Terry Robbins. Oughton had to be identified from the print on a severed fingertip and Robbins was only identified after a Weathermen communique confirmed his presence. Enough dynamite was uncovered to blow up a city block. Unfortunately, one of the young bombmakers failed to exercise proper safety procedures. Cathy Wilkerson, Kathy Boudin, and several other Weathermen escaped.[37] Peter Collier and David Horowitz provide this account of the actual event:

Terry had been building a bomb in the basement of the townhouse, an antipersonnel bomb he intended to plant at Fort Dix, New Jersey, and explode during an army dance. Diana, although haggard and sick, had been helping him.
    Ted Gold . . . had just gone out to the drugstore for cotton to muffle the ticking of the time-bomb clock. . . . Just as he started to open the basement door, Terry crossed two wires mistakenly; the bomb blew with such shattering force that the brownstone simply collapsed. The beam over the door fell on Gold, crushing his chest. Diana's body was so mangled that she was identified with certainty only when two of her fingers were found in the debris. Terry was torn into such small pieces that no sure identification could be made.[38]

Not long after this event most Weathermen—numbering perhaps two hundred— went underground.

This was not the end of the violence. In June 1970, an explosion rocked the second floor of New York City's police headquarters. Eight people were injured, but fortunately no one was badly hurt. A hand-printed letter gave the Weathermen credit for this act. The letter stated in part:

Tonight, at 7 P.M. we blew up the N.Y.C. Police headquarters. We called in a warning before the explosion. The pigs in this country are our enemies. . . . The pigs try to look invulnerable, but we keep finding their weaknesses. . . . Every time the pigs think they have stopped us, we come back a little stronger and a lot smarter. They guard their buildings and we walk right past their guards. . . . The time is now. Political power grows out of a gun, a Molotov, a riot, a commune . . . and from the soul of the people.

In late May 1970 the Weathermen had issued a "declaration of war" and promised to "attack a symbol or institution of American injustice" in the near future. Thus, it seems likely that they did plant the bomb in question.

In July 1970, the federal government indicted thirteen Weathermen on the charge that they planned to detonate bombs in four large cities: Berkeley, Chicago, Detroit, and New York. Just one of these bombings had actually been attempted: at the Detroit Police Officers Association building, where the bomb failed to detonate. According to the indictment, the conspiracy originated at the December 1969 "war council" where Mark Rudd had supposedly stated that those at the meeting "should participate in bombings of police stations and banks throughout the country and killing police to further the revolution."[39] The Weather Underground toll was impressive, although ultimately not particularly damaging.

There were later Weather Underground bombings of the United States Capitol in March 1971 and of the Pentagon in May 1972. No one was injured due to warning phone calls.

In its six years as a functioning clandestine organization, the Weather Underground claimed responsibility for about two dozen bombings. Only two of them, the bombs in the bathroom of the Capitol and in the bathroom of the Pentagon . . . did more than negligible damage.[40]

According to Hugh Davis Graham and Ted Robert Gurr, in 1969–70 the Bureau of Alcohol, Tobacco and Firearms Division of the Treasury Department conducted a thorough canvass of information on bombings from reports gathered from state and local law enforcement agencies.

In 15½ months, beginning January 1969, those agencies recorded 975 bomb explosions and 3,355 incendiaries, 1,175 bombs that failed to go off, and more than 35,000 bomb threats.[41]

Graham and Gurr found that 20 percent of the bombings occurred during campus disturbances, 7 percent were attributed to black extremists, and 5 percent were attributed to white extremists. Sixty-four percent arose from unknown causes. The authors further noted:

If we suppose that most bombings of unknown cause had private motives, the evidence suggests that at most a quarter of American bombings during this period had political objectives—most of the campus bombings and some of the racial ones.[42]

From this and other studies it becomes clear that the great majority of the bombings and their accompanying destruction during the late 1960s and early 1970s period of florid leftist (primarily SDS and its successors) activity on the campus can be attributed to that movement and the passions that it so carefully justified and cultivated. Although much attention has been paid to radical right violence during the 1980s, it has proven relatively mild—with far less property damage and loss of life—when compared to the violence-prone movements that grew out of the sixties.

Only a few of the indicted Weathermen were actually captured. The others eventually turned themselves in after years at large. Most notable were Bernardine Dohrn, who replaced Communist party stalwart Angela Davis on the FBI's "Most Wanted" list, and Bill Ayers, who surfaced together in 1980. They were subsequently married in 1982. According to Sam Roberts in the *New York Times:*

> After spending 11 years as a fugitive on charges of rioting and related accusations, she surfaced in 1980 and pleaded guilty to two counts of aggravated battery and two counts of bail-jumping stemming from protests against the Vietnam War in 1969. She was fined $1,500 and placed on three years probation.
>
> In 1982, she spent seven months in the Metropolitan Correctional Center in Manhattan for refusing to cooperate with a Grand Jury investigating the 1981 robbery of a Brinks armored truck and murders in Rockland County.[43]

Dohrn had given up none of her sixties radicalism. Her loyalties remained much as they were when she disappeared underground. Peter Collier and David Horowitz remark:

> More than anyone else, Ayers and Dohrn embody the odd mix of characters and politics that propelled the Weathermen onto the center stage of the American scene in the late sixties. . . . They seem oddly unchanged by the intervening years, as if life in the previously undiscovered country of the American underground, where they lived for a decade, kept them from aging. . . . The two of them were on the run for ten years, setting off bombs, issuing "communiques," and making themselves into legendary figures. When they negotiated their way back aboveground late in 1980, they were unlike some of the others who freely admitted that their gods of revolution had failed.[44]

In 1985 Dohrn, who had been working in the New York litigation office of Sidley & Allen, a prestigious Chicago law firm, was attempting to be admitted to the bar in New York state. Sam Roberts reported:

> As recently as 1982, her own lawyer described her in an affidavit as having "a view of the law and a view of life and her rights that is myopic, convoluted, unrealistic, childish, and inexplicable" and as a woman who "is intractable in her views and beliefs to the point of fanaticism."
>
> "I would be very troubled as to the notion of fairness if she wasn't made a member of the bar now," Mr. Reuben (Ms. Dohrn's attorney) said. "This country makes a point of looking at people as they are and not visiting upon them their past silliness of their youth."[45]

In a related case, David S. Fine (not connected with the Weather Underground) applied for admission to the Oregon bar in 1986. Previously, Fine had pled guilty to third degree murder for a 1970 bombing at the University of Wisconsin in which a research physicist was killed. Jeffrey Kilmer, attorney for the Oregon bar, doubted Fine's remorse for the bombing, noting that its depth is about "the same as you or I stepping on a worm when we were fifteen years old."

> Kilmer said the bomb was made of six 55-gallon barrels filled with fertilizer and oil, which exploded with the force of 3,800 sticks of dynamite. Kilmer called it the "largest homemade bomb ever exploded anywhere until the Beirut bombing of the American barracks."[46]

Fine's attorney, on the other hand, said that he had "shown no trace of anti-social behavior" in the past ten years. The three-member trial panel heard five days and 1,566 pages of testimony on the issue and recommended that Fine be denied admission. The panel noted that Fine had participated in antiwar activities since he was thirteen years old, and had supplied the escape vehicle for his co-conspirators in the bombing. During his years as a fugitive Fine had created two phony identities and was in the process of creating a third when he was captured by the FBI on January 7, 1976. According to the panel, Fine continued to proclaim his innocence after his release on bail. And he has never publicly renounced his radical views, repudiated the bombing, or expressed contriteness or remorse over the results.[47]

On January 18, 1970, Silas Trim Bissell and his wife, Judith, were arrested with an explosive device they were attempting to place in an Air Force Reserve Officer Training Corps building at the University of Washington. The two disappeared while free on bond and became Weather Underground fugitives forfeiting $50,000 bail. Judith Bissell was apprehended in 1977, convicted, and served nearly two years in prison. Silas Bissell was not apprehended until 1987, while living under the assumed name of Terence Jackson. In May 1987 Silas Bissell pleaded guilty and was convicted of a reduced count of carrying an unregistered explosive device—a charge that carries a maximum charge of ten years in prison and a $10,000 fine—and sentenced to two years in prison, in spite of extensive special pleading.[48] Bissell said he

> went into the anti-war movement not out of anger but as a matter of conscience. It was a terribly stressful time for the nation. It was inordinately stressful for those of us who were involved in anti-war work because we felt so much responsibility to do the right thing to bring an end to the war.[49]

In handing out the sentence U.S. District Judge Walter McGovern was not impressed and said that moral or political justification is no excuse for a felony. Judge McGovern had been the recipient of some two hundred letters on behalf of Mr. Bissell.

\*    \*    \*

The Prairie Fire Organizing Committee (PFOC), formed in 1974, was the publishing arm of the Weather Underground Organization. Its first pamphlet was *Prairie Fire: The Politics of Revolutionary Anti-Imperialism,* written by Bernadine Dohrn, Bill Ayers, and Jeff Jones. According to Harvey Klehr:

> It announced that "we are communist men and women" and urged its supporters to form an above-ground arm of the WUO Chapters soon formed in several cities with perhaps a thousand members. Members of PFOC helped facilitate communication and logistics for WUO members living underground.[50]

The PFOC also published *Breakthrough,* a quarterly journal which routinely called for widespread resistance to U.S. imperialism, ran article after article praising third-world single-party Marxist-Leninist dictatorships as well as accounts of alleged "political repression" of leftist activists in the United States.

Another Weather Underground front, the John Brown Anti-Klan Committee (JBAKC), was formed in 1978 and soon had chapters in over a dozen cities with about 300 members.[51] It quickly took its place alongside other Marxism-Leninism-based anti-Klan organizations such as the Progressive Labor party's INCAR and the Workers World party's All Peoples Congress, and proceeded to stage violent confrontations with small Klan groups when they held marches or demonstrations. The JBAKC counter-demonstrators were almost always more violent than the Klansmen they protested. In 1983, for example, the JBAKC attempted to halt a parade of seventy Klansmen in Austin, Texas. Counter-demonstrators threw rocks injuring twelve people, including several police officers. Two members of the JBAKC—Elizabeth Ann Duke and Linda Evans—were among those involved in the May 19th Communist Organization.

\*    \*    \*

In commenting on such extremists as the Weathermen, Dr. Bruno Bettelheim stated that some very "sick" people in this country were doing exactly what the radical left in Germany did in facilitating the Nazis' rise to power. And philosopher Sidney Hook, discussing young leftists, has described attitudes that prevail among many types of extremists:

> They define the presence of the democratic process by whether or not they get their political way, and not by the presence or absence of democratic institutional processes. The rules of the game exist to enable them to win and if they lose that's sufficient proof the game is rigged and dishonest. The sincerity with which the position is held is not evidence whatsoever of its coherence. The right to petition does not carry with it the right to be heard if that means influence on those to whom it is addressed. . . . Petitions are weapons of criticism, and their failure doesn't justify appeal to other kinds of weapons.[52]

The Weather Underground went through a few more spasms before it finally died. On October 20, 1981, a Brinks armored truck was robbed outside Nyack, New York. The robbers simply opened fire on the guards, one of whom was killed; two others were wounded; two policemen died in a shootout during a fumbled getaway. Within a short time police had several suspects in custody along with information leading them to hideouts in New York and New Jersey, where they found quantities of weapons and explosives. Through a fingerprint check they discovered that they had captured Cathy Boudin, Judith Clark, David Gilbert, and several other 1960s radicals. Boudin and Clark had been indicted together in 1980 in connection with the Weathermen's "Days of Rage" demonstrations in Chicago.

Altogether the FBI linked seventeen persons—including the suspects in the $1.6 million Brinks holdup—to a wide-ranging conspiracy of murder, bank robberies, and explosives. These included Joanne Chesimard, a fugitive convicted of killing a New Jersey state police officer; Nathaniel Burns, Anthony LaBorde, and Donald Weems, all suspected "soldiers" in the Black Liberation Army (BLA); Marilyn Jean Buck, the only white BLA member and a fugitive; Cynthia Boston and Jessie Dixon, members of the Republic of New Afrika, a group advocating a separate black nation in the United States; William Johnson, Boston's husband and also a fugitive; Mutulu Shakir, founder of the Black Acupuncture Association of North America and a fugitive; Barbara Zeller, identified as the "spouse or ex-spouse of Alan Berkman, a physician jailed for refusing to cooperate with the grand jury"; Eve Rosahn, jailed for refusing to cooperate with the grand jury; and Cecil Ferguson, Edward Joseph, and Samuel Brown, not identified with any group.[53]

In April 1984, Boudin pleaded guilty to her role in the holdup. She said:

> I feel terrible about the lives that were lost. I have led a life of commitment to political principles and I think I can be true to those principles without engaging in violent acts.[54]

Boudin was sentenced to twenty years to life in prison. She will be eligible for parole in 2001. Among those present at the trial was Bernardine Dohrn. Judith Clark and David Gilbert, also convicted in the case, are both serving seventy-five years to life terms. (Ironically, it was the Weather Underground's armored car robbery that inspired a similar crime by The Order, a neo-Nazi group, in 1984. They didn't get away with it, either.)

In March 1985 Susan Rosenberg and Timothy Blunk were found guilty of eight counts each of possessing explosives, weapons, and fake identification cards. Blunk and Rosenberg were arrested in November 1984, at a rental storage unit that contained the items in question. Rosenberg was also charged with driving the getaway car used in the 1981 Brinks robbery in Nyack, New York.

On May 11, 1985, authorities apprehended Marilyn Jean Buck, who had accidentially shot herself in the leg while driving a getaway car during the 1981 robbery and who was treated by Alan Berkman. A few weeks later the FBI arrested Berkman and Elizabeth Duke, members of the May 19 Communist Cell, an offshoot of the Weather Underground and the Black Liberation Army. Berkman and Duke had stocked a building in Doylestown Township, Pennsylvania, with quantities of automatic weapons, bulletproof vests, explosives, and bomb-making components. They were arrested as they drove toward New York City with automatic weapons in their laps. Berkman was indicted in November 1982 on charges of being an accessory after the fact in the Brinks robbery. He had been a fugitive on a federal warrant since February 1983, when he failed to show up for a hearing in U.S. District Court.[55]

The original arrests in the Brinks case opened up a series of leads that ultimately led to the cracking of several cases of terrorism, robberies, and bombings committed by Weather Underground functionaries, including the "Ohio Seven" and their United Freedom Front, yet another of the overlapping groups that made up the Weather Underground complex. There was considerable overlap in these groups. Harvey Klehr observes:

Judy Clark and Eve Rosahn were actively involved in the Committee for the Suit Against Government Misconduct. Clark was also active in the PFOC and the May 19th Communist Organization. Rosahn, once a member of Columbia SDS, had been a PFOC activist, and was indicted for aiding the May 19th defendants in the Brinks robbery—although the charge was later dropped. Michelle Miller was a leader of the New Movement in Solidarity with Puerto Rican Independence and Socialism, a PFOC organizer, and active in the May 19th group. Miller's roommate, Sylvia Baraldini, was one of the leaders of the May 19th Communist Organization. She and Miller were found guilty of criminal contempt for refusing to testify before a federal grand jury investigating bombings committed by the Puerto Rican terrorist group, the FALN.[56]

Klehr also notes that:

May 19 was never a very large organization although it did have a rather unique social composition. A substantial proportion of its membership was white women, many of them committed to Lesbianism. Press reports estimated its membership at anywhere from forty to four hundred.[57]

*    *    *

While awaiting trial in September 1986 for the murder of a New Jersey state trooper in 1981, Thomas Manning and Richard Williams referred to themselves as "anti-imperialist revolutionary freedom fighters" in an underground war against the "military-industrial complex." "At a different time in history I would call myself a prisoner of war," said Manning. Williams said, "What differentiates us from criminals—what makes us political prisoners—is that criminal action is done for some type of personal gain."[58] Manning was subsequently convicted of the murder and given a life sentence and Williams was to be retried because the jury could not agree on a verdict.

In March 1988 the trial of the "Ohio Seven" began in Springfield, Massachusetts. The charge—plotting the violent overthrow of the U.S. government—has been used only a few times since it was first invoked to punish Confederate rebels in the Civil War. (In April 1987 a group of fifteen right-wing extremists were indicted in Fort Smith, Arkansas, on sedition charges stemming from their 1984 version of the Brinks holdup. They were acquitted a year later.) The defendants faced one count each of seditious conspiracy, racketeering conspiracy, and racketeering enterprise. According to press reports:

> The indictment accuses defendants Raymond Luc Levasseur and Thomas W. Manning of nearly 20 bombings and 10 robberies throughout the Northeast since 1975 to raise money to finance their radical political aims. Two others, Jaan K. Laaman and Richard C. Williams, allegedly joined them in their crimes.
>
> The wives of three defendants—Patricia Lavasseur, Carol A. Manning and Barbara J. Curzi-Laaman—are accused of harboring their husbands as fugitives, using false identification, and taking part in some bombings.[59]

The FBI's 1989 annual report, *Terrorism in the United States,* stated:

> The United Freedom Front (UFF) was a violent, left-wing terrorist group which claimed credit for numerous bombings in the New York metropolitan area from 1982 to 1984. Some members of the group were also involved in bank robberies, the murder of a New Jersey State Trooper in 1981, and the attempted murders of two Massachusetts State Troopers in 1982. Some members were also allegedly involved in an earlier terrorist group, the Sam Melville-Jonathan Jackson Unit, which claimed bombings in the Boston, Massachusetts, metropolitan area between 1976 and 1978.
>
> Originally eight UFF members were indicted in May, 1986, on charges of Racketeer Influences and Corrupt Organization (RICO) Act violations, RICO Conspiracy and Seditious Conspiracy. The eight individuals indicted were Raymond Lavasseur, Patricia Gros-Lavasseur, Thomas Manning, Carol Ann Manning, Richard Williams, Jaan Laaman, Barbara Curzi-Laaman, and Christopher King. In 1986, several of these individuals were convicted of murder and bombings. In 1988, Christopher King pleaded guilty and was sentenced to prison; charges were dropped against Thomas Manning and Jaan Laaman; and Barbara Curzi-Laaman was severed from the other defendants.
>
> On January 5, 1989, Carol Manning was sentenced to a total of 12 years imprisonment and a $300,000 fine pursuant to her December 29, 1988, plea of guilty to her RICO and related charges. Trial for the remaining three UFF members commenced on January 10, 1989. On November 27, 1989, the jury returned not guilty verdicts on several counts, but could not reach a decision on the remainder. On November 29, 1989, a mistrial was declared. All defendants are currently in prison, except for Patricia Gros-Levasseur who remains free on bail.[60]

In September 1990 three more radicals associated with the Weather Underground pleaded guilty to bombing charges. Laura Whitehorn, Linda S. Evans, and Marilyn Jean Buck admitted participating in a conspiracy to set off eight bombs at the U.S. Capitol and seven other sites. The November 7, 1983, blast blew a hole in a wall outside the Senate chambers. Bombs were also detonated outside the National War College, the Washington Navy Yard Computer Center, an FBI office on Staten Island, the Israeli Aircraft Industries building in New York, the South African Consulate in New York, and the New York Patrolman's Benevolent Association between 1983 and 1985. The government, in turn, agreed to drop bombing charges against three other group members (Susan Rosenberg, Timothy R. Blunk, and Alan Berkman) variously identified as the Armed Resistance Unit, the Revolutionary Fighting Group, or the Red Guerrilla Resistance Unit. A seventh defendant in the case, Elizabeth Duke, was a fugitive.

*    *    *

With the end of this string of Weather Underground trials SDS faded from the media and into the history books. For some, it remains a bad memory; for a few, the worst mistake they ever made; and for those ideologues who still cling to their 1960s fanaticism, it was their finest moment. For many sixties radicals, however, their memories of SDS are considerably more benign, depending upon their length and degree of involvement. They recall the good feelings and the bad realizations, the great gap between fine intentions and the reality that ill-advised policies usually engender.

Although SDS has been gone for nearly two decades, its influence is still being felt. A surprising number of college and university professors in their forties today were active in SDS and other radical movements of the 1960s and 1970s. Many critiques of the trend toward authoritarianism on some campuses ("political correctness") charge that these former radicals have played a major part in its development—their own little exercise in (apparently) legal intellectual oppression. The legacy lives on.

## Notes

1. Joseph Conlin, *The Troubles: A Jaundiced Glance Back at the Movement of the 60's* (New York: Franklin Watts, 1982), 89.

2. Paul Jacobs and Saul Landau, *The New Radicals* (New York: Vintage Books, 1966), 28.

3. Conlin, 92–93.

4. Ibid., 29.

5. Students for a Democratic Society, *Port Huron Statement* (Ann Arbor, Mich.: Students for a Democratic Society, 1962).

6. Quoted in Conlin, 96.

7. Ibid., 194.

8. Stanley Rothman and S. Robert Lichter, *Roots of Radicalism: Jews, Christians and the New Left* (New York: Oxford University Press, 1982), 81.

9. Ibid., 80.

10. Richard Braungart, "Status Politics and Student Politics," *Youth and Society* 3 (December 1971): 195–208. Quoted in Rothman and Lichter, 81.

11. Robert S. Berns, Daphne Bugental, and Geraldine Berns, "Research on Student Activism," *American Journal of Psychiatry* 128 (1972): 1499–1504. Quoted in Rothman and Lichter, 81–82.

12. This Harris poll is cited in Seymour Martin Lipset, *Rebellion in the University* (Boston: Little Brown, 1972), 86. Quoted in Rothman and Lichter, 52.

13. Conlin, 79–80.

14. Bayard Rustin, "From Protest to Politics," *Commentary* (February 1965): 29.

15. Steve Kelman, "The Feud Among Radicals," *Harper's* (July 1966).

16. Rothman and Lichter, 25.

17. Julian Foster and Durwood Long, eds., *Protest! Student Activism in America* (New York: William Morrow, 1970), 89ff., 365.

18. Conlin, 219.

19. Jack Newfield, *A Prophetic Minority* (New York: Signet Books, 1967), 150.

20. Students for a Democratic Society, *Port Huron Statement*.

21. Alan Adelson, *SDS: A Profile* (New York: Charles Scribner's, 1972), 225.

22. Statement, April 12, 1968. Quoted in Charles Kaiser, *1968 in America* (New York: Weidenfeld & Nicholson, 1988), 150.

23. Todd Gitlin, *The Sixties: Years of Hope, Days of Rage* (New York: Bantam Books, 1987), 307.

24. Gitlin, 326.

25. Kirkpatrick Sale, *SDS* (New York: Random House, 1973), 573.

26. Conlin, 278.

27. Undated press release.

28. "Where Ideas Are All": Tom Nairn, "Why It Happened," in Angelo Quattrochi and Tom Nairn, *The Beginning of the End* (London: Panther Books, 1968), 131–33, quoting from Antonio Gramsci.

29. Gitlin, 380.

30. Peter Collier and David Horowitz, *Destructive Generation: Second Thoughts about the '60's* (New York: Summit Books, 1989), 90.

31. Dan Georgakas in Mari Jo Buhle, Paul Buhle, and Dan Georgakas, *Encyclopedia of the American Left* (New York: Garland Publishing, Inc., 1990), 61.

32. Bernard L. Collier, "SDS: Is Radical Group Gaining or Losing Ground?" *Oklahoma City Times* (June 9, 1969), 24.

33. U.S. House of Representatives, Committee on Internal Security, *Investigations of Students for a Democratic Society* (Washington, D.C.: U.S. Government Printing Office, 1969).

34. Quoted in Adelson, 247.

35. Gitlin, 400.

36. Adelson, op. cit.

37. Gitlin, 400–401.

38. Collier and Horowitz, 100–101.

39. *Daily Oklahoman* (July 24, 1970), 2.

40. Collier and Horowitz, 106.

41. Hugh Davis Graham and Ted Robert Gurr, *Violence in America: Historical and Comparative Perspectives* (Beverly Hills: Sage Publications, 1979), 335.

42. Ibid.

43. Sam Roberts, "Bar Panel to Weigh Fitness of Bernardine Dohrn," *New York*

*Times* (August 26, 1985).

44. Collier and Horowitz, 68.

45. Roberts.

46. Fred Leeson, "Ex-Radicals Bar Hearing Under Way," *The Oregonian* (July 16, 1985).

47. John Painter, Jr., "Reason Detailed for Finding Fine Unfit as Laywer," *The Oregonian* (September 19, 1985); Fred Leeson, "Former Activist Pleads Case for Admission to Bar," *The Oregonian* (January 31, 1986).

48. "A War Radical Is Given 2 Years in a Bomb Case," *New York Times* (June 25, 1987).

49. "Ex-Weatherman Pleads Not Guilty to Bomb Charge," Associated Press (January 30, 1987).

50. Harvey Klehr, *Far Left of Center: The American Radical Left Today* (New Brunswick, N.J.: Transaction, 1988), 109. This book was commissioned by the Anti-Defamation League of B'nai B'rith.

51. *Montgomery Journal* (February 10, 1983).

52. Sidney Hook, "Social Protest and Civil Disobedience," *The Petal Paper* (November 1967).

53. Associated Press, "FBI Links 17 to Terrorist Conspiracy," *Kansas City Times* (July 22, 1982), A-14.

54. Jim Feron, "Kathy Boudin, in Reversal, Pleads Guilty to '81 Holdup and Slayings," *New York Times* (April 27, 1984), 1.

55. "FBI Arrests Doctor in '81 Brinks Case," *New York Times* (May 25, 1985); "FBI Seizes Revolutionary Cache," Associated Press (May 26, 1985).

56. Klehr, 112.

57. Klehr, 113.

58. "Jailed Radicals Defend Violent Acts," United Press International (September 28, 1986).

59. "Trial of 'Ohio 7' to Open in Massachusetts Courtroom," *Kansas City Times* (March 14, 1988).

60. *Terrorism in the United States, 1989,* (Washington, D.C.: Federal Bureau of Investigation, Terrorist Research and Analytical Center, 1989), 5.

# 8. Progressive Labor Party

The Progressive Labor party began as the Progressive Labor Movement in January of 1962 and began calling itself a party in 1965. Until June 1971, the PL followed the straight Chinese line, and therefore it could be argued that they were neither "progressive" nor connected in any way with the American labor movement. The "founding fathers" of the group, Milt Rosen and Mort Scheer, were kicked out of the Communist Party USA after making an unsuccessful attempt to keep that party solidly in the Stalinist camp. They later called the CP a hopeless apologist for imperialism. Another PL founder, Bill Epton, was expelled from the organization in 1970 for advocating black nationalism. Kirkpatrick Sale describes the founding of PL:

> On July 1, 1962, some fifty people meeting at the Hotel Diplomat in New York City established a new political organization on the left. Its fourteen-member coordinating committee consisted entirely of people who had been members of the Communist party and quit or were purged in late 1961 for being "ultra-leftists" and "agents of the Albania party"—i.e., "Maoists."[1]

Most of the early members of Progressive Labor were disaffected Communist party people. Joe Dogher, a contributor to the early issues of *Progressive Labor* magazine had quit the CPUSA in 1956. He had been an organizer for the United Mine Workers in Pennsylvania and had fought with the Lincoln Brigade in Spain. Lee Coe, West Coast editor of *Progressive Labor,* had been the labor editor of the West Coast CPUSA paper, *People's World.*

PL, as they call themselves, has always been a dynamic group with chapters on college campuses and offices in such cities as New York, Boston, Chicago, Houston, Los Angeles, Rochester, San Francisco, and Washington. They were the main force behind the mid-1960s "student" trips to Cuba, defying a State Department ban on travel to that country.

The role of PL in Students for a Democratic Society and its subsequent disillusion is detailed in the chapter on SDS. PL made a major attempt to capture a significant portion of the campus antiwar movement in 1964 when it established the May 2nd Movement. This account comes from the Socialist Workers party:

> In March 1964, a number of socialist tendencies, including the Socialist Workers Party, the Communist Party, and Progressive Labor participated in an east coast conference sponsored by the Yale Socialist Union. Out of that conference came plans for

demonstrations in several places around the country on May 2, calling for the withdrawal of troops from Vietnam. . . . Over 800 people participated in the New York demonstration, several hundred in San Francisco, and there were demonstrations in a number of other cities as well . . .

After the May 2 demonstrations in New York, however, the PLers in the committee held a closed meeting which excluded other tendencies . . . and decided to continue the organization on a permanent basis as the May 2nd Movement (M2M).

They mistakenly thought that the mass antiwar movement which was gestating could be controlled by one political tendency . . . the antiwar movement, of course, did not develop according to the PL blueprint . . .

As the mass antiwar movement became larger and larger, PL decided that M2M had obviously failed. In February, 1966, the east coast charters of M2M held a conference and decided to dissolve.[2]

\*    \*    \*

*Progressive Labor* magazine, complete with photographs and professional drawings, has been one of the better productions on the extreme left. The first issue appeared in January 1962. In May 1963 the first issue of its *Marxist-Leninist Quarterly* appeared. The lead article in that issue, "Where We Stand," was a statement of principles by the editors. They had the following about the Communist Party USA:

> The CPUSA has long been shackled by the liberal illusions of which we have spoken: that it has abandoned the fight for socialism, which is ostensibly "not on the agenda" . . . that it is no longer willing to take an uncompromising, principled struggle against class collaborationists in the labor movement and against liberal imperialists in the Democratic Party . . .[3]

Their criticism was not confined to the CPUSA. They attacked the Socialist Workers party as well:

> The Trotskyist SWP is dangerously wrong in its hostility to the Soviet Union and the socialist bloc and . . . its position is harmful to the struggle for a socialist world. We recognize that the SWP has generally defended the socialist bloc against the attacks of imperialism, but the extent and nature of its criticism has often done far more damage to our cause than its support could offset.[4]

Unlike the SWP, which has rhapsodized about Fidel Castro and his totalitarian Marxist-Leninist regime, PL found the "class character" of revolutionary Cuba somewhat wanting. A 1967 article in PL's quarterly, *World Revolution,* charged that "the greater part" of the land in Cuba "is in the hands of small owners who exploit the manual labor of others" and that "capitalist not socialist forms of agricultural production had developed." The article, reprinted from a pamphlet published by the Revolutionary Communist party of Chile, went on to say that "the bourgeoisie has not been relieved of its positions of leadership in the bureaucratic apparatus and cultural institutions." On the contrary, "the bourgeoisie is becoming more secure and gaining new positions of power."[5]

PL's weekly tabloid, *Challenge: The Revolutionary Communist Newspaper,* features half the pages printed in Spanish as an appeal to Hispanics.

While praising most black revolutionaries, PL publications have generally shown nothing but scorn for nonrevolutionary black leaders. They had this to say about Martin Luther King, Jr., about one year before his assassination:

> Martin Luther King in his book *Why We Can't Wait* does not tell us the reasons for the lack of progress in the movement for our freedom. He is a reactionary person who should like to be integrated into the corrupt society—so he could prosper from the misfortunes of his Black brothers, and later attempt to pacify them by preaching fatalism. . . . Comrades and friends we must beware! We must not collaborate with the Martin Luther Kings and his cronies and the imperialist press in condemning the Black rebellions. . . .[6]

One former PL leader, Fred Jerome, furnishes an interesting example typifying the mentality of this group. Son of a one-time Communist party leader, and an early member of the editorial board of *Progressive Labor* magazine, Jerome was evidently a convincing spokesman for his viewpoint. Jack Newfield, in his dated but interesting book, *A Prophetic Minority,* describes a conversation with Jerome:

> Pausing a long while before answering questions in a distracted monotone . . . Jerome, talking softly, looking right at you, can sound reasonable asserting that America is building up West Germany for a surprise attack on the Soviet Union, or "Of course the CIA had Kennedy assassinated," or "When America invaded North Korea . . ."[7]

Articles and cartoons in PL publications have always tried to convey the idea that every tragic event occurring in America follows a direct order from a high-ranking government official or labor leader. They also have had a problem seeing any difference between Nazis and liberals. *Challenge,* for example, had the following to say regarding the assassinations of the Kennedy brothers and Martin Luther King, Jr.:

> Marxist-Leninists know that assassinations are generally provocations by the ruling class. Assassinations are used against the people. This latest example is quite clear. U.S. imperialism will not be knocked down by the bullets of a few assassins. People in tens of millions must be won to the cause of revolution. Only the combined united action of the people, led by the working class, can defeat imperialism.
>
> The killing of Robert Kennedy—like the killing of Rev. King, and John Kennedy—is probably another reflection of differences within the ruling class. Of course, the killer looks like a "natural." Naturally, the big-boys will cover up whatever the trash is.
>
> It is the ruling class that used this individualistic violence as a means of solving problems. We should not be intimidated or diverted by this latest act of ruling-class violence. The money-men would like us to abandon the fight for our aspirations.

They would like us to ape their fake commiseration towards King and Kennedy. Yes, they want the people to surrender.

They will try to use this latest assassination to squelch us. We should never let this happen. Our march to liberation and socialism can only be won by the total defeat of this system. The ruling class will come up with a basketful of new Kennedy types to replace this one. To hell with their beauty contests! We are not fighting personalities—we are fighting a system.[8]

The involvement of PL in the disintegrating Students for a Democratic Society in 1968 is covered in another chapter. An important aspect of that involvement, however, was PL's use of both front groups and infiltration. PL had refined Leninist organizing tactics to a high degree, and the fanaticism of PL cadres made profound impressions on susceptible SDS members. According to Joseph Conlin:

By 1967, PL had carried its message deep into SDS which, through the May 2 Movement, a front group, its members were instructed to join . . . its members discovered that, armed with a coherent message and sharply honed apologetical skills, they easily converted impressionistic SDS rank-and-filers to their point of view.

Because they were disciplined as discipline went in the sixties, the PLers soon won some positions of power within SDS. In February 1968, PL elected four of the ten members of SDS's New York regional committee, and three of the remaining seven sometimes voted PL's way.[9]

*    *    *

No longer convinced Maoists, the Progressive Labor people long have maintained that they want to develop an American party and not follow any nation's line through every twist and turn. As independent communists, this group has continued to be as anti-civil-libertarian as when they were Maoists. Their front group InCAR (International Committee Against Racism), founded in 1973, has shouted down speakers on college campuses throughout the seventies and eighties. They also have shown no reluctance to employ violence against political "enemies." According to Harvey Klehr:

They have frequently challenged Ku Klux Klan and Nazi rallies with counter-demonstrations of their own, organized around the theme of smashing and destroying their opponents, not simply protesting against them. They have used rocks, bottles, and bricks, forced their way into radio stations and trashed movie theaters as part of their crusade.

In 1982 PLP and InCAR members broke through police lines and attacked Klansmen in Hannibal, Missouri. One hundred seventy-five attacked Klansmen in Rockville, Maryland, on the grounds that it was necessary to "squash these rodents physically."[10]

Militant antiracism engages many of the same behaviors as militant racism, i.e., the stereotyping and demonization of opponents, announcing that the end justifies the means, thinking in cliches and slogans, promoting censorship and repression, advocating double standards, and so on. In the case of InCAR this is manifestly evident. For example, in August 1978 a group of twelve to fifteen InCAR and PL members burst into a Kansas City, Kansas, radio station during a talk show in which two members of a neo-Nazi organization were being interviewed. According to news reports:

> Twelve to fifteen men, armed with pipes and clubs, disrupted an on-the-air 8 p.m. broadcast Sunday of the KCKN radio Community Hotline, which featured members of the Nazi or American White Peoples' Party. Five persons were injured, and the country music station's studio was damaged extensively.
>
> The attackers consisted of both black and white men. Armed with clubs and iron pipes, they got out of three cars and lined up single file near the station's side entrance. . . .
>
> A tape recording of the assault, which lasted only a few seconds, captured the sound of the studio door opening, shouts, screams, glass and equipment being smashed, then the voice of a man who said, "Let's go!"[11]

A subsequent article noted:

> The Kansas City chapters of the Committee against Racism and the Progressive Labor Party have claimed responsibility for the attack. . . . Both groups are engaged in a campaign against racism.
>
> Ms. Grace Moreno and Ms. Jane Duggan, local leaders for PL and InCAR respectively, reaffirmed their claim that their groups were responsible for the attack. They said the groups plan to confront Nazis whenever they attempt to air their views publicly.[12]

In 1986, PL member and InCAR leader at Northwestern University, Dr. Barbara Foley, led a group that prevented Nicaraguan contra leader Adolfo Calero from speaking and added injury to insult by throwing a red substance (blood or paint) on him. In typical fashion, Foley stated that Calero "should feel lucky to get out alive."[13] InCAR regularly participates in "anti-Klan" demonstrations where most of those arrested for violence are not Klansmen but demonstrators. InCAR publishes *Arrows,* a bimonthly. According to Klehr, in 1978 it had about 1,500 members.[14] Membership today is under five hundred.

Like other extremist groups, PL has had its share of problems with illegal and unconstitutional police harassment and surveillance, much of which was at the instigation of the FBI. Unlike the SWP, however, PL and InCAR had a legitimate reputation for violence. The disinformation and destabilization activities against the organization went far beyond any bona fide law enforcement interest, however, and it was one of a plethora of extremist groups targeted by the government seemingly on the basis of its perceived values, opinions, and beliefs.

At an estimated five hundred members in a society of 250 million people, only one person in 500,000 is a member of the Progressive Labor party, little more than the combined hardcore membership of neo-Nazi groups in the United States, which was estimated at 400 to 450 in 1987.[15] (It may be half that today.) From its inception in 1962, perhaps five thousand individuals have *been* members of the organization at one time or another.

Progressive Labor's impact on American society has been negligible, except to the small circle of fanatics and government agencies who take these "threats" seriously and who have a need to demonize and persecute political extremists.

Lofty abstractions about freedom of speech aside, the role some extremist groups play in their criticisms of society may be essential to good government. They may be the first to call attention to injustice, although they often advocate injustice themselves. They may raise issues the rest of us would prefer to avoid, although they avoid certain issues. They may provide a voice for an invisible minority, although they advocate silencing others. Because of their acute sensitivity to certain issues, they may see things in a way we don't.

## Notes

1. Kirkpatrick Sale, *SDS* (New York: Random House, 1973), 64.
2. Mary-Alice Waters, *Maoism in the U.S.: A Critical History of the Progressive Labor Party* (New York: Young Socialist Alliance, 1969), 12.
3. *Marxist-Leninist Quarterly* 1 (no. 1, Spring 1963).
4. *Marxist-Leninist Quarterly,* op cit.
5. Quoted in Mary-Alice Waters, 10.
6. *Progressive Labor* (February-March 1967): 143.
7. Jack Newfield, *A Prophetic Minority* (New York: New American Library, 1966), 118.
8. *Challenge* (June-July 1968).
9. Joseph Conlin, *The Troubles: A Jaundiced Glance Back at the Movement of the 60's* (New York: Franklin Watts, 1982), 279–80.
10. Harvey Klehr, *Far Left of Center: The American Radical Left Today* (New Brunswick, N.J.: Transaction Books, 1988), 89.
11. Lewis W. Diuguid and Stevenson O. Swanson, "Invade KCKN To Beat Nazis," *Kansas City Times* (August 14, 1978).
12. Greg Edwards and Howard S. Goller, "Leaders Say Attack On Nazis No Stunt," *Kansas City Times* (August 16, 1991).
13. Joseph Epstein, "A Case of Academic Freedom," *Commentary* (September 1986): 41.
14. Klehr, 89.
15. Irwin Suall and David Lowe, "Shaved for Battle—Skinheads Target America's Youth," *Political Communication and Persuasion* 5 (1988): 144.

# 9. **Workers World Party**

In 1958 a group of fewer than one hundred people left the Socialist Workers party because, by supporting a United Socialist ticket in the New York state elections that year, the SWP had given their blessing to social democrats (an unpardonable sin to the true revolutionary). This split actually began over the Hungarian Revolution, which the splitters claimed was led by social democrats ("The enemies of the people are everywhere!"); therefore, they said, Soviet intervention was certainly justified. This dissenting group became known as the Workers World party. The primary periodical of this group is a monthly tabloid, appropriately called *Workers World.*

According to Harvey Klehr:

> Some of its founders had been close to the Cochran faction of the SWP, expelled in 1953 for advocating "entrism," a tactic whereby Trotskyists were urged to disband their parties and enter communist or socialist parties in order to subvert them from within.[1]

Led by Vince Copeland and Sam Marcy, who, from the sixties into the nineties, have exercised strict discipline over a membership of about two hundred, the WWP always has been a very militant group. Quick to yell "fascist" and fill the air with unfounded accusations, WWP members might be included among the more dogmatic and opinionated on the extreme left. But, after all, as one young independent leftist told us in 1970, "What can you expect from a Maoist party built on a Trotskyist base?" The Workers World party of the late 1980s and the early 1990s, however, has been an independent communist organization claiming to support *all* Marxist nations.

Workers World has always conveyed the idea that the Central Intelligence Agency controls almost everything within the United States and most things abroad. Leaders have even gone so far as to link the CIA with George Lincoln Rockwell, the late commander of the American Nazi party, assassinated in 1967 by one of his fellow Nazis. Both organizations have had offices in Arlington, Virginia, and according to Workers World this somehow is a significant fact.

The Workers World party controls a youth group called Youth Against War and Fascism (YAWF). Not a membership group in the card carrying sense, YAWF consists of a few hundred young lefitsts willing to follow the leadership of Workers World party people who serve as the officers of YAWF. This organization has been one of the more direct-action-oriented youth groups in America. With only a few hours notice, YAWF has been able to produce one hundred pickets in almost any area of New York City, protected by a "Defense Guard" that has been extremely aggressive and known to attack hecklers at the slightest provocation. YAWFers always refer to hecklers as "pro-war hoodlums" and "fascists." One female leader of this group told us:

> If some fascist tries to give us trouble we make an example of him. We tell him, "Come on, we're not pacifists. If you want trouble you'll get it."

She illustrated this threat by doubling up her fists. Such mimicking of the nominally "fascist" style by antifascist groups is commonplace, but in few places is it as readily illustrated as in Youth Against War and Fascism. Yet another barely distinguishable front group controlled by the WWP is the All People's Congress, which specifically addresses issues of poverty and racism.

On November 27, 1982, the All People's Congress sponsored an anti-Klan rally in Washington, D.C., that degenerated into a riot in which store windows were broken, cars overturned, and looting took place. Between three thousand and five thousand anti-Klan demonstrators converged on the city, including many bused in by the APC. When police attempted to keep them from mobbing the handful of Klansmen who showed up, the demonstrators became violent. Police arrested forty people and twelve policemen were injured. Walter Fauntroy, the District of Columbia's representative in Congress, praised the APC for their order and discipline and blamed the violence on members of the Spartacist Youth League, another Marxist-Leninist splinter group. The Klansmen, protected by thousands of police, were led away safely.[2]

YAWF claims to have initiated many major far-left activities. The group maintains, for example, that they were the first to demonstrate against the Vietnam War (August 8, 1962), the only group to demonstrate for the Arab people at the time of the June 1967 war, and one of the first to view the Mideast struggle as a simple case of U.S.-Israel aggression. In a 1982 interview, Workers World spokesperson Deirdre Griswold dubbed the "Six Day War" as "the Israeli-provoked war in the Mideast."[3] Workers World also became the principal American supporter of Ethiopia's widely condemned Communist government in the 1980s. State actions against innocent Ethiopian citizens have been a concern of Amnesty International for more than a decade.

UN secretaries general have been, according to the WWP, puppets of U.S. imperialism, and for the UN they use Lenin's condemnation of its predecessor, the League of Nations. Lenin described that organization as "a den of thieves and robbers."[4]

The members of the Workers World party celebrated their thirtieth anniversary in March 1989, still dedicated to violent revolution. Most Americans found little joy in learning of this dedication, but they may have found consolation in the small size of the group's membership, which is estimated at roughly two hundred, about a third of whom are in the New York City area.

# Notes

1. Harvey Klehr, *Far Left of Center: The American Radical Left Today* (New Brunswick, N.J.: Transaction Publishers, 1988), 77.

2. Klehr, 81–82; *Washington Times* (November 30, 1982).

3. Frank Smallwood, *The Other Candidates: Third Parties in Presidential Elections* (Hanover: University Press of England, 1983), 121.

4. *Workers World* (July 16, 1970).

# 10. Revolutionary Action Movement

Robert F. Williams was honorably discharged from the U.S. Marine Corps in 1956 and returned to his home in Monroe, North Carolina, where he became leader of the local NAACP. Soon after assuming that position, he confronted the city powers-that-be with what now seems a modest request: allow blacks to use the local swimming pool one day per week. The city fathers vetoed this on grounds that they simply did not have the money to drain and refill the pool after each use by the "Nigras." No doubt exercising considerable self-control in containing their rage, the local NAACP people, with Williams as spokesman, called for total integration of the facility—a request that was, of course, *not* granted.[1]

This is but one illustration of the intransigence of that and other communities throughout the South and Southwest during the mid-1950s and 1960s. Throughout this time period, the Ku Klux Klan was active in the Monroe area and did its best to intimidate the black population, who could hardly turn for help to local law enforcement officials, because many police officers were themselves Klan members. Due in great part to this distressing situation, Williams organized segments of the black community into "self-defense units."[2]

In 1959, after a white jury acquitted a white of a brutal attack on a black, Williams told a reporter that violence should be met with violence. This resulted in his six-month suspension as head of the Monroe NAACP. All this turned out to be more than Williams could take, and he began to look outward, toward Marxist-Leninist states.

Journeying to Cuba a number of times in 1960, and disseminating favorable information about Fidel Castro and his government, Williams became even more unpopular with American black leaders than previously. He even went so far as to telegram Cuban foreign minister Raul Roa at the UN. The contents of this missive were read by Roa during a debate about the U.S.-backed 1961 invasion of Cuba known as the Bay of Pigs. The telegram stated:

> Now that the United States has proclaimed military support for people willing to rebel against oppression. . . . Negroes in the South urgently request tanks, artillery, arms, money, use of American airfields and white mercenaries to crush the racist tyrants who have betrayed the American Revolution and the Civil War. We also request prayers for this noble undertaking.

Thus Williams attracted the attention of the revolutionary left. So impressed was Milton Rosen, a Communist party functionary who later founded the Progressive Labor party, that he moved to Monroe to learn how to articulate and promote Williams's line among blacks.[3]

It was "an apparently trumped-up civil rights kidnaping charge" that caused Williams to flee to Cuba in 1961. At first he was treated very well by the Castro government and made broadcasts to the United States under the banner of "Radio Free Dixie." Due to a number of things, Williams grew disenchanted with Cuba. Probably ranking high on his disgruntlement list was Cuban insistence that they understood black American problems and solutions better than he.[4]

The Castroites pressured Williams to adopt the line that American blacks' "natural allies" were working class whites. He took strong issue with this: "The whites in the South who helped us were the intelligentsia. The farmers and millworkers . . . were the ones trying to kill us and standing on the sides jeering." Williams was also upset when the Cuban newspaper *Hoy* called Malcolm X a "black fascist." Further, he asked Castro for money to train blacks but was turned down. "Remember in the South," said Williams, "how they used to slap a black man on the back and give him a cigar? Well, it's the same in Cuba, only it's a Havana cigar."[5]

During the years he was based in Cuba (1961–66), Williams was the acknowledged leader (chairman-in-exile) of a small, violent American group known as the Revolutionary Action Movement (RAM), and he published a pamphlet-like newspaper, *The Crusader,* which was smuggled into the United States. All sorts of violent "revolutionary" acts were suggested in the RAM leader's writings, with booby-trapping police call boxes, firebombing, and burning down forests being among the more frequently mentioned.

> We must become adept in the methods of massive defense. The new concept of revolution defies military science and tactics. . . . [It means] lightning campaigns conducted in highly sensitive urban communities . . . [to] sustain a state of confusion and destruction of property [and] reduce the central power to the level of a helpless, sprawling octopus.[6]

Williams was also founder of the Republic of New Africa, which took a black nationalist line, something he adopted while based in Cuba. By mid-1966, Williams had "had it" with the Cubans and moved to the People's Republic of China, where he was to spend three years before returning to the United States in 1969. Continuing to publish *The Crusader,* Williams insisted that it was not subsidized by the Chinese government of Mao Tse-tung. Instead, he maintained, workers volunteered their services—evidently because they wanted to be part of what they deemed an important undertaking.

Over the eight years Williams lived in exile, he paid visits to North Korea, North Vietnam, and also Tanzania, the East African nation where President Julius Nyerere held more political prisoners than did the Republic of South Africa. Also taking place during his time out of the United States were strange plots by his followers. In 1965 there was a thwarted plan to blow up the Statue of Liberty and in 1967 a conspiracy to assassinate civil rights leaders Roy Wilkins (NAACP) and Whitney Young (Urban League). Wilkins commented, "Apparently anyone who doesn't believe in machine guns is an Uncle Tom." Young averred that previous threats had come "from the Ku Klux Klan."[7]

After Williams returned to the United States in 1969, he remained a black nationalist but mellowed in his attitude toward violence. He settled in Detroit and hit the church and school lecture circuit, no longer putting out *The Crusader*. In 1970, he testified in private before the Senate Internal Security Subcommittee. Finally, in early 1976, all charges were dropped in the North Carolina kidnaping case and Williams slipped from view.[8]

## Notes

1. Mari Jo Buhle, Paul Buhle, and Dan Georgakas, *Encyclopedia of the American Left* (New York: Garland Publishing, 1990), 57–58.

2. Robert F. Williams, *Negroes With Guns* (New York: Marzani and Munsell, 1962).

3. Methvin, Eugene H., *The Riot Makers* (New Rochelle, N.Y.: Arlington House, 1970), 283.

4. Georgie Anne Geyer, "The Odyssey of Robert Williams," *The New Republic* (March 20, 1971).

5. Geyer.

6. *New York Times* (August 18, 1969).

7. *Newsweek* (July 30, 1967), 30.

8. For more on Williams and RAM see *Workers World* (August 31, 1967); William Worthy, "The Red Chinese American Negro," *Esquire* (October 1964).

# 11. Revolutionary Communist Party

Originating in 1969 as the Bay Area Revolutionary Union (BARU), this group eventually became the Revolutionary Union (RU) and then the Revolutionary Communist party (RCP) in 1975, at which time it probably had under one thousand members and chapters in about twenty-five states. The principal founder, Bob Avakian, was still unquestioned leader in the 1990s, although for more than a decade he has been residing in Europe. An organizer for Students for a Democratic Society (SDS) in the San Francisco area and a writer for RU's newspaper, the *Bay Area Worker,* Avakian was elected to the eleven-member National Interim Committee of SDS at the organization's last convention in 1969, when he was in the thick of the fight for control. The Revolutionary Union, as it was known then, brought a large group to the convention to fend off a similar takeover attempt by the Progressive Labor party.

According to Noel Ignatiev in the *Encyclopedia of the American Left,* the RCP

> passed through several regroupments and splits, with some of the veterans of the Black Workers Congress (some of whom had earlier been influenced by the Revolutionary Action Movement) and with the Puerto Rican Revolutionary Workers Organization and the August 29th Movement in the Southwest, eventually emerging in 1975 as the Revolutionary Communist Party, which at its peak attained a membership of 500–700.[1]

A 1972 congressional report contained testimony from undercover informants in the Revolutionary Union. The FBI had identified branches in some twenty-five localities of nine states, and estimated the total membership at four hundred.[2] The Hoover Institution figured that the RCP's 1978 membership was 2,000, with chapters in eighteen states.[3] The difference between this last figure and Ignatiev's demonstrates the general unreliability of alleged membership figures for extremist organizations.

This organization is one of the few that has never wavered in singing the praises of Mao Tse-tung; it long has considered China's Great Proletarian Cultural Revolution of the mid-1960s to have been among the most positive events for true Communists everywhere. According to Francis M. Watson in *The Alternative Media:*

Avakian and a large group of Revolutionary Union members made a triumphant visit to Peking more than five months before President Nixon's visit. The warm reception by the Chinese leaders not only demonstrated to others on the U.S. left that China considered the Revolutionary Union to be the prime Maoist organization in the country, but set a pattern for subsequent trips by Americans who would come back to the U.S. singing the praises of the "New China" under the auspices of the U.S.-Chinese People's Friendship Association.[4]

The idealization of the Communist Chinese regime was a consistent thread among the more radical student Marxist-Leninist movements of the period. Another country with a host of such admirers at that time was Albania, perhaps the most intolerant, dogmatic, totalitarian dictatorship in the world. The Revolutionary Communist party and its predecessors joined in the admiration. According to Watson:

> Two ranking members of the Revolutionary Union subsequently held offices in the U.S.-China People's Friendship Association. One of these, William H. Hinton, influential in founding both RU and USCPFA, was the Friendship Association's chairman from its beginning in 1974 to 1976. His credentials as a Maoist were impressive. He had spent most of the Korean War years in the newly established People's Republic of China and had written several books on the subject. His contacts in China included his sister, Joan Hinton Engst, a nuclear physicist who defected to Peking in 1949 after having worked as a scientist at Los Alamos.
>
> Another prominent figure in the Revolutionary Union/U.S.-China People's Friendship Association was Clark Kissinger, who served in the association variously as national vice chairman and member of the national steering committee. His credentials as a "New Leftist" were impressive. He was, at three separate times, secretary of SDS, figured prominently in the battle that destroyed SDS, and headed up the staff of the Chicago bureau of the Maoist-oriented underground/alternative newspaper *Guardian*, before joining Revolutionary Union.[5]

In its literature the RCP has described itself as:

> a national communist organization made up mainly of workers and students, black, brown, Asian, Native American, and white. Our immediate program is to bring together, under the leadership of the working class, the main spearheads of struggle against the U.S. imperialist system. . . . The long-range goal of this United Front Against Imperialism, led by the working class, is to overthrow the dictatorship of the handful of monopoly capitalists (imperialists) and to establish the dictatorship of the working class, the great majority society, to build toward socialism and communism. . . . To do this, we must join together into a single Communist Party, with the discipline, division of labor, and strategy and tactics capable of leading the immediate struggle of the people to deal the death blow to the imperialist system.[6]

The stilted ideological language, filled with thought-stopping cliches, buzzwords, slogans, and epithets, is fairly typical of the hybrid Marxist-Leninist fringe groups that spun off from the original Students for a Democratic Society in the late

1960s and early 1970s. This language is used not because it necessarily explains anything, but because of the feeling it gives the user of having a "correct line," or in today's terms, a feeling of "political correctness."

In fact, these people can accurately be termed Stalinists. Of course, they have been slightly critical of Stalin, but they always claim that he never wavered from the true "revolutionary path."

Differing with many groups on the far left, the RCP has opposed busing for racial balance, the Equal Rights Amendment, and gay rights. In fact, they have been described as having "hostility" toward homosexuals.[7] While their newspaper, *Revolutionary Worker,* has featured articles complimentary to Albania and North Korea, no government on earth ever has been suitable to their taste. The Soviet Union, which was never acceptable, became worse under Gorbachev, who was classified (along with Reagan and French leader Francoise Mitterand) as a "bloodsucker."[8] The Berlin Wall never had anything to do with communism. Built by Khrushchev, "who restored capitalism" in the Soviet Union, the wall "has been testimony to the failure of revisionism and social-imperialism."[9]

Although members would deny any such assertions, the RCP, like a number of other far-left and far-right groups, seems to exhibit some cult-like traits. This is especially true with respect to the unquestioning allegiance given to leader Bob Avakian. A sub-headline in the *Revolutionary Worker* typifies the reverence for Avakian:

Our ideology is Marxism-Leninism-Maoism
Our vanguard is the Revolutionary Communist Party
Our leader is Chairman Avakian[10]

Perhaps most notable about Avakian are his long polemical articles in *Revolution,* the RCP's quarterly propaganda organ. Typical are "Upheaval in China: Mao More Than Ever" (Fall-Winter 1989, eighteen pages), and "The End of a Stage—The Beginning of a New Stage" (Fall 1990, twenty-five pages).

Still active in the early 1990s, the RCP sent Carl Dix, principal spokesperson in the United States, on a speaking tour. Billed as the "Yo! The World Is Being Turned Upside Down! Tour," its main aim was to place Dix in many different cities and expose his views to a wide audience. College campuses seemed to be the preferred setting.

What is unusual is the RCP's strong public support of the Sendero Luminoso— the Shining Path terrorists of Peru who have murdered both people and dogs in their efforts to control the countryside. Shining Path has also protected coca-growing farmers and thus supported the cocaine trade.

Eventually, the RCP fell out of favor with the Communist Chinese government, in part over the Avakian personality cult and in part due to the death of Mao Tse-tung and the following changes in the party leadership. In the late 1970s some of RCP's membership transferred their allegiance to the Communist Party (Marxist-Leninist), headed by Michael Klonsky and Lyn Wells. RCP membership in the 1990s is estimated at well under five hundred.

## Notes

1. Mari Jo Buhle, Paul Buhle, and Dan Georgakas, *Encyclopedia of the American Left* (New York: Garland Publishing, 1990), 49.

2. "America's Maoists—The Revolutionary Union," (House Internal Security Committee, U.S. Congress, 1972).

3. *1978 Yearbook on International Communist Affairs* (Stanford, Calif.: Hoover Institution, 1978).

4. Francis M. Watson, Jr., *The Alternative Media: Dismantling Two Centuries of Progress* (Rockford, Ill.: Rockford College Institute, 1979), 70.

5. Watson, 70–71.

6. *Red Papers 1, 2, 3* (a seventy-page RCP—then called Revolutionary Union—booklet not dated but believed to have been published in 1970).

7. Harvey Klehr, *Far Left of Center: The American Radical Left Today* (New Brunswick, N.J.: Transaction Books, 1988), 92.

8. *Revolutionary Worker* (November 4, 1985).

9. *Revolutionary Worker* (November 13, 1989).

10. *Revolutionary Worker* (November 7, 1988).

# 12. Communist Workers Party

On the evening of August 14, 1980, hopes were high for partisans of mainstream politics. The Democratic nominee, President James Earl Carter of Georgia, was making his acceptance speech at their national convention. It is unlikely that any of the Democrats present in Madison Square Garden that night imagined that an extremist attack was in the offing. Nor was this attack from the racist right, from people angry at Carter for being "soft on Communism" or a "nigger-lover." Instead, it was perpetrated by people who thought him a racist and a fascist—the Maoist militants of the Communist Workers party (CWP). Wearing riot gear and armed with mace and clubs, the CWPers tried to storm the hall, but they were parried by police and fifteen were taken into custody. Inside, one of their number ignited firecrackers while another yelled Communist slogans.[1]

Here was a group that had hailed the deeds of Stalin, Mao, even Pol Pot, and applauded the Iranian regime of the Ayatollah Khomeini for giving the death penalty to fourteen Trotskyists (whom they termed "counter-revolutionary dogs").[2] The Communist Workers party had first come to national attention on November 3, 1979, when five of their number were killed and nine others wounded in a shoot-out with Klansmen and Nazis in Greensboro, North Carolina. The CWP was staging a "Death to the Klan" rally when the violence occurred. (Previously, they had sought confrontations with the Klan and even stopped a screening of D. W. Griffith's classic film *Birth of a Nation* in China Grove, North Carolina, burning the Klan's confederate flag in the process.)

Two of the Communists killed were physicians, one of whom was educated at the University of Chicago, the other at Duke University. Another was a graduate of Harvard Divinity School and the fourth was a *magna cum laude* graduate in political science at Duke. The fifth was a former student body president at Bennett College in Greensboro. One of the two doctors had quit his practice in order to organize in the textile mills around Greensboro; he had become president of the local textile workers union. All of the victims had been devoted to a fanaticism so powerful and compelling that they sacrificed careers that most people idealize. Their choices were not dictated by any rational considerations, but rather by a cult-like subservience to Marxist-Leninist doctrine on the order of religious fanaticism.

Among the various causes that the organization, under its present or past names, had championed were elimination of student competency testing and opposition to forced busing in Boston.

\*     \*     \*

163

According to Harvey Klehr, a political science professor at Emory University in Atlanta who writes an annual profile of Communist groups in the United States, "Factionalism is endemic in the dozens of Maoist groups around the country and they all hate each other."[3]

Lindsey Gruson in the *Greensboro Daily News* notes that factionalism has been a serious problem in the CWP:

> The factionalism among the groups in Greensboro became apparent a few days before last Saturday's fatal shootings. Cindy Luiz, a member of the Revolutionary Communist Party, one of at least two area rivals of the WVO [Workers Viewpoint Organization, previous name of the CWP], charged Nelson Johnson, the organizer of the weekend rally, with cooperating with the Nazis and Klansmen.
>
> Johnson and other members of the WVO have repeatedly denied the charges and accused the Klan and the Nazis of murdering their leaders on orders from the government and multinational corporations.[4]

The Klan and Nazi groups involved in the incident were no better. Thoroughly steeped in racial hatred and bigotry, the various Nazi parties and Ku Klux Klan organizations (there are literally dozens, most very small) represent the farthest shores of the extreme right and are remarkably like the CWP in a number of respects, not the least of which is their tendency toward factionalism and internal discord. The CWP–Ku Klux Klan–Nazi party mixture was one just waiting for a spark to set it off.

Six months after the shootout, Terry Eastland, writing in *Commentary* magazine, assessed the CWP as having "at most 200 members in active chapters in New York City, Los Angeles, Durham and Greensboro, North Carolina, among other places." He also asserted:

> The CWP . . . is one of the small Maoist groups that have developed since the disintegration of the Students for a Democratic Society in 1969. . . . Although it had doctrinal differences with other Maoist groups, it agreed with them on the main goal, namely, the destruction of the American capitalist order by the working class.
>
> It is a common belief that yesterday's radicals have either "mellowed out," becoming consummate Me-Decaders or joining the establishment, or have become religious fanatics. The People's Temple of Jonestown should have placed this belief in doubt, and Greensboro now unambiguously proves it wrong. . . .
>
> The CWP can be faulted for another, potentially more deadly [form of racism]: manipulating blacks for its own political ends. The CWP went into a black community thinking that the poorer and less sophisticated of Greensboro's blacks might be successfully exploited in this campaign to abolish class in America: it did not appear to mind how many black lives thus might be endangered, even sacrificed. In this the CWP ironically made a kind of common cause with its avowed enemy, the Klan.[5]

Following the shoot-out the Klansmen and neo-Nazis were tried on two separate occasions, both of which resulted in acquittal. A state jury found the defendants not guilty of murder in 1980, and a federal panel acquitted them on charges of conspiring to violate the CWP demonstrators' civil rights in 1984.

During the trial CWP spokespersons, especially Signe Waller, widow of the slain James Waller, called the proceedings "nothing but a coverup for the conspiracy," which they claimed included federal, state, and local officials.[6] Another claimed to have been "wounded by the same Klan/Nazi/U.S. government agents that murdered the CWP members."[7] There were even accusations that North Carolina Governor Jim Hunt and President Jimmy Carter had cooperated in the killings. Additionally, the CWPers refused to testify.[8]

Among the revelations offered by the defense was that a federal agent— Bureau of Alcohol, Tobacco and Firearms agent Bernard Butkovich who had infiltrated the Forsyth County unit of the American Nazi party—knew of the planned confrontation two days before it occurred, yet failed to inform any police agency. Klan members testified that Butkovich actually encouraged them to commit a variety of illegal acts and offered to procure hand grenades. On another occasion, according to former Nazi R. L. Shannon, Butkovich "tried to get us into a plan to assassinate Joe Grady [a rival Klan leader]. He was going to drive the car and all."

Roland Wayne Wood, one of the KKK defendants, testified that Butkovich urged him to take a pistol to the rally where the shootout occurred. Wood said, "He tried to lead me into things, to make me give him orders." Nazi party leader Harold Covington said that Butkovich had offered to teach a course on how to make bombs. Gorrell Pierce, a former Klan leader, said that Butkovich had suggested that the Nazis take weapons to the rally in the trunks of their cars.[9]

Yet another informant in the Ku Klux Klan and Nazi party was Edward Dawson. According to Wyn Craig Wade in *The Fiery Cross: The Ku Klux Klan in America:*

> What CWP members didn't know was that the Greensboro police had a paid informer in the Klan—Edward Dawson, who had joined the Klan in 1964 and been a member in earnest for over ten years. As a Klan security guard, Dawson had been arrested and served time for the destruction of property in Alamance County and had also been involved in a 1969 Fourth of July fracas in which a black girl had been shot and a police car shot up. After serving nine months in prison, Dawson had become an informant for the FBI and now for the Greensboro police. . . .
>
> For reasons that are not clear, Dawson began a vigorous campaign to entice scattered Klan groups in the Greensboro area to attend the rally. . . . One Klansman later told the *Greensboro Daily News,* "We'd never have come to Greensboro if it wasn't for Ed Dawson berating us."[10]

Elizabeth Wheaton has commented on Dawson's FBI activities:

> The pattern especially prevalent in the agency's dealings with the Klan and Nazi groups was to use an informant or undercover agent to create a split to draw members away from an existing group and form a new faction. Dawson was involved in just such a split.[11]

Such a strategy is not without precedent. A *New York Times* dispatch of July 11, 1978, tells of former FBI informant Gary Thomas Rowe, Jr., a Ku Klux Klan infiltrator who has now admitted shooting a black man to death and keeping quiet about the incident at the instruction of an FBI agent. The FBI has denied the charge. However, Alabama authorities have revealed that investigative documents show that Rowe has twice failed polygraph tests in which he denied direct involvement in a 1963 Birmingham church bombing and in two other bombings. According to the *New York Times* article:

> As a result of those tests, according to sources close to the renewed investigation into racial violence in Alabama in the 1960s, Rowe is now suspected of having acted as an agent-provocateur, participating in and helping to plan the violent activity that the FBI had hired him to monitor.

The Bureau of Alcohol, Tobacco and Firearms (BATF) is second only to the FBI in tracking and harassing extreme rightists. A division of the U.S. Treasury Department, the BATF is not normally thought of as law enforcement in the same sense as the FBI or Secret Service. Supposedly it is involved in collecting taxes on alcohol, tobacco and firearms, but since some extreme rightists tend to promote—and use—illegal firearms, the BATF fell into this specialty and applied its talents with considerable abandon.

From the BATF's perspective most firearms and explosives cases are simple possession cases. That is, one need only be in possession of a particular item to break the law; how the possession occurred is a secondary matter. In a Kansas City–area case, the BATF was accused of attempting to coerce a local policeman into planting a pipe bomb in the house trailer of a local Klansman. The police officer refused.[12] In yet another case, at a training seminar the BATF circulated a list of "paramilitary groups" which included a number of clearly nonparamilitary organizations such as the John Birch Society, and wound up withdrawing it when some of the groups protested.[13] Many similar incidents have occurred.

An article by Martha Woodall in the *Greensboro Record* at the time of the KKK/neo-Nazi trial notes:

> Although tighter surveillance restrictions were placed on the FBI and CIA in recent years, most of the limitations have not been extended to the Treasury Department's Bureau of Alcohol, Tobacco and Firearms.[14]

Ms. Woodall also notes that BATF officials claimed that they "strictly forbid the type of provocation ATF agent Bernard Butkovich is accused of attempting." Regarding a later civil lawsuit brought by the survivors of the slain CWP members, a *Newsweek* article said:

> Also in the dock is Bernard Butkovich, an Ohio-based agent of the U.S. Bureau of Alcohol, Tobacco and Firearms who infiltrated the North Carolina Nazis as part of a gun investigation. The plaintiffs argue that in seeking the Nazis' confidence,

Butkovich became a *provocateur,* at one point telling them, "I wouldn't go (to Greensboro) without a gun." He says he had no reason to expect violence.[15]

In the federal criminal case, *U.S.* v. *Virgil Griffin,* in which nine Klansmen and neo-Nazis were indicted under section 371, title 18, U.S. Code (conspiracy to violate federal law),[16] Elizabeth Wheaton noted in her book on the incident, *Code Name Greenkil:*

The prosecutors presented seventy-seven witnesses and an overwhelming array of technical evidence: charts, graphs, models, analyses, and the videotapes —run in forward, reverse, slow motion, stop action, and with elaborate Hollywood produced highlights. No one would venture to estimate the cost of obtaining evidence and prosecuting the case, but $1 million is probably a conservative figure.[17]

Nevertheless, as Ms. Wheaton notes, at the end of the trial, "forty-eight times the clerk read the name and the charge. Forty-eight times he read, "The jury finds the defendant not guilty."

According to the *Greensboro Record* of November 3, 1980, "The prosecution sent more items, more than 2,000, to the FBI for analysis than any other trial with the exception of the Kennedy assassination and the Wounded Knee case." Over six hundred pieces of evidence were actually introduced.

In both cases the deciding factors appeared to be an awareness of at least partial CWP responsibility for the confrontation as well as the fact that CWP members were armed, too. A CWP directive of November 3, 1979, noted, "The main content of the anti-Klan campaign should be militant, direct action—a confrontation with the Klan would be best if we can get it." Ku Klux Klan member David Matthews had testified that he had fired five shotgun blasts at three black men pointing guns at him. A widely circulated photograph of the incident showed CWP member Rand Manzella kneeling with a pistol in his hand. CWP members were tried, and in some cases convicted, of lesser charges surrounding the incident. These factors, along with the "beyond a reasonable doubt" consideration inherent in criminal trials, resulted in acquittals for the Klansmen and neo-Nazis in spite of the enormous resources that went into the prosecutions, including grants of immunity to several key witnesses in exchange for their testimony.

On balance, it seems incredible that Ku Klux Klan and neo-Nazi killers of five individuals, even Marxist-Leninist extremists, could go unpunished. Nevertheless, they were tried and acquitted. The CWP immediately charged a conspiracy was afoot. Following the first acquittals on state charges, the survivors of the slain CWP members filed a civil suit against virtually everyone connected with the event in any way, including the city of Greensboro, the BATF, and the previously indicted and acquitted Klansmen and neo-Nazis. *Waller* v. *Butkovich* asked for $48 million in damages. In that suit the plaintiffs contended:

The Greensboro police and agents of the FBI and the firearm bureau learned of plans by the Klan and the Nazis to disrupt the march by blacks and union organizers and either encouraged those plans or, at the least, looked the other way.[18]

While the defendants (except for law enforcement and city officials) had to rely on their own resources for legal counsel, the plaintiffs had the resources of their Civil Rights Fund, which raised over $600,000 for the civil suit and generated support from the American Civil Liberties Union, the NAACP, the National Council of Churches, and the Congressional Black Caucus, among others. As in most civil suits, it was largely a contest of resources to pay attorneys and cover legal costs.

On November 6, 1985, a settlement was announced. A total of $394,959.55 was awarded, and the major part of that consisted of the $351,500 that the city of Greensboro paid to the estate of Michael Nathan. According to a *New York Times* article:

> Found liable in Dr. Nathan's death were Eddie Dawson, a Klansman and Greensboro police informer who was charged with helping organize and leading the caravan of Klansmen and Nazis to the demonstration; David Wayne Matthews and Jerry Paul Smith, Klansmen; Roland Wayne Wood and Mark Scherer, Nazi Party members; Jack Fowler, a former Nazi Party member; Greensboro Police Lieut. P. W. Spoon, and Greensboro Detective J. H. Cooper.[19]

The jury also found all forty-five defendants not guilty of engaging in a conspiracy to violate the plaintiffs' civil rights; seventeen city and police defendants were found not guilty of a charge that they failed to provide adequate protection for the demonstrators.

\*    \*    \*

Chinese-born Jerry Tung was the main founder of the Communist Workers party in 1973. Originally called the Asian Study Group and based in New York City, it became the Workers Viewpoint Organization in 1976. The WVO organized the Trade Union Educational League, which infiltrated and moved into the leadership in several local unions in North Carolina and covertly participated in several labor strikes in 1978 and 1979. WVO became the Communist Workers party in late 1979. Under its various names the organization has always been populated by a large percentage of well-educated Asian members. According to Blanche McCrary Boyd in *The Village Voice:*

> The CWP "line" includes unqualified admiration for Chairman Mao, qualified support for Pol Pot, and enthusiasm for the Zimbabwe and Iranian revolutions. Members like to talk about the objective laws of history and the science of MLMTT, Marxism-Leninism–Mao Tse-tung Thought. They call each other comrade. They see feminism as a bourgeoisie trickery, homosexuality as sickness, and revolution as necessary surgery on the social structure.
>
> The communists I interviewed lead rigidly normal lives. Marriage is correct, children is correct, hard work is admirable. Drugs and unsanctioned sex are decadent. They live in unpretentious houses in unpretentious neighborhoods. They try not to make too much money.[20]

In 1985, the group again underwent changes in both name and tactics. Becoming the New Democratic Movement, they decided to work within the Democratic party because, as Jerry Tung put it, "We can get funding from the Democrats to sustain our struggle."[21] Estimates of the group's numbers had fallen to between five hundred and two thousand by the mid-1980s. We doubt that CWP membership has ever exceeded five hundred.

Nelson Johnson, a former CWP member who helped organize the "Death to the Klan" march in 1979, is now a minister at one of Greensboro's largest black churches, Shiloh Baptist. Eddie Dawson is no longer an undercover operative in the Ku Klux Klan. He works as a self-employed carpenter in Greensboro. Paul Bermanzohn, a CWP member wounded in the shoot-out, is now a psychiatrist in Queens, New York. Martha Nathan, wife of the slain Dr. Michael Nathan, is remarried and a doctor in a rural health clinic. Signe Waller, widow of James Waller, holds a Ph.D. in philosophy and lives in Milwaukee.[22]

## Notes

1. *New York Times* (August 25, 1980).

2. Mark Pinsky, "Greensboro Massacre," *The Progressive* (January 1980); *Greensboro Daily News* (November 6, 1979), A-1, 17, 18.

3. Quoted in Lindsey Gruson, "They All Hate Each Other, Professor Says of Leftists," *Greensboro Daily News* (November 6, 1979), A-18.

4. Gruson, op. cit.

5. Terry Eastland, "The Communists and the Klan," *Commentary* (May 1980): 65–66.

6. "The Dream Is Shattered," *Oklahoma Journal* (October 24, 1980).

7. *Guardian* (September 24, 1980).

8. *Guardian* (June 19, 1985).

9. Martha Woodall, "Nazis Say Federal Agent Infiltrated Unit, Knew of Plans for Nov. 3 Motorcade," *Greensboro Record* (July 14, 1980), A-1, A-2.

10. Wyn Craig Wade, *The Fiery Cross: The Ku Klux Klan in America* (New York: Simon & Schuster, 1987), 380–81.

11. Elizabeth Wheaton, *Code Name Greenkil* (Athens: University of Georgia Press, 1987), 12.

12. Bill Norton, "The Convert," *Star Magazine* (October 3, 1988).

13. List circulated at a BATF-sponsored "Extremism and Terrorism School," Lodge of the Four Seasons, Lake of the Ozarks, Mo., February 8 and 9, 1984. BATF form letter dated September 28, 1984, advising that recipients "disregard the paramilitary caption, and refrain from any redistribution of this material."

14. Martha Woodall, "Rules Differ for ATF Agents Involved in Undercover Work," *Greensboro Record* (July 14, 1980).

15. "Greensboro Shoot-Out: Round 3," *Newsweek* (April 8, 1985), 87.

16. Defendants were Virgil Griffin, Edward Dawson, David Matthews, Roland Wayne Wood, Jerry Smith, Jack Fowler, Roy Toney, John Pridmore, and Milano Caudle. They were also charged with conspiring to violate the civil rights of persons because of their race or religion.

17. Wheaton, 272.

18. Paul Wenske, "Suit Puts Klan, Nazis, Federal Agents on Same Side of Table," *Kansas City Times* (May 20, 1985), B–4.

19. "8 Found Liable in Slaying at Anti-Klan Rally in 1979," *New York Times* (June 8, 1975).

20. Blanche McCrary Boyd, "Ambush: An Inquiry Into the Holy War in Greensboro," *The Village Voice* (May 26, 1980).

21. Harvey Klehr, "Maoist Nose Enters Democratic Tent," *New York Post* (August 22, 1987).

22. Jim Schlosser, "Klan Shootings—10 Years Later," *Greensboro News & Record* (October 29, 1989).

# Part III. **The Far Right**

The core values of the American right are individualism, capitalism, religiosity, and nationalism. This has been consistent for most of the twentieth century.

The great majority of far right organizations and individuals tend to adhere to an ideology that includes: strong support for religion (primarily Christianity), intense nationalism/patriotism, anti-Marxism, antiliberalism, anti-social-democracy, and support for nations that are traditional authoritarian dictatorships. In addition, a number of extreme right organizations have developed convoluted conspiracy theories that embrace some elements of superstition and mysticism, such as the "Illuminati" and Masonic conspiracies.

Many right extremist groups focus on ethnic/racial chauvinism as the main component of their ideology—Aryan Nations, the various Ku Klux Klans, the Nation of Islam, and the New Order, for example. Others, such as the John Birch Society and Christian Crusade, eschew ethnic/racial prejudice as part of their ideology. The tendency of many writers to regard the entire right wing, from moderate conservative to neo-Nazi, as objectively "racist" is simply not justified.

# 13. Reverend Billy James Hargis and His Christian Crusade

> God called me for this service. I did not choose it; God called me. It is nothing
> short of miraculous the way the Lord has used my friends and my enemies to create
> the ministry of Christian Crusade.
>
> Billy James Hargis[1]

The large, well-dressed black man at the podium arranged his notes carefully
before looking around at the auditorium filled with attentive white faces. Introductory remarks concluded, he began to attack prominent black organizations
and leaders. Swelling applause and enthusiastic amens came from the audience,
hungry for his startling pronouncements. The purpose of the pro-Communist civil
rights movement, the speaker declared, had been to create hatred between Negro
and Caucasian Americans and to destroy the free enterprise system.

The speaker was Dr. Donald Jackson of Buffalo, New York; the place, the
large central auditorium of the Christian Crusade Cathedral in Tulsa, Oklahoma;
the occasion, the annual national convention of Reverend Dr. Billy James Hargis's
Christian Crusade; and the date was August 1, 1970.

Outside, in the stifling 104-degree temperature, traffic jammed Sheridan
Avenue, which separates the large cathedral from the construction site of Hargis's
American Christian College. Signs directing visitors from all parts of the country
flanked the streets and entrances to the cathedral parking lot, filled to overflowing
with cars bearing license plates from such places as California, Florida, and
Montana. Although a few pickup trucks could be seen, the parking lot was packed
mostly with expensive, late-model automobiles, emblazoned with flag decals and
bumper-sticker slogans of the far right.

Up the wide steps leading to the cathedral entrance, late-arriving groups of
middle-aged visitors passed between two large eagles, poised wings akimbo like
Old Testament cherubim, guarding the cathedral's "God and Country" treasures
from the "Satanic forces" Hargis had inveighed against for more than two decades.
Just inside the double-doored entrance, visitors moved across the wide, curving
foyer, past the registration desk into the rear of the auditorium, where Donald
Jackson was now well into his speech.

Jackson's voice was piped into all parts of the cathedral through an elaborate
sound system. Many first-time pilgrims to the Christian Crusade International
Headquarters listened while they paused in the foyer to view the religious and

military displays in the area Hargis called his "Christian Crusade Religious and Americanism Museum." Near the front were mementoes and artifacts of Hargis's early career, and against one wall stood the pulpit from the Rose Hill Christian Church of Texarkana, Texas, from which Hargis preached his first sermon in 1943. There were also large photographs of him clasping the hands of such favorites as Nationalist Chinese leader Chiang Kai-Shek and former South Korean leader Syngman Rhee.

The museum, Hargis said, "embraces both the religious and the Americanism aspects," and it says to "one and all that there is a relationship between Christ and Americanism. Were it not for Christ, we would not have America." To one side near the end of the foyer stood the Cathedral Bookshop containing racks and shelves of Hargis publications, together with works of the Birch Society, Dan Smoot, Clarence Manion, Taylor Caldwell, and a host of other far-right authors and publishers, plus all kinds of items to help Christian Crusaders in their unending struggle to "save America."

Inside the large Tulsa auditorium, Jackson continued his speech, discoursing on the terrors of racial intermarriage, the evil of the civil-rights movement, and the machinations of "pro-Communist" NAACP leader Roy Wilkins, who only *seemed* to be moderate. In Jackson's view, black militants schemed to make Wilkins and those like him appear acceptable. The audience agreed wholeheartedly.

From a back-row position, it was possible to see the leader himself. He had entered from a side door and taken one of the temporary seats placed against the back wall for ushers and police officers. Perched on the yellow plastic seat, Billy James Hargis beamed at all who glanced his way, radiating strength and a special kind of holy warmth. He was dressed in a natty, lightweight summer suit and a blue striped shirt. His well-groomed black hair showed no trace of gray or thinness, and the flashing smile set in his rotund baby face transmitted radiant joy. His ponderous weight rested lightly on the edge of the seat as he bent his hands in applause and shouted exhortations to the black speaker. The audience recognized the voice and caught his enthusiasm. Victory was in the air, victory over the devil, with the Christian Crusade's leader in command.

In 1970, Billy James Hargis, founder-director of Christian Crusade, was the epitome of success. After more than twenty years of struggle, he could view the reward of his accomplishments with considerable pride. By most standards of measurement in twentieth-century America, he had "arrived." He was a man of means, director or owner of much property and wealth, recipient of honors and monetary donations large and small. His views on every subject could be carried instantly to every part of the United States and much of Canada and Mexico by hundreds of radio stations or by his own newspaper. Various educators, evangelists, nationally known industrialists, and even a few governors and congressmen had beaten a path to his cathedral door to deliver speeches and lectures; a few American military men such as Major General Edwin A. Walker, Major General Charles A. Willoughby and Lieutenant General Pedro A. Del Valle were his supporters or companions on tour; even rulers of various countries around the world were numbered among his personal friends and admirers.

Hargis had labored hard to put Christian Crusade in a position of prominence among the hundreds of far-right organizations in America. Outside the Ku Klux Klan, largely discredited for obvious reasons, only the John Birch Society was better known than his organization.

Billy James Hargis was born in 1925 in Texarkana, Texas. An only child, he grew up strongly attached to his parents, especially his mother. They were poor; indeed, for some time the elder Hargis worked for a dollar a day as a truck driver. The family was very active in the Rose Hill church. It was always an independent church, but through the years Hargis was often erroneously reported as belonging to either the Church of Christ or the Disciples of Christ. This conflict may have occurred because both these churches were once joined together with various independent Christian churches in the Restoration Movement, a nineteenth-century religious effort that stressed a strong liberalist tradition.

Young Hargis was so caught up in religious activities that he decided at the age of nine that it was time to be "saved." Even at age forty, Hargis was still insisting that his very early conversion was entirely proper and not the childish action that some might have considered it.

A poor student in high school, Hargis wrote later that he never really studied until he entered Bible college.[2] Shortly after high school, Hargis decided he had received a "call" from the Lord. It was, after all, a time when most of his generation were having to make serious decisions and, it can be safely assumed, because he was unmarried and of the proper age, young Hargis would soon have become a prime candidate for induction into the armed services.

Having opted to become a preacher and forego the opportunity to serve in World War II, Hargis decided to enter Ozark Bible College (Bentonville, Arkansas) immediately and arrived there in March of 1943. With fewer than a dozen students in an educational plant that could boast of little more than a roof over the heads of its first class, Ozark Bible College was hardly an institution that could inspire much hope in a young man anxious to be successful. Hargis was unquestionably a highly motivated student; indeed, it appears that he was so concerned to become a minister that, less than three months after enrolling at the Bible college, Hargis made a weekend trip to Texarkana, where he was ordained by the pastor of the Rose Hill Christian Church. His ordination followed the general pattern of rural lay ministers and was made possible because the pastor and elders of his church approved of it. It could not have been based on either experience or education. But Hargis's ordination had the immediate effect of placing him beyond the reach of the military draft, although there is no evidence whatsoever that that was his motive. Corpulent even as a young man, his weight alone would almost certainly have been enough to make him unfit for the service.

After attending for less than a year and a half, Hargis quit Ozark Bible College. (Later he wrote that he was forced to leave for financial reasons.) Hargis pastored several small churches in Arkansas, Oklahoma, and Missouri before accepting the pulpit of a fairly large Christian Church in Sapulpa, Oklahoma, a growing community a few miles south of Tulsa.

It was but a matter of time before Hargis was convinced that he should be preaching his newly found convictions to all of America. He expressed his ambition in prose that blended patriotism with religious sentimentality:

> By this time I was twenty-five years of age. I had become concerned about communists and religious apostasy. Would I volunteer to God as a prophet and crusader or would I remain as a comfortable pastor? I realized what my decision meant to my future life. I made it and stepped out in faith for the harder service as a crusader.[3]

This "harder service" involved setting up an organization in 1948 to propagate his views and withdrawing from the church to devote all of his time to his "crusade." He incorporated the movement under the name of Christian Echoes Ministry, Inc. (later Christian Echoes National Ministry, Inc.), but the organization became better known as Christian Crusade. It was, like similar movements of the day, a nonprofit, religious organization that enjoyed tax-exempt status. Hargis claimed it was a movement directed by God to save America. Right away he began to use local radio to get out his message, heavily larded as it was with attacks on politicians and the activities of large, mainstream Protestant churches. Hargis was soon progressing very well in many small towns and backwoods communities. But his message went largely unnoticed by the news media in big cities, where it was generally indistinguishable from the doomsday sermons of legions of other right-wing fundamentalist preachers who had followed their congregations into cities beckoned by higher wages and the "good life."

What Billy James called his "first big break" came in 1953, when the Reverend Carl McIntire, president of the International Council of Christian Churches, an organization set up in opposition to the National Council of Churches, appointed Hargis chairman of a committee to initiate the "Bible Balloon Project." This effort was designed to send thousands of portions of the Bible into countries behind the Iron Curtain by means of balloons launched from Western Europe. The project attracted an unusual amount of attention from the press, so much so that the balloon effort was extended for some five years. It was the first real publicity for Hargis.

Many observers have wondered how McIntire, one of the country's best known extremist preachers of the day, came to select a little-known backwoods minister from Oklahoma to run the Bible Balloon Project. The most probable answer is that Hargis impressed him as an articulate, political soulmate with considerable potential. In an early-1960s book, *Men of the Far Right,* Richard Dudman described the Christian Crusade operation:

> [Its main office] occupies an entire floor in a downtown Tulsa office building and has 55 employees. Three of them, on a recent day, were busy opening the 2000 letters a day that pour in responding to speeches and appeals by Hargis and his disciples on radio and television and in leaflets and magazines. They were taking the money

out and forwarding the letters for further processing. In the next room, five girls sorted the letters and recorded their contents. In a third, clerks filled orders for Hargis pamphlets and other materials. Seven automatic typewriters typed form letters to be signed by an automatic signer. Hargis himself handles about 4500 letters a month.

Hargis's message goes out commercially over 250 radio and nine television stations across the country. . . . The Crusade publishes *The Weekly Crusader* . . . the monthly . . . *Christian Crusade Magazine,* with a circulation of 100,000; and a weekly column by Hargis distributed to newspapers.[4]

Despite Hargis's high-sounding commitment to save America, he had done nothing more than leave his Sapulpa pulpit to join that segment of the rightist political fringe that has specialized in blending political ideology with fundamentalist religion. The blending of politics and religion is hardly new, however. For example, the civil rights movement has looked almost exclusively to the leadership of black preachers, not the least of whom was Rev. Martin Luther King, Jr. Some socialist leaders, such as Norman Thomas and Francis Bellamy (author of the Pledge of Allegiance, 1892) came from the pulpit, and religious influence has been strongly felt in the peace and antinuclear movements. Virtually every religious denomination has taken positions on one political issue or another.

*       *       *

Like all political extremists, Hargis has been vulnerable to guilt by association. It's appropriate to recall similar situations with leftists where early associations with Communist party members, for example, haunted them throughout their careers. Some of the most articulate objections to this tactic came from the far left; such circumstantial evidence is of limited value. Often political extremists may share an interest in a subject area or they may agree in some areas and not in others. The fact that members of the Communist Party USA were active in the civil rights movement does not make the civil rights movement a Communist movement, although many far rightists, including Hargis, have stated otherwise. Although Hargis himself used guilt by association to attack his enemies, we run the risk of legitimizing it as a tactic when we use it against him.

On the other hand, associations are not entirely irrelevant. Occasionally, a person may be trying to conceal a hidden agenda and one's associations may be a significant clue to that fact. Short of this, associations may represent an influence that isn't readily apparent. It may be that the individual or organization is being used and may not be aware of it, or that an effort at infiltration is underway.

Some critical judgment is necessary to assign proper weight to a particular association. A number of factors have to be considered. If the association involves an individual, did it involve membership in an organization or was it merely an association with someone who was a member? Did it last for a long period of time or was it fleeting? Did it occur frequently or only once or twice? Was the relationship a close one? Is it a current relationship or in the distant past?

Most importantly, what *demonstrable consequence* did it have, and what evidence is there to support such a conclusion?

Finally, is it even necessary to cite a particular association to prove a point? If a person is some kind of communist or Nazi there is probably enough evidence in his own writings or speeches to determine that; the use of guilt by association is really unnecessary. Caution is essential in combatting or exposing political extremism in order to avoid becoming what one claims to oppose.

Guilt by association could also be used in support of Hargis. In 1971 a book by Soviet journalist Vyacheslav Nikitin, entitled *The Ultras in the USA,* featured Hargis prominently and targeted him for a considerable amount of invective:

> Christian Crusade's annual gatherings invariably turn into orgies of hatred and fanaticism. The usual targets include not only the socialist countries but also democratic institutions within the USA. . . .
>
> By appealing to the superstitions and ignorance of provincial audiences, to the emotions of people ridden by doubt and fear, Hargis has made ultra-rightist propaganda a big business.[5]

Some of the people Hargis associated with or sought advice from during the earliest days of his career in the political far right often had compromising backgrounds. Among the more notable of his associations was that with Reverend Gerald Burton Winrod, widely known as a leading pro-Nazi apologist. Winrod's views are dealt with in another chapter, but his role as a spokesman for the Nazi regime is well-documented. By the end of the thirties, the Kansas preacher had been branded as the "Jayhawk Nazi." He was indicted three times for sedition during World War II. Ignoring First Amendment considerations, the government charged that Winrod's publication, the *Defender,* was essentially a Nazi propaganda organ put out to undermine the American form of government—a charge that sounds like a "conspiracy theory" itself. In Winrod's trial the government even named Adolf Hitler as a coconspirator. After the death of the judge, a higher court dismissed the indictment, censuring the Justice Department for "lack of diligence in prosecuting the defendants."[6] In point of fact, the case was based largely on the attitudes, opinions, and beliefs of the defendants and was poorly prosecuted because it was quite weak.

Writing in the October 1959 issue of *Christian Crusade,* Hargis recalled that he once called on Winrod for guidance in beginning his radio programs: "Dr. Winrod explained the operations of an office and the use of letters to underwrite the cost of such an expensive operation," he said. (He did not mention that articles and letters written by Billy James Hargis appeared in Winrod's magazine.) In the March 1962 issue of *Christian Crusade,* Hargis said: "We will not publicly criticize anybody on our side in this fight against Communism," echoing a sentiment also found in "progressive" left movements relative to their causes. Hargis has generally remained true to that 1962 pledge.

Even though Hargis had moved his headquarters to Tulsa and garnered some publicity from his Bible Balloon Project, Christian Crusade still limped along without spectacular growth. In 1955, however, he hired L. E. "Pete" White, Jr., and things began to change. White owned a Tulsa advertising company and specialized in the promotion of preachers. His public relations magic had turned the backwoods preacher Oral Roberts into a nationally known faith-healer and his church into a million-dollar success in a few short years. White's price was a 15 percent commission plus an agreed-upon fee, and within six years he had improved Hargis's financial position by a factor of ten. But it was not Pete White alone who kept Hargis's organization alive and growing during those early years. Like most preachers who make a successful transition into the radical right, Hargis found an "angel." He was W. I. Foster, a Tulsan who had made millions investing in oil leases and who had supported Gerald L. K. Smith, dean of the pre-World War II American Jew-baiters.

According to *The Thunderbolt* (organ of the neo-Nazi National States Rights party), Hargis once tried to obtain a job with Smith:

> Years ago Gerald L. K. Smith of the "Christian Nationalist Crusade" announced that "Billy James Hargis once sought employment from him." Dr. Hargis later decided to drop the word "Nationalist" and form "Christian Crusade." He patterned the organization basically after that of Gerald L. K. Smith, whom he admired so much. . . . Later in the 1960's Billy James Hargis met with Dr. Edward R. Fields (NSRP leader) and an assistant in a downtown hotel in Birmingham, Alabama. Hargis told us that he knew the Jews were the primary forces promoting racial integration and a Marxist revolution in America, but he did not want to openly profess this knowledge.[7]

Whether the NSRP version of Hargis's views can be believed is open to debate. While Hargis made efforts to avoid racism, he did publish a pamphlet called "The Truth About Segregation," in which he called segregation one "of Nature's universal laws," and insisted that no intermingling or crossbreeding with animals of widely different characteristics takes place except under abnormal or artificial conditions. "It is my conviction," he said, "that God ordained segregation."

Professor John Redekop, in his excellent 1968 study of Hargis, insisted that the Tulsa preacher repudiated his early racist pamphlet. (Redekop did admit that Hargis continued to show some segregationist tendencies.[8]) Redekop sought to prove his contention by citing Hargis's *Weekly Crusader* of March 30, 1962. In that issue, Hargis discussed his letter inviting some one hundred organizations to a unity conference and proudly wrote that he had included this sentence in his letter: "Organizations that are anti-Catholic, anti-Jew, anti-Protestant, anti-Negro are not welcome at this meeting."

In February 1960, Hargis received what he has called his "biggest break." This was the "Air Force manual incident," for it became front-page news all across the country that the Air Force had distributed a training manual containing charges that the National Council of Churches had been infiltrated by Communists. Homer T. Hyde, a civil-service worker for the Air Force, was the technical writer who started this strange incident. At his minister's suggestion, Hyde contacted Hargis for some information about Communism. The material he received was integrated into the text of the training manual for noncommissioned officers in the Air Force Reserve, much to the chagrin and embarrassment of Thomas Gates, the secretary of defense. The manual was quickly withdrawn, but not before Hargis reaped considerable publicity from the scandal. Some observers date Christian Crusade's rapid growth from the manual incident.[9]

Another Hargis associate also had his abortive attempt at indoctrination in the military. Major General Edwin A. Walker had been relieved of his duties while commander of an American army division in Germany after it was found that he had used John Birch Society and other right-wing materials to conduct seminars on communism.[10] Walker was reprimanded for exceeding his authority and transferred to Hawaii. In November 1961 he tendered his resignation and it was accepted.

The lecture program, a six-hour presentation entitled "Citizen in Service," was largely the work of Walker's information officer, Major Archibald E. Roberts, who wrote or compiled most of the material. It was intended to replicate the World War II "Why We Fight" series, only substituting Soviet Communism for German Nazism. Its most controversial aspect was its reference to alleged Soviet infiltration and subversion in America. Numerous segments extolled faith in God, the Bible, and Christian principles. The slant of the program as well as its frankly propagandistic nature were obvious and not convincingly disputed by any of the principals involved.[11] Roberts was relieved of his duties as an information officer and later reassigned to a stateside tour.

A special Senate subcommittee, headed by John Stennis, was created to investigate the activities of right-wing extremists in the armed forces. The John Birch Society, Hargis's Christian Crusade, and other groups launched a letter-writing campaign that produced 147,000 pieces of mail in three days protesting the treatment of Gen. Walker. Walker was called upon to testify on April 4, 1962, and he made no secret of his connections to the John Birch Society and declared that the case against him was concocted by the Communists.

In September 1962 Walker went to Mississippi to observe the military forces sent to occupy Oxford to enable the enrollment of James Meredith, a black man, in the University of Mississippi. Walker was arrested by military authorities on October 1 and charged with inciting a riot, sedition against the United States and other crimes. Nearly four months later, after having been confined in a mental hospital at the direction of a government psychiatrist who had never examined or seen him,[12] the federal grand jury in Oxford refused to indict Walker and all charges were dropped. Civil libertarians opposed to Walker's views felt his rights had been violated.

Walker, a popular figure in the far right, teamed up with Hargis in 1963 to make a sweep through seventeen states and twenty-seven cities on a speaking tour dubbed "Operation Midnight Ride." On the evening of April 3, 1963, Hargis and Walker completed their tour at the Shrine Auditorium in Los Angeles, where they spoke to an audience of 4,500 mostly middle-aged men and women.

Following his reassignment Major Archibald E. Roberts again ran afoul of military brass for stating his views. An editorial entitled "One Man's Battle" in a September 1965 issue of the *Chicago Tribune* recounts his story:

Three years ago Maj. Arch E. Roberts was removed from active duty for making a speech before the Daughters of the American Revolution which offended army censorship and government officials. Roberts, after 18 years' service, stood to lose his service pension as well as his place in the Army.

He went to court and finally won a verdict that he should be restored to duty with "all rights, privileges, and emoluments" he had previously enjoyed. The ruling will protect all army reservists with 18 or more years service from summary separation in the future without a hearing.[13]

Hargis regularly received criticism because of the source of the doctor of divinity degree that made him "Dr." Billy James Hargis. He first donned the title after an honorary doctor of divinity degree was conferred on him by the Defender Seminary in Puerto Rico, a little missionary effort erected by the previously mentioned Gerald B. Winrod. Apart from any considerations of the source of the degree, its bestowal might be considered unusual since it was granted before Hargis had obtained a bachelor's degree. This he acquired in 1956 from Burton College and Seminary of Manitou Springs, Colorado, an institution labeled a "degree mill" by the Department of Health, Education and Welfare. Additionally, he obtained an honorary doctor of law degree in 1957 from Berlin Memorial University in Chillicothe, Missouri, another "degree mill" (according to the federal government).

Public commentary on his degrees seemed to rankle the Tulsa crusader a great deal. He explained why he obtained the controversial degrees in his "official biography," a collection of reminiscences called *Crusading Preacher From the West: The Story of Billy James Hargis,* by Fernando Penabaz. In this book, Hargis noted that "many of my critics have said that I am not qualified, educationally speaking, to do what I am doing." He pointed to the late Reverend Billy Sunday and observed, "God used a ballplayer and made of him the greatest evangelist of all time. . . . God has used me with my one year and two and a half months of formal education. Why, I don't know but he has." Hargis's degrees were explained as follows:

> After starting Christian Crusade, I realized that I needed a formal education. I wrote around to different schools in the country and asked them if I could get a degree by correspondence. They turned a deaf ear to me for two reasons; one, Ozark Bible College, which I had attended, was not accredited; second, I was asking for a degree strictly on the basis of correspondence and thesis without resident work and they were unwilling to grant a degree on this basis. . . .

Hargis's critics have charged that his career has been largely one of contradictions and distortions. His reasons for accepting the degree conferred on him by Winrod's Defender Seminary constitute a masterpiece of glossing over, since Winrod is a subject he skirted as much as possible:

> My critics have made a lot of this. They claim that Dr. Gerald Winrod was the main supporter of Defender Seminary; therefore, using their "guilt-by-association"

technique, I must be anti-Semitic since they alleged that Winrod was anti-Semitic. These critics conveniently overlook the fact that Dr. J. F. Rodrigues was President of the Seminary and gave me the degree, not because of any association with Winrod, but because of the successful Bible Balloon project.

If other forms of name-calling were not enough, most of the spate of books and articles attacking Christian Crusade in the sixties usually included in their descriptions references to Hargis's weight. Chubby even as a teenager, he ballooned to enormous size as an adult, and critics estimated his weight at 260 to 290 pounds. Many writers mentioned his condition only briefly and some resorted to euphemistic words or phrases to avoid appearing unfair. A few, of course, dwelt at unusual length on the subject. Some called him "portly," "beefy," "stout," and "Oklahoma Fats." Peter Schrag, who interviewed him in August 1970, described Hargis as being so huge that he "found it impossible that day to fit his belly into a restaurant booth."

If his own sensibilities were shocked by such personal references, Hargis did not seem concerned when the sword was in his own hand. He appeared to tolerate a double standard about personal ridicule. In a booklet he described former Soviet Premier Nikita Khrushchev as the "ugly roly-poly paragon of satanic Communism" and American labor leader Walter Reuther thus:

> He is a smart, smug, arrogant labor boss. He is a bold, shrewd, foul-mouthed agitator. He is a vile perveyor [sic] of vicious slander. He is a ruthless, reckless, lawless labor goon. He is a persistent prevaricator. He is a cunning conspirator. He is a rabid anti-anti-Communist. He is a slick, sordid, conniving politician. He is a double-talking, rabble-rousing opportunist who glibly repeats the fallacious fulminations of his Red-tinged ghostwriters.[14]

\*    \*    \*

In the latter part of the sixties Hargis began pioneering in the publication and distribution of tiny, right-wing books that varied in length from about thirty to fifty pages. These booklets were written on the various controversial issues of the day and were offered to his radio audience in order to stimulate interest in Christian Crusade programs. He also invited Professor John Redekop, author of a book-length study of Hargis, to debate the chief Hargis aide, David Noebel, at the 1968 Christian Crusade National Convention. Critic Redekop (an evangelical Christian and a "real" conservative, as opposed to Hargis's pseudoconservatism) turned the debate into a one-sided affair in front of a packed "Hargis audience."[15] There were no more celebrated debates held at Christian Crusade Cathedral.

In March 1971, Hargis suddenly became an expert on the occult and quickly distributed one of his dollar minibooks, *Satanism—Diabolical Religion of Darkness,* to warn of the assault on morality and Christianity by the world of psychic phenomena and the occult in general. He condemned witchcraft, fortune telling, ESP, astrology, and all the related parapsychological elements, although with little of the sophistication of academic critics of the practices. They weren't wrong because they were superstitious and unproven, but simply because they were anti-Christian, according to Hargis. But within two months he was embracing Haiti's Arthur Bonhomme, ignoring his past connections with "Papa Doc" Duvalier and Haiti as the capital of the voodoo world.

This attack on the world of the occult rang hollow. Hargis was, after all, indirectly assisting the best-known occult figure in America, the so-called seeress Jeane Dixon. One of the members of the board of regents of Hargis's tiny American Christian College, the late General Clyde Watts, had been friendly with her. Hargis neither repudiated Watts nor condemned Jeane Dixon. Further, Hargis's biographer, Jess Pedigo, author of *Satanism—Diabolical Religion of Darkness,* wrote of Dixon's "regular church attendance" and noted that she claimed "to look to God for her knowledge." Pedigo also mentioned "the world-wide acclaim that has been given to her for her predictions."[16]

Although the Head Crusader indulged in numerous political twists, turns, and contradictions, a February 10, 1973, memorandum from H. R. Haldeman to John Dean certainly jelled with his thought patterns. Read before the Senate "Watergate Committee," the memo stated: "We need to get our people to put out the story on the foreign or Communist money that was used in support of demonstrations against the President in 1972." Indeed, as late as October 7, 1973, Hargis was asserting that President Nixon had every right to bug Democratic headquarters:

> If he was knowledgeable of the bugging, as I personally believe he was, he should have called a press conference and told the American people what many of us already know, namely that there was a rumor circulating around Washington during the McGovern campaign that the Senator from South Dakota running for the Presidency on the Democratic ticket was getting campaign funds from such Communist governments as Castro's Cuba.

While many critics declared Hargis bereft of most humanitarian virtues and short on ideological consistency, no one denied his shrewdness in relation to political opportunism.

\*   \*   \*

In early 1976, the Reverend Billy James Hargis followed Nixon into ignominy, albeit for dramatically different reasons. *Time* magazine carried a story entitled "The Sins of Billy James," which revealed that Hargis, who had railed against homosexuality for over twenty-five years and had attacked sex education as programmed perversion, had had sexual relationships with at least four boys at his American Christian College. Three of the boys (one of them a minor) stated their homosexual encounters with Hargis had lasted for a three-year period. At an October 1974 meeting between college Vice President David Noebel, other college officials, Hargis, and his lawyers, the Head Crusader and college president admitted guilt and attributed his behavior to "genes and chromosomes." Hargis later announced he was retiring to his farm in Neosho, Missouri, due to ill health.[17]

Hargis's homosexuality was not entirely a secret, nor was he the only one among his colleagues to embrace this behavior. (General Edwin A. Walker was later indicted for soliciting homosexual contact in Dallas.) Other right-wing leaders had been aware of Hargis's proclivities. Robert B. DePugh, leader of the Minutemen, who knew Hargis, had reported on his behavior at least a year prior to the news accounts. A number of students at American Christian College stated that they had heard rumors to this effect for some time.[18]

Although he later tried a couple of comebacks and even appeared as a guest on a few Christian TV shows in the early eighties, Hargis's star had fallen and he faded into obscurity. There really wasn't very much media coverage of his plight. The only publication that attacked him mercilessly was as irresponsible as Hargis himself: *Hustler* magazine. Editor Larry Flynt called Hargis a "lecherous bag of pus," a "pig," a "gutless maggot," a "filthy, steaming pile of shit," an "unctuous faggot," a "despicable creature," and a "miserable turd."[19]—not exactly the language of moderation with which to effectively combat extremism.

Hargis and his empire are gone from the American scene, having left hardly a ripple on the political profile of the nation. For many years he was a source of some anxiety to extremist-watchers and provided journalists and a few authors with some interesting copy. Eventually that little self-destructive time bomb that ticks away in most political extremists went off and it proved far more ruinous to him than all of the attacks and exposés combined. Like most extremists, Reverend Billy James Hargis spent his life cultivating enemies and tended to define himself in those terms, contrasting their "badness" with his "goodness." In the end his biggest enemy proved to be himself.

In the 1990s, he was again running his ministry from his farm in Neosho, Missouri, and publishing *Billy James Hargis' Christian Crusade*. He was still calling himself "Dr." and still insisting, "All I want to do is preach Christ and save America."

## Notes

1. Fernando Penabaz, *Crusading Preacher From the West* (Tulsa, Okla.: Christian Crusade, 1962).

2. Penabaz, 41. For an interesting account of Hargis, see James Morris, *The Preachers* (New York: St. Martin's Press, 1973).

3. Penabaz, 55.

4. Richard Dudman, *Men of the Far Right* (New York: Pyramid Books, 1962), 88–89.

5. Vyacheslav Nikitin, *The Ultras in the USA* (Moscow: Progress Publishers, 1971), 155.

6. Ralph Lord Roy, *Apostles of Discord* (Boston: Beacon Press, 1953).

7. *The Thunderbolt* (June 1971).

8. John Redekop, *The American Far Right: A Case Study of Billy James Hargis*

*and His Christian Crusade* (Grand Rapids, Mich.: William Eerdmans, 1968), 193–94.

9. Morris, 265–66.

10. *Overseas Weekly* (April 12, 1961).

11. *Congressional Record* (August 1961), 17457–573. Sen. Strom Thurmond inserted the entire transcript of the program.

12. *Washington Star* (October 7, 1962).

13. Editorial, "One Man's Battle," *Chicago Tribune* (September 4, 1965).

14. Billy James Hargis, *Walter Reuther's Secret Memorandum* (Tulsa, Okla.: Christian Crusade, n.d.), 27.

15. John George attended the convention and took notes of the debate in addition to taping it. Rev. David Noebel didn't even address the debate question, which was "Can Christians Support the Philosophy and Anticommunist Activity of Christian Crusade?" It was less a debate than a rout with Redekop coming across as an intellectual conservative confronting an intelligent, but ignorant, right extremist. For an excellent description of the debate see Morris, 283–89.

16. Morris, 310–11.

17. *Time* (February 16, 1976), 52.

18. Ed Kelley, "Hargis Story Not New At ACC," *Daily Oklahoman* (February 29, 1979). See also, "Hargis College Nearly Broke," *Daily Oklahoman* (April 12, 1976), 1.

19. *Hustler* (May 1976).

# 14. The John Birch Society: A Plot to Sell Books?

> Robert Welch never prepared for the role of political leader, is remarkably ignorant of the nature of the communist conspiracy . . . ever since he founded the Society, he has done more to injure the cause of responsible conservatism than to act effectively against communism.
>
> Russell Kirk, conservative commentator
> *America,* February 17, 1962

"The United States is a huge insane asylum, and the worst patients are running the place."[1] Thus spoke Robert H. W. Welch, Jr., retired candy-maker, former vice president of the National Association of Manufacturers, founder and, from 1958 until his death in 1985, "grand wazir" of the John Birch Society. Considering the increased turmoil and polarization in the country since Welch made that statement in 1965, it is not unreasonable to assume that some people have come to view the United States and the world as somewhat "insane," but only a small percentage has been likely to agree with Welch's viewpoint that the "worst patients are running the place." On the other hand, a fairly large segment of adult Americans has long considered the John Birch Society as part of the political "lunatic fringe."[2]

Robert Welch was born in 1899 in North Carolina. He attended both Harvard and the University of North Carolina and spent two years at the U.S. Naval Academy. Later he entered the business world and became successful as a candy tycoon. Active in the National Association of Manufacturers, Welch served as a director and vice president of that organization. After World War II, he began devoting more and more of his time to a study of the "Communist conspiracy," and made trips to various countries. He also made one attempt at politics, running unsuccessfully for lieutenant governor of Massachusetts.[3]

Early in 1957 Welch withdrew from the business world to contemplate the conspiracy full time. He became convinced that only dynamic personal leadership could deter the Red menace, and that he was the man to provide that leadership. Thus, in December 1958, he summoned eleven friends from various parts of the nation to meet with him in Indianapolis. These men came to sit for two days, listening to Welch's appraisal of the success of the international Communist conspiracy. In his opening remarks Welch declared that before the next day was over he hoped "to have all of you feeling that you are taking part, here and now, in the beginning of a movement of historical importance." On the second day Welch and friends founded the John Birch Society. Subsequently the text of Welch's two-day soliloquy was printed up in a volume entitled *The Blue Book of The John Birch Society*. Unlike many far-right leaders, Welch minced no words, and made clear to the whole world that he favored the rigid, authoritarian form of organizational structure:

> The John Birch Society is to be a monolithic body. A 'republican' form of government or of organization has many attractions and advantages, under certain favorable conditions. But under less happy circumstances it lends itself too readily to infiltration, distortion and disruption. And democracy, of course, in government or organization, as the Greeks and Romans both found out, and as I believe every man in this room clearly recognizes—democracy is merely a deceptive phrase, a weapon of demagoguery, and a perennial fraud.[4]

This organization, Welch said, would be both revolutionary and religious. It would welcome people of all religions into its chapters, which would consist of from ten to twenty "patriots." It would be a dues-paying group that would exert an impact at the community level to awaken and change the pattern of American thinking. It would be an educational rather than a political movement, a group that means "business every step of the way." As an organization it would be devoted to fighting Communism, and only Communism, and would be ruled by Welch, who in theory would be advised by a twenty-five-man Council of Advisors. The only paid members would be the coordinators who, at the middle level of the society, would assume responsibility for a specified geographical area. They would appoint section leaders, who would in turn be responsible for overseeing the activities of several chapter leaders. Neither the ordinary members of the society nor anyone at the very top—including Welch—would draw a salary.

The society was named after John Birch, a young fundamentalist Baptist preacher who was killed by Chinese Communists after the close of World War II. Welch considered Birch the first casualty of World War III and believed the twenty-six-year-old soldier "possessed in his own character all of those noble traits and ideals which we should like to see become symbolized by the John Birch Society."

According to *Time* magazine of April 14, 1961, John Birch was born in Landour, India, to a husband-and-wife team of missionaries. He was raised in New Jersey and Georgia and graduated in 1939 from Georgia's Baptist-controlled Mercer University. Top in his class, Birch was remembered by a classmate as "always an angry young man, always a zealot. He felt he was called to defend the faith, and he alone knew what it was." A Mercer psychology professor said, "He was like a one-way valve: everything coming out and no room to take anything in." During his senior year, Birch organized a secret "fellowship group" to suppress a mildly liberal trend at Mercer. His group collected examples of "heresy" uttered by faculty members and even succeeded in forcing the university to try five men on that charge. The cases were dismissed, but Dr. John D. Freeman, a world-famous Baptist leader, was admonished for using a theologically "unsound" textbook. That summer Freeman quietly retired from Mercer. Said one professor: "It broke him."

A missionary in China during World War II, Birch located and guided to safety Colonel Jimmy Doolittle and some of his Tokyo raiders who had landed by parachute. Later he joined General Claire Chennault's Fourteenth Air Force and began a career in air combat intelligence, which often involved work behind enemy lines. He was considered a pioneer in field-intelligence work and was decorated for some of his activities. In spite of his professional successes in China, a number of people Birch worked with considered him a loner with overbearing manners. Even Major Gustav Krause (the commanding officer of the base) noted that "Birch was a good officer, but I'm afraid he is too brash and may run into trouble." He did.

After the war, the young captain led a mission to ascertain how far south in China the Communists had penetrated. He stumbled onto a Communist force and argued violently with the Chinese officer who tried to disarm him; he was seized, tied, and shot. The Communists bayoneted him repeatedly and then threw his body on a garbage heap. When asked about the incident, Krause said: "My instructions were to act with diplomacy. Birch made the Communist lieutenant lose face before his own men. Militarily, John Birch brought about his own death." Army records released in 1972 confirmed Krause's version of the sad demise of Captain Birch.

*    *    *

Robert Welch outlines his blueprint for turning back the Communist conspiracy in *The Blue Book*. The society would establish reading rooms, somewhat similar to the Christian Science reading rooms, in cities and towns all across America in order to extend the circulation of "conservative" literature. Welch also advocated a campaign to "start shocking the American people into a realization of what is happening; for example, expose the reasons the Communists just had to get rid of Sen. Joseph McCarthy, and went to such extreme lengths to do so." Further, Welch suggested means and methods of harassing those people who would attempt to obstruct the society's efforts.

Soon after the society began to gather strength at the beginning of the 1960s for its stated mission of saving America, FBI Director J. Edgar Hoover made it clear he did not need the aid of such groups to help him control the Communists. In the February 1962 *American Bar Association Journal,* Hoover said:

> Today, far too many self-styled experts on communism are plying the highways of America, giving erroneous and distorted information. This causes hysteria, false alarms, misplaced apprehension by many of our citizens. We need enlightenment about communism—but this information must be factual, accurate and not tailored to echo personal idiosyncrasies.

Hoover was more specific in a November 1964 news conference when he stated: "I have no respect for the head of the Society, Robert Welch." The Birch Society was hardly out of swaddling clothes when trouble appeared—a skeleton from Welch's past. Sometime after December 1954, he had written a long letter to a few of his close friends, explaining "parts of Mr. Eisenhower's record." Originally a document of some nine thousand words, this "letter" grew to more than two hundred pages and became a manuscript, which Welch entitled *The Politician,* later published by the Society.[5]

In August 1960, a columnist of the *Chicago Daily News,* Jack Mabley, acquired one of the copies of the manuscript and let the rest of the world know the nature of Welch's fantastic allegations. The John Birch Society and its founder would never again be able to "work quietly" toward their goal, for America was shocked to learn that Welch had labeled President Dwight Eisenhower a "dedicated, conscious agent of the Communist conspiracy." A paragraph from the book provides a picture of Welch's reasoning:

At this stage of the manuscript, however, perhaps it is permissible for me to take just a couple of paragraphs to support my own belief. And it seems to me that the explanation of sheer political opportunism, to account for Eisenhower's Communist-aiding career, stems merely from a deeprooted aversion of any American to recognizing the horrible truth. Most of the doubters, who go all the way with me except the final logical conclusion, appear to have no trouble whatever in suspecting that Milton Eisenhower is an outright Communist. Yet they draw back from attaching the same suspicion to his brother, for no other real reason than that one is a professor and the other a president. While I too think that Milton Eisenhower is a Communist, and has been for 30 years, this opinion is based largely on general circumstances of his conduct. But my firm belief that Dwight Eisenhower is a dedicated, conscious agent of the Communist conspiracy is based on an accumulation of detailed evidence so extensive and so palpable that it seems to me to put this conviction beyond any reasonable doubt.[6]

Later editions of *The Politician* omit some of the above, but according to Welch, it was not only the Eisenhower brothers who were traitors. Since sometime in the late 1930s General George Marshall had also been a conscious, deliberate, dedicated agent of the Soviet conspiracy. Furthermore, Welch declared, "for many reasons and after a lot of study, I personally believe [former Secretary of State John Foster] Dulles to be a Communist agent." And Allen Dulles, head of the CIA, Welch warned, was "the most protected and untouchable supporter of Communism, next to Eisenhower himself, in Washington."[7] An outraged response arose across the nation and a few of the most stunned, no doubt, were prominent members of Welch's own society. The Birch chieftain's explanation, quickly picked up and spread about by leaders in this movement, was that the manuscript was actually a letter to his close and sympathetic friends; it had nothing at all to do with the John Birch Society or its policy. But this line was dropped in the latter half of 1962. *The Politician,* Welch announced, would now be published to let everyone read and judge for himself. He spoke of an "increasing stream of letters from individuals . . . resolutions passed at meetings of patriotic organizations . . . personal pleas from many friends," as reasons for publishing the manuscript.

In the midst of the speculation surrounding his wild statements, Welch attempted clarification. At a "Ladies of the Press" interview in 1963, Welch was asked if he still believed his remark from *The Politician* that only the word "treason" could describe Eisenhower's purpose and action. "Yes," replied Welch, and he willingly reiterated that John Foster Dulles was a Communist. On the West Coast, Paul Choates of the *Los Angeles Times* considered Welch, whom he described as "the pudgy, pink-cheeked poobah of the extreme right," a stain on the fabric of reason. He noted that the Lectures and Concerts Board of San Diego State College had denied Welch permission to speak on campus. This, he felt, was a mistake, the sort of thing Welch would do if he should ever gain the power to grant or deny the right of free expression. One of the essential proofs of our nation's strengths, Choates emphasized, is that we can afford to let everyone say what he wishes, even though what he wishes is to destroy democracy.

The Eisenhower and Dulles brothers were not the only public figures attacked in *The Politician*. For instance, concerning U.S. Supreme Court Justice William J. Brennan, Jr., Welch had this to say:

> The plain truth is that Brennan's pro-Communist leanings were so clearly established in his record that we do not believe he could possibly have been confirmed for the Supreme Court only three or four years ago.

"Our opinion is that Robert Welch is damaging the cause of anti-communism," noted William F. Buckley. And Senator Barry Goldwater demanded that this "political silliness" stop. Some columnists pointed to the Birch Society's opposition to the UN intervention in the Congo in the early 1960s, and noted that this coincided with the Soviet line. With Robert Welch setting the tone from the late 1950s until his death in the mid-1980s, the John Birch Society gained a reputation as a group that would make wild, unfounded charges and employ character assassination as readily as any on the American scene.

But a most interesting change in belief within the society appeared in the November 1966 issue of *American Opinion* magazine. Welch wrote that he had become convinced that the root of the problem wasn't simply communists, but a two-hundred-year-old conspiracy that controls communism and nearly every other political movement. Welch dubbed this sinister group The Insiders, and linked it to the Illuminati (formed in 1776, abolished in 1785), a "conspiracy" many extreme rightists believe has been in operation continuously since (at least) the late eighteenth century:

> But the Communist movement is only a tool of the total conspiracy. As secret as the Communist activities and organizations generally appear, they are an open book compared to the secrecy enveloping some higher degree of this diabolical force.[8]

In 1985 Charles Armour, the society's western district governor headquartered in San Marino, California, explained the conspiracy issue this way:

> The difference, I think, between conservatives and liberals literally is that a conservative sees a series of events and uses that evidence to come to a conclusion. We're not satisfied today to simply say, "Well, this is just ineptitude or stupidity or coincidence." The coincidence is far too consistent for it to be coincidence. So we take the conspiratorial view.[9]

During the decades of the sixties and seventies numerous prominent people were named by Welch as part of this giant conspiracy: William F. Buckley, Henry Kissinger, Charles DeGaulle, Zbigniew Brzezinski, George Bush, Jimmy Carter, Gerald Ford, Richard Nixon, Pierre Elliot Trudeau, Harold Wilson, Francoise Mitterand, George Schultz, and many others. Due in great measure to such accusations, many Americans have refused to take the John Birch Society seriously. One wag has charged that the organization is actually an elaborate plot "to sell crummy books."

After Welch's death in January 1985, the Birch Society fell on hard times and a large number of members resigned. No doubt many factors contributed to this deterioration, but the one element that seemed most bothersome to the dropouts was the ascension to power of John McManus, for many years publicity director of the society. McManus had become de facto leader of the group some months prior to Welch's demise and was especially suspect due to his traditionalist Catholic views. McManus aroused still more ire when he claimed that Welch, who had held nonorthodox, even Unitarian-like religious views for most of his adult life, converted to Roman Catholicism during his last days. Former Birch writer Gary Allen, author of *None Dare Call It Conspiracy,* commented angrily in a letter of August 19, 1985:

> About the lowest, most vulgar stunt I've ever heard of was when Jack McManus slithered into Mrs. Welch's office just two days after Mr. Welch's death to gloat to her that her husband had converted to Feeneyite Catholicism on his deathbed, after having taken instructions in the faith. This is a damnable lie. During the last months of his life he didn't even recognize his wife most of the time. He couldn't take instructions in anything. You may think this stunt is beneath contempt, but I have a lot of contempt for it.
>
> The Feeneyites believe the Pope, whom the KGB tried to assassinate, is a Communist and that all non-Feeneyites are going to Hell. Outside of Tom Hill and (A. Clifford) Barker, this cult virtually runs Belmont. If the general membership ever found out about Feeneyite control of the Belmont bureaucracy, there would be revolt in the ranks.

Membership figures for the John Birch Society have been a matter of some controversy. Welch sometimes gave the dubious range of "between 60,000 and 80,000." Many authorities doubt this, however. Boston's long-time extremist-watcher, Gordon Hall, estimates a figure in the neighborhood of half that, based on second-class mailing figures for the society's publications. However, a significant portion of the membership was in the form of dual husband-wife arrangements where only one copy of the *Bulletin of The John Birch Society,* the society's internal publication, was mailed. Also, not all members received *American Opinion* and/or *Review of the News,* the society's magazines. According to Arnold Forster and Benjamin R. Epstein in *Danger on the Right,* the society's financial statements to the attorney general of Massachusetts suggest that the highest possible membership at the close of 1962 would have been 24,000.[10]

*Los Angeles Times* feature writer John Kendall stated membership had peaked at 90,000 to 95,000 and that it had declined to 40,000 by 1985, figures that are probably too high. He quoted Stanford University political sociologist Seymour Martin Lipset as saying, "I never saw any evidence of their having a mass appeal. . . . Their problem is how to get people to listen." He also noted that the society "was an interesting media event" back in the 1960s.[11]

A later estimate by David H. Bennett in *The Party of Fear* gives the figure of 80,000 members and four hundred chapters in 1967, which was during the society's most influential period. Bennett also says:

> Welch's overheated conspiracy theories, the bizarre world he constructed in which famous conservatives were secret enemy agents, were too much even for those who had championed the anticommunist activities of [Sen. Joe] McCarthy and others. He went too far in accusing Eisenhower of being a Red. He compounded his problems by asserting that the CIA "is on the Communist side" and by alleging, in 1962, that the United States is "50 to 70 per cent under Communist control."[12]

Society membership probably peaked in the mid-1960s, perhaps at 50,000 to 60,000, and began a steady decline that has continued to the present day, where it has leveled off at perhaps 15,000 to 20,000. Interestingly, we estimate that over the thirty-three years of its existence perhaps as many as 250,000 Americans have been members of the John Birch Society, most for only a few years. In our contacts with former Birchers over the years, we found a large number who were members only briefly, and who also knew many others who had similarly fleeting attachments with the society. One subject put it thus: "One helluva lot of mainstream conservatives were Birchers for a year or two, and then returned to the real world. It was an experiment for them, not unlike the Communist Party was an experiment for many liberals. A brush with extremism is sometimes part of the process of finding yourself." Birch "loyalists" tend to be those with ten or twenty continuous years of membership, and although prominent in the leadership on all levels of the organization, their numbers are modest.

The society began to have serious internal difficulties in the 1980s, although there has been a steady trickle of expulsions and resignations over policy issues virtually from the beginning. In the late 1960s, for example, founding council member Robert D. Love of Wichita quit the society to pursue more libertarian and less authoritarian goals. On the other hand, Revilo P. Oliver, a founding council member and professor of classics at the University of Illinois, became unwelcome in the society because of his increasing anti-Semitism. Oliver's 1964 *American Opinion* article on the assassination of John F. Kennedy, in which he said Kennedy was killed because he wasn't delivering America into the hands of the Communists fast enough, brought a whirlwind of scorn on the society.[13] Always outspoken and reluctant to conceal his true convictions, at a 1959 Illinois Daughters of the American Revolution function, Oliver had made the following observation:

> The Batista government in Cuba was not, to be sure, a perfect government, but it probably was as good a government as one could reasonably expect to find in an island largely populated by mongrels.

On July 4, 1966, Oliver formally resigned from the John Birch Society. His statement to the press read, in part, as follows:

> I have resigned from the Council of the John Birch Society (and from the Society itself) because I can no longer in conscience remain a member. Although I helped found the Birch Society in December 1958, it was not until 1964 that I began to suspect that behind Welch there was a secret and powerful force that was using the Society to paralyze patriotic Americans. I began a very painstaking and delicate investigation. It took more than two years for me, with my limited resources, to discover the incredible truth about the Society I had helped found. It took me even longer to reach the conclusion that Welch was not, as I had supposed, the helpless captive of that sinister and alien force, but was instead its cunning and willing agent.

There have been numerous schisms in the society over the years, most of them involving a relatively small number of individuals. In 1979 Bill Murray, a full-time Birch coordinator for nearly nine years, published an exposé detailing his disillusionment with the rigidity and hide-bound "conservativism" of the leadership, which he maintains was subverting the society's goals. In *The Belmont Syndrome* Murray observed:

> Gradually at first, but with increasing intensity, my growing concern over nine years became an unshakable conviction: the John Birch Society's Achilles Heel is that Belmont considers all criticism to be heresy. I have always found that the slightest suggestion— the slightest implication—the slightest innuendo—that Belmont may not be all-knowing in all matters within its purview, is instantly met with fierce hostility and immediate rejection.[14]

Murray goes on to complain of "Belmont's paranoia" and proceeds to offer numerous specific criticisms and suggestions, all of which deal with the apparently innate incapacity of the society for objective self-criticism. He also announced the formation of his own organization, CONGRES, INC., which was an acronym for Citizens Organization for the National Grass Roots Education of Society.

In 1985, following Welch's death, Dr. Charles A. Provan, a twenty-one-year member of the society, issued a long and detailed letter outlining his disillusionment with recent developments, including the alleged promotion of a "K.G.B. agent" in the form of Abdul H. Shams, an Afghan refugee, on the cover of *The New American*. Provan also complained of an ad for the English translation of *Pravda,* the Soviet newspaper, claiming that "Mr. Welch . . . had an *absolute* policy of never publishing leftist ads in our publications."

Dr. Provan noted with alarm the exodus from the society of top writers such as Gary Allen, Scott Stanley, Alan Stang, Medford Evans, and John Rees, as well as the resignations of council members William H. Cies and Thomas Parker. Shortly afterward Provan formed the New American Movement, an organization composed largely of former Birchers.

Although frequently accused of harboring anti-Semites, the society has made a deliberate effort to purge them from its ranks. Welch's 1963 speech, "The Neutralizers," specifically disavows any form of anti-Semitism as a counterproductive "neutralizing" influence. Numerous members have complained of being expelled over alleged anti-Semitism, but a fair number of bona fide anti-Semites have been members of the society at one time or another, usually quitting when they found the society uncongenial to their views. Nevertheless, the association of the society with racism and anti-Semitism has persisted.[15]

On occasion the society may have been the subject of a dirty tricks campaign. In the 1971 documentary, *This Is The John Birch Society,* G. Edward Griffin, an eleven-year member, describes an incident where a letter writer in the *San Diego Union* received correspondence from someone claiming that "the Kennedy administration is riddled, not only with Catholics, but with Niggers and Jews, too!" It was signed, no name, but merely: "Member, local chapter of the John Birch Society." Griffin noted that at that time there had been no meetings of the society in San Diego. Also, according to Griffin, in 1966 Leonard Fairorth, an employee of the city of Philadelphia, forged the signature of a society coordinator and wrote a letter with racist overtones threatening to kill Governor William Scranton. Interestingly, this same individual had written a letter to the editor complaining of the tactics of the John Birch Society.[16]

In 1980 the society issued a "Memorandum on *The Spotlight,*" referring to the weekly tabloid publication of Liberty Lobby, which has been roundly accused of anti-Semitism. The memorandum notes that, "The John Birch Society is not now and never has been so much as associated with either *The Spotlight* or its publisher, Liberty Lobby, Inc."

One former society member, "Brig. Gen." Gordon "Jack" Mohr, a regular on the American Opinion Speaker's Bureau circuit for eleven years, resigned following what he termed in a publicly circulated letter of September 17, 1979, as a "gradual movement underway to phase me out as a speaker." Mohr noted that, "My high Christian standards have not made me popular with certain persons in the Society." Mohr formed his own organization, the Crusade for Christ and Country, and within a few years was lecturing at seminars sponsored by the Christian Patriot's Defense League on the role of Jews in subversive movements. Soon, he had a well-deserved reputation as an outspoken anti-Semite.

The 1983 death of Georgia Congressman Larry McDonald (who had become head of the society) on Korean Air Lines flight 007 on September 1, 1983, was a blow from which the society never recovered. In typical fashion, it denounced the tragedy as an assassination plot.

Following Robert Welch's death in 1985, the society folded *American Opinion* and *Review Of The News* and began a weekly publication, *The New American*. One of the casualties of this new arrangement was Mrs. Robert Welch, who had been assistant managing editor of *American Opinion*. In an August 1986 Associated Press story, she complained of the way the new publication was treating President Ronald Reagan. "They are tearing him apart," said Marian P. Welch, in her eighties and living in a retirement home in Weston, Massachusetts.

In November 1985 a new chairman, A. Clifford Barker, undertook a comeback campaign to help relieve the debts that the society had accumulated and to stop the increasingly severe membership plunge. In June 1986 he was replaced by Charles R. Armour, a twenty-three-year society employee, following an executive council meeting in Cincinnati.

In mid-1989 the society moved its headquarters from Belmont, Massachusetts, to Appleton, Wisconsin, home of the society's long-time hero, Senator Joseph McCarthy. Former insurance executive G. Allen Babolz became chairman in late 1988, though few doubted that John McManus was the society's most influential member. Babolz once stated, "To call [George Bush] a leftist is to give him more credit than he deserves."[17]

The John Birch Society may be labeled the most successful far-right organization in American history, in the quality of organization, the time, effort, and resources at its disposal, and the number and quality of people it attracted. Nominally "conservative" groups such as the American Legion are larger and have lasted longer but are hardly "far right" in nature. Despite its success, the internal squabbles of the society eventually wore it down and this demise illustrates the problems that rightist organizations tend to have because of dogmatism, rampant "individualism," and the inability to shift to meet a changing situation. In the final analysis, it's difficult to find any significant, enduring effect the society has had upon the United States. The John Birch Society will probably linger for a few decades longer and then fade into the history books.

## Notes

1. *Daily Oklahoman* (October 5, 1965), 12.

2. According to Alan Westin in Daniel Bell, ed., *The Radical Right* (New York: Doubleday, 1963), 239, the April 1961 Gallup poll "indicated that 39 million persons . . . had read or heard of the Birchers. Of these 44 percent had an unfavorable estimate of the Society, 9 percent were favorable and 47 percent had not yet reached a judgment." This was probably the peak of John Birch Society acceptance.

3. G. Edward Griffin, *The Life and Works of Robert Welch, Founder of the John Birch Society* (Thousand Oaks, Calif.: American Media, 1975).

4. Robert Welch, *The Blue Book of the John Birch Society* (Belmont, Mass.: The

John Birch Society, 1961), 159.

5. Robert Welch, *The Politician* (Belmont, Mass.: Privately printed, 1963).

6. From the original version of *The Politician*. Quoted by John Birch Society writer Medford Evans in *American Opinion* (March 1985): 55.

7. Welch, *The Politician,* 223, 227.

8. Robert Welch, "The Truth in Time," *American Opinion* (November 1966).

9. John Kendall, "John Birch Society Mounts Campaign to Revitalize, Rebuild," *Los Angeles Times,* appearing in the *Kansas City Times* (November 28, 1985).

10. Arnold Forster and Benjamin R. Epstein, *Danger on the Right* (New York: Random House, 1964), 11.

11. Kendall, op cit.

12. David H. Bennett, *The Party of Fear* (Chapel Hill: University of North Carolina Press, 1988), 319.

13. Revilo P. Oliver, "Marxmanship in Dallas," *American Opinion* (February 1964): 13–24.

14. Bill Murray, *The Belmont Syndrome* (Sea Girt, N.J.: The Author, 1979).

15. Among these are Tom Metzger, leader of the White Aryan Resistance in Fallbrook, California, who was recently sued by Morris Dees over the death of an Ethiopian killed by skinheads associated with Metzger's group.

16. "F.B.I. Accuses City Worker of Threats," *Philadelphia Evening Bulletin* (August 19, 1966); "City Employee Held in Threat to Johnson," *Philadelphia Inquirer* (August 20, 1969).

17. *Newsweek* (September 17, 1990), 36.

# 15. The Christian Right

Theoretically, religion and politics are supposed to be separate in the United States. In reality, throughout our history, they have usually been mingled. Thomas Jefferson's oft-repeated dictum that there should be a "wall of separation" between church and state has not been taken too seriously by the majority in a literal sense, but rather as a metaphor suggesting a general principle; most Americans believe that religious values have a place in the laws and government of the country.[1]

Article Six of the Constitution contains the phrase that "no religious Test shall ever be required as a Qualification to any Office or public Trust under the United States." This means that the government may not require a "religious test" (to demonstrate church membership or adherence to a particular religious doctrine) for one to run for or be appointed to office. It does *not* mean that it's unconstitutional for individuals or groups to take a candidate's religious views into account with respect to his fitness for office. American political campaigns—from presidential to school board—have raised issues of the morality and ethics of the respective candidates, and reasonably so. Who wants candidates who are "immoral" and "unethical?" The problem is that the public generally understands these terms in their religious context, as if religion were the only vehicle for morality and ethics. Christianity being the dominant religion in the United States by quite a large margin, it is Christian morality and ethics that have dominated the controversy.[2]

In a free society where one has choices about religion and politics, and where interest groups are allowed to organize and promote their views, religious as well as political controversies are bound to flourish, and they should. We have more to fear from *stifling* these controversies than we do *allowing* them, although it's also true that the volatility inherent in religious belief, combined with its metaphysical nature, does not lend itself well to rational discourse.

\*     \*     \*

The most recent manifestation of the blending of religion and politics in American life began to form in the late seventies and got into high gear at the beginning of the eighties. This movement became known as the Christian Right, Fundamentalist Right, or Religious Radical Right. We prefer the least pejorative term and will refer to it merely as the Christian Right. While focusing on most of the same issues as the fundamentalist radio preachers of the twenties through the sixties (such as Bob Schuler, Charles E. Fuller, Paul Rader, Billy James Hargis,

Carl McIntire, C. W. Burpo, etc.), the prime-time preachers of the seventies, eighties, and nineties have had considerably more attention drawn to them.

The success of the Christian Right has been due in great measure to three factors: first, the new preachers have made extensive use of "show-biz" and advertising techniques via television and other media; second, for a number of years they have worked hand in glove with direct mail wizards and have adapted techniques originally developed for political campaigns; and third, our nation's rapidly changing mores in such areas as sexual behavior, explicit books, movies and plays, and the use of illegal drugs have been catalysts that caused many citizens (who otherwise might have paid scant attention) to turn to the Christian Right for answers. One needed only to turn on television during the eighties to observe that "solutions" to pressing problems were being offered on a multitude of programs.

Quentin J. Schultze, professor of communication arts and sciences at Calvin College, and author of *Television: Manna From Hollywood,* has noted:

> In the late 1970s, when the "New Right" was given front-page status, the term electric church was coined to help explain the "sudden" rise of religio-political conservatism. . . .
> The truth is that little in contemporary evangelical broadcasting (except some of the technology employed) lacks historical precedent. Today's methods and personalities are remarkably similar to those of 60 years ago. The good and the bad, the extravagant and the simple, the authentic and the counterfeit, have existed side-by-side in evangelical broadcasting from the earliest days.[3]

According to Schultze, "there is no evidence that a greater percentage of the population today watches or listens to evangelical broadcasts than at any time in the last 50 years." He adds, "Religious broadcasting has always had its champions of conservative ideology. In the 1920s Rev. Robert "Fighting Bob" Shuler lost his station license because of his sermons directed at public officials, one of which got the Los Angeles police chief fired for drunkenness. His fundraising techniques were rather creative as well:

> "I know a man listening in," Shuler told listeners. "If he does not give a hundred dollars I will go on the air next Tuesday night and tell what I know about him." Many hundreds of dollars were raised.[4]

Another view is voiced by Clyde Wilcox in *God's Warriors: The Christian Right in Twentieth Century America*:

> The New Christian Right attracted a good deal more media attention than had earlier manifestations of the fundamentalist right. The new communication channels that the fundamentalists had established, particularly the televised sermons of sympathetic preachers, served to alert potential converts. Moreover, new technology, such as computerized direct mail, enabled the organizations to more accurately target sympathetic individuals and approach them with carefully designed messages. . . . The net result of all of these factors was that the general public was significantly more aware of

the existence and message of the New Christian Right than it had been of its predecessors.[5]

Support for the Christian Right in the 1970s and 1980s, according to Wilcox, was not particularly widespread. Citing a study by Emmett Buell and Lee Sigelman in 1985,[6] among others, he says, "Among the general public, support hovered between 10 percent and 15 percent of the population."[7]

The impact of the Christian Right on the electoral system has been a subject for debate, and the data have been subject to various interpretations; however the claim by certain fundamentalist leaders such as Reverend Jerry Falwell that his now-defunct organization, the Moral Majority, and others caused a significant rise in turnout by "Bible-believing Christians" in the 1980 election gained wide acceptance. On the other hand, three researchers using Survey Research Center–Center for Political Studies data "found very little evidence that fundamentalist attitudes were related to turnout, despite the promise of the Moral Majority to deliver millions of votes."[8] While this finding may be disappointing to Christian rightists, it should also calm the fears of their more alarmist critics. Few topics have caused as much furor in the American left and liberal communities as the rise of the "Religious Radical Right."

Like all movements with extremist tendencies—right, left, or otherwise—the Christian Right often has claimed privileged access to the truth, to moral certainty. For example, former Moral Majority leader Jerry Falwell stated that he has had no doubts whatsoever that he is right.[9] But statements by Christian Right spokespersons often have been simply not factual, and more often have been half-truths and therefore misleading. In short, leaders of Christian Right groups put out a considerable amount of incorrect information. Examples follow.

The Reverend Tim LaHaye of the Moral Majority and the American Coalition for Traditional Values wrote *The Battle for the Mind,*[10] a perfunctory perusal of which reveals not only questionable assertions but a number of statements that simply are factually wrong. For instance, LaHaye informs us that Australia and Brazil are larger in area than the United States (they aren't).[11] He states that Sweden has the world's highest suicide rate, which has not been true for at least fifty years.[12] (One year it ranked as high as fourth, while other years it was not in the top fifteen. Actually, Hungary has led the world in suicide— often by huge margins—for the past thirty years in a row.) LaHaye also writes that humanists are amoral, one-world socialists.[13] Although LaHaye doesn't differentiate between religious and secular humanists, the latter became the new bogeymen for the Christian Right beginning in the late seventies. In fact, "secular humanism" is the only genuinely new issue they have raised. Radio preachers of the sixties—Billy James Hargis, Carl McIntire, C. W. Burpo, etc.—also focused on the majority of the issues that have dominated the far-right political preachers of the eighties: abortion, anti-Americanism, Communism, homosexuality, por- nography, and sex education.

Incorrect information can be a two-way street, however. In June 1991 a federal judge in Philadelphia ordered the general counsel for the National Endowment for the Arts to stop making false statements about Reverend Donald Wildmon of the American Family Association, a crusading anti-pornography organization, or pay him $100,000 in damages. The NEA acknowledged that Julianne Ross Davis had "erroneously attributed to the AFA certain extremist policy positions when, in fact, they are not directly attributable to the AFA."[14] Relying on an article in *Mother Jones* magazine, Davis had attributed to Wildmon a statement of his desire that "astrologers, adulterers, blasphemers, homosexuals and incorrigible children be executed, preferably by stoning."[15] The error was readily discovered but it took the threat of a lawsuit to get a retraction and a public apology.

According to premier survey researcher Daniel Yankelovich in his 1981 tome *New Rules: Searching for Self-Fulfillment in a World Turned Upside Down*,[16] what the Christian rightists have been battling under the name "secular humanism" may actually be described as "social pluralism." This term is defined generally as the right to choose one's own lifestyle within the relatively broad boundaries available in American culture. With this in mind, we might speculate that Reverend Tim LaHaye and his cohorts never have really understood what actually constitutes secular humanism. This speculation may be bolstered by returning to LaHaye's *Battle for the Mind* with its host of misleading and nonfactual statements, especially those regarding humanism.

LaHaye's charge that humanists are amoral is a rather serious one, since very few Americans are without morals. Whether one agrees with the "morality" expressed in "A Secular Humanist Declaration" (1980) or *The Battle for the Mind* is another topic. Suffice it to say that the overwhelming majority of charges of amorality by anyone are open to argument and debate.

LaHaye's "one-world socialism" assertion that "all committed humanists are one-worlders first and Americans second"[17] is questionable for at least two reasons: one-world socialism long has been such a passé ideology that only a small percentage of Americans still entertain it as even a possibility, and probably the most over-represented political philosophy among secular humanists in the United States is libertarianism. Although LaHaye and other spokesmen on the Christian Right never have been too pleased with that mode of thought, it is nevertheless rather removed from "one-world socialism." While the secular humanist camp still has a few socialists, they are democratic socialists in the mold of one of the world's leading secular humanists, the late Sidney Hook—a hero to many political conservatives due to his long-standing anti-Communism.

LaHaye writes that humanists ridicule the "work ethic, free enterprise, private ownership of land, and capitalism,"[18] but there is simply no evidence that a clear majority of secular humanists do not accept *all* of these. (It strains credulity to imagine such people as Isaac Asimov, Carl Sagan, and Andrei Sakharov being opposed to the work ethic.) What LaHaye is implying is that most humanists are socialists, and there is no evidence to support this.

In his discussion of abortion, LaHaye writes that because so many have been performed in the United States, "we will soon have to apologize to Adolf Hitler."[19] In the manner of so many others who feel as he does on this issue, LaHaye seems unaware that Hitler was avidly anti-abortion, and that abortion was not legal in Nazi Germany, just as it was not for years in Stalin's Russia. (The pro-choice movement, of course, should not use this fact to do a "LaHaye" of its own, and equate anti-abortionists with Adolf Hitler.)

The two most prominent leaders of the Christian Right have been the Reverends Jerry Falwell and Pat Robertson. While both of these gentlemen have demonstrated some capacity to learn from their experiences, it was Falwell who demonstrated that ability more completely. After he folded his Moral Majority organization to return to his own church, an editorial in *Christian Century* noted that for a fundamentalist Falwell was remarkably ecumenical:

> Perhaps Falwell's greatest accomplishment, however, was getting Protestants, Catholics, and Jews to work together on common causes. . . .
> That such a foray into the dangerous waters of ecumenical action should come from a fundamentalist pastor is remarkable.[20]

Nevertheless, both Falwell and Robertson would quite possibly be embarrassed today if they looked back on some of the unfounded charges and irresponsible accusations they made during the eighties, seventies, and before. Falwell, for instance, in 1980, used the Gus Hall strangulation fake quote (see appendix I on fake quotes), although he was probably unaware it was bogus, and also warned his congregation against reading anything but the Bible and church-prescribed literature.[21] He also stated, "Many women have not accepted their God-given roles. They live in disobedience to God's laws and have promoted their godless philosophy throughout our society." Further, he said, "Christians, like slaves and soldiers, ask no questions." In 1958 he used scripture to illustrate that the 1954 Supreme Court integration decision (*Brown* v. *Board of Education of Topeka*) was a satanic plot.[22] Finally, there is Falwell's famous lie about what he said to President Carter in the White House. Falwell claimed he asked the president why he had so many homosexuals working there and Carter supposedly replied that this was the case because he represented all Americans. No such conversation ever took place, and Falwell later apologized and called it an anecdote.[23]

Pat Robertson claimed that God commanded him to run for president in 1988. Robertson tried to skewer the *Humanist Manifesto II* (1973) for stating that "unbridled sexuality is not immoral. In fact it is healthful and good." This *Manifesto* contains no such words (see appendix I). Robertson also passed on an urban legend about a small girl in El Paso who was praying her rosary while riding the school bus. The driver stopped the bus, came back to her, and told her to stop praying, insisting that it was not allowed because of separation of church and state. Robertson also publicized the false story that Texas Attorney General Jim Mattox made these assertions in 1988: "The state owns your children. And it owns you, too."

Perhaps the most embarrassing aspect of Robertson's past, however, occurred in 1988 as he was preparing to run for president. It turned out that in spite of Robertson's gung-ho anti-Communism in his "700 Club" TV broadcasts and his references to being a combat veteran, he had, according to former seven-term Republican Congressman Paul "Pete" McClosky of California, been given preferential treatment in the army during the Korean War at the request of his father, A. Willis Robertson, a U.S. senator from Virginia at the time. According to McClosky and others, Robertson had told them his father was having him reassigned. "The most distinct memory I have of this," said McClosky, "is Pat standing on the dock in Kobe (Japan) with this big grin on his face, saying, 'So long, you guys—good luck.' " Robertson sued McClosky for defamation and then withdrew the suit.[24]

Rev. Robertson's conspiracy-oriented book, *The New World Order* (1991), contains a rehash of Illuminati legends (see section on the Illuminati in the chapter on Motivations). In typical Robertson style, the book features three fake quotes and at least one other that is probably fake. Most interesting among these is the Adolf Hitler "Law and Order" quote (see Appendix 1) which, until employed by Mr. Robertson, had only been used by people on the political left (usually Marxists). *The New World Order* also features the Rowan Gaither "comfortably merge with the Soviet Union" phony (see Appendix 1), and an Abraham Lincoln fake about "corporations [being] enthroned and an era of corruption in high places" which will result in the destruction of the United States. Finally, the current Master of Doubtful Quotes attributes one to Masonic leader Albert Pike about "Lucifer, God of Light . . . struggling for humanity against Adonay, the God of Darkness and Evil."

Other big guns of the Christian Right included Jimmy Swaggart and Jim and Tammy Faye Bakker. Swaggart has been an inveterate fake quote user and purveyor of misinformation. He used a phony Charles Darwin quote on more than one occasion (see Appendix 1). Jim Bakker illustrated his ignorance by agreeing with a guest on his PTL (Praise the Lord) program that the Russians had a machine that would bore a hole forty-five feet in diameter into the side of a mountain.[25] The personal problems of Swaggart and Bakker were well publicized and are not within the purview of this book. Whatever the case, however, one must support the principle that these people be treated fairly and evenhandedly. The position that they should be "made examples of" is entirely wrongheaded. Perhaps the best example we can make is to judge them with more compassion than they have judged others.

James Dobson and Bob Jones III have been conspicuous in the Christian Right. Dobson has asserted that human fetuses are served as delicacies in Chinese restaurants, while Jones's displays of irresponsibility have, perhaps, exceeded those of any other prominent figure. President of Bob Jones University (Greenville, South Carolina), which has conferred honorary doctorates upon Jerry Falwell, Tim LaHaye, and others, Jones called George Bush a "devil" and the United States a "God-hating, devilistic country that I can't be loyal to anymore." He also asked God to smite Alexander Haig "hip and thigh, bone and marrow, heart and lungs," and said that Pope John Paul was a "perfect example of the anti-Christ."[26]

A number of Christian Right leaders showed signs of anti-Catholicism while others attacked the idea of a pluralist society. Jimmy Swaggart occasionally didn't conceal his anti-Catholicism, and Daniel Fore, a former Moral Majority leader in New York, insisted in 1981 that Catholics were not really Christians. On the other hand, Gary Potter of Catholics for Christian Political Action averred, "After the Christian majority takes control, pluralism will be seen as immoral and evil, and the state will not permit anyone to practice evil."[27]

As the present-day Christian Right began to form in the late 1970s many Jewish leaders were concerned about anti-Semitism. This proved to be a non-issue, however, as most of the major Christian Right spokesmen have proven to be strong and often uncritical supporters of Israel—so much so, in fact, that Grace Halsell, in *Prophecy and Politics: Militant Evangelists on the Road to Nuclear War,* has charged that their hawkish views have put the world at risk of a global confrontation.[28]

One such supporter is Senator Jesse Helms, perhaps the contemporary political figure most thoroughly identified with the Christian Right. In the summer of 1987 Helms was honored at a dinner in New York sponsored by the ultra-Orthodox Lubavitch leaders of Moshav Kiryat Gat and their U.S.-based supporters. Journalist Wolf Blitzer, writing in *Jewish Week,* noted:

> For years, Helms was strongly disliked by the mainstream of the U.S. Jewish community, both because of his extremely conservative view on such issues as prayer in the public schools and abortion and for his opposition to foreign aid to Israel. Lately, however, he seems to have undergone a political conversion as far as Israel is concerned, and this has led some Jewish activists here to turn a blind eye to his right-wing views.
>
> "I believe that Israel is vital to the survival of Western Civilization," Helms said last May. And responding to allegations that he was anti-Israel, the Christian fundamentalist said: "Let me ask you this: How can someone who is named after King David's father be anti-Israel?"[29]

What has been bothersome to many, but especially to people considering themselves Christians, is the Christian Right's use of positions on political issues as a measuring stick to determine the extent of one's Christian commitment. They forget that segments of the "religious left" have done this as well. For example, the backbone of the leadership of the civil rights movement has been black ministers, and the sermons of Reverend Martin Luther King, Jr., among others, readily demonstrate how they have tended to reframe legal, political, and social issues surrounding desegregation and equal opportunity into religious ones, and perhaps rightly so. The antiwar movement has been similarly populated with liberal and leftist religious activists, ranging from the Berrigan brothers to countless Christian pacifists. The pacifist Catholic Worker movement has concerned itself with explicitly political topics ranging from foreign affairs to domestic policies. There is also the "liberation theology" movement with its neo-Marxist economic and social theories combined with Catholic doctrine. This is a growing movement in Central and South America, where it has been closely linked with radical leftist revolutionary movements, and it is beginning to develop a following here.[30] Moreover, if one were looking for bad examples to tar the Christian Left, one could cite Reverend Jim Jones and his People's Temple, whose atrocities the Christian Right has yet to match.

Both the Christian Right and the Christian Left have taken broad positions on national issues. Major denominations are veritable hotbeds of debate over gay rights, the environment, and other of the very issues the Christian Right has focused on:

abortion, sex education in public schools, and censorship. There were even "Christian" sides to be taken regarding the selling of AWACS to Saudi Arabia, aid to the Nicaraguan Contras, sanctions on South Africa, aid to Jonas Savimbi's guerrilla force in Angola, whether Jerusalem should be recognized as Israel's capital, recognition of the government of Mozambique, and a whole range of others. Previously, the majority of American Christians seemed to believe that religious commitment had little to do with the position taken on political issues, but this may no longer be the case. Religion in the United States seems to have become more politically partisan, and the Christian Right is hardly the only offender.

To add a bit of perspective, it's important to note that nontraditional religions are also active in nominally "political" issues. The influence of neo-paganism ("womyn's religion") in radical feminism is surprisingly strong, as is its role in radical environmental and the animal rights movements such as Earth First! and the Animal Liberation Front, both of which contain terrorist elements. Large portions of the heterogeneous "New Age" movement, with its polyglot of metaphysical and spiritual jargon and beliefs, have been active in many social causes, including those mentioned above.

Because of its rather large size and the capacity of its doctrine to engage individuals in every aspect of their lives, the Christian Right has produced a growing number of "defectors." Some of these have congregated around groups like Fundamentalists Anonymous, which purports to deal with the emotional damage done by the rigidity and dogmatism of the movement. Rod L. Evans and Irwin M. Berent write of this in *Fundamentalism: Hazards and Heartbreaks*.[31] The authors deal with the conflict between technology, science, growing religious pluralism and the belief that the Bible is the literal word of God which must not be questioned. They note the enormous attraction of easy solutions to complex problems.[32]

According to Clyde Wilcox, psychologizing accounts of the appeal of the Christian Right are as off-base as they often are with other nominally "extremist" movements. He says:

> There is no evidence that support for the Christian Right is linked to alienation, at least as this term is conceived by mass-society theorists. Supporters were as attached to social groups and involved in politics as nonsupporters, and they were not the isolated individuals that some theorists have portrayed as "easy prey" for right-wing groups. . . . The tests for social-status inconsistency were quite direct and show no evidence to support this hypothesis.
>
> The best predictors of support for the Christian Right are religious identities, doctrines, affiliations, and political beliefs. Conservative religious identities, orthodox doctrine, high levels of public and private religiosity, and affiliation with conservative denominations are all positive predictors of support for the Christian Right.[33]

What is objectionable about the Christian Right (or the Christian Left, for that matter) is not necessarily the views that they hold—i.e., their version of "political correctness"—but that they would thrust them upon others who have their own vision of morality and ethics. This objection can be leveled at all moralizing crusades, including those with which we might agree. To paraphrase John Stuart Mill: it's the principle of dogmatic religion, dogmatic morality and dogmatic philosophy that needs to be rejected, and not necessarily any particular manifestation of that principle.

## Notes

1. Harry Holloway and John George, *Public Opinion: Coalitions, Elites and Masses* (New York: St. Martin's Press, 1979), chapter 7, "Religion: A Nation of Believers."

2. Of potential significance is the growing Jewish "religious right," a blend of religious traditionalism and "neoconservative" politics.

3. Quentin J. Schultze, "The Wireless Gospel," *Christianity Today* (January 15, 1988): 18.

4. Schultze, 21.

5. Clyde Wilcox, *God's Warriors: The Christian Right in Twentieth-Century America* (Baltimore: Johns Hopkins, 1992), 13.

6. Emmett Buell and Lee Sigelman, "An Army That Meets Every Sunday? Popular Support for the Moral Majority in 1980," *Social Science Quarterly* 66 (1985): 426–34.

7. Wilcox, op. cit.

8. Paul R. Abramson, John Aldrich, and David W. Rohde, *Change and Continuity in the 1980 Elections* (Washington, D.C.: Congressional Quarterly Press, 1982), 84.

9. Interview, *Penthouse* (March 1981).

10. Timothy LaHaye, *Battle for the Mind* (Old Tappan, N.Y.: Revell, 1980).

11. Ibid., 37.

12. Ibid., 115.

13. Ibid., 83, 92.

14. Joyce Price and George Archibald, "NEA Counsel Settles in Wildmon Lawsuit," *Washington Times* (June 5, 1991), A3,

15. Fred Clarkson, "Wildmon Kingdom: Traditional Values? Try Private Armies, Stoning Kids and No Public Schools," *Mother Jones* (November-December 1990), 11.

16. Daniel Yankelovich, *New Rules: Searching for Self-Fulfillment in a World Turned Upside Down* (New York: Random House, 1981).

17. LaHaye, 76.

18. Ibid., 39.

19. Ibid., 119.

20. "Home to Lynchburg," *Christianity Today* (February 15, 1988): 16–17.

21. Flo Conway and Jim Siegelman, *Holy Terror* (Garden City, N.Y.: Doubleday, 1982), 70; *New Yorker* (May 18, 1981); *San Francisco Examiner* (May 26, 1981).

22. *Inquiry* (August 3 and 24, 1981).

23. Ibid.

24. William Plummer, with Dirk Methison, "A Lawsuit Over Pat Robertson's War Record Has Ex-Marine Pete McClosky Fighting Mad," *People* (March 14, 1988): 44–46.

25. *PTL* (September 15, 1982).

26. *Focus on the Family* (August 1995); *Edmond* (Oklahoma) *Sun* (March 3, 1982); *Inquiry* (May 17, 1982); *Buffalo News* (April 4, 1982).

27. *Oklahoma Observer* (February 10, 1982); *Inquiry* (May 17, 1982); *Buffalo News* (April 4, 1982).

28. Grace Halsell, *Prophecy and Politics: Militant Evangelists on the Road to Nuclear War* (Westport, Conn.: Lawrence Hill, 1986).

29. Wolf Blitzer, "Israel Gains 'Convert' in Christian Rightist Helms," *Jewish Week* (February 13, 1987).

30. Paul E. Sigmund, *Liberation Theology at the Crossroads: Democracy or Revolution?* (New York: Oxford University Press, 1990).

31. Rod L. Evans and Irwin M. Berent, *Fundamentalism: Hazards and Heartbreaks* (LaSalle, Ill.: Open Court Publishing Co., 1988).

32. Other significant works on the Christian Right include: Steve Bruce, *The Rise and Fall of the New Christian Right* (Oxford: Oxford University Press, 1988); Sharon Georgianna, *The Moral Majority and Fundamentalism: Plausibility and Dissonance* (Lewiston, N.Y.: Edwin Mellon Press, 1989); Erling Jorstad, *The New Christian Right, 1981–1988* (Lewiston, N.Y.: Edwin Mellon Press, 1987); R. Liebman and R. Wuthnow, eds., *The New Christian Right* (New York: Aldine, 1983); Matthew Moen, *The Christian Right and Congress* (Tuscaloosa: University of Alabama Press, 1989); and Robert Zwier, *Born-Again Politics: The New Christian Right in America* (Downes Grove, Ill.: InterVarsity Press, 1982).

33. Wilcox, 225.

# 16. Willis Carto and Liberty Lobby

The period from 1955 to 1959 marked a low point in the activities of the extreme right in America. Senator Joseph McCarthy had finished a poor second in his nationally televised duel with the U.S. Army and its counsel, Joseph Welch, and his career in the headlines came to a dismal finish when his fellow senators condemned him in late 1954. The John Birch Society was organized in December 1958 but had not yet achieved national notoriety. Merwin K. Hart, Billy James Hargis, Carl McIntire, and many other right-wing stalwarts were busy during this period, but they received comparatively little publicity and the ordinary citizen hardly knew they existed.

It was during this period of relative quiescence that a California businessman named Willis Carto started a monthly newsletter called *Right*. With the organization "Liberty and Property" listed as publisher, it lasted only about five years, from late 1955 to late 1960. Summarizing materials from a large number of right-wing sources, throughout most of its existence the ideological line of *Right* placed major emphasis on anti-Communism and conspiracy theories, delivered in a style that prevails in Liberty Lobby publications today.

Frank P. Mintz, in his detailed *Liberty Lobby and the American Right,* describes the publication:

> *Right,* in the five years of its existence . . . drew not only from racial theories but from the wider stock of conspiracy and culture doctrine to fashion a propaganda style which anticipated the tactical and ideological tenor of Liberty Lobby.[1]

*Right* had strong anti-Semitic overtones, claiming, for example, that the "Bolshevik conspiracy was hatched and led by Bronx Jews and financed to a great extent by Wall Street Jews." The November 1956 issue claimed that the interests supporting the Eisenhower administration were

> closely associated with the big international banks which have brought so much grief to the world by their financing of the Russian bolshevik revolution and their unsuccessful agitation for wars which have all but destroyed Western civilization.[2]

Other issues railed against the Wall Street "Communist-Zionist financiers," contained articles by Ernest Sevier Cox on racial theories, opposed racial "mongrelization," and carried alarmist accounts of the "Communist conspiracy," which Carto said "should be outlawed and all Communists given the traditional penalty for traitors, since all Communists are consciously in the service of the Soviet Union."[3]

*Right* has been defunct since September 1960, and there would be little reason to review the history of one of the countless publications that come and go, except that this particular newsletter marked the start of the political career of one of the most influential personalities in the American far right. Beginning as executive director of Liberty and Property in 1955, Willis A. Carto has for many years wielded considerable power in the world of right-wing extremism. The August 1957 issue of *Right* announced the formation of Liberty Lobby while the January 1958 issue contained an article by noted novelist Taylor Caldwell, entitled "Unite With Liberty Lobby." With the demise of his newsletter in 1960, Carto was free to devote energies to his new project and Liberty Lobby began its rocky ride.

Carto had been involved in far-right activities briefly before starting his newsletter. In 1954 he was an officer of the Congress of Freedom, an organization headed for some time by Glenn O. Young of Sapulpa, Oklahoma. But the factor that evidently helped form Carto's eventual blend of right-wing conservatism and not-so-vague sympathy for National Socialism was his short personal association with Francis Parker Yockey, a 1941 honors graduate of the University of Notre Dame law school. The Yockey story represents a fascinating look into the bizarre and colorful personalities that show up in the sometimes shadowy world of political extremism, where things are often not what they seem. Let us take a closer look at Yockey and examine a possible explanation for his activities.

Though brilliant, Yockey was unstable and disturbed. He received a medical discharge in 1942 from the U.S. Army, which described him as a "dementia praecox, paranoid type."[4] After World War II he became an assistant to a team of lawyers preparing for the prosecution in some of the Nuremberg trials. Yockey, who is alleged to have believed that the United States should have fought the Soviet Union rather than Germany, quit his job after less than a year. The papers he prepared were said to have revealed his pro-Nazi feelings.

Late in 1947, Yockey went to Brittas Bay, Ireland, where, supposedly working for only six months, he wrote a 619-page tome entitled *Imperium,* using the pseudonym Ulick Varange. Published in London in 1948, the book was dedicated "To the hero of the Second World War," i.e., Adolf Hitler. The American edition of the book, pubished by Carto's Noontide Press, features a lengthy introduction by Carto himself.

*Imperium,* which has been called a "neo–*Mein Kampf* for neo-Nazis," is heavy reading by any standard. Parts of it are difficult to comprehend and in some respects it has a "flight of ideas" character about it that suggests instability and disorganization. The rambling discourse ranges from "constancy of inter-organismic power" to attacks upon Jews as "cultural distorters." Much of the book's enduring reputation lies in its incomprehensibility. Many neo-Nazi and other extreme right booksellers have offered it for sale and copies exist in the tens of thousands, yet it is unusual to encounter a Carto follower or rightist of racial nationalist persuasion who claims to understand it, and many have tried. In the tiny community of neo-Nazism, *Imperium* is the "bible" few people have thoroughly read and almost nobody understands.

Yockey was turned down when he attempted to renew his passport, so he traveled throughout Europe and the United States for eleven years by using forged papers. During this time he didn't work, and some rightists have maintained he was supported by sympathizers and followers, domestic and foreign.

On a trip to San Francisco in June 1960, Yockey inadvertently left a suitcase in Ft. Worth. It was opened by airline employees who discovered seven birth certificates, German press credentials, and American, Canadian, and British passports bearing the same photo of Yockey but with different names. Yockey was arrested while attempting to claim the suitcase and held on $50,000 bond, inordinantly high at that time for a passport violation.

Yockey spent a week and a half in jail before committing suicide by swallowing a cyanide capsule. The last person to visit him, with the exception of his attorney, was Willis Carto. According to sources on the far right, Yockey feared he would be forced to reveal his activities with the European Liberation Front, a group he organized in 1949. Carto published a commentary on Yockey's death in the July 1960 issue of *Right,* in which he wrote that a "great creative genius" had been "persecuted" until he chose suicide. He also praised the book *Imperium,* prophesying that it would "live a thousand years."

When he was arrested, Yockey was visiting the residence of one Alexander Scharf (a Jew, ironically). He had supposedly told Scharf, "I'm the top fascist in the world. There is nobody bigger than me."[5] His cellmate, Adam Nieman, said Yockey boasted he was "the number one Nazi here."[6]

Most people who knew Yockey shared the view that he actually believed what he said about himself, but there may have been even more to the man than we suspect. Recent documents acquired from East German intelligence reveal that the East German Stasi—their equivalent of the Soviet KGB—ran double agents posing as neo-Nazis and even organized neo-Nazi groups and engaged in anti-Semitic activity and violence in West Germany. We are acquainted with an individual who was quite close to Yockey. In a mid-1970 interview, this individual revealed little-known information:

Author: Did you know Yockey very well?

X: He was a rather shadowy figure. Yes, I knew him quite well for a rather brief time. He was a remarkable guy. I did know and like Yockey as a man.

Author: Why was the FBI after him so much? They had him under surveillance for about eleven years. Did he really have that kind of Nazi connections in Europe, or not?

X: He had Soviet connections.

Author: Oh, he did?

X: Yeh. The current bunch who exploit him don't want to hear about that angle.

Author: What was he doing with the Soviets?

X: I think he was a coordinator of some sort. I think the Russians, particularly in Germany, were encouraging some of those radical rightist groups and parties, for their own purposes.

The assertion of Yockey's Soviet connections is supported by other data suggesting that not only was he flirting with the Soviets but that he was also quite anti-American. According to a letter written in January 1953 by a German rightist named Wolfgang Sarg, director of a far-right organization called NAT-INFORM (Nationalist Information Service) located in Oldenburg, Germany, Yockey "prais(ed) the Soviet policy in Germany."

A. Raven Thompson, secretary of the British fascist organization (led by Oswald Mosley) known as the Union Movement, described Yockey in a letter written in March 1953:

Yockey [has] a strong anti-American phobia . . . taking the view that the present American influence in Europe is more damaging to European culture than the direct alien threat of Communism from the east.

Peter J. Huxley-Blythe, another British extremist, who once edited Yockey's *Front Fighter,* and later *Northern World and Folk,* wrote in 1954 that Yockey had Eastern connections:

Now to Yockey. I now know, for the first time, of his contacts with the East, and this explains many things. In Europe his propaganda has left a decided mark and only recently a manifestation of his pro-Communist propaganda was heard at the "National Forces of Europe" congress in Brussels. His propaganda must be countered.

In his perceptive monograph entitled *The National Renaissance Party* (1970), William Goring states that although he had "no proof," it was his "suspicion that the work of [Yockey's] European Liberation Front was secretly encouraged and, possibly, financed in part by the Soviet Union." Goring further speculated:

Yockey never seemed to lack money in his travels. It is, of course, possible that he was financed by a wealthy Nazi sympathizer. On the other hand, there is no way to explain the fact that the Russians let these people travel in their country. . . . There is also the problem of getting passports; someone was furnishing these fascists with forged passports and papers. Had a rightist authoritarian group . . . ever taken over a European country, it would certainly have been beneficial to the Soviet Union to have a few European Liberation Front sympathizers in the top ranks. This, however, is only conjecture.

Conjecture, indeed, but it was well-reasoned and (apparently unknown to Goring) supported by other evidence. It is possible that Yockey was so vehemently anti-American that he would cooperate with any group or individual who shared his feelings. If he *did* in fact work for the Soviets, his efforts were well paid. Both an informant and his sister stated that he usually had plenty of money and never worked. The sister also told the *San Francisco Chronicle* (June 18, 1960) that "he was not anti-communist. He felt Russia had a role to play in world history."

\* \* \*

Liberty Lobby, Carto's flagship operation, was founded in 1957, and by the end of the 1960s the organization's monthly, *Liberty Letter,* had a circulation of more than 200,000, although it is not known how many subscribers were actually members of the organization. Another publication, *Liberty Lowdown,* was sent to pledgers or contributors. Two other Carto publications, *Western Destiny* and *Washington Observer,* appeared in 1964. In 1966 Carto obtained the old *American Mercury* magazine (founded by H. L. Mencken and George Jean Nathan) and folded *Western Destiny.*

Notables of the extreme right who wrote for the *Mercury* during the late fifties and early sixties included Russell Maguire, once the magazine's chairman of the board; Harold Lord Varney, who also wrote for the John Birch Society publication *American Opinion* for several years; Karl Hess, a former speechwriter for Barry Goldwater and right-wing anarchist who moved to the far left, then back to the right, calling himself a "new right" libertarian; John A. Lovell, a leading British Israelite and health faddist; Myron C. Fagan, who wrote extensively on alleged "reds" in Hollywood; Gerald L. K. Smith; Helaire du Berrier, another writer for *American Opinion;* Kenneth Goff, a former member of the Communist party and leader of the Minutemen affiliate, Soldiers of the Cross; Billy James Hargis, discussed fully in chapter 20; Prof. Revilo P. Oliver, former Birch Society council member; Gen. Pedro A. del Valle, who praised Mussolini and once co-owned the now defunct anti-Semitic newspaper *Common Sense.*

In the winter 1970 issue of *American Mercury* Ian MacLeod, who once wrote for Carto's *Right,* revealed the response elicited from a number of American publishers whom he approached regarding the publication of Yockey's *Imperium.* Apparently chagrined by refusals on every hand, MacLeod decided that book publishers do not practice freedom of the press. The rejection by Joseph Greene, managing editor of Grosset and Dunlap, Inc., was extremely candid:

> I can assure you that I read this book as carefully as I read the works of Hitler, Towenberg, Streicher, and others 35 years ago. I cannot see how you can claim not to be a Neo-Nazi movement. For example, the comments on "Mongrelization" prepare the philosophical rationalization for extermination camps. In my opinion, there is little in *Imperium* that has not been said better by the Nazis 40 years ago.

An article entitled "The Way It Might Have Been" appeared in the summer 1973 *American Mercury.* This strange journey into nostalgia depicted the situation that would have existed had Germany defeated America and her allies in World War II. The article approvingly states:

Americans, in order to try and understand the victory of Germany, would be forced to study the nationalist philosophy and White Studies would be taught in schools instead of sex education, sensitivity training and Black Studies.

Considering all factors, *American Mercury* was always written on a higher intellectual level than almost any other publication of the extreme right, but then Willis Carto certainly would not fit H. L. Mencken's "Boobus americanus," a term Mencken applied to the average American, whom he considered rather ignorant.

Word of Carto's clandestine activities first hit the news in a 1966 Drew Pearson column. A Liberty Lobby employee, Jeremy Horne, inadvertently discovered a box containing copies of letters Carto had written to various right extremists, including a couple of black nationalists. One of these letters contained plans for shipping blacks back to Africa. In another, Carto stated:

> Hitler's defeat was the defeat of Europe and America. How could we have been so blind? The blame, it seems, must be laid at the door of the international Jews. It was their propaganda, lies, and demands which blinded the West to what Germany was doing. If Satan himself . . . had tried to create a permanent . . . force for the destruction of all nations, he could have done no better than to invent the Jews.[7]

Horne turned all his information over to the FBI (although it turned out that no laws were broken) and later to Drew Pearson, who published segments of the letters in his columns. Liberty Lobby twice sued Pearson, once for libel and once for publishing the letter which contained the foregoing quote. They lost on both occasions, going all the way to the U.S. Supreme Court. Carto claimed that Horne was a spy for Drew Pearson all along. Horne denied this and told us that he got the Liberty Lobby job by answering a newspaper ad.

\*    \*    \*

The February 1969 *Liberty Letter* reported the founding of the National Youth Alliance, which came together following a November 1968 meeting of the remnants of the Youth for Wallace movement. John Acord, chairman of the Wallace group, initially went along with the transformation. According to Drew Pearson and his associate, Jack Anderson (who secured affidavits from six former leaders of Youth for Wallace concerning "Carto's Nazi activities"), an NYA regional conference was held on January 25, 1969, near Monroeville, Pennsylvania, at Conley's Motel. The meeting hall featured Nazi flags. Carto, who had given the group financial backing, was the evening speaker. Shortly afterward Acord and a colleague, Dennis McMahon, were summarily dismissed when they objected to the highly authoritarian character the group had acquired. Acord was embittered by the experience and charged that Liberty Lobby was in fact a front for Nazis and anti-Semites. He recounted the whole affair in a May 14, 1969, notarized statement to Group Research, a Washington, D.C.-based organization formed to monitor rightist activity.

Carto's NYA won the participation of Dr. William Pierce, a former associate of American Nazi leader George Lincoln Rockwell, and Louis Byers, who had left the John Birch Society largely because of its opposition to anti-Semitism. Another influence in the NYA was a group of supporters of the publication *Statecraft,* an anti-black and anti-Jewish newsletter in Virginia. As is so often the case, however, the NYA fell apart in fratricidal conflict, having been the usual amalgam of unstable and idiosyncratic personalities.

Claiming that the NYA had become a branch of his Action Associates, Carto demanded that the group's assets be turned over to him and, according to an affidavit by former NYA chairman John Acord, even broke into the organization's office and removed a file cabinet. He then informed the post office that NYA's new mailing address was his office in the building with Liberty Lobby. Fifteen of the seventeen former NYA leaders tried to regain what seemed rightfully theirs, but they were unable to raise funds for the necessary legal battle and soon admitted defeat.

The group most closely associated with Carto and *Statecraft* became Youth Action (in 1971), which is still around as *Youth Action News,* published by C. B. Baker. The dissident group, associated with Pierce, became the National Alliance and also survives today. Pierce acquired some fame in the mid-1980s as the author of *The Turner Diaries,* a fictional account of a right-wing racist takeover of the United States. This is the book alleged to have inspired the paramilitary group The Order (or Bruder Schwiegen) in its armored car holdup and assassination of a Denver talk show host in 1984.

Liberty Lobby's position on the Vietnam War was originally critical of intervention, but by 1967 it began calling for an American victory. Other positions were typically isolationist, noninterventionist, anti-Communist, anti-Zionist, patriotic, and populist. In terms of legislative impact, Liberty Lobby influence probably peaked in the mid-1970s. From that point on it was effectively blacklisted as anti-Semitic and racist, largely through the efforts of the Anti-Defamation League of B'nai B'rith, the "watchdog" organization that monitors anti-Semitic opinions and activities.

*   *   *

Kansas City was the site for Liberty Lobby's third national convention in October 1973. A testimonial dinner was sponsored in behalf of Minuteman founder Robert DePugh, who had been released from prison in May, having served three years and ten months for firearms violations and bond jumping. Speakers for the occasion included such far-right bigwigs as John Birch Society member and American Party candidate Tom Anderson, *Councilor* editor Ned Touchstone, retired General Pedro A. del Valle, and *Herald of Freedom* editor Frank Capell.

In August 1975 Liberty Lobby terminated publication of *Liberty Letter* and commenced publication of *National Spotlight,* later renamed *The Spotlight,* which continues to this day. In 1980 both *American Mercury* and the *Washington Observer* were folded. One of the best descriptions of *The Spotlight* and its readership comes from Kevin Flynn and Gary Gerhardt, reporters for Denver's *Rocky Mountain News:*

> The weekly paper was [in 1982] one of the right wing's most widely read publications, with a circulation of a quarter million. It regularly featured articles on such topics as Bible analysis, taxes and fighting the IRS, bankers and how they bleed the middle class, and how the nation is manipulated by the Trilateral Commission and the Council on Foreign Relations. The paper attracted a huge diversity of readers, from survivalists and enthusiasts of unorthodox medical treatments to fundamentalist Christians and anti-Zionists.[8]

The ADL's campaign against Carto and his organization was at its peak effectiveness in getting the radio program *This Is Liberty Lobby* off the air. Heard for the first time in March 1973 over four stations (by November the number had reached 107), the program was sponsored by local Liberty Lobby supporters and businesses owned by them.[9] During 1974 and 1975 the program had aired several broadcasts attacking the ADL and had expressed views highly critical of Israel and Zionism, so the ADL's interest in the program was understandable.

The ADL did not confine its response to the normal channels of communication and debate, however. On June 18, 1974, David Brody, an ADL operative in Washington, D.C., wrote to Irwin Suall, the ADL's fact-finding director, with the suggestion that the ADL file a petition to deny the renewal license of radio station WAVA, which carried "This Is Liberty Lobby." He added:

> I don't think we can succeed with such a petition if carrying the Liberty Lobby broadcast is the only issue. However, if there is a station among those which carry the broadcast which has a generally bad record of serving the public interest, then I think that would be an added factor and if we were successful--although as you know it would be a long and arduous effort—it might have the effect of discouraging other stations from carrying the broadcast.

On July 23, 1974, Irwin Suall sent a directive to all ADL regional offices with the following "recommendations for action" against the Liberty Lobby broadcasts:

> Regional directors should communicate directly with the management of each of the radio stations in their respective areas carrying the Liberty Lobby program by mailing to them a copy of the reprint from the June, 1974 *ADL Bulletin* with a brief covering letter. The letter should state only that it has come to our attention that the station is carrying the Liberty Lobby program and that we are sending the enclosed article for their information, so that they may gain a better understanding of the organization which is responsible for the radio program.
>
> Attached are guidelines for concerned individuals to write directly to stations carrying the Liberty Lobby program. You should urge regional directors to distribute copies of these guidelines, together with the *ADL Bulletin* reprint, to their regional

board members, lodges, rabbis, etc. Businessmen should be encouraged to write on their business stationery. Non-Jews, especially clergymen, should be asked to write.

The ADL lobbying effort was generally successful and many radio stations cancelled the program. In April 1974 Liberty Lobby had signed a contract with the Mutual Broadcasting System to begin carrying the program on their extensive network of six hundred stations. On July 8, 1974, *Broadcasting Magazine* ran an article under the head, "Liberty Lobby's Radio Commentary Under Attack for Anti-Jewish Bias." The article noted:

> John L. Goldwater, chairman of ADL's national fact-finding committee . . . said "This Is Liberty Lobby" made "daily attacks" on Israel and American Jews, calling Israel "a bastard state," and accusing American Jews of being subversive, in broadcasts during and immediately following the October Arab-Israeli war. Such attacks, he said, were "typical" of the program's point of view.

Ranier K. Kraus, an attorney consulted by radio station WVOX-FM, responded on January 16, 1975, with a letter to Donald J. Flamm regarding the pressures brought by the ADL:

> WVOX believes that it has an obligation to present all responsible sides of public issues, even when it may disagree with the positions taken or disapprove of non-broadcast activities of the speaker or sponsoring organization. Despite the pressures I referred to earlier, WVOX has refused to remove "Liberty Lobby" from the air simply because some or many of the non-broadcast activities of its sponsor may be described as "offensive."
>
> For WVOX, the test is whether the "Liberty Lobby" program itself is conducted within broad but reasonable bounds of propriety. I know that Bill [William F. O'Shaughnessy, president of WVOX] has had a number of discussions with officials of the American Civil Liberties Union and it is my understanding that the ACLU believes that attempts to remove it from the air represent a classic example of attempts to suppress freedom of speech.
>
> WVOX has offered daily and weekly time to the ADL to rebut or comment about specific Liberty Lobby programs and the series in general. These offers have not been accepted—but they remain outstanding. I do not see how there can in fact be serious substantive complaints about this program by the ADL under the circumstances.

In response to an extremely intense campaign, which we have only touched upon here, Mutual Broadcasting Network cancelled its contract with Liberty Lobby effective January 31, 1975. Shortly thereafter Liberty Lobby filed suit in federal court against the Anti-Defamation League alleging interference with its First Amendment rights. It also charged that the ADL and Mutual Broadcasting conspired to restrain trade or commerce in violation of federal antitrust laws. In August 1976 the court dismissed the suit. Liberty Lobby appealed to the U.S. Court of Appeals for the Fifth District, but on June 1, 1978, it unanimously affirmed the district court's dismissal.

Liberty Lobby remained off the air for nearly a decade and then began broadcasting a regular program over a satellite linkup, which initially reached only a few thousand homes—mainly those in the farm belt with satellite disks. In 1989 its program, entitled "Radio Free America," hosted by Tom Valentine, acquired shortwave and conventional outlets as well. Valentine has featured a wide variety of guests, most of them nonpolitical, discussing subjects ranging from mercury in dental fillings to the Gerson cancer therapy.

*The Spotlight* peaked with a circulation of 315,000 in 1981 and is currently in the 90,000 range. Today, Liberty Lobby itself has on its rolls an estimated 25,000 "members," but this number is not particularly meaningful. One of the authors was listed as a Liberty Lobby "Board of Policy" member for several years for nothing more than mailing in a couple dollars for information.

Carto's political arm was the Populist party, founded in 1984, but in recent years the party has gone an independent course as the result of one of those fratricidal range wars that plague the far right. Bob Richards, a former Olympic pole-vaulting champion, was the party's first presidential candidate in 1984, only to be sued by Carto for money expended on his candidacy after the Federal Election Commission filed complaints of funding irregularities.

The party's 1988 candidate, David Duke, received only 47,047 votes, coming in behind the candidates of the Libertarian Party (432,116) and the New Alliance Party (217,219), not to mention the Democratic and Republican parties. As has been the case with the Communist party, however, some of this poor showing is due to restrictive regulations that tend to keep third parties off the ballot in many states. Third party ballot access can be quite difficult and in many cases requires the collection of tens of thousands of signatures.

David Duke's ill-fated presidential race apparently whetted his appetite for other ventures into electoral politics, however, and he was subsequently elected to the Louisiana legislature. In 1991 he ran for governor of Louisiana against former Governor Edwin Edwards, and managed to get 38 percent of the vote. His 1992 effort for the Republican presidential nomination proved to be a dismal flop, however.

Recent issues of Carto's *Spotlight* and the Populist party's *Populist Observer* have contained charges and countercharges concerning the parting of the ways between the two groups. Carto claims that Bill Shearer, long-time leader of the small, California-based American Independent party and a former Populist party leader, has played a "wrecker's" role, which Shearer denies. It was by making Shearer's American Independent party an affiliate of the Populist party that Carto was able to get on the California ballot in 1984.

In a February 28, 1991, letter to the Populist party executive committee, Carto suggests some "vitally important guidelines which are absolutely essential to be observed by the leaders of any successful new party":

> For instance, the elimination of a Platform Committee, purging yo-yos and hobbyists from party leadership and avoiding the mistakes which every new party effort has

succumbed to heretofore, such as getting bogged down in speechifying rather than action and the playing of musical chairs for titles rather than organizing.

. . . If the party had continued according to my plan of 1984, today there would be populists in Congress and elected officials all over the nation.

Carto also noted that Richard Winger, editor of *Ballot Access News,* which reports on the problems of third parties across the political spectrum, had dropped the Populist party from his list of those seeking ballot access in 1992. According to Winger, there were nineteen states where the party could already have been working to get on the ballot during the period of April to October 1991 but, under Populist party chairman Don Wassall's leadership, they declined. Wassall also changed the colors of the party and substituted an eagle for Carto's original falcon/phoenix logo, much to Carto's dismay.

Don Wassall has been highly critical of the party's fortunes when it was under Carto's control and has tried to disassociate the party from the racist and neofascist onus that Carto and Liberty Lobby have acquired. A lengthy "editor's note" appearing in the March 1991 issue of the *Populist Observer* read:

Carto is a totalitarian who wants only lackeys working for him. Due to his questionable political judgment and the tremendous mismanagement associated with the 1984 Populist Party when it was under the Liberty Lobby's control, Wassall and the current Executive Committee have made sure that the Populist Party of America remains independent and sovereign in all ways.

In a subsequent issue of the *Populist Observer* Wassall went even further, devoting five full pages to attacking Carto. Of particular interest was an article entitled "Carto's Endless Feuds":

Although probably not more than one in a hundred *Spotlight* readers is even aware of who he is, the shadowy Carto has clashed with an impressive list of conservatives, nationalists, populists, racialists, and religious conservatives. Although the following list is not complete, it gives a good idea of some of the individuals and organizations Carto has clashed with or attacked over the years:

    Eustace Mullins, Harold Covington, Tom Metzger, George Dietz, Dr. Revilo Oliver, Dr. Edward Fields, Ben Klassen, David McCalden, Michael Hoffman, Robert DePugh, Dr. William Pierce, the John Birch Society, John Rees, William F. Buckley, Robert Bork, Reed Irvine, *Human Events,* Richard Vigurie, Rep. Vin Weber, Rep. Robert K. Dornan, Rep. Newt Gingrich, Jerry Falwell, Moral Majority, Pat Robertson, Jim Yarborough, Bob Richards, Don Kimball, Don Wassall, Pat Buchanan, and David Duke.[10]

Another Carto project—this time marginally successful—is the Institute for Historical Review, founded in 1978. The IHR is dedicated to historical "revisionism," in practice largely Holocaust "revisionism," attacking widely accepted accounts of the extermination of Jews at the hands of Adolf Hitler. In addition to articles by bona fide and obvious anti-Semites like Francis Parker Yockey, Major Robert

H. Williams, and Michael A. Hoffman, *The Journal of Historical Review* has had contributions by the British historian David Irving, the civil war historian William B. Hesseltine, China authority Anthony B. Kubek, former CIA agent Victor Marchetti, and Pulitzer Prize–winning historian John Toland. In spite of this mix, however, there is a tendency toward Hitler apologism in the *Journal,* and a general contempt for Zionism and Jewish institutions is evident in many articles.

Like most Carto ventures, the IHR has had its share of internal feuding and controversy. David McCalden, who by his account was the actual "founder" of the IHR under the name "Lewis Brandon," had a disagreeable parting of the ways with Carto in the spring of 1981. McCalden had been active in British neofascist groups and had founded the British National party in 1975. He was notoriously difficult to get along with and his experience with Carto was merely a repeat of similar experiences with others. A talented writer, he went on to publish over a hundred issues of *David McCalden's Revisionist Newsletter,* which devoted inordinate space to attacking Carto and his "lackeys." McCalden died of AIDS in 1990.

At McCalden's request in 1981 the IHR offered $50,000 to anyone who could provide satisfactory proof that execution gas chambers actually existed in any of Hitler's concentration camps. The idea was to force that claim to undergo the rigorous examination of proof and evidence that one customarily associates with a trial. Los Angeles businessman Mel Mermelstein, an Auschwitz survivor, made a claim on the $50,000. When the IHR rejected his evidence, Mermelstein instituted a breach of contract lawsuit against the institute. The case went to trial with the IHR people confident of a day in court. To their amazement, however, on October 9, 1981, Thomas T. Johnston, a Los Angeles County Superior Court judge, took "judicial notice" that Jews were gassed in Auschwitz during the summer of 1944 without hearing any evidence to the contrary and Mermelstein was awarded $50,000. The IHR appealed but learned that potential satisfaction in the courts was going to be prohibitively expensive and eventually settled with Mermelstein for $90,000 to avoid more litigation.

In 1984 arson destroyed the IHR headquarters in Torrance, California. No one was indicted for the crime, but there were suspicions of Jewish Defense League involvement. The IHR regrouped, resumed publishing its *Journal,* and holding annual conferences. Circulation is in the 2,500 range and the organization survives on subscriptions, donations, and profits from Carto's Noontide Press (a publishing and mail order bookselling operation), which it manages. Bradley Smith, a libertarian, is media director of the IHR and a regular radio talk show guest in its behalf.

Under Bradley Smith the IHR's latest publicity efforts have been directed at publishing full-page advertisements in college and university newspapers around the country. Several campus papers have accepted the ads, always amid enormous controversy before and after the fact. Among these have been papers at Cornell, Ohio State, Vanderbilt, Louisiana State, and Rutgers. According to Smith, the ads produce few campus inquiries but the publicity brought about by the protests have "put the IHR on the map." Smith, sometimes accused of being a "racist" by virtue of his association with the IHR, is married to a Hispanic lady by whom he has a daughter.

*     *     *

In the spring of 1981 Health and Human Services Secretary Richard Schweiker nominated Warren Richardson, a Washington attorney, to the post of assistant secretary for legislation of that department. The Anti-Defamation League brought out its dossiers and exposed the fact that Richardson had served as general counsel for Liberty Lobby from 1969 to 1973 before severing his connections to the group. Following the predictable surge of media publicity, Richardson withdrew his name from consideration to avoid further embarrassment to Secretary Schweiker. Richardson explained that he was not anti-Semitic and that he had worked for Liberty Lobby because he had needed the money.[11] Later, Richardson said that the incident was an attempt to destroy his career for a past political indiscretion. Some civil libertarians commented that the Richardson affair was a kind of "reverse McCarthyism"—where individuals with distant right-wing connections were persecuted and blackballed. However one looks at it, the message got out: associate with Liberty Lobby and you're a marked man.

A recent Liberty Lobby convention was populated mostly by people in their sixties or older; people under thirty were conspicuously absent. The organization will probably suffer the fate of similar groups and slowly die by a process of attrition as its philosophy continues to fall out of favor and its members pass away.

*     *     *

How much influence has Willis Carto had? In the American far right, quite a bit—but in the total scheme of things, he has had almost none at all. There is one Liberty Lobby member per 10,000 Americans. IHR *Journal* subscribers are one per 100,000 Americans, while about one American in 2,800 subscribes to *The Spotlight*. The political philosophy that Carto and Liberty Lobby represent today would have had more appeal back in the 1930s, and perhaps even as recently as the 1950s and early 1960s. Today, however, the organization is hopelessly antiquated and has been so marginalized by a steady stream of attacks and exposés in the press and through private channels that only an incautious politician would be identified with it.

Nevertheless, whatever else one can say of Willis Carto, it is clear that he, more than any other individual, has been responsible for giving form to the ragtag band of citizens who make up the rightist fringe. Carto has attempted to ride herd on a very difficult and contentious band of rugged individualists, prima donnas, loners, and nut cases with predictably marginal results. Some critics on the right say that Carto's failures have been caused by his autocratic personality, but it's doubtful anyone else could have done better. Far rightists simply do not work well together. As one rightist who must remain nameless put it, the far right "is full of generals and privates with very little in between, because every rising buck sergeant soon sees himself as a potential general and that's when another organization forms or an existing organization splits apart."

\*    \*    \*

From 1953 until 1974 Carto published more-or-less semiannual directories called *"Rightist" Groups, Publications and Some Individuals in the United States (and Some Foreign Countries)* under the imprint of the Alert Americans Association, a letterhead group.[12] What is not generally known about the 3,000-plus listings Carto accumulated is that the majority of them have been basically "one man" organizations— i.e., the sole operation of a single individual, or perhaps what has become known as "two guys and a post office box."

For the past twenty-two years one of the authors (Wilcox) has published a similar directory (and a companion directory on the political left) and can attest that the pattern persists. Much of the alleged proliferation in the radical right is in the form of very small, marginal groups with their xeroxed and mimeographed publications. "National" Ku Klux Klan organizations with six members are not particularly uncommon, and at least three neo-Nazi "parties" consisting of fewer than five individuals are in existence today. When one understands this characteristic of the extreme right, it becomes clearer how remarkable Liberty Lobby has been in its relative success—and how difficult a prospect it remains to keep it, or any other extreme right group, together.[13]

## Notes

1. Frank P. Mintz, *Liberty Lobby and the American Right: Race, Conspiracy and Culture* (Westport, Conn.: Greenwood Press, 1985), 70.

2. *Right* (November 1956): 3–6.

3. "The Right Line," *Right* (May 1956).

4. *San Francisco Chronicle* (June 11, 1960).

5. Joseph Trento and Joseph Spear, "How Nazi Nut Power Has Invaded Capitol Hill," *True* (November 1969): 38.

6. *San Francisco Examiner* (June 18, 1960).

7. Anti-Defamation League of B'nai B'rith, *Extremism on the Right* (New York: Anti-Defamation League, 1983), 64.

8. Kevin Flynn and Gary Gerhardt, *The Silent Brotherhood* (New York: The Free Press, 1989), 85.

9. Liberty Lobby Staff, *Conspiracy Against Freedom* (Washington, D.C.: Liberty Lobby, 1986).

10. *Populist Observer* (April 1991): 8–12.

11. "Liberty Lobby and the Carto Network of Hate," *ADL Facts* (Winter 1982): 6.

12. This series was revived in the early 1980s under the editorship of Steve Goodyear.

13. Laird Wilcox, *Guide to the American Right: Directory and Bibliography* (Olathe, Kan.: Editorial Research Service, 1969–91); Laird Wilcox, *Guide to the American Left: Directory and Bibliography* (Olathe, Kan.: Editorial Research Service, 1970–91).

# 17. **Robert Bolivar DePugh and the Minutemen**

See that old man at the corner where you buy your papers? He may have a silencer-equipped pistol under his coat. That fountain pen in the pocket of the insurance salesman that calls on you might be a cyanide gas gun. What about your milkman? Arsenic works slow but sure. Your automobile mechanic may stay up nights studying booby traps. These patriots are not going to let you take their freedom away from them. They have learned the silent knife, the strangler's cord, the target rifle that hits sparrows at 200 yards. Only their leaders restrain them. Traitors, beware! Even now the crosshairs are on the back of your necks.

Printed on black-bordered letterhead entitled "In Memoriam," this message has been distributed by the Minutemen, an extreme-right para-military organization. Along with other groups such as the Ku Klux Klans, neo-Nazis, and organizations identified with the extreme left such as the Black Panthers, the Minutemen created a climate of fear and apprehension during the 1960s and afterwards.

The disconcerting quotation (originally published in the March 15, 1963, issue of the Minutemen newsletter, *On Target*) became a part of the organization's logo and was printed on three-inch-square stickers under the outline of a rifle's crosshairs and the slogan "Traitors, Beware." It was but one example of the group's talent for attracting attention and sending panic through the ranks of its enemies. No other modern extremist group, except perhaps the Ku Klux Klan, engaged the imagination of its opposition more thoroughly. It was but an example of the genius demonstrated by its leader for generating law enforcement attention and journalistic scrutiny. But like almost everything else the Minutemen did in its roughly ten years of active existence, it was entirely counterproductive.

\* \* \*

The Minutemen organization was founded in 1960 by Robert Bolivar DePugh, then a thirty-seven-year-old chemist from Norborne, Missouri. The story has often been repeated that the impetus for the group developed out of a conversation between DePugh and his friends while on a duck-hunting trip. Supposedly, one hunter remarked jokingly, in reference to world events, that if the Communists ever invaded the United States, outdoor groups like DePugh's hunting party could easily turn into guerrilla bands and fight from the hills. This led to a sober discussion of how important it was that Americans know how to defend themselves. From that point, it was a short distance to the formation of a study group and later a movement organized to become familiar with guerrilla tactics, paramilitary maneuvers in the countryside, and the caching of guns and ammunition. This official explanation of how the Minutemen began was included in *Minutemen: America's Last Line of Defense Against Communism,* published by the group in the early 1960s.

As is so often the case with extremist groups, the real story is much different from the official myth. According to J. Harry Jones, Jr., a *Kansas City Star* reporter who made a detailed study on DePugh and his organization, it was also literature from organizations like the John Birch Society and the House Committee on Un-American Activities that supposedly gave DePugh his rationale.[1] It's questionable whether the duck hunting incident ever occurred as described, but it's also questionable that exposure to any particular literature was responsible, either. To attribute it to literature leaves unexplained why the hundreds of thousands of other individuals who read this same literature also didn't go out and form paramilitary organizations. Always a one-man show with a small following, the Minutemen organization was an extension of Robert Bolivar DePugh's personality. Had there been no Robert Bolivar DePugh, there would have been no Minutemen; he was able to find a few individuals who shared his rather complex delusional system.

There was no relationship whatsoever between DePugh's Minutemen and Minutewomen, USA, a superpatriotic group that peaked in the early 1950s. In 1925 a group of Ku Klux Klansmen formed the Minute Men of America in Denver, Colorado. The group folded in 1926 and was unknown to DePugh. The term "Minutemen" has appeared from time to time over the years but never in connection with DePugh. The head Minuteman was probably inspired by Colonel William Gale (whom he knew well) and Gale's minuscule California Rangers, but in most respects the group was a DePugh original.

The Minutemen organization deserves more than passing interest, even though it was small and lasted only a short time. It illustrates the considerable impact— largely through the media—a single extremist (DePugh) can have, and it demonstrates the enormous extent of government infiltration into extremist organizations. It's also a fascinating study in intrigue, duplicity, and betrayal.

It was Walter Reuther, president of the United Auto Workers, and his brother, Victor, head of the UAW's international affairs section, who were responsible for the intense attention focused on the Minutemen in the early days, well before its extensive legal difficulties. Alarmed at the influence of radical right-wing groups, U.S. Attorney General Robert F. Kennedy asked the two brothers for suggestions on dealing with them. According to Phillip Finch:

> The Reuthers replied on December 19, 1961, with a memorandum that was supposed to have remained confidential, but which somehow was leaked to the press shortly afterward.
> The document is not one of the nobler legacies of the Kennedy administration.

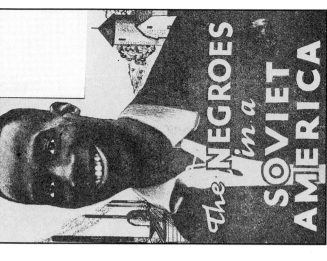

the NEGROES in a SOVIET AMERICA

A 1935 publication of the CPUSA. During the Depression era, Communist party membership grew considerably in the United States (ch. 4).

What is
the
Communist Party
of the
United States
of America?

CPUSA
66
1919 1985

*WE INVITE YOU TO*
**JOIN THE**
**COMMUNIST PARTY!**

Fill out and mail this coupon.

Name

Address

City

State/Zip

**COMMUNIST PARTY, USA**
235 West 23 Street
New York, NY 10011
(212) 989-4994

BE A BETTER FIGHTER
IN THE STRUGGLE FOR:
· PEOPLE BEFORE PROFITS
· PEACE, NOT WAR ·
· EQUALITY, NOT RACISM
· JOBS, NOT UNEMPLOYMENT
· FOR SOCIALISM

A 1985 brochure from the Communist Party USA (CPUSA), which states: "In eliminating private profit, socialism will end the cause of national and racial oppression of the Black, Chicano, Puerto Rican, Native American Indian, Asian Pacific and all other specially oppressed and foreign born peoples."

THE BLACK PANTHER    WEDNESDAY, JANUARY 15, 1969    PAGE

HUEY NEWTON
MINISTER OF DEFENSE
BLACK PANTHER PARTY

Party cofounder Huey Newton.

Front page of *The Black Panther*, the weekly tabloid of the Black Panther party (ch. 6).

# The Crusader

## MONTHLY NEWSLETTER

**ROBERT F. WILLIAMS, Publisher —IN EXILE—**

**VOL. 6 — No. 1**      **JULY - AUGUST 1964**

### IMPARTIAL LEADERS OF A PARTISAN STRUGGLE

THE STRUGGLE of our people in the social jungle of racist America is more than just a struggle for civil rights. It is a

### Sundown for Martin Luther King

struggle for survival. The white racists of America are savage beasts displaying no more capacity for human traits towards black people than the very lowest of jungle beasts. The jungle beast selects its prey of the basis of substance or the law of survival. The racist American selects his prey on the basis of blood or pigmentation. He kills, maims, terrorizes an dehumanizes black humanity for the gratification of his sadistical cravings.

Front page of *The Crusader*, published by the Revolutionary Action Movement. Founder Robert F. Williams promotes a black nationalist movement and urges readers to commit violent revolutionary acts to further the cause (ch. 10).

# Workers, unite!

# MAY 1st

## International working class day

Fight Reagan and the Contragate criminals!

Support the revolutions of the poor in Central America!

Defend the immigrant workers!

Beat back racism from Howard Beach to South Africa!

Say NO! to layoffs and concessions!

Rally to the Marxist-Leninist Party,
Party of class struggle and socialism!

May Day Events

RCP

# REVOLUTIONARY WORKER

Voice of the
Revolutionary Communist Party, USA

No. 584    (Vol. 12, No. 32)    December 9, 1990    Editions in English and Spanish published weekly    $1.00

## Stop the U.S. War Machine, No Matter What It Takes!

# U.N. Green Light for Gulf War

*Left:* Front page of the *Revolutionary Worker*, published by the Maoist Revolutionary Communist party. This group has consistently idealized The People's Republic of China (ch.11). *Right:* An advertisement for May Day celebrations sponsored by the Marxist-Leninist Party, USA, a long-time supporter of Enver Hoxha's dictatorship in Albania.

## Christian Crusade Weekly

AN INTERNATIONAL CHRISTIAN NEWSPAPER

Vol. 14—No. 35     TULSA, OKLAHOMA 74102     July 21, 1974—$2.00 per year

# Grade School Boys and Girls Are Exposed to Sex Education

By Dr. Billy James Hargis
Founder-Director, Christian Crusade

### Publishing *Christian Crusade Weekly*

**The Most Important Mission**

We will write each one to over a quarter million readers in the next 30 days, asking each one to renew his subscription to the *Christian Crusade Weekly*. In addition, we are asking each subscriber to send the name of local Christian and conservative leaders who need to be alerted to the facts contained in this important newspaper.

It is Dr. Hargis' desire to increase the circulation of the *Christian Crusade Weekly* by half a million in the next 90 days. He has asked the cooperation of every reader in order to make this most necessary dream become a reality.

Dr. Hargis said today: "I have

The Department of Health, Education and Welfare has reopened the sex education issue by an incredible bureaucratic ruling — accompanied by the threat of reprisals if it is not complied with.

As a father of school-age children, and a minister of the gospel, I intend to protest this latest ruling and I urge all of the readers of *Christian Crusade Weekly* to voice their concern as well — to the right people, that is, to local school boards and to their representatives in the U.S. Congress.

According to the Associated Press of June 19, HEW announced that *grade school boys and girls will be required to attend sex education classes together.* Notice, it's our children in

the elementary grades whose lives are being tampered with.

The bureaucratic regulations, the AP story said, are in compliance with a two-year-old law supposedly aimed at eliminating sex discrimination in the schools. What a lot of destructive nonsense is being foisted upon our people (and now our children) in the name of sexual equality.

The HEW regulations will not take effect until Oct. 15, being held in the meantime "open to public comment." And when a HEW spokesman admit there are "some understandable concerns," he expresses the understatement of the year.

After Oct. 15, the ruling goes to the

— See Education, page 2

---

*Left:* The Reverend Billy James Hargis, founder-director of Christian Crusade, in 1976. *Inset:* Rev. Hargis delivering a radio sermon. *Right:* Front page of Hargis's newspaper.

# Muhammad  Speaks

Dedicated to Freedom, Justice and Equality for the so - called Negro. The Earth Belongs to Allah.

Vol. 10-No.3 - 2 Sections 48 Pages     OCTOBER 2, 1970     20c—OUTSIDE ILLINOIS—25c

**MUHAMMAD ON RADIO IN CHICAGO EVERY SUNDAY, WJOB 1230 kc, 5:30 P.M. AND WEAW - 1330 (AM), 4:15 P.M. TO 4:45 P.M.**

# WARNING!

# A message to the believers

### by Minister Louis Farrakhan

The NATION OF ISLAM is under attack by the enemies of Allah (God) from within and without.

From 1977 to 1983, problems were limited and was easily solved, even with the new laborers' limited experience in handling people and problems. However, in August of 1983, during the 20th anniversary of the March on Washington, we came to the attention of the media and general white public.

Since 1984 and our emergence on the national and international scene with the Rev. Jesse Jackson campaign, it has been and is the wicked intent of the United States Government and certain groups within the United States to destroy the Nation of Islam, with a particular focus on its leadership.

In 1957, just prior to the Nation of Islam's coming to national attention, the Honorable Elijah Muhammad wrote in an article which appeared in the *Pittsburg Courier*, that "My followers are honeycombed with rotten characters," such as stool pigeons and agents of the government, whose aim it was to destroy the Nation from within by sifting the Believers for their weaknesses and then using their weaknesses to further the ultimate aim of the government which was to destroy the leadership and the person of the Honorable Elijah Muhammad.

Excerpts from the newspaper of the Nation of Islam, a group widely known as the Black Muslims (ch.22).

National Socialist Party of America leader Harold Covington (ch. 23).

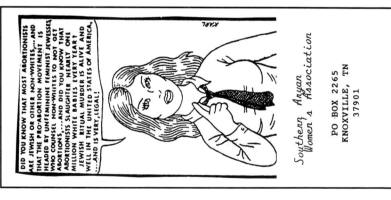

Typical publications of the Ku Klux Klan (ch. 25).

It is, in fact, a suggested agenda for using presidential influence to destroy nettlesome political opponents, and is disturbingly similar in approach to the "enemies list" that would be drafted in the Nixon White House a decade later.

It suggests, among other tactics, the revocation of tax-exempt status for some right-wing groups; IRS scrutiny of right-wingers' tax returns and of contributions by businesses to the offending organizations; use of the Federal Communications Commission to discourage the free time being given to right-wing speakers; and FBI infiltration of right-wing groups.[2]

The "Reuther Memorandum," as it became known, targeted groups and individuals much less extreme than the Minutemen, including Billy James Hargis, Fred Schwarz and his Christian Anti-Communism Crusade, the John Birch Society, and the "Life Line" radio programs of H. L. Hunt. In the second half of the memo, the Reuthers made several suggestions for action against the far right, including "steps to end the Minutemen." This "official" recognition of his organization was evidence to DePugh that he had become a very important figure on the American scene.

\* \* \*

According to Minutemen lore, the basic unit of the organization is the squad. The individual squads, composed of between five and twenty-five members, were to have no knowledge of each other. Only the state commanders knew who the squad leaders were and no records were to be kept of the individual members. The national organization had no control over the squads, each one of which was to operate as a little army. The only real function of the national organization was to recruit members through the distribution of literature and to generate publicity for the organization. The rationale behind all of this decentralization and secrecy was to preclude "neutralization" in the event of a communist takeover. Theoretically, only a handful of members would be known to intelligence agencies, such as the FBI, and any move against the organization would be of very limited effectiveness.

In reality, most Minutemen members were quickly known to authorities, often within days of their recruitment. The primary reason for this was their own indiscretion coupled with government infiltration and neutralization. The kind of individual attracted to such a marginal enterprise was often the typical compulsive extremist who had been active in other groups ranging from the John Birch Society—which was of little interest to the FBI—to the Ku Klux Klan and the American Nazi party—which the FBI had heavily infiltrated and monitored.

Whenever individual Minutemen were in trouble with the authorities, which was fairly often, they usually tried to buy their way out by telling everything they knew. Inasmuch as the organization affected the image of a mixture of James Bond, green beret, and western sheriff, it tended to attract individuals profoundly moved by authority figures. "Flip a badge on these guys and you can't shut them up. What most of them want to be is a policeman," one federal agent said. A surprising number of former Minutemen, when questioned about their involvement, advanced the notion that they were merely "investigating" the group. There were also professional informants in the organization, including some of DePugh's closest associates. A former member once described the organization as "the damnedest collection of blabbermouths, paranoids, ding-a-lings and fuckups you have ever seen."[3] Finally, DePugh and his group were followed closely by several journalists, who delighted in digging up anything they could find. DePugh, however, described the group as

> an organization of 100,000 men and women with one thing in common—they are loyal American citizens who are tired of being pushed around by the communists and want to do something to stem the tide of their advance.[4]

On other occasions DePugh gave figures ranging from 25,000 to 46,000. In 1964 he said he believed a "membership close to 1,000,000 is possible in the near future." On the other hand, DePugh admitted at that time that he regularly sent out only 2,000 copies of *On Target,* the biweekly newsletter. He also claimed that the Minutemen had a membership of 3,500 in California, New York, Michigan, and Pennsylvania.[5] Clearly, the prospect of a large underground army was a haunting one and no one knew this more than DePugh himself. Psychologically speaking, the inflated figures represented a kind of shield for DePugh. In his mind, he was a very important patriotic man surrounded and protected by an immense secret army.

All of these figures, however, are highly suspect. According to the Anti-Defamation League of B'nai B'rith:

> At first DePugh claimed to have 25,000 members in the organization, with a national goal of 1,000,000 armed men. Subsequent investigations found little substance to De-Pugh's claim, and DePugh himself later admitted that in 1961 there were fewer than 600 members. Law enforcement officials from several states reported during the mid 1960s a total of only a few hundred active Minutemen. In addition, the FBI estimated the entire national membership of the Minutemen in early 1968 at less than 500.[6]

Further comment on the Minutemen numbers was given by FBI Director J. Edgar Hoover in his testimony before Congress in 1965:

> DePugh is the only known leader of the group. He is, therefore, its sole spokesman and some of the things he says are, indeed, hard to believe. While he has placed the membership of the Minutemen at "more than 25,000," there is little real evidence that the Minutemen are anything more than essentially a paper organization, with just enough followers over the country so they can occasionally attract a headline, usually because of their preoccupation with violence, or weapons of war. We have penetrated this organization and our sources are keeping us advised of developments.[7]

According to J. Harry Jones, Jr., by February 1968 Hoover had stated that "recent information indicates there are less than fifty persons upon whom Minutemen leaders can call for overt action."[8]

The actual number of genuine, active, committed Minutemen was in the neighborhood of two hundred, with a group of perhaps four hundred more on the periphery at the organization's peak, most of whom only contributed money and received literature. Altogether perhaps as many as a thousand individuals had been "members" of the organization at one time or another, many for only a few years. Some members were drummed out by DePugh on "security" grounds. Several former Minutemen remain active in extreme right groups today.

An early disinformation effort by DePugh concerned the organizational structure of the Minutemen. Claiming it was governed by a ten-member "Council," DePugh even supplied occupations for each of the council members (fireman, electrical engineer, etc.). In point of fact, a council existed on paper only, although some individuals were told they were "members." In 1966, however, DePugh said he had testified before a federal grand jury that the council didn't even exist, which confirmed the suspicions of various DePugh watchers. Harry Jones says:

> The numerous inconsistencies noted . . . in the birth and infancy of the Minutemen and in the reality or fiction of the Minutemen's council leadership may suggest that DePugh is none too reliable as a source of information about his organization.[9]

Another myth about the Minutemen, and other extremist groups for that matter, is that they are just confidence games to raise money. This may happen, but in our experience not very often. In the case of the Minutemen, the out-of-pocket cost to DePugh of his various activities almost certainly exceeded any funds coming in, not to mention the value of the time taken away from a relatively profitable business and devoted to his numerous right-wing projects. J. Harry Jones has noted, "Most con men do not take the risks he has."[10]

\* \* \*

Having read quite a bit of Lenin, Mao Tse-tung and other revolutionary leaders, DePugh had an approach to organization that seemed to owe more than a little to Leninist doctrine. According to Jones, when confronted with the apparent counterproductivity of some of his actions DePugh replied, "The purpose is to provoke the government into taking harsh and repressive measures against the general population so people will be turned against the government"—an incredible assertion from the leader of a supposedly "ultraconservative" group.[11]

The organization had its internal problems early on. In 1962 Richard Lauchli, one of DePugh's first disciples, left the Minutemen to clone his own group— the Counter-Insurgency Council—because he regarded DePugh as erratic. Lauchli had his own run-ins with the law, however. According to George Thayer:

> Lauchli has been arrested a number of times on violations of firearms laws. He was fined $100 in 1957 for possessing firearms unlawfully transferred or made, and he was fined $500 in 1960 for stealing twenty-three bazookas.[12]

It didn't end there. In 1964 Lauchli was indicted on charges of making and transporting illegal firearms after he tried to sell some guns to a federal agent who posed as an anti-Castro Cuban general. He was convicted of making and transporting illegal firearms, conspiracy, and interstate transportation of firearms by a convicted felon. Two months out of prison he was arrested again when federal agents raided his home and found a thousand Thompson submachine guns and a large quantity of ammunition.

DePugh's knack for making hair-raising statements was evident in several news stories that appeared about the Minutemen in the early 1960s. Projecting a scenario for the future, in April 1963 DePugh told a newspaper editor:

> There may be a long period of assassination and counter assassination, of terror and counter terror. In this I feel we have one big edge because we feel that our knowledge of the left wing is far greater than their knowledge of the right wing, so far as identities are concerned.
>
> If something happened to spark this thing off—if for example it should be known that I was killed by a Communist, our organization would take immediate reprisal against the other side and, in turn, they would take reprisal against the ones of us that they know and it could spread like wildfire to the point where there would be mass murder on both sides.[13]

Following the defeat of Senator Barry Goldwater in the 1964 presidential election, the Minutemen were quoted as saying:

> The time is past when the American people might have saved themselves by traditional political processes. The hopes of millions of Americans that the Communist tide could be stopped with ballots instead of bullets have turned to dust.[14]

In an article appearing in the *San Francisco Chronicle* in November 1964, J. Harry Jones said of DePugh:

> He . . . acknowledges that by the very nature of the Minutemen—with no tight chain of command, little discipline, strict secretiveness even within the organization—few safeguards have been provided to prevent some mentally unstable follower from using Minutemen gospel as a "patriotic" justification for just about any act.[15]

Alarm over the Minutemen and similar groups grew to such an extent that bona fide sportsmen's groups were beginning to feel some heat from the fallout. In September 1965, a spokesperson for the National Rifle Association wrote:

> By lies and insinuations, coupled with exaggerated presentations of minor incidents involving firearms, the American people have been led to believe that private armies are being formed by "fanatics" and "extremists." It is alleged that these people are being supplied with guns and ammunition by the U.S. Government through the director of civilian marksmanship. This is not true.[16]

In 1966 DePugh drafted what was probably his most successful publication, *Blueprint For Victory,* a kind of superpatriotic manual on how to fight communism. It consisted of a collection of articles from *On Target,* various Minutemen pamphlets, and some of DePugh's own speeches. During the weekend of July Fourth, DePugh launched his Patriotic party, which was to be the political arm of the Minutemen. Over the years, tens of thousands of copies of *Blueprint For Victory* have been distributed. It and a later publication, *Can You Survive?,* are still sold by far-right book dealers today.

The Patriotic party lasted a few years. In 1967, a year after it was formed, DePugh claimed a membership of three thousand. A party convention held at the Town House Motor Inn in Kansas City, Kansas, again over the Fourth of July weekend brought only 150 members out of six hundred expected. Speakers included far-right radio commentator Richard Cotten; Myron Fagan, who claimed to monitor "reds" in the film industry; and the Reverend Kenneth Goff, a long-time Jew-hater and leader of the small, extreme right Soldiers of the Cross organization, often cited as a Minutemen "affiliate."

\*     \*     \*

In 1966 DePugh was indicted for possession of bombs (a felony) and contributing to the delinquency of a minor, a misdemeanor. The bomb possession charge was eventually dismissed a year and a half later, but not before DePugh was also indicted (and later convicted) for possession of firearms while under indictment for bomb possession. On March 9, 1967, a judge ruled that the bomb possession indictment was "fatally defective." The misdemeanor charge was dismissed when a review of the case showed that it would also have probably resulted in acquittal.

In the meantime, however, a major issue had surfaced. The grand jury that had indicted DePugh on the above charges also issued a subpoena demanding Minutemen records, including a list of *On Target* subscribers and contributors between 1961 and 1965. DePugh refused, and with the quiet help of the Kansas City chapter of the American Civil Liberties Union, it was determined that a 1958 U.S. Supreme Court case, which upheld the refusal of the NAACP to hand over its membership records to state officials, applied to the Minutemen as well. The court ruled that such a request was intended to restrain the NAACP from exercising its right of freedom of association. Once again the principle demonstrated that in providing for the civil liberties of an unpopular minority in one case, you provide for civil liberties in all cases. Nevertheless, it was great irony that a case protecting the NAACP should protect the Minutemen as well.

In November 1966, Robert DePugh, Wally Peyson, and Troy Houghton were convicted in federal court on firearms charges. All three defendants were charged in the first count, accusing them of conspiracy to violate the National Firearms Act by "transferring, making, receiving, and possessing" automatic weapons and silencers. Only DePugh and Peyson were charged in the two other counts, which accused them of illegally possessing a machine gun, failing to pay the $200 tax required under the act, and having possessed two additional machine guns and a machine pistol. The government's star witnesses included former Minutemen who were in legal jeopardy themselves: Jerry Milton Brooks (who later repudiated his testimony) and James Moore, an undercover BATF agent. The three defendants were subsequently convicted and on January 17, 1967, DePugh, Houghton, and Peyson were sentenced to four, three, and two years in prison respectively. The convictions were appealed, with two counts being dismissed and the third remanded for retrial.[17]

"I have been indicted twelve times," DePugh stated while awaiting trial in an Albuquerque jail cell in early 1970. "Out of these twelve indictments, the Government has managed to get two convictions. They have dropped the other charges." This statement was made after DePugh and his top aide, Walter Peyson, were arrested by the FBI in July 1969, when agents raided a house near the little town of Truth or Consequences, New Mexico. Along with DePugh and Peyson, the FBI found a massive arms cache that included silencers, homemade bombs, grenades, and various types of rifles and handguns.

DePugh was sentenced to one year in prison in Missouri for transporting a firearm across a state line while under indictment on another charge. Later he was convicted on a three-count firearms charge (mentioned above), which was appealed. During this period of appeal, a federal warrant was issued on February 20, 1968, in Seattle for DePugh and Peyson charging them with conspiracy to commit bank robbery in Washington, a charge that was also eventually dropped. Shortly before the warrant was issued, DePugh and Peyson disappeared to spend most of the next year and a half as federal fugitives. "It was as if two Catholics held up a filling station and they indicted the Pope. That's how far removed I was," DePugh said in 1979.[18]

According to sympathizers, DePugh and his family were desperately trying to make bond, but each time it seemed they would be able to raise the required funds, the amount was increased. The Minutemen claim this was the principle reason for DePugh's flight.

> The excessive bond set by the court, difficulty in obtaining bond because of "mysterious" interferences discouraging bondsmen and a fear for his personal safety caused Mr. DePugh to go "underground" or into "self-imposed exile."[19]

DePugh himself explained it to Phillip Finch:

> I was indicted on one charge after another—some of them totally without foundation, tentative hearsay evidence. But every time I was indicted I had to go to the bank, put up a bigger and bigger share of my company, money to make bond. When I finally went into hiding, I jumped bond on $480,000. That was money that went down the drain, and I never saw another dime of it.[20]

For seventeen months DePugh and Peyson eluded the FBI, prompting a massive manhunt that consumed thousands of hours and hundreds of thousands of dollars. After they were captured in July 1969, DePugh was held in Albuquerque, while Peyson was sent to the federal correctional institution at Marion, Illinois, a maximum-security facility. On February 20, 1970, DePugh stood before the bench in a Kansas City federal court and received a sentence of four years in prison for jumping bond. DePugh claimed he was not guilty, that he had not received notice of the trial and did not know the date on which it was to be held.

On the following morning, DePugh was given an opportunity to make a statement. He began by reviewing his own record: "I am forty-six years old. For the first forty-one years of my life I was a completely law-abiding citizen." He had always worked hard for others, he claimed, and had been fair to those who had worked for him. DePugh indicated that he had received honorary memberships in scientific societies, and that many new medical products had resulted from his work as a research chemist. He had always lived by a rigid code of personal conduct, so strict that it did not permit him to gossip, use profanity, drink, or smoke. But during the past five years, he had been repeatedly accused of crimes—crimes, he emphasized, that he had not committed. This forced him to marshall his limited resources time after time to defend himself against the awesome power of the state and federal governments. He continued:

> Now, your honor, for the other side of the coin. I stand before the court tried and found guilty. At this point it is no doubt traditional for the prisoner to offer some expression of repentance, but in all sincerity I cannot do so. To make matters worse, I cannot, in good conscience, give the court the slightest assurance that I will ever change my ways. . . . I would appreciate justice. But if I am not given justice, then I will accept injustice, and I will fashion even that into a weapon to continue the fight for principle, for pride, for honor. I will never give that up.[21]

Seven months later DePugh was again found guilty in a federal court, this time on nine counts of violating federal firearms regulations. On October 10, 1970, he was sentenced in Albuquerque to ten years in federal prison. This time the prison gates had slammed shut with a vengeance on Robert DePugh.

\*     \*     \*

While serving his one-year term in Leavenworth Penitentiary, DePugh was allowed to mingle with the general prison population. He reported, "There is a right philosophy—an ultra-right philosophy, if you prefer—that is very easily accepted by the convict population." He had been surprised, he said, at the intellectual abilities and character of many prisoners:

> I would say there are far more political prisoners in this country than the people of the United States realize. These political prisoners are perhaps far left as well as far right, and always the government has some excuse for convicting them. The government doesn't say you are a political prisoner. They say you are a bank robber. . . . From the past history of political prisoners, it is pretty obvious that the real reason the government wants to keep them confined is not because of their character but because of their political ideologies.[22]

While in prison DePugh wrote a surprising book, *Behind the Iron Mask,* in which he advocated measures for liberal prison reform. He also became a strong advocate of rehabilitation—somewhat out of character for a hide-bound right-winger. An example of his approach describes a prisoner's preparations for a new life:

> The formation of a new sense of personal identity involves more than just the way the prisoner sees himself. A real and permanent change involves the formation of new social bonds. While he is still in prison, it may be desirable to help the prisoner's family move to another city entirely. Thus, on his release, the prisoner need not return to the same old friends and neighborhood where all his social bonds involve a criminal's sense of personal identity.[23]

From sounding like a liberal social worker DePugh shifts to his usual social Darwinism in other essays in *Behind the Iron Mask,* and from there to a critique of law enforcement practices that would do credit to an ACLU attorney. This complex book by a complex and contradictory man is illustrated by his own line drawings, which have a vague Rockwell Kent quality about them. There is far more to DePugh than originally meets the eye. He is no ordinary right-wing nut case.

*    *    *

In the winter 1970 issue, the extreme right *American Mercury* magazine included another prison message from the incarcerated Minutemen leader that revealed a new development in his political outlook:

> Sometimes we refer to ourselves as the "right-wing." At other times we call ourselves anti-communists, or conservatives, or nationalists, or patriots. We may laughingly label ourselves "extremists" or "racists." We have let our enemies give us these names and in so doing we have allowed them to describe our philosophical-political identity.

Was it any wonder, he asked, that rightists were "divided and splintered, quarreling among ourselves. How can we have a unified philosophy when we don't even know who we are?" What was needed, DePugh declared, was a unified philosophical foundation. He felt that several good books had approached the problem, among them John Stormer's *None Dare Call It Treason,* John Beatty's *Iron Curtain Over America,* Barry Goldwater's *Conscience of a Conservative,* and *The Blue Book of the John Birch Society.* But these books still missed the mark, he felt. More to his liking was Francis Parker Yockey's *Imperium,* which he called "a remarkable achievement" to be rated almost as high as the *Critique of Pure Reason,* by Immanuel Kant. But it, too, contained certain defects. What was needed, according to DePugh, was a work outlining a strong philosophical foundation for the "beliefs, ideals and objectives" of rightists.

DePugh had actually started such a work during his period "underground," he said, only to have the FBI seize the half-finished manuscript when he was arrested. He had started again, realizing the task—if it would be completed at all—might require years. "But sooner or later it must come, if not from me then from someone else. . . . Only then will 'we' be welded together in a solid defense as they are welded together to plot their evil against us." This new approach represented a deviation from his earlier Birch-like philosophy, which did not include open anti-Semitism.

There were indications that the Minutemen organization was badly divided and that others had attempted to take over the leadership position. A leaflet purporting to be a Minutemen *Bulletin* was distributed early in 1971 from Elgin, Illinois. The one-page document said:

> The headquarters staff at Norborne have been stealing defense funds for some time and spending this money on luxury items for their own personal use. Also some of this money has been used for . . . drugs which are used quite heavily by persons on the staff. . . . Bob DePugh is no longer able to run the organization, and his attempts to do so from jail are tearing us apart. . . . Patriots . . . have been sold out by the pimps and dupes who now control the operations at Norborne.[24]

Because of these conditions, the writer of the *Bulletin* declared, the Norborne office would no longer be recognized as the national headquarters of the organization and the people working there would no longer be recognized as members. Further, the continental United States had been divided into ten regions, and coordinators for these regions were being appointed. Members were urged to write to a box number in Brentwood, Maryland, and were warned not to put a return address on the outside of the letter.

The Brentwood post office box belonged to a J. C. Stephens, alias George Van Ness, who had emerged as an eastern spokesman attempting to reorganize the Minutemen, according to a *Washington Post* news item of December 22, 1970. Another eastern group, the promoters of *Statecraft,* also seemed to hold similar ideas about the leaderless Minutemen. Meanwhile, flyers prepared under the aegis of Minutemen in San Diego had been distributed around the country. Adding to the confusion, DePugh's old publication, *On Target,* was still being published in late 1970 by a group calling itself the Minutemen–Patriotic Party–Committee of Correspondence.

Quite probably two different things were occurring. Splinters from the foundering Minutemen, which was highly decentralized to begin with, were attempting to keep the organization's mystique alive. Moreover, other right extremists no doubt saw an opening to create a "new" Minutemen. At the same time the FBI was utilizing its Counterintelligence Program (COINTELPRO) to destabilize what was left of the group. According to DePugh, the bulletin published in Illinois was in fact published by the FBI. This would be consistent with other FBI COINTELPRO activities against other left and right extremist groups. This view is also supported by Phillip Finch, who obtained a large volume of documents related to FBI disruption and destabilization of right-wing organizations. Discussing the FBI's COINTELPRO activities against the far right, Finch notes its actions against the Minutemen:

> Some were petty disruptions—like mailing 850 copies of a faked letter, apparently from the national office of the Minutemen, requesting that members of the group withhold their dues and contributions because of a security leak.[25]

The Minutemen, in fact, were among the most thoroughly infiltrated of all domestic far right groups. According to Eric Norden, in his long essay on the paramilitary right appearing in the June 1969 issue of *Playboy* magazine, virtually all of the major Minutemen cases were cracked with the assistance of government infiltrators and informants.

One of these informants was a nightmare named Roy Frankhauser, a professional government infiltrator whose alliance with DePugh began in the early 1960s, shortly after the organization was formed. Frankhauser was well-known for having taken the Fifth Amendment thirty-three times when questioned about his Ku Klux Klan involvement by the House Un-American Activities Committee in 1965. Unaware of Frankhauser's role, Norden interviewed him extensively for his article. Frankhauser, whom DePugh had made a regional coordinator, portrayed the Minutemen to Norden as a neo-Nazi organization to be feared and reckoned with:

> Hitler had the Jews; we've got the niggers. We have to put our main stress on the nigger question, of course, because that's what preoccupies the masses—but we're not forgetting the Jew. If the Jews knew what was coming—and believe me, it's coming as surely as the dawn—they'd realize that what's going to happen in America will make Nazi Germany look like a Sunday-school picnic. We'll build better gas chambers, and more of them, and this time there won't be any refugees.[26]

Norden notes that Frankhauser, having made this statement, "paused and seemed to brood for a few seconds," and then continued:

> Of course, there are some good Jews, you know, Jews like Dan Burros, who was a friend of mine. Yeah, print that some of my best friends are Jews. Dan Burros was one of the most patriotic, dedicated Americans you'll ever meet in your life.

Norden commented:

> Frankhauser fell silent. Burros was a fanatic American Nazi who served as [George Lincoln] Rockwell's [American Nazi party] lieutenant for years, then resigned in 1962 to edit a magazine called *Kill!*[27] and finally became a Klan leader. He had rushed into Frankhauser's house in October 1965 brandishing an issue of the *New York Times* that exposed his Jewish ancestry, snatched a loaded pistol from the wall and blew his brains out.[28]

What Norden did not say is that some conspiracy buffs believe that Frankhauser may have had more than a casual involvement in the killing, although no determination of that fact was ever made and the death was ruled a suicide. Another theory, also not confirmed, is that Frankhauser may have encouraged Burros's suicide inasmuch as his cover had been blown. Burros died from three bullet wounds, unusual in a bona fide suicide. DePugh, who examined the gun, said it was unlikely that Burros killed himself. Other Frankhauser associates have ventured related opinions. What is also possible is that in 1965 Frankhauser was working as a government informant and that Dan Burros was too, perhaps reporting to Frankhauser. At the time of this writing Frankhauser still resides in the Reading, Pennsylvania, house where the death occurred; blood stains are still imbedded in the ceiling.[29]

But was Frankhauser a government informant and agent provocateur so early in his career? Frankhauser denies it, but his own U.S. Army records suggest otherwise. During an extensive interview under oath that took place during the period July 13 to 18, 1957, Army records reveal the following:

> (FRANKHAUSER) made a decision to infiltrate organizations such as the Neo-Nazi Party, the Communist Party, and the Ku Klux Klan, to determine their motives, identify the leaders, and report this information to the proper intelligence agency of the United States Government if their aims were ascertained to be inimical to the interest of the United States. FRANKHAUSER advised he had created a cover story which included causing people to think he was a true Communist or Nazi and the creation of an organization which was to be a large, well-organized unit, but which was composed of only one man—FRANKHAUSER. FRANKHAUSER'S aim at Fort Bragg was to get the Klans of the North together with the Klans of the South to give the United States government the opportunity to destroy these organizations.[30]

During the 1960s, Minutemen were involved in three major terrorist acts in which Frankhauser was the possible informant, directly or indirectly, who tipped off the FBI. According to Norden:

> In the predawn hours of October 30, 1966, 19 heavily armed Minutemen, divided into three bands, were intercepted by staked-out police (tipped off by an FBI informant) as they zeroed in on left-wing camps in a three-state area. Targets of the coordinated forays were Camp Webatuck at Wingdale, New York, where fire bombs with detonators had already been set in place; Camp Midvale in New Jersey; and a pacifist community at Voluntown, Connecticut, established by the New England Committee for Nonviolent Action.[31]
>
> In June 1967, five New York City Minutemen organized an assassination attempt against Herbert Aptheker, director of the American Institute of Marxist Studies and a member of the U.S. Communist Party, whose Brooklyn headquarters had already been the target of an abortive Minuteman fire-bombing. . . . The Minuteman plotters were swiftly apprehended.[32]

In 1968 six Minutemen attempted a second attack on the pacifist encampment in Voluntown. According to Norden:

Once again, FBI infiltrators in their ranks had tipped off local authorities—but this time the warning came too late. . . . The Minutemen opened fire and a brief gun battle ensued before they threw down their weapons and surrendered. Six people were shot in the melee—one state trooper, four raiders and one of the women residents, who was wounded in the hip when a trooper's shotgun discharged as he sidestepped a Minuteman's bayonet thrust.[33]

In 1973, after DePugh was released from prison, Frankhauser became head of Minutemen intelligence. An article in the *Philadelphia Inquirer* describes Frankhauser's "discovery" of a piece of fake dog feces with a hidden listening device embedded in it. The article, by John Hilferty, begins:

A few weeks ago a member of the ultra-right Minutemen was mowing the lawn of the organization's training camp hidden in the woods of the Blue Mountains in Schuykill County.

With a clang, the blade struck what appeared to be the leavings of a dog. But why the clang?

Close examination showed that what appeared to be the work of a dog was actually a man-made replica. Inside the four-inch object was a tiny electronic listening device.

Two more similar devices were found on the grounds, each containing three tiny batteries, a small microphone, and a small antenna. The transmitters had a range of up to six miles and a life of three months. Hilferty continued:

Last week in his home in Reading, national Minuteman Intelligence chief Roy Frankhauser acknowledged that the three devices were found at the Schuykill County camp but refused to comment or speculate on their origin.

"I don't know who put them there," said Frankhauser, 32, a widely-known extremist who also doubles as Grand Kockard, or second in command of the Pennsylvania Ku Klux Klan.

However, a source close to Frankhauser said the belief among Minutemen is that the devices were planted by either the FBI or the U.S. Treasury Department's Bureau of Alcohol, Tobacco and Firearms (ATF), which has conducted at least two futile searches for arms and ammunition at the deeply wooded camp.

A search warrant issued on September 9, 1970, on the Schuykill County Minuteman location revealed an unsuccessful raid by the ATF to find material for making hand grenades.[34]

In fact, Frankhauser was instrumental in placing the listening devices on the property himself, in cooperation with the Alcohol, Firearms and Tobacco office in Reading, Pennsylvania.

*    *    *

During October 1973 DePugh was a featured speaker at Liberty Lobby's annual Board of Policy meeting in Kansas City, Missouri. He had been released from prison six months earlier. Frankhauser, as security director, was his constant companion and lived with the DePugh family in Norborne for several weeks—all the time working for the ATF as an undercover informant.

Interestingly, Frankhauser and DePugh were both discharged from military service for somewhat similar psychiatric problems—problems that have a bearing on their extremist political tendencies.

J. Harry Jones confirmed that during DePugh's 1966 arraignment the government made a motion to have him examined by a psychiatrist to determine whether he was mentally able to stand trial:

> The government said he had been discharged on August 31, 1944, for "medical" reasons after a board of medical examiners had concluded he was unfit for military service because he suffered from "psychoneurosis, mixed type, severe, manifested by anxiety and depressive features and schizoid personality."
>
> "Soldier is unable to perform duty due to anxiety, nervousness and mental depression," the report said. "This condition is chronic and for three years has been attended with vague hallucinations and mild ideas of reference."[35]

According to Jones, a more detailed report said, "There is a paranoid trend in his thinking." DePugh's response to this report was to state that the examination in question had only lasted ten minutes and was routine for anyone discharged for medical reasons. Judge Elmo B. Hunter found that DePugh was competent to stand trial in spite of these findings.

Roy Frankhauser's background is much more convoluted. According to U.S. Army documents released under the Freedom of Information Act in 1988, Frankhauser was enmeshed in deep personal problems long before he entered the army. The victim of a broken home and an alcoholic mother, and regarded by school officials and various employers as emotionally unstable and unreliable, he enlisted in the U.S. Army on November 6, 1956. Long a collector of Nazi memorabilia and a Ku Klux Klan sympathizer even as a young man, he was engaged in a number of half-baked plots that immediately brought him to the attention of army authorities.

Military reports specified that Frankhauser joined the army and volunteered for airborne duty in order to be assigned to Germany. He developed a scheme to have himself declared officially dead so he could leave the army and join the neo-Nazi movement, hoping to rise to a position of prominence. On July 2, 1957, Frankhauser stated that he planned to desert the U.S. Army and join the revolutionary forces in Cuba. In fact, he went AWOL and arrived in Miami, Florida, on July 5, 1957, to do precisely that. He was taken into custody shortly thereafter and returned to his military unit.[36] Army records reflect that Frankhauser was discharged on November 18, 1957, under the provisions of AR-635-209 (unfit for military service).[37]

Frankhauser's rather incredible role as a government informant is well-documented. It first came to light in July 1975 when the *Washington Star* reported on his role in an undercover operation in Canada authorized by the top-secret National Security Council.[38] Frankhauser was assigned to infiltrate the "Black

September" terrorist organization. The "CBS Evening News" of July 28, 1975, did a feature on Frankhauser during which announcer Fred Graham noted that:

> Sworn testimony by federal agents [maintains] that Frankhauser has carried out a series of undercover missions for the government, including one approved by the National Security Council in the White House.
>
> One government source said Frankhauser had an uncanny ability to penetrate both right- and left-wing groups, that he could still help convict those who supplied the explosives that blew up school buses in Pontiac, Michigan, in 1971.

Frankhauser eventually ran afoul of his ATF superiors by going too far with his entrapment schemes and not clearing them with the ATF beforehand. This brought about his eventual indictment on February 28, 1974, on charges of stealing explosives, at which time he used his relationship with the agency as a defense. He was eventually convicted and sentenced to a period of probation, after which the ATF had a way of enforcing his cooperation and curbing his erratic behavior (or so it thought). An FBI teletype dated June 17, 1974, revealed:

> Frankhauser has proposed through his attorney that if allowed to plead guilty and receive probation on current bombing charges he will introduce federal agents to individuals who have approached him regarding his activities.[39]

Frankhauser's ATF "handler," Edward N. Slamon, had written several internal memos describing Frankhauser as "an excellent infiltrator and confidential informant," according to the *Washington Star*. The article described other undercover activities in which Frankhauser participated:

> Frankhauser spied—on behalf of government prosecutors—on Robert Miles, a Ku Klux Klansman and fundamentalist preacher who was convicted of bombing school buses to prevent school integration in Pontiac, Michigan, four years ago.[40]

Miles had been an associate of DePugh, who had regular correspondence and other contacts with him. According to Frankhauser, in his 403-page affidavit in his case:

> Affiant [Frankhauser] was directed by agents of said Alcohol, Tobacco and Firearms Bureau to monitor conversations by means of a tape recorder between Robert Miles and four other defendants in the Pontiac bus bombing conspiracy . . . between said defendants and their attorney, James E. Wells, and that affiant did further understand that such information was given to . . . the Federal Bureau of Investigation and the United States Department of Justice.[41]

Other accounts of Frankhauser's role as an informant abound. Patsy Sims's 1978 book *The Klan* discusses his undercover work.[42] Frank Donner, in his 1981 work on domestic political spying, *The Age of Surveillance,* refers to Frankhauser thusly:

The uncrowned king of ATF informers is surely Roy E. Frankhauser, former Pennsylvania Grand Dragon of the United Klans of America, organizer of the National States Rights Party, a Minutemen activist, and a member of more than thirty other right-wing groups. Frankhauser reveled in spookery and claimed he was in fact a double agent, using his role as an ATF informer to obtain access to intelligence in the agency's files about his right-wing associates.[43]

Roy Frankhauser's involvement as a government undercover operative and agent provocateur began in the 1960s and continued sporadically until 1986, when he was indicted along with Lyndon LaRouche and several other defendants in the Boston LaRouche case involving credit card fraud and other charges. Frankhauser, who made his first contact with the LaRouche organization in 1975, had become their director of security![44] On December 10, 1987, Frankhauser was convicted of plotting to obstruct a federal investigation of the group. This is covered in depth in the chapter on Lyndon LaRouche, although a couple of points have bearing with respect to the Minutemen period.

According to Dennis King, author of *Lyndon LaRouche and the New American Fascism,* much of Frankhauser's work as an informant against Robert Miles, the Michigan Ku Klux Klan leader convicted of the 1971 Pontiac school bus bombings, was for Miles's benefit. According to King:

> Although Roy's maneuverings during this period are extremely murky, the best bet is that he was fishing for information about the Miles case and trying to compromise the feds so Miles could charge federal misconduct. Miles himself certainly believes this.[45]

\*  \*  \*

Frankhauser was not the only FBI or ATF informant in the Minutemen. Michael Sadewhite, an ATF informant in both the KKK and the Minutemen, was well-known to Frankhauser and is dealt with at length by Jones.[46] Another was Jerry Milton Brooks, also discussed by Jones. Among Brooks's allegations was the celebrated plot to put cyanide in the air conditioning system at the United Nations building. Brooks told Eric Norden that the idea developed during a training session in the summer of 1965.[47] In fact, it was entirely Brooks's idea and was suggested to another member while they were washing an automobile. Brooks, who had worked for a licensed exterminator, began relating the story over and over, embellishing it with more detail and seriousness each time, until it found its way into the literature on the Minutemen. Yet another Brooks fabrication was that DePugh sent him on a bus trip around the country with three vials of strychnine to knock off "Communists."[48] He was sent on a $99 bus tour but it was to gather "intelligence," Brooks said later, and no such strychnine ever existed.

Former FBI agent William Turner interviewed Brooks in 1966. The subsequent story, which appeared in *Ramparts* magazine in January 1967, relates Brooks's claim that he was "DePugh's intelligence officer until he became squeamish over the Minutemen's intent to overthrow the government." Brooks said he was picked because he had a criminal record and was going to "shoot a few people" and shake a few people down. Among other fantastic claims, he placed Minutemen membership at eight thousand—roughly twenty to forty times its actual number.[49]

\*    \*    \*

Another covert paramilitary group with vague ties to the Minutemen was the Secret Army Organization (SAO), which functioned in Southern California from 1967 to 1972. Unlike the Minutemen, it engaged in surveillance of suspects, infiltration, occasional burglaries, and physical violence. It targeted local leftists, particularly the San Diego *Street Journal,* and its members stockpiled quantities of legal and illegal weapons and ammunition.[50]

What distinguished the SAO from the Minutemen, however, is that while the Minutemen were heavily infiltrated by federal authorities, the FBI and ATF had much greater direct control of the SAO through a key agent, one Howard Barry Godfrey, who had been recruited as an informant–agent provocateur following his arrest in 1967 on possession of explosives. In a familiar trade-off similar to Roy Frankhauser's, the charges were dropped in exchange for services. Godfrey, however, was not just another informant but was instrumental, with FBI approval, in setting SAO policy, which included a wide variety of criminal activities. According to Frank Donner:

> While Godfrey subsequently claimed that he was instructed to reduce his own involvement to the minimum required to preserve his cover, the evidence is overwhelming that he was quite at home in SAO circles, initiated and led its most aggressive activities . . . and that the Bureau was fully informed about his involvements and protected him from their consequences.[51]

Another interesting account of Godfrey and the SAO appears in *The Glass House Tapes,* which purports to be a series of transcripts of tape recordings of Louis E. Tackwood, an undercover operative for various police agencies and the FBI. According to the account, Godfrey was actually cofounder of the organization.[52]

The Minutemen represented a certain level of danger and when left entirely to their own devices they were quite capable of getting into enough trouble without any help, or without anyone fabricating stories about them. Typically, the FBI and ATF utilized a considerable degree of overkill and in the process wound up flubbing cases or engaging in illegal entrapment. Also in line with FBI COINTELPRO policies in effect at the time, the agency used friendly media contacts to generate alarm and opposition to the group (as if this weren't going to happen anyway).

DePugh's scraps with other extreme right leaders were legendary. His attempts to recruit members from John Birch Society ranks, only minimally successful, resulted in his being ousted from the society, according to Robert Welch, JBS founder. Welch complained:

> Mr. DePugh has made the most continuous and determined effort to bring about the extensive collaboration of the Minutemen with the John Birch Society that we have ever experienced with any other group.[53]

Mainline conservative groups regarded DePugh and his Minutemen as far too radical for them. His most fertile recruiting grounds were among fringe elements in the John Birch Society, radical tax protesters, the Ku Klux Klan, and neo-Nazi organizations such as the National States Rights party. A small percentage of his members had no previous affiliations.

Following DePugh's release from prison in May 1973, the Minutemen remained moribund. Although they technically still existed, DePugh's efforts were directed at other "patriotic" enterprises. He took a stab at coordinating the activities of a number of right-wing groups at a "Patriots Leadership Conference" in September 1974. To this end, he established a coordinating operation, the Patriots Inter-Organizational Communications Center, in Norborne. The effort failed when the members took to squabbling among themselves and attempted to steal each other's mailing lists.

It was during this period that the Bureau of Alcohol, Tobacco and Firearms took another stab at infiltration and possible entrapment. They recruited the father of a DePugh employee, Robert Foote, to accompany his daughter to Norborne and spy on DePugh. ATF agent Jim Moore, who testified against DePugh in his 1966 trial, had convinced Foote that his daughter Roberta Owens might be in danger. After eleven days Foote came to the conclusion that not only was his daughter not in danger but that DePugh was being harassed for his beliefs. According to Foote:

> I weighed all the evidence up . . . and I decided that the only thing he [DePugh] was guilty of is working his tail off trying to make a living. It looked to me like he was being hounded, so I called Roberta up and told her just exactly what the hell was going on.[54]

DePugh was aggravated by the news, in part because he had learned that records of his long-distance telephone calls between January and November 1974, had been subpoenaed by the government, and because Owens had found a high-powered rifle in one of his buildings. He claimed the rifle had been planted. According to J. Harry Jones, Jr., in the *Kansas City Star:*

> DePugh speculated that the ATF planted it in anticipation of Foote's arrival in an undercover role. Foote said he had been instructed to write down the serial number of any weapon he saw and report it to Moore. That information, presumably, would have been sufficient for the government to obtain a search warrant and confiscate the weapon.[55]

ATF agent Jim Moore denied having planted the weapon. He did admit to having recruited Foote and engaging in heavy surveillance of DePugh over a period of time. The incident soon passed, leaving DePugh a little more wary and apprehensive.

In July 1976 DePugh engaged in a bit of COINTELPRO-type activity of his own. Phillip Finch describes it as follows:

> In July 1976, a nightmare in a manila envelope arrived in the mailboxes of Radical Right leaders and contributors. Within was a fifty-four page typewritten document titled *Deguello,* purportedly written by a group of international intelligence officers sympathetic to the cause. After some preliminary rehashing of socialist history and conspiracy theory, *Deguello* proceeded to accuse virtually every notable on the radical right of being either a Jew, a secret collectivist, or a closet homosexual. . . .
>
> The paper named more than thirty leading conservative and right-wing figures as infiltrators who were deliberately destroying the movement. That was the nightmare: the fear non-pareil on the Radical Right that the enemy is everywhere, and that nobody can be trusted. In a way, that is implicit in the Radical Right's rampant squabbling, but nobody had ever said it so flatly before. Nobody had ever put into words the paranoia underlying so much of what the Radical Right is about.[56]

Although he attempted to deny it, the *Deguello* report bore Robert Bolivar DePugh's psychological fingerprints. The text read as if it were a virtual transcript of conversations DePugh had over coffee with many friends and acquaintances. More to the point, it had just enough truth in it to make the entire document seem credible to uncritical readers.

There were, in fact, several prominent figures on the far right who indulged in homosexual behavior. Reverend Billy James Hargis of Christian Crusade and Major Edgar Bundy of the Church League of America are but two examples. The *Deguello* report, however, named dozens of individuals in an eighteen-page section devoted to the subject. Careful checking with numerous sources inside and outside the extreme right confirms that DePugh was wrong on this score as often as not. In some cases he was so far off base that it's obvious the report was really nothing more than name calling at its worst. Essentially, DePugh was getting back at his enemies, real and imagined, which by this time included most of the extreme right.

The report caused quite a stir, though—particularly among associates of those named in it. Few people bought the cover story of a group of international intelligence officers having produced it, and some even suspected DePugh from the outset, but it didn't really matter. The *Deguello* report appealed to the paranoia buried deep within the extremist psyche. Its primary effect was to demoralize and a chorus of "Ain't it awful!" arose from the ranks as copies were circulated from group to group. Within a few years it wasn't mentioned except on rare occasions. There were more immediate things to worry about.

In 1977 DePugh purchased the old Eaton-Cunningham printing business in Kansas City, including its physical plant—an impressive turn-of-the-century, three-story industrial building. He had hoped that ownership of a printing business would give his activities a boost, but its antiquated technology proved a considerable liability. He published the tabloid *Controversy,* which he hoped would find its way onto supermarket checkout stalls. It got nowhere as it aired charges and countercharges between DePugh and his former associates, and soon folded.

Although DePugh surrounded himself with racists and anti-Semites, many people who knew him said he was never particularly outspoken against blacks and Jews; anti-Semitism was a relatively late development in his political rhetoric, appearing in a major form for the first time in the *Deguello* report. His primary preoccupation was always Communist subversion and disloyalty.

* * *

By the late 1970s DePugh had managed to alienate himself from virtually every far-right leader. His attacks on Willis Carto of Liberty Lobby were vitriolic, and Carto replied in kind. By 1981 his isolation was nearly complete and his desperation increased. Late that year Bradley J. Smith,[57] an acquaintance who had invested in some of DePugh's ventures, accused him of misrepresentation and fraud, claiming that the state of Missouri had revoked the charters for both the Biolab Corporation and Private Enterprise, Ltd., and that DePugh had misstated the par value of the shares in these corporations. In the end DePugh's credibility was damaged even further.

A humorous incident occurred in 1979 when DePugh attempted an alliance with one Reverend Robert LeRoy, a far-right preacher who possessed a legitimate church tax exemption, something DePugh coveted greatly. LeRoy had previously held the title of "chaplain" to the Minutemen and had quit the organization more than once over some disagreement. The arrangement, in part, was that DePugh would pay LeRoy so much for "services" and cover certain expenses in exchange for use of LeRoy's mailing privileges at greatly reduced rates.

This went along well until LeRoy, a married man with several children, developed a crush on one of DePugh's daughters and began sending her mash notes, which DePugh obtained and published. After a brief spat of charges and countercharges the two parted ways.

DePugh's Committee of Ten Million, founded in 1976, had been offering lifetime memberships for $5 and provided easily $5 worth of printed matter to each new member (including *Blueprint for Victory*). It folded in 1981 for obvious reasons. It was largely an attempt to build a mailing list for later ventures. However, DePugh's last mailing of the list in 1982 cost him $7,000 and raised only $5,000. He held a few "Patriots Leadership Conferences" in Kansas City, one of which drew slightly over a hundred attendees in 1980. At this meeting DePugh accused a number of prominent figures of Communist, Jewish, or homosexual connections, to the amazement of some members of his audience. Otherwise, he spent much of the time huddled in private meetings agonizing over how to handle "infiltrators" who had shown up. One attendee was a black man who had reserved space for a table to distribute tax protest literature. DePugh's last effort before giving up entirely in 1982 was another tabloid, *The American Patriot*. It came to the usual untimely end.

One of DePugh's more peculiar character traits was an almost desperate need to surround himself with attractive young women. This was evident during his Minutemen days and remained with him into the 1980s. One way he accomplished this was through the hiring of a seemingly endless number of secretaries and telephone girls, all pretty, who never stayed around for more than a few months.

An even more obvious example, however, was his modeling school and agency, resembling what is widely known as the scam where a "student," almost always a young woman, pays a set fee of several hundred or a thousand dollars for a modeling "course" which includes a photographic portfolio and a promise of help finding modeling jobs. DePugh's Ad-Art agency was precisely such a school and over several years he sold his course to a couple hundred young women, few of whom actually got substantial modeling jobs. A DePugh associate became suspicious of the operation. Working in the building while DePugh was away, he examined the photograph collection in detail but found only typical cheesecake poses—no nudes or anything close to pornography. When questioned about his agency, DePugh said having beautiful young women around made him feel young.

In late 1981, DePugh sold Biolab, his printing company, and by 1983 he had retired from right-wing activity altogether. Moving to Iowa, he attempted to start another business on the order of Biolab. A local community virtually donated the land and he built a plant which, at last report, had gone belly up after a brief existence.

Little more was heard from the Minutemen leader until September 1991, when newspapers announced that he had been jailed on charges of sexual exploitation of a minor. The case stemmed from photographs he had allegedly taken of underage girls who had modeled for him. This met the strict Iowa definition of taking "sexually explicit" pictures of a minor—a felony. After sifting through tens of thousands of photos, investigators came up with a handful that they felt merited prosecution.[58] A subsequent search of his estranged wife's home in Norborne surfaced a large number of rusting weapons, including a mortar and nineteen practice rounds—evidently left over from his Minutemen days in the 1960s.[59]

DePugh was indicted by a federal grand jury on October 8, 1991, on four counts of firearms violations. In February 1992 his trial was held in Kansas City, and he was convicted on three counts and acquitted on the fourth, despite testimony by his son John, who claimed responsibility for the weapons.[60] Sentencing is pending at the time of this writing. DePugh faces a potential twenty years in prison, which, at his age of sixty-eight, would amount to a life sentence. Although his attorneys plan to appeal, he is being held without bail.

DePugh is an enigma to those who know him. He is highly intelligent, a virtual renaissance man of talents. He is equally adept at changing engines in automobiles, repairing a printing press, editing complicated copy, and managing a sophisticated business. On a one-to-one basis he can be extremely personable and likable. He often speaks of his family and expresses affection for his parents. There is a very real human being behind the image of a far-right political extremist and paramilitary fanatic.

DePugh is also a virtual encyclopedia of the American extreme right and able to expound at great length on this organization or that individual. Had his personality been different he might have been considerably more successful. In the end it was his deep and darkly suspicious nature that rendered him ineffective, totally enmeshed in the tangled knots of the paranoid processes.

Paranoid thinking involves extensive use of the self-fulfilling prophecy whereby the individual suspects or predicts hostility on the part of others and then, perhaps unconsciously, proceeds to behave in such a way as to encourage it. It's difficult to imagine anything that would provoke law enforcement and various interest groups more than a right-wing paramilitary operation like the Minutemen. DePugh's attention-getting statements reinforced this and within no time at all he had the enemies he always knew were out there.

The political career of Robert B. DePugh lasted roughly twenty years, including prison time, and added up to zilch in terms of his stated objectives. DePugh, however, did not see it that way in 1981. In a long interview with Phillip Finch, he took credit for playing a role in a conservative movement that ultimately elected Ronald Reagan president.[61] Now, more than ten years after the fact, it's apparent that the extreme right wing, with its racist and neo-Nazi elements, probably never had a worse enemy than Ronald Reagan and his Justice Department. It was during the Reagan administration that a major government program would form (known as Operation Clean Sweep), and antiparamilitary laws would be enacted in the legislatures of over a dozen states with Justice Department approval. Also, the neoconservative movement (including many Reagan administration figures) grew by leaps and bounds and proved as hostile to the extreme right as to the extreme left. If DePugh's claim of partial credit for the election of Ronald Reagan is accurate, the Minutemen leader made a miscalculation of monstrous proportions.

## Notes

1. J. Harry Jones, Jr., *The Minutemen* (Garden City, N.Y.: Doubleday, 1968), 39.

2. Phillip Finch, *God, Guts and Guns: A Close Look at the Radical Right* (New York: Seaview/Putnam, 1983), 119.

3. Interview with Jerry Brooks, Kansas City, Mo. (July 1968).

4. "Minutemen," *Kansas City Times* (October 23, 1961), 1.

5. Interview with Robert B. DePugh (November 25, 1964), in John S. Perkins, *The Minutemen: An Example of a Pressure Group,* paper, University of Kansas, December 11, 1964.

6. Anti-Defamation League of B'nai B'rith, *Extremism on the Right: A Handbook* (New York: The League, 1983), 65.

7. J. Edgar Hoover, testimony before the House Appropriations Committee, May 19, 1965.

8. Jones, 133.

9. Ibid., 42.

10. Ibid., 47.

11. Ibid., 54.

12. George Thayer, *The Farther Shores of Politics* (New York: Simon and Schuster, 1967), 142.

13. Wayne Nichols, "Founder Explains Army of Minutemen," *The Richmond* (Missouri) *News* (April 22, 1963), 1, 9.

14. *On Target* (November 1964).

15. J. Harry Jones, Jr., "Minutemen's Violent Schemes," *San Francisco Chronicle* (November 22, 1964).

16. National Rifle Association, editorial, *The American Rifleman* (September 1965).

17. Houghton later disappeared before reporting to serve his sentence, never to be found. It is widely suspected that DePugh may have had something to do with his disappearance.

18. Finch, 201.

19. Mrs. Robert DePugh, *Robert B. DePugh—Patriot,* one-page flier, n.d.

20. Finch, op. cit.

21. *A Patriot Speaks Up,* one-page flier, Minutemen, n.d.

22. Robert B. DePugh, *Behind the Iron Mask* (Norborne, Mass.: Salon Publishing Company, 1974).

23. Ibid., 394.

24. The Minutemen, *Bulletin,* December 15, 1970.

25. Finch, 158.

26. Eric Norden, "The Paramilitary Right," *Playboy* (June 1969), 248.

27. Cooperating with Burros in the publication of *Kill!* was John Patler, who was subsequently convicted for the assassination of American Nazi party leader George Lincoln Rockwell in 1967. Patler was freed after serving a relatively short sentence.

28. Norden, op. cit.

29. A detailed account of the Burros affair is contained in A. M. Rosenthal and Arthur Gelb, *One More Victim: The Life and Death of a Jewish American Nazi* (New York: Signet Books, 1967), much of the information for which was supplied by Roy Frankhauser. The authors note that Burros had established an informant relationship with various police agencies at the time of his death.

30. U.S. Army, Roy Everett Frankhauser, Jr., RA 13595185, Report of Investigation (2 August 1957), AJSEC-4.5 G3003924.

31. Norden, 104.

32. Ibid., 146.

33. Ibid.

34. John Hilferty, "Were Rightists Bugged? Minutemen Find Devices on Grounds," *Philadelphia Inquirer* (August 23, 1973), 1–A, 2–A.

35. Jones, 27.

36. U.S. Army, op. cit.

37. U.S. Army, Roy E. Frankhauser, RA 13595185, Agent Report (DA Form 341), (25 November 1957), AJSEC-4.5–G3003924.

38. John Hilferty, "Man in Jackboots, Swastika Was Secret Agent for U.S.," *Washington Star* (July 20, 1975), A–6.

39. Federal Bureau of Investigation, "Teletype," (June 17, 1974), from Director, FBI, to RUEHSE/U.S. Secret Service (PID).

40. Norman Kempster, "Informer's Trial: He Says Uncle Sam Was His Partner in Crime," *Washington Star* (September 15, 1974), A–1, A–10.

41. Ibid.

42. Patsy Sims, *The Klan* (New York: Stein & Day, 1978), 71–72.

43. Frank J. Donner, *The Age of Surveillance: The Aims and Methods of America's Political Intelligence System* (New York: Random House, 1981), 346.

44. Matthew L. Wald, "LaRouche Taken in By Aide, Trial Told," *New York Times* (December 10, 1987).

45. Dennis King, *Lyndon LaRouche and the New American Fascism* (New York: Doubleday, 1989), 199.

46. Jones, 358–64.

47. Norden, 104.

48. Jones, 21.

49. William W. Turner, "The Minutemen," *Ramparts* (January 1967), 72.

50. Detailed accounts of various aspects of the SAO are contained in Milton Viorst, "FBI Mayhem," *New York Review of Books* (March 18, 1976); Richard Popkin, "The Strange Tale of the Secret Army Organization (USA)," *Ramparts* (October 1973); and Peter Biskind, "The FBI's Secret Soldiers," *New Times* (January 9, 1976).

51. Donner, 443.

52. Donald Freed, ed., *The Glass House Tapes* (New York: Avon Books, 1973), 162.

53. "Birch Society," *Kansas City Times* (September 16, 1964), 11.

54. J. Harry Jones, Jr., "Spy on DePugh Uncovers Zealous Federal Detective," *Kansas City Star* (January 5, 1975).

55. Ibid.

56. Finch, 155.

57. This is *not* the same Bradley Smith associated with the Institute for Historical Review.

58. Bill Norton, "Head of Rightist Army Charged in Sex Case," *Kansas City Star* (September 14, 1991).

59. John T. Dauner, "Search After Sex Charge Reveals Arsenal," *Kansas City Star* (September 17, 1991).

60. Tom Jackman, "DePugh Is Convicted on Gun Charges," *Kansas City Star* (February 21, 1992).

61. Finch, 198–99.

# 18 The Militias

The blast that destroyed the Murrah Federal Building in Oklahoma City on April 19, 1995, was felt by John George thirteen miles to the north in Edmond. When the dust cleared it became apparent that the worst instance of domestic terrorism in the history of the United States had just occurred. The final tally of dead was 168 with hundreds more wounded, many seriously.

Initial speculation concerning the perpetrators focused on Arabs inasmuch as the bombing was quite similar in both scale and type of explosive to the 1993 bombing of the World Trade Center in New York City, which was committed by a radical Muslim sect. According to *Newsweek*:

> The low point came on Thursday (April 20th) when CNN reported that two suspects had been arrested in Dallas and one in Oklahoma City. The network actually named the Arabs who had been detained even though there was no confirmation of any connection to the case.[1]

Within twenty-four hours, however, a new suspect emerged: the small right-wing civilian "militia" movement. Militias were obsessed with guns and their right to own them, they possessed army manuals on weapons and explosives, and they were "right-wing," which meant that they were bad guys.

Intuitively, the militias seemed to fill the bill. Timothy McVeigh and Terry Nichols, two former soldiers, had been apprehended and were the main suspects in the bombing. It was rumored they had "links" and "ties" to the shadowy antigovernment militia movement. The militias had the apparent means, an apparent motive, and some members whose demeanor and statements were very suspicious. Over the next several weeks the public became witness to an incautious and generally misdirected feeding frenzy.

The spate of disinformation went unabated. Every group even vaguely identified with militias and every individual that could be "linked" with them were investigated and subjected to the harsh glare of adversarial publicity. Writing in the liberal *Progressive* magazine, June Jordan said:

It has taken the tragedy of Oklahoma City to understand that "The Aryan Nation" is not the name of an organization of some sort. "The Aryan Nation" is the goal of the Christian Coalition and the Patriot Militias and the Contract with America and Governor Pete Wilson.[2]

Writing in the *New York Times,* liberal columnist Tom Reiss observed:

The white extremist subculture that has come to light since the Oklahoma City bombing spreads its message of hate mostly through newsletters, talk radio and the Internet.[3]

Josh Sugarmann, executive director of the Violence Policy Center asserted:

We think the tragedy in Oklahoma City is the inevitable result of a concerted campaign led by the National Rifle Association attacking the Clinton administration and the BATF for their gun control policies.[4]

James Ridgeway, who writes on right-wing politics for various liberal and leftist publications, and Leonard Zeskind, a former Marxist-Leninist activist and researcher for the Center For Democratic Renewal, produced a piece on the militias, complete with a conspiracy theory of their very own. Writing in the *Village Voice* two weeks after the bombing, they said:

There is every reason to believe that the attack was a call for revolution by the far right wing of this country, organized through the widespread militia movement and carried out by one of the leaderless terror cells created by that movement.

It is probable that the three men being held in connection with the bombing—Timothy McVeigh, James Nichols, and his brother Terry Nichols—are all members of that same militia cell.[5]

None of this proved true, of course, and one of the most intensive investigations in FBI history failed to link these three to any militia organization in any significant way.

The Ridgeway/Zeskind article also refers to the Posse Comitatus as a precursor to the militias.

Kansas is an old center for the posse. During the 1980's federal law enforcement sources said that as many as one-third of all Kansas state sheriffs were either involved in, or sympathetic to, the posse. Posse doctrine holds that the highest law of the land is the county sheriff.[6]

Checking with the Kansas Attorney General's office and officers of the Kansas Sheriff's Association, we were informed that they did not know of a single sheriff who had been in any way "involved in or sympathetic to" the posse comitatus. In point of fact, Kansas sheriffs, and presumably sheriffs elsewhere, tended to view posse members as "idiots" and troublemakers who were more of a nuisance than a bona fide threat. The occasional posse member who seriously ran afoul of the law was swiftly dealt with by Kansas or other law enforcement officers.

The posse held a strange fascination for anti-extremist groups, most of which vastly exaggerated its membership and influence. According to Jeffrey Kaplan, writing in the scholarly journal, *Terrorism and Political Violence*:

> The Posse, it turned out, was composed of a small group of high profile "leaders" backed by a membership no more substantial than a mailing list peopled by an anonymous group of correspondents who, for the cost of a stamp and perhaps a contribution of a few dollars, could become the proud owners of a Posse Comitatus membership and a stack of literature which the putative new local Posse leader was invited to reproduce and distribute at will.[7]

## McVeigh's Explosives Training

It was not any right-wing militia or explosives manual from the Internet that acquainted Timothy McVeigh with bombing and mayhem. Rather, it was the U.S. Army, which McVeigh entered in May 1988. A gung-ho recruit, McVeigh quickly became a model soldier who rose to the rank of sergeant in less than three years. Trained as a gunner on the Bradley Fighting Vehicle, McVeigh experienced his first taste of blood during Desert Storm, where he won a Bronze Star and other medals for his actions leading to "the liberation of Kuwait and the ultimate defeat of the Iraqi Army." Sheffield Anderson, a fellow soldier, relates:

> He was a good shot. I remember when he reported shooting an Iraqi from 1000 meters. He took off the guy's head with a cannon shell, which you're really not supposed to do. I remember he was very pleased.[8]

Robin Littleton, who shared a room with McVeigh, said McVeigh felt let down that the United States didn't overthrow Iraqi President Saddam Hussein. "He was upset that we didn't go all the way. . . . He really believed the government had stopped short of what they really needed to do."[9] McVeigh's sentiments were, of course, widely held in the United States.

If there was any event in McVeigh's life that might have contributed to his alleged crime, it was his training and experience with the highly lethal weaponry of modern warfare in the armed forces of the United States of America in its war against the premier Arab bad guy of our time. It had nothing to do with any militia or other rightist organization. A book did seem to influence McVeigh's thinking, however: *The Turner Diaries* by neo-Nazi William Pierce (pseudonym Andrew MacDonald). He avidly recommended this fictional account of a violent racial nationalist takeover of the United States.

## Militia Roots

The civilian militia movement is a relatively recent phenomenon in the American right. Small paramilitary groups, such as the Minutemen, existed in the sixties, but none were as open, as up front with their ideas, or as apparently popular as the current militia movement. Racist groups like the various Ku Klux Klans and Aryan Nations maintained small paramilitary contingents, and a few communal paramilitary groups flourished briefly in the early 1980s, such as the the Covenant, Sword and the Arm of the Lord (CSA) in southern Missouri. The Minutemen and the CSA are long since defunct, and the KKK, Aryan Nations and other racist groups struggle along with a fraction of their 1980 membership.

The ideological roots of the militias are somewhat obscured by the highly individualistic nature of their adherents. The movement consists primarily of white males between thirty and sixty, although a surprising number of women are active, too. Several blacks have been identified with militias, along with a few Asians, American Indians, and even some Jews. Most militia activists appear to have roots in their communities, with families, jobs, and children in school.

As far as we can ascertain, most militia members are political neophytes. Those with a political past were active in the so-called patriot movement, which consists of a hodgepodge of small tax protest, parents rights, anti–gun control, constitutionalist, monetary reform, and radical libertarian groups. Some of the modern civilian militias have their roots in the survivalist movement that developed in the late 1970s. A few activists have been members of "hate groups" like the Ku Klux Klan, but these are generally weeded out soon after they're discovered.

If one were to select at random a group of actual members of militias, five categories would probably be represented in the following order of frequency:

1.  People generally conservative in outlook, although not very ideological, who are worried about what they see as a repressive government imposing all manner of strictures on them from unfair taxes to gun control.

2.  Would-be adventurers—generally nonideological weekend-warrior types who like to wear camouflage and play soldier in the woods. They watch movies with western and military themes and like to hunt and fish.

3.  Libertarian-conservatives who accept some government on the local or state level, but who oppose federal regulations of almost all kinds.

4.  Anarcho-libertarians who consider virtually all government as repressive and overbearing. They refer to themselves as "freemen" or "sovereigns."

5.  Hard-core extremists who harbor an obsessive conviction that the United States, indeed the world, is in the grip of an all-powerful conspiracy.

James Aho, a professor of sociology at Idaho State University and author of *The Politics of Righteousness: Idaho Christian Patriotism*[10] feels that a primary function of the militias is as a social activity involving like-minded friends.

> You get to dress up, you get to play army, you're reading compasses and maps and crawling under logs, setting up your tent and building a fire, and then you go out and shoot your gun and you come back and have a meal together. It's probably kind of fun. . . . For the most part it's harmless.[11]

Although fund-raising letters by antiracist groups state otherwise, the alleged "links" between the modern civilian militias and the neo-Nazi and other racist paramilitary groups seem few and far between. These mostly consist of charges that some militia members had attended racist meetings or had spoken with KKK or neo-Nazi representatives.

Unable to demonstrate rampant racism and anti-Semitism in the militias, the Anti-Defamation League and Southern Poverty Law Center have claimed that the KKK and neo-Nazi groups have "infiltrated" the militias, but these claims are based on only a few incidents. Another claim is that the conspiracy theories espoused by militias parallel those of racist groups on several points. This is often true, but as we shall see, they occasionally parallel those of the far left as well. An editorial in *New York Newsday* a week after the bombing noted:

> Even the initial suspicions of racism and anti-Semitism don't hold up across the board. . . . And even though militias have their share of white supremacists and separatists, not all of them share these sentiments. Others have actively recruited blacks and Hispanics. Some militias are rabidly anti-Zionist but others have recruited Jews. Many militia members are Christian fundamentalists, but a fair share are non-believers.[12]

The real impetus for most of these groups, however, was the controversy over gun control and most particularly a 1994 federal law which requires a five-day waiting period for the purchase of handguns, and which outlaws the manufacture or importation of a number of semiautomatic firearms. Fiercely protective of their "right to keep and bear arms," some militias were organized as a way to prevent the government from disarming the American people.

> They are spurred by passage of the Brady law, which applies waiting periods to gun purchases; they fear the law is the first step toward Big Brother's confiscation of their guns. . . . Their agenda is to thwart gun restrictions and fight most government intervention in their lives.[13]

Jim Dupont, sheriff of Flathead County, Montana, said:

> I'd say 95 percent of the people who are interested in a militia are good, honest, hardworking people who were concerned about the Federal Government dictating to the states about gun control. This is a big issue in this county.[14]

Militia members, along with most libertarians and a minority of constitutional scholars, feel that under the Second Amendment to the United States Constitution the right of "the people" to keep and bear arms means just that—that individual "people" have an unqualified right to possess firearms. Gun control groups and most of the legal community disagree, claiming that the Second Amendment guarantees only state governments the right to organize state-sponsored militias, such as the National Guard. Given this ambiguity, some people felt that by forming something called a "militia," the suggested constitutional requirement of "militia" membership might be met.

One source for their interpretation of the right to bear arms is Sanford Levinson, a University of Texas Law Professor, who has defended private gun ownership. In a December 1989 *Yale Law Journal* article Levinson quoted Judge Thomas Cooley, a recognized constitutional expert. Cooley wrote:

> The right of people to bear arms in their own defense and to form and drill military organizations in defense of the state . . . is significant as having been reserved by the people as a possible and necessary resort for the protection of self-government against usurpation.[15]

Although scholars championing this interpretation of the Second Amendment are in a clear minority, Cooley is not alone. Another is William Van Alstyne, a leading constitutional scholar at Duke University. According to Scott Heller, writing in the *Chronicle of Higher Education*:

> In his article [in the *Duke Law Review*], Mr. Van Alstyne turns to the history of federalism and anti-federalism, arguing that the right to bear arms explicitly applied to the whole body of citizens, not merely to trained soldiers, and was meant to protect people against the incursions of the federal government. Furthermore, he reads the adoption of the 14th Amendment as bolstering the individual rights position, since it restricts state governments' power to limit personal rights.[16]

Two other major "radicalizing" issues for militia members are the August 1992 FBI killings at Ruby Ridge, Idaho, which took the lives of Randy Weaver's son and wife, and the April 19, 1993, FBI assault on the Branch Davidian compound in Waco, Texas, in which seventy-four members of the sect died.

## Randy Weaver and Ruby Ridge

Weaver had been charged with selling two shotguns with a barrel one-quarter inch less than the legal length. In pursuing the case, the Bureau of Alcohol, Tobacco and Firearms (BATF) fabricated accounts of Weaver's dangerousness by claiming he had been convicted of crimes and was suspected in bank robberies. Weaver had never been convicted of and was not a suspect in any crime.[17] They also claimed he was a member of the neo-Nazi Aryan Nations when, in fact, he was not. After an extensive surveillance of eighteen months, BATF agents were spotted on Weaver's land. A shootout occurred and a U.S. Marshall killed fourteen-year-old Sammy Weaver, while Kevin Harris, who lived with the Weavers, killed U.S. Marshall William Degan in turn. Later, an FBI sniper shot and wounded Randy Weaver and Kevin Harris, and then killed Weaver's wife, Vicky, who was unarmed and carrying her baby.[18]

Weaver and Harris, both seriously wounded, surrendered to the FBI after several days, following the intervention of Col. Bo Gritz, a retired Special Forces officer and a major figure in the patriot movement. Weaver and Harris were charged with several crimes, including murder, conspiracy, and assault. According to *U.S. News and World Report*:

The 12 week trial in Boise in 1993 was a disaster for the government: the jury acquitted Harris of all charges and convicted Weaver only of failing to appear on the original firearms charge. The government effort was plagued by repeatedly tardy deliveries of crucial documents to the defense team. The delays so angered Judge Edward Lodge that he fined the government $1,920 and declared that the FBI had shown a "callous disregard for the rights of the defendants and the interests of justice" and a "complete lack of respect" for the court.[19]

Weaver and his remaining family wound up collecting $3.1 million in damages against the government. Following congressional hearings on the event several FBI officials were suspended or reassigned.[20]

## The Branch Davidians and Waco

The BATF raid on the Branch Davidian headquarters at Waco, Texas, on February 28, 1993, should have been a fire bell in the night for civil libertarians and proponents of religious freedom everywhere. The Branch Davidians are an offshoot of the Seventh Day Adventist Church. A small, multicultural sect headquartered in Waco, the Davidians had a worldwide membership of between one thousand and two thousand.

Acting on what it called reliable tips that the Branch Davidians were manufacturing drugs and stockpiling illegal weapons, BATF staged a paramilitary-style raid on their headquarters, which the Davidians called "Mount Carmel." The raid was badly bungled and the ensuing gunfight left six Branch Davidians and four BATF agents dead and many more wounded. Following the raid, the Davidians held out for fifty-one days, during which time both BATF and the FBI demonstrated astounding incompetence in dealing with them at virtually every turn.

Finally, U.S. Attorney General Janet Reno, believing reports that "child abuse" was happening in the building, authorized a final assault with an army tank converted to force a form of tear gas (banned by international agreement six months earlier) into the structure.[21] During that assault the building caught fire and burned to the ground killing 104 members of the group. Evidence suggests that the fire may have been set by the Davidians themselves.

Writing two years after the Waco fire, sociologist Stuart A. Wright detailed some of the troubling findings that had emerged from various investigations.

> The initial raid by the Bureau of Alcohol, Tobacco and Firearms (BATF) was unnecessary. The forceful assault was based on faulty intelligence.
>
> In an attempt to hide the bungled siege, federal agents painted an exaggerated and sinister portrait of the Branch Davidians.
>
> The FBI prematurely terminated peaceful negotiations, ignoring the advice of its own behavioral scientists.
>
> The FBI manipulated the media by controlling all information at Mount Carmel.
>
> Federal agents in charge dismissed Mr. Koresh's religion as nonsense ("Bible-babble"), ignored advice from outside religion experts familiar with the sect leader's apocalyptic theology.

The final assault on April 19 was predicated on inaccurate information. Attorney General Janet Reno claimed that the assault was prompted by evidence of ongoing child abuse. This statement proved to be groundless.[22]

Wright also said that the Branch Davidians posed no threat to themselves or their neighbors. He added:

> They lived in an insulated community, had voluntarily withdrawn from mainstream society, and enjoyed a social world constructed to their own liking. What was their crime? Faith in a living prophet? Belief in an apocalypse? Polygamy? Evidently these insidious features were sufficient to prompt the stigma-inducing label of "cult," a slippery and politically loaded term.[23]

Following a long investigation, on September 30, 1993, the Treasury Department, which oversees the BATF, released a 220-page report of the debacle in which they observed that "law-enforcement officials botched virtually every aspect of their plan to capture David Koresh . . . and then misled investigators and congress about their mistakes."[24]

On February 26, 1994, a jury acquitted eleven Branch Davidians of murder, rejecting claims that they ambushed federal agents. Five were convicted of voluntary manslaughter, two were convicted of weapons charges, and four were acquitted of all charges. Most of the guilty received maximum prison sentences.

What was most puzzling about both Ruby Ridge and Waco was that traditional civil-liberties groups found little to complain about in either case. After all, Weaver was some kind of mad-dog right-winger and Koresh was a religious nut. Many rightists felt that had Randy Weaver been a Black Panther or David Koresh a feminist neo-pagan some civil libertarians might have shown more interest. It has been the populist right—the patriot movement, militias, talk-show hosts, and libertarians on the internet—that have kept the issue alive.

An early player in the militia movement was Linda Thompson, a self-described "dumpy broad from the Midwest," who founded the American Justice Federation in Indianapolis, Indiana, and acts as the "adjutant general of the Unorganized Militia of the United States of America." Thompson is the author of two videos that circulate widely in the militia-patriot milieu: *Waco: The Big Lie* contains footage purporting to show that the FBI actually started the fire that engulfed the Branch Davidians; and *America Under Siege,* which describes her conspiracy theories about the New World Order.

In April 1994, Thompson issued an "alert" for a massive march on Washington, D.C., to "deliver a New Declaration of Independence to the White House." Thompson also said the militia will arrest congressmen "who have failed to uphold their oaths of office and will have them tried for treason by citizens courts."[25]

Thompson cited as examples of federal misconduct searches without warrants, that a cashless society is imminent so that citizens can be tracked, and that detention camps are already built nationwide to "house dissidents" who oppose these plans.[26]

The alert caused some alarm among more conventional rightist groups, includ-

•

ing the John Birch Society, which has viewed Thompson with considerable suspicion. The Society issued a position paper in which it advised against Thompson's march. Even the Liberty Lobby tabloid, *The Spotlight*, advised its readers not to take part. To the everlasting relief of many, the march was called off. According to Adam Parfrey and Jim Redden, writing in the *Village Voice*:

> Thompson is now convinced that the [*Spotlight*] is a "government operation." Ditto the John Birch Society. . . . The American Patriot Fax Network, which disseminates news to approximately 1000 Patriot fax machines nationally, is characterized by Thompson as a government con job. [Thompson] believes *Contact,* the weirdo alien-channeling Patriot newspaper, is a CIA front. Populist presidential candidate Bo Gritz [is a] government stooge, warns Linda Thompson.[27]

But what about Linda Thompson? Parfrey and Redden observe that in order to log on to her Associated Electronic Network computer bulletin board

> one must type in one's name, address, phone number, vow to an armed battle against the wicked, and supply questions regarding the supply of a safe house, guns, or ammunition— damning evidence if the government decided to use this information in a conspiracy or RICO charge against the Patriots. And although Thompson boasts that the FBI is likely bugging her bulletin board, she attacks other Patriot bulletin boards as being a method for the government to suck up names, addresses and phone numbers.[28]

This could easily be a case of the bad judgment that "patriots" are notorious for, and we have no evidence to implicate Linda Thompson in anything of this nature. However, such schemes by government agencies are not unheard of, and fighting "terrorism" provides an easily accepted rationale. For example, the Canadian Security Intelligence Service (CSIS) was embroiled in a major scandal in 1993 when it was revealed that one of their informants in right-wing groups was actually an agent provocateur who was directing a campaign of terrorism against Jews and other minorities. According to the *Toronto Sun*:

> A *Sun* probe has revealed that Grant Bristow, the white racist group's intelligence and security chief, has been a paid informant for the CSIS since early 1989—six months before the formation of the Heritage Front. And in addition to helping found the avowed neo-Nazi group, Bristow directed a harassment campaign that may have sparked street clashes between racists and anti-racists.[29]

In addition to trying to promote racial violence, the CSIS agent tried to "link" the conservative Reform Party to neo-Nazis in order to discredit it. When Reform Party officials discovered Heritage Front supporters among their members, they kicked them out.[30] Typically, this tactic is used to "discover" neo-Nazis or racists in a group in order to stigmatize the entire organization. In yet another case, Bristow attempted to derail the defense of an alleged World War II Nazi war criminal by spying on his attorney.[31]

But do such things happen in the United States? Of course they do. We've documented several cases elsewhere in this book. Extremist groups on the left and right are under constant threat of infiltration, destabilization, and disinformation tactics of the kind exposed in Canada.

Also in 1993, the Anti-Defamation League, which has a reputation of close cooperation with law enforcement agencies on all levels, was involved in a serious scandal in California. According to news reports:

> After a yearlong investigation into charges that the Anti-Defamation League built a national intelligence network using illegal spying, [San Francisco] District Attorney Arlo Smith agreed Monday not to prosecute the organization in exchange for its payment of up to $75,000 to fight hate crime.
>
> The [ADL] had been accused of illegally receiving confidential data from police sources. As part of the agreement, the group pledged not to engage in improper information-gathering in California. The case highlighted the Anti-Defamation League's intelligence operation and its infiltration of political and ethnic groups.[32]

The ADL's operations against anti-Semitic groups were widely known but what was surprising is that they were involved in spying on left-oriented groups, some of which had been their allies on various occasions.[33]

## Militia Membership

Estimates of militia membership range from fairly realistic to the patently absurd. Marc Cooper, writing in *The Nation* immediately after the Oklahoma City bombing, claims that militias have "signed up maybe 20,000 active volunteers who network by fax, phone, talk-radio and the Internet."[34] Chip Berlet and Matthew N. Lyons opined in *The Progressive* that "the number of militia members ranges from 10,000 to 40,000."[35] Several months earlier, Mark Potok, writing in *USA Today* in January 1995, stated that militias "have appeared in at least 24 states, drawing up to 50,000 members."[36]

In June 1995 the Anti-Defamation League issued a report putting the figure at 15,000.[37] In September 1995 the "militia task force" of the Southern Poverty Law Center (SPLC) issued a report that identified seventy-three "militias or militia support groups nationwide, with a total of 30,000 to 40,000 members." The SPLC also claimed that about forty-five have "ties to the Ku Klux Klan."[38] In the SPLC's *Klanwatch Intelligence Report* of June 1995, however, they claimed that "Over 200 Militias and Support Groups Operate Nationwide."[39]

In June 1995 the *Montgomery Advertiser* published a report on the SPLC's fundraising tactics as part of a continuing series of articles examining the organization. Entitled "Marketing the Militias," by Dan Morse, the report noted that "Morris Dees and the Southern Poverty Law Center are using the militia controversy to raise funds, but not all donors approve of their methods." The article quoted a former donor to the SPLC who had learned that the organization had amassed $60 million in reserves.

"It's almost like jumping on whatever shameful thing has happened in the country to so-licit funds," said Harvy Aronson, a Long Island man who has sent about $1,000 to the cen-ter. He quit giving last year when he found out about the millions in reserves. "My im-pression always was that they needed money. Some little group working out of practically a storefront," he said.[40]

The SPLC began a massive mailing fourteen days after the Oklahoma City bombing. This was followed up two weeks later by letters stating, "We need your help now with the most generous special gift you can make to help us expand our Militia Task Force." Another SPLC mailing dated April 27 and which appears to have been prepared before the bombing also asks for funds for their Militia Task Force. "You know, that's interesting. That was timely wasn't it. I mean, we didn't know the bomb was going to go off," Dees is quoted as saying.[41]

Groups that monitor charities and former SPLC employees have questioned the SPLC's fundraising tactics, claiming that the center misleads its donors with desper-ate pleas for money. In 1993, the American Institute for Philanthropy ranked the SPLC as the "fourth least-needy charity in the nation."[42]

If figures given by militia critics seem high, militia spokesmen themselves have given figures of 100,000 in Texas, 12,000 to 15,000 in Michigan, and have claimed that the "militias could field more than one million men and women."[43] Mark Ko-ernike, a voracious self-publicist identified with the Michigan Militia and who calls himself "Mark From Michigan," said that "as many as 2,070 such groups cooperate around the country with up to 4 million members."[44] Every side to this controversy, it seems, has a motive in inflating membership figures, either to emphasize danger-ousness or to underscore an alleged mass following.

## What Is a Militia?

The actual number of militia groups depends on several questions, and foremost among these is "what is a militia?" The answer is obvious if we restrict our definition to groups that use "militia" as part of their name or who engage in actual physical paramilitary training. However, groups like the small Christian Patriots Defense League, which once conducted paramilitary training in the early 1980s, but which is now nothing more than a postal ministry, are often included, as are various tax protest, gun rights, and so-called patriot groups, most of which are in no way paramilitary. Some writers make this distinction, others don't, claiming that they are merely militia "support groups."

The SPLC did this in their September 1995 report, when they claimed that Col-orado had twenty "militia" groups, an estimate that is the third highest in the nation after the estimates for Michigan and California. Among those listed as militias or mili-tia "support groups" were the American Agricultural Movement, the National Com-modities and Barter Exchange, the Tenth Amendment Committee, and Financial and Monetary Consultants. Most of the groups labeled by the SPLC denied they were as-sociated with militias in any way. According to Jim Abbott, founder of the Tenth Amendment Committee:

We were formed for one purpose. When [Colorado] state Senator Charles Duke introduced his [1994] resolution to ask the federal government to obey the law, the Tenth Amendment Committee was formed to lobby the legislature to get that resolution passed.[45]

Another Colorado group listed as a "militia" by the SPLC, Guardians For American Liberty (GOAL), was also identified as a militia group by the BATF in a 1994 report, which said that GOAL "incorporates many diverse, radical ideals." What was the basis for it being labeled a militia group? The BATF report said that when two right-wing extremists were arrested on firearms charges in Las Vegas, Nevada, applications for GOAL membership were found in their clothing.[46]

In short, the SPLC inflates its militia figures by listing every group, no matter how small, that shares similar conspiracy theories or beliefs about the role of government. SPLC Militia Task Force Director Michael Reynolds linked these groups to neo-Nazis and the KKK:[47]

The organization of some of these militias [is] exploited and led by white supremacists and anti-Semites that have moved out of the Klan, Posse Comitatus, Christian Identity, who have generated this movement for a variety of reasons. Mainly it is anti-federal government.[48]

The SPLC is not alone in inflating the membership figures of groups they oppose. In September 1966 the Anti-Defamation League published a statement in the *New York Times* in which they claimed that Ku Klux Klan membership was 29,500. An internal FBI memorandum dated September 22, 1966, from F. J. Baumgardner to William J. Sullivan, director of the FBI Domestic Intelligence Division, stated:

The Anti-Defamation League of B'nai B'rith released a statement to the effect that membership in the Ku Klux Klan has increased by about 10,000 members since the first of the year. They estimated Klan strength in the nation at about 29,500. These figures are exaggerated.

The present Klan membership is between 14,000 and 15,000 active members. . . . Klan leaders have always exaggerated the strength of their organizations in an effort to give the impression that they have substantial influence and power.

The Anti-Defamation League has vested interest in discovering and exposing anti-Semitic organizations such as the Klan and other hate groups.[49]

In the 1950s similar tactics were used to dramatically inflate the number of Communists in the United States. In addition to actual party members, there were "crypto-Communists," "fellow travelers," "Communist sympathizers," and "dupes." There were even "state-of-mind Communists." At a time when Communist party membership was under 6,000, irresponsible anti-Communist watchdog organizations claimed figures many times that as well as vast Communist influence reaching into every aspect of our lives.

## What Is a Member?

When we ask the question, What is a member? do we mean someone who has taken a pledge, filled out an application, and paid dues, or do we mean someone who has merely gotten on a mailing list? If we mean the former, then militias are probably quite small. If we mean the latter, then a larger figure is certain. That figure, however, often includes anyone who ever wrote for information, including the authors.

Our estimate, based on several factors including law enforcement sources, reliable informants in the militias, and the observations of several other researchers, is that at the time of the Oklahoma City bombing actual bona fide militia membership was probably under five thousand. In addition to this, a roughly equal number of wives, girlfriends, fishing buddies, coworkers, and curiosity seekers have attended meetings or gone on maneuvers on an irregular basis.

Some large groups, like the Michigan Militia and the Militia of Montana, had two or three hundred real members in April 1995. At the opposite extreme is the two or three buddies, often with some military or law enforcement background, who like to fish and hunt and have designated themselves the "militia" of whatever county they happen to live in.

In the case of the Kansas Militia, which we are intimately familiar with, early estimates from reporters calling the authors immediately after the bombing suggested a dozen militia groups with an aggregate membership of over a thousand, and one imaginative reporter claimed inside information supporting ten thousand gun-toting extremists in "dozens" of militias in Kansas. In fact, there were three tiny groups each calling themselves a militia in Kansas, the largest of which may have had fifty members, according to Kansas Attorney General Carla Stovall.[50] Not surprisingly, the Kansas militias themselves have claimed their numbers exceed two thousand.[51]

When the *Syracuse New Times* went looking for militias in New York State, the second most populous state in the union, writer Spider Rybaak reported:

> Our research uncovered two in New York State: the Second Amendment Militia (2AM) in Johnson City, which claims about a half-dozen members, and the CCCM (Chemung County Citizens Militia), which has had meetings attended by several dozen.[52]

When a national militia organization announced a March 1995 rally of militia members from around the country in Montana, they were sorely disappointed.

> What was supposed to be a national rally of . . . the North American Volunteer Militia in Hamilton earlier this year fizzled when only about 125 local residents showed up for a constitutionalist's lecture at the Corvallis Grange Hall.
> "People attend out of curiosity," said Mike Batista, head of the [Montana State attorney general's] law enforcement services division.[53]

Curiosity about the militias or general sympathy with their essential message of individualism and local government does not necessarily translate into membership or even a serious following. Moreover, we have good reason to dispute claims that militia membership has risen enormously after the bombing. In fact, a large number of militia members quit within days, as they found themselves being called "baby killers" and their families being shunned by friends and neighbors. Then when the FBI came knocking in response to "tips" to their widely publicized "hot line," the attrition was accelerated. Neighborhood busybodies had a field day performing their civic duties by turning in their suspicious neighbors in camouflage.

By June the "hot line" had produced over forty thousand calls and "more than 39 million nuggets of information had been dumped into computer files."[54] In addition, the FBI interviewed thousands of sources and questioned the suspect's friends and acquaintances extensively, often to the point of harassment. In the case of the Michigan militia, dozens of members were interrogated at length and some placed under surveillance for a time. The same was true in Oklahoma and Arizona.

If the FBI knew little about the militia movement before the bombing, they certainly rectified this afterwards. It was one of the biggest fishing expeditions in FBI history. "Watchdog" groups were disappointed, however. The result: no significant links turned up between any militia or other right-wing organizations and the Oklahoma City bombing. It would be left to imaginative staff writers and fundraisers to make that case minus hard evidence.

The initial publicity surrounding the militias brought about a large number of inquiries, often from reporters and investigators, but few new members despite claims to the contrary. People who may have been attracted to the militia message were frightened by the alleged "links" with the bombing.

The Michigan Militia, for example, found itself split into several small groups as some members attempted to distance themselves from the absurd conspiracy pronouncements of "Commander" Norman Olson, who had claimed that the bombing was a Japanese plot. For bean counters in the "anti-extremist" community we now have the Northern Michigan Regional Militia, the Wolverines, the Straits Area Militia, the Upper Peninsula Militia, the Central Michigan Militia, and the Southern Michigan Militia.[55]

Other changes have taken place in the months after the bombing. Fearing the link with extremists, several militias have shut off the conspiratorial rhetoric and reorganized in the civil defense model. Numerous militias have folded up completely. Doug Christiansen, a former Utah Highway Patrolman, said the association with Oklahoma City caused him to disband his fifty-member Box Elder Militia, which was set up to support local law enforcement.[56] Claiming that "vague ties between the bombing suspects and militia groups were too much to overcome," Commander Morris Wilson said he was disbanding the Kansas Citizens Militia.[57] Dozens of other small groups followed suit.

"I think the movement is done," said Bob Johansen, a 66-year old former Marine who commands the Florida Militia's 2nd Regiment in St. Lucie County on Florida's east coast, considered one of the strongest units in the state.

"The [militia members] don't even want to come to a meeting. . . . They don't want to get together. . . . The man who let us use his land for a firing range told us we're not welcome there anymore," said Johansen, who blames the media for painting militias with the same broad brush he says Senator Joseph McCarthy used to smear those on the left in the 1950s.[58]

In October 1995 some one hundred militia members and leaders met near Dallas to plan strategy in the aftermath of the bombing. Some twenty states were represented. Seven militia leaders met with Dallas FBI chief Jim Adams in what was described as a "cordial meeting." The press was welcomed to hear speakers. Colorado State Senator Charles Duke stated, "What I'm about is peaceful solutions, lawful solutions, constitutional solutions."[59]

Mike Vanderboegh of Jews For Preservation of Firearms Ownership spoke, urging the crowd to avoid racial and religious animosities. According to news reports:

> When the chief of a Midwestern militia federation was asked by another man in fatigues what rules he followed in admitting groups for membership, he replied: "No Aryans, no anti-Semites, no wing nuts. . . . The first time I hear the word 'nigger,' the first time I hear the word 'Jew' in a bad way, that's it. They're out. They're done," he declared.[60]

On the other hand, there is evidence to suggest that some groups did add to their membership rosters, although not by the margin suggested by watchdog groups, and a few new groups have been formed. How much these gains have offset losses is not known, but probably not by much. Giving every factor the benefit of the doubt, we feel it is possible that bona fide committed militia membership by January 1996 may have reached six or seven thousand with a similar number of marginal supporters of the type previously mentioned.

After the initial losses, which devastated some groups, militias found themselves the beneficiaries of the growing public awareness that their movement had nothing to do with the Oklahoma City bombing. "It's kind of like being charged with a terrible crime, being demonized in the media and then it begins to develop that you were more-or-less framed," one militia leader said. "Now everybody knows who we are, and we're seen as underdogs and victims ourselves."

In Missouri, a group calling itself the First Missouri Volunteers has responded to several emergencies, including the floods and tornadoes that ravaged parts of the state earlier in the year. According to news reports:

> Their critics call it an attempt to bolster their sagging public image. But organizers say emergency public service has long been part of the militia mission, right up there with defending the Second Amendment and keeping an eye on the federal government.[61]

Stephanie Selemen of the ADL responded that the militias "are using the flood and the tornado to boost their image. There's no doubt that they've jumped at the chance to legitimize themselves."[62] But Harold Sheil, a retired firefighter and spokesman for the Missouri 51st Militia, said, "Almost every one of us has been involved in this effort before we were in the militias—we have floods all the time."[63]

## The Government and the Militias

The militias, such as they are, range enormously in character. Some are little more than an armed neighborhood watch, who are known to and cooperate with local police. Others are heavily into extreme antigovernment, tax protest, and conspiratorial "freemen" rhetoric that more or less conforms to the media stereotype. Like all extreme marginal movements, the militias attract their share of sociopaths. When someone stops paying taxes, buying license plates, and insists on carrying a gun everywhere, sooner or later the authorities are going to have to respond to the challenge. Left to its own devices, law enforcement is likely to act with reasonable restraint. But when politicians and watchdog groups are lobbying for a maximum response policy in order to make examples out of "hate groups," disaster is often just around the corner.

The line of demarcation between militia members and so-called freemen is murky. "Freeman" is a euphemism for a kind of anarcho-libertarian lifestyle devoid of taxes, gun control, and other encroachments from the state, such as compulsory education and building codes. Freemen frequently refer to themselves as "sovereigns" who are not subject to the federal jurisdiction of the United States and, in some cases, state and local laws. Of course, not all militia members are freemen, in spite of the similarity of their rhetoric. When legal problems arise, it's often the doing of the freemen much to the dismay of most rank-and-file militia members, who tend to be law-abiding, albeit extremely critical of overreaching authority.

In Montana, for example, Ronald Fulbright, a Lewistown rancher, was convicted in June 1994 on three federal felony counts of "conspiracy to injure, impede or influence federal officials." He was accused of operating a scam under the name of "We, The People," which promised large settlements from the federal government in return for a $300 fee. Ironically, many of his victims were other tax protesters and "freemen."

Red Beckman, a Billings tax protester, was removed from his home by sheriff's deputies in May culminating a twenty-year battle with the IRS. Beckman is the founder of the "Fully Informed Jury Amendment" organization and author of several related books.

In Garfield County, wanted posters appeared in March offering a $1 million bounty for the arrest and conviction of several state, county, and other officials associated with the foreclosure of Brusett rancher Ralph Clark. The *Billings Gazette* reported on the government response to the posters:

> Garfield County law enforcement agents responded by charging 15 "freemen" with criminal misdemeanors relating to the impersonation of public officials. Clark is charged with a felony stemming from the bounty.[64]

This, however, is not a case where a family lost their small farm they had built up from nothing because they owed a few thousand dollars as in novelist John Steinbeck's *Grapes of Wrath*. Clark had owed $1.8 million in federal loans on one of his ranches and hadn't made a payment since 1981. The property brought $493,000 at auction. Clark says he was "swindled."[65] Perhaps he felt better after he had been appointed "marshall" of "Justus Township," a freeman enclave of "a half-dozen fortified houses and ranches" in Northern Montana. Many of the freemen living there have outstanding warrants on various charges relating to their noncompliance with taxes and regulations.

> The Freemen have set up their own government . . . which has its own laws, currency and officials. . . . Their system is based on the Bible, the Magna Carta, common law, the U.S. Constitution, parts of the Montana Constitution and the Uniform Commercial Code. For more than a year, Justus Township has issued its own writs, liens and money.[66]

Critics of the freemen say their financial plight largely boils down to financial incompetence, having overextended themselves on easy credit or mismanaged their holdings. If so, this is not the first case of political dissidents rationalizing their own bad decisions and failures into an ideological belief system complete with the pre-requisite conspiracy theory. Now it's somebody else's fault.

A few isolated exceptions aside, in cases like these freemen and tax protesters in-evitably lose and are inevitably bitter about losing, usually attributing it to a con-spiracy against them. So often is this the case that one wonders if freemen aren't en-gaging in some kind of masochistic self-fulfilling prophecy. In the case of Fulbright, who was clearly running an illegal confidence game, U.S. Attorney Sherry Matteucci said:

> The followers of Ron Fulbright and his ilk are seriously misled about the protections of the laws and their requirements. I hope that the message they receive [is that] in this coun-try, we all follow the same law, not something they make up because they feel like it.[67]

Although some freeman offenses are clearly and unequivocally criminal, others seem ambiguous, as in "wanted posters" against government officials that are clearly a political statement. Similar wanted posters appeared during the civil rights, and an-tiwar movements of the 1960s. However, as it was with leftist groups during the Vietnam War, tolerance of right-wing protesters is low. Montana Governor Marc Racicot announced, in a statement reminiscent of a southern governor in the 1960s, "Any civil disobedience of any kind is not something that a civil, organized society can tolerate."[68]

In another case, seven freemen associated with the Militia of Montana, includ-ing cofounder John Trochmann, were arrested in March 1995 in Roundup, Montana. Five were charged with felony intimidation, two with misdemeanor counts of carry-ing a concealed weapon. The incident arose out of a protest against the sentence given to freeman William L. Stanton, who was given ten years for "having committed criminal syndicalism." According to news reports:

> Stanton is believed to be the first ever prosecuted in Montana for that offense, defined as the advocacy of crime, malicious damage or injury to property, violence or terrorism to accomplish industrial or political ends.[69]

Bail was initially set at $100,000 for each defendant, including those charged with misdemeanors.[70] Following an investigation the Montana attorney general's office de-termined that the felony charges were unfounded. Apparently sheriff's deputies had stated that the defendants had planned to rob banks and kidnap local officials, which was not true. All felony charges and all but two misdemeanor charges were subse-quently dismissed.

Many criminal cases against political extremists, left or right, involve alleged conspiracies and not actual physical crimes in the sense we ordinarily think of them. These conspirators *rarely* kill or bomb or overthrow anything. They are charged with contemplating these deeds (perhaps over a couple of beers) and this often is related by a paid government informant or somebody trying to buy a reduced sentence by cooperating.

Criminal syndicalism laws were intended as weapons against "reds" and labor radicals during the 1920s' red scare. It is ironic that they are increasingly used today against dissidents associated with the far right.

In Roanoke, Virginia, four members of the Blue Ridge Hunt Club, which the government characterized as a militia, were charged with "plotting an armed insurrection . . . if gun control laws became overbearing." The U.S. attorney presented jurors with an elaborate conspiracy theory based largely on the testimony of a government informant. Defendant William Stump admitted firing a .22 caliber squirrel rifle equipped with a silencer that the club's leader, James Mullins, brought to a meeting. Stump was acquitted on a conspiracy charge but convicted of possessing two rifles with silencers that had no serial numbers. In addition to Stump, one man was acquitted and two others convicted. No actual act of violence was alleged against any defendant. William Lindsey, a juror in the case, said that Stump "seemed to be in the wrong place at the wrong time." Stump, thirty-five, faces a possible twenty years in prison.[71]

## Militias Are Soft Targets

Gregory Walker is unique among terrorism experts in that he has actually served in America's armed forces. A bona fide former Army Ranger and Green Beret, Walker is also editor of a U.S. Special Operations journal called *Behind The Lines.* In an interview that appeared in the *San Jose Mercury News,* Walker expressed his dissent to the "hysteria" that has swept the nation. He views the militias as "soft targets" for law enforcement officials to infiltrate and journalists looking for "sound-bite solutions and bumper-sticker rhetoric." According to Walker:

> The militias are soft targets because they are very easy to identify. They make themselves available to literally anybody and everybody who wants to listen to them. . . . It's made up primarily of law-abiding citizens who make no attempt to conceal their identities or (ideology). . . . 80 percent of militia members have no military experience, and just an infinitesimally small percentage have any kind of combat experience.[72]

Walker had been approached before the bombing by the new Oregon Militia to verify the credentials of a would-be trainer who claimed to be a decorated Vietnam-era Navy Seal. The guy turned out to be a fraud. When the militia asked Walker to train them, he refused and told them to "keep out of the camouflage and lock up the guns." "Right now," he said, "you're seen as lunatics."[73] The Oregon Militia was one of many that disbanded after the Oklahoma City bombing.

## The Militias and the Government

The militias managed to embarrass the Treasury Department's BATF when members of the small Gadsden Minutemen exposed the "Good Old Boys Roundup," held in Polk County, Tennessee. The Roundup, an annual gathering of some three hundred law enforcement officers, including several agents of the BATF and FBI, had regularly condoned openly racist behavior of the sort that both agencies investigate.[74]

Militia members released a videotape of the 1990 Roundup that showed attendees wearing T-shirts with racist themes and a large sign that said, "Nigger Check Point" and "Any Niggers In That Car?"[75] The gathering had been organized every year since 1979 by former BATF agent Gene Rightmeyer. The telephone number of the Greenville, South Carolina, office of BATF appears on the invitation to the roundup as a point of contact for inquiries.[76] When confronted with the video, BATF officials suggested that the tapes had been altered, presumably by the militia.

> Civil rights leaders and the organizer of the annual roundups, a former BATF agent, have said they believe the 90-second tape may have been doctored, particularly the part showing a banner proclaiming a racial epithet.[77]

After an investigation by the FBI laboratory, the tape was found to be genuine and an "unedited original."[78]

## Senate Hearings on the Militias

In June 1995 the Senate held hearings on the militias. During their ninety minutes of testimony militia leaders amused their hosts with conspiracy theories that Japan might have had a hand in the Oklahoma bombing in retaliation for a nerve gas attack on Tokyo's subway earlier in the year, that the government was tampering with the weather, and that it "defines human beings as a biological resource under the United Nations ecosystem management program" and "allows our military to be ordered and controlled by foreigners."[79]

Things became more serious when senators hinted that the militias were racist. "I am getting awfully tired of being called a racist," said James Johnson, who is black. "This movement is not about guns and skin color. It is about freedom." Bob Fletcher of the Militia of Montana called the racism charges "garbage." When Senator Diane Feinstein asked, "Why do I read constantly these violent quotes, this hatred for other people . . . ?" Fletcher erupted:

> My wife of 35 years is Jewish and Italian. My business partners for four or five different years were blacks, and my granddaughter is half American Indian. So if I'm a racist, I'm doing a lousy job of it.[80]

Daniel Levitas, a director of Leonard Zeskind's "Institute For Research and Education on Human Rights, Inc.," produced documents indicating that John Trochmann, cofounder of the Militia of Montana, had spoken at a racist meeting in 1990. Trochmann admitted attending the meeting. The participants at the meeting were drunk, he said, and he returned later that year to "speak to them about their immorality."[81]

Mack Tanner, writing in the libertarian *Reason* magazine, described Trochmann as follows:

> A devout Christian, John Trochmann is a strong advocate of New World Order conspiracy theories. But he adamantly denied he is a member of any racist organization. He readily admitted that he and his family twice visited the Aryan Nation compound in Hayden Lake, Idaho, several years ago, but insisted that he had gone there as part of a home-school learning project. "I am not on their mailing list, I have never signed any of their statements, and I certainly never joined the organization," he told me in loud, angry tones.[82]

Charges that the militias are sexist are also on shaky ground, although it can't be denied that their macho image certainly evokes that assumption. Writing in *USA Today,* Katy Kelly reported:

> Although the militia movement still is dominated by men, women are playing increasingly active roles. In Idaho, one of the most active states, one-third of all militia members reportedly are women.[83]

Attempts to stereotype militias have had varying degrees of success. It didn't work in the San Francisco Bay Area where the Alameda County Free Militia was founded by Larens Imanyuel, a black man who lives in Berkeley. A staunch believer in conspiracy, Imanyuel believes that "it is carried out by a plutocracy of rich people, international corporations and the United Nations, and its aim is to keep the lower middle class as almost slave labor."[84] This statement could pass for Marxist organizing rhetoric. Imanyuel notes that it is not a coincidence that the recently formed group is comprised mostly of lower-middle-class workers, including computer people, a warehouse worker, and a recycler/scavenger.

Annastasia Steinberg, a local Anti-Defamation League official, attended a meeting of the group in December 1994. Observing that the attendees appeared "mainstream," she observed, "In fact, it concerns me how kind of normal they appear to be."[85] She added: "I think it's a feeling that the government is out of control, that the average citizen is under siege. And they think that the government is out to get them."[86]

Alfred Adask, head of Citizens For Legal Reform, a "constitutionalist" organization and publisher of the like-minded *Anti-Shyster* magazine, says:

> It is the first time I've seen evidence of something that I would call class consciousness. I don't like the term because of its Marxist connotations, but it seems to me we have a class of people who are making it, including the government and the media, and they are living in their own world, and there is a whole other world down here that is paying for it.[87]

## Conspiracy Theories

Perhaps the most bizarre, and sometimes entertaining, aspect of the militia movement is the wide range of conspiracy theories credited to them. These range from the barely plausible to the downright ridiculous. Among these are the perfidious machinations of the more than two centuries old Illuminati (see "Sinister Plots Abound" in chapter 3), the Trilateral Commission, the United Nations, the Federal Reserve System, the International Monetary Fund, Globalism, and something called the "New World Order." Add to this assassination plots, fluoridation of drinking water, black helicopters, concentration camps, UFO coverups, mind control, weather control, and gun control. Then there are conspiracies involving child molesters, Satanists, Neo-Pagans, Zionists, Rosicrucians, and the pope, and this is just the tip of the iceberg.

We also have conspiracies involving the Hong Kong police coming to the United States to aid in firearms confiscation, the World Health Organization deliberately creating the AIDS virus to depopulate parts of the earth, Russian and Chinese Troops being smuggled into Mexico to assist in a takeover of the United States, and massive crematoriums built to accommodate the planned liquidation of millions of resisting American patriots.

Even Col. Robert Brown, publisher of *Soldier Of Fortune* magazine, which has been identified with the militia movement, is critical of the militias on this account:

> They [the militia leaders], while selling their wild-ass tales that fuel the fire, are also selling their tapes and making their speeches. Maybe they believe what they're saying. Maybe they're simply opportunists, or some combination of the two. Who knows what motivates them, but they're full of [blank].[88]

The range of conspiracy theories may be almost encyclopedic, but they all have one thing in common: some kind of diabolical plot by the dark forces to do in the champions of righteousness and freedom. The details vary considerably, but they usually involve secrecy and deception, complicated scenarios by which the people are fooled, sometimes even by those claiming to oppose the plotters. All this ends with the control or enslavement of the masses by a self-appointed elite.

The great appeal of conspiracy theories is much the same as the appeal of ideologies; i.e., they attempt, usually through some convoluted circular reasoning, to explain everything and in a way that is psychologically satisfying.

The philosopher Karl Popper was a studious observer of belief systems and their various snares and pitfalls. Speaking of ideological belief systems he said that the acceptance of one of these theories has

> The effect of an intellectual conversion or revelation, opening your eyes to a new truth hidden from those not yet initiated. Once your eyes were thus opened you saw confirming instances everywhere: the world was full of verifications of the theory. Whatever happened always confirmed it. Thus its truth appeared manifest; and unbelievers were clearly people who did not want to see the manifest truth, who refused to see it.[89]

Of course, not every element of an ideology is fallacious and some ideologies work better than others. Conspiracy theories, too, range from the more-or-less bona fide to the utterly fanciful. It would not be absurd to say that there was a conspiracy to murder Jews during World War II, or that certain Marxist-Leninists have conspired to undermine non-Communist societies.

The issue, of course, is the quality of the evidence that backs up the particular theory, and most of the conspiracy theories championed by the far left and far right lack the kind of evidence necessary to lend substantial credibility. Most of these conspiracy theories are basically unproven (and often utterly unprovable) tautalogical arguments.

Complicating this is the fact that it's much easier to identify a bona fide conspiracy after the fact, especially if it is successful. The American Revolution (and all revolutions, for that matter) had many elements of a conspiracy. Many assassinations involve some kind of a conspiracy, although rarely on the level conspiracists claim. Modern politics sometimes has a conspiratorial flavor, as we learn from the many scandals that emerge, but such conspiracies are limited in scope.

One place where real conspiracies exist, and are often proven, is in the criminal justice system. How often do we read of someone convicted of "conspiring to commit" one crime or another? But these differ from the broad-ranging political conspiracies in that they are small in scale, usually pertaining to a single event or issue.

Political conspiracy theories are always much more complicated and sometimes cover an immense range of time and events connected by tenuous "linkages" that often exist only in the mind of the conspiracist. Post hoc and ad hominem fallacies are commonplace. Conspiracy theories of this type involve great intuitive leaps and a kind of credulousness that seems surprising, given the high intelligence of many conspiracists. There's a kind of bone-headedness among people who advance most of these theories and those who argue with them will usually find themselves viewed as dupes or apologists for the conspirators.

Far leftist Michael Parenti made the case for conspiratorial thinking at a 1994 convention of political assassination buffs:

> Many people suffer from what I would call "conspiracy phobia." They treat anyone who investigates actual conspiracies as oddballs. . . . The conspiracy phobics believe—as an article of faith—that conspiracies do not exist.
>
> Often the term "conspiracy" is applied in a dismissive way whenever one tries to ascribe any kind of human agency to elite power. If you suggest that people who occupy positions of political and economic power are willfully dedicated to advancing their elite interests, someone will derisively ask, "Oh, what do you have, a conspiracy theory?"[90]

Both the far right and far left are obsessed with the machinations of the intelligence community, particularly the C.I.A. Both camps believe there is a broad conspiracy to stamp out dissidents of their own political stripe and they weave complicated scenarios concerning international financial interests, transnational corporations, and the plottings of a shadowy world elite which, depending on which conspiracist one encounters, controls events even down to the local level.

Some conspiracy theories are neither left nor right in origin. Consider a 1990 poll administered to about a thousand black church members, which found that more than one-third of them believed the AIDS virus is a germ warfare conspiracy to commit genocide against blacks.[91] An April 1995 Gallup Poll determined that fully 39 percent of Americans think that the federal government "poses an immediate threat to the rights of ordinary Americans."[92]

Michael Kelly, writing in *The New Yorker,* uses the term "fusion paranoia" to denote conspiracy themes common to the far right and left.

> Although fusion paranoia draws from, and plays to, the left and the right, it rejects that bipolar model for a more primal polarity: Us versus Them. In this construct, the Us are the American people and the Them are the people who control the people—an elite comprising the forces of the state, the money-political-legal class, and the producers of the news and entertainment in the mass media.
>
> At its broadest level, fusion paranoia is entirely rational. There is a governing elite. Its interests and values are often radically different from those of the ordinary citizens, and this elite does indeed work to advance those interests in antidemocratic fashion.[93]

Kelly cites three "cutting edge" conspiracy publishers and book-sellers: Paranoia, Flatland, and Steamshovel Press. He notes that these sources are "essentially of the left, but they publish and advertise much of what the right has to offer, as long as it is conspiracist, radical and anti-government." Among leftist authors represented in their pages are Noam Chomsky, Jerry Rubin, Timothy Leary, Oliver Stone, Ramsey Clark, and Allen Ginsberg—hardly writers the far right would favor.

Kelly also states that Bob Fletcher, a major figure in the Militia of Montana, once found a soulmate in Danny Sheehan, a radical lawyer who ran the far-left Christic Institute. They shared a complex of conspiracy theories involving CIA operations.[94]

One of the major sources of combined left-right conspiracy theories is Dave Emory, heir to the exhaustive conspiracy files of the late Mae Brussell, the grand dame of conspiricism. Emory is by virtually every standard a leftist. An antiracist, antihomophobe advocate of multiculturalism, he prefers to refer to himself as an "antifascist researcher." According to news reports:

> Emory, 46, sees in the web of corporate-industrial lies, government coverups, covert military operations, political assassinations and international espionage the imminent triumph of worldwide fascism, no less.[95]

Among his favorite conspiracy themes are Watergate, the Kennedy assassination, Corporatism, Iran/Contragate, and a theory that the space shuttle causes earthquakes! Emory said:

> The right wing would love to destroy the Bay Area. It would certainly give the Christian right a chance to point to this as God's punishment for the sodomizers and fornicators who have violated the will of the Lord.[96]

Emory also suggests that the Oklahoma City bombing might have been a government setup—a conspiracy theme common to the militias. "The intelligence community and the FBI have infiltrated the paramilitary right to an extraordinary extent," he says.[97]
According to Mack Tanner:

> If those in the militia movement thought they had good reason to fear the government before, they are now even more convinced that powerful forces are planning to take away their freedoms. New conspiracy theories are already spreading via the Internet, the fax machines, and the shortwave radio stations. These theories describe the Oklahoma tragedy as one more piece of the conspiracy, perhaps deliberately planned and executed by federal agents to destroy the patriot movement and regain the power lost in the last election.[98]

## Civil Liberties Issues

In response to the Oklahoma City tragedy, President Clinton and other politicians advocated far more intrusive surveillance of extremist activities, including the introduction of the "Omnibus Counterterrorism Act." Since no groups, extremist or otherwise, were involved in the Oklahoma City bombing, the bill would have done nothing to prevent it.

Among provisions of the bill that are especially troublesome to civil libertarians are those that make certain kinds of political association criminal in and of themselves, and thus subject to the whole array of repressive government responses. *New York Times* columnist Anthony Lewis remarked:

> The legislation would let the President designate any foreign organization as a terrorist group, and similarly to designate individual Americans and organizations that raise funds for or otherwise support such a foreign group. The bill would make it a crime to give money to, or raise it for, such a group—even if the money goes to peaceful, political or humanitarian activities.[99]

Lewis also noted that under the bill a President could easily label one side or another in any country's conflicts as "terrorist" and thus make its supporters in the United States criminally liable.

The history of government surveillance of political groups is long and sordid. The COINTELPRO revelations of 1974 established that the FBI had conducted a campaign of infiltration and harassment against the Socialist Workers party, the Black Panthers, the Communist Party USA, and the Ku Klux Klan, among others. This included the use of thousands of informants, fabrication of news reports hostile to group leaders, break-ins and burglaries, and other forms of intimidation. In August 1975 Attorney General Edward Levi issued guidelines that sharply curtailed FBI abuses, including the requirement that the groups targeted were "engaged in activities involving the use of force and violence and that the group's activities would involve a violation of federal law."[100]

Some of the more sober and rational analyses of the militia "threat" came from surprising sources. One of these was Barbara Dority, president of Humanists of Washington and executive director of the Washington Coalition Against Censorship. Writing in the *American Humanist* magazine she observed:

> Much of the readily available "information" about militias and the patriot movement is being disseminated by "anti-hate" organizations with their own agenda. One such group is the Southern Poverty Law Center [which] has recently established a massive computer database of "hate groups" including reports on 14,000 individuals who have "committed hate acts" or who are "affiliated with hate groups," as well as "extensive intelligence" on more than 3,200 "hate and militia organizations."
>
> From a civil liberties standpoint, these tactics are a little too reminiscent of organizations like the John Birch Society, which kept extensive records on "communists and communist sympathizers." Moreover, the SPLC campaigns for laws that will effectively deny free speech and freedom of association to certain groups of Americans on the basis of their beliefs.[101]

Dority also quotes Clark McCauley, professor of psychology at Bryn Mawr College, who states:

> If you think these [militia] people are crazy, you have to ask [if] there [is] anything the federal government could do that would make you willing to take up arms against it. If you can answer no, then you're entitled to think these people are crazy. But if you say yes, then you'd better hazard a thought that [militia members] are human beings just like you.[102]

A number of groups, including the Anti-Defamation League, the American Jewish Committee, the Southern Poverty Law Center, and the Simon Wiesenthal Center, called on Congress to enact laws to criminalize paramilitary training. Following their testimony in support of these laws, Congressman Robert Barr said he was flabbergasted to hear them "dealing so cavalierly" with civil liberties. He complained of "such a pell-mell rush to outlaw more activity, to cut off people from doing things" that are disagreeable. In a statement that could have come from any militia leader referring to the FBI and BATF, Kenneth Stern of the AJC testified that the real threat to free speech is the atmosphere that armed "thugs" create, which "makes people afraid to speak their minds."[103]

Even Alexander Cockburn, a veteran leftist of long standing, wrote in *The Nation*:

> It's been . . . disheartening to find out how many on the liberal/left end of the spectrum hope earnestly for a ferocious pogrom against the militias and all those "linked" to them by the Justice Department, the F.B.I., Congressional committees working along HUAC lines with the full arsenal of conspiracy and RICO laws relentlessly deployed.[104]

As disquieting as the militia movement and similar organizations are to most Americans, it would be easy to justify policies and procedures we would instantly recognize as wrong if they were directed at organizations whose goals we approved of.

Significant criminal acts need to be addressed, no matter who commits them, but unremitting surveillance and special efforts to prosecute members of any political or social minority is frightening. Terrorism expert Jeffrey Kaplan observes:

> The manichaean "us against them" ethos which characterizes the radical right could well engulf those whose task it is to enforce the law. . . .
> While it is true that most Americans would shed few tears were there to be fewer denizens of the . . . radical right . . . it is also true that, as the siege of the Branch Davidian compound demonstrates, state violence once unleashed can acquire a momentum of its own. The consequences of this are surely considerably more deleterious than the disquieting views espoused by the radical right.[105]

## Notes

1. Jonathan Alter, "Jumping to Conclusions," *Newsweek* (May 1, 1995): 55.
2. June Jordan, "In the Land of White Supremacy," *The Progressive* (June 1995): 21.
3. Tom Reiss, "Home on the Range," *New York Times* (May 26, 1995).
4. Quoted in Samuel Francis, "A Little Terror from the Left," *Washington Times* (April 28, 1995).
5. James Ridgeway and Leonard Zeskind, "Revolution U.S.A.," *Village Voice* (May 2, 1995).
6. Ibid.
7. Jeffrey Kaplan, "Right Wing Violence in North America," *Terrorism and Political Violence* 7, no. 1 (Spring 1995).
8. Jonathan Franklin, "Timothy McVeigh, Soldier," *Playboy* (October 1995).
9. Reuters dispatch (May 14, 1995).
10. James A. Aho, *The Politics of Righteousness: Idaho Christian Patriotism* (Seattle: University of Washington Press, 1990).
11. Mark Potok and Katy Kelly, "Members Feel a Sense of Community," *USA Today* (May 16. 1995).
12. Editorial, *New York Newsday* (June 25, 1995).
13. Mike Tharp, "The Rise of the Citizen Militias," *U.S. News & World Report* (August 15, 1994): 34–35.
14. Keith Schneider, "Fearing a Conspiracy, Some Heed Call to Arms," *New York Times* (November 14, 1994).
15. Sanford Levinson, "The Embarrassing Second Amendment," *Yale Law Journal* (December 1989).
16. Scott Heller, "The Right to Bear Arms," *Chronicle of Higher Education* (July 21, 1995).
17. Linnet Myers, "Weaver Painted as Extremist," *Chicago Tribune* (September 9, 1995).
18. Neil A. Lewis, "Before Skeptical Senators, 8 FBI Agents Defend Tactics in Idaho Shootout," *New York Times* (September 15, 1995).
19. Gordon Witkin, "The Nightmare of Idaho's Ruby Ridge," *U.S. News and World Report* (September 11, 1995).
20. Tribune News Service, "U.S. Bill for Fatal Idaho Siege: $3.1 Million," *Chicago Tribune* (August 16, 1995); David S. Jackson and Elaine Shannon, "The FBI: Anatomy of a Disaster," *Time* (August 28, 1995).

21. Laune Kellman, "Reno Denies Knowing of Ban on Waco Gas," *Washington Times* (June 28, 1995).

22. Stuart A. Wright, "Two Years after the Waco Fire," *Washington Times* (April 19, 1995); *Armageddon in Waco* (Chicago: University of Chicago Press, 1995).

23. Ibid.

24. Stephen Labaton, "Report on Initial Raid on Cult Finds Officials Erred and Lied," *New York Times* (October 1, 1993).

25. Clair Johnson, "Armed Militias Called to D.C.," *Billings Gazette* (July 11, 1994).

26. Ibid.

27. Adam Parfrey and Jim Redden, "Patriot Games," *Village Voice* (October 11, 1994).

28. Ibid.

29. Don Wanagas, "Expose Sparks Outrage," *The Toronto Sun* (August 15, 1994).

30. Rosemary Speirs and David Vienneau, "Who's Watching Who," *The Toronto Star* (August 27, 1994).

31. Kirk Makin, "Lawyers Assail Bristow Tactics," *The Globe and Mail* (December 8, 1994).

32. Los Angeles Times, "Deal Lets Anti-Defamation League Escape Trial On Spy Charges," *St. Louis Post-Dispatch* (November 17, 1993).

33. Tom Tugent, "ADL Probed on Charge of Operating 'Spy Network,' " *Queens Jewish Week* (April 9, 1995); Ken Hoover, "Anti-Defamation League Raided by S.F. Cops," *San Francisco Examiner* (April 9, 1993); Richard C. Paddock, "Spy: 40 Years of Undercover Work for the ADL," *Los Angeles Times* (April 13, 1995); Robert I. Friedman, "The Anti-Defamation League Is Spying on You," *Village Voice* (May 11, 1993).

34. Marc Cooper, "Montana's Mother of All Militias," *The Nation* (May 22, 1995): 714–21.

35. Chip Berlet and Matthew N. Lyons, "Militia Nation," *The Progressive* (June 1995).

36. Mark Potok, "American Movement of Arms and Ideology," *USA Today* (January 30, 1995): 7A.

37. "Report: Militia Groups Growing," *Montgomery County Observer* (June 21, 1995).

38. Dick Foster, "10 Militias at Home in Colorado," *Rocky Mountain News* (September 6, 1995).

39. Southern Poverty Law Center, "Over 200 Militias and Support Groups Operate Nationwide," *Klanwatch Intelligence Report* (June 1995).

40. Dan Morse, "Marketing the Militias," *Montgomery Advertiser* (June 26, 1995).

41. Ibid.

42. Ibid.

43. David Eugene Frese, "Feds Accused by State Militia," *Salina Journal* (April 23, 1995).

44. Michael Janofsky, "Report Says Membership in Militias Increasing," *St. Paul Pioneer Press* (June 18, 1995).

45. Dick Foster, "Groups Deny Militia Connections," *Rocky Mountain News* (September 7, 1995).

46. Charlie Brennan, "Colorado's 'Patriots,' " *Rocky Mountain News* (April 30, 1995).

47. Dick Foster, "20 Militias at Home in Colorado," *Rocky Mountain News* (September 6, 1995).

48. Ibid.

49. United States Government Memorandum, F. J. Baumgardner to W. C. Sullivan (FBI), Subject: Investigation of Klan Organizations; Racial Matters—Klan. (September 22, 1966).

50. David Eugene Frese, "Kansas Commander: Militia an Insurance Policy," *Salina Journal* (May 14, 1995).

51. Rick Montgomery, Matthew Schofield, and Karen Uhlenhuth, "Area Groups Have Grown in the Last Year," *Kansas City Star* (May 6, 1995).

52. Spider Rybaak, "Onward Christian Soldiers: New York's Militias Battle a Godless New World Order," *Syracuse New Times* (July 5–12, 1995): 9.

53. Carol Bradley, "The Militia in Montana," *Great Falls Tribune* (April 30, 1995).

54. Kevin Johnson, "Tip-off Tally: 40,000 leads in Bomb Probe," *USA Today* (June 5, 1995).

55. "Whatever Happened to the Michigan Militia?" *Michigan Monthly* (November 1995).

56. "Group That Was Formed to Assist Law Officers Disbands in Utah," *Great Falls Tribune* (April 30, 1995): 7A.

57. Kevin Q. Murphy, "Kansas Militia Dissolves after Oklahoma Bombing," *Kansas City Star* (November 29, 1995).

58. Rogers Worthington, "Militia Members May Have Spun One Conspiracy Theory Too Many," *Chicago Tribune* (May 1, 1995).

59. Dick J. Reavis, "Militia Leaders Polishing Image Instead of Rifles," *Christian Science Monitor* (October 18, 1995).

60. Ibid.

61. Valerie Richardson, "Militias Hear Call of Public Service," *Washington Times* (May 27, 1995).

62. Ibid.

63. Ibid.

64. Clair Johnson, "Freemen Lose Battles against Justice System," *Billings Gazette* (July 2, 1994).

65. Mike Tharp, "In the Shadow of Ruby Ridge," *U.S. News & World Report* (December 4, 1955): 59–60.

66. Ibid.

67. Johnson, op. cit.

68. Associated Press, "Racicot Warns Protest Groups," (March 11, 1995).

69. Dennis Gaub, "Stanton Receives 10 Years," *Billings Gazette* (March 2, 1995).

70. Matt Bender, "Freeman Packed Firepower," *Billings Gazette* (May 3, 1995).

71. David Reed, "Fourth Conviction Wraps Up Probe of Militia," Associated Press (September 24, 1995).

72. Nina Martin, "The Militias Are 'Soft Targets,' " *San Jose Mercury News* (May 22, 1995).

73. Ibid.

74. Mercury News Wire Services, "Militias Plotted ATF Sucker Punch," *San Jose Mercury News* (July 21, 1995).

75. Kevin Johnson, "Racist Rally Reviewed Today," *USA Today* (July 21, 1995).

76. Tom Weiner, "FBI Says at Least 7 Agents Attended Gathering Displaying Racist Paraphernalia," *New York Times* (July 19, 1995): C18.

77. Associated Press, "Doubts Surface in Racism Claim at 'Ol' Boys' Rally," *Kansas City Star* (August 28, 1995): A–4.

78. Jerry Seper, "Good Old Boys Roundup Video Genuine," *Washington Times* (December 7, 1995).

79. Michael Janofsky, "Five Paramilitary Leaders Tell Senate They Pose No Threat," *New York Times* (June 16, 1995); "Militia Leaders Go On the Defensive," *Kansas City Star* (June 16, 1995).

80. Laurie Kellman, "Militias Decry Oklahoma Bombing," *Washington Times* (June 16, 1995).

81. Ibid.

82. Mack Tanner, "Extreme Prejudice: How The Media Misrepresented the Militia Movement," *Reason* (July 1995).

83. Katy Kelly, "Women Find Niche in Militias," *USA Today* (May 16, 1995).

84. Dan Strober, "Militia Sees World Conspiracy Group," *San Jose Mercury News* (April 26, 1995).

85. Ibid.

86. Ibid.

87. Victoria Pope, "Notes from Underground," *U.S. News & World Report* (June 5, 1995).

88. Joe Murray, "Soldier of Fortune Editor Says Militias 'Driven by Conspiracy Theories,'" *San Jose Mercury News* (September 30, 1995).

89. Karl Popper, *Conjectures and Refutations: The Growth of Scientific Knowledge* (New York: Harper & Row, 1961).

90. Michael Parenti, remarks at the Three Decades of Doubt Conference, sponsored by the Coalition on Political Assassinations in Washington, DC, October 7–10, 1994.

91. "One-Third of Blacks: AIDS Manufactured to Kill Them," Associated Press (November 2, 1995).

92. Victoria Pope, "Notes from the Underground," *U.S. News & World Report* (June 5, 1995): 24-27.

93. Michael Kelly, "The Road to Paranoia," *New Yorker* (June 19, 1995): 60-75.

94. Ibid.

95. Ken Kelley, "Tuned in to Possible Conspiracies," *San Jose Mercury News* (October 27, 1995).

96. Ibid.

97. Ibid.

98. Tanner, op. cit.

99. Anthony Lewis, "This Is America," *New York Times* (May 1, 1995).

100. George Archibald, "The Left, Once Foe of FBI Monitoring of Groups, Now Favors It," *Washington Times* (May 11, 1995).

101. Barbara Dority, "Is the Extremist Right Entirely Wrong?" *American Humanist* (November/December 1995): 12–15.

102. Ibid.

103. Daniel Kurtzman, "Putting a Foot Down," *Washington Jewish Week* (November 15, 1995).

104. Alexander Cockburn, "Beat the Devil: Neither 'Left' nor 'Right,' " *The Nation* (July 17/24, 1995).

105. Kaplan, op. cit.

# 19. Gerald L. K. Smith and Christian Nationalist Crusade

"I need Help!! Liberty at Stake!!! Jews Move in for the Kill!!! History is Being Made!!!!" This headline, hand-written in large, bold strokes across one-third of the front page was all that regular observers of the radical right from the forties to the mid-seventies needed to identify its source: a special newsletter from the Los Angeles and later Eureka Springs, Arkansas–based Christian Nationalist Crusade, conveying a typical appeal (predominantly for contributions) from one of America's most enduring radical rightists, Reverend Gerald Lyman Kenneth Smith.

A large man with a magnetic personality, Smith had an oratorical style that eventually earned him the reputation as one of the greatest speakers who had ever leaned over a pulpit. The former dean of intolerance was a phenomenon of American extremism almost defying description. He was one of the few rightist leaders in the sixties and seventies with campaign ribbons from the tumultuous far-right battles during the Depression days of the thirties. Some might say that there was no one quite like him in America.

As mentioned in an earlier chapter, in 1942 Smith launched Christian Nationalist Crusade, his main vehicle for dispensing anti-Semitic and racist propaganda. He also formed the Christian Nationalist party in St. Louis in 1948, and became its candidate on a platform pledged to deport Zionists, destroy "Jewish Gestapo Organizations" and the United Nations, and ship Negroes to Africa. In 1952, from his Tulsa office Smith launched an anti-Eisenhower drive that culminated in a special meeting of "patriots" who held their own separate convention in Chicago. For president, they nominated General Douglas MacArthur, who took no notice of their action. Smith had once distributed a chart demonstrating Franklin D. Roosevelt's "Jewish ancestry." Now he found evidence that Eisenhower was also Jewish. Needless to say, his efforts to stop Eisenhower were hardly noticed.

Smith eventually made Los Angeles the main headquarters for his crusade, operating out of a post office box. He also maintained an "east" office in Tulsa. From Los Angeles *The Cross and the Flag* was mailed monthly to virtually all parts of the country. His front groups included the Nationalist News Service, Christian Youth Against Communism, American League Against Communism, Citizens Congressional Committee, Patriotic Strategy Committee, and the Henry Ford Memorial Commission.

In addition to *The Cross and the Flag,* which had a circulation of about

30,000 in the early 1960s, Smith periodically bombarded his subscribers with gaudy newsletters dwelling on the same subjects as his magazine. There were also special in-depth reports that could be obtained for a contributon. The last three or four pages of Smith's magazine usually listed his "Crusading Literature." Many items were tracts, single copies of which were offered free. One example is "The Hidden Hand of the Anti-Christ," which Smith described as a "summary based on personal experiences of Gerald L. K. Smith." Other examples: "The Popes and the Jews," "Poison Water" (a tract on fluoridation), "God and the Moon—Man's dominion confirmed by Gerald L. K. Smith," and "What About Gerald L. K. Smith? Rogue? or Patriot?" The last-named tract could be had free by the bundles.

Smith's literature list also included a special box of four pieces that he felt should be in every home. This list consisted of his monthly magazine, of course, *The Protocols of the Learned Elders of Zion, Iron Curtain Over America,* and *The International Jew.* Smith was one of the bigger purveyors of the discredited *Protocols* in America. The last two volumes are highly polemical Jew-baiting "histories" consisting of themes woven around the framework made from the *Protocols. The Cross and the Flag* was loud and sensational, its major theme anti-Semitism. There were usually one or two articles, a section entitled "Smith Missiles," and another called "News Letter Items." One of these items explained how to have your will made out to Gerald L. K. Smith.

For years Smith flooded the country with magazines, books, pamphlets, newsletters, leaflets, manuscripts, photostats, brochures, squibs, folders, appeals, and "special reminders." All observers believe that his operation was profitable. Much of the success could be attributed to the constant stream of letters appealing for contributions. These letters, as well as his monthly magazine, were written in a style that has been best described by H. Keith Thompson as a "delicate balance between fundamentalism, anti-Communism, financial appeals, anti-Jewish-Negro sermons, and the most cloying, smug approach that has ever been seen."[1] This "delicate balance" has been imitated but never successfully duplicated by others on the far right.

While Smith's style was "cloying" to the average intelligent American, it was also, for reasons only a psychologist could venture to fathom, extremely satisfying to hardcore anti-Semites. Here, for example, is the heading of Smith's newsletter for October 8, 1970: "My Saddest Letter—I Weep!!" Then the letter begins: "Dear Friend: My throat swells, my eyes moisten—I sob. I am almost as sad as if there had been a death in my family. Why? Why? Why?"

The reasons for his sobbing are then listed in several numbered paragraphs. Paragraph one reveals, "Our Nation is about to surrender to the enemy in the Orient." Paragraph two laments, "The President of the United States has paid tribute to one of the most bloody Communist dictators that ever lived (Tito of Yugoslavia)." The third paragraph is more positive: "My research reveals that the slaughter in Jordan was a Jewish conspiracy to wipe out the heroic patriots who threatened to re-establish the State of Palestine." Farther on, the newsletter announces that Smith has written a report on what went on in Jordan which could cost me my life, or my liberty. Men will try to kill me, and they will try to imprison me for writing what I have written. It has gone to press and a copy will be sent to all who answer this letter.

A recurring theme in Smith's requests for money was the assertion that, as head of the Christian Nationalist Crusade, he was standing on the firing line absorbing abuse and torture for "conservatives" luxuriating in comfort and security at home. Thus, a 1961 letter was entitled "Holding the Line With Blistered Hands." Another, for December 6, 1967, was written in red: "No Vacation for Me. No Holiday for the Front Line." Sometimes his newsletters begin with questions: "Are We Losing America? Is It Too Late?" At other times Smith urged followers to be brave and persevering: "Face The Music! Hold The Line! Endure Victoriously!" Periodically, he felt constrained to show that "our side" is making progress: "The Blind Are Beginning To See—The Sleepy Are Beginning To Awaken—The Cowards Are Crying For Help—Even the Stupid Are Beginning To See The Light—The Day of the Christian Patriot Is At Hand."

Smith also complimented himself regularly in the headlines of his newsletters: "Men with less courage would weep! Men with less faith would quit! Men with less hope would complain!" Of course, all the newsletters end with an appeal for contributions, which patriots should be eager to make because of the sacrifice on Smith's part:

> Give until it hurts. Give money until you feel the pain of sacrifice. If those of us who stand in the front line trenches of the battle and take social ostracism can become outcasts in conventional society and face death and prison every day of our lives, if we can take it without compromise while moving steadily forward, then *the least you can do is give us the money with which to fight.*

Smith's use of sensationalism in reporting rather ordinary events so devalued the imagery ordinarily evoked by strong adjectives that the effect was soon dulled or burned out. His topic headings often became more descriptive phrases such as "A Tearful Disgrace," "Shocking Truth," "A Pitiful Situation," and "UNBE-LIEVABLE! UNBELIEVABLE! UNBELIEVABLE!" While using *The Cross and the Flag* and periodic newsletters to exaggerate, shock, and heighten fears and tension, Smith accused the regular news media of doing much the same thing.

His October 1970 issue of *The Cross and the Flag* urged readers to use the Ninety-first Psalm as a panacea for the effects created by the "scaremongers and panic button pushers. The news media is in the business of 'scaring everybody to death' every morning." In the manner of many extreme right leaders, Smith possessed such an inflated ego that he apparently could not discern the level of modesty the ordinary American maintains. As a result, there were almost constant references to himself and his accomplishments.

\* \* \*

In the May 18, 1961, newsletter Smith discussed a number of his "victories." One was the preservation of the Immigration Act, "protecting our Nation against wholesale invasion by undesirables." He also noted that the "Jewish conspiracy to involve us in a war with the Arabs in order to extend their bandit-gained borders in the Middle East has failed." He insisted that "over 100 vital patriotic groups with as many different names have grown out of the patriotic soil created by this Crusade." One evidence of this was the number of leaders in the John Birch Society who had been trained in Christian Nationalist Crusade.

By 1970 Smith was claiming that the number of "patriotic" groups spawned directly or indirectly by him had grown to some two thousand. And whenever the Supreme Court took over the headlines, Smith would distribute this special reminder on a black, index-sized card:

> Please be reminded that the Christian Nationalist Crusade has been largely responsible for much of the sentiment that is building up in America demanding a purging of the Supreme Court of the United States. We were the first to circulate a petition demanding the impeachment of numerous members of the Court.

Much to the chagrin of John Birch leader Robert Welch, Smith never quit talking about the Birchers. The September 1966 issue of *The Cross and the Flag* featured his reply to an attack by Welch:

> Mr. Welch knows that my followers make up a substantial portion of his membership. People who are alert to the Jewish question are in every segment of the John Birch Society. . . . All honor to Robert Welch and all honor to the John Birch Society, but as a veteran in this fight may I admonish the officers of the John Birch Society and the members of the John Birch Society not to panic in their attempt to escape the scorn of the Jew.

Again, in the October 1966 issue of his magazine, Smith reproved Welch: "Wake up, Mr. Welch, and identify your enemies. The organized Jew is out to destroy the John Birch Society and all organizations which are doing an effective job of fighting Communism."

The old canard that "Communism is Jewish," that the Jews established the Communist regime in Russia, was one of the main slogans of the extreme right in the thirties when Smith began his task of "saving America." Later events made the argument (that Jews control Russia) almost an embarrassment, and many gutter-level hate sheets on the far right felt compelled to modify their stories. Smith, however, took this position:

> We do not know whether the Russians are governed by those who seem to be their public officials, or by a "hidden hand" of secret authority. The factor remains, however, that the Soviet Union Government was established by Jews. The American Military Intelligence revealed that at the time more than 30-odd commissars which became the government of the Soviet Union following the revolution were Jews who came from the United States of America.[2]

This hoary old tale and others quite similar have been exposed as fraudulent countless times since the 1930s, when they enjoyed a wide circulation in the United States. There is not now nor has there ever been an institution of the United States government or the military services called "American Military Intelligence."

Smith's opposition to Jews and to the nation of Israel moved him to a pro-Arab position. In his newsletter of June 27, 1967, he revealed, "The Jews inside the Russian government, working with the Jews inside the U.S.A. government, are indulging in . . . doubletalk designed to . . . enslave 100,000,000 Arabs."

His antagonism toward any politician favorable to a Middle East solution that guaranteed the integrity of Israel was overwhelming. This was especially true of his attitude toward Robert Kennedy. His newsletter of March 21, 1968, showed concern that Kennedy could become president:

> The election of Bobby Kennedy to the Presidency would be the most catastrophic misfortune that could befall the U.S.A. . . . Bobby Kennedy is completely committed to the political and economic conspiracies of international Jewry. If the Jews demand it, he would withdraw troops from the Orient where they resist Communism and transplant them to the Middle East where they could slaughter the Arabs. . . . Anti-Semitism . . . would under Bobby Kennedy become a crime, punishable by prison or death.

By April 4, 1968, Smith was asking, "Will Bobby Kennedy become our dictator? . . . Does George Wallace hold the balance of power that can save America?" In a May 1st letter, Smith answered his own questions: "The Kennedy blight symbolizes a political and sociological disease. . . . A deadly document has come to my desk [that] refers to Robert F. Kennedy as an emerging American dictator." Two weeks later his newsletter disregarded all candidates except Kennedy:

> All candidates look good compared to Bobby Kennedy, who must be stopped. If we get him as the President we will have a complete, ruthless psychopathic, sadistic dictatorship. He will liquidate all his enemies.

By May 28, Smith's special packet on Kennedy was ready. His newsletter advised:

> The most dangerous political victory we could experience . . . would be for Bobby Kennedy to become President. . . . He must not be nominated as a Democrat, and all who answer this letter will receive a packet of tracts entitled "Stop Kennedy."

Smith was one of the anti-Semitic extremists who did not attack J. Edgar Hoover, but he did attack President Richard Nixon with a vengeance. Random criticism of Nixon stopped with the March 5, 1969, newsletter, when Smith mounted a frontal assault on the president. He never really did have confidence in the integrity of Richard Nixon, he said, but he did think that the president would be smart enough to implement George Wallace's program after he was elected by stealing Wallace's "law and order" issue. Smith had supported Wallace through-out the campaign and now revealed that he had helped him for a much longer time:

> As my friends know, I supported George Wallace from the very beginning. In fact, I supported him back in 1964, when I sent my personal secretary and paid her salary to direct the clerical work in his Indianapolis headquarters and in his Baltimore, Maryland, headquarters. I believed in George Wallace back in the days when he was an object of ridicule before millions began to take him seriously.

Smith claimed he clandestinely helped Republicans beat off Harold Stassen's bid for Nixon's vice-presidential place on the ticket in the 1956 campaign. For his efforts, he said, Nixon repaid him by stating, "There is no place for Gerald L. K. Smith and his ilk in the Republican Party." Nixon was now a "crazy demagogue," posing as a right-winger to get elected in order to doublecross the people who elected him. He had hated to write this letter exposing Nixon because many of his friends still had confidence in the new president. He said, "I would rather have been flogged with my face down until I spilled my blood on the ground than to have written this letter."

*       *       *

In the mid-sixties, Smith cast his eye on the little village of Eureka Springs, Arkansas. A tourist center known as the "Queen of the Ozarks" in the early 1900s, it had become a sleepy little town after the fad of mineral baths died out. Its main attractions were those of a retirement community because of the low real estate prices and the scenic beauty of the surrounding Ozarks. Smith picked this community as a restful site in which to spend his declining years. He also had in mind a few projects he felt would fit nicely into such an unspoiled rural area.

By the end of the 1960s he had constructed a whole collection of what he called "sacred projects." The most obvious is a seven-story mortar statue of Jesus with outstretched arms. This he erected on Magnetic Mountain, just outside the city limits of Eureka Springs. In the valley below the giant statue, he built an amphitheater, where he staged a Passion play during part of the year. He found support from local businessmen who felt that such a tourist attraction would be an economic shot in the arm for the town. Few, if any, people in the little village had ever heard of Smith, but they soon found out.

When the *Arkansas Gazette* learned that America's most infamous anti-Semite was moving into the state, a series of articles was published on his background. This began a division of the community of Eureka Springs that existed until Smith's death in 1976. Unperturbed, Smith expanded his activities and purchased one of the most expensive homes in the area, an old stone dwelling known as "Penn Castle." New attractions were continually added to his Eureka Springs complex: a "Garden of Gethsemane," a "Mount of Olives," "Pilate's Judgment Court," the "Upper Room," and even the streets of Jerusalem as part of the stage for his Passion play. He also built the "Christ Only Art Gallery," exhibiting his "lifetime collection."

Admission was charged to all of Smith's projects with the exception of the "Christ of the Ozarks" statue. The latter was built by the Elna M. Smith Foundation (named for Gerald's wife). When his projects were going nicely and tourists were pouring into the rural area, Smith discovered that a new road was needed to prevent traffic jams. It's been said that few people reach for government aid faster than those whose dogma normally calls for individual initiative, and Smith proved to be no exception. He applied to the Ozarks Regional Commission, a creation of the Commerce Department, for a grant to build the road. He was quite willing to let the taxpayers pay for it. When Jack Anderson broke the story in his syndicated column, the proposed road was described as a "highway to hate," and the statue as "a mockery to all the Savior taught." After headlines proclaimed that "Bigot Taps U.S. Funds," Secretary of Transportation John Volpe, under whose jurisdiction the road was finally placed, canceled the project.

Smith had good reason to suspect that his views and reputation were responsible for the furor. He screamed that the "hidden hand" of the Jews had struck again, and while reporters were pointing out that Secretary Volpe was a devout Catholic, he hurriedly got off a newsletter, vowing to fight:

> I weep as I write this letter. My throat swells, my heartbeat has been quickened. I have a feeling that we are on the border of Gethsemane, and I must be willing to imitate my Master. . . . These are deadly, trying days. The Jews have moved in for the kill. . . . Only a short while ago I received a letter from a man who signed his name and said: "The first time I see you, I'll kill you." I am not intimidated but I do know that without the hovering hand of God Almighty, I cannot be spared.

And so it went. Gerald L. K. Smith died in 1976 at age seventy-eight. He was buried at the foot of his seven-story, ivory-white, cross-shaped statue, Christ of the Ozarks. For over fifty years he had spread the message of hatred, bigotry, righteous indignation, and moral superiority. He had become even more shrill in the midst of the nation's polarization during the seventies. The Jews, he claimed, had gotten the atom and hydrogen bombs and intended to bring under their control the Caucasian capitals of the world: "America cannot be saved without concentration camps. At least a million of our people must be rounded up, isolated, and put away."

\*    \*    \*

Two years after Smith's death came publication of *Besieged Patriot,* described on its cover as "Autobiographical episodes exposing Communism, Traitorism and Zionism from the life of Gerald L. K. Smith, Gifted Speaker, Social Commentator, Servant of God." His style lived on.[3]

In analyzing the decline of Smith's popularity over the years, Glen Jeansonne observed:

People might go once to hear Smith out of curiosity, but he could not compete with television to lure people out of their homes on a regular basis. Political oratory in general was waning because of competition from television, and Smith never learned to exploit the medium. His rambling speeches were too long and disorganized for an effective television presentation. At his best among screaming zealots, he was out of his element before more sophisticated audiences. The more he raved, the more ridiculous he appeared; even his homilies seemed corny.[4]

Jeansonne commented at length on Smith's personality and what he thought was the driving force behind his fanaticism. Some of his observations:

Despite his obvious gifts, Smith was a troubled individual, tortured by guilt and his own desire for importance. As to sources of his guilt we can only conjecture. . . .

To give meaning to his life and to overcome the tremendous guilt he felt, Smith created out of his own imagination his mission to save civilization and give it God's stamp of approval.

By exaggerating the strength of his enemies and imagining conspiracies against himself, Smith elevated his own importance and that of his movement.

Because he manipulated others, it was easy for Smith to believe that others plotted to manipulate him. He used the "ruthlessness" of his enemies to justify his own.[5]

What appears obvious to us is that Smith had much in common with extremist fanatics all over the political spectrum. Jeansonne's general description of Smith's personality could account for dozens of extremists we have known from the far left and far right. This reminds us of Eric Hoffer's admonition that the real goal of the fanatic is to give meaning to an otherwise threadbare life—to feel worthwhile and important in spite of deep-seated feelings of worthlessness.

As with nearly all American political extremists, the net effect of Smith's life work was essentially zero. His projects in Eureka Springs will be seen predominantly as a novelty for tourists. If Smith is remembered at all, it will be as an example of what not to be. Even without the sometimes heavy-handed efforts to contain his influence, he probably would have ultimately been no more successful than he was. He remains a curiosity of American history.

## Notes

1. Keith Thompson, "A Survey of the Right Wing," *The Independent* (August 1962): 10.

2. *The Cross and the Flag* (October 1970): 9.

3. Gerald L. K. Smith, *Besieged Patriot* (Eureka Springs, Ark.: Elna M. Smith Foundation, 1978).

4. Glen Jeansonne, "The Case of Gerald L. K. Smith," in David A. Gerber, ed., *Anti-Semitism in American History* (Urbana: University of Illinois Press, 1986), 161.

5. Glen Jeansonne, *Gerald L. K. Smith: Minister of Hate* (New Haven, Conn.: Yale University Press, 1988), 172–73.

# 20. The LaRouche Network

During the 1970s and 1980s it often seemed that the media had given the man two extra names. Most common references to him began: "Political extremist Lyndon H. LaRouche." Few would deny that the label was warranted—LaRouche's pronouncements and demeanor, as well as those of his associates, virtually personify the extremist style. He is one of the most accomplished and inventive conspiracy theorists on the entire political spectrum, and his organization has a well-deserved reputation for conducting smear campaigns against various targets, among whom have been Walter Mondale, Henry Kissinger, David Rockefeller, and the queen of England.

Other appellations applied to LaRouche have included "Communist," "Trotskyist," "former leftist," "neo-Nazi," "Stalinist," "Democratic candidate," "Marxist-Leninist," "cult leader," "small-time Hitler," "demagogue," "kook," "Hitlerian hate-monger," and "anti-Semite." (Ironically, most of these labels came from LaRouche opponents who object to his penchant for name-calling.) Depending upon what one focuses on and what one ignores it would be possible to make a case for each of the above epithets. It could also be argued that to one degree or another LaRouche contains elements of all of them. One thing is very certain: Lyndon LaRouche has spent much of the past twenty years cultivating a vast array of enemies, some of them not much less "extremist" than he. On the other hand, his distorted view of the world and his demonstrated hostility toward various groups, including Jews, has produced some justifiable alarm.

Lyndon Hermyle LaRouche, Jr., was born in 1922 to Quaker parents and grew up in Lynn, Massachusetts. He entered the U.S. Army as a conscientious objector in World War II, during which he served as a medic in Burma. While in Calcutta, India, he joined the Communist party. After the war he was a Communist Party USA (CPUSA) member for a few years; in 1949 he joined the Socialist Workers party (SWP), the principal U.S. Trotskyist group. He used the party name, Lyn Marcus. In all, he spent seventeen years in the SWP. His first wife, Janice Neuberger, was also a member. After their divorce he lived with another SWP member, Carol Schnitzer, who was still with him during the early years of his National Caucus of Labor Committees.[1]

Although a committed Marxist-Leninist, LaRouche was always contentious and restless. He was secretly involved with embittered former SWP members, including Tim Wohlforth and his American Committee for the Fourth International, a small Trotskyist splinter group. In 1966 LaRouche was expelled from the SWP for working to organize a schism in the Trotskyist movement with Gerald Healy, leader of the (British) Socialist Labor League. Typically, LaRouche later broke with Healy and Wohlforth and went his own way. He began teaching Marxist economics at the Free School of New York, where he organized a following of young new leftists, including members of the Columbia University chapter of the Progressive Labor party (PLP), a Maoist group founded by former members of the CPUSA. During the student strike in 1968 LaRouche and his followers— many of whom were in the PLP—organized their own faction within Students for a Democratic Society (SDS), which they called the SDS Labor Committee.

During the 1968–69 period, the SDS national office found itself increasingly under attack by the PLP-oriented faction within SDS ranks. By the end of 1968 the LaRouche faction, now known as the National Caucus of SDS Labor Committees, was expelled over policy differences in the New York City teachers' strike. At the 1969 SDS convention in Chicago, the organization split into three factions and soon disintegrated, with the PLP-dominated Worker-Student Alliance in sharp opposition to LaRouche's group. Dennis King, author of *Lyndon LaRouche and the New American Fascism,* had been a Marxist-Leninst and a PLP member from 1963 until 1972, although he does not mention this anywhere in his book.[2] His bitterness at LaRouche is suggested in his comments:

> The main cause of the split was the sectarianism and ideological extremism of the two major factions, not the actions of LaRouche's followers, who were reviled as elitists by both camps. But LaRouche's 1967–68 raid on the PLP had definitely helped to tip the balance. It was his first lesson in how a small but adroitly led group, through the right tactics at the right time and place, can help to produce a "manifold shift" in the larger political arena.[3]

The NCLC remained small and little was heard from the group until 1973. Then, from May to September of that year, the NCLC engaged in what it described as "Operation Mop-Up," a series of violent confrontations with SWP and CPUSA members in which several people were injured. In the following years the NCLC began to transform itself from a more-or-less traditional—if somewhat kooky —Marxist-Leninist organization into a conspiracy-oriented political cult. La-Rouche's obsession with the Rockefeller family is an example of this shift. An article from a 1975 issue of the NCLC publication, the *Campaigner,* noted:

> At this moment, the human race stands closer to destruction than at any time in its history. The remaining loyal elements of the Rockefeller political-financial machine— which once bestrode the world like a colossus but now rages in the mortal terror of its impending extinction as a species—are determined to salvage what they can by bringing the world to the brink of nuclear war. Under present military-strategic circumstances, such desperate folly means the total thermonuclear destruction of North America and major destruction in Europe and the Soviet Union.[4]

The NCLC published the twice-weekly *New Solidarity* until 1986, at which time it reappeared as the *New Federalist.* In addition, it published another weekly,

*Executive Intelligence Review* at $400 per year, and two monthlies, *Campaigner* and *Fusion*. In addition to these, the organization also put out numerous private "intelligence reports" (some of which sold for several hundred dollars a copy), and a selection of books on LaRouche themes, including the widely circulated *Dope, Inc.,* which blames narcotics trafficking on "Zionists" and British intelligence circles.

*     *     *

The LaRouche group is best known for its peculiar ideological postures. The general confusion over whether it is "right" or "left" revolves around the group's novel approach to political theory. Lewis and Oddone explain:

> NCLC literature reflects LaRouche's strange theory of history, in which he posits three groups: the conspirators ("oligarchs"), LaRouche supporters ("humanists") and everyone else (variously described as "sheep" or "subhuman").
>
> Just who the oligarchs are is never clearly stated, but the "British Monarchy" is mentioned again and again. Among their plans is "genocide," a reduction of the world's population "to as little as 1 billion persons" by the end of the century. This will be accomplished with the aid of limits-to-growth organizations like the Club of Rome, "satanic promoters of Nazi-like euthanasia and global genocide." Also supporting this or other plans of the oligarchs are said to be UNESCO, the Jesuits, the Zionists, the National Council of Churches, most leftist organizations, many conservative organizations, Great Britain, and the Women's Christian Temperance Union ("founded by bands of axe-wielding lesbians").[5]

One of the best descriptions of the LaRouche complex of conspiracy theories is found in George Johnson's *Architects of Fear:*

> Not all believers in vast, apocalyptic conspiracies are right-wingers. One of the best-funded of the conspiracy-theory think tanks, the National Democratic Policy Committee, is run by conspiracy theorist Lyndon LaRouche, whose politics are so complex that he has been simultaneously accused of being funded by the KGB and the CIA. LaRouche counts among his enemies not only international bankers, the Federal Reserve System, and the Trilateralists, but also Ken Kesey, Bertrand Russell, *Playboy* magazine, Isaac Newton, the Nazis, the Jesuits, the Zionists, the Socialist International, and the Ku Klux Klan.[6]

According to Johnson, the line separating the good guys from the bad guys in the LaRouchean world is whether they are on the side of Aristotle or on the side of Plato in the battle over how one views reality. One camp has a relativistic view of the world (Aristotelian), in which reality, i.e., the evidence of the senses, is primary and empiricism reigns; the other camp embraces an absolutist view of the world (Platonic), in which ideas exist in a metaphysical realm, and idealism and utopianism reign. Because of their particular idealistic perspective, LaRouche's followers believe themselves to be the equivalent of the philosopher-kings described in Plato's *Republic.*

LaRouche's animus against the British greatly stems from his view that Aristotelianism (as advocated by the British empiricists Hume, Locke, Bentham, Russell, Berkeley, and others) is responsible for many of the ills of society:

> LaRouche believes that by emphasizing the empirical over the metaphysical, society has lost its moral bearings. Apply Aristotelianism to ethics, he says, and the results are moral relativism; in anthropology, cultural relativism; in religion, the idea that one system of belief is as valid as another—whatever works for the believer.[7]

According to LaRouche, the "oligarchs," the wealthy British families, are disciples of Aristotle and his intellectual tradition. They use his methodology in a conspiracy to keep the masses uninformed about the true nature of reality and helpless against their nefarious machinations. This bizarre conspiracy theory applies to virtually every aspect of the world and is extended and twisted to apply to situations and examples that seem ridiculous on the surface but that make "sense" if one accepts LaRouchean premises. LaRouchean thinking is profoundly ideological. Johnson says:

> For LaRouche's followers, the crowning touch of their conspiracy theory is that it offers an epistemology that seeks to justify paranoid thinking. . . .
> "It's done through ideas, not mechanistic control," Paul Goldstein explained. In LaRouchean Neoplatonism, causal links are unnecessary. Because ideas are more real than facts, influencing another's thinking is, by their definition, conspiracy. According to this logic, some of the weird juxtapositions in LaRouche's world view make their own kind of sense.[8]

In his early years, LaRouche had been intimately acquainted with the three largest Marxist-Leninist parties in the United States—the CPUSA, SWP, and PLP—and he had become aware that they were going nowhere. There were, he felt, serious flaws in Marxist-Leninist theory. It simply wasn't working in the United States. Further, like most political fanatics, he invested his entire ego in the drive for political power. He was a gifted and articulate, if also a somewhat cranky and contentious, ideologue. He had good persuasive skills and an almost diabolical talent for organization. He believed he *must* be a leader.

*     *     *

In 1973 LaRouche founded the U.S. Labor Party as the "electoral" arm of his operation. In 1976 he undertook his first presidential campaign. His platform included traditional Marxist-Leninist conspiracy theories and rhetoric, but with an added twist—LaRouche threw in some of the conspiracy slogans and buzzwords common to the far right. This marked the beginning of attempts to infiltrate and compromise rightist groups. In the process he managed to alienate the few Marxist-Leninists outside his orbit who still favored him. Some of this was probably rivalry and jealousy—because, like it or not, Lyndon LaRouche ran a tight ship. Typically, the Marxist-Leninist left began accusing him of becoming a right-winger and a fascist, as they have routinely labeled their renegades.

LaRouche has managed to pull together some of the brightest and best-credentialed young people an American extremist group had ever seen, including a disproportionate number of college-educated Jews (to the consternation of mainstream Jewish organizations). While other radical groups with roots in the left tended to idealize the working class, LaRouche and his followers concentrated on intellectuals. He demanded complete loyalty and usually got it. Many of his staffers received no pay and actually gave money to the organization. Those who needed subsistence usually received little more than that, except for a tight circle of top aides who received modest salaries. In terms of talent—the ability to write and speak, to organize and carry through projects—the LaRouche people, although fewer in number, were a considerable cut above other radical groups and on a one-to-one basis were much more efficient at their mission.

In point of fact, aware of the limited appeal of Marxist-Leninist rhetoric and principles to Americans, LaRouche wisely realized that in order to attain any success whatsoever, his program would have to embrace certain symbols and elements more congenial to the average American, whom he perceived as being on the political right. LaRouche's extremist style—strident, authoritarian, moralizing, and intolerant—was generically extremist. Given the correct "spin," it could be perceived as being either "right wing" or "left wing," depending upon what was needed. He believed, for example, that it was possible to form opportunistic alliances with right-wing groups on specific issues. According to Gregory Rose, a former NCLC member whose exposé of the organization appeared in the conservative *National Review* magazine in 1979, an NCLC "Security Memorandum" from the spring of 1975 set out LaRouche's rationale:

> Right-wing organizations offer four opportunities: 1) sources for fund-raising (especially related to our organizing); 2) political contacts to circulate our perspective in anti-Rocky political-financial-military circles; 3) opportunity to expose and discredit Rocky's Buckley-FBI-CIA penetration of the Right; 4) potential USLP members and periphery.
>
> Cadres should be firmly fixed on the politics underlying this move: the real enemy is Rocky's fascism with a democratic face, the liberals, and social fascists. We can cooperate with the right to defeat this common enemy. Once we have won this battle, eliminating our right-wing opposition will be comparatively easy.[9]

The mainstream conservative right nibbled at the bait but almost uniformly rejected it. LaRouche would occasionally reel in individuals, often the result of intensive recruiting campaigns targeting them on the basis of a shared hatred for drug peddlers, for example. In 1981 the conservative tabloid *Human Events* ran an extensive exposé of the LaRouche operation:

> In a series of lectures given in 1976, "What Only Communists Know," LaRouche described his network as a part of the "world's Marxist labor movement" which together

with "allied Communist forces within the capitalist sector generally are working overnight, constantly, to bring into being a new Communist international."

In that same year, however, LaRouche appeared to reverse course, ordering his followers to pursue "tactical alliances" with conservatives. LaRouche became critical of the drug lobby, the anti-nuclear movement, and the left-wing Institute for Policy Studies.

LaRouche also concocted conspiracy theories involving the Trilateral Commission, the Council on Foreign Relations, the Rockefellers, the British, and "Zionist agents."[10]

The article noted, with chagrin, that the Conservative Book Club had taken out advertisements in LaRouche's *Fusion* magazine and that the Freedoms Foundation had given an award to *Fusion* for a series of pro-nuclear articles. (It also noted that after learning of LaRouche's connection with *Fusion,* the foundation acknowledged making a mistake.)

Of particular interest was a *Human Events* account of the brief involvement of the far-right Liberty Lobby with the LaRouche operation. Acknowledging that Liberty Lobby and its publication *Spotlight* happen to share LaRouche's fascination with the Rockefellers and various conspiracy theories, the article told of their disillusionment with LaRouche's views, particularly his softness on "the major Zionist groups." Their common interest in certain conspiracy theories motivated *Spotlight* to comment that the USLP was "probably the only 'honest' Marxist group in the U.S. because it is not controlled by Rockefeller money, as are all similar groups."[11]

Gregory Rose had been an FBI informant within the USLP. His previously mentioned article in *National Review* was in retaliation for a series on the Buckley family in the *Campaigner,* which attempted to link the Buckleys to the "Rockefeller-CIA conspiracy." Rose responded with some heavy linking of his own and charged that there was extensive collaboration between LaRouche and Willis Carto:

> Carto was a conduit for extremist right-wing contributions to LaRouche's USLP campaign for the presidency, including part of the more than $90,000 used to purchase a half-hour prime-time commercial on NBC on the eve of the 1976 elections.[12]

On the other hand, Rose also linked the LaRouchies to the Soviets, stating: "The NCLC is avowedly pro-Soviet, as even a cursory examination of *New Solidarity* will show." Rose asserted:

> The NCLC is in a position to promote a pro-Soviet line on such issues as U.S. defense posture within certain conservative circles, whereas the Soviets could not make such an approach directly. It is equally obvious that information on conservative attitudes and personalities gained from NCLC contacts would be helpful to Soviet intelligence.
>
> Much of the Left regards the NCLC as a police-provocateur organization. There is little evidence, if any, to support such a hypothesis. However, the evidence of a Soviet connection is extensive and well-founded.[13]

In retrospect, we now know that LaRouche was definitely not a Soviet agent and also went nowhere with either the conservatives or the radical right.

*     *     *

The relationship, such as it was, between the USLP and Willis Carto's Liberty Lobby was marked by a good deal of mutual suspicion. Carto found LaRouche's writings too obscure and convoluted for his liking. Put simply, he was no more adept at understanding them than anyone else. Nor was he particularly happy with the large number of Jews associated with the USLP. The LaRouche people, on the other hand, regarded the Liberty Lobby crowd as "red-necks" and "idiots." Carto acknowledged some exploratory talks with LaRouche, particularly concerning his proposal that LaRouche

> assist us in fighting the IRS, pushing for legislation against the IRS and putting his organization in a more populist stance, and they refused that. Their derivations are entirely different from ours. They've never dropped their basic socialist positions. Every socialist likes high taxes and every populist hates high taxes. There's a fundamental difference there.
>
> I think they've gone very far afield by, for instance, their support of Alexander Hamilton. That's an anomaly. I just can't feature that. Alexander Hamilton was a royalist, he was a pro-aristocrat, he was for a central bank. For Christ's sake, this is anathema as far as I'm concerned. We are pro-Jackson and pro-Thomas Jefferson. To us central banking is really the core of the evil so I can't go along with that.[14]

Although the transient relationship is frequently mentioned to illustrate "links" and "ties" between LaRouche and the extreme right, it was brief and fleeting. Given their respective personalities, a union of LaRouche and Carto would be a miracle under any circumstances.

There was, however, one legitimate and enduring "link" between the LaRouche group and the racist, anti-Semitic right. This was the "Typhoid Mary" of political extremism, Roy Frankhauser, whom we dealt with extensively in the chapter on the Minutemen. A talented informant and con man, Frankhauser pulled off one of the biggest hoaxes in the annals of political extremism on LaRouche and his staff. This would not have been possible had it not been for LaRouche's obsession with conspiracy theories and his relentless foraging for "intelligence" information on his enemies—who by this time had become legion.

Roy Frankhauser had been an informant for one government entity or another since the early 1960s. During the early 1970s he worked for the Bureau of Alcohol, Tobacco and Firearms of the U.S. Treasury Department on cases involving right-wing extremists. In addition, he proved a prolific source for journalists and others who traded information. He affected the demeanor of a self-made master spy, albeit a rather dissheveled and unorthodox one, and always regarded his activities as "intelligence work."

Frankhauser came to the attention of LaRouche after he was indicted on charges of stealing explosives in 1974. Frankhauser's defense was that he was acting as an ATF informant at the time. He wound up being sentenced to a period of probation instead of the several years in prison that was customary in cases like his. In July 1975 the *Washington Star* reported on his role in a Canadian undercover operation authorized by the top-secret National Security Council.[15] Frankhauser was assigned to infiltrate the notorious "Black September" terrorist organization on grounds that it was plotting to kidnap Jewish Americans. On July 28, 1975, he gave an interview arranged by the USLP that was covered by *CBS Evening News*. During that program, CBS newsman Fred Graham revealed:

> One government source said Frankhauser had an uncanny ability to penetrate both right- and left-wing groups, that he could still help convict those who supplied the explosives that blew up school buses in Pontiac, Michigan in 1971.[16]

The occasion for the interview was a press conference arranged by LaRouche's USLP. The LaRouche people were thrilled to have an actual government agent in their clutches. They assisted Frankhauser in the preparation of a long, rambling "Press Statement" in which he made the following claims:

> From my experience as an undercover agent for the following agencies of the Federal Government—the Central Intelligence Agency (CIA), the Federal Bureau of Investigation (FBI), the Alcohol, Tobacco and Firearms (ATF) division of the U.S. Treasury—I have concluded that the wide spectrum of terrorist and criminal activity in this country is the creation of the National Security Council and the covert intelligence community which functions under NSC control.
>
> It became obvious to me as a result of my investigation that various Maoist, Anarchist, and right-wing extremist groups in this operation were under the control of the FBI, LEAA (Law Enforcement Assistance Administration) and other Federal Agencies.[17]

Frankhauser's disjointed 3,500-word statement continued with several implausible and fantastic allegations implicating numerous law enforcement officials, politicians, and political activists in one form of perfidy after another. Included was an account of his own "brainwashing," in which he said:

> Drugs were put into my food and I was taken to an interrogation room where more drugs were given to me through injections. The effect of the drug was to promote a sensation of receding into a tunnel. I also experienced at other points a cessation of breathing and also an overwhelming sense of drowning and loss of consciousness. While I was strapped in the medical chair I was asked questions relating to Canada in the form of: "Do you remember? That didn't happen, this happened," etc.
>
> I know beyond a doubt that I was subjected to "behavior modification" or, as it is more commonly known, "brainwashing" during my incarceration. There could have been no purpose for this other than the fear on the part of the CIA and the National Security Council that I possessed incriminating evidence as to the nature of the so-called Black September terrorist venture.[18]

Following this encounter with the LaRouche operation, Frankhauser gradually worked his way into its "intelligence" and "security" apparatus. Far from being put off by his associations (with racist and anti-Semitic groups ranging from the Ku Klux Klan to the American Nazi party), they simply regarded it as part of his cover as an intelligence operative. Referring to the LaRoucheans as the "comrades," he soon acquired a reputation as a reliable source with LaRouche security officers Jeff Steinberg and Paul Goldstein. They paid his fare and expenses to travel to New York City for consultations. In time Frankhauser was a handsomely paid full-time security consultant.

Beginning in 1977 Frankhauser started his imposture as the conduit for "Mr. Ed," allegedly a CIA contact who was funneling information and advice to LaRouche. Over the years until 1984 Frankhauser created dozens of memos from "Mr. Ed" to LaRouche, all seemingly well-informed and authentic. So realistic did the memos appear that when their existence leaked out of LaRouche circles through defectors from the security staff, there was speculation among journalists and others about who "Mr. Ed" might be, and a number of past and present CIA figures were suggested. "Mr. Ed" was actually the skillful creation of Roy Frankhauser.

Frankhauser brought in a confederate, Forrest Lee Fick, whom he had known in KKK circles. Fick was placed on the LaRouche payroll and the two of them worked closely to continue the deception. Although intelligent and cagey, Frankhauser always had a very difficult time writing. He would dictate material to Fick, who would dutifully transcribe it for him. Among their many deceptions were the weekly "COMSTA-C" reports. These, like the messages from "Mr. Ed," were entirely the product of Roy Frankhauser, who had learned from years of observation exactly what the LaRouche people wanted to hear. In addition, Frankhauser cultivated a relationship with a media source in New York City so he would have access to wire service information before it was printed or broadcast. Hence he was able to give "tips" to LaRouche that something was imminent just prior to its being reported—a rather impressive trick that "confirmed" his intelligence ties as far as the NCLC security staff was concerned.

Many of LaRouche's alleged "links" to right-wingers were made at the suggestion of Frankhauser. One of these was Mitchell WerBell, a former contract CIA agent and arms manufacturer with a flair for self-promotion. WerBell, an acquaintance of Willis Carto, operated Cobray International, a counterterrorism training school. Dennis King alludes to this in the following observation:

> It was Roy who first suggested that the LaRoucheans should link up with Mitch WerBell. Claiming to have worked with WerBell on CIA assignments, Roy helped them compile a detailed dossier on him."[19]

King also notes that it was a warning from Frankhauser's "Mr. Ed" on August 1, 1977, that LaRouche was being considered for assassination, which prompted LaRouche to hire WerBell as his security leader. After a period of observation, WerBell learned that the key to keeping LaRouche on the hook was to feed his monstrous ego while jerking on his paranoia chain from time to time. LaRouche, on the other hand, dealt with WerBell in characteristic fashion, by jerking *him* around on fees for services performed.

Frankhauser was also responsible for the meetings between Robert Miles (whom he had earlier informed on for the ATF) and the LaRouche staff. They were led to believe that Miles had "intelligence" connections. When it finally dawned on them that Miles was a real neo-Nazi, they broke contact. Dennis King acknowledges Frankhauser's role in deceiving the LaRouche people:

> There was a good reason for Roy's success as a secret agent: He was making up most of it. "It was bullshit," Fick said. "Roy would make up a source A, then a Source B, C, and D. I'd be sitting right beside him when he did it." Internal reports from LaRouche's security staff in 1984 confirmed Fick's story.[20]

Although LaRouche and his staff must assume full legal responsibility for their actions, King acknowledges that Frankhauser's assurances that their (illegal) activities would be protected by the CIA did encourage their endeavors.

> Meanwhile the LaRoucheans blithely continued with their credit-card and loan schemes. They believed Roy's assurances of support from "down the way," the cumulative faith built up by a decade of transmissions from Mister Ed and the Source. When almost four hundred federal agents and state and local police officers swooped down on the NCLC's Leesburg headquarters in October, 1986, the LaRoucheans could blame it in no small part on the misleading advice of their Ku Klux Klan scout.[21]

By the time LaRouche was running for president in 1984 he was referring to himself as a "conservative Democrat" and claiming he had never been a leftist, but was merely opposed to the excesses of Wisconsin Senator Joseph McCarthy. In typical LaRouche fashion, he had "forgotten" previous references to himself as the American Lenin.

A February 1988 broadcast by his campaign organization over CBS TV claimed that LaRouche had played a key role in gaining support among America's allies and neutral nations for President Reagan's Strategic Defense Initiative. The LaRouche broadcast claimed that the Soviets declared the former "American Lenin" to be "Soviet public enemy number one." Ironically, this "Soviet public enemy" had previously characterized the dissident Andrei Sakharov as a KGB agent whose job it was to manipulate the United States.[22]

*    *    *

Dennis King goes to considerable lengths to paint LaRouche as a neo-Nazi, even engaging in a little conspiracy-mongering of his own. King maintains, for example, that words like "British" were really code words for "Jew." Obviously, people of good will can disagree on the relative "threat" LaRouche and his crew have represented to the republic, but we feel that King goes too far. There are numerous

LaRouchean political indiscretions and the courts will take care of the criminal matters. Questionable assertions are unnecessary.

In a review of King's book which appeared in the *New Republic,* John Judis says that King overrated LaRouche. Judis notes historian Richard Hofstadter's observation that "populist anti-Semitism functioned in America as a rhetorical style, not a tactic or program." He also observes, "If there is to be a 'new American fascism,' it will probably not come from a crackpot like LaRouche."[23]

Ricky Cooper, publisher of *NSV Report,* organ of the neo-Nazi National Socialist Vanguard, has been active in groups of that nature for some twenty years. Cooper has a reputation for being highly critical of his own movement and also as a reliable media source. He knows of no instance where LaRouche "ever cooperated with or had any positive relationship with anyone that could be considered neo-Nazi besides Roy Frankhauser." Cooper did mention a positive comment on LaRouche in Robert Miles's newsletter, *From the Mountain.*[24] Miles— a former Ku Klux Klansman, acquitted defendant in the 1988 Fort Smith sedition trial, and neo-Nazi guru—acknowledged having talked to LaRouche but confirmed that there was "no tie and no sympathy whatsoever" between himself and the man.[25] Miles's praise of LaRouche for causing consternation in Jewish circles was simply an application of the principle of "The enemy of my enemy is my friend" (and a momentary friend at that).

Former California KKK leader and founder of the White Aryan Resistance, Tom Metzger (see neo-Nazi chapter), has asserted that charges of Nazism against LaRouche are "ridiculous." According to Metzger, no one in the neo-Nazi movement has regarded LaRouche as even vaguely sympathetic, and those who have paid him any attention have been suspicious of the large number of Jews and other minorities in his organization.[26] Other professional neo-Nazis say essentially the same thing. If Lyndon LaRouche is a neo-Nazi, that fact is apparently unknown to leaders of the American neo-Nazi movement.

On the other hand, LaRouche's general antiestablishment views, often expressed with nastiness and stridency, clearly have been designed to defame, degrade, and offend. To the extent that this has included Zionism, Israel, the "Zionist lobby," and Jews as a class of people, hostility toward Jews has been plainly evident.

The charge of racism against LaRouche is similarly problematic. On October 24, 1984, the leader of the Congress of Racial Equality, Roy Innis, took the stand as a character witness for LaRouche in his slander suit against NBC News. Innis stated under oath that LaRouche's attitude toward racism was consistent with his own. In response to the question, "Have you seen any indication of any racism at all in Mr. LaRouche's associates?" Innis replied, "I have not." When asked whether he had seen any indication that LaRouche or his associates were anti-Semitic, Innis replied: "I have seen no such evidence."[27] Numerous black and other candidates "of color" have appeared on election ballots under the LaRouche banner over the years and Reverend James Bevel, a former Martin Luther King, Jr., associate, has written for the *New Federalist.*

Other prominent black figures who have identified with LaRouche include

Amelia Robinson Boynton, a leader in the original civil rights movement who took part in the historic 1965 march in Selma, Alabama. She currently works with LaRouche's Schiller Institute, which recently published her autobiography, *A Bridge Across Jordan*. Another is the late Hulan Jack, the first black elected president of the borough of Manhattan. Jack worked closely with the National Democratic Policy Committee, a LaRouche operation, and nominated LaRouche for president of the United States in 1980.

*    *    *

A Mike Royko column in April 1986 addresses the confusion surrounding LaRouche and his strange ideology. He asks, "Are they right-wingers or left-wingers or just plain nuts? How can they be anti-Semitic when so many of them are Jews?" He concludes that "they still function more like Stalin-era communists than anything else." Why the appeal to the far right? Royko says: "The answer is that there's not much of a market in this country for communism. But there are a lot of people on the far right. So they tailored their pitch to that market."[28]

Whatever can be said about the ideological basis of the LaRouche phenomenon, one action put him on the wrong side of virtually everyone: the credit card and loan fraud schemes. Beginning in the 1970s LaRouche fundraisers were resorting to unsavory pressure tactics to get money for their leader's increasingly expensive election campaigns and burgeoning intelligence-gathering apparatus. These tactics quickly escalated to fraud in the form of raising the amounts charged for subscriptions to LaRouche publications paid for by credit card. When subscribers complained about a ten- or hundredfold increase in their charges, LaRouche fundraisers would attempt to negotiate the overcharge into a contribution or, if all else failed, a loan. They were successful in a surprising number of cases. Literally hundreds of thousands of dollars were "raised" this way.

John Mintz, writing in the *Washington Post* in October 1987, commented on the mentality that permitted this kind of thing to occur. Quoting former NCLC Member Charles Tate, he said:

> "Outsiders are considered morally inferior to people inside the group," ex-member Tate said. "It's [seen as] practically a favor [to outsiders] if they're made instrumentalities of the organization. If you have $20,000 in your bank account, you're better off if you give it to the group to use for an important purpose. You'd probably just do something self-degrading with it anyway, like go off to Hawaii."
>
> That kind of attitude, investigators and ex-members charge, led the group to stall interminably when people complained about not getting their money. . . .
>
> Former LaRouche associates say that because the organization got away with so much for so long, group members believed they would never be held responsible.[29]

Gradually, however, victims of this fraud began filing complaints with various agencies, and a few even initiated lawsuits to recover their funds. These complaints reached a flood stage and several states began undertaking investigations and issuing indictments. In December 1986 LaRouche and six of his aides went on trial in Boston for a massive credit card scam. The case, however, became so muddled when evidence of government misdeeds began cropping up that the judge declared a mistrial. In 1988, however, LaRouche et al. were tried in federal court in Virginia and convicted on several similar counts. LaRouche and some of his associates are currently in federal prison. State prosecutions also resulted in convictions of other LaRouche officials.

In analyzing the failings of the LaRouche group, it becomes woefully apparent that this organization has been prone to the problem of "groupthink," a behavior described by Irving L. Janis as:

> a mode of thinking that people engage in when they are deeply involved in a cohesive in-group, when the members' strivings for unanimity override their motivation to realistically appraise alternative ways of action.
>
> Groupthink refers to a deterioration of mental efficiency, reality testing, and moral judgment that results from ingroup pressures.[30]

A case can be made that the LaRouche organization represents a certain level of "danger" to society, but how much? As much as drunk drivers in Cleveland last July, or as much as dope dealers in New York City on any given weekend? As emphasized throughout this book, we believe that indiscriminate or unfair repression of this and other extremist groups also represents a danger. It's probably true that LaRouche could not have happened in an authoritarian state. The price we pay for a free society is that some people will behave badly. Another aspect of that freedom is that other individuals and groups are free to organize and propagandize against the LaRouche operation, and in this way contain its influence.

Although mainstream figures are legitimately concerned with the LaRouche organization, a good number of his harshest detractors come from extremist ranks themselves. A writer who has spent considerable time on LaRouche is John Foster "Chip" Berlet, of Political Research Associates (PRA) in Boston. His articles on LaRouche go back into the 1970s. Berlet is also a veteran of the 1960s student left, and currently serves as the National Lawyers Guild (NLG) representative to the National Committee Against Repressive Legislation. Harvey Klehr confirms:

> The NLG is an affiliate of the Soviet-controlled International Association of Democratic Lawyers (IADL), founded in 1946. Expelled from France in 1949, the IADL is now headquartered in Brussels. Over the years it has supported every twist and turn in Soviet foreign policy, including the invasions of Hungary, Czechoslovakia, and Afghanistan. The American Association of Jurists, the regional affiliate of the IADL, is headquartered in Havana. Its president, Ann Fagan Ginger, is a long-time NLG activist.[31]

In 1987, when Berlet moved with his organization to Boston from Chicago, the Chicago Area Friends of Albania gave him a special sendoff, noting that, "Chip was one of our founding members, and a steadfast friend of Albania through thick and thin." King gives Berlet credit for considerable assistance, and Berlet in turn reviewed King's book for the Marxist-Leninist *Guardian*.[32]

The primary evil of the LaRouche organization and groups like it lies not so much in their particular ideological pronouncements or the positions they take on various issues, but in how they treat their opponents and in the vision they maintain of the civil liberties of all Americans. Here the antidemocratic and anti–civil libertarian nature of LaRouche and his followers is manifest, and it is primarily on *these* grounds that they should be opposed.

## Notes

1. Biographical information on LaRouche comes from a variety of sources including: Dennis King, *Lyndon LaRouche and the New American Fascism* (New York: Doubleday, 1989); Chip Berlet and Joel Bellman, "Who Is This Guy?" *Reader* (December 12, 1986); and Lyndon H. LaRouche, Jr., *The Power of Reason: A Kind of an Autobiography* (New York: New Benjamin Franklin Publishing House, 1979).

2. Dennis King says he has not concealed his past PLP membership and has spoken of it on a number of occasions but did not think it was relevant for his book. We disagree.

3. King, 16.

4. *Campaigner* (December 1975).

5. Sasha Lewis and Mareen Oddone, "The Strange History and Curious Persecution of Lyndon LaRouche and the U.S. Labor Party, Lately Arrived in California," *New West* (March 24, 1980): 76.

6. George Johnson, *Architects of Fear: Conspiracy Theories and Paranoia in American Politics* (Los Angeles: Jeremy Thatcher, 1982), 22.

7. Johnson, 195.

8. Johnson, 198.

9. Quoted in Gregory Rose, "The Swarmy Life and Times of the NCLC," *National Review* (March 30, 1979): 409–413.

10. "Who and What Is Lyndon LaRouche?" *Human Events* (February 7, 1981): 5–6.

11. Ibid.

12. Rose, 411.

13. Rose, 413.

14. Willis Carto telephone interview (September, 11, 1991).

15. John Hilferty, "Man in Jackboots, Swastika Was Secret Agent for U.S.," *Washington Star* (July 20, 1975), A–6.

16. Fred Graham, "CBS Evening News" (July 28, 1975).

17. Roy Frankhauser, "Press Statement" (July 1975).

18. Ibid.

19. King, 201.

20. King, 204.

21. King, 206.

22. *Richmond Times Dispatch* (October 5, 1984).

23. John Judis, "The Making of a Madman," review of *Lyndon LaRouche and the New American Fascism,* by Dennis King, *New Republic* (May 29, 1991), 39.

24. Ricky Cooper telephone interview (September 11, 1991).

25. Robert Miles telephone interview (September 11, 1991).

26. Tom Metzger telephone interview (September 11, 1991).

27. William Bastone, "Runnin' Scared," *Village Voice* (July 12, 1986), 11.

28. Mike Royko, "LaRouchites Are More Like Stalin-Era Communists Than Anything Else," Tribune Media Services (April 17, 1986).

29. John Mintz, "A New Menace in the Demon-Filled World," *Washington Post National Weekly Edition* (October 5, 1987), 24–25.

30. Irving L. Janis, *Victims of Groupthink* (Boston: Houghton-Mifflin, 1972).

31. Harvey Klehr, *Far Left of Center: The American Radical Left Today* (New Brunswick, N.J.: Transaction Publishers, 1991), 161.

32. Berlet and Bellman, op. cit.; Chip Berlet, "LaRouche's Bizarre Brand of Fascism," *Guardian* (August 2, 1989).

# 21 Jewish Defense League

In 1994 Baruch Goldstein, an Orthodox Jew and member of the Jewish Defense League, sprayed automatic weapon fire into a mosque in Hebron, Israel, killing 29 and wounding 125. He was beaten to death on the spot by a mob of survivors. People belonging to his group (and sympathizers) called him a hero and claimed this violent act was motivated by his love for the Jewish people. Normal humans recoiled at such sentiments and wondered at the lack of empathy and humanity of those affiliated with such an organization.

Jewish Defense League members consider themselves the heirs of Vladimir Zeev Jabotinsky (1860–1940), a radical Zionist of the 1920s and 1930s. In the manner of those Marxist-Leninists who have continued to commune with the ghost of Leon Trotsky (1879–1940), leaders of the JDL have regarded Jabotinsky as their "spiritual founder."

The JDL's actual founder was an Orthodox rabbi named Meir Kahane (Ka-HAH-nee), who organized the group among predominantly Orthodox Jews in lower-middle and working class areas of Brooklyn in 1968. Born Martin David Kahane in 1932, the future champion of Jewish ethnocentrism was a "revolutionary from a young age," according to an uncle who was convinced his nephew always had a "messianic complex" that led him to believe that he would be instrumental "in the revival of the Jewish people."[1] It seems quite natural that Kahane's beliefs would develop as they did. In the manner of "red diaper babies" who become Communists, his ideas were, to a great extent, those of his father, who admired the aforementioned Jabotinsky. The elder Kahane pushed his son to join Betar, the youth organization of Jabotinsky's nonsocialist Revisionist party, the postwar successor of which was Menachem Begin's Herut party. As a young Betar member, Kahane "spent his spare time at the docks of Bayonne and Hoboken, N.J., smuggling guns on freighters bound for the rebels seeking to establish Israel as an independent State."[2]

By the mid to late 1960s Kahane, who had become associate editor of the *Jewish Press,* began to be concerned about what he interpreted as rapidly growing anti-Jewish attitudes in America and the world. He also believed that muggers were preying on Jewish neighborhoods not only because they hated Jews, but because Jews were seen at patsies while other ethnics, especially Italians, were seen as tough. Kahane set about to change this outlook by forming the Jewish Defense League, and soon his group had a reputation for being not only "tough," but dangerous.

Interestingly, during this period Kahane also served as an undercover informant for the FBI in, of all groups, the John Birch Society. He found relatively little to inform on. Using the pseudonym Michael King, Kahane promoted the pro-Vietnam "Fourth of July Movement," and with Joseph Churba he coauthored a booklet, *The Jewish Stake in Vietnam.* According to an article published in *The Jewish Week* following Kahane's death in 1990:

> As Michael King, he led a double life in the 1960s, allegedly carrying on a relationship with a Christian woman named Gloria Jean D'Argenio. D'Argenio, who worked as a model, jumped to her death from the Queensborough Bridge in 1966, reportedly distraught over the relationship.[3]

\*    \*    \*

By 1971 the JDL claimed chapters in a dozen cities and a list of contributors who numbered over 10,000. In its early days the JDL focused on the plight of Soviet Jews. Tactics included picketing and "camping" outside Soviet institutions, such as the Soviet UN mission, the embassy, TASS and AMTORG offices—all legitimate and accepted protest activities. But JDL actions soon revealed a dark side of the organization when members began roughing up Soviet (and Arab) diplomats in public. In January 1971 JDL activists set off a bomb at the Soviet cultural offices in Washington, their first real venture into terrorism. JDL violence soon became a source of concern to Soviet officials. At one point Soviet Ambassador Anatoly F. Dobrynin abruptly left Washington for Moscow in apparent protest. Soviet officials accused the United States of "connivance" in the attacks. Mark R. Arnold in *The National Observer* noted:

> Far from denying its militancy, JDL flaunts it. In full-page newspapers showing teenagers armed with bats, it asks: "Is this the way for nice Jewish boys to behave?" and answers in the affirmative, arguing that if Jewish people don't look out for themselves, no one will.[4]

Late that same year the JDL launched a "massive campaign to encourage aliyah" (Jewish immigration to Israel). Kahane pushed the message that Jews had no future in the United States, but only in a Jewish state. He set an example by moving to Israel in September 1971. Near the end of the 1970s the group mounted a terror campaign against "Arab residents of the Israeli occupied West Bank" of the Jordan River. According to the *FBI Analysis of Terrorist Incidents in the United States, 1983,* the JDL also had defended "Jewish rights" by attacking Egyptian, French, German, Iranian, Iraqi, Lebanese, and Palestinian "targets in the U.S."[5]

One of the several offshoots from the JDL was a small group called the Jewish Armed Resistance, led by a Steven Rombom. During the period of its existence, pipe bombs exploded outside several diplomatic offices (including Soviet, Iraqi, and Polish). Shots were fired into the homes of several Soviet diplomats. On May 2, 1976, pipe bombs exploded outside Communist Party USA headquarters in New York. The violence stopped when the FBI arrested Rombom (seventeen), Steven Ehrlich (twenty), and Thomas MacIntosh (thirty-six), a Jewish convert. MacIntosh testified for the prosecution and the others were convicted. Rombom spent twenty months in prison. His psychiatric report noted that he "needs long psychiatric treatment in a disciplined and structured environment."[6]

*    *    *

The late 1970s was a time of considerable JDL activity, particularly in southern California. In October 1977 three JDL members—Irv Rubin (thirty), the West Coast coordinator, and two executive board members, Earl Krugel (thirty-four) and Robert Manning (twenty-five)—were apprehended by Los Angeles police following an explosion at the Beth Star Shalom Religious Center in North Hollywood. News reports described the event:

> Investigators said patrolling officers heard the blasts . . . just before a car containing the three men pulled away from the curb. The vehicle was stopped a short distance away.[7]

All three men were released on $5,000 bond. The blast caused only minor damage to the sidewalk. The charges were later dropped, presumably for lack of evidence.

In 1978 the New York City chapter of the JDL had offered (through its telephone message service) a $500 bounty on "every Nazi lawfully killed during an attack on a Jew."[8] Los Angeles-based JDL leader Irv Rubin topped that at a press conference by offering $1,000 to the person who turned in a Nazi's ears. Rubin was charged with solicitation of murder for making the statement. He was later tried and acquitted.[9]

The JDL was often suspected of staging anti-Semitic incidents in order to win sympathy and publicity. JDLers were caught redhanded in Philadelphia in February 1979 when James Guttman, who later proved to be none other than Mordechai Levy, applied for a permit to hold a neo-Nazi rally in Independence National Historical Park. The permit application made a considerable stir in the Philadelphia media. Guttman (Levy), who had identified himself as an official of the American Nazis, in the portion of the application indicating how many participants were expected, wrote: "100 fo us, Oh how many niggers and Jews [sic]." News reports indicated:

> Channel 6 anchorman Jim Gardner last night said he had asked Mayor Rizzo about the situation. "He [Rizzo] said if the permit is granted and the feds ask for police protection, he'll tell them to go get the Marines. Rizzo also said the city would go to court to stop the rally."
>
> Hilda Silverman of the American Civil Liberties Union said today that she had received no complaints about the rally as yet. "We support the rights of groups to demonstrate and march," she said.[10]

Jewish organizations mobilized to protest the permit. The Jewish Community Relations Council announced it would "call upon all appropriate governmental officials to investigate these events fully and completely." A Michael Guttman was located but he knew nothing about the Nazi party or the rally. He had lost his passport and identification cards two years previously. Slowly, the investigation began to focus on Levy. New York State Police advised that the telephone number given by James Guttman had been used by a "Mordechai Levy."[11]

The permit was rescinded because of irregularities, mainly the difficulty in identifying the applicant. Finally, a *New York Times* article revealed:

> Court testimony suggested that the man identified as James Guttman may have been using a stolen identification when he sought the permit. A Philadelphia police sergeant said another man, identified as Mordechai Levy, had once been arrested in New York using information from the card. Mr. Levy had been associated with the Jewish Defense League.
>
> The permit was challenged by the Association of Jewish New Americans. Its attorney, David Ferleger, contended that there was evidence that the applicant was indeed a Nazi, and added, "I'm very upset and angry at attempts to haggle this around and blame Jews."[12]

According to Dennis King in *Lyndon LaRouche and the New American Fascism,* Mordechai Levy first encountered the LaRouche group in 1980, became one of their "secret operatives," and immediately began doublecrossing them.

> Given the code name "Leviticus," he carried out various assignments in Los Angeles and made frequent trips to New York. . . . This relationship lasted for four years, with the LaRoucheans paying tens of thousands of dollars for his meals, airfare, and hotel rooms. To maintain his cover, *New Solidarity* [a LaRouche newspaper] occasionally attacked him as a Zionist terrorist.
>
> Mordechai was supposed to collect intelligence on LaRouche's enemies and run operations against them. What he actually did was compose fictitious information . . . while passing along tips about LaRouche's plans to journalists, the ADL, and Jewish community leaders. . . . After dropping his double-agent role in 1984, he agreed to be a witness for the Boston prosecution of LaRouche for obstruction of justice.[13]

\* \* \*

The JDL often protested and threatened violence when pro-Arab speakers appeared. For example, in November 1979 Irv Rubin appeared on the campus of the University of California at Northridge to protest Dr. Halem I. Hussaini, of the Palestine Information Office, who was scheduled to speak at the university during Human Rights Week. Accompanying Rubin's appearance was a telephone threat to student president Bill Imada, during which a man identifying himself as a member of the JDL said that "a bomb would be placed on campus where the speaking engagement was to be held." News reports stated that other individuals had been threatened by the JDL over the incident. Hussaini spoke as planned and no bombing occurred.[14]

In September 1979 the JDL picketed a California talk by the Reverend Jesse Jackson outside the Garden Grove Community Church. Jackson had told church members that the United States should work toward ending "warmongering" in the Middle East.

While Jackson was speaking, a band of 11 "Jewish fighters" dressed in army fatigues and brandishing baseball bats, sauntered about or stood in the shade telling passers-by that Jackson was "anti-Semitic."

"Jackson is an anti-Semite; he's proven that by his political stand," said one JDL member. JDL National Director Irv Rubin said: "This is a show of strength; to show that we are tired of dying and, if we are kicked, we will kick back. Anyone who is for the PLO hates Jews and we are against them."[15]

What did "kicking back" entail? In the October 18, 1980, issue of the Jewish Defense League newsletter, JDL national director Brett Becker made the following threatening pronouncement:

I believe what is needed for our survival in America is the establishment of a secret, Jewish strike-force: an underground, that will quietly and professionally eliminate those Jew-haters that are both a threat and a danger to our existence. It should be led by sane individuals who realize that such a group would not have an office or a phone and not even take credit for their actions. To do what must be done yet say nothing.[16]

Under Rubin's leadership, the JDL forged an image of itself as a guardian of Jewish interests. For example, in April 1980 the JDL gained much publicity following an alleged synagogue desecration:

Five to 10 Jewish Defense League members, some armed with semi-automatic weapons, others with handguns, patrolled a small Orthodox Jewish seminary in North Hollywood last night to ward off a possible second attack of anti-Semitic vandals.

Irv Rubin, the No. 2 man in the JDL below Rabbi Meir Kahane, and league member Earl Krugel, stood behind the Aish Hatorah College for Jewish Studies on Chandler Boulevard. Rubin carried a .308 caliber carbine rifle on his shoulder and Krugel carried a replica Thompson semi-automatic rifle.

The seminary was the target of a Passover Eve vandalism attack Monday night. Black spray-painted swastikas and slogans such as "Death to Jews" and "Hitler is Alive" were left behind on walls, fences, and cars around the building. Vandals also broke one car window and a building window.[17]

In March 1981 the JDL picketed and threatened the offices of the Institute for Historical Review, an organization noted for its publications questioning the Jewish Holocaust in World War II. Chanting "Never again" and "Jewish justice," some fifteen JDL members demonstrated in front of the IHR offices in a small industrial park. According to news reports:

"We are here to expose the Institute for Hysterical Review," said Irv Rubin, JDL leader. "As sure as the sun rises tomorrow, 6 million Jews died. We want to show that this cancer exists in Torrance, and we want them to know that we will be back."

Mordechai Levy and other demonstrators attacked the car of a man claiming to be the landlord and ordering the JDL off the property. Levy smashed the right passenger window of the man's car as he drove off. "Unless he wants us down here every week, he better evict him," Rubin said.[18]

In June 1981, a Molotov cocktail was thrown through the window of the IHR's offices. It did little damage. News reports noted:

> Shortly before the pre-dawn explosion at the Institute for Historical Review, a caller identifying himself as a member of the "Jewish Defenders" called United Press International and threatened to bomb the group's headquarters.[19]

A considerable number of people who should have known better were attracted to the organization due to its militance and Kahane's charismatic personality— and also because of the group's slogan: "Never again." But perhaps the most important attraction to many seems to have been Kahane's adoption of the cause of Soviet Jewry. If, as has been charged, this "cause" was predominantly a ploy to gain support for the JDL, it worked. Such well-known personalities as comedian Jackie Mason, Haagen-Daz ice cream magnate Reuben Matteus, and author and country and western singer Kinky Friedman of "Kinky Friedman and His Texas Jewboys" all lent support.

The mainstream Jewish response to Kahane and the JDL has been a combination of revulsion and embarrassment. In November 1981 the national office of B'nai B'rith Hillel sent a directive to all its college chapters requiring them to bar Kahane from appearing under their auspices. Kahane replied:

> The national directive is only written confirmation of a previous unwritten policy of censorship by the feudal barons of B'nai B'rith and Hillel. Hillel bears direct responsibility for the tragic spiritual holocaust destroying Jewish youth on the campuses. The tragedy is that, rather than humbly accepting criticism, they—as all tiny totalitarians—attempt to silence the speakers of truth.[20]

The Anti-Defamation League has regularly denounced Kahane, the Jewish Defense League, and its various spinoffs. The ADL has made it clear that the group does not represent the greater Jewish community and that it unequivocally disapproves of JDL philosophy and tactics.

\*     \*     \*

The JDL's relationship with other extremist groups is a matter of some interest. INCAR (International Committee Against Racism) is a front group for the Progressive Labor party, an independent communist organization. In January 1982 one of its members, then living in Israel, wrote this of the JDL in the PLP newspaper *Challenge:*

> Without the serious backing of the bourgeoisie, they are nothing more than a few marginal fascist activists, kept alive by nickels and dimes. But when the interests of the bourgeoisie are threatened, these dormant fascists are showered with money and publicity in the hopes that they will become a "popular" movement capable of protecting their masters' interests.

What should be expected from this "new and improved" JDL? First, they will attempt to intervene in all popular struggles against the KKK, Nazis and other fascists. When they do, they will be stridently anti-communist, much more concerned about stopping INCAR and PLP than the Klan or Nazis.[21] (Wording and punctuation original.)

The Black Panther party had confrontations with the JDL as well. On May 7, 1970, the JDL staged demonstrations in front of two BPP headquarters in New York. In Harlem, thirty-five JDL members reportedly scuffled with Panthers. According to the Revolutionary Communist party, the cause of these altercations was the FBI. In a July 1982 issue of *Revolutionary Worker,* the RCP reported on FBI records acquired under the Freedom of Information Act dealing with the JDL:

> In a Memorandum between the New York City office of the FBI and J. Edgar Hoover, the idea of using the JEDEL [the JDL's original acronym] against the New York chapter of the Panthers was headlined, "Operations Under Consideration." The following proposal ran:
> "The (New York office of the FBI) is presently considering an attempt to contact and establish some rapport with the Jewish Defense League in order to be in a position to furnish JEDEL with information the Bureau wishes to see utilized in a counter-intelligence technique."
> The memo is dated September 5, 1969. For the next 8 months the FBI fed anti-Semitic letters, purportedly from the Black Panthers and other "Black organizations" to the JDL.[22]

These documents cannot be authenticated, but the practice described is consistent with numerous other descriptions of FBI disinformation and destabilization activities against what it has termed racial "hate groups."

\*     \*     \*

In 1981 twenty-year-old Mordechai Levy, who once served as the JDL's security chief, broke with the group to found his own, the Jewish Defense Organization (JDO). At a press conference in June 1981 Levy met with reporters at the Los Angeles Press Club to announce the opening of a guerrilla training camp north of Los Angeles which he called "Camp JUDO" (Jews United to Defend Ourselves). He brandished a collection of two semi-automatic rifles, two other rifles, and a shotgun. The event produced seven arrests:

> An unimpressed Los Angeles Police Department responded by arresting seven members of the three-month-old Jewish Defense Organization in the press club parking lot.
> The police later released JDO leader Mordechai Levy and his followers after determining that the weapons were not loaded. But the officers held on to the weapons, reportedly to check their registration, a police spokesman said.
> "The time has come to launch physical attacks on nazis and the Ku Klux Klan

when they become a threat to the Jewish community," Levy said. "God help any nazis who vandalize synagogues because there is going to be nazi blood."

At the press conference Levy called [Irv] Rubin a "sellout" and said that the JDL has become "ineffective."[23]

In 1982 the American-Arab Anti-Discrimination Committee published a report entitled *The Jewish Defense League: A Cult of Racism and Terror, A Threat to Arab-Americans.* The report detailed several specific incidents where JDL terrorists were allegedly responsible for acts of violence directed at Arab-Americans. These incidents, beginning in 1970, ran from telephone threats to arson and pipe bombs. No convictions for these crimes have occurred so far.[24]

Arab-Americans had reason to worry. The JDL made no attempt to soften its rhetoric. During his years in Israel, Kahane wrote a regular column for the *Jewish Press,* a tabloid newspaper serving the Orthodox Jewish community of New York City. In a 1983 "Kahane Speaks" column he called upon the Jewish Defense League to "declare war on the physical enemies of the Jewish people." Specific recommendations included, in part:

> To create a specially trained, uniformed Jewish Defense Corps of physically strong Jewish expert fighters and weapons users. This will be on instant call to react to or act upon acts of Jew-hatred and their perpetrators.
>
> To monitor and infiltrate the hate groups on every level.
>
> To create classes in Jewish identity, Judaism and pride so that every JDL member will grow both in Jewish spirit as well as body. . . .
>
> To use the news media cleverly and proficiently to publicize the declarations and to warn our enemies that we do not seek their love—only their cautious decision to leave Jews alone. . . .
>
> And, with every opportunity, to cry ever more loudly: Jews go home![25]

During Kahane's campaign for the Knesset in 1984 he was outspoken about his plans for Arabs in Israel. Referred to as "the most electrifying candidate in Israel's July 23 election, as well as the most passionately revered and despised," Kahane promised:

> One day after I get elected to the Knesset I will go to the Arab village of Um-el-Fakhm with a sheet of paper and a pen in my hand. I will say to the Arabs, "Whoever signs his name on this paper that he is ready to leave Israel voluntarily will be given financial compensation. Those who do not will be forced to leave anyway, but will not be given a thing."[26]

In February 1984 a JDL spin-off calling itself Jewish Direct Action telephoned UPI offices in New York City and claimed responsibility for several bomb explosions that rocked a Soviet residence in the Bronx. The caller said, "There will be no easing of American-Soviet tensions until Anatole Schransky and other Soviet Jews are freed."[27] JDA leader Victor Vancier denied involvement. He did acknowledge that he had been jailed in similar bombings. News reports confirmed:

Jewish Direct Action, which had scheduled its news conference outside the Soviet mission in Manhattan before the bombing, plans to harass Soviet diplomats, tie up the mission's telephone lines and continue weekend rallies until Soviet Jews are permitted to emigrate, Vancier said.

A news release quoted Vancier as saying Soviets also faced "major acts of violence that will seriously endanger their lives," and that the assassination of Soviet officials was "absolutely inevitable" as long as Schransky and others were held."[28]

On July 4, 1984, the Institute for Historical Review was burned to the ground, the obvious work of arsonists. The JDL was widely suspected. The arson has not been solved at the time of this writing. The *New York Times* reported:

The early morning fire appeared to have been set by someone who hurled a firebomb into the building or doused the offices in gasoline and set them afire, Lieut. Jim Pabst of the police said. Damage to the one-story building occupied by the Institute was estimated at $400,000.[29]

The IHR was physically wiped out. Only small amounts of records and books were salvaged. The organization survived, however, and was able to eventually resume publication of its *Journal.*

\*    \*    \*

One of the odder developments in the JDL's history occurred when Irv Rubin formed an alliance with Michael Canale, a 285-pound neo-Nazi. Canale, who had been the southern California representative of Aryan Nations, spent thirty-two months in federal prison for setting fire to Temple Beth David in the San Gabriel Valley in 1980. After his release from prison he became an informant for the JDL. News reports described the liason:

A huge bear of a man, Canale has spent nearly half of his 36 years in prison for drug and burglary offenses. During one of those terms in the mid-1970s, he became involved in the neo-Nazi movement and the association lasted for the next eight years.

He credits his conversion to "a totally converted JDL ideologue" to the man he claims is the hate groups' most despised Jewish antagonist: West Coast JDL leader Irv Rubin, the target of an aborted KKK assassination plot in 1978.

[In prison] he began a correspondence with a skeptical Rubin, apologizing for the temple arson and renouncing his former beliefs. Despite frequent rebuffs from the JDL leader, Canale eventually convinced him of his sincerity and the two met in October [1983] and formulated plans for Canale to infiltrate the ranks of his former colleagues.[30]

Canale, thirty-six, was not to enjoy his new-found friendship for long. In September 1984, by then a JDL member, he was arrested and held in lieu of $50,000 bail on charges that he phoned in a false bomb threat against Dr. George Ashley, a director of the IHR.[31] Canale pled guilty.

In Israel, Meir Kahane was having his problems. Resistance to his admittedly racist views was mobilizing and he was encountering more and more opposition from liberal and moderate elements in Israeli society. Jerusalem Mayor Teddy Kollek had called Kahane's election to the Knesset "a stain on Israeli democracy." Even Menachem Begin issued a statement that he and his conservative backers "have nothing in common" with Kahane. A September 1984 issue of *Newsweek* related:

> At an anti-Arab rally in Haifa last week, Meir Kahane felt right at home. But suddenly some unexpected cries rang out from the crowd of 2,000. "Down with fascism" chanted hecklers, peppering the Brooklyn-born rabbi with catcalls and preventing him from speaking. "I'll deal with dogs like these," he snarled back. His manner and his campaign to oust all Arabs from the Jewish homeland have rubbed some very raw nerves in Israel."[32]

In August 1985, Kahane resigned as leader of the JDL. He named Irv Rubin as his successor. Rubin commented: "We are going to change the emphasis of the JDL to be more of an American-based organization. That's the way the JDL was created and that's the way we are most effective."[33]

Rubin was also quoted as saying that the JDL membership was thirteen thousand, a figure disputed by almost all observers. Jerome Bakst, director of research for the Anti-Defamation League, said that the organization in New York probably consisted of a few members meeting in homes. Informed estimates of JDL membership at this time were in the neighborhood of two hundred active members with perhaps two thousand supporters and contributors.[34]

An account of Kahane's resignation from the JDL that ran in the *New York Times* noted:

> The decision to make these changes comes at a time when the league and competing militant Jewish groups have become the focus of numerous federal and state investigations into recent bombings and assassinations on the East and West coasts. The FBI said Friday that the league was "the possible responsible group" in three bombings in the last three months, one in Santa Ana, Calif., one on Long Island and one in New Jersey. Rubin said the league had nothing to do with the bombings.
>
> Law enforcement officials on both coasts say they are concerned that the JDL may have formed a militant underground effort in the United States. . . .
>
> Four gunmen who fired on an Arab bus in the Israeli-occupied West Bank, wounding seven passengers, on March 4, 1984, were JDL members, Kahane has said. They were trained in the use of weapons at league camps in New York State and Los Angeles, according to Bruce Hoffman of the Rand Corp. in Santa Monica (CA).[35]

Terrorism attributed to the JDL went on unabated in 1985. Any person or group who offended the organization was subject to attack. In May an explosion ripped the front door off the home of a retired Los Angeles school teacher who had expressed doubts about popular accounts of the Holocaust. The initials "JDL" were painted on the sidewalk to George Ashley's house.[36] In June a German-American group was firebombed.

A $50,000 fire ignited by an arsonist broke out early at the Santa Monica offices of a group that claims the number of Jews exterminated during World War II is exaggerated.

In a tape-recorded message telephoned to United Press International, the voices of a man and woman claiming to be members of the Jewish Defense League said the militant group had "bombed" the offices of the German-American National Political Action Committee.[37]

JDL leader Irv Rubin said the recording was a fraud, "probably done by GANPAC itself."[38]

A priority target of the JDL had always been individuals in any way identified with Nazi war crimes. On August 13, 1985, Tscherim Soobzokov, sixty-one, a former SS officer, was injured in a pipe bomb explosion at his home in Paterson, New Jersey. He died a month later of wounds suffered in the explosion. Soobzokov had vigorously denied any participation in Nazi atrocities. On September 6, a pipe bomb directed at Elmars Sprogis, seventy, of Brentwood, Long Island, seriously injured another person. Sprogis had been accused of having been a Nazi. In 1983 he had been cleared by a federal judge of involvement in war crimes. According to press reports:

> The Jewish Defense League has claimed responsibility for yesterday's firebombing of the home of a Long Island man once accused of being a Nazi.
>
> Tom Scheer, FBI commander of the Joint Terrorist Task Force, said that shortly after the blast, a man who said he was from the Jewish Defense League called a newspaper and claimed responsibility.
>
> Probers said the blast, caused by a pipe bomb, resembled the August 15 explosion at the home of Tscherim Soobzokov. Investigators said that in both incidents a pipe bomb was set on the front porch of the houses and a diversionary fire was set to lure the victims outside.[39]

Nineteen eighty-five saw a wave of terror against Arab-Americans. In August a bomb was left on the front steps of the Boston office of the American-Arab Anti-Discrimination Committee. A policeman was seriously injured in disarming it. In October a bomb ripped apart the Santa Ana, California, offices of the group and killed its spokesman, Alex Odeh, who had received frequent threats from the JDL.[40] In November arson was blamed for a fire that destroyed the ADC's offices in Washington, D.C. The JDL was suspected in all three incidents. An Associated Press article published November 9, 1985, noted:

> The FBI on Friday attributed a California bombing that killed an official of an Arab-American group to the Jewish Defense League.
>
> Lane Bonner, the FBI's spokesman, said in answering a question that the bombing "has been classified as a terrorist attack and attributed to the JDL." The bombing is still being investigated, he said, and he declined further comment.
>
> Irv Rubin, who is national head of the JDL, said: "We are not responsible, although we do not shed tears for the death of Mr. Odeh. He was 100 percent in back of the PLO."[41]

Mordechai Levy of the JDO was also busy during 1985. A spate of window-smashing of Jewish-owned shops in the Boro Park and Flatbush neighborhoods of Brooklyn brought out his street patrols. Levy said he planned to "teach a lesson" to vandals that "Jews won't be pushed around."[42] An enormous amount of publicity was generated over the incidents, including a $10,000 reward offered by New York City, and a $5,000 reward offered by the Jewish Community Relations Council. In due course the perpetrator was nabbed: Gary Dworkin, a thirty-eight-year-old Jewish resident of Boro Park. No evidence developed to show any links between Levy and Dworkin, who was ordered to undergo psychiatric examination.[43]

In spite of increasing signs of opposition, Meir Kahane's stance was attracting a growing following in Israel. An article by Thomas L. Friedman for the New York Times News Service commented:

> When Rabbi Kahane was elected to the Israeli Parliament a year ago, most political commentators dismissed him as an "American import" and a "racist lunatic" who would never find a serious following in Israeli society. His election, they said, was a "fluke."
>
> Today, nobody is dismissing Kahane, who advocates ousting all Arabs from Israel and the occupied territories and turning the country into a purely Jewish state that would be run according to Jewish law. He is the most talked-about political figure in Israel and by all indications his popularity is soaring.[44]

Among Kahane's shocking proposals was the expulsion of Arabs from Israel. He warned that Arabs "breed like rabbits" and would take over the Israeli Knesset in twenty-five years. "I am not prepared to sacrifice Zionism to democracy. There is only one solution: The Arabs must leave Israel." An Israeli reporter asked: "How could you do that? Midnight deportations in cattle cars?" Missing the Naziesque implications, Kahane firmly answered, "Yes!"[45] A 1986 book in Hebrew, *Heil Kahane,* by Yair Kotler, draws parallels "between Kahane's legislative proposals" and laws targeting Jews in Nazi Germany.[46]

A fascinating insight into the JDL is provided by Robert I. Friedman in a long and detailed article in the *Village Voice* in May 1986, entitled "The Return of the JDL: Nice Jewish Boys With Bombs." Dealing largely with JDL internal matters, Friedman says that the JDL is fragmented and has degenerated into "competing bands of right-wing Jewish warlords." Noting that Kahane appointed Victor Vancier, a JDL member since 1971, to head the organization's East Coast operations, Friedman says:

> When Victor Vancier joined the JDL in 1971, he was a junior at Jamaica High School in Queens. Three years later he was convicted for his first felony—a JDL firebombing of a Soviet diplomat's car in Manhattan.
>
> Vancier was also one of the JDL's most notorious bombers. After committing a wave of bombings for which he says he was never arrested, in December 1978 Vancier and another JDL member were convicted for firebombing 11 Egyptian diplomatic targets in New York, Virginia, and Maryland. Vancier served 16 months of a 21-month sentence in federal prisons in New York and Florida.[47]

Friedman details the relationship between the JDL and Murray Wilson, who has contributed more than $350,000 in cash and equipment to the organization. When Kahane wrote a 1984 column in the *Jewish Press* calling for the liquidation of "Hellenist, spiritually sick [Jews] who threaten the existence of Judaism," Wilson became a bitter opponent of Kahane.

In a thorough account of the JDL underground, Friedman describes various crimes attributed to the JDL against Soviet, Arab, and former Nazi targets in the United States, as well as numerous incidents in Israel—many involving Americans who went to Israel to work with Kahane. Of considerable interest is Friedman's account of Bob Jacobs, whom he describes as "one of Kahane's most fanatical supporters," a man who contributed $20,000 for his 1984 Knesset campaign and who has raised money on behalf of convicted Jewish terrorists. Jacobs, it seems, has also provided money for his "close friend, North Carolina Senator Jesse Helms, who made his first journey to the Holy Land with Jacobs last summer." Helms, an "extreme conservative" and lifelong critic of Israel, completely reversed position during his 1984 election campaign and now supports Israeli occupation of the West Bank.

In the United States, Kahane continued to experience rejection from mainstream Jewish leaders, who often used the questionable tactic of attempting to deny him a forum. In Seattle a Kahane supporter accused the *Jewish Transcript* and the Jewish Federation of Greater Seattle of trying to keep Kahane's views from the local Jewish community. The paper had declined to run an ad for Kahane's November Seattle speech, while the federation had adopted a resolution opposing Kahane's visit.[48]

During a November 1986 talk at the National Press Club in Washington, Kahane was splattered with red dye by a man who left behind a typewritten statement signed, "Jews Against Zionism." The man was arrested and charged with simple assault. Kahane was unharmed. During the talk he had applauded the fact that Israel had nuclear weapons.[49]

In April 1987 the FBI arrested Murray Young. Agents found evidence in his home linking him to the JDL and to "recent bombings and terrorist acts." Among the items seized were seventeen firearms, materials and tools used to make explosives, and JDL records and documents. He was charged with possession of a pistol silencer and was released after he made $1 million bond.[50]

In May 1987 *The Jewish Week* reported that three JDL members had been arrested by FBI agents on six pipe bomb and grenade incidents in the New York metropolitan area between 1984 and 1986. Four of the incidents were against Soviet targets. The paper said:

> Victor Vancier, alias Chaim Ben Yosef, 30, of Queens, Jay Cohen, 23, also of Queens and Sharon Katz, 44, of Manhattan, were arraigned before U.S. District Judge John Caden. . . .
> Vancier . . . was arrested as he was mailing a letter to JDL member Murray Young. . . . Vancier's letter warned Young "to keep his mouth shut because the government doesn't have enough evidence and if everyone keeps his mouth shut, everything will be all right."[51]

In September 1987, Vancier, Cohen, and Katz pleaded guilty to federal racketeering charges. Cohen, who faced up to twenty years in prison and $25,000 in fines, tragically committed suicide with an overdose of prescription drugs prior to sentencing. The three had confessed to several acts of terrorism: the 1986 fire-bombing before a performance by the Moscow State Symphony at Avery Fisher Hall, the 1986 firebombing of a Pan Am landing dock, and the 1984 firebombing of the Soviet diplomatic residence in Riverdale, New York.[52]

In November 1987 the FBI announced that Israel was obstructing its investigation of the 1985 bomb slaying of Alex Odeh and several other terrorist acts linked to the JDL. The FBI has repeatedly asked for "telephone subscriber information, criminal background information, prison contacts, associates, resident status and travel documentation," according to the memo.[53] A Robert I. Friedman article in the *Village Voice* stated:

> The primary murder suspects come from a group of about 35 hardcore JDL members, primarily from the New York area, who routinely ferry back and forth between the U.S. and Israel, where they are involved in Rabbi Kahane's violently anti-Arab Kach Party. . . . The suspects often travel here on Israeli passports under their Hebrew names, making it more difficult for U.S. authorities to track their movements.[54]

In 1988 it became public knowledge that the FBI had identified three individuals who were prime suspects in the 1985 bombings of Alex Odeh, Tscherim Soobzokov, and a bystander in the attempted bombing of Elmars Sprogis. All were Americans living in Israel and all were members of the Jewish Defense League. They were Robert Manning, thirty-six, who had been arrested along with Irv Rubin in 1977 outside a Los Angeles area Jewish center immediately following an explosion; Keith Fuchs, twenty-four, who was sentenced to thirty-nine months in prison in Israel for shooting up an Arab automobile; and Andy Green, thirty, a violence-prone fanatic who worked as a cult "deprogrammer" with Manning for a time.[55]

In July 1988 the *Los Angeles Times* did a background story on Manning, documenting his violence-prone personality, his militant Zionism, and his early affiliation with the Jewish Defense League. In 1972 Manning was charged with setting off a bomb at the home of an Arab activist in Hollywood. He was convicted and received the remarkably light sentence of three years probation. The story noted:

> One JDL associate said Manning had a reputation as a "not very well educated" man. The story is told of a friend reading aloud several quotations from Martin Luther that had anti-Semitic overtones. Manning got the point, so the story goes, too well.
>
> "He doesn't like Jews too much, does he?" he quoted Manning as saying. "Where can I find his ass?"[56]

In a related case, William Ross, a fifty-one-year-old Los Angeles real estate broker and supporter of the JDL, was arraigned in August 1988 for his part in what was described as a "murder-for-profit scheme over a bitter real estate dispute." A *Jewish Week* article reported:

> To carry out the scheme, Ross allegedly enlisted the help of two fellow Jewish Defense League members, Robert Steven Manning and his wife, Rochelle.
> Robert Manning's fingerprints were found on the bomb's wrapper and Rochelle Manning's on the enclosed letter, according to U.S. postal authorities.[57]

Rochelle Manning and Ross were tried for the crime, but in January 1989 a mistrial was declared. The prosecution decided not to call for a retrial until it could extradite Robert Manning to the United States. Mrs. Manning promptly joined her husband in the occupied territories. The U.S. State Department, interestingly, maintains that it cannot extradite Manning from the occupied territories—only from Israel proper! (The rationale behind this reasoning is that if it were to insist on extraditing from the occupied territories, it would amount to recognizing Israeli sovereignty over the West Bank and Gaza.)

Pat McDonnell Twair, an American woman married to a Syrian-American man, describes the frustration this situation presents to the Arab-American community:

> There is a pervasive sense among Arab Americans that they are not accorded equal protection by law enforcement officials in Southern California, and that this is one reason that serious crimes against Arab Americans go unpunished.[58]

Twair relates the case of her husband, who was assaulted by a man during an American-Arab Anti-Discrimination Committee demonstration against the Haagen-Daz ice cream chain, whose former owner, Reuben Matteus, was a financial supporter of the JDL. The man called her husband a "PLO lover" and hit him on the chest and exclaimed, "You're a dead man." A police report was filed, but assault and battery charges were dropped by the city attorney. The assailant turned out to be the president of the National Screen Directors Guild. Twair wrote:

> One wonders what the city attorney's office might have done if the situation had been reversed and a Syrian American had twice punched the president of the National Screen Directors Guild in the chest, and then threatened his life.[59]

This raises an important issue. In surveying the history of the JDL, one finds that prosecutions against members were surprisingly few in light of the supposed number and gravity of their alleged crimes. Moreover, the sentences upon conviction—particularly in the early days of the group—seem disproportionately light. For example, Robert Manning's three years probation for bombing an Arab activist's home in 1972 was incredible. A satisfactory explanation for this situation needs to be found.

*    *    *

Mordechai Levy and Irv Rubin clashed again in June 1989; they spat in one another's faces during an altercation at Los Angeles International Airport following Levy's arrival from New York to "tell Jews how to arm against attacks by skinheads." Rubin said Levy "only comes out here to stir up trouble, then he leaves." Rubin's followers shouted, "You're a punk. We don't need you. Go back to New York." They prevented him from holding a news conference.

On August 10, 1989, the tension between Rubin and Levy came to a head. Rubin, accompanied by Steven Rombom (who spent eight years of his youth in psychiatric institutions) and Allan Klebanoff (an Israeli army veteran) showed up at Levy's apartment in New York City's East Village to serve court papers in a $1 million slander suit. Levy had accused Rubin of drug dealing on a radio talk show. Levy, convinced that Rubin and Rombom were there to kill him, opened fire on the street below with a semi-automatic rifle, seriously wounding a bystander. Levy then barricaded himself in his apartment for two and a half hours, until a police hostage negotiating team got him to surrender. He was charged with four counts of attempted murder, assault, and criminal possession of a weapon.[60]

With Levy in jail and the JDL under intense scrutiny by law enforcement, the organization became almost quiescent in 1990. JDL activities had been winding down steadily since 1985. Many of the most militant members were now living in Israel and among those still in the United States, many were getting involved with careers and families. The campaign against the group within the Jewish community had also taken its toll. Once looked upon as a protector of Jewish interests, the JDL was viewed more and more as a potential threat to them. Over the years perhaps one to two thousand individuals had *been* active members of the JDL, the JDO, or one of the other splinter groups. It was the kind of thing grandparents might brag to their grandchildren about thirty or forty years later.

In the meantime, Kahane was having varying degrees of success with his program in Israel. Upon the realization that his Kach party might actually garner 3 percent of the vote, the Israeli government—including many elements who were thought to privately sympathize with Kahane—attempted to squelch him. The move was prompted by the realization that any significant success by Kahane and his followers in Israeli politics could become a public relations disaster. In February 1987, for example, the Knesset stripped Kahane of free mailing privileges on the grounds that his missives were racist. The government backed a law to actually ban the Kach party as racist. The very kind of anti–civil libertarian repression Kahane had advocated against Arabs wound up being used against him.

> After one term in the Knesset, Kahane involuntarily maintained a lower profile. An Israeli law, adopted specifically to exclude him from the parliament, removed his legitimacy as a legislator. The Israeli media, by common agreement, largely ignored his activities.[61]

Kahane was also involved in numerous legal problems, including two cases pending in Israel, where he had been charged with refusing to disperse a rally in May 1989 and also for calling the Arabs "a cancer in our midst" during a speech on July 4, 1989. He was also awaiting a decision on his U.S. citizenship which had been taken away following his election to the Knesset.[62]

In November 1990 Kahane spoke to about sixty members of the Zionist Emergency Evacuation Rescue Organization at a New York hotel. While mingling with the crowd afterward, the imprudent Kahane, who had seldom taken wise security measures, was gunned down by a naturalized Egyptian-American, El Sayyid al-Nosair, who evidently acted alone. Official spokesmen at al-Nosair's mosque did, however, have good words for the murder of Kahane.[63] Nosair was later acquitted of the murder charge but convicted of weapons and civil rights violations.

Kahane's death will probably not affect the immediate future of the Jewish Defense League in the United States. The group was in a period of decline anyway as the result of increasing police surveillance and growing opposition from the mainstream Jewish community. It is doubtful, however, that the JDL will ever attain the level of support it did in its early days. In Israel, Kahane's Kach party was banned in the mid 1980s. A spinoff group, Eyal, spawned Yigal Amir, assassin of Prime Minister Yitzhak Rabin. A JDL spinoff is Kahane Chai (Kahane Lives), founded by the rabbi's son, Benyamin. Its U.S. leader, Mike Guzofsky, has stated that Rabin was a traitor and deserved what he received. Guzofsky described his group as right wing freedom fighters.[64] Most Jews consider such people despicable and aver that there is no place in Judaism for such ethnic bigotry and intolerance. Would that it were so.

## Notes

1. Robert I. Friedman, "The Mission of Meir Kahane," *Inside* (Spring 1988). See also: Friedman, *The False Prophet: Meir Kahane, From FBI Informant to Knesset Member* (Chicago: Lawrence Hill, 1990).

2. Mark R. Arnold, "Militant Defense League Cries: Jewish Is Beautiful," *The National Observer* (January 18, 1971).

3. Steve Lipman, "A Voice Silenced: Thousands Mourn Meir Kahane, Slain Militant Leader," *The Jewish Week* (November 9, 1990), 3, 48.

4. Arnold, op. cit.

5. Bruce Hoffman, "The Jewish Defense League," *TVI Journal* (Summer 1984): 10–15.

6. Robert I. Friedman, "Oy Vey, Make My Day: Fear and Loathing in the Jewish Underground," *Village Voice* (August 22, 1989), 16.

7. "3 JDL Members Held in Connection with Center Blasts," *Evening Outlook* (October 27, 1977), 7.

8. "$500 Nazi Bounty Offered by N.Y. Jewish League," Associated Press (February 18, 1978).

9. Robert Ballenger, "Rubin to Seek Assembly Post," *Daily News* (February 21, 1982), 18.

10. Nels Nelson, "Nazis to Hold Rally at Independence Hall," *Philadelphia Daily News* (February 15, 1979), 15.

11. Jim Nicholson and Maria Gallagher, "Mystery Person's Nazi Rally Called Off," *Philadelphia Daily News* (February 23, 1979), 3.

12. "Park Service Rescinds Permit for Nazi Rally at Independence Hall," *New York Times* (February 24, 1979).

13. Dennis King, *Lyndon LaRouche and the New American Fascism* (New York: Doubleday, 1989), 245.

14. Mary A. Thompson, "Imada Reveals Threats," *Daily Sundial* (November 4, 1979).

15. Mark C. Smith, "Jackson Talk Picketed," *Long Beach Independent* (September 10, 1979), section B.

16. Brett Becker, "Needed: A Jewish Underground," *Update* (October 1980).

17. Art Hertin, "JDL Guards Seminary from Attack," *Los Angeles Herald Examiner* (April 8, 1980), A6.

18. Jane Glenn Haas, "JDL: 'Never Again': Jewish Group Demonstrates Against Anti-Holocaust Institute," *The Daily Breeze* (March 20, 1981).

19. 'Blast Hits Right-Wing Group's Office," *Evening Outlook* (June 26, 1981).

20. "Hillel National Office Orders Chapter to Bar Kahane," *Jewish Press* (November 27, 1981), 60.

21. "Jewish Nazis Backed by Bosses," *Challenge* (January 27, 1982): 5.

22. "JDL Produced 'Tangible Results' for FBI," *Revolutionary Worker* (July 30, 1982): 14.

23. "Super-Militants Learn Who's Boss in L.A.—The Police," *San Diego Jewish Press Heritage* (June 18, 1981).

24. *The Jewish Defense League: A Cult of Racism and Terror, A Threat to Arab-Americans,* ADC Issue Paper No. 9, American-Arab Anti-Discrimination Committee (1982).

25. Meir Kahane, "Kahane Speaks," *Jewish Press* (February 4, 1983).

26. "American Extremist Meir Kahane Campaigns for Israel's Knesset on a Platform of Racial Hate," *People* (July 30, 1984), 39.

27. "Explosions Rock Soviet Residence in New York," United Press International (February 23, 1984).

28. Gary Langer, "Soviet Living Compound Bombed," *The Oregonian* (February 24, 1984).

29. "Coast Fire Destroys Offices of Group Doubting Holocaust," *New York Times* (July 6, 1984).

30. Michael D. Harris, "Former Neo-Nazi Defects to Local Jewish Defense League," *Los Angeles Daily Journal* (March 2, 1984), 1.

31. "Ex Neo-Nazi Faces Trial as JDL Member," *Los Angeles Times* (September 23, 1984).

32. "Racism From the Right," *Newsweek* (September 3, 1984).

33. David Bird, "Kahane Resigns as Jewish Defense League Chief," *New York Times* (August 20, 1985).

34. Ibid.

35. Marcia Chambers, "New Leader Plans Changes for Jewish Defense League," *New York Times,* reprinted in the *Tampa Tribune* (November 12, 1985), 3 A.

36. "JDL Denies Setting Fire to Offices," *Los Angeles Daily News* (June 6, 1985).

37. "Fire Causes $50,000 in Damage to Santa Monica Building; Arson Blamed," *Santa Monica Evening Outlook* (June 5, 1985).

38. "JDL Denies Office Firebombing," *Los Angeles Times* (June 5, 1985).

39. Michael Hurewitz and Peter Moses, "JDL Owns Up to Bloody Bombing at 'Nazi' Home," *New York Post* (September 7, 1985), 11.

40. Timothy Carlson and Mark S. Warnick, "Bomb in Santa Ana Kills Prominent Arab-American," *Los Angeles Herald Examiner* (October 12, 1985).

41. "FBI Blames Jewish League in Fatal Bombing," *The Oregonian* (November 9, 1985), A14.

42. "Jewish Defense Group Organizes Patrols," *Kansas City Jewish Chronicle* (December 6, 1985), 24a.

43. "NY Jewish Vandal Nabbed," *Kansas City Jewish Chronicle* (December 20,1985).

44. Thomas L. Friedman, "Kahane's Zionist Stance Attracts Growing Following in Israel," *The Oregonian* (August 5, 1985).

45. *Kansas City Times* (June 2, 1981); Robert I. Friedman, "The Sayings of Rabbi Kahane," *New York Review of Books* (February 3, 1986); *Washington Post Weekly* (November 23, *1987*); *A Message to the Young Jew: Don't Date Gentiles*, updated one-page flier from Meir Kahane, head of the Koch movement.

46. Henry Wall (Anti-Defamation League), "Rabbi Kahane: Problem for All," *Seattle Times* (November 20,1986).

47. Robert I. Friedman, "The Return of the JDL: Nice Jewish Boys with Bombs," *Village Voice* (May 6, 1986).

48. S. L. Sanger, "Jewish Federation Accused of Bid to Muzzle Kahane," *Seattle Post-Intelligencer* (November 13, 1986), A7.

49. "Red Dye Dumped on Israeli Extremist," *Albany Democrat-Herald* (November 13, 1986), 15.

50. "JDL Bombing Suspect Is Released on Bond," *New York Times* (April 4, 1987).

51. "3 JDLers Seized by FBI in Bombings," *The Jewish Week* (May 15, 1987), 9.

52. "JDL Leader's Death Is Ruled Suicide," *The Jewish Week* (September 18, 1987), 59.

53. "FBI Says Israel Blocking Terrorism Probe," *The News and Observer* (November 20, 1987): 16A.

54. Robert I. Friedman, "Who Killed Alex Odeh?: FBI Probe of JDL Bombers Gets No Help From Israelis," *Village Voice* (November 24, 1987).

55. Robert I. Friedman, "Did This Man Kill Alex Odeh?: On the Trail of the JDL Terrorists," *Village Voice* (July 12, 1988), 19-21.

56. John Spano and George Ramos, "Incident as Youth Led Man into Jewish Activism," *Los Angeles Times,* Valley edition (July 17, 1988).

57. Tom Tugend, "JDL Supporter Accused in Mail-Bomb Murder," *The Jewish Week* (August 19, 1988), 8.

58. Pat McDonnell Twair, "Pressure Budding in California for Action on Odeh Murder Case," *Washington Report on Middle East Affairs* (April 1989): 34.

59. Ibid.

60. "Head of One Militant Jewish Group Fires Shots at Rival," *Los Angeles Herald Examiner* (August 11, 1989); Robert I. Friedman, "Oy Vey, Make My Day: Fear and Loathing in the Jewish Underground."

61. Lipman, op. cit.

62. Ibid.

63. Chris Hedges, "Zealots Investigated in Kahane Killing," *New York Times* (November 13, 1990).

64. CBS, "60 Minutes" (Nov. 5, 1995).

# 22. The Nation of Islam

Only those who wish to be led to hell, or to their doom, will follow Malcolm. The die is set and Malcolm shall not escape, especially after such foolish talk about his benefactor in trying to rob him of the divine glory which Allah has bestowed upon him. Such a man as Malcolm is worthy of death—and would have met with death if it had not been for Muhammad's confidence in Allah for victory over the enemies.[1]

In late 1964 these words appeared in *Muhammad Speaks,* newspaper of the Nation of Islam, a group known widely as the Black Muslims. The author was one Louis X, who was to become infamous under the name Louis Farrakhan. Two months later, on the first day of National Brotherhood Week in 1965, Malcolm X, who had left the Nation of Islam in March 1964 after failing to sway the narrow racist thinking of its leader, Elijah Muhammad, was gunned down by three black men. He was speaking to an audience of over four hundred at the Audubon Ballroom in New York at the time. Two of the three convicted of Malcolm's murder were members of the Nation of Islam. All received life sentences. Whether any of them had participated in the firebombing of Malcolm's home two weeks earlier was never established, but he had accused Nation members in that assault.

Louis Farrakhan's threat had been carried out, although not necessarily by him or at his direction. Nor did death spare Malcolm from attacks by Farrakhan; twenty-five years later he was charging that the renewed attention to the life of Malcolm X was part of "a conspiracy aimed at undermining his [Farrakhan's] mission."[2] Evidence strongly suggests that Louis Farrakhan long hated and envied both Malcolm the man and his memory. Let us further examine these two dynamic leaders and also the man both once followed, Elijah Muhammad nee Poole.

In the early thirties, a door-to-door salesman of silk and cheap clothing named Wallace D. Fard (also known as W. Farad Muhammad) told blacks in Detroit that he was sent from Mecca on a mission to awaken that "dead nation in the West; to teach them the truth about the white man."[3] But Fard disappeared without a trace in 1934 and his mantle was taken by Elijah Muhammad, who added his own twists to Fard's already distorted version of the religion of Islam. Elijah Muhammad preached that the black man was created by the Supreme Being, the white man by an evil wizard-scientist named Yacub who, though he lived to age 152, never saw the "bleached out devil race" he created; Elijah Muhammad claimed he was a prophet, but orthodox Islam insists that the seventh-century Muhammad was the final prophet; Elijah Muhammad proclaimed blacks to be superior to whites in all ways, while orthodox Islam eschews racism; Elijah allowed only blacks in his religion, while orthodox Islam has been open to all. Interestingly, the Nation of Islam and the Jehovah's Witnesses, who may well have had some influence on Elijah's beliefs, seem to be the only religions that put the earth's age at 42,000 years—literalist Christians say it's about six thousand while most scientists use a figure of more than four billion. (Elijah Muhammad probably picked up this idea from Jehovah's Witnesses who were proselytizing in black areas of cities during the 1930s.)

Along with their bizarre religious views, the "Lost-Found Nation of Islam" under Elijah Muhammad forwarded a message of black pride. He advised his followers to discard their "slave names," often in favor of a simple X. In addition, the eating of pork and other "unclean" food was forbidden, as were alcohol, tobacco, illegal drugs, movies, dancing, and sporting events. These group norms were enforced by a combat-trained, intimidating bunch called the Fruit of Islam, a sort of well-dressed thug squad. Also strongly stressed were competitive private enterprise, self-reliance, and strict separation of the races. In fact, the Nation of Islam wanted the U.S. government to give them at least one state where only blacks would be allowed to live. (Needless to say, a considerable number of white racists thought this one damn fine idea.)

Elijah Muhammad's views are best expressed in his book, *Message To The Blackman*. In it, he conveys the rationale for his strident black nationalism:

> The worse kind of crime has been committed against us, for we were robbed of our desire to even want to think and do for ourselves. We are often pictured by the slavemaster as a lazy and trifling people who are without thoughts of advancement. I say, this is a condition which the slavemaster very cleverly wanted and created within and among the so-called Negroes.[4]
>
> To The Lost-Found members of the tribe of Shabazz (the so-called Negroes), I warn you my people and especially the women. Be aware of the tricks the devils are using to instill the idea of a false birth control in their clinics and hospitals. STERILIZATION IS NOT BIRTH CONTROL, BUT THE END OF ALL POSSIBILITY TO BEAR CHILDREN.[5]
>
> America desires to keep us a subjected people. So she, therefore, wants to stop our birth (as Pharaoh did). The Birth Control Law or Act of today is directed directly at the so-called Negroes and not at the American whites. The story of Moses and the Pharaoh is a warning to you today. They are seeking to destroy our race by the birth control law, just as Pharaoh sought to stop Moses's race by killing off all the male babies at birth. They are seeking to destroy our race through our women. DO NOT LET THEM TRICK YOU.[6]

\*     \*     \*

In the early 1950s, one Malcolm Little, formerly known as Detroit Red, later to become famous as Malcolm X, joined the Nation of Islam. A former street hustler—numbers, dope, etc.—who did prison time for burglary, Malcolm became one of the fiercest and most impressive orators of the 1960s, promoting Elijah

Muhammad's message, especially in black urban settings.[7] Dan Georgakas recorded in the *Encyclopedia of the American Left*:

> Although the formal leader was Elijah Muhammad, an aged figure who spent most of his time in Chicago, the charismatic leader of the Black Muslims was Malcolm X. Like many Black Muslims, Malcolm X had been a criminal. Under his direction the Nation of Islam intensified an already vigorous recruitment in urban ghettoes and prisons.
>
> Malcolm X developed a speaking style that provided a systematic critique of U.S. foreign and domestic policies in terms easily comprehended by urban audiences of limited formal education. His speeches also began to attract the admiration of radicals.[8]

But much to the chagrin of the messenger of Allah, Malcolm made a pilgrimage to Mecca and came back with an entirely different outlook: that of an orthodox Muslim. Since he had been unable to make headway in changing the dogmatic and ignorant Elijah, Malcolm defected from the Nation of Islam and later formed the Organization of Afro-American Unity. (He also had been troubled by Elijah's fathering over a dozen children out of wedlock.) Gone was the hatred of Caucasians, and the narrow belief that only Muslims could be moral people. Malcolm X repudiated bigotry and this led to his untimely end. In one of the last speeches before his assassination he said:

> We don't judge a man because of the color of his skin. We don't judge you because you're white; we don't judge you because you're black. We judge you because of what you do and what you practice. . . . So we're not against people because they're white. We're against people who practice racism.[9]

During the last few years of his life, Malcolm X was enthusiastically courted by Marxist-Leninists, particularly by the Socialist Workers party, who regularly sponsored forums where he spoke. Following his assassination, the SWP attempted to claim him as one of their own. Pathfinder Press, the publishing house of the SWP, issued two books on the event.[10]

In contradistinction to Malcolm X, Louis X—formerly Louis Eugene Wolcott, later Abdul Haleem Farrakhan, still later Louis Farrakhan—strictly adhered to the message of his "peerless leader," Elijah Muhammad. Even the peerless die, however, and 1975 was Elijah's year; he was succeeded by his son, Warith Deen (formerly Wallace Dean), more of a businessman than an ideologue. Warith continued to pursue what the Nation of Islam had been trying to do since the early 1970s: attract the better educated to the cause. This met with rather limited success for a number of reasons, but especially because college-educated people would be unlikely to embrace as a tenet of their religion that the final result of interbreeding of the dog, cat, and rat is none other than the "unclean" and abhorrent pig.

Warith Deen Muhammad repudiated most of the religious beliefs of his father and changed the name of the Nation of Islam to the World Community of Islam in the West. In 1985 he disbanded the group and told his followers to affiliate with orthodox Islamic organizations. Warith always liked Malcolm X and in 1976 had renamed the mosque in Harlem after Malcolm. Further, it seems that many if not most of the beliefs he came to hold were those of Malcolm at the time of his murder. Followers of Warith were still publishing *Muslim Journal* (a weekly) in the 1990s.

As might have been expected, Louis Farrakhan rejected Warith's moves, and in 1978 he left the World Community of Islam in the West and formed his own group, taking with him the original name, Nation of Islam, and the beliefs of Elijah Muhammad. The group's newspaper, *The Final Call,* seems much like the defunct *Muhammad Speaks.*

The new Nation of Islam has received a considerable amount of publicity due to Farrakhan's questionable associations and his outlandish pronouncements. Like his mentor, Elijah Muhammad, Farrakhan secured a large, interest-free loan ($5 million) from Libya's Muammar Kaddafi. And, no surprise to observers of rightist black separatist movements, he has been on good terms with such white racial supremacists as the editors of Willis Carto's *Spotlight* and former KKK leader Tom Metzger, founder of the White Aryan Resistance (WAR). These black and white racists long have had a similar goal: total involuntary segregation of the races. This is reminiscent of times during the 1960s and 1970s when numerous white racial nationalists told us that the only black leader they respected (in a few cases even "liked") was Elijah Muhammad. Indeed, Elijah invited George Lincoln Rockwell to address a 1962 Nation of Islam convention in Chicago. The five thousand Muslims gathered there gave the Nazi leader a generally good reception, booing only his references to Hitler.

Among Minister Farrakhan's more extreme statements have been charges that the American government has "poured drugs into" cities with large black populations; that AIDS in Africa has been part and parcel of a white plot to gain control of that continent's minerals;[11] that Jews are wicked and practice a "dirty religion" (not "gutter religion" as often reported);[12] and that "Hitler was a great man."[13] In 1993 he even justified the murder of Malcolm X. In a speech to Nation of Islam faithful, Farrakhan rhetorically asked outsiders: ". . . if we dealt with him like a nation deals with a traitor, what the hell business is it of yours?"[14]

If these were not enough, Farrakhan also threatened black *Washington Post* writer Milton Coleman with death for revealing an unflattering item about Jesse Jackson, whom Farrakhan supported in the 1984 presidential race. When publicly questioned about such utterances, Farrakhan has employed hate, obfuscation, and numerous evasions in addition to counterattacking with the common complaint that the media has always treated him unfairly. This last charge is not entirely untrue, for leaders of extreme movements are often the target of sloppy media exposés.

Some commentators, including reporters, have labeled the Nation of Islam as far leftist. This simply doesn't fit. The group and its members exhibit a number of essential characteristics generally associated with social movements of the right. For example, they are highly religious, stress ethnocentricity, and advocate racial separatism and nationalism. They also advocate (and practice) capitalism and self-reliance. It seems clear to us that this movement is more at home on the "right" side of the political spectrum than on the "left."

In October 1995 Farrakhan and his minions organized a black men's March on Washington. More than three-quarter million attended, the overwhelming majority having no ties of any kind to the Nation of Islam. Why did so many participate in a situation that might be compared with a well-known leader of a *white* racist group calling for a white men's march to focus attention on unemployment? Why, asked black intellectual Ellis Cose, were so many

> willing to pay homage to a self-righteous demagogue whose message is marinated in mysticism and intolerance? Why, given the massive amount of black oratorical and intellectual talent available did it take such a divisive figure to bring black men—and not only the openly disaffected—together?

Cose answered that much can be traced to Farrakhan's style and his eagerness to speak "'truths" about various groups. That these "truths" have often been slanderous "nonsense and misinformation" has not lessened his appeal. Where traditional black leaders have been perceived as ineffective, Farrakhan has been seen as "a strong black man unbeholden to white power."[15]

Other observers stressed that Farrakhan was saying black men should behave responsibly. Who would disagree with this emphasis? But is it not similar to a Klan leader stating that white men should behave well? Should it impress us that Stalin favored healthy diets for children, or that Hitler believed milk is good for babies?

## Notes

1. *Muhammad Speaks* (December 1964).

2. Adolph Reed, Jr., "False Prophet—II: All For One and None For All," *The Nation* (January 28, 1991).

3. Bill Peterson, "Black Muslims: Organization Full of Inter-religious Conflict," *Washington Post* (March 11, 1977).

4. Elijah Muhammad, *Message To The Blackman* (Newport News, Va.: United Brothers Communications Systems, 1965), 37.

5. Muhammad, 64.

6. Muhammad, 67.

7. See Alex Haley, *The Autobiography of Malcolm X* ( New York: Grove Press, 1965). See also Bruce Perry, *Malcolm: The Life of a Man Who Changed Black America* (Barrytown: Station Hill Press, 1991); and Michael Eric Dyson, *Making Malcolm: The Myth and Meaning of Malcolm X* (New York: Oxford University Press, 1995).

8. Mari Jo Buhle, Paul Buhle, and Dan Georgakas, *Encyclopedia of the American Left* (New York: Garland Publishing, Inc., 1990), 139.

9. Malcolm X, speech in Rochester, N.Y., February 16, 1965, quoted in *Malcolm X: The Last Speeches* (New York: Pathfinder Press, 1989).

10. George Breitman, *The Last Years of Malcolm X: The Evolution of a Revolutionary* (New York: Pathfinder Press, 1967); George Breitman, Herman Porter, and Baxter Smith, *The Assassination of Malcolm X* (New York: Pathfinder Press, 1976).

11. "The Return of the Paranoid Style in American Politics," *U.S. News & World Report* (March 2, 1990).

12. Farrakhan Convention Center speech, Washington, D.C., July 22, 1985; Farrakhan radio broadcast, June 23, 1984; Associated Press release, June 29, 1984.

13. United Press International release, November 15, 1985.

14. From the film *Brother Minister,* 1994.

15. Ellis Cose, "The Key to Farrakhan's Middle-Class Appeal," *Newsweek* (October 30, 1995), 42.

# 23. **Assorted Neo-Nazis**

The neo-Nazi movement in the United States is characterized by two outstanding traits: small size and large capacity to generate media coverage. Estimates vary, but it's unlikely that at any time the various post–World War II "Nazi" parties ever exceeded two thousand members aggregate, and a more reasonable figure is half of that. According to Irwin Suall and David Lowe of the Anti-Defamation League: "Hard-core membership in the avowedly neo-Nazi groups in the U.S. has declined steadily over the past decade, from a peak of 1,000–1,200 in 1978 to no more than 400–500 in 1987."[1] A substantial percentage of these were informants from various government and private agencies, probably exceeding the 6 percent figure attributed to informants in the Ku Klux Klan in the 1960s. (It's worth noting, incidentally, that 450 neo-Nazis amount to one for every half million Americans.)

The term "neo-Nazi" is probably used too freely and quite often merely as an epithet. In some cases it is used as a synonym for anti-Semite and racist. However, not all anti-Semitic or racist groups affect the recognizable Nazi style and symbolism, nor do they necessarily identify with Nazism *per se*. Such indiscriminate usage is irresponsible and only distorts an already murky and difficult problem of definition. For our purposes "neo-Nazi" means an organization or party that generally adopts or advocates traditional Nazi symbolism, including the swastika or approximate equivalent; the wearing of uniforms or other paraphernalia, the use of the terms "Nazi," "Nationalist Socialist," or some variation in its name; and a demonstrated reverence for or appreciation of Adolf Hitler and the Third Reich. (Two rather unique groups—the National States Rights party and National Christian Publishers—are discussed in separate chapters.)

Post–World War II revelations about the nature of Nazi Germany and the Holocaust dramatically erased any possibility of a significant American Nazi movement. Uniform hostility to Nazi values in the culture, a wholly unsympathetic news media, the gradually increasing participation of minorities in the politics of the nation, and many other factors have virtually assured that any neo-Nazi movement would remain highly marginalized. Nevertheless, several small groups have formed. Their history tends to consist of two elements: a biography of their leaders (since virtually all of them have revolved around the personality of a single individual), and an account of their troubles (with infiltrators, FBI informants, local law enforcement, and one another). Successes, if one could call them that, have been trivial and fleeting.

In December 1954 the House Committee on Un-American Activities issued its *Preliminary Report on Neo-Fascist and Hate Groups*.[2] It read much like HCUA reports on leftist groups, utilizing many of the same rhetorical devices leftists complained about—exposure for exposure's sake, "linking" of individuals with various organizations, and lots of names.[3] There was a bit of irony in the report: for years right-wing extremists had successfully used HCUA to attack and vilify leftists, and now it was their turn.

This *Preliminary Report* focused on two extreme right entities: a minuscule neo-Nazi organization headquartered in New York City named the National Renaissance party, and a tabloid newspaper published in Union City, New Jersey, called *Common Sense* (dealt with in another chapter). The document began:

> Communism's present threat to the very survival of the United States and the rest of the free world has placed heavy burdens on the defenders of human freedom and dignity. The Committee on Un-American Activities is concerned to observe that this burden is being aggravated by certain individuals and organizations unscrupulously exploiting the menace of communism to promote other activities equally subversive and totally un-American. Such activities would destroy the very foundation work of the American Republic, if permitted to operate unnoticed or unchallenged.[4]

*    *    *

## National Renaissance Party

The first American neo-Nazi organization to form after World War II, the National Renaissance party (NRP), was led by James Madole of Beacon, New York, from its founding in 1949 until his death in 1978. The NRP grew out of an early Madole project, the Animist party, which he organized in 1947. Although quite small, the NRP is significant because it set the pattern for the "comic book" neo-Nazi style of subsequent groups and also because several later neo-Nazis got their start in the group.

The NRP received considerable publicity in the early 1950s due both to its vociferous and outrageous demonstrations and to pamphlets containing such flagrant messages as: "You are being brainwashed by a pro-Communist, Jew-controlled press; *New York Times—New York Post—Time—Look—Coronet—*radio—TV—and decadent Hollywood movies."

According to contemporary observers, a typical NRP event would consist of Madole haranguing a hostile crowd of a couple hundred or so while a dozen uniformed NRP members nervously protected him from being torn to shreds. The shouting and epithets would sometimes completely drown out Madole, who seemed oblivious to that fact.

The NRP brought together a strange bunch of fanatics, adventurers, and informants. With respect to the latter, one of the prime examples was Emmanuel Trujillo, who went by the name Mana Truhill. According to long-time extremist-watcher Gordon Hall, Truhill was "one of those guys like [Roy] Frankhauser . . .

in that he was all over the place. He was an informant, did some work for the ADL, and was also . . . a really way-out type himself."[5] Truhill was widely suspected to be an informant by other far rightists. Veteran right-wing ideologue Joseph P. Kamp attacked Truhill claiming:

> By 1953 Truhill had practically taken over the Renaissance Party. His apartment became the New York headquarters. He created an "overseas office" and put himself in charge, after which he proceeded to correspond with "Nazis," "Nationalists," and "anti-Semites" all over the world."[6]

According to Kamp, it was Truhill who was responsible for the use of swastikas and other Nazi symbolism by the NRP, including the formation of its "elite guard," whose job was to protect Madole. It's unlikely that this was entirely the case, for Madole obviously had neo-Nazi propensities on his own. Nevertheless, Truhill's influence was considerable and less biased sources than Kamp have arrived at similar conclusions.

Often a speaker at NRP rallies was group organizer James R. White. Although Madole had claimed that White "had already organized a fully uniformed group in his city and distributed thousands of copies of the *National Renaissance Bulletin*," this was apparently based only on White's misrepresentations. In its *Preliminary Report*, the HCUA noted:

> A youth in his early twenties, White was publisher of his own newsletter, *Reason*, in 1952. Committee information shows that several years prior to his involvement in neo-fascist activities, White had been a member of the Spartacus Club of American Youth for Democracy—a front organization of the Communist Party. It might be noted at this point that Mana Truhill, previously mentioned as head of the NRP overseas bureau, had admitted having attended the Communist-operated Jefferson School of Social Science in New York. This is another illustration of the common ground often reached by fascists on the extreme right and Communists on the extreme left.[7]

Meetings of the New York–based group drew more people than would have been expected. With regard to the NRP's size, Gordon Hall says, "If it ever got beyond 50 or 75 members I would be surprised . . . and that might be a little generous if you're talking about guys who paid dues and all that."[8] In its thirty years of existence, the NRP never exceeded that ceiling, and sometimes it was down to a mere dozen or so diehards.

The *National Renaissance Bulletin* was published on an irregular basis, usually in mimeographed form, and was always a typical anti-Semitic screed—except that it often had a few kind words for the Soviet Union. The rationale for this was that the Soviet Union was anti-Jewish and the Jews were trying to destroy that nation, hence it couldn't be all bad.

James Madole himself ran afoul of the law on occasion and was convicted of riot, conspiracy to riot, and illegal possession of arms. Probably the worst publicity, from Madole's point of view, was the suicide of former NRP activist Dan Burros after the revelation that this "fascist" had Jewish parents. Among those individuals who passed through the NRP on their way to later neo-Nazi involvements were Matt Koehl, who became second-in-command and later leader of the American Nazi party; H. Keith Thompson, active in numerous neo-Nazi organizations, including his own American Committee for the Advancement of Western Culture; and Eustace Mullins, who joined Madole in his street-corner propagandizing and went on to prominence in the extreme right as an author and "leader" of several letterhead organizations.[9]

The NRP often cooperated with other racist and neo-Nazi groups. In 1972 the *Nationalist Renaissance Bulletin* announced:

> The NRP collaborated with its political allies, the Ku Klux Klan and White Action Movement, in celebrating the birthday of Adolf Hitler, founder of National Socialism and creator of the first historically-recorded government whose policies were based exclusively on RACIAL considerations.[10]

Over the years, under Madole's leadership, the NRP drifted more and more toward occultism. The last issue of the *NRP Bulletin* published before Madole's death in 1978 featured a photo of NRP officers attending a "Pagan 'May Eve' Banquet at Temple of Baal." Literature sold by the NRP during this period featured such titles as *ISIS Revealed,* by Helena Blavatsky; *The Occult and the Third Reich,* by Jean-Michel Angebert; *A Practical Guide to Quabalistic Symbolism,* by Gareth Knight; and *The Occult Science in Atlantis,* by Lewis Spence.[11]

## American Nazi Party

Founded in 1959 by George Lincoln Rockwell, a former Navy commander, the American Nazi party quickly caught the attention of the U.S. public. As one Nazi told us in the mid-1960s, "Before I became a Nazi, no one seemed to notice me, didn't even seem to know I was around. Well, they sure notice me now."

Commander Rockwell, as he preferred to be known, was tall, rather good-looking, and had an assertive, military bearing. Intelligent and doggedly fanatic, he was a formidable street orator. As a strident and outspoken racist and Jew-hater, he mangled facts, openly lied and distorted, and was known for bullying and bellowing at opponents, including other neo-Nazis. Rockwell, in short, was a comic-book Nazi, almost scrupulously following the stereotype down to the uniform and paramilitary trappings.

Rockwell was the son of vaudevillian actor George (Doc) Rockwell. He attended Brown University and later studied commercial art at the Pratt Institute. In 1948 he won a $1,000 prize in a nationwide art contest sponsored by the National Society of Illustrators. He served in the U.S. Navy during World War II and the Korean War, rising to the rank of commander. Leaving the navy, he launched *U.S. Lady,* a magazine for service wives, which failed. He was married twice and had a total of seven children.[12] His second wife, Thora, was the daughter of Iceland's ambassador to the United States.

The American Nazi party was never large. At its peak it may have had one hundred active members, its high point being in the late 1960s, with a couple hundred more subscribing to its publications, *The Stormtrooper* and the *Rockwell Report*. On the other hand, during its lifetime perhaps two hundred to three hundred individuals were members at one time or another, some for only a few weeks. Quite a few of Rockwell's former "stormtroopers" are active in neo-Nazi groups today. Life at ANP "barracks" in Arlington, Virginia, also known as "Hatemonger Hill," was spartan and marked by intensive conflict as individual "stormtroopers" vied for Rockwell's attention and got into one kind of trouble after another. Rockwell had frequent temper tantrums, and over a period of time virtually every member was disciplined, suspended, or expelled.[13]

In 1962 Rockwell wheedled an appearance before a meeting of the Nation of Islam in Chicago. It was a major publicity coup. Elijah Muhammad, leader of the organization, was in attendance, as was Malcolm X. Rockwell reportedly drew a warm response. Also in 1962 he traveled to England, where he met with British neo-Nazis, including Colin Jordan, leader of the National Socialist Movement. His visit caused an enormous stir in the British press and efforts were undertaken to have him deported.[14]

Rockwell had considerable disdain for cowardly sympathizers and the mainstream right wing:

> I learned from bitter experience that the human material of the right wing consists 90 percent of cowards, dopes, nuts, one-track minds, blabbermouths, boobs, incurable tight-wads and—worst of all—hobbyists: people who have come to enjoy a perverted, masochistic pleasure in telling each other forever how we are all being raped by the "shh—you-know-who," but, who, under no conditions would think of risking their two cars, landscaped homes or juicy jobs to DO something about it.[15]

Rockwell had several benefactors, most of them quite modest: the exception was Harold Arrowsmith, Jr., a wealthy Baltimorean.

> Arrowsmith assembled some printing equipment across the river from the capital in Arlington, put Rockwell in charge, and called his new venture the "National Committee to Free America from Jewish Domination." This partnership soon splintered when things began to get tough. The bombing of an Atlanta synagogue in October, 1958, was associated in the public's mind with Rockwell and his recent anti-Jewish activities. . . . The full force of the law and public opinion descended upon the organization. The police and FBI raided his premises, anonymous telephone threats were made, home-made bombs were thrown at the house, shots were fired. . . . Even though Rockwell was cleared of any complicity in the bombings, the notoriety was too much for Arrowsmith; he took back his presses and fled.[16]

The party was primarily funded by dues and small contributions. On one occasion Rockwell said he had received money from Jewish groups, but that was never corroborated.

During 1963 and 1964 Rockwell spoke on several university campuses, including the Universities of Colorado, Hawaii, Kansas, and Montana. At the University of Kansas he addressed a crowd of some 2,000 students on February 20, 1964. He was sponsored by a recognized campus organization, the Minority Opinion Forum, which arranged controversial speakers from across the political spectrum. Demonstrators carried placards expressing disagreement with what he said but supporting his right to speak. KU Chancellor W. Clarke Wescoe issued a statement concerning the upcoming speech:

> I cannot recommend Rockwell to you. I despise his principles. I am convinced, however, that no one can be harmed by listening to him and that, conversely, his very presence may serve to make us all more dedicated to the principles of brotherhood as we come face to face with his repugnant views.[17]

After his talk, which was widely publicized, students left the building smirking and shaking their heads. Contrary to alarmist fears, Rockwell made absolutely no inroads among students and his message fell upon deaf ears. Appearances such as these tended to demystify and thereby neutralize any potential impact he might have had. Students invariably saw him as he was—a hateful fanatic.

In 1965 Rockwell ran for governor of Virginia and got a few thousand votes. That same year the IRS padlocked the ANP headquarters over a $5,000 tax debt. Rockwell raised the money and paid it off.

Rockwell's artistic side showed in the cartoons featured in *The Stormtrooper* and the *Rockwell Report*. He also possessed what might be called a cruel sense of humor. A pamphlet he distributed was entitled "Nigger! You too can be a Jew." This, the pamphlet vowed, could be achieved through the utilization of the "New Sammy the Kosher Coon Correspondence Course," obviously in reference to Sammy Davis, Jr., who was of the Jewish faith. One John Patler also contributed his artistic skills to ANP publications.

*The Stormtrooper* featured ads for Rockwell's autobiography, *This Time the World,* which sold for an outlandish price ($10 in 1964). Much more of a bargain (at fifty cents) was *How to Get Out and Stay Out of an Insane Asylum,* the story of the commander's battle against the "Jew Mental Health Attack."

In 1966 Rockwell changed the name of the ANP to the National Socialist White People's party (NSWPP). That same year he transferred the leader of the Chicago unit, Matt Koehl, to Arlington to work on the headquarters staff. Shortly afterward Deputy Commander Alan J. Welch resigned and Koehl assumed his position.

In April 1966, Rockwell achieved the publicity he had hoped for. Black writer Alex Haley, later to be known for his immensely popular book *Roots,* interviewed him for *Playboy* magazine. Rockwell said:

> With the economy coming apart at the seams, with the niggers pushing, with the Communists agitating, with all this cowardice and betrayal by our government, the

masses of common, ordinary white people will have had it up to here. . . . They'll be looking for a white leader . . . with the guts to stand up and say, "I'm going to completely separate the black and white races and preserve white Christian domination in this country, and I'm going to have the Jew Communists and any other traitors gassed for treason. And if you don't like it, you know what you can do about it."[18]

* * *

In August 1967, at the age of forty-nine, George Lincoln Rockwell was assassinated in a laundromat parking lot by John Patler, twenty-nine, a disgruntled member Rockwell had recently expelled.[19] Following Rockwell's death, NSWPP leadership was assumed by thirty-three-year-old Matt Koehl, who was also the executor of Rockwell's estate. Formerly a member of the National Renaissance party and National States Rights party, Koehl had spent all of his adulthood in one neo-Nazi group or another. Lacking Rockwell's dynamic personality, Koehl depended heavily on two national officers, Robert Lloyd and William Pierce. The NSWPP experienced a period of stability and modest growth under their command, in spite of the usual squabbling and defections. In 1968 it moved into a new building in Arlington.[20]

Rockwell was regarded with considerable suspicion by other right-wing leaders, suspicion that was heightened with the release of COINTELPRO data on the campaign against white hate groups, which revealed that the FBI had contemplated planting information in a *Rockwell Report* in order to discredit KKK leader Robert Shelton. An FBI document of February 4, 1966, to the special agent in charge of the Birmingham, Alabama, office from the director of the FBI, said:

> The Bureau is contemplating increasing its counter-intelligence effort against Robert Shelton, Imperial Wizard, United Klans of America, Knights of the Ku Klux Klan. In order to have necessary information, the Birmingham office is requested to review its files for specific background data on Robert Shelton. . . .
>
> In addition, the Bureau desires a summary of information concerning Shelton's close associates. . . . [including] any information concerning Shelton's relationship with his wife, any other females or males, any unusual behavior patterns and general Klan talk concerning his use or misuse of Klan funds, what motivates him, etc.
>
> The reason for this information is to begin with the planning of a "Rockwell Report," put out by George Lincoln Rockwell of the American Nazi party, "exposing" some information about Shelton which would tend to discredit him.

The memo, widely circulated in right-wing circles, was rather ambiguous. It was not clear whether this was information the FBI would covertly feed to an unsuspecting Rockwell to use in his campaign against a rival, or whether Rockwell was actually cooperating with the FBI. Depending upon what one wanted to believe, either case seemed plausible.

Conspiracy theories flourished and some far rightists believed that Rockwell was really an FBI or ADL agent whose revival of Nazism was a ploy to alert the American people to a bogus danger of anti-Semitism and thus encourage persecution of "patriots." The far-right tabloid *The Councilor* devoted several articles to this theme in a December 1977 issue, none of which offered any particularly compelling evidence.[21]

In 1986 a small alternative agriculture newspaper, *ACRES USA* (whose editor, Charlie Walters, is a student of political movements and an admirer of Eric Hoffer), ran an in-depth interview with one of Rockwell's early followers, who used the pseudonym "Smith." Among Smith's observations:

> Rockwell had a type of charisma, he had the ability to attract people like a magnet, and I admit I was one of them. . . . And there are basically a lot of people like me out there. They're basically born followers, or born lieutenants. . . .
> Eric Hoffer said it all. The revolutionary has to be totally ignorant of the task. That's why they sometimes succeed. If they knew what they were doing, they wouldn't even try. George Lincoln Rockwell was dangerous. It's just that they took him out before he really got his hands on some serious money or power.[22]

In the spring of 1970 Frank Collin, the NSWPP's midwestern coordinator, was dismissed by Koehl and went on to found the National Socialist Party of America. During the early 1970s a number of former members started neo-Nazi parties of their own. Karl Allen formed the White party of America in Washington, D.C.; John Bishop started a new American Nazi Party in Iowa; and Charles White established the National White Peoples party in Asheville, North Carolina. All were defunct after a few years.

In July 1970 William Pierce was dismissed and Robert Lloyd resigned shortly afterward. Pierce subsequently went on to form the National Alliance. John Beattie, a Canadian neo-Nazi who had been active on the NSWPP's behalf, was also out. It was later revealed that Beattie has been an informant for the Royal Canadian Mounted Police intelligence unit.[23]

*        *        *

During the 1970s the NSWPP made some attempts at electoral politics. In 1975 NSWPP member Art Jones polled 5.5 percent of the vote in Milwaukee's primary election for mayor. Other neo-Nazi candidates garnered much publicity and a few votes during the period.[24]

With the departure of Pierce and Lloyd, the NSWPP headquarters was understaffed. In 1972 Martin Kerr was appointed second-in-command and general spokesman when Koehl wasn't there, which was much of the time. Kerr had been a member of the National Renaissance party and a student at Hofstra University, where he was in frequent conflict with school authorities over his views. In 1977 he was made editor of *White Power* and the quarterly *National Socialist,* the publication of the World Union of National Socialists (a letterhead organization).[25]

In 1976 *Crawdaddy* magazine did an article entitled, "The American Reich," which featured both Koehl and Collin. Koehl had this to say about blacks:

The white man brought the blacks over here against their wills and tried to put them in a white society. . . . It was a terrible mistake. It is the source of so much of our headache today. It can be solved when we undertake a serious repatriation program.[26]

And about Jews:

In the future Aryan America there will be no room for a Jewish parasite colony. Therefore we are going to remove them from our presence. . . . Maybe we can find a big island somewhere in the middle of the ocean where they can go and perform hard and honest work just like anyone else, and if it kills them, well then it is their tough luck. The world of the future will have no room for parasites.[27]

Under Koehl the NSWPP continued to experience difficulties. In 1981 disgruntled ANP member Ricky E. Cooper protested the sale of "Victory Certificates" by the NSWPP. The certificates were "redeemable for cash payments after the Nazis assume 'national political power.' "[28] Cooper had sued to recover $888 he paid for the certificate. He lost the lawsuit but the party ceased sales following an investigation and warning by the Securities and Exchange Commission. In 1982 the IRS put a $37,000 lien on the party headquarters for unpaid taxes, which the party claims was negotiated down to $26,000.[29] That same year a name change was announced. The NSWPP would now be known as the "New Order."

With its membership embarrassingly small and splinter groups beginning to form—such as the Chico Area National Socialists (CANS) in California, which broke away in 1981—the secretarian Koehl decided to work with like-minded groups, a radical departure from past traditions.

In the past, the New Order/NSWPP has been very hesitant to hold joint activities with other racialist organizations. But, as part of our new outreach, we felt that this occasion would be a perfect one in which not merely to give lip-service to White Unity, but rather to give a practical demonstration of it.[30]

It was to no avail. Personality and doctrinal differences prevailed, as always, and each neo-Nazi group retained its little fiefdom of supporters, with defections from one to another being major events, almost like gossip about divorces and affairs among suburbanites. By 1984 publication of *White Power* ceased and only the *NS Bulletin* was appearing regularly.

In 1983 the party moved to New Berlin, Wisconsin, close to Koehl's home town of Milwaukee. The present-day New Order is very small, tightly organized, and relatively stable by neo-Nazi standards. In 1984 the ADL estimated that "The New Order today has an active hard core cadre of about 25 and a membership of about 100 who pay dues and receive its publication, the *NS Bulletin*."[31]

## Nationalist Socialist Party of America

Frank Collin's NSPA remained small, consisting mostly of young men and adolescents. Collin attained a fair degree of notoriety when it was publicized that his father, a retired furniture store owner named Max Cohn, had been an inmate at the Dachau concentration camp during World War II.[32] This fact cost him considerable support among neo-Nazis. According to Elizabeth Wheaton in *Code Name Greenkil*:

> Frank Collin was ousted from the NSWPP in 1970 as the result of an FBI-instigated smear campaign. For a Nazi, it was the ultimate smear: Frank Collin's real name was Frank Cohn—and he was half Jewish.[33]

In 1975 Collin ran for alderman in a Chicago ward, polling 16 percent of the total vote cast. In 1978 Matt Koehl of the NSWPP offered a $10,000 reward to anyone who could "prove conclusively" that Collin was not Jewish. It was also Collin's NSPA that sparked the controversy when he announced plans to hold a 1977 rally in Skokie, Illinois, a predominantly Jewish town with a large population of Holocaust survivors. According to the ADL:

> The NSPA subsequently received reams of publicity when new local ordinances in Skokie prohibited the group from holding a rally. The ordinances required would-be marchers to obtain $350,000 in insurance policies and prohibited the wearing of military-style uniforms and the dissemination of hate literature.[34]

Perceiving a blatant First Amendment violation, in January 1978 the Illinois Supreme Court ruled on behalf of the marchers and declared that the swastika was "symbolic political speech to convey to the public the beliefs of those who display it." The city of Skokie appealed. Backed by the American Civil Liberties Union, Collin and his Nazis basked in the glow of media coverage as the case worked its way to the U.S. Supreme Court, which refused to prohibit the march.[35] The case was a major watershed for the ACLU, many of whose members were Jewish:

> Collin's attorney, David Goldberger, 36, is Jewish. Goldberger, who is the ACLU legal director, is proud of his heritage. But his links with Collin have caused trouble for him. "Most of my friends have criticized me and I've received several threats against my life," he said.
> The final irony is that Collin did not decide to march through Skokie until after Chicago, through its Parks District, banned the Nazis from demonstrating.[36]

After the legal victory Collin rescheduled his march. Instead of Skokie, however, the NSPA decided to hold a rally in the plaza of the Federal Building in Chicago. On June 24, 1978, Collin, Harold Covington, and a few other NSPA members showed up to find several thousand counter-demonstrators waiting for them. After trying to speak for a brief time, they were escorted by police back to their headquarters.

On July 9, 1978, Collin and twenty-five NSPA members and associates held a rally in Chicago's Marquette Park in the face of 2,500 spectators and several hundred counter-demonstrators who were held back by riot-helmeted policemen. Skokie was the galvanizing event that marked the beginning of the "counter-hate" movement in which small groups of neo-Nazis and Ku Klux Klansmen were routinely overwhelmed by violence-prone counter-demonstrators virtually everywhere they went to speak, march, or hold rallies.

Covington, a twenty-three-year-old NSPA member and a former NSWPP member, also made the news. A contentious and articulate spokesman, Covington took advantage of the Skokie controversy to publicize his NSPA activities in Raleigh, North Carolina. He announced his 1977 candidacy for city council and was the subject of numerous local articles. During 1978 and 1979 Covington was busy organizing NSPA activities and recruiting new members, largely from the ranks of the local KKK.

In 1979, while Covington was still leader of the North Carolina unit of the NSPA, the infamous shootout took place between members of the Communist Workers party and the KKK in Greensboro; five CWP members died. Two of the Klansmen were also NSPA members. The media gave heavy coverage of the incident and subsequent trial, and Covington quickly became the most recognizable neo-Nazi in the country. However, his rise to the leadership of the NSPA was not a product of his new-found notoriety. In 1979 he went to NSPA headquarters in Chicago while Collin was away.

> In Frank Collin's absence, the Nazis discovered "films, pictures and addresses of some little boys," Covington said, in Collin's room in the Nazi headquarters building. Covington responded by buying the building, "an urgently necessary tactic in order to remove my regrettable predecessor from the scene," he told party leaders in a confidential memo.
>
> On Collin's return to Chicago, detectives from Chicago's Youth Division placed him under arrest for taking indecent liberties with adolescent boys. Collin, in astonishing stupidity, had taken photographs of himself and the boys he victimized. And he left the evidence in Nazi headquarters. "Quite frankly," Covington bragged, "we handed Frank Collin to the cops on a silver platter."[38]

In 1980 Harold Covington assumed the leadership of the NSPA. It was a banner year for him in other respects as well. He had caused quite a local stir when he filed in the Republican primary for attorney general, but when he won an incredible 43 percent of the vote it made national headlines. His streak of successes was short-lived, however. Events during the trials of Klansmen and NSPA members led some of his followers to suspect that he was an undercover informant. Faced with internal revolt and what he later called "harassment and threats" by the ATF, Covington announced he was going underground. In March 1981 he appointed St. Louis NSPA leader Michael Allen, twenty-nine, as his successor and disappeared shortly thereafter. He wound up on the Isle of Man, living there for several years before returning to the United States. He currently resides in Raleigh, North Carolina, and puts out the newsletter *Resistance.*

Allen, it turns out, was a bona fide ATF informant. According to Elizabeth Wheaton, an ATF memo that surfaced in the Greensboro trials referred to an NSPA party leader in St. Louis—none other than Michael Allen.

> Allen supplied the ATF with Nazi membership lists, organizational rules and structures, and "eyes only" memos to party leaders from Covington. One of those memos detailed his method for ousting Frank Collin, which he dubbed "Operation Bobby Brown."[39]

After the assassination attempt on President Reagan by John W. Hinckley in 1981, Allen made the news with the claim that Hinckley had been a member of the NSPA who was kicked out because of violent tendencies.[40]

Following his exposure as an ATF informant, Allen was replaced by Jim Burford in 1982, and the NSPA folded shortly thereafter. A group of former members resurrected the name American Nazi party and yet another tiny neo-Nazi group was born (or reborn). The group then split into two factions, the new ANP led by Dennis Milam and the America First Committee headed by Art Jones.

*    *    *

For other stories about the American neo-Nazi movement, we refer the reader to a 1987 book by Andy Oakley, an investigative reporter for the Chicago-area *Mundelein Herald* who infiltrated the NSWPP and other groups over a period of six years. The account of his adventures appears in *"88": An Undercover News Reporter's Exposé of American Nazis and the Ku Klux Klan.* Oakley announces in the front of the book that "all author's proceeds from this book will be donated to the Anti-Defamation League of B'nai B'rith, the Southern Poverty Law Center's Klanwatch Project and the Simon Wiesenthal Center."[41]

The book is a fascinating and readable account of Oakley's experiences with Chicago-area groups and individuals. He provides a rich amount of detail and relates numerous conversations as he remembers them. There are no footnotes. The book is clearly adversarial. His major coup is the exposé and destruction of the career of a KKK member who worked as an operator at a nuclear power plant.

# Neo-Nazi Splinters and Sects

Numerous small neo-Nazi organizations came and went during the 1970s and 1980s; several still marginally survive. The following is a brief account of some of them. Four others—somewhat more substantial—Aryan Nations, the Mountain Church, the Posse Comitatus, and White Aryan Resistance, will be dealt with separately, as will The Order, a criminal group.

### AMERICA FIRST COMMITTEE

This very small Chicago organization was headed by Art Jones, a former NSWPP member who ran for mayor of Milwaukee under the party's banner. Jones is a Vietnam veteran and a former student in political science and journalism at the University of Wisconsin. Founded in 1980, the committee published several issues of a newspaper called *The American Lancer.* A typical one-man operation with a mailing list, the "committee" is now defunct, although Jones remains active in extreme right politics. His most recent effort was to raise money for neo-Nazi causes with a 900 telephone number. The messages were vintage Nazi and little money was raised.

### AMERICAN WHITE NATIONALIST PARTY

Formally incorporated in Columbus, Ohio, in 1972, the AWNP was led by brothers John and Edward Gerhardt. They published a newsletter called the *White Nationalist,* later renamed *White Unity.* In 1979 both were convicted of conspiring to bomb a Columbus school in protest against court-ordered busing. Sentenced to six years in prison, they were paroled in 1983.

The conviction came about as the result of an undercover police informant, George Giammarino, who had infiltrated white supremacy groups. For two years he was in charge of internal security for the Gerhardt organization. He was paid $200 cash per week for his services, but news reports stated that he had been a professional informant for the FBI, ATF, and various police departments for ten years. According to the defense, the surreptitious tape recordings produced as evidence against the Gerhardt brothers conveniently contained gaps where conversation that would be exculpatory took place. John Gerhardt asserted that one critical omission was his statement to Giammarino, "Wait a minute. How did your idea become my idea?"[42]

The conviction was for conspiracy to commit the act, not the act itself, since it never happened. Conspiracy charges often have been used against political dissidents of the left and right because of the ease with which cases can be built. A discussion of this phenomenon is contained in Pat Watter's and Stephen Gillers's book, *Investigating the FBI*. A featured essay, "Political Informers," by Frank Donner, notes, "The undercover man may also induce others to commit a crime." With respect to informants and conspiracy cases, they say:

> Informers play a particularly important role in conspiracy cases. The vague character of the conspiracy charge and the atmosphere of plotting and hidden guilt which accompanies it make a perfect foil for the undercover agent who surfaces on the witness stand. Besides, group crimes like conspiracy offer the maximum punitive return for the smallest commitment of intelligence resources.[43]

With the Gerhardt convictions and jail sentences, the AWNP folded. An appeal of the convictions was unsuccessful. The brothers still publish an occasional mailing piece, which extols their views.

## EURO-AMERICAN ALLIANCE

Active since the mid-1970s, the EAA is a tiny neo-Nazi group founded by "Major" Donald V. Clerkin, who serves as both commander and chairman. He publishes two small newsletters, *The Talon* (monthly) and the *Euro-American Quarterly*. A recent issue of *The Talon* begins with an article entitled "Constructive Hatred":

> When you see a White woman in the company of a non-White man, which one should you hate? The non-white male is carrying out his race's imperative: he is debauching a willing victim. What do you do when you come across a White mother coddling a child who is a race alien? Hate her and shun her.[44]

Clerkin's group has about two dozen hardcore "members" and supporters and a mailing fist of a few hundred. He was still publishing in 1991.

## NATIONAL ALLIANCE

The NA was founded in 1974 by Dr. William Pierce, a former physics professor at the University of Oregon. Pierce had been active in George Lincoln Rockwell's American Nazi party and in the NSWPP under Matt Koehl after Rockwell was assassinated. He was editor of *National Socialist World*, but was purged by Koehl in 1970. Originally located in Arlington, Virginia, the NA moved to Mill Point,

West Virginia, in 1985. Pierce also used a religious front, the Cosmotheist Community Church, and was granted tax-exempt status by the IRS in 1978. Following protests by the ADL, the IRS revoked the status, and that revocation was upheld by a federal appeals court in 1983 on the basis of the church's white supremacist beliefs.

NA originally published the tabloid *Attack,* which became a bimonthly magazine retitled *National Vanguard.* Unlike most neo-Nazi publications, *National Vanguard* is intellectual and readable. Not an action organization, the NA has a membership estimated at two hundred (less than one per million Americans) with several hundred more subscribing to its publication. It also conducts a mail-order bookselling operation. Pierce received national notoriety in 1984 when it was revealed that he was the author of *The Turner Diaries* (under the pseudonym Andrew McDonald), a fictional account of a white revolution that allegedly inspired the neo-Nazi group The Order. Several members of The Order were also involved with the NA. The group was still active in 1991.

## NATIONAL DEMOCRATIC FRONT

Founded in 1985 by Gary Gallo, the NDF originated in Maryland but moved to Knoxville, Tennessee, a few years later. Gallo operates a bookstore out of his headquarters, a remodeled residence, and publishes a monthly newsletter, *The Nationalist.* Gallo is a lawyer who ran a chain of legal clinics in the Washington, D.C., area in the early 1980s. The group has between fifty and one hundred mail-order members and a mailing fist of several hundred.

## NATIONAL SOCIALIST LEAGUE/WORLD SERVICE

The United States's only homophile neo-Nazi group was organized in 1974 by Russell Veh, who had earlier headed the Ohio White Nationalist party in Toledo. It published the NS *Mobilizer,* a newsletter. The publishing arm of the NSL is World Service, also headed by Veh in Los Angeles, which publishes *Race and Nation.* WS sells a wide selection of Nazi-oriented movies, such as *Triumph of the Will, Jude Suss,* and other titles. Still active in the 1990s, it has consisted predominantly of a mailing fist.

## NATIONAL SOCIALIST LIBERATION FRONT

Originally founded in 1969 by Joseph Tomassi, a former member of the original American Nazi party, the California-based NSLF acquired a reputation as one of the more violent neo-Nazi factions. Tomassi himself was killed in a dispute with an NSWPP member as a result of a feud between the two groups. The NSLF was noted for a heavy, but only marginally effective, recruitment drive in prisons.

In 1981 Karl Hand, a former KKK member and one of David Duke's Grand Dragons, assumed the leadership. Hand moved the headquarters to Metairie,

Louisiana, where he published *Defiance,* a tabloid, and coordinated the activities of a dozen or so tiny chapters. Hand was convicted of firing shots into the home of black neighbors in February 1980, for which he served three months in jail. In 1985 he was involved in a violent altercation, which he claims was a setup, and was sentenced to fifteen years in prison for attempted murder. The organization folded shortly after Hand's incarceration.

## NATIONALIST SOCIALIST MOVEMENT

Based in Cincinnati, Ohio, the NSM was founded in 1975 by James Mason and Robert Brannen, a former member of Rockwell's American Nazi party. It published the *National Socialist Bulletin* and had "units" in Cincinnati and Detroit. Actual membership was around a dozen. The organization merged with the National Socialist Liberation Front in the early 1980s. Mason has written articles for various neo-Nazi publications in recent years.

## NATIONAL SOCIALIST VANGUARD

The NSV was formed in January 1983. Originally located in Salinas, California, it moved to The Dalles, Oregon, in August 1986 and is headed by Rickey Cooper and Dan Stewart, both of whom are past members of the NSWPP under Matt Koehl. The group's publication, *NSV Report,* is full of gossipy information on various other neo-Nazi organizations and personalities. Still active in the nineties, NSV has no structure and no members besides Cooper and Stewart.

## NATIONALIST SOCIALIST WHITE AMERICA PARTY

Founded in the early 1980s in Pacific Palisades, California, the NSWAP is a one-man operation run by James Karl. His publications include the *NSWAP Newsletter* and a series of flyers and stickers designed to shock readers with emblazoned swastikas and slogans like "Nigger Get Out!" and "Death To Race-Mixing." The "group" was still functioning in 1991.

## NSDAP/AO

Known principally by this acronym, the National Sozialistiche Deutsche Arbeiter Partei/Auslands Organisation (National Socialist German Workers Party/Overseas Organization) is the creation of Gary Rex Lauck, who uses the pseudonym Gerhard Lauck. Lauck was associated with Frank Collin's NSPA until it folded. NSDAP/AO is the primary publisher of neo-Nazi literature exported from the United States to Germany, where its publication is illegal. Operating out of a post office box in Lincoln, Nebraska, Lauck founded the NSDAP/AO in 1974, after he was expelled from West Germany for giving a speech on Nazism in the United States. German authorities arrested him again two years later when he was caught with a large quantity of neo-Nazi posters. He spent over four months in jail and was subsequently deported and banned from entering West Germany for the remainder of his life. Lauck reportedly maintains ties with German neo-Nazi groups.[45]

NSDAP/AO publishes a well-written (occasional) tabloid called *The New Order* in English, and a German-language newsletter, *NS Kampfruf,* in addition to a large selection of books on white racist and neo-Nazi themes. The September/October 1990 issue of *The New Order* listed about 125 books and a large selection of paraphernalia, including swastika stickers, patches, badges, and cassette tapes.[46] Like many neo-Nazi groups, it is strictly a mail-order operation, holding no meetings or rallies, and having no "membership" in the participatory sense. Its serials are circulated to subscribers, mail-order book customers, contributors, other neo-Nazi organizations, and anyone requesting a sample copy.

## NATIONAL SOCIALIST WHITE WORKERS PARTY

Allen Vincent, an early member of Rockwell's American Nazi party, founded the San Francisco-based NSWWP in 1976. Vincent has described himself as a "graduate of California's penal institutions." The organization had roughly fifty members, including an active group in Houston, Texas, where NSWWP member Michael Ange announced his candidacy for mayor in 1977.[47]

The first issue of the NSWWP's journal, *Stormer,* was published in September 1977. In addition to Allen Vincent as editor, it listed James Mason, of the Nationalist Socialist Movement, as a member of the editorial staff, and contained articles by Gerhard Lauck and Frank Collin.[48]

Vincent attained considerable notoriety when he opened the Rudolph Hess Bookstore near a Jewish neighborhood in San Francisco. On April 1, 1977, the store was attacked and burned by a mob armed with sledgehammers and crowbars. Morris and Allan Weiss were arrested and charged with malicious mischief. Morris Weiss was also charged with aggravated assault. Charges against the two were dropped, however, "because of substantial evidentiary problems and in the interest of justice," according to San Francisco District Attorney Joseph Freitas.[49] The group is now defunct.

## SOCIAL NATIONALIST ARYAN PEOPLES PARTY

A one-man neo-Nazi "party," the SNAPP was headed by Keith Gilbert, a former member of the Minutemen during the 1960s and a veteran of several KKK and neo-Nazi groups, including Aryan Nations. Gilbert once spent five years in San Quentin for possession of almost three-fourths of a ton of dynamite. In 1985 Gilbert was convicted of numerous counts of welfare fraud and tax evasion and is serving a term in Idaho State Prison.

## SS ACTION GROUP

In 1979 John Morierty and Edward Dunn broke with Casey Kalemba's United White People's party and formed their own neo-Nazi group, the SSAG. The organization has been deliberately confrontational and its publications, *S.S. Action Group Michigan Briefing and Aryans Awake,* often feature news stories of its clashes with counter-demonstrators and rescue by police. In March 1983, for example, fifteen of the group showed up in Ann Arbor in full Nazi uniform and immediately confronted some two hundred counter-demonstrators, including members of the Progressive Labor party front, INCAR (International Committee Against Racism), and other Marxist-Leninist groups. Police arrested nine of the counter-demonstrators and escorted the SSAG members out of town. During a similar incident in March 1988 two dozen neo-Nazis faced two hundred counter-demonstrators:

> Despite the presence of about 50 police officers, the counter-demonstrators, wielding clubs, bottles, eggs and chunks of concrete, smashed several large plate glass windows at the Federal Building, which houses a post office, a federal courtroom and offices for the Federal Bureau of Investigation and the Internal Revenue Service.[50]

Based on the small turnout at demonstrations, membership in the SSAG is estimated to have peaked at less than fifty, with considerable turnover. The group was still functioning in 1991.

UNITED WHITE PEOPLES PARTY

The UWPP, based in Cleveland, Ohio, was headed by Casey Kalemba. It operated out of a storefront location and had twenty to thirty "members" in the Cleveland area. Kalemba attempted to forge a coalition among neo-Nazi groups; he called it the "White Confederacy." Several leaders said they would participate, but the confederacy was ineffective. The group is defunct.

# Major Groups of the 1980s

The 1980s saw the growth of entirely new groups, hybrid organizations embracing what might be called "nontraditional" neo-Nazi doctrines.

ARYAN NATIONS

Headed by Richard Butler, few political organizations have received as much publicity in the last ten years as Aryan Nations. The group coalesced during the late 1970s around Butler's "Church of Jesus Christ—Christian" and peaked in the early 1980s at perhaps two hundred bona fide members and a mailing list of about two thousand. Attendance at the group's World Aryan "Congress" had routinely been in the neighborhood of 150 until 1988, when it declined precipitously. Active membership is restricted partly because of the requirement that members tithe and the geographic remoteness of the group's northern Idaho compound at Hayden Lake. Butler has issued military-type uniforms and advocates paramilitary training. For a far-right group, the organization is eclectic and includes members of the various Ku Klux Klans, the Posse Comitatus, neo-Nazi groups and other Identity churches. Publications include *Calling Our Nation* and *Aryan Nations Newsletter.* Butler's religious views are as unorthodox as his politics.

> Butler's church is a proponent of the Identity doctrine, a relic from a 19th-century movement in Great Britain that identified white Anglo Saxons as one of the 10 lost tribes of Israel, and England and America—particularly the Pacific Northwest—as the promised land referred to in the Bible.
>
> Identity followers believe whites are the true children of Israel, that Jesus was a white man who descended from the same line that produced the Germanic and Scandinavian peoples. The modern founder of the Identity movement was Wesley Swift—who, in establishing his church in Southern California after World War II, publicly called for the destruction of all American Jews by the end of 1953. Butler was one of Swift's proteges and claims to carry the mantle of the Identity movement since Swift's death in 1970.[51]

Issue number 60 (1989) of *Calling Our Nation* contains a long article on Adolf Hitler by Manfred Roeder entitled "The Greatest Revolutionary of All Time." Roeder asserts:

> Hitler had solved all the pressing problems of our time. He and his work were destroyed because his opponents did not want to accept that some of his ideas were universal and valid for every man. He was destroyed because his enemies succeeded in the use of the superpower USA for their purposes, just like the Pharisees succeeded in using the superpower of Rome to crush the idea of Jesus 2000 years ago.[52]

Aryan Nations maintains a prison ministry headed by Janet Housell, a woman in her sixties who corresponds with a large number of white inmates. The ministry publishes *The Way,* a newsletter that antiracist groups have attempted to have banned from prisons on grounds of its alleged offensiveness. The May-July 1989 issue addresses this litigation in its "Legal Corner" column:

> Several Christian Identity brethren have filed litigation in the U.S. District Court, Southern District of Texas (Galveston), Case No. G-87-298, alleging the denial of First Amendment rights of worship and religion. William Bryan Sorens . . . is presently gathering evidence regarding the denial and/or delay of correspondence and publications from our brethren or each other. Other things are being litigated as well, including prejudicial treatment from [prison] officials because of our faith.[53]

As one of the more militant and notorious of all neo-Nazi groups, Aryan Nations has tended to attract particularly fanatic devotees, including a fair number who subsequently ran afoul of the law. Many of the twenty-three indicted members of The Order had been involved with Aryan Nations, as were several defendants in the 1988 Fort Smith sedition trial (in which all were acquitted). Today, under constant surveillance, Aryan Nations is a shell of its former self. Meetings are sparsely attended, with the requisite number of undercover agents always present, and income and circulation of publications is a fraction of its previous level.

An outstanding study of Aryan Nations and related groups in Idaho was undertaken by Idaho State University sociology professor James A. Aho. Published in 1990, *The Politics of Righteousness: Idaho Christian Patriotism* is a detailed and scholarly account of this phenomenon.[54] Aho makes insightful comments, which could be applied to all political and social movements:

> The Christian Patriots studied here come in one of two forms. They are either "hedge-hogs" or "foxes" (to borrow an image from Isaiah Berlin), grand theorists or empiricists. To say it more precisely, some patriots derive their positions on specific issues from explicit theories of history and society, and are able to fit events as diverse as earthquakes, venereal disease, and commodity prices into an overarching theoretical scheme. Others are concerned with a specific problem such as school textbooks, abortion, or sex education, but are disinclined and/or unable to theoretically justify their responses beyond catch phrases like "secular humanism."[55]

Butler is in poor health, having had open-heart surgery and being over seventy years of age. It's likely that when he dies his church and Aryan Nations will soon follow, although they may hang on for a few years.

## THE MOUNTAIN CHURCH

The Mountain Church of Jesus Christ was founded in 1971 by Robert Miles, former Grand Dragon of the United Klans of America's Michigan Realm. A New York native, Miles was formerly an insurance company manager but lost his job due to his Klan affiliation. In October of that same year he was indicted along with four others for conspiracy to violate civil rights and possession of explosives for the bombings of ten empty school buses used for integration purposes in Pontiac, Michigan. Sentenced to nine years in prison, he was paroled after serving six.

Over the years Miles built up a following culled largely from Ku Klux Klan, neo-Nazi, and Christian Identity groups. His own religious theology, which he calls "dualism," differs from traditional Christian fundamentalism in a number of respects, but he doesn't regard those differences as particularly important. The out-standing characteristic of dualism is its Manicheanism. In the context of Christian Identity beliefs, James Aho describes it in this way: "At the most theoretical level the world division is symbolized by the familiar 'God and Devil,' 'good and evil,' 'truth and deception,' 'light and darkness,' 'life and death.' "[56]

Miles is as comfortable with neopagans and Odinists (those who worship the Norse god Odin) as with Christians. The church has been a regular meeting place for right-wing racists of all types, and events there were regarded as high points in the neo-Nazi and white racist movement.

Miles has published a newsletter, *From the Mountain,* in which he expounds on his philosophy and carries newsy items about individuals and groups associated with his interests. The tone is that of a patriarchal semi-intellectual philosopher, as distinguished from the harsh racist rhetoric of other neo-Nazi leaders, in which he only occasionally indulges.

Miles was a star attraction at the 1988 Fort Smith sedition trial in which he and all the other defendants were acquitted. In 1990 he folded *From the Mountain,* ostensibly to retire from the fight and take care of his wife, who has numerous health problems.

## THE ORDER

In October 1983 a group of extreme right-wing racists led by Robert Matthews, including many from Aryan Nations, formed a secret society known as The Order (also as The Silent Brotherhood). During 1983 and 1984 members of The Order participated in a series of sometimes violent crimes, largely to raise money (in the Leninist tradition) for their operations, including armored car and bank robbery and counterfeiting. Other crimes were the murders of Denver talk show host Alan Berg and their own member Walter West, whom they suspected of betraying them.

In many respects the crimes of The Order resembled those of the far-left Weather Underground. James Coates drew attention to this in *Armed and Dangerous: The Rise of the Survivalist Right:*

> Between 1971 and 1981 . . . the Weather Underground alone claimed responsibility for twenty-five bombings, including those of the U.S. Capitol in 1971 and the Pentagon in 1972. In 1981 a half dozen Weather Underground radicals were charged with the commando-style attack against a Brink's truck in Nyack, New York, in which $1.6 million was taken and two policemen and a guard were shot to death.[57]

Eventually all members of The Order were apprehended, except for Matthews, who died in a shootout with FBI agents in December 1984. James Aho described the expensive operation:

> After a cost of over $1 million, the presentation of 1,538 pieces of evidence, and the appearance of 280 witnesses, the U.S. Justice Department completed its successful prosecution of the Order in Seattle in late 1985. . . . The investigation is said to have involved one-quarter of the total manpower resources of the FBI, which followed a trail of sixty-seven separate crimes including robberies, arson, bombings, counterfeit schemes, and murders throughout the country.[58]

In April 1987 a federal grand jury in Denver indicted four defendants on the grounds they had "willfully injured and interfered with Alan Berg . . . because he was Jewish . . . resulting in [his] death by gunfire." Berg, a talk-show host, was murdered in June 1984. Named in that indictment were Jean Craig, David Lane, Bruce Pierce, and Richard Scutari. In November 1987 a jury convicted Lane and Pierce and acquitted Craig and Scutari. Both were sentenced to 150 years in prison.

Also in April 1987 a federal grand jury in Fort Smith, Arkansas, indicted Aryan Nations leader Richard Butler and nine others for "seditious conspiracy between July 1983 and March 1985, to overthrow the government." Indicted with Butler were Andrew V. Barnhill, Louis R. Beam, Ardie McBrearty, David E. Lane, Robert Miles, Bruce Pierce, Robert J. Scutari, Robert N. Smalley, and Richard W. Snell. Charges against Smalley were dismissed during the trial for lack of evidence. In addition, Snell and four others were charged with conspiring to murder a federal judge. Charged with Snell were William H. Wade, Ivan R. Wade, Lambert Miller, and David M. McGuire.

A year later, on April 7, 1988, to the dismay of prosecutors, the jury found all of the remaining thirteen defendants not guilty. Evidence strongly suggests that it was a politically motivated case, including the fact that sedition charges are extremely rare in the American legal system. The defendants had the services of DeDay LaRene, an exceptional defense attorney hired by Miles.[59]

## POSSE COMITATUS

Originally founded in 1969 by Henry Beach and William P. Gale, a retired army colonel who led World War II guerrilla units in the Philippines for General MacArthur,[60] the Posse received little attention until the late 1970s, when it experienced a rush of publicity. Posse philosophy states that the only legitimate government is located at the county level. Local, virtually autonomous Posse units claim the right to perform citizens' arrests, use "Posse Comitatus" badges as symbols of authority, and refrain from paying federal income taxes.

Although not neo-Nazi in the sense of the small Nazi parties, the Posse nevertheless has articulated similar anti-Jewish conspiracy theories and has had a number of Klansmen and neo-Nazis involved in its work. Most journalistic accounts treat the Posse as part of that genre. More properly, it represents radical fringe of the tax protest movement that blossomed in the late 1970s.

Jim Wickstrom became the Posse spokesman and published a newsletter, *The Posse Noose,* in which he made the usual inflammatory statements extreme rightists are noted for. Some Posse members wore tiny gold hangman's nooses on their lapels. Virtually every law enforcement agency in the country became involved in a campaign to ferret out and prosecute Posse members, including the criminal investigation division of the Internal Revenue Service.

Wickstrom himself was imprisoned in March 1984 on two counts of impersonating a public official and one count of bail jumping. The Posse had formed its own township consisting of a couple dozen house trailers and a tavern. "Tigerton Dells," as it was known, was located adjacent to Tigerton, Wisconsin, Wickstrom's home town. The charges arose because Wickstrom had declared himself municipal judge and town clerk.

Concern about the Posse reached a fever pitch in February 1983 when Gordon Kahl, a Posse activist, killed two federal marshals in a shootout at his North Dakota farm and became a fugitive. The marshals were attempting to serve a warrant for probation violation. In a March 1983 letter to Jim Wickstrom, Kahl said that he took "no pleasure in the death or injury of any of these people," adding that he "would have liked nothing other than to be left alone." He had also made comments such as, "We are a conquered and occupied nation . . . conquered and occupied by the Jews." Kahl was tracked down in a nationwide manhunt and killed in another shootout in the mountains of Arkansas in June 1983. He thus became a hero and a martyr to the radical tax protest movement.[61]

The Posse was only one of dozens of radical tax protest groups active in the late 1970s and early 1980s. In 1986 Ruth E. Schweizer of the Criminal Investigation Division of the IRS Office of Intelligence prepared the *Illegal Tax Protester Information Handbook,* which contained profiles of ten organizations and several individuals. On pages 36 to 39 are listed some forty-eight organizations under a heading, "Organizations with a Propensity for Violence." No explanation for this belief is given and although some groups like the Posse fit the description, many of the organizations are only ephemerally involved in tax protest and have little or no record of violence. Some are extremely small, such as the one-man Farmers Liberation Army in Kansas.[62] The index lists eighty-four names of individuals. The tone of the handbook is superficial and alarmist on the order of an exposé. The treatment of each group is too brief to be of use to a field agent. It reads more like a hit list.[63] Following complaints from several individuals listed, including Lois Peterson of Liberty Lobby, the IRS was forced to withdraw the publication. Peterson received notice from the IRS on August 25, 1986, that "the office that originated Document 7072 (I–86) has sent a memorandum to those offices having the document in their possession to destroy the document completely."[64]

This was not the only case where a government agency had to withdraw a manual because of inaccuracy and potential legal action and embarrassment. On February 18, 1984, the ATF conducted an "Extremism and Terrorism School" at the Lodge of the Four Seasons on the Lake of the Ozarks in Missouri. A manual bearing the insignia of the Bureau of Alcohol, Tobacco and Firearms and a replica of a U.S. Department of the Treasury special agents' badge, designated "Terrorism and Extremism School," was distributed to the attendees. Much of the information appeared to be lifted from journalistic sources and the publications of "antiextremist" groups. Appended to the ATF manual, however, was a list entitled "Paramilitary Groups Nationwide," which included, in addition to obvious cases such as the Ku Klux Klan and Minutemen, such nonviolent and non-paramilitary groups as the John Birch Society, the Committee to Restore the Constitution, Liberty Lobby, and the Institute for Historical Review.

The implications of such an "official" designation were rather stark. It could mean law enforcement surveillance, harassment, introduction of informants and undercover agents, and other difficulties one can only imagine. "Extremist" is one thing. "Paramilitary" is another.

A flood of protests descended on ATF headquarters, including threats of legal action. At least one victim actually hired an attorney to pursue the matter. Flushed with embarrassment, in September 1984 James W. Elder of the ATF office in St. Louis, Missouri, issued a letter to all attendees of the conference:

It has been brought to my attention that one page of the handout contains a list of organizations under the caption, "Paramilitary Groups Nationwide". . . . The list includes a wide range of groups from the John Birch Society, Citizens Council, and the Liberty Lobby to the Ku Klux Klan and the Posse Comitatus and could erroneously be viewed as reflecting a law enforcement interest by the Bureau of Alcohol, Tobacco and Firearms in all of these groups. The Bureau of Alcohol, Tobacco and Firearms has no evidence these groups are "paramilitary" in the general sense of the term.

We, therefore, would ask that you disregard the paramilitary caption, and refrain from any redistribution of this material.[65]

The tax protest movement involved tens of thousands of taxpayers at its peak. According to James Coates:

In the mid-1970s the Internal Revenue Service assigned a number of its best agents to a newly formed Illegal Tax Protester Program to seek out Posse members and bring charges against them. In 1980, the IRS was able to identify 17,222 tax protesters who either stated their views on tax forms or did not file forms as a specific protest. . . . By 1982 the figure for protesters had nearly tripled to 49,213 and it jumped again to 57,754 in 1983. Despite vigorous prosecution by the new unit, the number of protesters had only declined to 52,000 by 1986.[66]

It should be noted that these figures also include nominally left-wing tax protesters in the form of War Resisters League members, religious objectors, and others who refuse to pay taxes to support the military. The WRL claims between 3,000 and 5,000 active cases of war tax resistance.

Posse Comitatus membership has been a matter of some controversy. Wickstrom, an inveterate publicity hound, claimed figures of a million or more, which is sheer fantasy. The difficulty in determining membership numbers is compounded by the fact that Posse "groups" were highly autonomous and there was virtually no central authority. The headquarters in Tigerton sold publications and published the newsletter and little else. Various "anti-extremist" groups have come up with figures of several thousand, often citing other tax protest organizations they claim are Posse "fronts." The *Posse Noose* claimed a circulation of 2,500 at its peak, but that included sample copies, complimentary and exchange subscriptions, and hundreds of free copies distributed at tax protest meetings. Posse literature was reprinted freely. Our estimate is that the Posse Comitatus never had more than one thousand bona fide members at any given time, although two or three thousand individuals may have been members at one time or another. Like many extremist groups, it existed largely on the basis of its reputation and the antics of a few of its members.

## WHITE ARYAN RESISTANCE

WAR is essentially an extension of Tom Metzger, a former Grand Dragon in David Duke's Knights of the Ku Klux Klan. Formerly called the White American Poetical Association, Metzger's group assumed its current name in 1983 and has always operated out of his home in Fallbrook, California. Metzger publishes a tabloid entitled *WAR*. In its pages Metzger and other writers engage in some of the most outspoken and vehement racist and anti-Jewish rhetoric in the neo-Nazi movement. There are no subtleties or nuances. Metzger's views are right up front.

In September 1980 two men affiliated with the National Alliance Against Racist and Political Repression, a Communist Party USA affiliate, were arrested after one attempted to pull a gun during a Democratic County Central Committee meeting in San Diego. In attendance was Tom Metzger, who had won a Democratic primary election for the 43rd Congressional District (he received 14 percent of the vote in the general election). One of the leftists was charged with carrying a concealed weapon, assaulting a police officer, and assault with a deadly weapon. The other was charged with assault and resisting arrest. Metzger was unharmed.

WAR has made extensive use of new technology in getting its message across. Metzger has used computerized bulletin boards as an organizational tool and has produced a videotape series for cable television entitled *Race and Reason,* which is noted largely for its antiminority rhetoric and attempts to stifle it. Other Metzger innovations have included taped telephone messages at various locations around the country.

Metzger has attempted to reach students and young people on a scale exceeding all other neo-Nazi groups. He helped form White Student Unions at both the high school and college levels, although with very limited success. WSU leader Greg Withrow turned on Metzger in 1986 and gave a series of news interviews denouncing him and apologizing for his own racist activities. Withrow was subsequently attacked, slashed, and nailed to a six-foot plank. In 1987 Metzger's son, John Metzger, became WSU president.

More than any other neo-Nazi or Klan leader, Metzger has promoted the growth of the "Skinhead" movement, an openly racist import from Great Britain. In 1989 the ADL estimated the number of Skinheads at three thousand. Noting that "much of the Skinhead organizing has centered around a number of charismatic figures," the ADL says:

> The most successful of these has been John Metzger (himself not a Skinhead), whose WAR Youth works in tandem with John's father Tom of the White Aryan Resistance to organize Skinheads throughout the country.[67]

It's important to note that not all Skinheads are racists. The ADL acknowledges that "non-racist Skinheads (often called 'baldies' or 'two-tones') considerably outnumber racist ones in most areas of the country." Some Skinheads are actually militantly antiracist.

Much of the violence associated with white racist groups in the late 1980s and early 1990s was attributed to Skinheads. There have been numerous incidents of racial harassment, name-calling, and occasional serious violence by members of Skinhead organizations. One of these proved to have serious consequences for the victim, the perpetrators, and also for Tom and John Metzger.

On the morning of November 13, 1988, in Portland, Oregon, three Skinheads—Kenneth Mieske, Kyle Brewster, and Steven Strasser—got into a violent altercation with three Ethiopians—Mulugeta Seraw, Wondwosen Tesfaye, and Tilahun Antneh. All parties apparently had been drinking. When it was over, Mulugeta Seraw was dead. The three Skinheads pleaded guilty: Mieske to murder, and Brewster and Strasser to manslaughter. They are all serving long prison sentences It was a senseless, stupid tragedy.[68]

This was not the end of the matter, however. The Southern Poverty Law Center and the Anti-Defamation League filed a $10 million lawsuit on behalf of Seraw's estate against Mieske and Brewster. The suit attempted to link John and Tom Metzger to the killing through the questionable doctrine of "vicarious liability." Morris Dees, head attorney for the SPLC, argued that the Metzgers, through a Skinhead organizer named Dave Mazella, were responsible for the killing by virtue of their alleged instructions to Mazella and his subsequent actions in organizing and motivating the Portland Skinheads. The case has been a worrisome one to civil libertarians.

After a long trial (before a judge with one year's experience) in which Mazella himself was the star witness, the jury returned a verdict against the Metzgers in October 1990. Although they represented themselves during the trial, the Metzgers hired Chicago civil liberties lawyer Michael Null for their appeal.[69] In the meantime, Dees has taken judgment against the Metzgers and their assets have been seized. At one point, when Metzger attempted to pay for a transcript of the trial in order to prepare their appeal, Dees garnished the payment, thus impeding their efforts.

What is interesting about this case is not that the Metzgers' racist and neo-Nazi allies have rallied to their defense, but that liberal and leftist publications have expressed doubt about the verdict, too. The *Williamette* (Oregon) *Weekly,* a local alternative tabloid, editorialized:

> In the wake of last week's stunning legal victory over California's white supremacist Tom Metzger at the hands of crusading civil rights lawyer Morris Dees, a number of courthouse observers are quietly raising questions about a little-mentioned development in the trial. It is now clear that Dave Mazella, the star witness who provided Dees with the crucial link between Metzger and the racist Skinheads who murdered Mulugeta Seraw on the streets of Portland in November, 1988, perjured himself on the witness stand.
>
> "If definite proof can be presented that Mazella committed perjury, it may be possible for the Court of Appeals to order a new trial," says Michael Simon, a local lawyer who monitored the case on behalf of the Oregon chapter of the American Civil Liberties Union.
>
> Such proof does, in fact, exist. Not only are there witnesses who insist that Mazella was lying on the stand, but there are also letters by Mazella himself that contradict his sworn testimony.[70]

In a column appearing under the banner of the Los Angeles Times/Washington Post News Service, Ray Jenkins, a writer for the *Baltimore Sun,* noted, "A wise judge once observed that great constitutional rights often are established in the cases that involve 'not very nice people.' " He also observed that while the state of Oregon lacked the evidence to put Metzger on trial for murder in the Seraw case, what Morris Dees did was to

> convert the civil law, whose basic purpose it is to settle disputes between individuals, into an arm of the criminal law. In legal abracadabra, the standard of proof in civil cases—usually only "preponderance of evidence"—is a good deal easier to meet than the higher standard of "guilt beyond a reasonable doubt" required in a criminal prosecution.
>
> Let's not forget, there are cases on record where civil law was tortured into criminal law to punish Communists in the 1950's, then civil rights groups, including the National Association for the Advancement of Colored People, in the 1960's. There was even one celebrated case in which an Alabama jury attempted to destroy the *New York Times* by using the civil action of libel as a criminal action. The U.S. Supreme Court swiftly put a stop to that nonsense.[71]

The moderate leftist *In These Times* opined, "Jurors in a West Coast white-supremacy trial struck a blow for social justice last week but may have bruised some vital civil liberties in the process." *In These Times* writer John Shragg questioned the credibility of Mazella's testimony and pointed out:

> Dees was backed by his center's multi-million-dollar bankroll and its cadre of lawyers along with the equally impressive resources of the Anti-Defamation League of B'nai B'rith and the complete cooperation of federal, state and local authorities. The Metzgers represented themselves.[72]

Shragg also quoted ACLU attorney Michael Simon to the effect that holding organizations liable for the unauthorized acts of their representatives would have a "chilling effect" on political activity.

Even with a successful appeal of the Seraw decision, the Metzgers would probably wind up with a new trial, which would strain their limited resources even more. Tom Metzger is presently collecting welfare, since the judgment ruined his business. In the meantime, a successful attempt was made to convict him for a 1983 felony cross burning on private property which had already been dismissed in the courts twice.

## Summary

An often overlooked aspect of the neo-Nazi movement is the personal tragedy it has brought to so many lives. Some people who have joined such groups were unstable to begin with; others less afflicted soon found themselves virtual outcasts in a society almost uniformly hostile to their views. Either way, the psychological pressures on the average active neo-Nazi are strong and unrelenting, which is undoubtedly why so few people have stayed with Nazi groups for more than a couple of years.

In September 1978 two young U.S. Marines were discharged from the service for "distributing [neo-Nazi] literature to the Yuma [Arizona] civilian community and engaging in other Nazi-related activities." One of these was nineteen-year-old Lance Corporal Dominic Lewitzke, who subsequently went to work in the head-quarters of the National Socialist White People's Party in Arlington, Virginia. On July 23, 1980, Lewitzke shot himself in the head with a "party weapon" at the headquarters and died several hours later.

According to NSWPP spokesman Martin Kerr, Lewitzke was "troubled by personal circumstances and given to bouts of severe depression." He praised Lewitzke as "an upstanding member of his race and a dedicated National Socialist revolutionary" and noted that his party affiliation "was the central thing in his life." However, sources close to the case reveal that Lewitzke was disillusioned by the social cost of his Nazi activities, and was shocked and depressed by the conduct and character of party officials. Far from being a heroic band of fighters for their race and ideals—as Nazi propaganda asserts—it was a collection of deeply troubled people acting out their inner torments through membership in a group espousing the most hated ideology in American society. Lewitzke came to realize he had made a terrible mistake, including the sacrifice of a Marine Corps career, and subsequently took his own life.

There is good reason to look at membership in an outcast group like the Nazis as a symbolic suicide. When one joins such a group, and becomes publicly identified with it, the old life effectively ends. All but the most loyal of friends and family disassociate themselves, and often marriages and jobs are lost as well. Membership in a Nazi organization is incompatible with family fife and career, as numerous former members have attested. One ex-Nazi likened his period of membership to being "like a part of me died when I joined and didn't come back to life again until I got out."[73]

The neo-Nazi movement today, such as it is, is highly fragmented, infinitesimally small relative to the population, and heavily watched by everyone from the news media to "watchdog" groups to the U.S. Justice Department and local police. It represents no threat to our political system and probably never did. As is usually the case with extremist movements of the left or right, we as a nation have far more to lose in terms of civil liberties by ruthlessly suppressing the domestic neo-Nazis than we risk by essentially leaving them alone (subject, of course, to the laws that govern us all).

## Notes

1. Irwin Suall and David Lowe, "Shaved for Battle—Skinheads Target America's Youth," *Political Communication and Persuasion* 5 (1988): 144.

2. *Preliminary Report on Neo-Fascist and Hate Groups,* Committee on Un-American Activities, U.S. House of Representatives (December 17, 1954).

3. The tactics used against extreme rightists were similar to those used against the radical left, and no less unfair. For a detailed account of HCUA tactics see: David Caute,

*The Great Fear* (New York: Simon & Schuster, 1978); Frank Donner, *The UnAmericans* (New York: Ballantine Books, 1961); Walter Goodman, *The Committee* (New York: Farrar, Straus, 1968); Telford Taylor, *Grand Inquest* (New York: Ballantine Books, 1955).

4. *Preliminary Report,* 1.

5. Gordon Hall, telephone interview, August 23, 1991.

6. Joseph P. Kamp, *The Bigots Behind the Swastika Spree* (Westport, Conn.: Headlincs, 1966), 30–31.

7. *Preliminary Report,* 9.

8. Hall, op. cit.

9. *Preliminary Report,* 5–11.

10. "First Racial Government," *National Renaissance Bulletin* (January and February 1972).

11. *National Renaissance Bulletin* 29, nos. 4, 5, 6 (April/ May/June 1978).

12. "Der Tag," *Newsweek* (September 4, 1967), 30–3 1.

13. For a detailed account of life at Nazi headquarters under Rockwell see: A. M. Rosenthal and Arthur Gelb, *One More Victim: The Life and Death of a Jewish American Nazi* (New York: Signet Books, 1967).

14. George Thayer, *The Farther Shores of Politics* (New York: Simon and Schuster, 1967), 25–26.

15. George Lincoln Rockwell, *This Time the World* (Arlington, Va.: Parliament House, 1963), 193.

16. Thayer, 19–20.

17. W. Clarke Wescoe, quoted in Franklin S. Haiman, *Freedom of Speech: Issues and Cases* (New York: Random House, 1965), 184.

18. Alex Haley, "Playboy Interview, George Lincoln Rockwell," *Playboy* (April 1966).

19. "Radicals: Finis for the Fuhrer," *Time* (September 1, 1967), 12.

20. James Mason, *Facts in Regard to the Matt Koehl Question* (Ohio: Privately published, 1976).

21. "Criminals on Federal Payroll Engineered Rockwell Hoax on America," *The Councilor* (December 30, 1977): 1–3.

22. "An Insider Talks About Fringe Organizations," *ACRES USA* (September 1986): 24–27.

23. Kathleen Griffin, "Ex-Nazi Leader Cop Informant, Writer Claims," *Toronto Sun* (June 17, 1989); Richard Campbell, "OPP Paid Ex-Nazi $15 a Week to Inform," *Toronto Star* (December 27, 1972).

24. Anti-Defamation League, *Hate Groups in America* (New York: Anti-Defamation League, 1988), 35.

25. Andy Oakley, *"88,"* *An Undercover News Reporter's Exposé of American Nazis and the Ku Klux Klan* (Skokie, Ill.: P.O. Publishing Co., 1987), 66.

26. Bill Martin, "The American Reich," *Crawdaddy* (August 1976): 46.

27. Ibid.

28. Lee Michael Katz, "Nazis Probed in Stock Deal," *Arlington Journal* (May 15, 1981); "Cooper Loses Nazi Bond Suit," *Arlington Journal* (May 22, 1981).

29. Mary Battiata, "IRS Moves to Seize Home of White People's Party," *Washington Post* (March 9, 1982); Len Boselovic, "IRS May Seize Nazi Offices," *Arlington Journal* (March 8, 1982); "Nazis Claim to Have Stalled IRS," *Northern Virginia Sun* (March 10, 1982).

30. *NS Bulletin* (November 1982).

31. *Hate Groups,* 49.

32. William Sherman, "Skokie Once Quiet Town But Nazis Changed All That," *New York News* (April 28, 1978), 3-A, 8-A.

33. Elizabeth Wheaton, *Code Name Greenkil* (Athens, Ga.: University of Georgia Press, 1987), 46.

34. *Hate Groups* (1988), 34.

35. David Hamlin, *The Nazi/Skokie Conflict: A Civil Liberties Battle* (Boston: Beacon Press, 1980).

36. Sherman, op. cit.

37. Wheaton, 81.

38. Wheaton, 190–91.

39. Wheaton, 209.

40. *Extremism on the Right* (New York: Anti-Defamation League, 1983), 36.

41. Oakley, op. cit.

42. *Columbus Dispatch* (December 16, 1979); *Columbus Citizen-Journal* (October 11, 1979).

43. Pat Watters and Stephen Gillers, *Investigating the FBI* (New York: Ballantine Books, 1973), 317.

44. "Construction Hatred," *The Talon* 12, no. 140 (June 1988): 1.

45. Anti-Defamation League, *Extremism on the Right: A Handbook* (New York: Anti-Defamation League, 1988), 118–19.

46. Book List, *The New Order*, no. 101 (September/ October 1990).

47. Dean Calbreath, "Nazi Party Thriving in Bay Area," *The Daily Californian* (March 21, 1977), 1, 3; "Isle's Nazi Leader Files Mayoral Bid," *Houston Chronicle* (February 11, 1977).

48. *Stormer* 1, no. 1 (September 1977).

49. Tom Hall, "Nazi Store Charges Dropped," *San Francisco Examiner* (June 14, 1977), 8.

50. "Four Arrested Protesting Neo-Nazis," *Ann Arbor News* (March 21, 1988).

51. John Snell, "Meeting Draws Leaders of Neo-Nazi Groups," *The Oregonian* (July 12, 1986), B–6.

52. Manfred Roeder, *Calling Our Nation* no. 60 (1989): 4.

53. "Legal Corner," *The Way* (May–July 1989): 12.

54. James A. Aho, *The Politics of Righteousness: Idaho Christian Patriotism* (Seattle: University of Washington Press, 1990).

55. Aho, 17.

56. Aho, 85.

57. James Coates, *Armed and Dangerous: The Rise of the Survivalist Right* (New York: Hill & Wang, 1987),19.

58. Aho, 61.

59. "Sedition Trial Ends With 13 Acquittals," Associated Press (April 8, 1988).

60. Cheri Seymour, *Committee of the States: Inside the Radical Right* (Mariposa, Calif.: Camden Place Communications, 1991). A surprisingly objective account of Gale and his work, including the demise of a later venture, the Committee of the States, a Posse-like organization.

61. Anti-Defamation League, *Extremism on the Right: A Handbook,* 106–107. For a sympathetic account of Kahl see: Capstan Turner and A. J. Lowrey, *There Was a Man: The Saga of Gordon Kahl* (Nashville, Tenn.: Sozo Publishing Co., 1985).

62. Bruce Maxwell, "'Far-Right Group Ready to Fight for Farmers," *Rochester Post-Bulletin* (November 13, 1984).

63. Ruth E. Schweizer, *Illegal Tax Protester Information Handbook,* Document 7072 (1–86), (Washington, D.C.: Internal Revenue Service, 1986).

64. Letter to Lois Peterson of Liberty Lobby from A. W. Parretta, tax law specialist, Public Services Branch, Internal Revenue Service, August 25, 1986 (PM:S:DS:P:2).

65. Form letter, Department of the Treasury, Bureau of Alcohol, Tobacco and Firearms, Room 611, 1114 Market St., St. Louis, Mo. (September 28, 1984).

66. Coates, 111.

67. *Skinheads Target the Schools* (New York: Anti-Defamation League, 1989).

68. Elinor Langer, "The American Neo-Nazi Movement Today," *The Nation* (July 16/23, 1990), 98.

69. No. CA A67833, In the Court of Appeals of the State of Oregon.

70. "Everything But the Truth: Dave Mazella's Perjury Could Be Tom Metzger's Salvation," editorial, *Williamette Weekly* (October 29, 1990).

71. Ray Jenkins, "Even a Scoundrel Is Due a Fair Trial," Los Angeles Times/ Washington Post Service (November 1990).

72. John Schrag, "Supremacy Verdict Hurts Civil Liberties," *In These Times* (October 31–November 6, 1990), 2.

73. Lee Michael Katz, "Death of a Nazi: Discharged Marine Shoots Himself," *Arlington Journal and Globe* (July 25, 1980).

# 24. National States Rights Party

Formed in 1958, the National States Rights party was the lineal descendant of three other organizations: the Columbians (1946), which appeared on the now defunct U.S. attorney general's list of "subversive" organizations; the Christian Anti-Jewish party (1952); and the United White party (1956). Instrumental in the organization's formation were Edward Fields, a boyishly handsome chiropractor, and Jesse B. Stoner, lawyer and Ku Klux Klan organizer who, on more than one occasion, referred to Adolf Hitler as "a moderate." (Commenting on this, one rightist stated, "Compared to Stoner, Hitler probably was a moderate.") Both Stoner and Fields were officers in the Christian Anti-Jewish party, holding the posts of "Archleader" and "Chief Secretary," respectively. According to George Thayer,

> Jesse Stoner originally came from Chattanooga, Tennessee, where his family used to own Rock City, a well-known tourist attraction on top of Lookout Mountain, south of the city. In his youth, Stoner suffered an attack of polio which has left one leg shorter than the other.[1]

The group's first headquarters was located in Jeffersonville, Indiana, but the organization soon relocated to Birmingham, Alabama, then to Augusta, Georgia, before finally settling in Marietta, Georgia. Not only has the organization been geographically mobile, it has also managed to absorb several other extreme right groups. Included among these are a Florida group headed by Dewey Taft called the Conservative party, the National White American party, the North Carolina Knights of the Ku Klux Klan, and the Seaboard Citizens' Council led by John Kasper, who ran for president on the NSRP ticket in 1964. NSRP leaders that same year were Ned Dupes, an elderly arch-segregationist, and two women: Mrs. E. L. Bishop, vice chairman, and Bernice Settle, secretary.

J. B. Stoner began his political career in the 1940s as a Ku Klux Klan Kleagle (organizer) and founder of the Anti-Jewish party, which distributed *The Protocols of the Learned Elders of Zion,* the notorious anti-Semitic forgery. Perhaps the most outspoken and obsessive anti-Semite in American history, Stoner said that the aim of his party was to "make being a Jew a crime, punishable by death."[2]

In February 1966 Stoner appeared before a Congressional committee investigating the Ku Klux Klan; taking the Fifth Amendment, he refused to answer all questions. An attorney, Stoner frequently represented Klansmen in criminal cases. In 1969 he was one of the attorneys handling James Earl Ray's appeal of his conviction in the assassination of Martin Luther King. Ray's brother, Jerry, was a frequent fixture around NSRP headquarters.[3]

Stoner has run for public office several times. In 1948 he ran for Congress in Tennessee under the banner of the Stoner Anti-Jewish party and received over 500 votes of the 30,000 cast. In 1970 he garnered 18,000 votes in Georgia's Democratic gubernatorial primary against Jimmy Carter and seven other candidates (Carter won). In 1972 he campaigned in the Democratic primary for U.S. Senate on the slogan "You cannot have law and order and niggers too. . . . Vote white!" He received 40,000 votes. In 1974 he ran for lieutenant governor in the Democratic primary, receiving 71,000 votes. Stoner finished third in the 1978 Democratic primary for governor.

In 1977, however, Stoner was indicted by an Alabama grand jury and charged as a "conspirator" with an "unknown person" in the 1958 bombing of a Birmingham church. Although it was widely reported that the church was one in which several black children were killed, the indictment makes it clear that the church was empty at the time. The fact that the indictment came nearly twenty years after the event raised some legal questions, but Stoner was convicted and in April 1982 his conviction was upheld by the Alabama Appellate Court. In January 1983 the U.S. Supreme Court refused to hear his case and Stoner, fearing persecution at the hands of blacks in prison, failed to appear in Birmingham to begin serving his sentence. Four months later he surrendered to authorities. He served three and a half years and was released in December 1986.

Dr. Edward R. Fields has been the primary figure responsible for the NSRP, serving as national secretary of the party and editor of its publication, *The Thunderbolt*. During the late 1970s he also formed a Ku Klux Klan group in Georgia called New Order–Knights of the Ku Klux Klan, but it was short-lived.

Fields, with the NSRP, put together probably the most successful post–World War II neo-Nazi organization. At its peak it was larger than any similar group and has enjoyed a longevity and stability not found elsewhere in the U.S. neo-Nazi movement.

Fields and Stoner were united in the intensity of their disdain for Jews and blacks and their relationship was a symbiotic one of two distinctly different personality styles. Stoner, ever the flamboyant politician and stump speaker, was a necessary complement to an organization as controversial as the NSRP. Fields, with his business sense and organizing ability, kept the party running on a day-to-day basis. It was his responsibility to edit and handle the details of publishing *The Thunderbolt*, of which some 348 issues had been published by early 1991.

Fields's strident anti-Semitism has been abundantly reflected in the editorial content of his paper. In a 1972 article entitled "The Enemy Within," Fields said: "What is required? Every Jew who holds a position of power or authority must be removed from that position. If this does not work, then we must establish (the) Final Solution!!" The constitution and by-laws of the NSRP leave little doubt about their views:

Jew-devils have no place in a White Christian nation. When our party is elected . . . the Government will expel the Jews and confiscate their ill-gotten wealth for the benefit of the American people. When the Jews are gone, we Americans will own rich America.

Communism is Jewish! Communism is one of the Jew plans, along with the United Nations organization and other world government schemes, to destroy us and conquer the world. Revolutions, no-win wars, internationalism, economic chaos, inflations, starvations, unemployment and depressions are deliberately designed by the Jews to promote their communistic plans. In every communist country, the Jews are the ruling race. Almost all communist spies are Jews. Our Party proposes for the Government to expel all communists from this Nation. Without the Jews, there would be NO communism!

Fields has traveled abroad and has been widely known throughout neo-Nazi circles in Europe and elsewhere. In 1980 a group of leaders of a Flemish neo-Nazi movement came to Atlanta to meet with Stoner and Fields. The U.S. government, in a questionable action, revoked their visas and ordered them to return to Belgium. Fields has also conferred with neo-Nazi leaders from England, Germany, and France at one time or another.

Other individuals who were once closely associated with the NSRP in its early days are Matt Koehl, who worked as an organizer briefly before joining the American Nazi party, and later headed its successor, the National Socialist White People's party, now renamed the New Order; and James K. Warner, who joined the NSRP after falling out with George Lincoln Rockwell of the American Nazi party. Warner then moved on to form the Sons of Liberty and Christian Defense League, both of which function today.

Admiral John Crommelin (once an advisor for Willis Carto's National Youth Alliance) ran for senator and vice president on the NSRP ticket. Instrumental in his 1962 Senate campaign was the Reverend Gordon Winrod, NSRP chaplain and son of the late Gerald B. Winrod of Kansas. In addition to Fields and Stoner, other long-time mainstays of the NSRP included Ned Dupes and the Reverend Connie Lynch, a militant segregationist.

We have personally observed Lynch in action and the man almost defies description. He made George Wallace, at his fieriest, seem a pillar of moderation. Lynch would whisper, scream, bellow, rave, turn red, and even slobber occasionally. Audience size seemingly had little or no effect on his performance. On one occasion he had only seventeen listeners, including two police officers sent to maintain order, but he performed as though addressing a capacity crowd in Yankee Stadium. "Kikes," "niggers," "race mixers," and the FBI always received very rough treatment in Lynch's speeches.

In St. Augustine, Florida, in 1964, Lynch addressed a crowd after an attack on civil rights demonstrators by a club-wielding mob. He told the eight hundred assembled whites: "I favor violence to preserve the white race. . . . Now I grant you, some niggers are going to get killed in the process."[4] Lynch continued:

I spoke to the white people, the white people rallied behind it and we kicked the livin' hell out of the niggers—sent the out-of-town niggers to hospitals and out of state to their own home town where they oughta been. And the niggers of St. Augustine got quiet and went back home to nigger-town where they belong.[5]

Regarding the FBI, the NSRP's position was clear for over three decades. Here is a typical statement from *The Thunderbolt:*

The FBI stands for the "civil rights" of a nigger to rape your wife, daughter or sister. To be effective, a conspiracy must camouflage itself and its true purpose and pretend to be the opposite of what it really is. That is the method of J. Edgar Hoover, the Master of Deceit, and the Communist-Jewish conspiracy which placed him at the head of the FBI.[6]

Lynch, who certainly embraced this attitude, had several run-ins with the law. In 1964 he was found guilty of disturbing the peace in San Bernardino, California, in an altercation involving high school students and several NSRP members who were wearing Nazi-like uniforms. One of the NSRPers shot Emilio Parker, a young Mexican-American, with a pellet gun. According to Michael Upton, an acquaintance of ours and a close friend of Parker, the high school boys were under the impression that the group called itself the "White Supremist party."

In September 1968 NSRP members were involved in a shootout with a group of blacks just outside Berea, Kentucky (Connie Lynch's hometown). According to Fields, the blacks opened fire on an NSRP meeting. One black, John Boggs, and one NSRPer, Elza Rucker, were killed. Among those sent to prison in connection with this incident was Connie Lynch.

\*　　\*　　\*

The NSRP differed from most other right-extremist groups in that it never opposed government spending programs such as Medicare, social security, etc., which are said to benefit the "common man." The group's main appeal, its leaders claimed, was to workers and farmers, whom they urged to "fight communism and race mixing." According to Fields, around 1970 the NSRP had twelve full-time employees and a membership in excess of two thousand. Available evidence strongly indicates that national membership was probably somewhat less than that, spread out among some thirty "chapters," ten of which had their own newsletters. Membership was drawn almost exclusively from people of working-class and lower-class backgrounds.

Several extreme right groups who reject anti-Semitism have looked with great disfavor on the NSRP, which they have viewed as an embarrassment. The John Birch Society even went so far as to accuse the organization of being communist because, among other things, NSRP members allowed the American Civil Liberties Union to defend them. The NSRP filed a libel suit and the Birchers quickly retracted the accusation and apologized. While it is highly doubtful that the NSRP is any kind of "black operation" (in this case, a bogus operation designed to discredit and neutralize its unwitting supporters), it should be noted that such groups are ready-made for the operations of *agents provocateur* as well as "watchdog" organizations who use them to justify their own existence and perhaps to advance a repressive agenda.

The National States Rights party occasionally has been one of the more comical organizations on the extreme right. Whereas George Lincoln Rockwell (the late Nazi leader) tried to be funny, the NSRP often has appeared ridiculous while trying to be serious. The group's publication, formerly *The Thunderbolt,* is almost satirical after one surmounts the initial shock of its coarseness and strident racism. An unprepared reader can be dismayed and outraged upon first examination, and the paper, now entitled *The Truth At Last,* far surpasses the limits of racial and religious decency with its rhetorical overkill and anti-Jewish conspiratorialism. Indeed, the obsession with alleged Jewish perfidy is so overdone that it's almost a parody of anti-Semitism.

*The Thunderbolt* reached a circulation of twenty-five thousand in the late 1960s. Fields has claimed that in 1970 the publication had subscribers in all fifty states, with Alabama leading the list, followed by California and Florida.

Writers for *The Thunderbolt,* principally Fields, spent considerable energy trying to prove that virtually everyone the NSRP didn't like and who wasn't black was really a crypto-Jew. Among those "exposed" were Attorney General Nicholas Katzenbach, Press Secretary Pierre Salinger, and Communist party leader Gus Hall. Many issues featured a special page for regular readers called "Jews in the News." Some of *The Thunderbolt*'s "gentility" may be conveyed by reviewing a collection of its headlines and article titles through the years:

"Negroes Have Diseased Blood" (August 1963); "Jesus Christ Not a Jew" (September 1964); "Jews Want Millions of Chinese Brought Here" (October-November 1964); "Scientists Say Negro Still in Ape Stage—Races Positively Not Equal" (December-January 1965); "FBI Agents Led Selma March—Not King" (May 1965); "Jews Behind Race Mixing" (September 1965); "Gerald Smith Reports New Evidence on Katzenbach Being a Jew" (September 1965); "Communism Is Still Jewish" (November 1965); "Is Mrs. Katzenbach a Negress?" (February 1965); "Jews Take Over U.S. Government" (December 1966); "Jews Invade Germany Again" (February 1967); "Anti-Riot Bill Would Be Used Against Right-Wing" (August 1967)—a reference to what later became known as the "Rap Brown Law," an antiriot bill opposed by most of the far left, much of the far right, and virtually all civil libertarians; "Sen. Jack Tenney, Former Un-American Activities Committee Chairman, Says Communism Is Directed By Jews" (June 1969)—an article about the late California state senator and long-time anti-Semite who was once closely associated with Gerald L. K. Smith and other extreme right luminaries.

In the 1969 issue of *The Thunderbolt* an article appeared by "Miss Jane Arnold, NSRP Headquarters Staff Worker." The title of the attractive Miss Arnold's article: "Duties of the Thunderbolt Man." It reveals the megalomania that seems to permeate extremist groups on both ends of the spectrum, as well as their dedication to "political correctness." The last paragraph states:

> The bold new Thunderbolt man is shaping the future. His clear eye reflects the strength of his ancestors as he stands ready, united with his White racial comrades. The revolution has begun and the White race must be saved. There is but one goal. History awaits the action of the Thunderbolt man as he steps forward to hail victory for his race and nation.[7]

The NSRP has distributed copies of the "Jewish Ritual Murder" edition of *Der Sturmer,* a newspaper published in the 1930s by Nazi propagandist and cartoonist Julius Streicher. Streicher's work was reputed to be so distasteful that even the leading Nazis looked down on him. In this paper, printed in German except for a few paragraphs on the back page, are drawings of Jews slitting the throats of Gentiles and drinking their blood. The NSRP introduction to "Jewish Ritual Murder" stated:

> Julius Streicher, pioneer anti-Jewish Patriot. Let this new edition of his most famous issue be a living monument to his courage and fortitude in expressing the Jew menace, even though it cost him his life. We salute Julius Streicher, Patron Saint of World Anti-Jewism.
>
> In memory of Julius Streicher who was murdered to appease the Jews. His only "crime" was to publish this newspaper, to enlighten Christian people of the fiendish crimes of the Jews.

Fields's smooth personality and alleged womanizing have not sat well with all NSRP members. In the spring of 1983, when J. B. Stoner was incarcerated and a controversy over his succession developed, a group of dissident members voted Fields out of the party and began a rift that ultimately led to the party's demise in 1984. The dissident group, called the States' Rights Voters League, published various allegations against Fields along with copies of correspondence Fields had exchanged with several individuals. Jerry Ray, brother of James Earl Ray and editor of the league's *Quarterly Report,* had the following to say:

> The one thing I noticed during my fifteen years with Ed Fields and J. B. Stoner was that Fields called the shots. He ordered J. B. around like a puppy and refused to do his share of the work and constantly raided the treasury to satisfy his every whim. J. B. tried his best to control Fields which culminated in 1983, when an open break between Fields and J. B. started to splinter the party. J. B. finally wrestled control of the building from him and placed it in Christian Rights, Inc., to prevent Fields from declaring it a headquarters for his klan organization.[8]

Jerry Ray commented that J. B. Stoner apparently did an about-face with respect to Fields while he was in prison and that he demanded that Fields be returned to control of the NSRP. There is reason to believe that Stoner's break with Fields may have been largely due to the stress of his impending imprisonment. Stoner, who had spent much of his life denigrating blacks and Jews, strongly believed that he would be killed in prison—not an entirely unrealistic fear. However, once he got to prison he was kept in virtual solitary confinement during his entire stay, largely for his own safety. According to Ray:

> J. B. has taken prison life very badly. Even before reporting to prison, after his much publicized disappearance, J. B. broke down and was unable to eat or sleep. He sobbed uncontrollably at the thought that he would be murdered in prison.*

Fields was apparently not immune to the fratricidal warfare that has plagued the majority of extreme right leadership. Ray commented on this as well:

> Fields has had a running feud with almost every leader in the right wing since he began operation. He attacked George Lincoln [Rockwell] for years before Mr. Rockwell sued him and made him admit on the front page of *The Thunderbolt* that he was a liar. He has attacked the heads of the *White Sentinel* falsely accusing them of being Jews. He has attacked the head of the Minutemen accusing him of being an FBI pimp and an ADL agent. He has even attacked Willis Carto who is the mastermind behind the *Spotlight.*

Due largely to this turmoil, the National States Rights party disbanded in 1984 after some twenty-six years of operation. With Stoner in jail, Fields was simply not able to reconstruct the party and decided to devote his energies to *The Thunderbolt.* Early that year Fields had filed suit against the officers of the party in order to retain publishing rights to *The Thunderbolt,* which he subsequently received in an out-of-court settlement.

On May 21, 1984, Fields was arrested for allegedly burglarizing the home of J. B. Stoner in an attempt to retrieve some belongings. The original complaint had been filed by Jerry Ray, who had assumed the role of "caretaker" of the Stoner house. The case was dropped when Stoner refused to prosecute.

Of particular interest in the States Rights' Voters League and its campaign against Fields was one Jerry Dutton, who had been a close associate of Bill Wilkinson, leader of the Invisible Empire, Knights of the Ku Klux Klan. Wilkinson had been uncovered as an informant for the FBI in a 1982 article in the *Nashville Tennessean,* a charge he admitted. In 1983 Wilkinson folded up his operation and faded away. Fields believes to this day that Dutton was also an FBI operative and had moved into his organization in a successful effort to destroy it.

Wilkinson, incidentally, was best known for staging media events in which the Klan invariably received a great deal of negative publicity. According to Wyn Craig Wade in *The Fiery Cross: The Ku Klux Klan in America,* "By the end of 1980 [Wilkinson] had perfected a technique that other Klan leaders belittled as 'ambulance chasing.' He traveled to any part of the country where he saw exploitable racial tensions or serious blue-collar unemployment."[9]

Released from jail in 1986, Stoner immediately formed a new organization.

---

*J. B. Stoner disputes this characterization.

His Crusade Against Corruption is a typical extreme right one-man operation. His rallying cry is "PRAISE GOD FOR AIDS!" He says, "God is intervening in earthly affairs with AIDS to destroy his enemies. . . . AIDS is a racial disease of jews and negroids that also exterminates sodomites." Crusade Aganist Corruption was still functioning in the early nineties.

\*    \*    \*

At the end of 1988, Fields changed the name of *The Thunderbolt,* which was closely associated with the old NSRP, to *The Truth At Last,* thus breaking its link with the past. In terms of editorial content, however, there is virtually no difference. For many years *The Thunderbolt* was undated, simply numbered, and *The Truth At Last* has continued this practice. According to Fields, he and Stoner are once again close friends.

The NSRP was so "far out" that many right extremists were careful to avoid it. After more than twenty-six years of trying to win Americans to its cause, the net effect of the National States Rights party has been to outrage its opponents, amuse extremist-watchers with its rhetoric, and provide a diversion for a small number of working class white racists who otherwise might have gone fishing. It cannot be said that it left any significant or permanent impact on society.

J. B. Stoner will continue with one form of racist agitation or another until he drops, given the degree of his fanaticism. Edward Fields will probably continue with *The Truth At Last,* dutifully mailing copies out to a declining subscription list until he is unable to continue. Between the two of them, they will supply enough copy to keep an unknown number of FBI agents, state and local police, and private "antiextremist" operatives employed for some time.

## Notes

1. George Thayer, *The Farther Shores of Politics* (New York: Simon & Schuster, 1967), 35.

2. *Atlanta Constitution* (July 5, 1946).

3. Anti-Defamation League, *Extremism On The Right: A Handbook* (New York: The League, 1988), 159–60.

4. Anti-Defamation League, *Hate Groups in America* (New York: The League, 1988), 37.

5. Thayer, 46.

6. *The Thunderbolt* (February 1960).

7. *The Thunderbolt* (July 1969).

8. States' Rights Voters League, *Quarterly Report* (Summer 1984): 3.

9. Wyn Craig Wade, *The Fiery Cross: The Ku Klux in America* (New York: Simon & Schuster, 1987), 383–96.

# 25. Ku Klux Klans

In 1944 the Ku Klux Klan was in effect temporarily shut down. Its charter was revoked, the Internal Revenue Service placed a $685,000 tax lien on its assets, and the organization disbanded. Following World War II, however, there was still considerable sympathy for traditional KKK values, particularly in the South. Various local KKK groups began to spring up, many of them headed by former Klan members, and in Georgia, Samuel Green, an Atlanta physician, formed the Association of Georgia Klans in 1946. These "new" KKK organizations were, for all intents and purposes, identical to the previous one.

An enterprising young man named Stetson Kennedy was particularly alarmed by the postwar resurgence of the Klan, and he undertook to infiltrate the organization. Kennedy had become the southeast research director for the Anti-Defamation League of B'nai B'rith, which funded his project. He also reported to Georgia Assistant Attorney General Dan Duke, who was looking for a way to revoke the new Klan's charter. Outside of Georgia the KKK was encountering fierce opposition, as several states—including California and New York—banned the organization outright. Kennedy's detailed account, *Southern Exposure,*[1] was a major factor in militating opposition to the Klan, so much so that in 1947 U.S. Attorney General Tom Clark put the organization on his "subversives list" along with numerous other groups of the far left and far right. The state of Georgia revoked the Association of Georgia Klans' charter.

Kennedy, in a highly creative move, hatched a plan to recharter the KKK himself and turn it into an antiracist organization, while keeping bona fide KKK types from using the name or any of the symbols associated with it. His application for a new charter was turned down in Illinois, and he abandoned the plan.[2]

Various other small Klans formed in the 1950s but no mass movement developed. Still, KKK violence occurred from time to time. In 1951 a series of bombings occurred in Miami. Another case, in which seven blacks were flogged by a large group of Klansmen, brought about the first prosecutions in the twentieth century under the Civil War–era Reconstruction Enforcement Act of 1870-71; a sheriff and one of his deputies were prosecuted and convicted. Several states adopted legislation effectively outlawing the KKK.

Had it not been for the U.S. Supreme Court decision on May 17, 1954—*Brown* v. *Board of Education*—the Klan might have again faded into obscurity. Two other events helped kick off a KKK revival of grand proportions: the 1955 Montgomery bus boycott led by Martin Luther King, Jr., and the integration of Little Rock High School, backed by federal troops, on September 23, 1957.

Few events were as objectively necessary and as justified as these, but also so tailor-made to evoke a reaction.[3]

In September 1957 a particularly brutal example of Klan violence occurred when six members of a small KKK group, Ku Klux Klan of the Confederacy, abducted a black man named Judge Aron and castrated him. Six members of the group were subsequently tried and convicted. Incidents of Klan violence multiplied during the late 1950s. George Thayer recorded:

> Between 1 January 1956 and 1 June 1963, for instance, there were 138 cases of dyna-mitings in the South associated with the Klan. There were 29 bombings in Birmingham alone between 1957 and 1965. Among all the rubble were Negro homes, churches and integrated schools.[4]

Also with respect to Klan violence, Thayer has observed:

> Most Klans . . . have an inner group, unknown to other Klansmen, which is composed of the most dedicated and fanatical members. They often plan and carry out the acts of violence and terrorism. Since the ordinary Klansman is not privy to their secrets, he can say with a straight face that the Klan is nonviolent.[5]

\*     \*     \*

There are few organizations as extensively studied as the Ku Klux Klan. Over a hundred books and thousands of newspaper and serial articles have appeared on the subject. It's hard to imagine writing anything particularly new about it. To go through a litany of Klan atrocities and acts of violence would consume this entire book.[6] Instead our focus will emphasize the following four elements:

1. The growth and general thrust of the post-1960 KKK. The postwar KKK grew by leaps and bounds during the early to mid-1960s and then faded rapidly. How did this happen?

2. A brief account of the major KKK personalities between 1960 and 1980. Klan leaders were in it for various reasons. There were the fanatics, the opportunists, and the double agents. Who were which?

3. The internal politics and dissension within the various Klan organizations. Klansmen have been a cranky and contentious lot. This is almost axiomatic. When they're not plotting against their opponents, they almost invariably focus on one another.

4. Government activities against the KKK. The FBI and state and local law enforcement agencies focused on the KKK to an enormous degree, and active measures ranging from infiltration to disinformation and destabilization activities have been used against it.

Also, it's rather important to bear in mind that there is no single Ku Klux Klan. Rather, there are many Ku Klux Klans, each headed by a different leader. The importance of this will become apparent as we go along.

## The Rise and Fall of the Post-World War II Ku Klux Klan

According to the Anti-Defamation League, "provable hardcore Klan membership was estimated at 10,000" in 1965. This estimate is repeated in Wyn Craig Wade's *The Fiery Cross: The Ku Klux Klan in America.*[7] The ADL adds that "the Invisible Empire includes an additional 25,000 to 35,000 likeminded racists who belong to an assortment of Klan type groups or 'gun clubs,' plus others who, without any formal Klan affiliation, stand ready to do its work of terror."[8] A number of objections to this estimate could be made. In some ways it's reminiscent of estimates of Communist Party USA membership that included all the "sympathizers" and "fellow travelers," which produced sharply inflated numbers. The figure was widely quoted and in 1984 the ADL simply stated flatly, "In mid-1965 the Klans in the South had an estimated strength of approximately 42,000 adherents."[9] The difference between "membership" and "adherents" may be a distinction without a difference to some, but it reflects the frequent use of rough estimates in determining KKK strength. Estimates became considerably more accurate over the years, in part due to the strategic placement of informants within the various Klans.

In 1959 approximately half of all Klansmen belonged to U.S. Klans, headed by Eldon Lee Edwards, an automobile spray-painter. Many of the remaining groups were part of a loose confederation called National Knights of the Ku Klux Klan. An independent state Klan group called the Alabama Knights of the Ku Klux Klan was headed by Robert Shelton, a former official in the U.S. Klans who had been ousted by Edwards.

A natural organizer, Shelton rapidly consolidated local Klans into his Alabama Knights. Edwards died in August 1960 and was replaced by Robert Davidson. The infighting and bickering among rival groups in the U.S. Klans was so great, however, that Davidson and Calvin Craig quit and formed an entirely new Klan organization: Invisible Empire, United Klans, Knights of the Ku Klux Klan of America, Inc. Later the name was shortened to United Klans of America (UKA). Davidson resigned as Imperial Wizard in 1961. In July 1961, the UKA united with Shelton's Alabama Knights and Shelton emerged as the new Imperial Wizard of the UKA. Calvin Craig became Grand Dragon of UKA's Georgia realm. Shelton's UKA remained the largest Klan in the United States into the 1980s. According to Wade:

> In one respect, Imperial Wizard Shelton was like the new President [John F. Kennedy] he detested: each was the youngest man ever elected to his respective office. In 1961, Shelton was only thirty-two years old.
>     A lean, long-faced, emotionless man, Shelton impressed reporters with his bright blue eyes. He carried himself with conscious pride and was seldom seen to smile.[10]

Shelton was particularly close to Robert B. DePugh, leader of the Minutemen organization. Their suspicious and wary view of other right-wing leaders was quite similar in that they tended to confuse disagreement with disloyalty. An insightful account of Shelton's formative years is contained in a laudatory biography, *They Say—Blood On My Hands,* by Robert M. Mikell. It contains Shelton's account of his 1965 appearance before the House Committee on Un-American Activities, in which he offers the following:

> First of all, the main purpose of the investigation of the Klan by the committee was for political power.
> The liberal element has gained control over the committee and it is their purpose to utilize the Klan and to force the Klan to join forces with the liberal, as well as the Communist groups, in bringing about the destruction of the committee itself.[11]

The primary rival to the UKA was the National Knights of the Ku Klux Klan, headquartered in Tucker, Georgia, and headed by James Venable, an Atlanta attorney. It was about one-fourth the size of the UKA.[12] In addition, there were numerous smaller Klans with memberships ranging from the hundreds to only a few dozen, and, in one case, a Klan with a single member. George Thayer gives a lengthy accounting:

> There is Earl E. George's Improved Order of U.S. Klans based in Litonia, Georgia; there is Houston P. Martin's thousand-member Original Knights of the Ku Klux Klan . . . in Louisiana; there is Imperial Wizard A. E. Bolen's Association of South Carolina Klans; Jason Kersey's 35-Klavern United Florida Ku Klux Klan; Grand Dragon Charles Maddox's Association of Georgia Klans from Savannah; Imperial Wizard H. J. Jones' U.S. Klan Knights of the Ku Klux Klan; William H. Morris' Federated Knights of the Ku Klux Klan from Buchanan, Georgia; and finally, Dixie Klans, Inc., from Chattanooga.
> In addition there are some unaffiliated Klans. There is Sam Bowers' militant and secretive White Knights of the Ku Klux Klan, located in Mississippi . . . ; there is the small Association of Arkansas Klans; the Militant Knights of the Ku Klux Klan, located in Florida; the Mississippi Knights of the Ku Klux Klan, run by Walter A. Bailey; and the one man Aryan Knights of the Ku Klux Klan run by a crippled World War I veteran named Horace Sherman Miller from Waco, Texas.[13]

Thayer also notes that the popular stereotype of the Ku Klux Klan as a rural phenomenon is inaccurate. He says:

> With a few notable exceptions, the Klan is an urban movement, not a rural one as it is often thought to be. The Klan is filled with "rednecks" and "wool hats" but mostly those who have recently moved to town. Klan strength, for instance, is found more in northern Georgia and between Atlanta and Augusta, not in the rural south; it is found in central Alabama between Birmingham and Montgomery where the industry is located, not in the northern or southern farm belts of the state.[14]

The major KKK events of the sixties included the September 1963 bombing of the 16th Street Baptist Church in Birmingham, Alabama, in which four teenaged black girls were killed. Three men, two with KKK affiliations, were arrested. In June 1964, civil rights workers James Chaney, Andrew Goodman, and Michael Schwerner were slain near Philadelphia, Mississippi. Seven men were eventually convicted for the crime, including Sam Bowers, head of the White Knights of the KKK, and Cecil Ray Price, chief deputy sheriff of Neshoba County. In July 1964, Lieutenant Colonel Lemuel Penn, a black Army Reserve officer, was shot and killed from a passing automobile as he was driving from Fort Benning, Georgia. Two Klansmen were tried and acquitted. In 1966 the same two were convicted in federal court of conspiracy to violate the civil rights of blacks.

In McComb, Mississippi, eighteen bombs were detonated at black churches and homes during 1964. In October, four Klansmen were arrested in connection with the bombings and they, together with five others, pleaded either guilty or "no contest." The court sentenced the nine men and then suspended the sentences. In February 1964 a black home was bombed in Jacksonville, Florida, because a six-year-old boy who lived there had entered a previously all-white school. One Klansman was convicted in the case; another five were tried but acquitted.

In March 1965 civil rights worker Viola Liuzzo was murdered on a Loundes County, Alabama, highway. Three Klansmen were convicted on federal civil rights charges and sentenced to ten years in prison. It was later learned that one of those who may have been responsible for the killing was an undercover FBI informant.[15] In January 1966 Vernon Dahmer, an official of the Hattiesburg, Mississippi, chapter of the NAACP, died as a result of burns in the firebombing of his home. In March 1966 a jury found a reputed Klansman guilty.

*    *    *

A major blow to Klan activity occurred when the House Committee on Un-American Activities plied the talents it had used to intimidate and harass extreme leftists over the years against the hooded organization. Between October 1965 and February 1966, one hundred eighty-seven witnesses were paraded before the HCUA, and thousands of documents and other evidence were gathered by committee investigators. Officers of the seven major Klan organizations, including Robert Shelton, were interrogated. Most of these pleaded the Fifth Amendment, including Roy Frankhauser (discussed elsewhere in this book). Shelton refused to produce subpoenaed Klan records and he, along with six other Klan leaders, was subsequently convicted of contempt of Congress. Shelton and two others paid $1,000 fines and were sentenced to a year in prison.

The final HCUA document, *The Present Day Ku Klux Klan Movement,* was released in December 1967.[16] It was one of the most detailed and complete studies of the KKK ever undertaken. Among the findings were that the Klan used "front" organizations in somewhat the same fashion as the CPUSA, calling theirs hunting clubs, rescue squads, or even ladies sewing circles. It also detailed paramilitary training and numerous cases of improper use of Klan funds.

*   *   *

Klan growth was considerable until 1967, but within a few years it declined fully 75 percent. In 1967 the ADL reported KKK membership at a postwar peak of 55,000. Of these, Shelton's UKA had over 44,000, Venable's National Knights had 6,800, and independent Klans made up nearly 4,000. The total included over 16,000 in Georgia, 12,400 in Alabama, and 9,800 in North Carolina. From this point on, the KKK lost members rapidly, dwindling to a mere 5,000 by 1973.[17]

What caused the rapid decline in Klan membership and influence in the late 1960s? The FBI is responsible, for the most part. FBI Counterintelligence Program (COINTELPRO) activities against the Klan and other extreme right groups have received only a fraction of the attention as such actions against the extreme left. The only books to give the operation more than a passing reference have been Phillip Finch's *God, Guts and Guns: A Close Look at the Radical Right*, and Kenneth O'Reilly's *Racial Matters: The FBI's Secret File on Black America, 1960– 1972*. Even Wyn Craig Wade's *The Fiery Cross* devotes only two and a half pages to the subject.[18]

According to several sources, it was the COINTELPRO program against the 1960s Klan that put a rapid stop to its growth and popularity. O'Reilly quotes FBI Major Case Inspector Joseph A. Sullivan as follows:

> In five years we blew them to hell. . . . By the time I left the South in 1966 an entire society had resolved to suppress outlawry in racial matters. . . .Hoover did his job well.[19]

O'Reilly comments:

> Within six months of the Liuzzo murder, the FBI operated nearly 2,000 informants, 20 percent of overall Klan and other white hate group membership, including a grand dragon in one southern state.[20]

Phillip Finch notes that beginning in 1964 the FBI proposed over four hundred COINTELPRO actions against seventeen KKK groups and nine other white racist outfits then under investigation. Of these, 289 were actually approved. One included the publication of an issue of American Nazi party leader George Lincoln Rockwell's *Rockwell Report* exposing UKA leader Robert Shelton. Another was the formation of the bogus "National Committee for Domestic Tranquility," a nominally right-wing group with a strong anti-Klan message. According to Finch:

> It was an elaborate hoax. The Bureau's exhibits section designed a letterhead, and agents in more than a dozen cities discreetly rented post office boxes. Regularly, new chapters were added to the letterhead to demonstrate the organization's rapid growth. . . . Using information developed by infiltrators, the FBI tried to target the committee's mailings to specific Klansmen who were considered receptive to its patriotic appeal. . . . The committee never held a public rally, never even called a meeting,

but that wasn't considered unusual; many small right-wing groups have their headquarters in post office boxes.[21]

Other strategies to subvert the Klan included sending postcards with the message: "You received this—somebody knows who you are!" and "Is your job safe after everyone finds out you're a Klansman?" There is little doubt that the operation was quite successful.

Wade conceded that "COINTELPRO was essentially a Hoover-backed scheme of cheap psychological warfare and dirty tricks. At innocuous levels, the program was simply schoolboy mischief." He added:

> At more serious levels, agents gave money to Klansmen to form independent Klans, splintering the UKA from within. Agents "leaned on" Klansmen's employers, and a number of Klansmen lost their jobs. Consistent with Hoover's favorite obsession, much of COINTELPRO's harassment was of a sexual nature. Informers were requested, whenever possible, to sleep with the wives of other Klansmen in order to learn new information and to alienate the affections of the Klansman's spouse.[22]

An example of a "serious level" COINTELPRO operation occurred when the ADL gave the FBI $38,000 to pay two informants to "set up" Tommy Tarrants, a twenty-one-year-old Klansman, following the bombing of a Meridian, Mississippi, synagogue. The two informants coaxed Tarrants into bombing the home of a local Jewish businessman. Tarrants, accompanied by Kathy Ainsworth, an elementary schoolteacher and KKK supporter, arrived at the home of Meyer Davidson and stepped into a hail of police bullets as he left his car. Ainsworth was killed outright. Tarrants was nearly killed, suffering numerous bullet wounds, and several lawmen were also injured.[23]

Wade also says that after developing the COINTELPRO for use on the KKK, the FBI proceeded to use it "against the Black Panthers, civil rights leaders, and anti-war demonstrators."[24] In point of fact, the disruptive tactics used against the Klan were in some cases almost identical to those used against radical left groups in the 1960s. The Klan provided an opportunity for the FBI to develop and refine its skills. As they say, what goes around, comes around.

O'Reilly observed that this anti-Klan program was actually the "third COINTELPRO, the first two having been launched in 1956 against the Communist Party and in 1961 against the Socialist Workers Party. Like its predecessors," he says,

> the Bureau designed the new program "to expose, disrupt, discredit or otherwise neutralize" the targeted group. Individual counter-intelligence operations (dirty tricks) often violated federal criminal statutes relating to mail fraud and incited violence, and sometimes involved the sending of obscene mail and extortion. But neither the COINTELPRO against the Klan nor any of the other programs had the solitary goal of invoking sanctions against dissidents. They had an explicitly "educational purpose" of bringing Klansmen or communists or Trotskyites "into disrepute before the American public."[25]

In the case of Viola Liuzzo, riding in the car of Klansmen who shot and killed her was Gary Thomas Rowe, a major FBI informant. Rowe was notoriously violence-prone, but the FBI protected him because of his usefulness. Apparently, more than one person may have been killed because of this decision. In 1987 the *New York Times* broke the following news:

> The Federal Bureau of Investigation's chief paid informant in the Ku Klux Klan in the early 1960's has told Alabama authorities that, while on the bureau payroll, he shot a black man to death, then kept quiet about the killing at the instruction of an FBI agent, according to investigative documents.[26]

The FBI denied the charge. Rowe was indicted in 1978 for the Liuzzo slaying along with Eugene Thomas, Collie Leroy Wilkins, and William O. Eaton. Rowe was never tried because Alabama authorities granted him immunity in exchange for testimony against the other defendants. Thomas, Wilkins, and Eaton were convicted of federal civil rights violations. Wilkins and Thomas were acquitted of murder charges in Alabama courts. A 1982 Associated Press story reported:

> The Justice Department has revealed that FBI agents covered up the violent activities of Gary Thomas Rowe, Jr., its key informant in the Ku Klux Klan in the early 1960s. . . . Department investigators said the agents protected Rowe because "he was simply too valuable to abandon."[27]

In 1982 the five surviving children of Viola Lizzuo filed a $5 million lawsuit against the federal government for not controlling the violent activities of Rowe.

Whatever the ethical issues involved, the simple fact is that the FBI's COINTELPRO campaign against the KKK was probably the most significant factor in its decline (aside from vigorous prosecution of actual KKK crimes, which is another matter altogether). Most Americans would rejoice that the FBI was largely successful and that an unquestionably violence-prone movement was at least partially derailed by whatever means necessary. On the other hand, most COINTELPRO operations, whether against left or right, were not directed at violent or even illegal acts, but rather against legal actions—publication and public speaking—of a radical protest movement.

\*     \*     \*

The six-year period from 1967 to 1973 was devastating for the KKK. Many klaverns folded up, the Klan lost immense prestige, its image as an outlaw organization was doubly reinforced, and a generational change took place within the organization. The 1960s Klan had a share of businessmen, homeowners, minor professionals, politicians, policemen, and individuals with roots in the community. Beginning in the 1970s a dramatic change in Klan membership occurred. The average age plummeted as older members died or dropped out and much younger members were recruited.

A great many 1960s Klan members were World War II veterans and had an uneasy feeling about open association with neo-Nazis, although they may have shared many of their values. In the 1970s these inhibitions gradually disappeared and by the late 1970s a Nazi-Klan alliance had developed.

*    *    *

In addition to the FBI, another factor in the Klan decline was that legal segregation became a lost cause in the United States. During the 1960s federal civil rights laws were enacted and were enforced by the Justice Department. Resistance to integration brought severe legal penalties. Ethnic intimidation also brought increasingly severe retaliation, and the list of imprisoned Klansmen was growing longer. In short, it was no longer a viable organization. Its capacity to recruit members from the general population was almost nil; it was left with only fanatics and fringe elements to draw upon. Nevertheless, the 1970s' Klan was also left with a number of FBI informants in its ranks just in case something should develop.

A period of regrouping, the 1970s was also a period of increased rivalry and dissension for the various Klans, not all of which was caused by the FBI. The ADL reported a slow but steady increase in Klan membership after it bottomed out in 1973. By 1975 ADL reported 6,500 members; between 6,000 and 8,000 in 1978; 9,000 to 10,500 in 1979; and another peak membership of 9,700 to 11,500 in 1982.[28]

In 1974 a new Klan organization appeared on the scene. David Duke incorporated his Knights of the Ku Klux Klan in Louisiana. Duke, a charismatic and polished speaker, had been a Klan member since 1973, before which he had been briefly active in the National Socialist White People's party. Photographs of Duke wearing a Nazi uniform would haunt him throughout his career. Duke's Klan was spectacularly successful, holding the largest Klan rally ever in Walker, Louisiana, with an attendance of 2,700 in 1975.

Also in 1975 Bill Wilkinson, a Duke lieutenant, quit Duke's Knights to form his own Klan, Invisible Empire, Knights of the Ku Klux Klan. Duke and Wilkinson almost immediately began sniping at one another, with Wilkinson the more aggressive of the two. The differences between them revolved around style more than content, as noted by Guy Martin:

> Wilkinson felt that Duke—with his soft semi-intellectual approach to the middle and upper-middle classes—just wasn't providing the old kick. He became the gun-toting, cigar-chewing, cow-pasture Klansman, a man unafraid of action. Sure he was a redneck, and the inference was, if he was a redneck, Duke was nothing but a slick-talking pansy.[29]

In September 1976 Duke and James K. Warner, a long-time neo-Nazi now in Duke's Klan, were arrested and convicted for inciting to riot during a Klan convention near New Orleans. Duke sent out an appeal letter to members to raise defense money. Wilkinson sent his own letter charging that all of the money actually went to Duke, while other Klansmen arrested (including Warner) had to pay their own legal expenses. He made charges suggesting other financial improprieties as well.[30]

Duke responded with another letter. He emphasized that his conviction for "incitement to riot" was his first offense, and his six-month jail sentence with no suspension or probation and $250 fine was highly unusual. "Not one person convicted of a first-offense misdemeanor in a thousand is sentenced to jail," he said. He also noted that the prosecution

> spent very little time on the incident itself and instead tried to attack the political beliefs of the defendants and the Ku Klux Klan organization in general. All defense objections as to this conduct were overruled by the Judge.[31]

Duke went on to charge that "a couple of individuals calling themselves 'Klansmen' have sent out a vile smear letter against me and our movement." He also suggested that the letter may have been sent to "the mailing list that Jerry Dutton stole from our organization when he worked for us last October." Dutton had been accused of stealing a similar list from the National States Rights party. Duke then accused Dutton of taking the list and going into business with Wilkinson, commenting, "Anyone who wishes to have any dealings with these traitors to our Movement is no friend of ours."

Charges flew back and forth between Wilkinson and Duke virtually the entire time either of them was a Klan leader. The animosity between the two Klan organizations became quite intense at times, as was often the case between other Klan factions. In March 1980, for example:

> An Internal Ku Klux Klan skirmish that erupted in gunfire . . . in east Orange County may have flared when a Central Florida group decided to break from the Klan and set up a chapter of the Christian Patriots Defense League.
>
> About 20 armed and robed men . . . burst into the concrete block meeting hall. . . . About 25 men were inside. The raiders beat the men at the meeting, shooting at the ones who tried to duck out of the one-room hall and escape to nearby woods.[32]

Many observers of the Duke-Wilkinson feud feel that the main issue was the intense jealousy Wilkinson felt toward Duke. Whatever the case, Duke was initially unfazed by it. The best asset Duke's Klan had was Duke himself, as noted by Wade:

> He recruited on colleges and campuses and tried to enlist "other intellectuals." . . . For the first time, women were accepted in Duke's Klan on equal terms with men— Duke had far too much appeal to women to restrict their membership in any way. Catholics were more than welcome.
>
> Since he was the only Klansman able to capture media attention, Duke drew hundreds into his organization, which reached a peak of thirty-five hundred members.[33]

In October 1977, Duke announced that Klan members planned a border patrol in southern California to help curb the illegal alien problem. Second in command was Tom Metzger, Duke's California Grand Dragon. According to news dispatches, Duke

> said that Klansmen armed with citizens band radios and legally registered weapons planned to patrol the United States–Mexican border from Brownsville, Texas, to the Pacific Ocean to help cut the flow of illegal immigrants.[34]

The tactic was spectacularly successful. All television networks carried news of the event, with shots of Duke in an automobile patrolling the border at night. Metzger, incidentally, went on to win the Democratic party nomination for California's Forty-third Congressional district in 1980. He lost in the general election.

The Duke-Wilkinson feud was soon joined by UKA's Robert Shelton, who printed attacks on both in a 1978 issue of his tabloid, *The Fiery Cross*. He accused Duke of publishing a pornographic novel and a street-fighting manual for blacks entitled *African Atto*. His attack on Wilkinson (entitled "Bill Wilkerson Pollutes North Alabama") misspells his name and accuses him of attracting the "worst elements of the communities that he visits" with his "perverted Klan."[35]

In the spring of 1978 Duke undertook his celebrated London tour, reveling in attempts by Scotland Yard to find and deport him in the wake of considerable media attention. Despite his celebrity-like status, Duke did not have quite what it took to be a Klan leader. He was too polished, too media-conscious, too smooth, and too articulate for the typical Klansman. By 1979 Wilkinson had surpassed Duke in terms of members and influence. Duke, deciding that the Klan was not really his forte, turned his organization over to Alabama Grand Wizard Don Black and formed the National Association for the Advancement of White People in 1980. The NAAWP had a program virtually indistinguishable from the Klan. It did eliminate the robes and other ceremonial Klan trappings, though. Not surprisingly, Wilkinson has another account of Duke's departure from the Klan:

> Bill Wilkinson . . . told the press that he had forced Duke's resignation from the Knights of the KKK by secretly videotaping a meeting during which Duke offered to sell Wilkinson his membership list for $35,000.[36]

One of Wilkinson's more bizarre lieutenants was Jordan Gollub, the son of a Jewish physician in Philadelphia, Pennsylvania, and an honors graduate of Temple University. Gollub had served as editor of Wilkinson's monthly newspaper, *The Klansman,* from 1980 to 1984, and was a member of several different Klans after leaving Wilkinson's group. He was Grand Dragon of Georgia in the U.S. Klans and also had been a kleagle under R. E. Scoggin in South Carolina. He joined the Christian Knights of the Ku Klux Klan in 1985, becoming a Grand Dragon and editing its magazine, *The Christian Searchlight.* In May 1989 Gollub was removed from his post because of his Jewishness.[37] Gollub is rumored to have a brother who is active in the Socialist Workers party.

Wilkinson was creative in attracting media attention himself. During the 1976 presidential election, for example, he organized a Plains, Georgia, rally to impeach Andrew Young, narrowly escaping serious injury or death when an anti-Klan fanatic drove an automobile into the speakers' platform. All but one of the nineteen people injured were newsmen.[38] Wilkinson regularly and purposely confronted civil rights activists. It became routine for Wilkinson's Klansmen to engage in heated exchanges with opponents, and virtually everywhere Wilkinson's Klan demonstrated, counterdemonstrations occurred.

In 1978 Wilkinson began engaging in a strategy that would make his Invisible Empire the main Klan group in the United States. His method was to openly and unabashedly engage in violent rhetoric. He said that the Klan had tried a moderate approach for years, but it had failed to stop black advances and that it was time to try other methods, presumably including violence. One disquieting tactic was to pose for the media with weapons, including machine guns. He went out of his way to engage in confrontations where violence might occur, and regularly faced anti-Klan activists in situation after situation. According to the ADL, some of Wilkinson's Klansmen had complained that "Wilkinson's encouragement of media exposure, especially of Klan paramilitary activities, was inviting a crackdown by govenrment authorities."[39]

The reasons for Wilkinson's behavior became clear when it was revealed that he had been an FBI informant. According to FBI documents dated September 1975, the New Orleans FBI agent in charge of Wilkinson

> feels assured that his source will not take any action to embarrass the Bureau as he has always indicated a strong desire that his contact with the Bureau not come to the attention of his colleagues or anyone else and has sought assurances that this contact not be revealed in any way.[40]

When the fact of Wilkinson's long history as an FBI informant hit the papers, his response was that he only told the bureau what it could find out in newspapers anyway. It is unlikely, however, that the FBI would be interested in newspaper information alone and that this was all Wilkinson supplied them. In point of fact, Wilkinson was a most cooperative informant. Over a period of several years he orchestrated the activities of the Invisible Empire so as to maximize Justice Department objectives, namely to arouse public fears of a Klan ievival and Klan violence and to destabilize the various Klans by inciting rivalry and dissension. Virtually every major demonstration. march, or confrontation was cleared with the FBI beforehand. All Klan records, including membersl p lists, wound up in FBI hands.

Interestingly, a 408-page Justice Department study issued in November 1980 has concluded that Wilkinson's Invisible Empire was the most violence-prone Klan group. According to a *New York Times* account:

> A Justice Department spokesman . . . said the report would not be made public but that the agency considered Mr. Wilkinson "the most militant" of the Klan leaders.

The Justice Department review reportedly found that two other Klan groups, Robert Shelton's United Klans of America and David Duke's new organization, the National Association for the Advancement of White People, were less violent than Mr. Wilkinson's Klan.[41]

Nor was Wilkinson the only example of FBI involvement in 1970s Klan activity. COINTELPRO may have died in 1971, but the FBI continued to develop informants throughout the Klan movement. An almost incredible situation existed in Indiana, where virtually the entire leadership of the Indiana Klan was composed of FBI informants. A detailed account appeared in a November 1979 issue of the *Indianapolis Star:*

> From 1969 through 1976, William M. Chaney, the imperial wizard of the Ku Klux Klan in Indiana, was an informant for the FBI, receiving up to $500 a month to report on the activities of the brotherhood he directed. In fact, most of the officers of the Indiana Klan were on the FBI payroll.
>
> Sources said that the local FBI perpetuated a public "myth" about the strength of the Indiana KKK so agents could enhance their standing within the bureau by developing Klan informants.[42]

At one point, Indiana Klan officials administered polygraph tests to members in order to locate informants. The very officials administering the test were FBI informants themselves. The article noted that in reality the Indiana Klan "not only is a minor factor in Indiana but hasn't been much more than a minor shadow behind a lot of overblown publicity, particularly from television news stations, in the last decade."[43]

Chaney, incidentally, traveled widely on behalf of the Indiana Klan during this period, and regularly met with other Klan leaders to discuss internal affairs, strategy, and other matters. Presumably, all of this information wound up in FBI hands as well. In addition, he was also instrumental in developing other informants.

\*    \*    \*

On November 3, 1979, five Communist Workers party activists died in a shoot-out with Klansmen and neo-Nazis in Greensboro, North Carolina. This is covered in some detail in chapter 17. What is of interest here is the reaction it provoked.

Until the Greensboro incident, the private, nongovernmental anti-Klan effort was divided among a number of organizations, most of which could be considered of "moderate" or "liberal" persuasion. These included the ADL, the American Jewish Committee, and a number of civil rights organizations, such as the NAACP and CORE. These were all fairly effective in developing information and organizing community opposition to the Klan. A number of Marxist-Leninist groups—such as the Progressive Labor party and its International Committee Against Racism (INCAR), founded in 1973, and the Communist Party USA and its National Alliance Against Racist and Political Repression, founded in 1972—also actively opposed the Klan. The Marxist-Leninist groups were always quite marginal and some were violence-prone themselves, especially INCAR. The 1970s and 1980s were filled with anti-Klan counterdemonstrations by these and similar organizations, usually greatly outnumbering the Klansmen and often responsible for most of the violence. Following Greensboro, however, a new mood was in the air. Wade recorded the change:

> In response to the Klan's 1979 attack on its non-violent marchers in Decatur and the arrest of Curtis Robinson (a Black man convicted of shooting two Klansmen), the SCLC had soon afterward called a conference in Norfolk, Virginia. Thirty organizations had responded and, out of the conference, the National Anti-Klan Network was born. Based in Atlanta, Georgia, the Network began by matching the ADL's research, monitoring and reporting on Klan/Nazi activity. Under the leadership of its coordinator, Lyn Wells, it took a strong stand against the Klan's corruption of children and assisted the NEA in creating its curriculum guide.[44]

Not widely known is that many of the staff of the National Anti-Klan Network (NAKN) were as far out on the ideological spectrum as the Klan itself. Lyn Wells, for instance, is a former member of the Central Committee of the October League (OL), which evolved into the Communist Party, Marxist-Leninist (CPML). In 1972 Wells gave an address to an OL labor conference. Standing below photos of Marx, Engels, Lenin, Stalin, and Mao Tse-tung, she said:

> It is true that building a party requires conscious work on the part of communists. A party is the organized conscious expression of the working-class struggle and cannot develop out of the struggle spontaneously. It takes years of difficult work, developing an experienced core of cadre, raising the theoretical level and deepening ties with the masses. While being close to the united front, the communist organization is at the same time separate with an independent life of its own.[45]

Although quite small, the October League and its successor, the CPML, both of which are defunct, were among the most extreme Marxist-Leninist sects in the United States. Another NAKN activist with extremist "links" is Leonard Zeskind, an organizer for the Marxist-Leninist Sojourner Truth Organization (STO) during the early 1980s. On the editorial board of *Urgent Tasks: Journal of the Revolutionary Left,* the STO's journal, Zeskind routinely engaged in classical Marxist-Leninist rhetoric. Zeskind found the response to Marxism-Leninism lukewarm at best. He gradually shifted his emphasis toward antiracism and published his own journal, appropriately called *The Hammer* (with Lyn Wells on his board), before hooking up with the NAKN.[46] *Urgent Tasks* acquired its name from a pamphlet by Lenin that asserted the urgent task of party workers was:

> not to serve the working class at each of its stages, but to represent the interests of the movement as a whole, to point out to this movement its ultimate aim and its political tasks, and to safeguard its politics and ideological independence.[47]

The NAKN was initially regarded with skepticism by other Marxist-Leninist groups. A November 1982 article in *Worker's Vanguard,* journal of the Spartacist League (a Trotskyist sect), described it thus:

> NAKN is a loose coalition of the remnants of the pro-Peking Stalinists of Mike Klonsky/Lyn Wells' disintegrating "Communist Party Marxist Leninist" with Southern black ministers headed by SCLC's Rev. C. T. Vivian, who organized in 1979 to provide an "alternative" to the communists in the wake of outrage over Greensboro.[48]

In 1986 the NAKN changed its name to the Center for Democratic Renewal, perhaps an attempt to blur its radical roots. The masthead of its newsletter, *The Monitor,* however, continued to list Wells as executive director and Zeskind as director of research. In early 1987 Lynora Williams, a frequent writer for the Marxist-Leninist *Guardian,* took over as executive director.[49]

The symbiotic relationship between the Klan and its various tormentors bears notice. The anti-Klan movement achieved such momentum in the 1980s that it sometimes took hundreds of police to protect a half dozen Klansmen during counterdemonstrations. Precisely that happened in Chicago in December 1990 when "about 1,500 people jeered and threw things at six robed Ku Klux Klansmen who staged a rally downtown."[50] It became increasingly common for virtually all the violence and arrests on such occasions to be the product of radical anti-Klan forces. Like the anti-Communist movements of the 1960s, anti-Klan movements of the 1970s and 1980s existed only because of the coexistence of an "enemy."

Writing in the *New Republic* in September 1983, Phillip Finch addressed the problem of this relationship. Noting that "the Klan's hold on our national psyche is its most durable feature," he further commented:

> Most anti-Klan groups have an interest in making the Klans appear stronger. The stronger the Klans seem to be, the more pressing is the mission of their opponents.
>
> Their message is unequivocal: the Klan is a menace that must be stopped by any means necessary. From this a striking symbiosis has evolved.
>
> For radical leftists, the Klan is a way to get the attention of the otherwise unresponsive masses: blacks and Chicanos, white liberals, even conservatives—everybody who is against the Klan.[51]

Soon after the National Anti-Klan Network was formed, another group sprang up, this time from the Southern Poverty Law Center, founded in 1971 by Morris Dees, Joe Levin, and Julian Bond. In response to Greensboro and other cases of Klan violence, the center announced its "Klanwatch" project. Its function was to monitor every aspect of Klan activity, including the gathering of information on individual members. The purpose of this ambitious investigative effort was to enhance anti-Klan education, litigation and, when necessary, criminal prosecution. The project announced a nominally civil libertarian approach:

"Klansmen have the same rights as anyone else to march, protest and speak," center spokesmen said, "no matter how wrong or despicable their beliefs may be. But they must be stopped from harassing, killing and intimidating innocent people."[52]

In 1981 Klanwatch filed suit on behalf of Vietnamese fishermen harassed by Texas KKK Grand Dragon Louis Beam and his paramilitary forces. The fishermen alleged that the Klan was responsible for setting fire to some of their boats and burning crosses near their docks and homes. In May a court order was issued prohibiting Klansmen from even wearing robes within sight of the fishermen. In another case, Klanwatch invoked an obscure Texas statute to keep Beam and his Klansmen from engaging in paramilitary training.

As the Klan moved into the 1980s, it became more and more apparent that it was on the way out. Membership continued to drop, approaching a mere 3,500 in 1990, or one for every 71,000 Americans. Much Klan violence undoubtedly emanated from the fact that a substantial portion of its membership was made up of persons who were statistically violence-prone anyway: single males in their twenties. Moreover, most Klan violence came from just a few of its members, as is often the case with militant groups. The Klan was too small to be called a "movement" any longer, too disreputable to attract even remotely "normal" people as members, and too closely watched to make many mistakes without getting caught. There were several events in the 1980s of note, however, and for the Klan, nearly all of them were bad news.

Numerous Klansmen were arrested during the 1980s for offenses ranging from conspiring to overthrow the country of Dominica to murder and arson, and each instance was another nail in the coffin lid. Several of the defendants in the 1985 trial involving the neo-Nazi group The Order, who plotted and carried out a year-and-a-half series of robberies and two murders, were Klansmen or former Klansmen. That same year a massive FBI raid on the Covenant, Sword and Arm of the Lord (CSA) paramilitary commune in southern Missouri, led to several arrests. A number of CSA members were also past or present Klansmen.[53]

In February 1982 five black women collected $535,000 in damages in the first private lawsuit under the Civil Right Act of 1870, a Civil War–era anti-Klan statute. Four had been shot from a passing automobile and the fifth had been shot in a separate incident, all in April 1980. Three Klan members were arrested. In July 1980 two were acquitted, but the third was convicted of assault and battery. The civil suit, where the standards of evidence are much weaker than in a criminal case, was proving to be an effective weapon.

In 1986 it became known that armed forces personnel were participating in Ku Klux Klan activity. This brought a flood of protests to the Defense Department. In one case, three United States Marines were discharged for becoming involved in the activities of the White Patriot party, formerly known as the Confederate Knights of the Ku Klux Klan.[54] Reagan's defense secretary, Caspar Weinberger, issued a directive on September 5 concerning "Hate Groups," which states, "Active participation, including public demonstrations, recruiting and training members, and organizing or leading such organizations, is utterly incompatible with military service."[55]

The directive was sweeping. It gave commanders the authority to take disciplinary steps, including expulsion from the military. Commanders were told they could declare any facilities used by such groups or the events sponsored by them "off-limits." A *New York Times* article said that:

> Mr. Weinberger's directive does not actually bar membership in groups that promote discrimination, a step officials said would be overly intrusive and impossible to enforce. Servicemen could enroll in the groups and pay dues.[56]

*    *    *

In May 1987 Morris Dees of the Southern Poverty Law Center won a judgment against United Klans of America and six of its members for the 1981 slaying of a black teenager whose body was left hanging in a tree. The UKA was forced to turn over its heaquarters, which was then sold, the money being given to the mother of the deceased.

At issue in the trial was the liability of the UKA for the acts of its members, a particularly questionable concept to some civil libertarians. The Dees victory, although heartwarming to the mother of the slain boy and anti-Klan activists, may prove troublesome. Had this doctrine been established as a legal precedent in the 1960s, the civil rights movement, the early feminist movement, the gay rights movement, the anti-war movement, and even labor unions could easily have been crippled by lawsuits arising from the violent acts of some of their participants. Suppose that a militant black activist group had been hit with a $7 million judgment because one of its members killed someone in the Watts riots? This sounds far-fetched, but had the Dees precedent existed then it could have happened and, indeed, could happen now. It also could be contended that the group helped create a "state of mind" that influenced one of its members to riot, and thus shared responsibility for his or her crimes.

In 1988 the Justice Department brought sedition charges against thirteen individuals, most of whom were identified in some way with KKK or neo-Nazi groups, and many of whom were already in prison following convictions in The Order case. The specific indictment read "seditious conspiracy between July 1983 and March 1985 to overthrow the government." The seedy history of sedition prosecutions in the United States, used mostly against leftists, should have been enough to discourage their use again. Nevertheless, having called 113 witnesses and presented thousands of pages of documents, the Justice Department lost its case and all defendants were acquitted.

In 1991 the ADL issued a report stating that the KKK has been in decline for many years and that there was little chance it would ever become a significant force again. It credited both criminal and civil prosecutions. The report also noted:

> Additional major factors in the Klan's decline were the departure of three of its most effective leaders—Robert Shelton, David Duke and Bill Wilkinson—who were the

three top figures in the late seventies; the onset of a period of intense factionalism; and the tendency to divide into ever smaller groups.[57]

The report said the "combined total membership of all Klans today is approximately 4,000."

The Ku Klux Klan, with its philosophy of hatred toward minorities, its propensity for violence, and its total disregard for human rights and civil liberties, is an abomination that may soon come to an end. In the process of causing that to happen, we must not inflict wounds upon our democratic system that diminish constitutional protections. The worst thing the Klan or any other extremist group can do to us is what they make us do to ourselves in misguided attempts to contain them. Like the terrorist who succeeds in destroying the system by forcing it to institute repressive measures, the Klan could gain a measure of success in the same way.

## Notes

1. Stetson Kennedy, *Southern Exposure* (New York City: Garden City, 1946).

2. Wyn Craig Wade, *The Fiery Cross: The Ku Klux Klan in America* (New York: Simon & Schuster, 1987), 281–87.

3. Neil R. McMillen, *The Citizen's Council* (Urbana: University of Illinois Press, 1971).

4. George Thayer, *The Farther Shores of Politics* (New York: Simon & Schuster, 1967), 95.

5. Ibid.

6. Detailed chronological accounts of Klan violence can be obtained from the Anti-Defamation League in New York City and the Southern Poverty Law Center in Atlanta, Georgia.

7. Wade, 309.

8. "The Ku Klux Klans—1965," *Facts* (May 1965): 321.

9. *Hate Groups in America* (New York: Anti-Defamation League, 1984), 85.

10. Wade, 313–14.

11. Robert M. Mikell, *They Say—Blood On My Hands* (Huntsville, Ala.: Publishers Enterprise, Inc., 1966), 53.

12. Accounts of Venable include: *Life* (April 23, 1965); *New York Times* (February 25, 1965).

13. Thayer, 86–87.

14. Thayer, 88.

15. Johnny Green, "Did the FBI Kill Viola Liuzzo?" *Playboy* (October 1980).

16. U.S. Congress, Report: *The Present-Day Ku Klux Klan Movement,* 90 Congress, 1 Sess., House Committee on Un-American Activities (1967).

17. *Hate Groups in America,* 87, 12.

18. Phillip Finch, *God, Guts and Guns: A Close Look at the Radical Right* (New York: Seaview/Putnam, 1983); Kenneth O'Reilly, *Racial Matters: The FBI's Secret File on Black America, 1960–1972* (New York: Macmillan, 1989); Wade, 361–63.

19. O'Reilly, 225.

20. O'Reilly, 217.

21. Finch, 161.

22. Wade, 361–62.

23. Wade, 362–63.

24. Wade, 363.

25. O'Reilly, 198.

26. "Informant of FBI Says He Killed Black," *New York Times* dispatch (July 11, 1978).

27. "FBI Covered Up for KKK Informant," Associated Press (October 29, 1982).

28. *Hate Groups in America* (New York: Anti-Defamation League, 1988), 85.

29. Guy Martin, "Ain't Nothing You Can Do But Join the Klan," *Esquire* (March 1980), 36.

30. "Re: David Duke and James Warner Conviction in Jefferson Parish, Louisiana," form letter, Invisible Empire, Knights of the Ku Klux Klan, n.d.

31. "A Legal Lynching: A Personal Account by David Duke," form letter, Knights of the Ku Klux Klan, n.d. (ca. 1977).

32. Mike Fiedler, "Klan Fracas: Were Raiders Teaching Renegades a Lesson?" *Sentinal Star* (March 5, 1980).

33. Wade, 371.

34. "Ku Klux Klan Plans Border Patrol to Help Fight Illegal Alien Problem," Associated Press (October 17, 1977).

35. "David Duke: The Untold Author," and "Bill Wilkerson [sic] Pollutes North Alabama," *The Fiery Cross,* no. 13 (1978).

36. *Hate Groups in America* (1988), 3.

37. Bill Montgomery, "Strange Passions: Christ and Klan," *Atlanta Journal and Constitution* (June 18, 1989), A–8; Susan Birnbaum, "KKK Removed Grand Dragon Because He's Born a Jew," *Northern California Jewish Bulletin* (May 26, 1989), 32; statement, The Imperial Wizard's Office, Virgil L. Griffin, Christian Knights of the Ku Klux Klan (April 12, 1989).

38. Wayne King, "Violent Rebirth of the Klan," *New York Times Magazine* (December 7, 1980).

39. *Hate Groups in America* (1988), 7.

40. "Memorandum," Federal Bureau of Investigation (September 10, 1975); "Teletype," FBI (March 28, 1975).

41. "Klan Leader Criticizes U.S. Report and Asserts, 'We Violate No Law' " *New York Times* (November 25, 1980).

42. Donald Thrasher and James G. Newland, Jr., "Most of Klan Leaders in Indiana Were Paid by FBI as Informants," *Indianapolis Star* (November 11, 1979).

43. Ibid.

44. Wade, 391.

45. *The Call* (April 1973).

46. Leonard Zeskind, "Events in Afghanistan," *Urgent Tasks* (Spring 1980): 21–24; Bruce Rogers, "Radical Chic, Kansas City Style," *City* (January 1981), 23.

47. V. I. Lenin, *The Urgent Tasks of Our Movement,* pamphlet (n.d.).

48. "Killer Klan Must Be Smashed," *Workers Vanguard* (November 12, 1982), 1, 11–12.

49. *The Monitor* (January 1986); *The Monitor* (September 1987); *The Guardian* (October 25, 1989).

50. "1500 Harass Six KKK Members at Rally," Associated Press (December 23, 1990).

51. Phillip Finch, "Can the Klan Ride Again?," *New Republic* (September 5, 1983), 18, 20–21.

52. Wade, 392.

53. Both the Anti-Defamation League and Klanwatch keep detailed accounts of Klan violence. These are available to the general public upon request.

54. "Marines Discharged for Neo-Nazi Activities," *Washington Jewish Week* (August 7, 1986).

55. "Military Forbids Active Role of Soldiers in 'Hate Groups,' " *New York Times* (September 11, 1986).

56. Ibid.

57. *The KKK Today: A 1991 Special Status Report* (New York: Anti-Defamation League, 1991), 1.

# Appendix I. **Fake Quotes and Fabricated Documents: A Common Extremist Tactic**

Quoting the famous for polemical purposes has been done by people residing in all parts of the political spectrum. Distorting quotations or actually concocting quotes or documents out of whole cloth has been a much-employed tactic by extremists, especially those of the right. While American leftists have used spuriosities of that sort sparingly, groups and individuals on the far right have raised such utilizations to a high art form. Probably this is more often done in ignorance; that is, quote users believe that the words "fit the situation" and simply use them without checking on authenticity. It is also the case that spurious quotes and documents have been put into print by people knowing all too well of their phoniness. but who nevertheless thrust them on the public in the name of a great ideological cause. Senator Joseph McCarthy was known to have concocted at least two nonquotes. Receiving the widest circulation was his pseudo-Leninism: "The world cannot exist half slave and half free. It must be all slave."

The question arises as to how one determines whether a quote/document is fake. Some are not hard to spot because they border on the ridiculous: "There is only one way to kill capitalism—taxes, taxes, and more taxes," attributed to Karl Marx. Most, however, require at least a fair amount of research. Oft times the researcher cannot be certain and must be satisfied with the preponderance of the evidence. In some instances, however, one may be fortunate enough to discover the origin of a fake or find that a real quote has been distorted. Occasionally, the words were actually said, but not by the person to whom they have been attributed.

Two important points:

1. When the authenticity of a quotation is in question, the burden of proof is on the user, not on the questioner.
2. Quotes/documents should *never* be used unless they can be documented.

The following list of quotations/documents are coded in this manner:

C = Certain that the quote is fake.
P = Probable that the quote is fake.
Q = Questionable that the quote is real.
D = Distortion—words left out, changed or added; not in context.

## Beria, Lavrenti

> By psychopolitics create chaos. Leave a nation leaderless. Kill our enemies, and bring to Earth, through Communism, the greatest peace man has ever known. C

Appearing in a sixty-page booklet on "psychopolitics," this quote was probably concocted by science fiction writer and Scientology founder L. Ron Hubbard. The old Soviet secret police head didn't even live long enough to hear about it. Most instrumental in spreading the phony booklet, *Brain-Washing: A Synthesis of the Russian Textbook on Psychopolitics,* was veteran extremist Kenneth Goff. Paul F. Boller and John George, *They Never Said It: A Book of Fake Quotes, Misquotes, and Misleading Attributions* (Oxford University Press, 1989), 5.

> If we can effectively kill the national pride and patriotism of just one generation, we will have won that country. C

This non-Beriaism is also from the booklet *Brain-Washing: A Synthesis of the Russian Textbook on Psychopolitics.* Boller and George, 6.

## Bismarck, Otto

> The division of the United States into two federations of equal force was decided long before the Civil War by the High Financial Power of Europe. These bankers were afraid the United States, if they remained one bloc and as one nation, would attain economical and financial independence, which would upset their financial domination over the world. The voice of the Rothschilds predominated. They foresaw tremendous booty if they could substitute two feeble democracies, indebted to the *Jewish financiers,* to the vigorous Republic, confident and self-providing. Therefore, they started their emissaries in order to exploit the question of slavery and thus to dig an abyss between the two parts of the Republic.
> Lincoln . . . perceived that these sinister financiers of Europe, the Rothschilds, wished to make him the executioner of their designs. . . . But Lincoln read their plots and soon understood that the South was not the worst foe, but the *Jewish financiers.* He did not confide his apprehensions, he watched the gestures of the Hidden Hand; he did not wish to expose publicly the questions which would disconcert the ignorant masses. . . .
> The death of Lincoln was a disaster for Christendom. There was no man in the United States great enough to wear his boots. And Israel went anew to grab the riches of the world. I fear that *Jewish banks* with their craftiness and tortuous tricks will entirely control the exuberant riches of America, and use it to systematically corrupt modern civilization. The Jews will not hesitate to plunge the whole of Christendom into wars and chaos, in order that the "earth should become the inheritance of Israel." C

It shouldn't be surprising that this odd mouthful appeared in the June 1971 issue of Gerald L. K. Smith's *The Cross and the Flag*. Bismarck supposedly revealed this "great truth" to Conrad Siem in 1876, and Siem published it forty-five years later. Thus, no one ever heard of it until 1921! An intense search of eleven books on Bismarck produced much about Jews (nothing negative), and nothing on Lincoln nor the American Civil War. Bismarck not only bore Jews no malice, but was even attacked by anti-Semites as a dupe of Jewish financiers.

### Brady, Sarah

> Our task of creating a socialist America can only succeed when those who would resist us have been totally disarmed. C

Supposedly said to liberal Ohio Senator Howard Metzenbaum while Brady was lobbying for a bill to ban semiautomatic weapons, this "quote" is a solid phony. The wife of Ronald Reagan's former press secretary, Jim Brady, always has been a staunch capitalist. This strange missive evidently appeared in 1990.

### Brando, Marlon

> You've seen every single race besmirched, but you never saw an *unfavorable* image of the Kike because the Jews were ever so watchful for that. They never allowed it to be shown on the screen. (Emphasis ours.) D

This quote is a (probably deliberate) distortion by the anti-Semitic National States Rights Party (NSRP) from their pamphlet *Jewish Stars Over Hollywood.* The emphasized word, "unfavorable," was not used by Brando. In addition, after the word "that," Brando stated: "The Jews have done so much for the world that, I suppose, you get extra disappointed because they didn't pay attention to that."

Obviously, when viewed in proper context, Mr. Brando's statement does not support the anti-Jewish position of the NSRP. *Playboy,* January 1979, 134.

### Brezhnev, Leonid

> Our aim is to gain control of the two great treasure houses on which the West depends. . . . The energy treasure house of the Persian Gulf and the mineral treasure house of Central and Southern Africa. P

The Congressional Research Service of the Library of Congress says "no direct documentation" exists and traced the quote's origin to 1968 Czech defector, General Jan Sejna. Brezhnev supposedly said this in either 1968 or 1973. Sejna didn't mention it during late sixties or seventies interviews nor in his 1982 book *We Will Bury You.* Boller and George, 9.

## Bulganin, Nikolai

The American working man is too well fed; we cannot appeal to him, but when through inflation America has priced herself out of the world market and unemployment follows—then we will settle our debt with the United States. P

This is a Ronald Reagan favorite which he employed in his speeches during the 1960s along with other spurious quotes: Lenin Overripe Fruit and Pie Crust, Khrushchev Doses of Socialism, and, of course, the Win one for the Gipper phony. There is no evidence that former Soviet Premier Bulganin ever said anything like this.

## Burke, Edmund

All that is necessary for evil to triumph is for good men to do nothing. C

Widely used, especially by far rightists, this one fooled *Bartlett's*. The closest Burke came was: "When bad men combine, the good must associate; else they will fall, one by one, an unpitied sacrifice in a contemptible struggle." Boller and George, 10.

## Carter, Jimmy

Our concept of human rights is preserved in Poland. C

Carter never said it, according to Mark Green and Gail MacCall in *Ronald Reagan's Reign of Error* (1983).

## Chou En-Lai

The more troops they send to Vietnam, the happier we will be, for we feel that we shall have them in our power, we can have their blood. So if you want to help the Vietnamese you should encourage the Americans to throw more and more soldiers into Vietnam. . . . We are planting the best kind of opium especially for the American soldiers in Vietnam. P

We first encountered this chilling item in Billy James Hargis's *Christian Crusade Weekly* for March 3, 1974. China's premier supposedly said it in a conversation with Egyptian leader Gamal Abdel Nasser in 1965, about the time the United States started getting heavily involved in the Vietnam War. Brian Crozier, terrorism specialist, has traced it to Mohamed Heikal's book *Nasser: The Cairo Documents,* and believes Chou actually made the statement. But Heikal's book features no documentation and the Library of Congress could find none either. China specialist Ross Terrill commented that while the sentiments in the quote could be Mao's at the time, Chou was slow to follow Mao on this. Terrill said he would be surprised if the words were actually Chou's. Fox Butterfield, the *New York Times* resident China hand, called it out of character for Chou and pronounced the opium part "outrageous." P Letter to John George from Brian Crozier, September 26, 1985; letter to John George from Ross Terrill, November 22, 1985; letter to Senator David Boren from Irene Schubert, Congressional Research Service, Library of Congress, undated but written late 1985; phone conversation, Fox Butterfield with John George, November 16, 1987.

### Cicero, Marcus Tullius

> The budget should be balanced. The Treasury should be filled. Public debt should be reduced. The arrogance of officials should be tempered and controlled, and assistance to foreign lands should be curtailed lest we ourselves should become bankrupt. The people should be forced to work and not depend on government subsistence. P

The *Kansas City Star* (January 15, 1986) used this mouthful without documentation and could furnish none in response to our query. Like other quotes of the same genre, this attribution seems more like a criticism of the modern welfare state than a missive from a Roman statesman of the first century B.C.E.

### Cohen, Israel

> We must realize that our party's most powerful weapon is racial tension. By impounding into the consciousness of the dark races that for centuries they have been oppressed by the whites, we can mould them to the program of the Communist Party. In America we will aim for subtle victory. While inflaming the Negro minority against the whites, we will endeavor to instil in the whites a guilt complex for their exploitation of the Negroes. We will aid the Negroes to rise in prominence in every walk of life, in the professions and in the world of sports and entertainment. With this prestige, the Negro will be able to intermarry with the whites and begin a process which will deliver America to our cause. C

Here we have a phony quotation from a nonexistent book (*A Racial Program for the 20th Century*–1912) written by a fictitious British Communist. According to the *Washington Star* (February 18, 1958) this was concocted by the American fascist Eustace Mullins, who originated other phony quotes and attributed them to one Rabbi Rabinovich. It was read into the *Congressional Record* (June 7, 1957) by Congressman Thomas Abernathy (D-Mississippi) and exposed as fraudulent in the same publication (August 30, 1957). This did not much retard its later use by such rightists as Dan Smoot and the John Birch Society's *American Opinion* (October 1963). Both Smoot and *American Opinion* retracted it in 1964, but Bircher Tom Anderson used it in his "Straight Talk" later that same year.

Among the clues to spuriousness are:

1. "Communist Party"—There wasn't one in 1912—not in the United States, the United Kingdom, nor Russia.
2. "Aid the Negroes to rise in . . . the world of sports and entertainment." (1912?)
3. Early twentieth-century talk of black-white intermarriage.
4. The term "guilt complex" (1912?).
5. No record anywhere of a book entitled *A Racial Program for the 20th Century*. Boller and George, 14.

## Communist Party Directive (1943)

When certain obstructionists [to Communism] become too irritating, label them, after suitable buildups, as fascist or Nazi or anti-Semitic, and use the prestige of antifascist and tolerance organizations to discredit them.

In the public mind constantly associate those who oppose us with those names which already have a bad smell. . . . The association will, after enough repetition, become fact in the public mind. . . . Members and front organizations must continually embarrass, discredit and degrade our critics. Accuse them of being traitors to the war effort, fascists, Red-baiters, peace destroyers, Quislings, labor-baiters and anti-Semites. P

The Congressional Research Service of the Library of Congress could locate no such "directive" and Communism expert Abraham Brumberg called it "possible but doubtful," which seems rather reserved given the fact that in 1943 the CPUSA was heavily supporting the U.S.-Soviet wartime alliance and was therefore unlikely to issue such a "directive." Boller and George, 18.

## Darwin, Charles

How I wish I had not expressed my theory of evolution as I have done. C

A British evangelist named Lady Hope claimed to have been at Darwin's bedside shortly before he died. She wasn't—then or ever, but this didn't stop her from spreading her fabrication far and wide. Nor have far-right fundamentalists such as Jimmy Swaggart been deterred in the 1980s and 1990s. Boller and George, 19.

## DeGaulle, Charles

The evolution toward Communism is inevitable. C

In 1960, DeGaulle supposedly told General de Beaufort that "evolution toward Communism is inevitable" and allowed himself "two years after peace is established with Algeria to make France into a Communist country" and further that he had "the strongest reasons to believe that (John) Kennedy would accept a

Communist Europe." William F. Buckley's *National Review* exposed this fraud in the November 6, 1962, issue. Boller and George, 33.

### Dimitrov, Georgi

> As Soviet power goes, there will be a greater aversion to Communist parties everywhere. So we must practice the techniques of withdrawal. Never appear in the foreground; let our friends do the work. We must always remember that one sympathizer is generally worth more than a dozen militant Communists. A university professor, who without being a party member lends himself to the interests of the Soviet Union, is worth more than a hundred men with party cards. A writer of reputation, or a retired general, are worth more than 500 poor devils who don't know any better than to get themselves beaten up by the police. Every man has his value, his merit. The writer who without being a party member, defends the Soviet Union, the union leader who is outside our ranks but defends the Soviet international policy, is worth more than a thousand party members. (Supposedly stated at the Lenin School of Political Warfare, 1938.) P

The earliest known source for this concoction is *The Yenan Way* (1951) by Eudocio Ravines, a former Peruvian Communist active in the Comintern (which served predominantly as a tool of Soviet foreign policy) in the 1930s. We have nothing other than Ravines's assertion that he heard Dimitrov speak these words. His book is replete with long quotations attributed to Stalin, Manuilsky, Zinoviev, and other leading Bolsheviks. It seems likely that, writing more than a decade later, he could well have fabricated some quotes. A perusal of Dimitrov's writings reveals no style or thoughts resembling the above, as is the case in so many instances of spurious attributions to Communist leaders. So, the question arises, would wily old Dimitrov actually have believed (and stated) that one non-Communist writer or labor leader who defends Soviet international policy "is worth more than a thousand party members"? It seems rather silly on the face of it.

Finally, Dimitrov was Bulgarian, not Russian, and there has never been any such place as the Lenin School of Political Warfare. Eudocio Ravines, *The Yenan Way* (New York: Scribner's, 1951), 265–66; "Report of the American Bar Association Special Committee on Communist Tactics, Strategy, and Objectives," *Congressional Record* (August 1958).

### Disraeli, Benjamin

> Under this roof are the heads of the family of Rothschilds—a name famous in every capital of Europe and every division of the Globe. If you like, we shall divide the United States into two parts, one for you, James, and one for you, Lionel. Napoleon III will do exactly what . . . I shall advise him. C

While the first sentence is accurate, the rest is a fabrication by the old radio priest, Father Charles Coughlin, who cited John Reeves's *The Rothschilds,* out of print since 1887. Proving Coughlin a liar, the *Chicago Daily News* noted what

Disraeli actually said was, "a family not more regarded for its riches than esteemed for its honor, virtues, and public spirit." Boller and George, 21.

> The people of God co-operate with Communism . . . [the Jews] touch the hand of all the scum and low castes of Europe . . . because they want to destroy Christianity. C

Gerald L. K. Smith spread this one. It first surfaced in *The Church Times* (April 13, 1923) more than forty years after Disraeli's death, which occurred long before Communism became a "big deal." Boller and George, 22.

### Dukakis, Michael

> I do not believe in people owning guns, only police and military. I am going to do everything I can to disarm this state. C

The Massachusetts governor and 1988 Democratic presidential candidate made this statement in June 1986, according to *American Hunter* magazine (October 1988). Dukakis not only didn't say it, but had answered an NRA questionnaire that same year in which he supported private ownership of weapons "for sport and personal protection." What Dukakis did write to a constituent was that handguns should be restricted to "legitimate sports persons under licensed and controlled conditions," and, of course, to police and security personnel. *Washington Post Weekly* (October 3–9, 1988), 11.

### Eisenhower, Dwight

> The John Birch Society is a good, patriotic society. I don't agree with what its founder said about me but that does not detract from the fact that its membership is comprised of many fine Americans dedicated to the preservation of our libertarian Republic. C

This one was featured in a 1964 John Birch Society advertising supplement in the *Los Angeles Times.* Birch public relations man John Rousselot claimed he heard Ike say it on TV, but was unable to offer any documentation. A spokesperson for Eisenhower stated that the quotation was not authorized and was not correct. He added that the general was certain that among Birch members there "are many devoted citizens sincerely dedicated to the United States." Boller and George, 24.

### Franklin, Benjamin

> In whatever country Jews have settled in any great numbers, they have lowered the moral tone, depreciated the commercial integrity, have segregated themselves, and have not assimilated, have sneered at and tried to undermine the Christian religion,

have built up a state within a state, and have, when opposed, tried to strangle that country to death financially.

If you do not exclude them from the United States, in the Constitution, in less than 200 years they will have swarmed in such great numbers that they will dominate and devour the land and change our form of government. C

Featured in numerous anti-Semitic periodicals and pamphlets since the thirties, this "prophecy" evidently originated in the February 3, 1934, issue of *Liberation*. The publisher of the screed was William Dudley Pelley, founder and leader of the Nazi group, Silver Shirts, who attributed it to notes taken by Charles C. Pinckney at the Constitutional Convention. Supposedly including informal talk between sessions, this "Pinckney diary," entitled (by Pelley?) "Chit-Chats Around the Table During Intermissions," does not exist. Historian Charles Beard investigated the Franklin "prophecy" and called it a "crude forgery." Boller and George, 26.

> I fully agree with Gen. Washington that we must safeguard this young nation, as yet in its swaddling clothes, from the insidious influence and impenetration of the Roman Catholic Church which pauperizes and degrades all countries and people over whom it holds sway. C

The same lovely folks have tried to make Franklin both a Jew-hater and a Catholic-hater. This Papist-bashing utterance is sometimes presented as a lead-in to the more infamous Franklin anti-Semitic quote from an evidently nonexistent Charles Pinckney diary. Colonel E. N. Sanctuary, a native American fascist of the thirties and forties, featured this item in his *Exposure of the Franklin "Prophecy"* (1943), never published, but located with his papers in the Wilcox Collection, University of Kansas, Lawrence. (See Franklin anti-Semitic quote and Pinckney anti-Semitic quote.) Boller and George, 28.

## Gaither, Rowan

> The overall aim of the Ford Foundation is to so alter life in the U.S. that we can be comfortably merged with the Soviet Union. Q-P

Often when a source is given for this attribution it is *Tax Exempt Foundations, Hearings, 82nd Congress, 2nd Session on House Resolution 461,* Novem-18–December 30, 1952. Usually no source is given and, indeed, the statement most often is not attributed to Gaither or anyone else. John Birch Society leader Robert Welch used it in this manner in the JBS *Bulletin* (February 1971 and September 1973) and in *Wild Statements* (1965). In such cases the Ford Foundation is not mentioned either. In the September 1973 *Bulletin,* Welch wrote in reference to President Richard Nixon: "One basic directive under which he has been working, let us repeat and keep repeating is: 'So to change the economic and political structure of the United States that it can be comfortably merged with Soviet Russia.' "

Evidently first to link Gaither's name with the idea of merging with the Soviet Union was Norman Dodd, a friend of Welch, who claimed that in 1953 at Gaither's Ford Foundation office the following conversation occurred:

Gaither:    Mr. Dodd, we operate here under directives which emanate from the White House. Would you like to know what the substance of those directives is?

Dodd:    Indeed I would, Mr. Gaither.

Gaither:    We here operate and control our grant making policies in harmony with directives the substance of which is as follows: We shall use our grant making power so as to alter life in the United States that it can be comfortably merged with the Soviet Union.

The foregoing was part of Dodd's 1978 testimony before the Illinios Joint Legislative Committtee on Regional Government.

The main questions here are: (1) How credible was Mr. Dodd? (2) When did he first claim Gaither uttered this alarming mouthful? (3) Why didn't he publicize it before the mid-1960s?

People who knew Gaither find Dodd's claim preposterous. Letter to John George from Richard Magat, director, Office of Reports, Ford Foundation, July 16, 1970; *Bulletin*—Committee to Restore the Constitution, December 1989; *The Report of Norman Dodd, Director of Research of The Special Committee of The House of Representatives to Investigate Tax Exempt Foundations* for the six months period November 1, 1953–April 30, 1954 (New Canaan, Conn.: The Long House, 1954).

## Gorbachev, Mikhail

Gentlemen, comrades do not be concerned about all you hear about Glasnost and democracy. . . .These are primarily for outward consumption. . . . There will be no serious internal change within the Soviet Union other than for cosmetic purposes. . . . Our purpose is to disarm America and let them fall asleep. . . . We want to accomplish three things:

1) We want the Americans to withdraw conventional forces from Europe.
2) We want them to withdraw nuclear forces from Europe. . . .
3) We want the Americans to stop proceeding with the Strategic Defense Initiative. C

Soviet leader Gorbachev supposedly revealed this information to a meeting of the Politburo in November 1987. How or where the Cincinnati-based periodical *Criminal Politics* (December 1989) obtained it, they evidently did not seem to know. Their office manager's response to our inquiry stated that they had "files full of articles" and didn't "have the staff or time to go back and find" this rather amazing Gorbachevism. *Christian News* (January 8 and 29, and February 26, 1990); *Criminal Politics* (December 1989); letter to John George from Phyllis Theis of *Criminal Politics,* February 8, 1990.

## Gordon, Sol

> All that is good and commendable now existing would continue to exist if all marriage laws were repealed tomorrow. I have an inalienable constitutional and natural right to love whom I may . . . to change that love every day if I please. C

This statement does not appear in Gordon's *Facts About Sex for Today's Youth,* as some rightists have claimed. The origin seems to have been *The Unbelievable Truth About Your Public Schools,* distributed by the Council for National Righteousness, Buffalo, New York. Dr. Gordon has complained that those opposed to him merely used to quote him "out of context—now they blatantly compose their own statements."

Interestingly, Gordon is author of *Raising a Child Conservatively in a Sexually Permissive World* (New York: Simon and Schuster, 1983). Boller and George, 43.

## Hall, Gus

> I dream of the hour when the last Congressman is strangled to death on the guts of the last preacher—and since the Christians seem to love to sing about the blood, why not give them a little of it? Slit the throats of their children and drag them over the mourners' bench and the pulpit and allow them to drown in their own blood; and then see whether they enjoy singing these hymns. C

Supposedly stated at the 8th National Convention of the Young Communist League (1937) and at the funeral of Eugene Dennis (February 1961), this bloodcurdler most likely originated with Jean Meslier (1664-1729) from his will published by Voltaire in 1733: "I would like to see . . . the last king strangled with the guts of the last priest." Meslier's *Testament* was one of the most thorough assaults on Christianity ever written.

Whether variations of Meslier's wish have been attributed to others is not known, but the first denunciation of Gus Hall in this regard seems to have been by the old right extremist, Kenneth Goff, in his *Pilgrim Touch* (April 1961). Nineteen years later, Jerry Falwell's Moral Majority used it in their multimedia presentation, *America You're Too Young to Die.*

Of course, no Communist, Nazi, or any other party leader would make such a ridiculous statement and, if some loon did, certainly the print media would carry it. No reporters at Eugene Dennis's funeral heard any such words. Boller and George, 44.

## Hitler, Adolf

. . . basically National Socialism and Communism are the same. D

Hitler did say something very similar to this, but he used the word "Marxism" rather than "Communism" and went on to say that the Nazis did not come to power to defend class interests, but to bring about the unity of the German nation. Since Hitler attacked Marxism on numerous occasions, it is surprising he referred to it in this way. As Friedrich Hayek put it: "Whatever may have been his reasons, Hitler thought it expedient to declare in one of his public speeches as late as February 1941, that 'basically National Socialism and Marxism are the same.' "

In this regard, it is well to remember two facts:

1. The economic system of Nazi Germany was basically capitalist.
2. Virtually all Communists have considered themselves Marxists but *many* Marxists have not been Communists, and, indeed, some have been anti-Communists. *Bulletin of International News* 18(5): 269; Friedrich A. Hayek, *The Road to Serfdom* (Chicago: Phoenix Books, University of Chicago Press, 1944), 30.

Knowledge is the ruin to my young men. Q

The great strength of the totalitarian state is that it forces those who fear it to imitate it. Q–P

Question: Did the word "totalitarian" exist as a German word before World War II?

The most foolish mistake we could make would be to let the subjected races possess arms. Q–P

The magnitude of a lie always contains a certain factor of credibility, since the great masses of people . . . tend to be corrupted . . . they more easily fall victim to the big lie . . . since they themselves lie in little things, but would be ashamed of lies that were too big. D

Hitler and his pal Goebbels obviously followed this dictum, but in *Mein Kampf,* Adolf, ever the consummate anti-Semite, actually attributes this technique to "the Jews." As Lenin accused his enemies of believing that "promises, like pie crust, are made to be broken," Hitler accused "the Jews" of using the Big Lie technique. Ralph Manheim translation of *Mein Kampf* (Boston: Houghton Mifflin, 1943), 231–32.

The streets of our country are in turmoil. The universities are filled with students rebelling and rioting. Communists are seeking to destroy our country. Russia is threatening us with her might, and the republic is in danger. Yes, danger from within and from without. We need law and order! Yes, without law and order our nation cannot survive. . . . Elect us and we shall restore law and order. We shall by law and order be respected among the nations of the world. Without law and order our republic shall fall. (Excerpt from a campaign speech made in Hamburg in 1932.) C

Making its appearance during the presidential campaign of 1968, this fake had wide circulation in the late sixties and early seventies, especially among radical leftists. It was used in the 1971 movie *Billy Jack* and also was made into a poster. Intensive research into Hitler's works proved fruitless as did inquiries to the Library of Congress, the West German Embassy, the Institute for Contemporary History in Munich, and Justice William O. Douglas, who asked his publisher to remove the utterance from his book, *Points of Rebellion.* As philosopher Sidney Hook observed, the only German university "students rebelling and rioting" in 1932 were young Nazi types protesting against Jewish professors. Letter to John George from Joachim Schonbeck, acting press counselor, West German embassy, August 14, 1970, stating that the Institute for Contemporary History was not able to verify the Hitler quote; letter to John George from Terry Watts (undated, received in the early 1970s) reporting that Justice Douglas's secretary, Fay Aull, replied to his inquiry that the Library of Congress could not authenticate the Hitler quote; John George phone conversation with Sidney Hook, Janaury 31, 1988; Sidney Hook, *Out of Step: An Unquiet Life in the Twentieth Century* (New York: Harper & Row, 1987), 588.

### Humanist Manifesto II (1973)

There should be no restraint on any expression of human sexuality. Unbridled sexuality is not immoral. In fact it is healthful and good. C

This spurious utterance appeared in *Pat Robertson's Perspective* (Fall 1981). Since *Humanist Manifesto II* is only eleven pages long it is fairly easy to determine that no words resembling the ones used by Robertson appear. In fact, a key phrase is almost in diametric opposition: "Without countenancing mindless permissiveness or unbridled promiscuity, a civilized society should be a tolerant one." Boller and George, 51.

### Ickes, Harold

What we were striving for was a kind of modified form of communism. P

President Ronald Reagan used this saying in December 1981. But Arthur Schlesinger, who read all of Ickes's diaries, found nothing of this sort in them. Boller and George, 52.

### Ingersoll, Robert

I would rather be the humblest peasant that ever lived than the greatest Christian that ever lived. C

Bawl-and-jump evangelist Billy Sunday first used this on May 26, 1912, and it has been utilized by fundamentalists since that time. What Colonel Ingersoll actually said in his address at the tomb of Napoleon was that he "would rather have been a French peasant and worn wooden shoes . . . and gone down to the tongueless silence of the dreamless dust, than to have been that imperial impersonation of murder and force, known as 'Napoleon the Great.' " Boller and George, 52.

### Jefferson, Thomas

That government is best which governs least. C

While certainly an intriguing thought, there is no evidence linking it to Jefferson. Boller and George, 56.

### Khrushchev, Nikita

Deception and drugs are our first two strategic echelons in the war with capitalism. Q–P

Supposedly uttered by Mr. Khrushchev in 1963, this "admission" appears in quotation form on the back cover of *Red Cocaine: The Drugging of America* (1990), but not as a quotation in the book itself (p. 49). The author, Joseph Douglass, said that the source is General Jan Sejna, a 1968 Czech defector. Douglass stated that Sejna is a reliable source. Strangely, Sejna mentioned nothing about this startling Khrushchevian utterance in his *We Will Bury You* (1982), nor does there seem to be any mention of it by anyone prior to the 1980s. Soviet specialists Carl Linden (George Washington University), Sidney Ploss (State Department), Joseph Whalen (Library of Congress), Peter Rodman (Foreign Policy Institute), and V. Stanley Vardys (University of Oklahoma) all found such words by Khrushchev highly unlikely.

We cannot expect the Americans to jump from capitalism to communism, but we can aid their elected leaders in giving them small doses of socialism until they suddenly awake to find they have communism. C

Soviet leader Nikita Khrushchev, it has been alleged, made this statement to a secret party meeting three and a half months before leaving on his visit to the United States in 1959. How it leaked out never was made clear. But the statement was actually concocted early in 1960 by two radical rightists and a moderate conservative who had infiltrated their group. The rightists felt it explained Khrushchev's attitude, and the infiltrator collaborated with them just to see if the quote would catch on with the far right. It did. Senator Strom Thurmond of South Carolina read it into the *Congressional Record* for July 26, 1961, and former FBI informant Herbert Philbrick gave it wide distribution in the 1960s, printing it on a bright red sticker with the information that the pudgy premier had said it several months before coming to the United States. But the CIA, the Library of Congress, J. Edgar Hoover, Senator James Eastland (then chair of the Senate Internal Security Subcommittee), and Congressman Francis Walter (then chair of the House Un-American Activities Committee) were, of course, unable to find a source for it. *Congressional Record* (March 8, 1962), 3676, remarks of Senator Lee Metcalf of Montana; John George, in conversation with one of the originators of the quote in 1970; Donald Janson, "Rules for Revolt Viewed as Durable Fraud," *New York Times* (July 10, 1970), 30.

Iran is like an apple—when it is ripe it will fall into our lap. C

According to *Newsweek* (January 21, 1980, 37), Princess Ashraf of Iran claimed that Khrushchev made this statement to her. When queried, Peter Sprague of *Newsweek* stated: "We have grilled the two *Newsweek* correspondents who claim familiarity with the quote and both aver that it is genuine—though we're aware that journalists' memories, like the apple, ripen with age." The likely alternative is that Princess Ashraf imagined or concocted the utterance. Letter to John George from Peter Sprague, April 15, 1980.

We will take this nation without firing a shot. It will fall into our hands like an over-ripe fruit. (See Lenin Overripe Fruit) C

We will bury you. D

At the National Press Club in September 1959, Premier Khrushchev was questioned about this remark by conservative columnist and editor of *U.S. News and World Report,* David Lawrence. Khrushchev explained that he had said something of the sort but insisted that he had not meant "the physical burial of any people but the question of historical force of development." He then used a typical Marxist analysis to explain how his nation's economic system would, as it were, bury ours, or, as he put it, "capitalism thereby would be, so to speak, buried." Some Russian speakers have maintained that a better translation is "we will leave you in the dust." Either way, history has proved Khrushchev dead wrong. *New York Times* (September 17, 1959).

You Americans are so gullible. No, you won't accept Communism outright, but we'll keep feeding you small doses of Socialism until you'll finally wake up and find you already have Communism. We won't have to fight you. We'll so weaken your economy until you'll fall like an overripe fruit into our hands. C

This superb doublefake, along with other spurious utterances, is featured in *Wake-Up America* by Robert L. Preston, who cited former Agriculture Secretary Ezra Taft Benson as his source. Benson claimed he heard old Nikita say it during his 1959 visit to the United States.

Since 1954 when the spurious "overripe fruit" quote was first attributed to Lenin, it also has been assigned to Mao, Stalin, and Khrushchev. (See Lenin "overripe fruit" quote.) The Khrushchev "doses of socialism" quote was concocted by three Americans in 1960 several months *after* the Soviet leader's visit to the United States. (See Khrushchev "doses of socialism" quote.) Both quotes had wide usage in American rightist circles during the sixties and early seventies. Given these facts, does it not seem quite likely that Mr. Benson's memory became faulty and, writing nine years later, he simply imagined that Khrushchev combined two fake quotes (previously etched in Benson's mind)? This kind of mix-up in human recollection is common. Ezra Taft Benson, *An Enemy Hath Done This* (Salt Lake: Parliament Publishers, 1969), 320; *Congressional Record* (March 8, 1962), 3676, remarks of Senator Lee Metcalf of Montana; Donald Janson, "Rules for Revolt Viewed as Durable Fraud," *New York Times* (July 10, 1970), 30; Karl E. Meyer, "The Elusive Lenin," *New York Times* (October 8, 1985), 26; Harry and Bonaro Overstreet, *The Strange Tactics of Extremism* (New York: Norton, 1964), 68–74.

## Kissinger, Henry

The American people lack the will and stamina to do what is necessary to keep this country #1. P

Kissinger denied this statement on numerous occasions and no one ever showed evidence of his saying it, according to Green and MacCall in *Ronald Reagan's Reign of Error* (1983).

The day of the U.S. is past and today is the day of the Soviet Union. P

Kissinger strongly denied the quote and State Department counselor Lawrence Eagleburger called it "pure invention." Boller and George, 61.

## Knights of Columbus

I do further promise and declare that I will, when opportunity presents, make and wage relentless war, secretly and openly, against all heretics, Protestants, and Masons, as I am directed to do, to extirpate them from the face of the whole earth; and that I will spare neither age, sex, nor condition, and that I will hang, burn, waste, boil, flay, strangle, and bury alive those infamous heretics; rip up the stomachs and wombs of their women, and crush their infants' heads against the walls in order to annihilate their execrable race. C

Exposed as phony by a special congressional committee in 1913, the bogus oath continued to be used by anti-Catholics throughout the nation. It cropped up during the 1928 and 1960 elections to warn of such dangerous Catholics as Al Smith and John Kennedy. Boller and George, 62.

## Lenin, V. I.

As long as capitalism and socialism exist, we cannot live in peace; in the end one or the other will triumph—a funeral dirge will be sung over the Soviet Republic or over world capitalism. D

This is a classic example of a distorted quotation utilizing "contextomy," since the next two sentences are "This is a respite in war. The capitalists will seek pretexts for fighting." Hence Lenin was saying that the capitalist world would not leave Soviet Russia alone, not vice versa. V. I. Lenin, *Selected Works* (New York: International Publishers, 1943), 297.

The capitalists will sell us the rope with which to hang them. P

One of the most widely used questionable attributions, this was supposedly attributed to Uncle Vladimir by his extreme left hand man, Gregori Zinoviev, not long after an early 1920s Politburo gathering. Evidently no documentation exists and communism expert Abraham Brumberg has called it spurious. Boller and George, 64.

First, we will take eastern Europe, then the masses of Asia, then we will encircle the United States which will be the last bastion of capitalism. We will not have to attack. It will fall like an overripe fruit into our hands. C

Not the oldest, but probably the most widely utilized of all phony quotations, the "overripe fruit" made its first appearance during Soviet defector Nicholas Goncharoff's July 1954 testimony before the Senate Internal Security Subcommittee. Whether Goncharoff originated this classic may never be known, but extreme left claims that it was concocted by Joseph Goebbels are totally without supporting evidence. John Birch Society founder Robert Welch used to aver that, while not actual, the quote constituted a summary of Lenin's strategy. Thus far, no one has produced this alleged strategy.

The highest art of war is not to fight at all, but to subvert your enemy by destroying his moral principles, his religion, his culture, his whole tradition. When a country is demoralized, you can take it without firing a shot. C

Featured in the South African newsletter, *Signposts,* this puts another preface on the idea of takeover without violent conflict. These words are not found in Lenin's *Collected Works. Signposts* 6, no. 3 (1987): 2; letter to John George from

Alfred Kutzik, director of the Reference Center for Marxist Studies in New York, July 22, 1988.

> It is, in fact, you who will, through your own cupidity, give us the means wherewith to destroy you. P

Senator Daniel Patrick Moynihan used this one in 1986. Two inquiries, two and a half months apart, brought no answer from his office. Someone there did, however, start sending his newsletter. Nothing like this is found in Lenin's *Collected Works*. *Insight* (September 8, 1986), 9; letter to John George from Alfred Kutzik, director of the Reference Center for Marxist Studies in New York, July 22, 1988.

> Millions of sins, filthy deeds, acts of violence, and physical contagions are far less dangerous than the subtle idea of a god. D

Furnishing another example of the distorted quote, this one cut off the wily Vladimir Ilyich before the end of his sentence. Lenin was speaking of "the subtle spiritual idea of a god *decked out in the smartest 'ideological' costumes.*" (Emphasis ours.) V. I. Lenin, "Letters to A. M. Gorkii," *Selected Works* (New York: International Publishers, 1943), 412.

> The road to Paris lies through Peking. C

Although not nearly so popular as the "overripe fruit" quote this one has been around since at least the late 1950s. Abraham Brumberg, former editor of *Problems of Communism,* has placed it on his list of phony Leninisms. Boller and George, 72.

> To tell the truth—this is a petty bourgeoisie prejudice. A lie, on the other hand, often justifies the goal. The capitalists of the world and their governments, in pursuit of the Soviet Market, close their eyes to the actuality pointed out above and become deaf, dumb and blind. They open credits which help us maintain the communist party in their countries and, equipping us with materials and technology that are in short supply among us, they rehabilitate our war industry which we need for future victorious attacks against our providers. In other words, they will work for their own suicide. P

Found in none of Lenin's works, this mouthful seems the product of an artist named Yuri Annenkov, who claims to have copied it from notes in Lenin's handwriting at the Lenin Institute in Moscow. Yuri Annenkov, "Recollections of Lenin," *Novyi Zhurnal* (#65, 1961), 147; William Safire column entitled "Lenin May or May Not Have Said," distributed by New York Times News Service, undated, but received April 29, 1987.

> Those in the West who aid our cause are useful idiots. P

Actually, we were forced to construct the above quote with the exception of the words "useful idiots." This became necessary because although we often have encountered these two words attributed to Lenin, that is all. Arnold Beichman of the Hoover Institution, a conservative think tank at Stanford University, believes that an artist named Yuri Annenkov may have first put the phrase into general circulation. Boller and George, 76.

> We must hate—hatred is the basis of communism. Children may be taught to hate their parents if they are not communists. If they are, then the child need not respect them; need no longer worry about them. P

This is one of three probable phonies read into the *Congressional Record* by Senator Arthur Robinson of Indiana in 1933. No such words have been located in Lenin's writings. *Congressional Record* (April 12, 1933), 1539.

> We must secure the good will of teachers and professors, of liberal ministers of religion and of the pacifists and reformers of the world in order to create a mental barrage in the minds of capitalist youth, which shall forever bar them from participating in a carnal conflict with the Communist order. P

This attention-grabber appeared in the *Fourteenth Report of the Senate Investigating Committee on Education,* California Legislature, 1956 Budget Session (p. 25). It is actually a cut-down version of a series of quotes attributed to Lenin, Stalin, Rykoff, and Bukharin.

John Norpell, then director of research of the Senate Internal Security Subcommittee, stated that he was unable to verify the quote and that it was "unfamiliar to our former research director and personnel knowledgeable in the Soviet field at the Library of Congress." Gerald Hayward, assistant consultant for the Senate Committee on Education, California Legislature, wrote in 1970 that the Senate Investigating Committee on Education was defunct and that he thought the quote "spurious and perhaps a product of the McCarthy era." Boller and George, 75.

> The world cannot exist half slave and half free; it must be all slave. C

Concocted by Senator Joseph McCarthy in 1953.

> The best way to destroy capitalism is to debauch the currency. P

Boller and George, 64.

> When the capitalist world starts to trade with us—on that day they will begin to finance their own destruction. C

Boller and George, 64.

One would like to caress the masses, but one doesn't dare; like a dog they will turn and bite. C

Boller and George, 65.

Corrupt the young of a nation and the battle is won. C

Undermining a nation through corruption of the young is a recurring theme in concocted quotes attributed to Soviets. The spurious short document, *Rules for Revolution,* begins this way. Boller and George, 65.

If there had been in Petrograd in 1917 a group of only a thousand men who knew what they wanted, we could never have come to power in Russia. P

Boller and George, 66.

We will find our most fertile field for infiltration of Marxism within the field of religion, because religious people are the most gullible. C

Boller and George, 66.

The first step in overthrowing a government is to establish a firearms registration law. C

This one misses badly. Communists only want arms control in nations already under *their* control. In nations where they seek power, they oppose arms control.

If you have five enemies, first ally yourself with four to destroy the one most dangerous. Then ally with three to destroy the fourth, and so on until you have only one enemy left, and you can take care of him yourself. P

This Machiavellian homily is far older than Lenin.

Why should freedom of speech and press be allowed? Why should a government which is doing what it believes to be right allow itself to be criticized? P

Lenin very probably believed these ideas, but there is no evidence that he ever gave expression to them. Boller and George, 67.

Give me a child for eight years and it will be a Bolshevist forever. C

This one also has been attributed to Catholic and Nazi leaders. There is no evidence that any of them said it. Boller and George, 68.

Our immediate aim is world conquest. Soviet domination recognizes neither liberty nor justice. . . . Repression is our right. . . . we shall reduce humanity to a state of docile submission to our domination. C

Only people who believe that Lenin *knew* he was evil and the West was good could buy this one. Boller and George, 68.

It is inconceivable that communism and democracy can exist side by side in this world. Inevitably one must perish. C

Since Lenin actually claimed to believe that democracy and communism were compatible, it is most unlikely he would make such a "prediction." Boller and George, 69.

Destroying all opposition by invective, slander, smear, and blackmail is one of the techniques of communism. C

Billy James Hargis used this in the 1960s. His scrupulously honest research director, Julian Williams, told him Lenin said no such thing. Boller and George, 70.

Promises are like pie crust, made to be broken. D

This is a classic example of out-of-context usage. Lenin was saying his enemies, not he, believed this, just as Hitler attributed the Big Lie technique not to himself, but to "the Jews." Psychologists call this projection—accusing others of what you yourself believe. Boller and George, 72.

National health insurance is the keystone in the arch of the socialized state.

Or the alternative version:

The best way to communize any country is to socialize its medical profession. C

Boller and George, 73.

We shall force the U.S. to spend itself into destruction. C

This may have originated at the Timken Roller Bearing Co. in Ohio. Lenin never said it. Boller and George, 74.

What does it matter if three-fourths of the world perish, if the remaining one-fourth is Communist? C

The fertile mind of Soviet defector Nicholas T. Goncharoff may have created this scary utterance, since he seems to have been first to use it (in testimony before the Senate Internal Security Subcommittee in 1954). A variation has been atttibuted to Mao. Boller and George, 75.

> Give me an organization of professional revolutionaries and I will turn the world upside down. D

What Lenin actually wrote in *What Is To Be Done* was that his cohorts were "acting as amateurs at a moment in history when we might have been able to say: 'Give us an organization of revolutionaries, and we will overturn Russia.' " Boller and George, 76.

> We will win the Western world for Communism without shedding a drop of a single Russian soldier's blood. How? . . . We will create fear, suspicion . . . religious antagonisms. . . . We will inaugurate campaigns to hate Jews . . . Catholics . . . Negroes. . . . We will do these things. C

There is no evidence that Lenin believed stirring up such ethnic and religious animosity was the way to bring about Marxist revolution. Boller and George, 77.

> Once we have gained control of American newspapers, magazines, and communications, capitalism will die. C

Created in 1970 by a person known to us, this Leninism has not been widely circulated.

> To enslave people, first locate the guns. C

Lenin, to put it mildly, was not a very nice fellow, but he did not speak nor write of enslaving people.

> It is inconceivable that the Soviet Republic should continue to exist . . . side by side with imperialistic states. Ultimately one or the other must conquer. P

Ronald Reagan used this along with six other spurious quotes in a 1961 speech. It sounds somewhat like a real Leninism from his *Selected Works* (vol. 8, 297). But quote-distorters have used only the first part of it: "As long as capitalism and socialism exist, we cannot live in peace . . . a funeral dirge will be sung either over the Soviet Republic and communism or over world capitalism." Accurate so far, but the next lines change the meaning: "This is a respite in war. The capitalists will find the pretexts for fighting."

> The only way to control the masses is through mass terror. C

Lenin believed in the use of terror but it is unlikely he would write of using "mass terror" against the masses.

The West are wishful thinkers. We will give them what they want to think. P

We must be ready to employ trickery, deceit, law breaking, withholding and concealing the truth. We can and must write in a language which sows among the masses, hate, revulsion and scorn for those who disagree. D–C

This is partly distortion and partly concoction based on a passage from Lenin's *Left Wing Communism: An Infantile Disorder,* in which he gives instructions on joining right-wing trade unions whose leaders "resort to every trick . . . to prevent Communists from getting into" their organizations. Lenin wrote that revolutionaries should "resort to all sorts of devices . . . illegal methods . . . evasion and subterfuge . . . to carry on Communist work" inside such unions. Letter to John George from Alfred Kutzik, director of the Reference Center for Marxist Studies, July 22, 1988.

## Lincoln, Abraham

All that loves labor serves the nation. All that harms labor is treason to America. . . . There is no America without labor. C

Honest Abe has been falsely quoted with this item by far, and not so far, leftists. Boller and George, 77.

I do not pretend to be a prophet. But . . . I see a very dark cloud on our horizon . . . coming from Rome. It is filled with tears of blood. . . . After it is over, there will be long days of peace and prosperity: for Popery with its Jesuits and merciless Inquisition, will have been forever swept away from our country. C

Known as "Lincoln's Warning," this anti-Catholic quote was concocted by ex-priest Charles Chiniquy. Boller and George, 79.

You cannot bring prosperity by discouraging thrift.

You cannot further the brotherhood of man by encouraging class hatred.

You cannot help the poor by destroying the rich.

You cannot estabish sound security on borrowed money. C

These are but four "CANNOTS" written not by Lincoln but by the Reverend W. J. H. Boetcker between 1916 and 1945. Boller and George, 83.

From whence then will danger come? If this nation is to be destroyed, it will be destroyed from within. C

Senator Joseph McCarthy used this in 1953 and rightists followed his lead in ensuing years, implying that Lincoln foresaw Red infiltration. Boller and George, 85.

## Long, Huey

> When the U.S. gets fascism it will call it 100% Americanism. D

The far and not-so-far left has used this distortion. What Long said, though perhaps not exactly in these words, was, "When the U.S. gets fascism, it will call it anti-fascism." Boller and George, 94.

## Lunacharsky, Anatole

> We hate Christianity and Christians. Even the best of them must be considered our worst enemies. They preach love of one's neighbor and mercy which is contrary to our principles. Christian love is an obstacle to the development of the revolution. Down with love of our neighbor. What we want is hatred. We must know how to hate. Only thus will we conquer the universe. P

According to the incredibly questionable source, Nicholas T. Goncharoff, this brutal manifesto was set forth by Lunarcharsky in 1935 when he was Soviet minister of education. Goncharoff hit the Senate Internal Security Subcommittee with this zinger during the same testimony in which he put forward a number of spurious extractions: the Manuilsky "clinched fist," and the Lenin "overripe fruit," "three-quarters killed," and "road to Paris" quotes.

Perhaps the important question is how many of these did Goncharoff himself concoct? He did not originate the Lunacharsky item, as it had appeared in the *Congressional Record* as early as 1933, negating Goncharoff's claim that the crafty Anatole said it in 1935. *Congressional Record* (April 12, 1933), 1539; *Strategies and Tactics of World Communism,* testimony of Nicholas T. Goncharoff before the Senate Internal Security Subcommittee, July 15, 1954.

## Manuilsky, Dimitri

> War to the hilt between Capitalism and Communism is inevitable. . . . To win we will need the element of surprise. The bourgeoisie will have to be put to sleep. So we will begin by launching the most spectacular peace movement on record. There will be electrifying overtures and unheard of concessions. The capitalist countries, stupid and decadent, will rejoice to cooperate in their own destruction. They will leap at another chance to be friends. As soon as their guard is down we will smash them with our clenched fist. C

This "war to the hilt/clenched fist" statement was supposedly given by Manuilsky to a group of students at the "Lenin School of Political Warfare" in either 1930, 1931, or 1949. "Devious Dimitri" never said any such thing and the Lenin School of Political Warfare has never existed except in the minds of the uninformed. Boller and George, 97.

## Mao Tse-tung

> With Asia and Africa disconnected with the capitalist countries of Europe, there will be a total economic collapse in Western Europe. There [sic] capitulation will be a matter of course. P

This quote is from "An Outline of Mao Tse Tung's Memorandum on New Program for World Revolution" read into the *Congressional Record* in 1954 by Senator William Knowland of California. The memorandum is allegedly from a Mao letter to Stalin delivered by Chou En-Lai in March 1953, and is of highly questionable authenticity, especially in light of the fact that Stalin died on March 5 of that year. Mao was supposed to have been a fairly perceptive fellow. Would he really have believed that Western Europe would collapse if Asia and Africa were "disconnected" from it? *Congressional Record* (April 29, 1954), 5707-8.

> Even if 300,000,000 Chinese were killed in an atomic war, there would still remain 300,000,000. P

On the basis of this quotation, millions of Americans once believed that Mao was willing to risk—nay, would even welcome—a nuclear war because millions of Chinese would survive it. Similar statements have been attributed to Chou En-Lai and Foreign Minister Chen Yi. A variation has been attributed to Lenin.

A possible source for this Mao quote was a speech given by Yugoslavia's Marshal Tito in Belgrade in 1958 (at a time when Belgrade and Peking were snarling at each other), which Elie Abel reported in the *New York Times.* According to Abel's dispatch from Belgrade on June 16: "Without mentioning names or places Marshal Tito said the Chinese liked to boast that their population of 600,000,000 was a guarantee of victory in war."

In 1957, Mao wrote about nuclear war: "If . . . half of mankind died, the other half would remain, while imperialism would be razed to the ground, and the whole world would become socialist; in a number of years there would be 2.7 billion people again." *Time* (September 20, 1976), 38.

> Surround the U.S. in a Communist world. They will fall into our hands like a piece of overripe fruit. C

The source given for this Maoism is a probably nonexistent letter to Stalin, supposedly carried to Moscow by Chou En-Lai in March 1953. Interestingly, Stalin died on March 5 of that year. Senator William Knowland of California read into *Congressional Record* (April 29, 1954, 5708) not the letter (did it ever exist?) but "An Outline of Mao Tse Tung's Memorandum on New Program for World Revolution." This rather odd item does not contain the "surround the U.S." quote. It does, however, say that the "United States must be isolated by all means possible," which would not be an unusual statement for Mao, but there seems to be no evidence pointing toward authenticity for this memorandum. Indeed, one might ask how Senator Knowland acquired it, as he did not so state and it evidently has been edited since the second paragraph has these words in parenthesis: "Communist terminology is different, this represents what it really means."

What we are left with is an edited version of a Mao letter of highly questionable authenticity which doesn't even contain the claimed quote. And, of course, we have again that old "overripe fruit," which has been attached to Lenin, Stalin, and Khrushchev in addition to Mao.

## Marx, Karl

There is only one way to kill capitalism—by taxes, taxes and more taxes. C

This one is rather silly. Only one way? What of revolution?

## Mattox, Jim

The state owns your children. And it owns you too. C

Television evangelist and 1988 presidential candidate Pat Robertson attributed this Orwellian utterance to the Texas attorney general in 1988. Mattox's press secretary called the statement "outrageous." *Dallas Morning News* (March 7, 1988), 1 and 4.

## Menjinsky (Menzhinsky), Vyacheslav

As long as there are idiots who take our signature seriously, and put their trust in it, we must promise everything that is being asked, and as much as one likes, if we can only get something tangible in exchange. P

No shred of evidence exists that the old Soviet secret policeman ever came up with this "cousin" to the Lenin "useful idiots" phrase. *Congressional Record* (April 12, 1933), 1538–43.

## Niemoller, Martin

In Germany they came first for the Communists, and I didn't speak up because I wasn't a Communist. Then they came for the Jews, and I didn't speak up because I wasn't a Jew. Then they came for the trade unionists, and I didn't speak up because I wasn't a trade unionist. Then they came for the Catholics, and I didn't speak up because I was a Protestant. Then they came for me, but by that time no one was left to speak up. P

Used by people from all parts of the political spectrum but especially those on the left, this quote never has featured documentation, and even quotation books often place the word "attributed" under it. William F. Buckley used it in a November 1987 column, but left out the part about Communists.

One clue as to spuriousness is "they came for the Catholics." This, the Nazis did not do. Individual Catholics were taken away, but not for being Catholics, while Jews, Gypsies, and others were carted off en masse simply for being what they were.

## O'Hair, Madalyn Murray

If this petition is successful, we can stop all religious broadcasting in America. C

In the mid-seventies, a petition was filed with the FCC asking that no new applications be granted to religious groups for TV or FM channels reserved for educational stations. About eight months later the FCC denied the petition on First Amendment grounds. But for a considerable number of American fundamentalists this was only the beginning and during the next five years the FCC received over sixty million pieces of mail claiming that atheist Madalyn Murray O'Hair's petition should be denied. O'Hair has never made any statements in this regard nor filed any request with the FCC, but petitions against her *fictitious* petitions were still circulating in 1990. Flo Conway and Jim Siegelman, *Holy Terror* (New York: Doubleday, 1982), 237–39; Bob E. Mathews, "Gullible People Easily Hoodwinked," *The Baptist Messenger* (June 6, 1985); petitions received by John George, 1984 through 1990.

## Pike, Albert

The Masonic religion should be by all of us initiates of the high degrees, maintained in the purity of the Luciferian doctrine. If Lucifer were not God, would Adonay . . . calumniate him? Yes, Lucifer is God.
     Freemasonry entails the fall of all dogmas and the ruin of all churches. P

Rightists who have seen Masonry as an integral part of "The Conspiracy" have attributed all sorts of evil sayings to Pike.

## Pinckney, Charles Coatesworth

For my part I never see any of the dirty fellows but that I would like to spit him on my sword. In less than 200 years if we admit them, the scurry scoundrels will be calling US their ANCESTORS. C

From the same sources as the phony Ben Franklin anti-Jewish warning, this unlovely sentiment supposedly originated in a diary kept by Pinckney which seems never to have existed. American Jew-haters of the 1930s and 1940s maintained that many copies once populated South Carolina but were destroyed when General William T. Sherman razed the libraries in that state. Boller and George, 105; E. N. Sanctuary, *Exposure of the Franklin "Prophecy,"* unpublished, 1943, but located in the Wilcox Collection, University of Kansas, Lawrence.

**Protocols of the Learned Elders of Zion C**

One of, if not *the* most widespread of fabricated documents of the twentieth century, the *Protocols* are purported to be the minutes of a late-nineteenth-century meeting of the world's leading Jews. The ostensible purpose of this "secret" meeting was to plan a Jewish world takeover.

Older Americans who learned of the screed in the 1930s and 1940s may be surprised to discover that it has survived to the present day. Respectable publishers, knowing something of the story behind this concoction, tend to ignore it. Nevertheless, it was still being distributed in the United States and especially in nations such as Egypt, Iran, Iraq, Libya, Saudia Arabia, and Syria in the 1990s.

It is possible here only to hint at the long and complex history of the *Protocols*. Such a document probably would have been worthless as a piece of ideological propaganda prior to about 1870, when political anti-Semitism was beginning to be a factor in European politics, for it was only after the French Revolution that one European country followed another in removing the legal restrictions that bound Jews to the ghetto. Religious anti-Semitism had, of course, existed for many centuries and attacks on Jews for the practice of "ritual murder" were commonplace, as was the claim by some Catholics that Jews were guilty of torturing the consecrated wafer. But religious anti-Semitism was rapidly becoming a thing of the dark past, a medieval aberration, when far rightists introduced political anti-Semitism into European politics.

The modern myth of a Jewish world conspiracy may be traced to the time of the French Revolution, when it was adopted from the centuries-old belief that the Jews worshipped the devil and were masters of black magic.

Today's version of the *Protocols* was concocted by a Russian attorney and strong supporter of the czar named Sergus Nilus. Appearing in his 1905 book *The Great in the Small* and published in pamphlet form thereafter, the *Protocols* spread rapidly throughout Russia. The 1911 edition was the first one in which Nilus featured anything faintly resembling documentation: he claimed a person known to him had stolen the *Protocols* from Zionist headquarters in France. Perhaps due to the fact that Zionist headquarters were never located in France, Nilus changed his story in the 1917 edition and asserted that he received the *Protocols* from an unidentified woman who surreptitiously obtained it from Masonic headquarters.

Of course Nilus's stories are nonsense, as the source of this fabrication has been rather conclusively determined and, indeed, had nothing whatever to do with Jews. The *London Times,* after having been somewhat "taken in" by the document, published in 1921 a series of articles based on evidence obtained by correspondent Phillip Graves which demonstrated that the *Protocols* were a partly plagiarized concoction. The source was an 1865 book by French attorney Maurice Joly called *Dialogue in Hell Between Machiavelli and Montesquieu or The Politics of Machiavelli in the Nineteenth Century.* A satirical work jabbing at the reign of Napoleon III, the *Dialogue* did not fool that despot and Joly was fined 300 francs and sentenced to almost a year and a half in prison. But the Jew-haters grabbed his work and "ran with it," placing the words used by the *Dialogue*'s Machiavelli in the mouths of "Jewish conspirators."

Probably most instrumental in giving the *Protocols* wide distribution during the 1920s was Henry Ford, who serialized it in his paper, the *Dearborn Independent,* under the title "The International Jew." In 1927, however, Ford recanted his belief that the document was authentic.

Summarizing the *Protocols* is a most difficult task, but a commendable effort was made by Albert Chandler, who stated that the main difficulty lay in that document's "incoherent and fantastic nature." Chandler's summary appears in *The Clash of Political Ideals:*

> The Jews were said to have caused the French Revolution. They engineered the successes of Darwinism, Marxism, and Nietzscheism. They work through Masonic lodges everywhere, but kill Masons who know too much in ways that elude all suspicion. They control the world's gold. They control the world's press. Democratic catchwords such as liberty, equality, fraternity unloose the power of the blind mob. For the Jews, "Politics have nothing in common with morals," and "our right lies in might"; also, "our motto is Power and Hypocrisy." Constitutional government promotes wrangling and inefficiency and thus serves Jewish ends. The Jews pose as saviors of the common people by inducing them to join the Socialists, Anarchists, and Communists. They spread an all embracing terror and have persons of all opinions and all parties in their service. They distort laws through contradictory interpretations. They promote "insane, dirty and disgusting literature." They promote freedom of religion, undermine the churches by criticism and dissension, and expect to achieve the early collapse of Christianity. By promoting conflicts of opinion in politics, they will confuse the Gentiles to the point that they give up forming political opinions. They will cause dissension and hatred throughout Europe; if necessary they will provoke a world war in order to achieve universal power. They provoke financial panics. Hungry mobs will sweep away all opposition when the time comes for the Jewish universal rule to be crowned. They have kept their plan secret through many centuries. The Jews' government will have a large corps of economic, legal, and other experts to control the Gentiles by playing upon their tendencies, failings, vices, and virtues. "The King of Israel will become the real Pope of the Universe."

David Bell, "The Jews Left Behind," *The New Republic* (Feb. 18, 1985), 12–14, discusses how the Soviets have pushed the idea of a Jewish conspiracy; Norman Cohn, *Warrant for Genocide* (New York: Harper & Row, 1966); Albert Chandler, *The Clash of Political Ideals* (New York: Appleton Century Crofts, 1957), 190–91; John S. Curtiss, *An Appraisal of the Protocols of Zion* (New York: Columbia University Press, 1942); Kenneth Jacobson, *The Protocols: Myth and History* (New York: ADL, 1981); Albert Lee, *Henry Ford and the Jews* (New York: Stein & Day, 1980); Gustavus Myers, *History of Bigotry* (New York: Capricorn Books, 1960), 295–97; Hans Speier, "Maurice Joly on Modern Despotism," *Polity* (Fall 1977), 25–31; Hugo Valentin, *Antisemitism Historically and Critically Examined* (New York: Viking Press, 1936); Lucien Wolf, *The Truth About the Forged Protocols of the Elders of Zion* (New York: McMillan, 1921).

## Rabinovich, Rabbi Emanuel

> There will be no more religions. Not only would the existence of a priest class remain a constant danger to our rule, but belief in an afterlife would give spiritual strength to irreconcilable elements in many countries and enable them to resist us. C

This item provides not only an example of a fake quote, but also of a fake rabbi. From all evidence both are creations of longtime anti-Semite Eustace Mullins. An informant well acquainted with Mullins told us that the man "has a sense of humor" and has concocted a number of hoaxes including the Israel Cohen "Racial Program for the 20th Century" (see Cohen). Mullins was at one time strongly influenced by the famous fascist poet Ezra Pound.

The above Rabinovich quote and the one following were utilized by anti-Semitic organs throughout the fifties and sixties and still occasionally rear their ugly heads. "A Rabbi Speaks: Foretells Gentile Doom," *Common Sense* VI, 167 (August 1, 1952), 1; Frank P. Mintz, *The Liberty Lobby and the American Right* (Westport, Conn.: Greenhaven, 1985), 59; personal communication, John George with an informant who has known Eustace Mullins since the early fifties.

> We will openly reveal our identity with the races of Asia and Africa. I can state with assurance that the last generation of white children is now being born. Our Control Commissions will . . . forbid whites to mate with whites. . . . Thus the white race will disappear, for mixing the dark with the white means the end of the white man, and our most dangerous enemy will become only a memory. C

Thom Arthur Robb flier (1974) featuring Rabinovich quote; "A Rabbi Speaks: Foretells Gentile Doom," *Common Sense VI,* 167 (August 1, 1952), 1.

## Reuther, Walter

> Carry on the fight for a Soviet America. C

Allegedly from a letter written by the labor leader and his brother, Victor, while visiting the Soviet Union in 1934, this smear was evidently the creation of one Mel Bishop. The Reuthers could accurately be described as anti-Communists. Boller and George, 111.

## Roosevelt, Franklin

> There is nothing wrong with the Communists in this country; several of the best friends I have got are Communists. P

Representative Martin Dies (D-Texas), who chaired the Special Committee on Un-American Activities in the thirties and forties, claimed that Roosevelt said this to him in 1938. If so, why didn't he put it in his 1940 book, *Trojan Horse in America,* or tell someone of it before 1950? Boller and George, 113.

## Rothschild, Amschel

Give me control over a nation's currency and I care not who makes its laws. P

Robert Preston, *Wake Up America* (Salt Lake City: Hawkes Publications, 1972), 31.

Let me issue and control a nation's money and I care not who writes its laws. P

W. B. Venard, *The Federal Reserve Hoax* (Boston: Meador Publishing Co., no date). Venard gives no source. Preston cites Venard but misquotes him. The origin of this may well be the Scot Andrew Fletcher, who lived around the turn of the eighteenth century and who said something like this: "I care not who makes a country's laws, so long as I can write its songs." Letter to John George from John McClaughry, June 14, 1989.

## Rules for Revolution (1919) C

On a dark night in May, 1919, two lorries rumbled across a bridge and on into the town of Dusseldorf. Among the dozen rowdy, singing "Tommies" apparently headed for a gay evening were two representatives of the Allied military intelligence. These men had traced a wave of indiscipline, mutiny, and murder among the troops to the local headquarters of a revolutionary organization established in the town.

Pretending to be drunk, they brushed by the sentries and arrested the ringleaders—a group of thirteen men and women seated at a long table.

In the course of the raid the Allied officers emptied the contents of the safe. One of the documents found in it contained a specific outline of "Rules for Bringing About a Revolution." It is reprinted here to show the strategy of materialistic revolution, and how personal attitudes and habits of living affect the affairs of nations:

"A. Corrupt the young. Get them away from religion. Get them interested in sex. Make them superficial, destroy their ruggedness.

"B. Get control of all means of publicity and thereby:

1. Get people's minds off their government by focusing their attention on athletics, sexy books and plays, and other trivialities.
2. Divide the people into hostile groups by constantly harping on controversial matters of no importance.
3. Destroy the people's faith in their natural leaders by holding these latter up to ridicule, obloquy, and contempt.
4. Always preach true democracy, but seize power as fast and as ruthlessly as possible.
5. By encouraging government extravagance, destroy its credit, produce fear of inflation with rising prices and general discontent.
6. Foment unnecessary strikes in vital industries, encourage civil disorders and foster a lenient and soft attitude on the part of government toward such disorders.
7. By specious arguments cause the breakdown of the old moral virtues: honesty, sobriety, continence, faith in the pledged word, ruggedness.

"C. Cause the registration of all firearms on some pretext, with a view to help confiscating them and leaving the population helpless."

The above "setting" and quote (actually the "Rules" constitute a short document) have been thoroughly researched and found to have originated in the British publication *New World News* (February 1946), rather than in Dusseldorf, Germany, in 1919. Widely distributed since the mid-forties, the "Rules" have been trundled out at various times when they "fit" or "explain" the issues of the day. Especially have they been used to argue against firearms control and sex education. Such far-right luminaries as Dan Smoot, Frank Capell, Billy James Hargis, and the old John Birch Society publication *American Opinion* have featured them, replete with dire predictions for America's future.

The National Rifle Association got into the "Rules"-authenticating business in the January 1973 issue of its magazine *The American Rifleman*. Editor Ashley Halsey reported that Captain Thomas Hunter Barber (1889–1962) was the *New World News* source for the "Rules." This was confirmed by a 1970 letter from *News* editor John Sturdivant. Reportedly one of those who raided the "secret communist headquarters" (the Spartacists, according to Halsey) in Dussleldorf, Captain Barber left a copy of the document in his own handwriting (but, of course, no document). Additionally, according to the article, the information about Barber was sent to the History and Government Division of the Library of Congress in January 1962. Granting this to be true, it still proves nothing about the authenticity of the "Rules"—only that there was a Captain Barber and he may have written the "Rules for Revolution" in his own hand. As to the source from which he copied them, who knows? Where is the original document and why had neither our military nor security agencies ever heard of it until 1946? Consider the following:

1. Such well-known conservative commentators as William F. Buckley, M. Stanton Evans, and James J. Kilpatrick have branded the "Rules" a forgery. And the old anti-Communist newsletter *Combat* called it a "hoax on anticommunists."

2. An exhaustive search of files of the FBI, CIA, Senate Internal Security Subcommittee, and Library of Congress failed to find any trace of the "Rules."

3. The Directorate for Information Services in the Defense Department stated its inability to locate a document resembling the "Rules" and referred the problem to the National Archives and Records Service of the General Services Administration. Result: no such document in the old War Department records, but archivist Robert Bahmer stated that a report on Bolshevist propaganda written in 1920 features phraseology and aims "quite different from the overall tone of the so-called 'Communist Rules for Revolution.'"

4. Thomas Hunter Barber, who had become a major by 1919, wrote *Along the Road* (1924). This memoir mentioned nothing of his experiences in Europe after 1918. Since he failed to write of such an important action as raiding Spartacist headquarters, one might well speculate that it didn't happen—especially in light of the fact that the Spartacists were located in Berlin, not Dusseldorf.

5. Challenge: Produce a documented copy of the "Rules" in German written before World War II.

Due to the weight of evidence against authenticity, plus the fact that the "Rules" seem to carry no internal evidence of Communist origin, we must agree with the late FBI Director J. Edgar Hoover and "logically speculate that the document is spurious." Boller and George, 114; *Combat,* August 15, 1969; *Con-*

*gressional Record* (August 13, 1969), S9909–11; Ashley Halsey, "Ending the Mystery of the Rules," *The American Rifleman* (January 1973); Donald Janson, "Communist Rules for Revolt Viewed as Durable Fraud," *New York Times* (July 10, 1970), 1, 30; Morris Kominsky, *The Hoaxers* (Boston: Branden Press, 1970), 602–603; letter to Paul Boller from Bernard J. Sussman, June 1, 1990.

### Russell, Bertrand

Soviet Russia is a closed tyrannical bureaucracy with a spy system more elaborate than the Tsar's and an aristocracy as insolent and unfeeling, composed of Americanized Jews. P

Far rightists who have employed this quote give Russell's *The Practice and Theory of Bolshevism* (1920) as their source. Nothing even similar appears in the book.

### Russian-Jewish Periodical (1904)

Free Masons have become for Jews the great weapon for the realization of their political, social, and cultural demand. C

V. Pigalev, writing in *Soviet Soldier* (February 1982), declared that this utterance orignated in an unnamed 1904 Russian-Jewish periodical. He further commented: "Little has changed in the Masonic-Zionist strategy. Only its methods have become still more refined." As so often in the past, anti-Semitic cannards continually roll out of Russia. William Korey, "Anti-Semitism and the Soviet Military," *Freedom at Issue* (March-April 1982).

### Sanger, Margaret

Blacks, soldiers, and Jews are a menace to the race. C

Evidently concocted in the late 1980s for the purpose of trying to make the early birth control advocate seem a racist and anti-Semite, this fabrication has been kept in circulation by antiabortion and anti–birth control groups and individuals. When a source is given, it is *Birth Control Review,* April 1933. That particular issue contains neither an article nor a letter by Sanger. A tip-off as to the quote's lack of authenticity is the word "blacks," which was not in common usage until the mid-1960s. During the 1930s, the acceptable terms were "Negro" or "colored." While Margaret Sanger came to adopt some unsavory beliefs regarding eugenics, she was certainly less bigoted than the great majority of people of her day and would not have stereotyped all blacks, Jews, and soldiers in such a manner.

### Smith, Walter Bedell

Rockefeller is a communist. P

The source of this daring (foolhardy?) utterance is page 367 of *O.S.S.—The Secret History of the First Central Intelligence Agency,* by R. Harris Smith. But this is not what the book says. The quote is not from Walter Bedell Smith (ambassador to the Soviet Union, 1946–49) himself but instead from an unnamed ex-CIA operative as follows: "I know you won't believe this," an ex-CIA man told this writer, "but Smith once warned Eisenhower that Rockefeller was a communist." Blatant hearsay! Why not "An ex-CIA man told me that Rockefeller told Eisenhower that Walter Bedell Smith was a Communist"?

### Stalin, Josef

Give me Hollywood for six months and I'll rule the world. P

Words have no relation to actions—otherwise what kind of diplomacy is it? Words are one thing, actions are another. Good words are a mask for concealment of bad deeds. Sincere diplomacy is no more possible than dry water or wooden iron. D

Stalin actually said that when "bourgeois diplomats" prepare for war, they begin to shout "peace" and "friendly relations" and are not to be trusted. "A diplomat's words," therefore, "*must* contradict his deeds—otherwise, what sort of diplomat is he? Words are one thing—deeds something entirely different. Fine words are a mask to cover shady deeds. A sincere diplomat is like dry water or wooden iron." Boller and George, 120.

Take eastern Europe, the masses of Asia, surround the U.S. by taking Africa, Central and South America, and we will not have to fight for it. It will fall into our hands like ripe fruit. C

As in the case of Khrushchev and Mao, a variation of the Lenin "over-ripe fruit" quote has also been attributed to Josef Stalin. An organization called Christ Is All (of Vernon, Alabama) was distributing the most recent version of this concoction in the late 1980s.

The Western nations must render aid to backward countries in order to socialize their economies and prepare them for entry into the world socialist system. D

This quote appeared in a letter to the *Dallas Morning News* on March 11, 1966, with the comment that "the last four administrations seem to be in complete agreement." It cropped up in numerous papers throughout the 1970s and into the 1980s. The quote seems to have been concocted in the early 1960s by distorting something Stalin wrote in 1921 in *Marxism and the National and Colonial Question* (page 116): "The triumphant proletariat of the advanced countries should render aid . . . to the toiling masses of the backward nationalities in their cultural and economic development . . . Unless such aid is forthcoming it will be impossible to bring about the peaceful co-existence and fraternal collaboration of the toilers of the various nations and peoples within a single world economic system that are so essential for the final triumph of socialism." Boller and George, 119.

You can't make an omelet without breaking eggs. P

This is an old adage that may well date back to the eighteenth century. Boller and George, 120.

### Schweitzer, Albert

I have given my life to try to alleviate the sufferings of Africa. There is something that all white men who have lived here like I must learn and know: that these individuals are a sub-race. They have neither the intellectual, mental or emotional abilities to equate or to share equally with white men in any of the functions of our civilization.

I have given my life to try to bring unto them the advantages which our civilization must offer, but I have become well aware that we must retain this status: [white] the superior and they the inferior. For whenever a white man seeks to live among them as their equal they will either destroy him or devour him. And they will destroy all of his work.

Let white men from anywhere in the world, who would come to help Africa, remember that you must continually retain this status: you the master and they the inferior like children that you would help or teach. Never fraternize with them as equals. Never accept them as your social equals or they will devour you. They will destroy you. Q

This certainly doesn't sound like Schweitzer's paternalistic statements about Africans in the works we have consulted. It appeared in racist periodicals such as *The Councilor* (September 1977) during the seventies and eighties. Henry Clark, *The Ethical Mysticism of Albert Schweitzer* (Boston: Beacon, 1962); Jay E. Green, *Four Complete Biographies* (New York: Globe, 1962); Albert Schweitzer, *On the Edge of the Primeval Forest* and *More from the Primeval Forest* (New York: McMillan, 1945); *Out of My Life and Thought* (New York: New American Library, 1961); *Philosophy of Civilization* (New York: McMillan, 1953).

### Taft, Robert

The UN has become a trap. Let's go it alone. C

Boller and George, 121.

### Talmud

But it is permitted to cheat a goy, because cheating goyim at any time pleases the Lord. C

This is but one of the many concoctions and distortions linked to the Talmud by twentieth-century Jew-haters. Boller and George, 122.

## Washington, George

Continued deficit spending must ultimately endanger all governments. P

Few would deny the truth of this, but there is no evidence Washington ever said it. Its origin is probably mid-twentieth century.

Firearms stand next in importance to the Constitution itself. They are the American people's liberty teeth and keystone under independence. . . . From the hour the Pilgrims landed, to the present day, events, occurrences, and tendencies prove that to ensure peace, security, and happiness, the rifle and pistol are equally indispensable. . . . The very atmosphere of firearms everywhere restrains evil interference—they deserve a place of honor with all that's good. Q

Widely used by gun enthusiasts, this utterance could not be documented by marksman and director of the American Pistol Institute, Jeff Cooper. Nor could another user, *Soldier of Fortune* magazine, furnish a source.

The Jews work more effectively against us than the enemy's armies. They are a hundred times more dangerous to our Liberties and the great cause we are engaged in. It is much to be lamented that each State long ere this has not hunted them down as the pests of society, and the greatest Enemys we have to the happiness of America. C, D

Washington actually made a similar statement. He was not speaking of Jews, but of currency speculators. There is no evidence that the first president was anti-Semitic. Boller and George, 126.

## Wise, Rabbi Stephen

Some call it communism. I call it Judaism. C

*Playboy* (April 1966) researched this and came up blank. American Nazi party founder George Lincoln Rockwell retracted his allegation that Wise said it.

## Zeffirelli, Franco

The Last Temptation of Christ is a product of that Jewish cultural scum of Los Angeles which is always spoiling for a chance to attack the Christian world. C

The noted Italian director did criticize *The Last Temptation of Christ* but used only a few words above in a most different context. Zeffirelli said a reporter asked his opinion of Lew Wasserman, whom "a group of fundamentalists in the States referred to as being part of 'that larger group of Hollywood Jewish scum.'

That was the question posed to me. I said I didn't know anything about Mr. Wasserman being a Jew or being scum." *Religious Freedom Alert* (September 1988).

## Zinoviev, Grigori

> We hope the Party will step by step conquer the proletarian forces of America and in the not distant future raise the red flag over the White House. P

Exposed as probably fraudulent in the mid-1920s, this one seems to have originated in the Justice Department's Bureau of Investigation. Boller and George, 133.

The foregoing rather overwhelming array of fabrications, distortions, and questionable items might lead one to the incorrect conclusion that extremists never quote well-known people accurately. In fact, they sometimes do. It has been our experience, however, that the use of spurious quotes exceeds the use of genuine ones by a considerable margin. The reason seems obvious: the available phony quotes usually "fit the situation" so well, why should the ideologue search for others?

We end this discussion with what may be the ultimate fake quote. The setting of this one was Lenin's deathbed in January 1924. It was chanted in unison by Lenin, Stalin, Gus Hall, Khrushchev, Trostky, Brezhnev, Zinoviev, Lunarcharsky, Bukharin, Bulganin, Beria, Manuilsky, and Dimitrov:

> Like pie crusts, overripe fruit will strangle your guts and they will fall into your lap in small doses so that you will hate your parents who will finance their own destruction and inevitably corrupt those useful idiots, the young, who will furnish the rope, locate the guns, and perish through mass terror, wishful thinking, debauching the currency, war to the hilt and smashing with clenched fists.

This mass compendium of spuriousness, which attempts to close on a note of levity, was concocted by Laird Wilcox, modified by John George.

# Appendix II. **Principal Characteristics of the Extremes and the Mainstream in America: A Handy Guide for Extremist Watchers**

Copyright 1968, 9th. revision 1991 by John George

(Remember: Extremism is more a matter of style and tactics than of goals.)

---

### Common Characteristics of Left and Right Extremists

---

1. EXHIBIT ABSOLUTE CERTAINTY THEY HAVE THE TRUTH. Which, among other items, is that
2. AMERICA IS CONTROLLED TO A GREAT EXTENT BY A CONSPIRATORIAL GROUP. They believe this evil group to be very powerful and in control of most nations. Thus, it is not surprising that, due mainly to fear and frustration, extremists exhibit
3. HATRED OF OPPONENTS. Because these opponents (actually "enemies" in the extremists' eyes) are seen as part of or sympathizers with "The Conspiracy," they deserve hatred and contempt. Due to these factors it is not surprising that extremists have
4. LOW REGARD FOR OPEN SOCIETIES & THEREFORE LITTLE CONFIDENCE IN DEMOCRATIC PROCESSES. Since they believe "The Conspiracy" has control of the world's major nations, extremists spurn compromise and show a
5. WILLINGNESS TO DENY BASIC CIVIL LIBERTIES TO CERTAIN FELLOW CITIZENS, because enemies deserve no liberties. Therefore, extremists have no qualms about resorting to
6. CONSISTENT INDULGENCE IN IRRESPONSIBLE ACCUSATIONS AND CHARACTER ASSASSINATION, such as calling fellow citizens Communists, Insiders, Amoral Secular Humanists, Fascists, Nazis, Racists, etc., & constantly imputing wicked motives to those who oppose them.

**Differing Characteristics of Left Extremists, Right Extremists, and Non-Extremists**

| Left Extremism | Liberal-Conservative Spectrum | Right Extremism |
|---|---|---|
| 1. Favor destruction of existing system and replacement with some variant of Marxism. Most believe this can only come about through violent revolution. | 1. Accept at least gradual change within the existing system. | 1. Believe that the true system has been perverted and desire to return to the way they imagine it was in the past. |
| 2. Generally non-religious, but claim to love humanity. | 2. Seldom impugn motives or loyalty of opponents; instead question judgment, reasoning process, sources of information. | 2. Generally religious, but often promote religious and ethnic bigotry. |
| 3. Generally internationalist in outlook; some factions aligned with foreign powers. | 3. Some commitment to democratic ideals, including civil liberties for all. | 3. Intensely nationalist and, though not aligned with foreign powers, look with favor on many dictatorships. |

| Left Extremism | Liberal-Conservative Spectrum | Right Extremism |
|---|---|---|
| **Representative Organizations** | **Representative Organizations** | **Representative Organizations** |
| *Soviet Ideology*<br>Communist Party USA<br>Young Communist<br>   League | Am. Bar Assoc.<br>Am. Legion<br>Am. Medical Assoc.<br>Common Cause<br>Democratic Party | *Ideology Not Concerned<br>   With Ethnicity*<br>Am. Coalition for Tradi-<br>   tional Values<br>Christian Crusade |
| *Trotskyist Ideology*<br>Spartacist League<br>Workers League | League of Women<br>   Voters<br>NAACP<br>Nat'l Assoc. of<br>   Evangelicals | Christian Voice<br>Eagle Forum<br>John Birch Society |
| *Maoist/Hoxhaist/Kimist<br>   Ideology*<br>Communist Workers<br>   Party<br>Marxist-Leninist Party,<br>   USA<br>Revolutionary Commu-<br>   nist Party | Natl' Assoc. of<br>   Manufacturers<br>Nat'l Conference of<br>   Christians & Jews<br>Natl'l Council of<br>   Churches<br>Planned Parenthood | *Ideology Concerned<br>   With Ethnicity*<br>Aryan Nations<br>⌐Jewish Defense League<br>Ku Klux Klans<br>Nation of Islam<br>NAAWP<br>White Aryan Resistance |
| *Independent Ideology*<br>All African People's<br>   Revolutionary Party<br>Progressive Labor Party<br>   (Formerly Maoist)<br>Socialist Workers Party<br>   (Formerly<br>   Trotskyist)<br>Workers World Party<br>   (Formerly<br>   Trotskyist) | Republican Party<br>U.S. Catholic Conf. | |

# Index